Colonel Richard Irving Dodge

Colonel Richard Irving Dodge, 1881. Reprinted from Dodge, *Our Wild Indians* (1882), frontispiece.

Colonel Richard Irving Dodge
The Life and Times of a Career Army Officer

Wayne R. Kime

University of Oklahoma Press : Norman

Other works written or edited by Wayne R. Kime

Pierre M. Irving and Washington Irving: A Collaboration in Life and Letters (Waterloo, Ont., 1978)
(ed.) *Raising the Wind: The Legend of Lapland and Finland Wizards in Literature*, by Ernest J. Moyne (Newark, Del., 1981)
(ed.) *Miscellaneous Writings, 1803–1859*, by Washington Irving (Boston, 1981)
(ed. with Andrew B. Myers) *Journals and Notebooks, Volume IV, 1826–1859*, by Washington Irving (Boston, 1984)
Donald G. Mitchell (Boston, 1985)
(ed.) *The Plains of North America and Their Inhabitants: A Critical Edition*, by Richard Irving Dodge (Newark, Del., 1989)
(ed.) *The Black Hills Journals of Colonel Richard Irving Dodge* (Norman, 1996)
(ed.) *The Powder River Expedition Journals of Colonel Richard Irving Dodge* (Norman, 1997)
(ed.) *The Indian Territory Journals of Colonel Richard Irving Dodge* (Norman, 2000)
(ed.) *The Sherman Tour Journals of Colonel Richard Irving Dodge* (Norman, 2002)
(ed.) *Fitz-James O'Brien: Selected Literary Journalism, 1852–1860* (Selinsgrove, Penn, 2003.)
(with Ralph M. Aderman) *Advocate for America: The Life of James Kirke Paulding* (Selinsgrove, Penn., 2003)

Publication of this book is made possible through the generosity of Edith Kinney Gaylord.

Library of Congress Cataloging-in-Publication Data

Kime, Wayne R.
Colonel Richard Irving Dodge : the life and times of a career army officer / Wayne Raymond Kime.
p. cm.
Includes bibliographical references and index.
ISBN 0-8061-3709-6 (alk. paper)
1. Dodge, Richard Irving, 1827–1895. 2. United States. Army—Officers—Biography. I. Title.

U53.D64K56 2006
978'.02092—dc22

2005055457

The paper in this book meets the guidelines for permanence and durability of the Committee on Production Guidelines for Book Longevity of the Council on Library Resources, Inc. ∞

1 2 3 4 5 6 7 8 9 10

For Evan and Emily

Contents

Illustrations

Maps

Preface

During his forty-three years as a U.S. Army officer, Richard Irving Dodge (1827–1895) achieved prominence in military circles but remained known to the general public primarily as an author. His two major works, *The Plains of the Great West and Their Inhabitants* (1877) and *Our Wild Indians* (1882), established him as the premier popular authority of his time on the subjects they treated: the Great Plains environment, the game animals that inhabited it, and the Indian tribes that had once roamed freely over it. In a period when ethnographic study of Plains Indians had barely begun, Dodge's accounts of American Indian culture won praise on both sides of the Atlantic for their range and insight. Urging just treatment of these peoples, who were being removed from their home country to reservations, Dodge argued that their best hope for survival and eventual adaptation to American culture was supervision by the army rather than by the corrupt "Indian Bureau" of the Department of the Interior, under whose oversight they languished. In advocating this policy change, he concurred with the views of the army at large, and as a result its commanding general, William T. Sherman, lent *Our Wild Indians* a semiofficial character by associating his name and the prestige of his office with it.

During the twentieth century, Dodge's reputation as an author was sustained by reprintings of his works, including a third volume, *The Black Hills* (1876), but the facts of his military career were all but forgotten. Although he was involved in events and developments that later attracted the interest of historians, many of his endeavors took place just outside the focus of their attention. Eventually my own interest in Dodge's great uncle, the American prose writer Washington Irving, led me to learn more about this soldier-author. Initially I studied the genesis of *The Plains of the Great West and Their Inhabitants* while preparing a critical edition of that work, published under the title he originally intended, *The Plains of North America and Their Inhabitants* (University of Delaware Press, 1989). Later I edited the texts of twenty journals compiled by

Dodge, now part of the Everett D. Graff Collection of Western Americana at the Newberry Library, Chicago, Illinois. The first six of these, written between May and October 1875, are a record of Dodge's experiences as commander of the army escort to a geological surveying expedition in the Black Hills of Dakota Territory. The next four, written between October 1876 and January 1877, detail his activities as commander of the infantry and artillery battalions on the Powder River Expedition, under Brigadier General George Crook, against the Sioux and Northern Cheyenne Indians. The next eight, written at intervals between September 1878 and December 1880, record his varied service chiefly in Indian Territory, the expanse of land that later became the state of Oklahoma. And the final two describe his experiences in 1883 during what he then considered the high point of his career: participation in General Sherman's valedictory inspection tour of military forts, cities, and settlements in the western states and territories. The Dodge journals, which have been issued in four volumes by the University of Oklahoma Press, thus do not comprise a continuous chronological record, nor do they portray a common set of circumstances. However, they all deal with matters of permanent historical interest and do so lucidly, suggestively, sometimes memorably.

Drawing on these documents and other published and unpublished sources, including official records, I offer in the present volume a narrative of Dodge's personal history and military career. One salient feature of the chapters that follow is attention to the close interrelationship between his experiences as an army officer and the published writings that grew out of them. Another is description of the various duty assignments through which he developed into his mature stature as a military leader. A third is attention to General William T. Sherman, first as an architect of the federal policy for removing Indians from the path of westward development and later as commanding general. This coverage helps set forth the postwar history of the army as it affected Dodge and establishes a context for describing the contacts between him and Sherman that laid a basis for their later professional relationship.

At one time Dodge hoped to write an anecdotal treatment of a subject that he thought deserved wider recognition: the work of the army in the West before and after the Civil War. Wishing to present something more comprehensive than "simply a chapter of my own life," he invited contributions from officers, enlisted men, and other persons willing to share their recollections. To exemplify the wealth of material available for possible treatment, he named prewar military leaders—"Harney, Cooke, Heintzleman, Kendrick, Graham, Shepherd, Sykes, Sully, and many others"—whose exploits had gone unrecorded thus far. It was "not right or just," he wrote, "that the Army should lose the record of the experience of the men of those days."[1] However, Dodge did not succeed in bringing his ambitious project to fruition except in fragmentary fashion. Despite continuing interest in the frontier army, the stories of some of the men he named still remain to be told.

Colonel Richard Irving Dodge, the first book-length biography of Dodge, is based on the premise that his own eventful life story merits a place in the published history of the U.S. Army. His versatility as a senior duty officer brought him into working contact with top-level commanders, including Christopher C. Augur, John M. Schofield, George Crook, John Gibbon, John Pope, Philip H. Sheridan, Nelson A. Miles, Alfred H. Terry, and William T. Sherman, some of whom he came to know well and characterized in his published or unpublished writings. His sociable disposition and devotion to the service kept him in touch with junior officers, enlisted men, and civilians. His official duties brought him into contact with changing conditions on the frontier, including the practical consequences of some government policies that troubled him deeply. As an articulate man of independent mind and strongly held views, he attempted on occasion to influence events; for example, during the 1870s he repeatedly drew official attention to the wanton destruction of buffalo herds by rapacious citizens. Of course, he understood that the course of history was not his to determine and that his first duty as a soldier was to obey lawful orders. He was aware that by supporting the advance of settlement, the army he served was helping to open up the unspoiled western wilderness he had come to love. Still, Dodge was proud of his profession and remained confident that, however imperfectly, he was advancing the cause of progress during a significant stage of the nation's development.

Concurrently with the close of the army's campaign to suppress Indian resistance to occupation of the western states and territories, Dodge was transferred with his regiment to posts in northern New York. Unlike some senior officers, he remained innovative and busy during his final years of active duty, confirming his reputation as a "very wide-awake commander" as he rounded out an honorable life's work. Although not without its disappointments and dark passages, Dodge's career thus adds luster to the history of the U.S. Army. For some years after his death, his portrait hung in a place of honor: the officer's mess at his alma mater, the United States Military Academy at West Point, New York. Signifying as it did the affection and respect of his comrades, it was a fitting tribute.

In the chapters that follow, several symbols and abbreviations are used in quotations from Dodge's unpublished writings: [roman], editorial additions; [*italic*], editorial explanations; / and \, the beginning and end of interlineated text. Restorations of canceled matter, shown within angle brackets in my editions of Dodge's journals, are not reproduced here. Except to correct potentially confusing or distracting errors, I have allowed variant spellings and misspellings to stand. Abbreviations in quoted material have been spelled out within brackets only if they are otherwise unclear or if the passage in which they occur denotes speech.

For courtesies and assistance as I prepared this work I am indebted to many persons and institutions, not all of whom are mentioned here. Financial support over the years came from the sabbatical leave program at Fairmont State College—now University; the Fairmont State College Foundation; the West Virginia Humanities Council; the National Endowment for the Humanities; and the Newberry Library, to all of which I express sincere thanks. Sharon Mazure, in charge of interlibrary loans at Fairmont State College, obtained for me scarce material that proved of considerable value. Robert G. Masters and his successor as library director, Thelma Hutchins, provided other helpful support of various kinds. Robert Heffner, Jr., shared his expertise in preparing the maps; and John Piscitelli, in supplying photographs.

Institutions whose facilities and personnel have assisted me in my research include the Newberry Library, Chicago; the National Archives, Washington, D.C.; the U.S. Army Military History Institute, Carlisle Barracks, Pennsylvania; the U.S. Military Academy, West Point, New York; the Manuscript Division, Library of Congress, Washington, D.C.; the Western History Collection, University of Oklahoma, Norman; the Oklahoma Historical Society, Oklahoma City; the Kansas Historical Society, Topeka; the Beinecke Rare Book and Manuscript Library, Yale University, New Haven, Connecticut; the New York Public Library, New York City; Columbia University Library, New York City; Rutgers University Library, New Brunswick, New Jersey; Historic Hudson Valley, Tarrytown, New York; the University of Pennsylvania Library, Philadelphia; the University of Delaware Library, Newark; Towson State University Library, Baltimore, Maryland; the History Library, Museum of New Mexico, Santa Fe; Northwestern University Library, Evanston, Illinois; West Virginia University Library, Morgantown; the Vermont Historical Society, Montpelier; and Fairmont State College Library, Fairmont, West Virginia.

Persons who have offered me space in their homes during my expeditions in search of information include Wallace and Sue Jungers, Ron and Susan Hamilton, Charles and Cynthia Crow, Eleanore Hofstetter, Joe and Mary Jo Furgal, Kathleen Moyne, Jude Olsen, Kay Rosselot, and Peggy Wolivar. Among the supportive—and stoic—captive listeners during one-sided conversations while the work was taking shape, I mention my accomplished wife, Alicia, and my friend and running companion David Bohnke. Ralph M. Aderman afforded me valuable experience through his invitation to revise and condense his biographical study of James Kirke Paulding, since published under both our names as *Advocate for America: The Life of James Kirke Paulding* (Susquehanna University Press, 2003). I am grateful to Paul L. Hedren and an anonymous reviewer for their careful study of the present work when it was in manuscript form. Mr. Hedren has since shared with me a valuable item in his personal collection, an unpublished letter from Richard Irving Dodge to his son, Fred, for use in this study.

For permission to quote from unpublished or copyrighted material and to reproduce photographs, I thank Mr. Hedren and the Newberry Library, Chicago; the U.S. Army Military History Institute, Carlisle, Pennsylvania; the U.S. Military Academy Library, West Point, New York; the Manuscript Division, Library of Congress, Washington, D.C.; the Beinecke Rare Book and Manuscript Library, Yale University, New Haven, Connecticut; the History Library, Museum of New Mexico, Santa Fe; and Sleepy Hollow Restorations, Tarrytown, New York. Portions of chapter 12 are revised from passages in *The Black Hills Journals of Colonel Richard Irving Dodge*; portions of chapters 13 and 15 are revised from passages in *The Plains of North America and Their Inhabitants*; portions of chapter 14 are revised from passages in *The Powder River Expedition Journals of Colonel Richard Irving Dodge*; portions of chapters 16–21 are revised from passages in *The Indian Territory Journals of Colonel Richard Irving Dodge*; and portions of chapters 22–24 are revised from *The Sherman Tour Journals of Colonel Richard Irving Dodge*.

Finally, I extend grateful thanks to Patricia Heinicke, Jr., the copyeditor of this volume; to Steven Baker, who supervised the editing of the work; and for their cooperation throughout the publication of Dodge's journals and this volume, to the able staff of the University of Oklahoma Press.

Wayne R. Kime
Fairmont, West Virginia

Colonel Richard Irving Dodge

Part One

A Long Lieutenancy, 1848–1861

1

Frontier Apprenticeship

For James R. Dodge and his family in rural Surry County, in western North Carolina, the summer of 1848 was a time of good fortune. The Dodges' eldest child and only son, Richard, had just graduated from the U.S. Military Academy at West Point, New York, and was at home on a leave of absence. His three months of leisure would enable "Rich," a strapping twenty-one-year-old, to savor his new consequence as a brevet second lieutenant while also hunting, fishing, and trekking through the hilly back-country he had known since boyhood. To his parents, young Dodge was still "the Boy Baby," but to his three sisters, Susan, Ann, and Mary Helen (Molly), he was the object of fond admiration.[1] Theirs was a close-knit family, and his stay was tinged with regret, for in all probability Rich would not return home for several more years.

Like his son, James R. Dodge had recently secured new employment, which though welcome, would entail periods of absence from his wife and daughters. A New York man, Dodge had settled in North Carolina in 1826, at the time of his marriage to Susan Williams, a daughter of a family well known in the region for its tradition of public service. The young people had met through Susan's uncle Nicholas Williams, a former congressman and a friend of Dodge's uncle William Irving, then a congressman from New York. James Dodge practiced law, and as the years passed, he won a reputation among his colleagues for steady reliability, pleasant good sense, and literary tastes and abilities.[2] However, he preferred not to follow the circuit court from town to town, soliciting business as he went, which was the common practice of the time. As a result, his practice yielded only a modest income. Influential friends, including congressmen Anderson Mitchell and David S. Reid, helped secure for his son the appointment to West Point that promised a first-class education Dodge could not have afforded on his own.[3]

Indeed, he was in financial difficulty when, late in 1846, the North Carolina legislature created a branch of the state supreme court at Morganton, a county seat approximately seventy-five miles from his home. He applied for the clerkship of this court to another old friend, Chief Justice Thomas Ruffin, and was granted a probationary appointment. The position required his presence in Morganton during the late spring and summer months, but it yielded a steady income, and happily for Dodge he gave general satisfaction. In the summer of 1848 his appointment was confirmed,[4] and at fifty-three years of age he had at last secured a berth that assured him and his family modest prosperity.

The younger Dodge's stories of West Point, set amidst scenic country beside the Hudson River forty miles north of New York City, must have entranced his sisters, who had never visited these northern scenes. His parents were somewhat more cosmopolitan. As a young man James Dodge had been employed in New York City, as a clerk in the wholesale hardware concern of his uncle Ebenezer Irving. At the time of their wedding he and Susan had been guests at the home of this former employer, a visit fondly recalled in later years.[5] James Dodge was the only one of five brothers and sisters who went south, and a steady stream of correspondence kept him in touch with his immediate family and other relations. The close ties between several New York clans—Dodge, Irving, Paulding, Frothingham, Van Wart, Grinnell, and Kemble—yielded a harvest of cousins, aunts, and uncles, and the North Carolina Dodges were well known to many of these. For young Rich, the visits of his northern kinfolk to West Point and the fashionable hotels at Cold Spring, across the Hudson River, must occasionally have enlivened the years of his immurement as a cadet.[6] He took his middle name from the Irving family, several of whose members resided only a few miles south of West Point, at Tarrytown.

Richard Irving Dodge found much to enjoy during the four years of study and military training that imprinted on him his adult self-image as a soldier. Cadets of the era tended to group together along regional lines—southerners, New Englanders, and westerners. Dodge moved easily among his classmates, but probably he was most comfortable with young men whose experiences of the rural south resembled his own. Such a comrade was Richard W. "Sub" Johnson, a cadet from Kentucky. Like Johnson, Dodge was not one of those Southrons who formed a patrician clique. Rather, he enjoyed conversation and storytelling and had a wry sense of humor, qualities that made him an agreeable companion. "Dickie," his West Point nickname, suggests his hearty good spirits. Possibly the name also hinted at a streak of mischievousness, for "Dickie" was also the name in covert use for Captain J. Addison Thomas, the commandant of cadets. Undoubtedly Dodge's soldierly bearing attracted the attention of his superiors. Standing over six feet tall, he was selected as a cadet officer, a distinction envied by some classmates who did not possess the same physical gifts.[7]

In Dodge's day, the program of studies at West Point bulked large with technical studies central to the Engineering Department, which dominated the institution. Courses in military law, tactics, horsemanship ("equitation"), topographical drawing, and military history formed parts of the academic program, but the primary emphasis was on studies that produced professional engineers. Among these disciplines the one most feared by cadets was mathematics, for it was the rock that sank the fortunes of many otherwise well-qualified young men. Unsatisfactory performance in any subject could result in a suggestion that a cadet resign or in outright dismissal, and one or the other was the fate of most. Of the ninety-four cadets in Dodge's entering class, only thirty-eight managed to graduate four years later. Dodge completed the course at the middle of his class, ranked nineteenth.[8]

Graduating West Point cadets had the privilege of stating a preference for duty in one arm of the service or another, but it was understood that ordinarily a young officer's class rank would determine his assignment. The top academic performers received coveted appointments in the Engineer Bureau, devoting their energies to the design and construction of fortifications, bridges, and other capital projects. Students at the second level were assigned to the Topographical Engineers, who surveyed and mapped regions where military activity might be required. The remaining appointments, accounting for the greater part of the class, were to units of the army's field arms, the regiments of artillery, cavalry, infantry, and dragoons. Satisfactory performance in these areas of the service was assumed to demand a more modest level of intellectual capacity than in the technical fields. Dragoons were the bottom of the heap in the military caste system. The only real requirement for a dragoon, it was said, was a broad bottom that enabled one to sit a horse.[9]

Dodge understood that his assignment would be to the field service, and as he anticipated, General Order 43, dated August 7, 1848, at the Adjutant General's Office in Washington, directed him to report by September 30 to his temporary unit, the Eighth Regiment of Infantry, then at Jefferson Barracks, Missouri.[10] Although officially a matter of routine, to Dodge this order was a milestone, for it sent him to the western frontier and identified him as an infantryman. Despite periods of staff duty and special assignments, in the forty-three years of active service that remained to him, he would become associated with the army's operations in the West and would invariably be listed in the annual *Army Register* as an infantry officer.

An appointment to the Eighth Infantry was a coveted distinction to a West Point graduate, for that regiment had served with honor in the recent War with Mexico. In 1846 the unit had been conspicuous in battles at Palo Alto, Resaca de la Palma, and Monterrey, and in the following year it had been part of the American forces at other noted actions—Vera Cruz, Cerro Gordo, Molino del Rey, and Chapultepec. The Eighth Infantry had participated in the storming and capture of the City of Mexico on September 13 and 14, 1847, the final major action of the war.[11] For gallant conduct in these affairs, several of its officers were later awarded brevet commissions. Of course, members of the Class of 1848 would not enjoy the same opportunity to distinguish themselves in battle that had been presented men of the Class of 1846, such as First Lieutenant Thomas Jackson and Second Lieutenants Dabney Maury and George B. McClellan.[12] The Treaty of Guadalupe Hidalgo, signed on February 2, 1848, secured peace between the combatant nations. Still, Dodge and other officers newly assigned to regiments like the Eighth Infantry could bask in the glow of military renown and professional pride that still gathered around their comrades.

As ordered, Dodge reported for duty at Jefferson Barracks, on the west bank of the Mississippi River four miles south of Saint Louis, Missouri. The Eighth, then under command of Major Pitcairn Morrison, was awaiting a new posting. In the interval, Dodge was made junior officer of Company G, commanded by First Lieutenant Jacob Booker in the absence of its captain, Joseph Selden.[13] Presently the regiment was ordered to report at San Antonio, Texas, headquarters of the army's Eighth Military District, and on November 23 its ten companies, numbering approximately six hundred men, embarked on the steamer *Aleck Scott* for New Orleans, where they arrived eight days later. After a delay spent securing space aboard ships for the voyage across the Gulf of Mexico, on December 12 the *New Orleans* sailed with the headquarters staff and seven companies aboard, and the *Telegraph* with the other three. Arriving at Port Lavaca, on the southern coast of Texas, the troops disembarked and went into camp, preparing for a 110-mile midwinter march up the Guadalupe River valley to San Antonio.

The month that followed proved an inauspicious beginning to the regiment's years of duty in the region. To facilitate the march, Major Morrison divided his force into two wings, each of five companies.[14] On December 21 the right wing broke camp, traveling by slow stages as far inland as Victoria, Texas, where it arrived on December 29. Ominously, a few cases of cholera were confirmed on the march, but the contagion did not spread. However, a virulent outbreak occurred among the troops still in camp outside Port Lavaca. Within two days the potentially fatal disease was so widespread that the stricken companies were ordered back into the town, where two temporary hospitals were hastily set up. The able-bodied remnants of the left wing marched ahead and rejoined the right wing on January 2, remaining in camp together for two more weeks as detachments of recuperated men arrived. After more than a month in transit from the coast, on January 28 the Eighth Infantry encamped at Camp Worth, just outside San Antonio.[15] The regiment would soon take up the difficult task of controlling hostile Indians, but it had already experienced a bitter initiation to the conditions of frontier life.

Although Dodge was serving as an officer of the Eighth, he was as yet a second lieutenant by brevet only. He would not be offered a regular commission until a vacancy occurred at the rank of second lieutenant in some infantry regiment, and then, should he accept the assignment, he would join that organization. A series of failed communications during this placement process now further delayed his introduction to the frontier. When Second Lieutenant James A. Deaney, Eighth Infantry, died of cholera on December 24, 1848, Dodge had reason to expect that his present assignment to duty would be made permanent. However, he was aware that another vacancy would soon be filled in the Second Infantry, then serving in remote California. Since he wished to remain at his present station, early in January he requested of the adjutant general that he "not be appointed to . . . any other Regiment" than the Eighth.[16]

Probably this would have ended the matter, but before his letter had reached its destination, he received from Washington a letter of appointment—not to the Second but to the Fourth Infantry, whose companies were stationed at posts in Michigan and along the Great Lakes. These were desirable postings, and Dodge therefore wrote accepting the appointment and explaining that in his earlier statement he had meant only to express preference for the Eighth Infantry over the Second.[17] In April, following a journey of approximately eighteen hundred miles, he reported for duty at Fort Gratiot, a one-company post on the Saint Clair River in Michigan, near the outlet of Lake Huron. The post commander, Captain Benjamin Alvord, had particular need of a subaltern officer and welcomed his arrival; for his part, Dodge was quite willing to remain there. But by the time he arrived at the post, the earlier instructions had been rescinded. An order of March 15, 1849, announced that since Dodge had declined promotion out of the Eighth Infantry, he was to be promoted to the vacancy in that regiment. His West Point classmate Second Lieutenant William A. Slaughter, then serving with the Second Infantry in San Diego, California, would be transferred to the Fourth. Captain Alvord remonstrated with the Adjutant General's Office that months must elapse before Slaughter could complete the sea voyage to New Orleans and then make his way north to Fort Gratiot, while a willing Dodge was already at hand.[18] His appeal was reasonable but not successful, and Dodge was sent on his way back to Texas, where he rejoined his company at Camp Lincoln on July 3, 1849.[19]

Within days of his arrival, this two-company post was redesignated Fort Lincoln, signifying semipermanent status. Located approximately forty-five miles west of San Antonio near the settlement of D'Hanis, it was one of eight recently established outposts extending north from the Rio Grande at intervals of sixty to seventy-five miles, beginning with Fort Duncan and including in succession Forts Inge, Lincoln, Martin Scott, Croghan, Gates, Graham, and Worth.[20] Collectively the posts were intended to shield the advancing wave of settlers from Indian depredations, provide security for wagon trains and travelers along a trail to California, and help suppress attempts by Indians to conduct raids into Mexico. A line of posts along the Rio Grande extending as far north and west as Fort Bliss, at El Paso del Norte, would bear primary responsibility for the latter function, enforcing a provision of the Treaty of Guadalupe Hidalgo. Units of the Eighth Infantry occupied posts along the north-south corridor, often marching from one post to another to reconnoiter and assert a military presence.

Of the 12,000 men who then made up the U.S. Army, approximately 1,000 were assigned to posts in Texas.[21] Of course, so small a force could not serve as an effective deterrent over so extensive a territory. A program of scouting expeditions by detachments of twenty or more men proved the most effective—or least ineffective—means for the army to fulfill its mandate in the region. Unfortunately, until 1856 the federal military force deployed in Texas was mainly infantry, and in pursuit of mounted Indians, foot troops posed little threat.[22]

Though designated "forts," the primitive installations occupied by Dodge and his fellow infantrymen during these early years were hardly worthy of the name. They consisted of rude barracks and outbuildings fashioned by the troops themselves from whatever materials might be found in the vicinity, and they included no fortifications. To guard against thievery by Indians, stables and corrals were constructed and secured with great care. Likewise, the sheds for storage of provisions were more substantial than the mud-daubed log structures occupied by the men. Food was hauled in by wagon train, brought back to the posts after successful hunts, or purchased in the vicinity. Wives and children rarely accompanied men on this tour of duty, for the mode of life was harsh and raw, even without the threat from Indians. "Texas was a new country then, and certainly an aggressive country," Dodge later wrote. "Every bush had its thorn, every animal, reptile or insect its horn, tooth or sting, every male human his revolver, and each was ready to use his weapon of offense . . . without the smallest provocation."[23] Stories of scorpions, rattlesnakes, and wild cattle abounded.

The program of studies at West Point had provided no foretaste of conditions like these, and by his own admission Dodge was "perfectly 'green' in frontier service" at the time he reached Fort Lincoln.[24] His almost two years at this post were thus a period of practical apprenticeship. The post commander, First Lieutenant James Longstreet, was a southerner like himself who had seen more than a decade of varied duty. However, on the eve of Dodge's first scout after Indians, this experienced campaigner gave him no instructions beyond stating the task he was to perform. He would need to master the details of scouting, making camp, and ensuring the safety of his men and animals in his own way. Fortunately, the sergeant of the scouting party was well versed in the plains lore Dodge had yet to acquire, and during the first week away from the post the twenty cavalrymen under his charge encountered no difficulty.

One windy afternoon later in the scout, Dodge made camp on a grassy space of ground, and having designated positions for the squad and set out a picket line for the horses, he posted the guards and turned over the command to his sergeant. Hoping to catch some fish for supper, he was becoming engrossed in his sport when suddenly he heard exclamations of alarm behind him. The campground was ablaze, with fire surging through dry grass toward the horses. Shouting an order to some men to move the animals, he plunged into the flames with the others in an effort to save the arms and equipment. The carbines began to go off, cartridge boxes exploded, and as the heat grew unbearable, the men took cover wherever they could. Fortunately, the fire raced past the camp in the high wind. Some equipment was destroyed, including Dodge's bedding and all his clothes except what he was wearing, and some rations were damaged, but no one had been injured. Within twenty-four hours all the stampeded horses had been found and returned.

In all, Dodge recalled, "we got off remarkably well, better than we deserved."[25] He knew from textbook study that the essentials of a good camp were wood, water, and grass, but the tinder-dry summer plains had taught him the first of several supplementary lessons. Experiences in later years demonstrated to him the peril that attended the sudden flooding of "dry" river bottoms, the withering force of plains "northers," the incapacitating glare of sheet ice on moonlit nights, the addling effect of attempts to discern direction without aid of a compass, the threat posed by any change in weather when crossing a sandy desert, and other caveats. He developed what he termed, using the phrenological parlance of his time, "a very large 'bump' of prudence."[26]

Pedro Espinosa

Dodge's most accomplished instructor in plains knowledge was Pedro Espinosa, a scout employed at Fort Lincoln. Espinosa was born about 1810 to Mexican parents on the Rio Grande near Laredo, Texas. When he was nine years of age, his parents were killed in a raid on their village by Comanche Indians, and he was taken captive. He grew to adulthood as an adopted member of the tribe, participating in its ceremonies, marrying and raising a family, and becoming a respected warrior. However, probably because his captors sensed in him a smoldering resentment about the fate his mother and father had suffered, he was never permitted to take part in the annual raids into Mexico. In fact, Espinosa hated the Comanches and was determined eventually to escape from them. At last, at the age of twenty-eight, he seized the opportunity during a hunting expedition in the Guadalupe Mountains. One night, while his tribesmen lay asleep, he selected a fleet horse, crept away from their camp, and by the next morning was thirty miles away. Arriving at Laredo after a long, solitary journey, he established his identity and began a new life.

As one who knew from experience the customs and patterns of Indian life in the region, Espinosa was invaluable to army authorities. Indian raiding parties had used the Bandera Pass and other routes through the Guadalupe Mountains as staging areas and avenues for escape, but Espinosa's knowledge of their activities denied them the invulnerability to pursuit and capture by army patrols that they had earlier taken for granted. Dodge learned all he could from this expert plainsman, and years afterward he paid tribute to him as a man who, "though utterly ignorant of all civilized knowledge and to whom the letters of the Alphabet were as unintelligible as Egyptian hieroglyphics, was yet full of wisdom and knowledge in all that pertained to his own mode of life, who brought up a thief was yet honest and faithful."[27]

Espinosa earned the nickname Prince of Trailers for his ability to trace the escape routes and infer the condition and intentions of Indian parties that had attacked federal property or raided civilian settlements. He was preternaturally adept, even for an Indian, at reading the "sign" scattered across a range of ground that marked the passage of some living thing. Even in the absence of a discernible trail, by patient observation he could piece together patterns of sign that yielded confident knowledge. Through this skill, Espinosa gave crucial assistance to Dodge in his first fight against Indians.

The corral fence at Fort Lincoln was formidable, consisting of thorny chaparral brush pressed tightly between posts set upright by twos at short intervals. In the summer of 1849 Indian marauders would climb over this fence at night and attempt to break it down by stampeding the horses inside. But having no success, they changed their tactics. One night an Indian who had eluded the guard was attempting to break open the bolt that held together the arms of the corral gate. Being discovered by the post blacksmith, he shot the man at once, killing him, and absconded with the rest of his party. The next morning Dodge set out in pursuit of the raiders, accompanied by a company of Texas Rangers, the volunteer militia supported by the state.[28] The party soon gave over the chase as hopeless, but eight days later Dodge set out again, this time with a troop of regulars and Espinosa.

Following the trail of a single shod horse, the guide moved ahead on his own mount, silent and apparently noting nothing worth observation. Well into the mountains, he dismounted, walked to the foot of a tree, and picked up four horseshoes. Handing them to Dodge, he observed with a grim smile that the Indian had elected to hide his trail. For the next six days the party continued on through the broken country, unable to discern the slightest mark or sign that might help Espinosa direct himself. Several times Dodge demanded of him what he was following, but the impassive guide only replied, "*Poco tiempo*" (in a while). Shortly afterward, he would point out half obliterated hoofprints along a mountain brook or else a pile of horse droppings. Moving steadily forward, dismounting occasionally to examine the ground more closely, Espinosa led Dodge and his men more than one hundred miles to a point where numerous trails came together, revealing that the fugitive Indians had first followed diverging routes and then reunited. Fifty miles further, the pursuers came undetected upon the Indian camp and attacked it. The fleeing tribesmen left behind almost all their property, including rifles, which, Espinosa explained, they considered less reliable than their bows and arrows. The avenging party now made its way back to Fort Lincoln covered with glory, its mission a rare instance of unqualified success. Its dogged pursuit effectively ended harassment of the post by Indians, for thanks to Espinosa, the garrison's capacity for retaliation had been demonstrated decisively.[29]

On their hunts together Espinosa regaled Dodge with recollections of his earlier life, including some chilling tales of Indian cruelty. He never fired his last shot at game, he said; he saved it for use on himself as a last resort, should he ever be threatened with capture by Indians. The fiendish tortures he had seen or had heard of would make self-inflicted death seem a lucky escape. He told of a murderous prank played by men of his own camp during one of their raids into Mexico. Attempting to defend his rancho against attack, one of the besieged villagers had displayed fierce courage, dispatching some of his Indian assailants with a huge axe and holding the others at bay until he was subdued by a lasso and taken captive. On the long journey northward, this sole survivor was closely guarded but treated with kindness. He was complimented on his fighting prowess and given to understand that he would be adopted into the tribe on that account. Reaching the edge of the "Llano Estacado" (Staked Plains) near the head of the Nueces River, the Comanches stopped for a few days at a water hole, where, they informed the prisoner, they wished him a dig a deep pit so that they could perform a religious ceremony.

Working with a knife and his bare hands, he completed the task in a day or two, little suspecting his captors' real intent. Early the next morning they wound a rope around him from ankles to neck, tying his arms tightly to his sides so as to render him immobile. Next, they placed him in the hole he had dug, five feet deep by three wide, and filled it with dirt, ramming it down around him. Finally they scalped him, cut away his lips and eyelids, cut off his nose and ears, and danced around him mockingly before departing and leaving him to his fate. According to Espinosa, the deviser of this torture was much admired for his inventiveness. The man buried alive would survive for probably eight more days, tormented by hungry maggots that would fill his exposed wounds and maddened by the brilliant sunlight.[30]

Experiences of Indians

Dodge heard horrific tales of this sort too often, and from too many reliable sources, to doubt them. Still, many of the Indians he encountered seemed harmless enough. They visited the fort, or the camps when on scout, simply to trade or to beg. On one occasion a Lipan Apache man offered several wildcat skins in trade for a box of matches. Having completed the transaction, he sat down and lit match after match, holding each in his fingers until forced to drop it, until all were gone.[31] Some Indians seemed no less curious about the army men, and perhaps fearful of them, than the soldiers were in return. It was an uneasy interchange between alien cultures.

In April 1851 Dodge, then in command of his company, was transferred to Fort Martin Scott, another two-company post seventy miles northeast of Fort Lincoln and a short distance from Fredericksburg, a community of German immigrants.[32] This was in the heart of Comanche country, and since the European American settlements were pushing further into territory the Indians regarded as their own, from time to time violence broke out. It was understood that the bands of Comanches and other tribes that visited the fort were at best fickle friends. Nevertheless, shortly after his arrival at the post, Dodge set aside his prudent caution and allowed himself to be hoodwinked.

A party of Lipan Apaches camped near the post and gave every evidence of friendly feeling. One day Dodge, an ardent sportsman, was out after quail with his dog in the vicinity of the Indian camp. He had come upon a large covey in good cover and was thoroughly enjoying himself when he looked round to notice a half dozen admiring Indians not far behind him. They had never seen a shotgun, and being accustomed to hunting only larger game, they were amazed to witness his hitting so small a target, and what was more, on the wing. Pleased at their evident admiration, he showed them his gun and equipment, including the tiny No. 9 shot he was using. Thereupon the chief invited him to visit their main village, on the headwaters of the Padernales River, where he said an abundance of quail and *guacalotes* (turkeys) was to be found.

Dodge returned to the post, stated the case to his commander, Lieutenant Colonel Thomas Staniford, and was granted the necessary permission. Two days later, mounted on a good horse and accompanied by one soldier, he set out with the Lipans toward their main camp. Pitching his tent beside a clump of trees nearby, he enjoyed himself afield for almost a week. At last, however, the chief came to him and warned him in Spanish that some of his young men had "bad hearts" toward white men. Taking the hint, he returned to his post without incident. Not long afterward the scales fell from Dodge's eyes when he learned that during his visit to the Indian village, certain of his obliging hosts had been murdering settlers right and left. The chief's visit to Fort Martin Scott had been a reconnaissance mission to ascertain how much military force could be put into the field against him, and his invitation to Dodge was an impromptu diversionary tactic, to ward off suspicion until all preparations were complete.[33] The young lieutenant, an unwitting pawn in a game far from peaceable, was fortunate that the consequences to himself were no worse.

Dodge thus developed a wary distrust of the "friendly" Indians he encountered. He knew that as potential enemies they deserved his respect, for they were expert horsemen, wily tacticians who avoided battle except on their own terms, and heartless victimizers of those who fell into their hands. Noble savages, à la Rousseau and Chateaubriand, they were assuredly not. Still, some of the Indians who served as guides and scouts at Fort Martin Scott were natural gentlemen—honest, faithful, and courageous. Among these was a Delaware Indian named John Connor, who had traveled widely, alone, in the western territories as far north as the British possessions and also south deep into Mexico. This hardy adventurer seemed able to recall every detail of the terrain he had passed through as if it were written down in a book.[34] Another Delaware, Black Beaver, was a no less experienced traveler who gracefully bridged the cultural gap that separated his people from the Americans. He was a valuable source of information about the country north of the army posts in Texas and the Indian tribes that ranged through those lands. Equally faithful were the several Tonkaway Indians, from southeastern Texas, who were employed as army auxiliaries.[35]

Exposed continuously to sometimes reliable, sometimes apocryphal information about Plains Indians as well as to direct contact with bands of various tribes, Dodge built up a body of miscellaneous knowledge about them, the very sketchiness of which piqued his interest. In conversations with Major Robert S. Neighbors, the U.S. agent designated to maintain contact with tribes in the region, he discussed what little was then known about the Indians' conception of a deity and an afterlife.[36] Great chiefs, he knew, were dressed in ceremonial garb upon their death, food and implements being placed beside their bodies to ensure them a propitious journey into the next stage of existence. But new insight came when during a scout he happened onto an encampment that had been the site of burial rites for a Comanche war chief. All in due form, the man's face had been painted and the crown of his head covered with a hat and feather. Horses had been slain, and testimonial bloodlettings had occurred among the survivors, and yet, strangely, the dead chief's body had been mutilated as well, dragged from the village by a rope tied around its ankles and secured to the pommel of a saddle. The skin of the back, sides, and loins had been torn away by this seemingly contemptuous treatment. The ill-assorted details of this burial remained a conundrum until several months later, when Dodge learned that the chief, though loved and feared by his people, had died ignominiously in a fit of delirium tremens. His tribesmen had fitted him out for the afterlife in traditional fashion, but only after registering their disgust at the manner of his death.[37]

Although alien and sometimes fearsome to the Americans, Indians were far from ignorant, and they had their principles. What was more, they could be funny, intentionally or otherwise. Dodge and his comrades smiled at the behavior of a Delaware Indian scout who upon receiving his bimonthly pay would invariably spend it all on a flashy suit of clothes, make a round of social calls at the officers' quarters in his new regalia, then trade the finery for a supply of bad whisky and get drunk. Another source of amusement was the Comanches' addiction to gambling. In a card game one man lost all his possessions, his children, and his wife, but he accepted the result philosophically, setting out on a raid into Mexico to recruit his fortunes.[38] Dodge was confident that the "civilized" culture he knew was superior to the "savage" one that produced behaviors so bizarre as these, but he also comprehended that the scale of value expressed in the dichotomy between civilized and savage was not valid in every respect. After all, the man he had learned the most from was Espinosa, an offspring of "greaser"[39] Mexican parents who had passed the greater part of his life among the Comanches.

By the summer of 1851 Dodge was no longer an untested newcomer, and accordingly he was assigned a stint of yeoman's labor suitable for a reliable second lieutenant: supervising construction of a seventy-five-mile wagon road to connect Fort Martin Scott with San Antonio.[40] His potential was recognized again in October, when he was made a member of the escort to the department commander, Brevet Major General Persifor F. Smith, on a three-month reconnaissance tour. Three full regiments of infantry, eight companies of mounted rifles, six of dragoons, and four of artillery acting as infantry were now stationed in the state, reflecting its importance to the nation.[41]

The frontier of settlement had moved north and west of the line of posts that had been established in 1849, and the strategic value of those installations was decreasing rapidly. Because construction of a new military cordon would soon be necessary, General Smith wished to satisfy himself as to the best sites to support the next stage of development. Already the headquarters of the Eighth Infantry were being moved from place to place as needs dictated, occupying tents in temporary camps. The regiment was performing hard, dangerous duty. In his annual report for 1851–1852, Charles M. Conrad, the secretary of war, acknowledged the challenges being faced by the army in Texas. "The troops stationed on the frontier may justly be considered as in active service," he wrote, "a service, too, in which they are exposed to all the hardships and dangers of war without its excitement to stimulate, or its hopes of

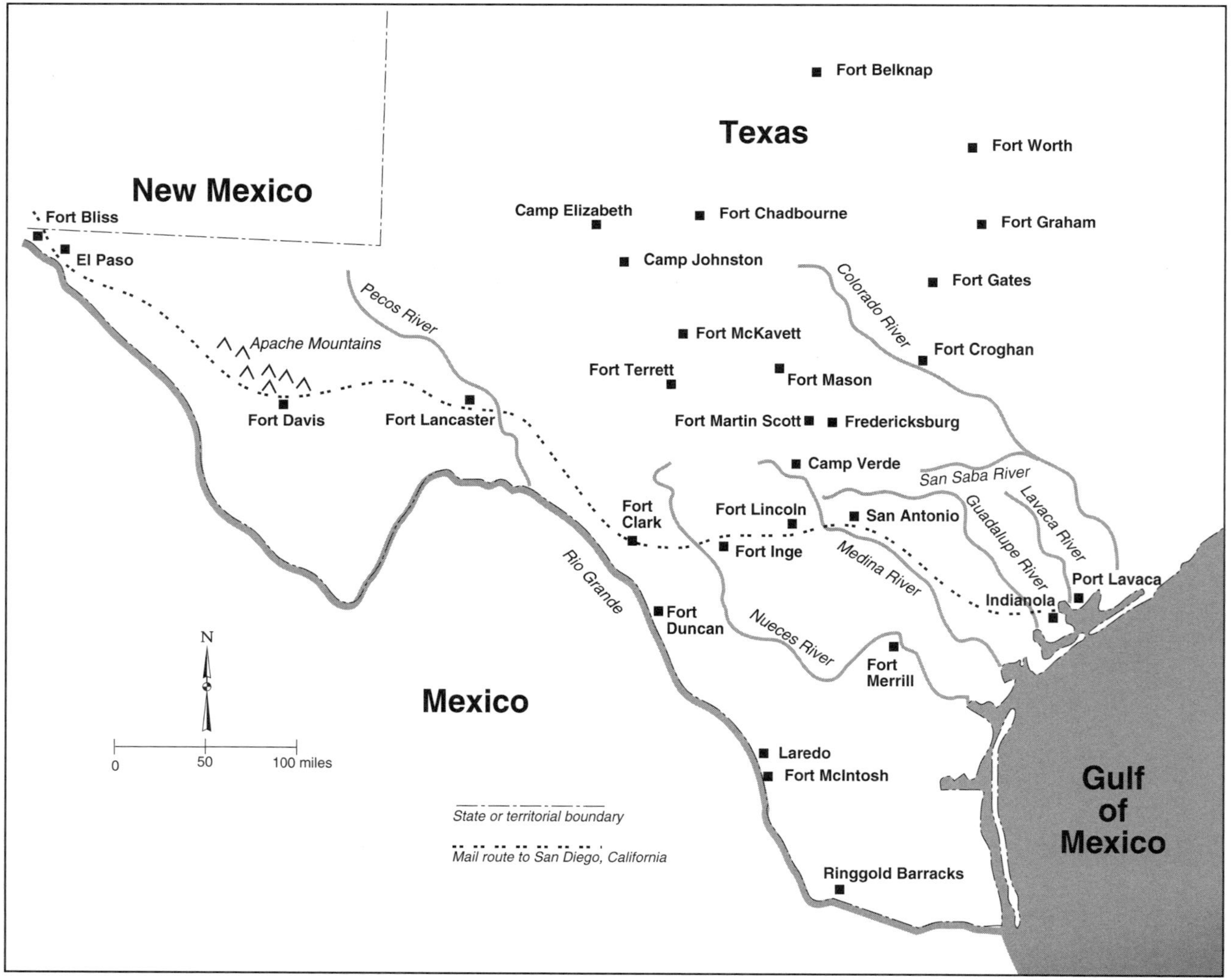

Region of Dodge's service in Texas, 1848–1856

honorable distinction to sustain them."[42] Inasmuch as Congress did not formally declare hostilities against the Indian tribes as it had against Mexico, the conflicts with Indians that now occupied the army were, paradoxically, sustained military actions but not "wars."

In a camp that later became the site of Fort Belknap, northernmost in the new line of posts, Second Lieutenant Dodge found himself overcome by a powerful new set of impressions. Then twenty-four years of age and possessed of what he later described as "a heart full of romance and head filled with Cooper's and other fictions of 'beautiful Indian maidens,'" he was stricken with love at first sight. Pa-ha-yu-ca, a prominent chief of the Northern Comanches who was peaceably inclined toward the Americans, paid a visit to General Smith, accompanied by a few warriors and his family, which consisted of several wives and one daughter. The girl, Dodge wrote years afterward, was "a vision of loveliness, apparently about fourteen, but ripened by the southern sun to perfect womanhood."

> Rather below the medium height, her form was slight and lithe, though rounded into utmost symmetry. Her features were regular, lips and teeth simply perfection, eyes black and sparkling with fun and the whole countenance beaming with good humor and bewitching coquetry. A tightly fitting tunic of the softest buckskin, reaching halfway between the hip and the knee, set off to admiration her rounded form. The bottom of the tunic was a continuous fringe of thin buckskin strings, from each of which dangled a little silver bell, not larger than the cup of a small acorn. Her lower limbs were encased in beautifully fringed leggings and her little feet in beaded mocassins of elaborate pattern. Her beautiful hair was plaited down her back, and adorned with huge silver buckles. The "part" of her hair was carefully marked with vermillion paint and a long gold (or brass) chain was twisted carelessly about her head and neck. What wonder, if with one look I literally tumbled into love. She saw my admiration, and with the innate coquetry of the sex in every clime and of every people, met my eager glances with a thousand winning airs and graces.
>
> We could not speak, but love has a language of its own. I haunted that Indian camp fire. Neither duty nor hunger could tear me away, and it was only when the Indians retired for the night, that I could return to my own tent and blankets to toss and muse, and dream of this vision of paradise. Next morning with the sun I was again with my fascination. The general gave the Indians a beef. Sometime after a warrior came and spoke to the girl. Rising from her seat, she gave me a look of invitation to accompany her. Proceeding a few yards into a little glade, we came to several Indians standing around the slaughtered beef, which was turned on its back, and the stomach split open. Taking a knife from one of the men my "beautiful Indian Maiden," plunged her lovely hand and rounded arm into the bowels of the beast, found and cut off some eight or ten feet of the "marrow-gut." Winding it about her arm she stepped to one side and giving the entrail a shake inserted one end in her

> beautiful mouth. Looking at me with ineffable content and happiness expressed in her beaming countenance, she slowly and without apparent mastication swallowed the whole disgusting mess.

Queasily, Dodge returned to his tent. His ardor had cooled, and the budding cross-cultural romance was at an end.[43]

Shortly after he rejoined his company at Fort Martin Scott, in January 1852, Dodge commanded a last winter scout from that post, which was about to be abandoned. On February 15 his company marched northwest with two other companies of his regiment, arriving two days later at a camp near Fort Mason, one of the new posts under construction. Two days later the seven other companies of the regiment arrived, and all remained in camp until the post could be made habitable. Even in the southern latitudes of Texas, exposure to the weather during winter service of this kind could be a severe trial. In mid-March Dodge and his men were at another new installation, Camp Johnston, on the North Concho River, preparing for the arrival of five more companies in mid-April.[44]

The physical strain of these duties aggravated a weakness of the lungs that had dogged Dodge even in his West Point days,[45] and by the end of April he was no longer able to remain with his company. Distressingly, as weeks passed he failed to improve. His condition was diagnosed at San Antonio as a severe attack of typhoid pneumonia, and on June 21 he was granted a sixty-day leave of absence that would permit him to recuperate at his family home in North Carolina. At the expiration of the leave period, he received an order to report to the superintendent of the General Recruiting Service at Fort Wood, New York harbor,[46] and he did so. However, a few days spent even in this physically undemanding duty weakened him noticeably. The post surgeon declared his health "not sufficiently re-established" to warrant his remaining at that station and recommended a transfer to some more southerly post.[47]

In response to that suggestion, the War Department directed Dodge to rejoin his company in Texas. However, knowing too well the dangers of such a course, he traveled to Washington, D.C. and applied there for a second medical leave of absence. Enclosing certificates of his condition from the physicians at Camp Johnston and Fort Wood, he declared his belief that a return to Texas at present "would only exagerate the disease," whereas "a few months in a propitious climate would entirely eradicate it."[48] Frustrated by his own weakness, he must have recalled the seemingly interminable weeks four years earlier, when he had traveled from south to north and back again in search of a regular regimental assignment. Fears for his life had not yet been expressed, but clearly a return to frontier duty might permanently weaken the health of this otherwise promising young officer. Upon being granted the six months' leave he had requested, Dodge returned to North Carolina to await events.[49] Fortunately, the indulgence of the authorities at Washington yielded the favorable results all had hoped for, and by spring he was back to full strength.

On June 4, 1853, he rejoined his company at Fort Chadbourne, Texas, another post that had been established the previous fall. He was still a second lieutenant, but in July he became the commander of Company G when First Lieutenant Longstreet was promoted to captain and assumed command of another company. Dodge was back in his element, and immediately he began making himself useful, leading a detachment of men on an examination of the country surrounding the post. Orders to undertake this survey had been issued from departmental headquarters in April, but until his arrival no officer had been available to complete the assignment.[50] Five years after his graduation from West Point, Dodge was thus becoming a valuable junior officer. A competent plainsman, a reliable leader who had seen service against hostile Indians, and a young man of good judgment and good nature, he had effectively completed his apprentice training. Men like Captains Longstreet, Arthur T. Lee, Larkin Smith, and Isaac V. D. Reeve were his comrades, brother officers despite their differences from him in rank and age. He had earned a place in their military family, and the Eighth Infantry was his clan.

Amusements Afield

Army life on the southern plains was not for the feeble or fainthearted,[51] but in the intervals of leisure from his duties, Dodge enjoyed comradely good times with fellow officers. Debauchery of the varieties to be found in San Antonio and El Paso del Norte was not to his taste. He was content to sip a few glasses of tolerable whisky in an evening of chat and storytelling, or as he termed it, "gassing." Reading material was scarce, but games like whist or dominoes helped pass the hours, as did letter writing and listening to music performed by soldiers or the Mexican laborers attached to the post. When on leave, or on duty in places where women were present, Dodge enjoyed dancing and flirting. At other times, the very remoteness of his duty stations and the primitive conditions there were sources of satisfaction to him. He loved the outdoors, and the unspoiled beauty of the Texas frontier was a powerful tonic.

Like other frontiersmen, Dodge smiled at the vagaries of those who had not yet acclimated themselves to life beyond the settlements. Once, for example, he was hunting with a citizen physician attached to his post when, after a few hours of travel, they encountered a heavy fog that obscured the sun and rendered landmarks invisible. Searching through their pockets, they discovered that neither had brought with him a compass. The physician, being nervous and excitable, grew alarmed at once and evinced signs of a classic plains malady—a senseless determination to keep moving. Dodge tried to calm him, explaining that they were not lost but were somewhere within a large triangle formed by two branches of a stream and a road that crossed them both. The doctor was not to be reasoned with, however, and insisted on letting his horse move forward without guidance, hopeful that the animal's instinct would carry them to safety. After hours of travel through the fog, the two men came upon the trail of two horses. Because Indians were known to be in the vicinity, Dodge thought it prudent to take a closer look. Dismounting, he at once recognized the hoofprints as their own; traveling by "instinct," they had been wandering in a great circle.

After much persuasion he convinced his companion to go into camp for the night and await a change in the weather. But the physician could not sleep and by morning was almost crazed with anxiety. Desperate to find water, that day he again insisted on letting his horse walk wherever it pleased. When he discovered that Dodge had killed a good-sized buck, he devoured chunks of its meat raw, not that he was especially hungry but that he feared he would become so. At 3:00 A.M. on that second night, Dodge was awakened by the physician, who with tears of relief in his eyes pointed out to him the stars shining brightly above them. They were saved! he cried, and insisted on breaking camp at once. By noon they had reached their post and established that they had wandered through the chaparral thickets to a point more than twenty-five miles distant.[52] But they had never been in danger, except through the panic of the man of science. He had not yet learned to keep a cool head when faced with one of the myriad vicissitudes of plains travel.

Whether the mental lapse of this tenderfoot became an object of general amusement at the time it occurred is doubtful, but on other occasions Dodge "rallied" his fellow officers when they made themselves fair targets. In later life, for example, he joked with a captain under his command about the doubtful courage of the soldiers in that officer's company. One of them had bolted in panic when he thought himself being pursued by an antelope—a proverbially timid animal.[53] Ribbing of this sort was the spice of comradeship, and those who engaged in it could expect to receive as well as to give. Once when Dodge was lost and alone on the Texas plains, he caught sight of smoke from a fire that he feared might indicate an Indian camp. Despite the considerable danger involved, rather than hurrying away, he moved forward cautiously to get a closer look, for he knew that the campfire might be that of his own party. If it was, and if it became known that he had run from it, a hailstorm of comments would be the result.[54]

Like his father, Dodge preferred humor among equals to the "quizzing" that could foment bad feeling. As a classmate of his once learned, to draw ridicule upon another could be positively dangerous. This was Second Lieutenant James M. Haynes, whom Dodge recalled as "a bright, intelligent, rollicking, roystering blade, full of kindly feeling and honorable in all his instincts, but so given to practical jokes, or 'fun,' as he called it, that he was cordially hated by many of his associates, and was a terror even to the friends who appreciated the worth hidden under all his curious foolishness." Haynes's brush with disaster occurred at Ringgold Barracks, on the Rio Grande, while he was being visited by a cousin, a physician who loved hunting but was ignorant of frontier life. Haynes stuffed the young gentleman with outrageous fables about Texas until on one morning he outdid himself, proposing for that day's activity an elephant hunt. "Do you have Elephants out here?" the cousin asked in amazement. "Plenty of them," responded his host. Shortly afterward a group of young men, parties to the prank, were afield in search of a likely herd.

Later that day the tables were turned against Haynes, almost mortally. After traveling five or six miles from the post, his guest was at a fever pitch of anticipation. Expecting much amusement, Haynes sent him out alone through a dense thicket of chaparral, when soon afterward a shot rang out, followed by loud cries for help. Galloping into an opening of an acre or two, he saw the physician being closely pursued on his horse by an angry wild bull in full charge. He hurried forward and fired his pistol, only to become the new object of the beast's rage. In one rush the bull gored his horse straight on, one horn passing completely through its body and the other being caught in the bones of its chest. Raised off the ground, the horse fell forward onto the head of the wild bull. Haynes, still astride, lay on the ground helpless, his leg wedged between the lifeless mount and the still vigorous bull. His companions feared shooting the bull, whose struggles might cause further injury, and instead they cut its jugular vein, causing it to die slowly. They then lifted the horse off Haynes, rigged a litter, and ferried him back to the post. For him and his cousin, that was the last elephant hunt.[55]

Further Experiences of Indians

At Fort Chadbourne, where Dodge was stationed from June through September 1853, he had additional opportunities to observe the Indians whose customs and beliefs so interested him. Sa-na-co, a leader of the Penateka Comanches, visited the fort several times with some of his people. He brought with him his family, which included several wives, one of whom was a girl ten years of age and another, an intelligent German woman whose husband and family had died in an Indian raid on the community of New Braunfels. When asked whether she did not wish to return to her own people, this woman replied that she no longer had friends among the whites. "Sa-na-co treats me well," she said, "and though my life is hard, it is no worse than to work for my living among strangers. I shall live the balance of my life with the Indians."[56]

Sa-na-co was peaceably disposed toward the Americans, but he wished to continue pursuing his nomadic mode of life so far as the changing conditions permitted. To that end, he used whatever means he could to obtain some of the tools, supplies, and provisions he saw at Fort Chadbourne. He would ask one officer or another to write out the name of some foodstuff, such as "sugar," then carefully put away the slip of paper he was given. He showed interest in the names of several articles of this sort, and naturally his inquiries attracted attention. The officers concluded that the old Indian was "making medicine" of some sort, as indeed he was. Several weeks after Sa-na-co had left the post, a runner from his camp arrived with a message for the post trader. It was a written order for "sugar," "coffee," and a dozen other items, each word on a line by itself and exactly counterfeited from the slips Sa-na-co had been given.[57] Enterprisingly, he was testing the power of these symbols to supply him some of the soldiers' bounty.

Another Indian leader who encamped near Fort Chadbourne was Mu-la-que-top, a Comanche who was then returning from a visit to the Kickapoo Indians far to the northeast, in present-day Oklahoma. Mu-la-que-top's people made themselves nuisances, begging incessantly, but the splendid herd of horses they had with them interested the officers, several of whom owned blooded stock. Knowing the Indians' love of gambling and proclivity for horse races, they urged Mu-la-que-top to authorize a contest, and after a few days a race was agreed to. It would pit the third-best horse of the garrison against any animal the Indians cared to match against him, at a distance of four hundred yards. According to Dodge, the Indians bet seventy dollars worth of robes and other wares against money, flour, sugar, and other American goods of equal value. "At the appointed time," he wrote in a published account, "all the Indians and most of the garrison were assembled at the track":

> The Indians "showed" a miserable sheep of a pony, with legs like churns, a three inch coat of rough hair stuck out all over his body, and a general expression of neglect, helplessness and patient suffering struck pity into the hearts of all beholders. The rider was a stalwart buck of one hundred and seventy pounds, looking big and strong enough to carry the poor beast on his shoulders. He was armed with a huge club with which, after the word was given he belaboured the miserable animal from start to finish. To the astonishment of all the whites the Indian won by a neck.
>
> Another race was proposed by the Officers and, after much "dickering," accepted by the Indians against the next best horse of the garrison. The bets were doubled and in less than an hour the second race was run by the same pony, with the same apparent exertion and with exactly the same result.
>
> The officers[,] thoroughly disgusted[,] proposed a third race and brought to the ground a magnificent Kentucky mare, of the true Lexington blood, and known to beat the best of the others at least forty yards in four hundred.
>
> The Indians accepted the race, and not only doubled bets as before, but piled up everything they could raise, seeming almost crazed with the excitement of their previous success. The riders mounted; the word was given. Throwing away his club, the Indian rider gave a whoop, at which the sheep-like pony pricked up his ears, and went away like the wind, almost two feet to the mare's one. The last fifty yards of the course was run by the pony, the rider sitting face to his tail making hideous grimaces and beckoning to the rider of the mare to come on.

The shaggy runt of a pony was an animal well known to Indians of the region. Its speed had enabled Mu-la-que-top to relieve the Kickapoos of some six hundred ponies, just as it helped his people acquire goods of all kinds from the confident folk at Fort Chadbourne.[58]

In September 1853 Dodge and his company were transferred four hundred miles south to Ringgold Barracks, where he was stationed through August 1854. Not far away was Rancho Las Laxas, adjacent to a crossing of the Rio Grande much in use by Comanche and Lipan Apache raiders. For a time Dodge occupied this position with a detachment of twenty men, charged with keeping Indians from crossing the river in either direction and also with watching for parties of American thieves said to haunt the vicinity. As protection against the fierce heat, he caused a ramada to be constructed over and around his tent, which he employed only for sleeping. His men, camped fifty yards away, protected themselves in similar fashion. The ramada permitted a free circulation of air while also securing privacy. It consisted of forked poles driven into the ground, with other poles set over the forks and leafy branches laid atop the resulting structure. For walls, poles were tied to the forks at angles, and straight sticks were woven between them.

Seated comfortably one night in his ramada, Dodge unwittingly had a narrow brush with death. With his dog lying at his feet, he was filling out quartermaster's papers when suddenly the dog made a furious rush at the door, as if to thwart an intruder. Startled, Dodge opened the door and looked out into the darkness. He called to the sentinel, who had seen and heard nothing. It appeared his dog had given a false alarm, so he scolded it, closed the door, and soon after went to bed. Later that night some Mexicans from the nearby ranch rushed into camp with the news that Indians had stolen all their horses, and the next morning Dodge sent out a guide to find the trail of the thieving party and work out the facts of the case. It was determined that on the night before, eight Indians had visited the soldiers' camp and then the ranch, all but one of them going directly to the latter place. Hoping to steal Dodge's horse, this man had crawled half a dozen times around the ramadas, watching carefully in the vain hope that the sentinel would grow careless for a moment. At one point he had come directly up to Dodge's door. Not six feet from the doorway were the prints of moccasins behind a little mesquite bush where the intruder had concealed himself when the dog made its rush.[59] The Indian could have killed the young officer, but the sound of a gunshot would have roused the entire command and probably ruined the raid on the ranch. Besides, he was in search of a more valuable prize than the life of a lone white man. As it was, the Indians got away with about twenty ponies; Dodge, with his life.

Between October 1854 and March 1855 Dodge was stationed at Fort Davis, a new post approximately 175 miles west of San Antonio on the trail to El Paso del Norte.[60] Named after Jefferson Davis, who was secretary of war between 1853 and 1857, this fort was picturesquely located near the mouth of a canyon in the Limpia Mountains. Its mission, a difficult one, was to protect emigrants and wagon trains along the trail, then in increasing use, and also to control the Comanche and Apache Indians who despoiled virtually at will in that mountainous country. Dodge's company was one of those selected to construct the five-company post, which housed the headquarters of the Eighth Infantry.[61] The approaching winter would bring severe weather, so rapid progress was at a premium. Each day from the 10th to the 30th of October, the post commander, Lieutenant Colonel Washington Seawell, ordered Dodge to search the surrounding country for timber, taking with him four soldiers as escort and also the guide, Sam Cherry. Signs of Indians were observed on several of these explorations, but since none indicated large parties, they caused little uneasiness.

At this time an episode of violence occurred that surely recalled to Dodge the warning of Pedro Espinosa against permitting oneself to be taken captive by Indians. Indeed, but for a break in the routine of duty, Dodge might easily have been the person captured. On the evening of October 30 he inquired of Lieutenant Colonel Seawell whether he should go out on scout the next day, as usual. When asked why he should put such a question, he replied that the last day of the month was muster day, the occasion of much routine administrative activity, and he thought Seawell might need him. "Of course I will," the colonel replied. "I had forgotten about muster. Detail a good sergeant to take your party tomorrow, and instruct him where you propose to go."

Duly instructed, on the next morning Sergeant Love of Dodge's company left the post as his substitute. Some concern was felt when the party failed to return that night, and early the next day the wagon master of an approaching supply train reached the post greatly excited, reporting that a man and a horse had been found dead on the road a few miles away. At once a full company of infantry was ordered out to investigate, and presently they came upon the dead body of Cherry, pinned to the ground by his horse. In a lateral canyon not far away were found Sergeant Love and three of the four privates, their bodies riddled with bullets and mutilated. Evidence scattered about made clear that they had given up their lives only after a hard fight. Thirty mounted Indians had swept down upon them at a point along Limpia Creek that precluded retreat toward the post, forcing them toward vulnerable positions in the canyon. Sensing the trap, Sam Cherry had turned and dashed through the Indians' line, galloping for his life. He was gaining distance on his pursuers when his horse stumbled and fell, breaking its neck and trapping him beneath it. In that almost helpless position he fired five of his six shots at the approaching Indians, then turned the muzzle to his own temple for the last.[62]

Dodge later learned more about this incident from a Mexican youth who had been made to interpret for the murderous Comanches when they interrogated the one surviving member of the luckless party, a drummer boy about twelve years old. His answers convinced the Indians that their plan to attack the new post would surely result in disaster to them. Angered, they turned over their informant to the squaws, who now sustained the reputation of their sex among Indians as experts at inflicting prolonged torture. Noisily reviling and tormenting the boy but taking care that he did not lose consciousness, they first stripped him and tied him securely to a tree. Next, they gathered resin-filled knots of pine and hacked them into splinters, pressing these into his flesh until he bristled like a porcupine. Setting fire to the splinters, they yelled with delight as the helpless boy screamed in pain. Insensible and near death, on the next morning the victim was bound to a horse and carried with the band as it changed position. Probably additional torments were in store for him, but after a few miles of travel he died. He was scalped and his body thrown among the rocks, where it was afterward discovered by the troops sent out in pursuit.[63]

Events of this kind were a heavy counterbalance to the satisfactions of life at a post like Fort Davis, whose surroundings Dodge's colleague Captain Arthur T. Lee described as "beautiful beyond description." Of an artistic spirit, Lee described in painterly fashion the deep canyon in which the fort was situated. The ground, he wrote, was "carpeted with the richest verdure, overshadowed by live oak, its lofty and precipitous sides festooned with perennial vines, and mantled with moss and flowers, looking out over smiling prairies and table lands, to miniature lakes, and lofty mountain peaks, that lost their summits in the clouds." Lee's appreciation of the post as an ideal "life long resting place," especially with the good company that congregated there,[64] makes macabre reading in light of the sufferings inflicted on the drummer boy. Perhaps the appeal of the scene to those who appreciated it most was the coexistence of breathtaking beauty and latent violence. In Yeats's phrase, it was "a terrible beauty."[65]

New Responsibilities

While in Texas, Dodge was assigned tasks not ordinarily considered as within the capacity of a young second lieutenant. Service at that rank and the one immediately above it, first lieutenant, was traditionally understood to be preparatory in nature, to afford an officer the experience and judgment he would eventually bring to bear as a captain, who commanded a full company of men. However, the army's limited resources necessitated compromise on that rule.[66] As early as January 1850, when he was only twenty-two years of age, Dodge commanded his company and had already served for a time as acting assistant quartermaster and acting assistant commissary of subsistence at Fort Lincoln.[67] In the first of these positions he had charge of all civilian employees at the post and of all supplies, animals, structures, and facilities for transportation sent and maintained there. In the second, he ordered, registered, and supervised the storage and distribution of all foodstuffs for consumption within the garrison. Requisitioning, receipting for, and securing all these varieties of material, issuing and monitoring the necessary contracts, and maintaining regular contact with regimental and departmental headquarters was demanding discipline for a junior officer, especially one who was also performing other duty.

The Quartermaster and Subsistence departments were separate bureaus within the army's organization, each with its own procedures and each presided over at the department level by an assistant quartermaster general or an assistant commissary general of subsistence. As the officer "acting" in their place at the post level, Dodge either worked within the administrative systems of their departments or else abided the consequences. It became a byword that, through trial and error, a post quartermaster and commissary must expect to sacrifice five hundred dollars in stoppages on his pay before he mastered the forms and procedures of these two departments.[68] However, Dodge possessed something of his father's respect for order and detail, and he seems to have performed his tasks ably. On more than one occasion following his tour of duty at Fort Lincoln he was ordered to San Antonio to serve temporarily as a quartermaster in preparation for some new initiative. Moreover, at several of his later stations he also served as post quartermaster and commissary. Once he left Texas, he was never again assigned these duties, but he understood them and comprehended their importance. He knew from experience that an able quartermaster and commissary were essential to the comfort and efficiency of a command, especially one in the field.[69]

Dodge also shared with his father the ability to perform reliably the tasks delegated to him by others. He was a good duty officer—a faithful subordinate who, without sacrificing the respect that was due him officially, worked energetically and with good judgment to comply with orders. In recognition of qualities like these, on September 1, 1854, he was appointed regimental adjutant, a responsible position ordinarily reserved for senior first lieutenants who had demonstrated unusual ability.[70] The adjutant—whether of a post, a regiment, a department, or the entire army—was the individual through whose office all official communications relating to the work of that military unit passed. Orders issued by the commanding officer—in the case of the Eighth Infantry in 1854, Lieutenant Colonel Seawell[71]—were promulgated through his adjutant. Reports and other communications directed to the commanding officer were addressed to his adjutant.

Depending upon the relationship between the adjutant and his commander and on the issues involved, the former was thus in a position to exercise considerable influence. More than any other officer in the unit where he was on duty, he was apprized of his colleagues' official activities. If, as was often said, the regiment was the true school of the soldier,[72] then the office of regimental adjutant was an advanced course of study in practical administration and executive assistantship. Dodge served in that capacity for one year, resigning it in October 1855, when he was transferred from Fort Davis to Fort Bliss, adjacent to El Paso, Texas. During that same period a vacancy at higher rank occurred within the Eighth Infantry and he was promoted to first lieutenant.[73]

Dodge had become accustomed to performing several official functions at once, and his duty at Fort Bliss continued the pattern. Besides engaging in stints of travel on "detached service," he was post quartermaster and commissary and also had charge of the regiment's recruiting depot in the growing town. Although extremely busy, he enjoyed his life at El Paso and in later years remembered it fondly.[74] He was serving under a company commander he respected, Captain Isaac V. D. Reeve, an officer seventeen years his senior who had been twice breveted for gallantry in the War with Mexico.[75] Among Dodge's military companions were First Lieutenant John P. Hatch, of the Mounted Rifles, and other congenial spirits.

A minor incident at Fort Bliss reveals something of Dodge's character and professional attitudes at this early stage of his career. Upon learning that a "grog-shop keeper" in the vicinity of the post was offering for sale quantities of coffee and sugar, neither of which commodity was then available for purchase in the public markets, he at once suspected that supplies in his care had been pilfered. Without revealing suspicion, he went through the post storehouse and confirmed the loss. The storehouse was secure, even at night, since he kept the keys to it in his own quarters. In the daytime the only person other than himself who had free access to it was an enlisted man of his company, Private George W. Reeves, whom he had detailed as acting commissary sergeant. He therefore confronted Reeves, and after much hesitation and confusion the man confessed to the theft, alleging that he had been subjected to terrible temptation in the form of rewards offered him by respectable citizens of the place. He begged Dodge not to punish him, but in vain. "As I consider that the only difference between good and bad men, is their power of resisting temptation," Dodge explained in a report, "his appeal had no effect. I immediately had all the stores counted and weighed, relieved Reeves from duty, placed him in the Guard House, and wrote out general charges against him."

Thus far the matter was straightforward: a theft of federal property had occurred, and the alleged perpetrator must be put to trial. However, it soon became clear that punishing Private Reeves through the usual system for administering military justice was impracticable. The man's term of enlistment would expire in one month, but twice that time would have to elapse before charges against him could be approved by the department commander and a general court martial be convened to hear the case. Unless something else could be done within one month, the post commander at Fort Bliss, Major Theophilus Holmes, Eighth Infantry, would be obliged to release Reeves from custody. The thief would escape punishment for his misdeed, not for lack of proof but for lack of time.

After consultation with Major Holmes, Dodge devised a plan that while not bringing upon Reeves the speedy judicial reckoning his theft deserved, would ensure an eventual investigation of it. In a garrison court-martial Reeves was found guilty of stealing goods to the value of $168 and sentenced to a brief confinement. This was the heaviest punishment within the power of a military court of the kind, which ordinarily met only to consider minor infractions. However, Reeves's guilt had been officially established, and when Dodge made out his discharge papers he wrote on the certificate that Reeves was indebted to the United States for the value of the goods he had stolen.[76] A copy of that notation would find its way to the Adjutant General's Office, and the certificate itself would accompany Reeves wherever he chose to take it. Dodge was satisfied "that in this way alone, could the matter, at that late day, be brought before higher authority for final examination and decision, and Reeves compelled to disgorge."[77]

The matter of the discharged soldier's indebtedness did eventually come before higher authority, though not exactly in the manner Dodge had intended. Later in the year the former soldier re-enlisted, this time in the Second Cavalry, and formally appealed against a stoppage that had been recorded against his future pay. Asked to comment on the merits of the case, Dodge expressed to the adjutant general his hope "that this man Reeves (who is a most unmitigated scoundrel, and should not now be in service having been convicted of stealing and dishonorably discharged) will not be allowed to profit by his unblushing robberies of the Govt. at Fort Bliss."[78] Probably he never learned that Reeves's attempt to lay claim to his ill-gotten gains proved unsuccessful, but he would have been pleased at the result. As he informed a colleague a few years afterward, he was not shy of a fight when the right and his sworn duty as an officer were on his side.[79] In the absence of an effective internal system to protect the army from the larceny of persons like Reeves, he was willing to devise an ad hoc solution and bear personal responsibility for it.

In July 1856 Dodge's youthful service in Texas came to a close when he and another officer, First Lieutenant Edward D. Blake, were assigned to duty with the General Recruiting Service in New York City as their regiment's quota of personnel for that purpose.[80] As he must have recognized, his years on the western frontier had exerted a powerful formative influence on him. Not only had he formed bonds of brotherhood with fellow officers, but he had come to respect the unique abilities of other persons who formed part of the military contingent in Texas—native guides like Pedro Espinosa, veteran noncommissioned officers like Sergeant Love, and the enlisted men who, unlike Private Reeves, shared his devotion to the service. He had become a thorough plainsman, an experienced combatant against Indians, a resourceful builder of posts, an explorer, an office administrator—in all, a versatile officer. Additionally, he had accumulated a fund of knowledge about Plains Indians and their sometimes admirable, amusing, or barbarous ways and beliefs, and he was interested in learning more. If army service had thus far denied him the satisfactions of marriage and a family, it had given him a great deal. It would be good to return east, but he had mixed feelings as he bid farewell to his comrades at El Paso.

2

Toward a Crossroads

On July 1, 1856, the authorized strength of the U.S. Army stood at 17,894 officers and men. This number represented a slight increase over the previous year that had been approved by Congress chiefly to facilitate operations in New Mexico and further west, in the Department of the Pacific. However, the army's actual strength was only 15,562,[1] an absurdly small force to protect an expanding nation that counted 30 million citizens. The General Recruiting Service, where Dodge was now assigned, bore major responsibility for overcoming the 2,000-man deficit in authorized manpower, but it faced serious obstacles to the effort. Not only did the American public consider full-time military duty a not particularly worthy pursuit, especially in the enlisted ranks, but more practical considerations also deterred potential recruits. Among the discouragements were a five-year term of enlistment, hard conditions of service in remote and dangerous localities, and monthly pay for an infantry private of only eleven dollars.[2] In many instances the ranks of the army were a place of refuge, or concealment, for men who had no other options. Dodge's thieving subordinate Private Reeves re-enlisted simply because he lacked the wherewithal to return East.[3]

Often the men who wished to enlist in the army were below the minimum age of eighteen years or else were unfit for service. Of 10,034 recruits who presented themselves in the twelve months ending September 30, 1856, more than half were declared ineligible. Meanwhile, the aggregate force was subject to constant attrition, through expiring terms of enlistment, death, and—by far the most frequent cause—desertion. Many absconded soldiers proved to have joined the army simply as a means to obtain an outfit of clothing and equipment and secure transportation to a duty station where they could desert and set off on their own. In 1856, "casualties"—that is, losses from the army rolls from all causes—included 6,090 men, of which 3,223 were by desertion.[4] Even among those men who kept their bargain with Uncle Sam and served out full terms of duty, devotion to the republican principles of the United

States often did not rank high among their motives. Throughout Dodge's era the army was weakened by poor morale within its enlisted force.

Recruiting stations were of two kinds: first, nineteen permanent rendezvous maintained by the General Recruiting Service, located in cities; and second, offices of the several regiments and of the mounted service, located at other points throughout the states and territories. Having recently had charge of the Eighth Infantry's recruiting station at El Paso,[5] Dodge was reasonably familiar with procedures when he reported in New York City to the superintendent of General Recruiting, Major Electus Backus, Third Infantry. The New York depot was the army's principal facility for the induction, training, and distribution of recruits.[6] While on duty in the city, Dodge divided his time between two stations, the first of which was Fort Columbus, on Governors Island, New York harbor. To ensure the comfort of men who occupied barracks there while they received preliminary instruction, this post was kept in first-class order. Dodge's living quarters were at the fort, its accommodations a princely contrast to the ramadas and mud-daubed huts that had been his lot before. At Fort Columbus he assumed some responsibility for training the recruits, but on occasion he also conducted groups of men who had completed the program to Fort Hamilton, at the entrance to the harbor, or to other military sites in the area.[7] His second duty station was the office of the General Recruiting Service in Chatham Street, Manhattan. Here he supervised the arrangements to supply information to interested persons and perform initial screening and mustering-in. The work was routine, but he was given considerable latitude in conducting office business in the manner he thought best.[8] Recruiting details were a necessary fact of life for brief terms in the careers of junior officers like himself.

In order "to attend to business which may be of the greatest importance to me," in November 1856 Dodge applied to the adjutant general for a two-month leave of absence. Probably the "business" he wished to transact related to an inheritance of property his mother stood to receive.[9] Major Backus did not support the application wholeheartedly, but he admitted that Dodge's presence was "not very necessary" just then, and as a result Dodge was granted an abbreviated leave of twenty days.[10] Evidently Backus was finding him useful at Chatham Street, for upon his return from leave he no longer took part in the instruction of recruits; instead, he reported for duty at the city recruiting office alone.

In January 1858, after almost ten years on the army rolls, Dodge drew the attention of the adjutant general to errors in the published identification of him in the annual *Army Register*. In recent issues his name had been listed as "Richard J. Dodge"—incorrect as to the middle initial. Lest there be continued confusion between the letters *I* and *J*—a real possibility, since the two resembled each other in cursive script and were often indexed as one—he emphasized that "the initial of my middle name is *I*, the *ninth* letter of the alphabet, *not* J as printed." Moreover, he continued, he was both "born in" North Carolina and also "appointed from" that state. These two details were ordinarily noted in *Register* entries for commissioned officers, but the latter had been omitted from the one on him. In response to his testy declaration, Colonel Samuel Cooper, the adjutant general, promised that the errors would be corrected in future editions.[11] The facts were shown properly in the 1859 *Register* and thereafter, but uncertainty about Dodge's name persisted for years to come. References to him in newspapers and magazines, and often in official records, specified *J* rather than *I* as his middle initial. But this proved only one facet of the lasting uncertainty about his name, and consequently his identity. Beginning in the mid-1860s and for the rest of his lifetime, he would be confused with a Civil War leader, Major General Grenville Mellen Dodge.[12]

Dodge's presence in New York City enabled him to visit often with members of his extended family who lived there and in communities to the north. In 1854 his aunt Helen Irving and her husband, who lived in Tarrytown, had visited James and Susan Dodge in North Carolina, and in 1857 the elder Dodges reciprocated. For a time they were guests at Sunnyside, the rural home of Washington Irving, where James Dodge's former employer Ebenezer Irving now resided.[13] First Lieutenant Dodge joined his parents in some of their reunions with family and friends, and on one of these occasions he introduced them to a young lady he had met, Julia Rhinelander Paulding. Coincidentally, this young woman's given name and surname were identical with that of a member of Dodge's family. The late Julia Paulding Irving had been a relation of James Dodge by marriage—the wife of his respected uncle, William Irving.[14] The happy coincidence instanced the network of relationships that bound together this group of families. Sons and daughters often married their cousins and named their offspring after forebears or elders. Thus First Lieutenant Dodge's Aunt Helen was married to her cousin, Pierre M. Irving, a son of William and Julia Irving. Julia Rhinelander Paulding was herself the daughter of two cousins, Frederick William Paulding and Maria Paulding.[15]

Like the Dodges and the Irvings, members of the Paulding family had a proud tradition as patriots in Revolutionary times and were known for their public service since. Julia's ancestor John Paulding was a Revolutionary hero, one of the captors of the British spy Major John André. Her uncle James Kirke Paulding was a leading American author who had served between 1838 and 1841 as secretary of the navy. Her paternal grandfather, William Paulding, had been mayor of New York City. Julia could thus appreciate the personal distinction of a young army officer like Dodge, and it presently became clear that he was impressed with her as well. Eleven years younger than he, she was a petite, bright-eyed brunette whose beauty and social graces utterly captivated him. Ebenezer Irving, writing to one of his daughters in November 1857, reported that Dodge and "Mr. Fredk Paulding's charming daughter Julia" were "so well pleased with each other that they have concluded to take each other for better or worse for life."[16]

A few days after Ebenezer Irving had written his pleasant announcement of the approaching marriage, Dodge's parents were obliged to end their New York visit. A portion of the Williams estate had fallen to Susan Williams Dodge, and arrangements connected with the bequest required their presence at home without delay. They and their daughters were therefore absent from New York City when, on March 3, 1858, the wedding of Dodge and Julia went off. The ceremony, at Calvary Church, was performed by the much admired Episcopal clergyman Dr. William Creighton of Tarrytown, and according to Ebenezer it was "quite a brilliant affair." Soon afterward the elder Dodges and the rest of the bride's new southern relations had an opportunity to greet Julia, for Richard and she traveled to North Carolina on their honeymoon.[17] For Dodge, the wedding journey was one part of an auspicious concurrence of events. Not only had he been granted a twenty-five-day leave of absence that took effect on the day of his marriage,[18] but in all probability he would no longer be attached to the General Recruiting Service upon his return to duty. If confirmed by the secretary of war, his new assignment would be a very desirable one, as instructor of infantry tactics at West Point. Maritally and militarily, his star was in the ascendant.

As he had hoped, by Special Order 61, issued at army headquarters on April 23, 1858, Dodge was assigned to duty at the military academy.[19] Colonel Richard Delafield, the superintendent of West Point, clearly welcomed the appointment, having in fact requested it the previous summer. Objection had since been voiced to the poor preparation of some officers detailed as assistants to the regular faculty, especially in the academic subjects, and the availability of Dodge would enable Delafield to replace an unseasoned instructor who had graduated only the previous year, Brevet Second Lieutenant James Claflin, with an officer of ten years' varied experience.[20] Of course, much of Dodge's field duty in Texas had taught him lessons about military tactics that lay outside the current curriculum, and the system of infantry tactics taught to cadets since 1854 differed somewhat from what Dodge had learned as a cadet.[21] Still, the changes were not so extensive as to cause him confusion, for like all infantry officers worthy their commissions, he knew his "Tactics" virtually by heart. That is, he knew in detail the evolutions for drill and deployment that were prescribed in printed manuals on the subject. The study of tactics might be unexciting in itself, but it was considered essential military training. It minimized the possibility of disorganization under battle conditions by supplying a known response to every contingency. His West Point classmate John C. Tidball likened an instructor of tactics with his text to a man of God with his testament, intimating that of the two, the former probably had the better command of his book.[22]

Dodge thrived during his more than two years of duty at West Point. His duties in the section room and on the parade ground brought him into regular contact chiefly with fourth-year cadets. James H. Wilson, a member of the Class of 1860, later remembered him with admiration as a "model instructor" and an "excellent disciplinarian" whose "magnificent presence" enhanced the air of authority he projected.[23] He was paid the salary and living allowance of a captain and was permitted to occupy one of the newly constructed stone cottages on the grounds.[24] He and Julia had access to the receptions and other entertainments that made up social life at the academy, and they won local notice when, on February 27, 1859, Julia gave birth to a son,

Frederick William Paulding Dodge, named after his maternal grandfather. A few months after the birth of Freddie, Julia and one of Dodge's North Carolina cousins called with the infant at Sunnyside, in Tarrytown. According to an observer on that occasion, there were "great demonstrations about the baby."[25]

Having acquitted himself well at West Point, by the summer of 1860 First Lieutenant Dodge had almost every reason to anticipate a bright future in the army. True, before many more months he would be ordered to rejoin his regiment, which would necessitate parting with his wife and son for a time, but quite possibly the separation would be brief. After all, the Eighth Infantry had done its share of hard frontier service and was due for a change of station. Dodge's sole cause for concern was political—namely, the growing antagonism between the northern and southern states. Sectional tension ran high at West Point,[26] and as the presidential election of 1860 drew near, the specter of perhaps violent political upheaval stalked behind it. Should the Republican candidate, Abraham Lincoln, be elected to the presidency, some states might secede from the Union in protest and to protect their sovereign rights. What consequences such an unprecedented fracturing of the federal union would have for the army was uncertain, but they could be grave.

By an order dated August 29, 1860, Dodge was relieved from duty at West Point upon the arrival there of his replacement, First Lieutenant John W. Forney, Tenth Infantry, and was directed to rejoin his company at that time.[27] Army authorities were keenly aware of the potential for violence in the eastern states, yet at the same time the prospect of a nationwide military emergency was as yet all but unthinkable in the Adjutant General's Office, as elsewhere. In any case, Dodge's return to the western frontier was necessary to help restore order within his own regiment. The proper commander of Company G, Captain Joseph Selden, had not served with it in the past thirteen years and still showed no inclination to join it.[28] Most recently the unit was commanded by Second Lieutenant James Van Horn, an 1858 graduate of West Point who had been unable to maintain due discipline acting alone. Riotous behavior had broken out in the ranks, resulting in the company's temporary disbandment and the transfer of its men elsewhere within the regiment.[29] It would be Dodge's task to restore order and reconstitute Company G.

Anticipating this assignment but also apprehensive about the threat to civil order in the nation at large, early in October Dodge applied to the adjutant general to be relieved from duty at West Point on November 1, well before the expected arrival of First Lieutenant Forney. By that date, he explained, his duties for the school term would be completed and he would be free to begin his usual thirty-day leave of absence. His not being present during November should cause no inconvenience to the academy, since Forney was expected to be on hand by December 1. Dodge went on to state three "reasons" for requesting this adjustment to his orders. First, breaking up housekeeping and removing his family from the military academy in the depth of winter would be difficult. Second, midwinter was the best time of year for travel to Texas, which he could do once he had provided for his wife and son. And third, he had "important private business which it is absolutely necessary to adjust before I go to the frontier, and which I cannot do while at the Military Academy." The latter consideration, though couched in general terms to the adjutant general, was the heart of the matter.[30] No doubt Dodge had detailed his concerns to Colonel Delafield and also to Lieutenant Colonel René de Russy, the commandant of cadets: he needed to make timely provision in North Carolina for the welfare of his parents and unmarried sisters during this period of threatened conflict.

The possibility that his rather detailed rationale for leaving West Point was a ruse to assist him in pursuing a disloyal purpose must have occurred to his commanding officers. The number of men, officers and cadets alike, breaking off their official relations to the army and returning to their homes in the South was already a cause for alarm. However, those who took that step almost invariably did so openly.[31] Dodge was a southerner, but he was not a man to skulk away under a false pretense, and moreover he was no friend of secession. Neither Delafield nor De Russy questioned his motives to the adjutant general, nor did they raise serious objection to compliance with his request. As a result, Dodge was granted a leave of absence through February 1, 1861, it being understood that upon his return to duty he would depart for Texas.[32]

The deteriorating political conditions that followed the election of Abraham Lincoln to the presidency rapidly altered many calculations, including the assessment of where First Lieutenant Dodge could be most useful. Outraged by the ascendancy of Lincoln, influential southerners vowed to repulse by whatever means necessary all efforts by the new administration to reduce their political influence and undermine their cherished way of life. Under the outgoing president, James Buchanan, the federal government pursued no policy to resolve the crisis other than to temporize. One after another of Buchanan's cabinet members resigned, and beginning with South Carolina on December 20, one southern state after another proclaimed its independence of the national union. The possibility of bridging the gulf of distrust and resentment that divided North from South grew remote. On February 4, 1861, a group of six disaffected states declared themselves the Confederate States of America, and two weeks afterward a former senator from Mississippi, Jefferson Davis, was inaugurated as president of the new nation. Within days, Davis had created a Confederate Department of War and issued a call, enthusiastically answered, for a military force of 100,000 men. Open hostilities had not broken out, but the determination of the Confederacy to defend itself by force if necessary was beyond question.

These were the political circumstances that evolved during Dodge's extended stay in North Carolina. His home state had not yet seceded, nor had Virginia, but the strong possibility of their doing so was clear. His reunion with some family members and friends must have been strained, for as an army officer he represented to some of them the tyrannical force of the federal government. His close relations were deeply divided in their allegiances. His father naturally identified to a degree with the northern states, and moreover he favored preserving the national union. Susan Williams Dodge's extensive family, the Williamses, were deeply committed to their home state and would support armed defense of North Carolina against invasion from the north. Chalmers Glenn, First Lieutenant Dodge's brother-in-law and a promising lawyer, favored secession and would soon be elected first lieutenant of a volunteer company, the Rockingham Rangers.[33] An uncle, James R. Chalmers, would become a Confederate general.[34] Dodge could not set aside his attachment to his home and fond regard for many of its inhabitants, but at the same time he knew himself to be virtually in enemy territory. His parents, peaceable folk who were secure in their Episcopal faith, did not wish to leave their longtime home. He could only hope that their standing in out-of-the-way Surry County would protect them from violence, should it break out. But as events took their course, after this visit he would not see them again for six more years.

Dodge's leave of absence was extended twice, through March 20, 1861.[35] During that confused period he was offered a commission as brigadier general in the Confederate army—a flattering recognition of his potential as a military leader, but he declined it.[36] Committed to the Union cause, he reported for duty on schedule, at Fort Wood, Bedloe's Island, New York harbor.[37] By that time the folly of sending him to Texas, fifteen hundred miles distant from a verging crisis in the eastern states, was manifest. The wiser course was to bring the Eighth Infantry east as soon as possible, so as to prepare it for operations there. In fact, authorities in Texas were already insisting on this transfer. On February 1 a convention of delegates voted overwhelmingly to dissolve the state's ties to the Union, and shortly afterward the commissioners of the former state demanded that all military posts and other property of the federal government be delivered into the possession of their representatives. In an act generally considered treasonous by supporters of the Union, Brigadier General David E. Twiggs, commander of the Department of Texas, capitulated. He ordered the almost 3,000 troops then stationed in his department to march without delay to the Gulf Coast, where they could be transported back to federal soil.[38]

In dismay, but in compliance with the general's order, the widely dispersed units of the Eighth Infantry thus formed themselves into three battalions and began marches from as far west as El Paso toward San Antonio, and thence to the seaport of Indianola. The Texas commissioners guaranteed that the departing troops would not be interfered with in any way. They declared that the men of the Eighth had become "our friends" through their years of service to the state, and that "every consideration" was due them.[39] In a manner that typified these strange weeks before the outbreak of war, the commissioners thus bade a gracious farewell to the armed forces of a potential enemy nation. If the departure of the regiment from Texas could be accomplished as planned, ships carrying its troops should arrive at New York harbor in late April.

Coincidentally, before leaving West Point, Dodge had applied for an appointment as assistant adjutant general at any one of the army's departmental headquarters, which would in all likelihood have resulted in his being assigned elsewhere than in Texas.[40] This was an effort to reconcile his commitment to army service with his responsibilities as a husband and father, and possibly also to satisfy Julia's taste for genteel surroundings. The Adjutant General's Office took no action on the initiative, but on March 18, two days before Dodge returned to duty at Fort Wood, it received a forwarded letter in support of the appointment. Moses Hicks Grinnell, a former Republican congressman from New York and a relation of Dodge's by marriage, had taken up the matter with his friend the secretary of state, William H. Seward. Grinnell praised Dodge as "a man of as high toned character as any in the army, and for reputation as an officer . . . distinguished for marked ability and cleverness." He also noted that Dodge "has a large circle of friends" in New York City who would be "exceedingly gratified" if a suitable position could be found for him at some headquarters.[41] However, by the time this statement of friendly support was received, both Dodge and his army superiors had formed other plans.

Anticipating the early arrival of his regiment, Dodge applied to Washington for authority to reorganize his disbanded company at once, using new recruits. Because Fort Wood housed "every facility . . . for the organization and instruction" of troops, he hoped to have a new company ready for service as soon as the rest of the Eighth Infantry reached New York City. Any effort to make up for the army's lamentable lack of manpower seemed desirable,[42] and Dodge was promptly authorized to move ahead with his plan. Brevet Lieutenant General Winfield Scott, the general in chief, cautioned that Dodge must make use of whatever recruits were forwarded to him by the General Recruiting Service rather than attempting to fashion an elite unit. But when Dodge asked to select his noncommissioned officers from the pool of "reserved recruits," those identified as possessing special competencies, his request was again speedily approved.[43] Thus in the early days of April 1861 he assumed command of the new Company G, Eighth Infantry, and set about molding it into an efficient fighting unit.

Dodge's thirteen years of experience had well prepared him to perform that task, but what duty might follow remained a matter for uneasy concern. To fight Indians and outlaws in Texas was one matter, but to take up arms against his neighbors, friends, and relations, quite another. He found that the comfortable security he had enjoyed only months before had been transformed into a limbo of rootless apprehension. Dodge was now cut off from part of his family, from his regimental comrades, and from his expectation of an honorable military career free from painful moral choices such as those he now faced. He stood on the verge of promotion to a captaincy just as the army he was proud to serve made hasty preparations for fratricidal war. On an island in the harbor of Charleston, South Carolina, the Union garrison of Fort Sumter was by now all but helpless, being surrounded by Confederate artillery and running low on supplies. Meanwhile, on Bedloe's Island in New York harbor Dodge drilled his men, in that small way helping the Union army prepare for fight.

Part Two

The Civil War and Its Aftermath, 1861–1867

The threat of war between the states had forced upon Dodge a choice between the region that had nurtured him in youth and the nation that claimed his allegiance as an army officer. The outbreak of hostilities confronted him with another painful dilemma. His devotion to the Union cause and to the army were firm, and an opportunity now lay open to distinguish himself as a soldier in the field. However, an experience of battle against the Confederate foe brought home to him the "horrid necessity" of mortal combat against friends and family members.[1] How was he to reconcile his personal feelings with his military duty?

In communication with his superior officers, Dodge fashioned a practical solution to this problem. During the greater part of the war, he served behind the lines, participating in programs to train, recruit, and reinforce the Union armies. These duties denied him the military glory that might have led to rapid elevation in rank, but they did allow him to contribute significantly to the war effort. As years passed, attracting new recruits grew increasingly difficult, owing to the resistance of disloyal elements, the unwillingness of citizens to perform military service, and political infighting. Dodge's effort to realize the goals of the embattled Union government within a deeply flawed system for recruitment tested his energy and sometimes his patience, even as it sharpened his organizational skills. Meanwhile, his effective imposition of federal authority in places where state and local leaders were jealous of their own sway brought him to the attention of the War Department as a useful official. As the conflict neared its close, he was assigned to duty in New York City, a center of population and wealth that remained vitally important to the Union but where powerful interests continued to resist the recruitment of volunteers and the "dreaded draft."[2]

In the aftermath of the Civil War, Dodge's familiarity with the processes of mustering-in and organizing the volunteer armies proved valuable to the government as it mustered them out again. His skills as a frontiersman lay in abeyance during the war years, but he added to his credentials as an army officer by his demonstrated flair as an administrator and his energetic approach to the duties assigned him.

3

"The Horrid Necessity"

Open conflict between the Union and the Confederate States of America broke out on April 13, 1861, with the firing of Confederate artillery on Fort Sumter. Two days later President Lincoln issued a call for the loyal states to supply 75,000 volunteers for three months of service to help quell the armed rebellion. Added to the regular army's puny complement of 15,215 men,[1] the volunteer force would signify by its existence the resolution of the several Union states to fight together as one. An undeclared war now existed, with volunteer regiments rapidly being organized in both the North and the South.

Under these altered circumstances, the Confederate state of Texas reneged on the pledge of its commissioners to offer unimpeded exit to the federal troops formerly stationed within its boundaries. Detachments of its state militia or Confederate troops surrounded the three commands of the Eighth Infantry one by one and forced them to surrender. On April 22, Company C, with the headquarters staff and regimental band, were captured in San Antonio and made prisoners of war. Unaware of the events at Fort Sumter, the officer in command had marched into town without suspecting that enemies awaited him. Two days later Companies A and D were taken prisoner at Indianola, and on May 9 the six remaining companies, under command of Captain Isaac V. D. Reeve, were suddenly confronted by a large force west of San Antonio and forced to surrender. Moving with his men along a public road, Reeve was also unacquainted with the imminent danger.[2] A message of warning had been sent to him in care of Pedro Espinosa, Dodge's former guide and tutor, but Espinosa was captured. The incriminating note being discovered on his person, he was summarily shot.[3]

On May 3, 1861, Dodge was promoted to captain, Eighth Infantry, but within a few days of that action his regiment effectively ceased to exist. Only those few of its officers who, like him, were on detached service or leave of absence in the Union states were available for duty.[4] Worse yet, the greater number of Dodge's regimental comrades cast their lots with the Confederate cause. Fourteen of the regiment's thirty-three officers, including Captain James Longstreet and First Lieutenant George E. Pickett, had resigned before the war and would accept commissions in the rebel army. Eleven others, among them Dodge's former company commander, Captain Joseph Selden, and his former post commander at Fort Bliss, Major Theophilus W. Holmes, would eventually take the same action.[5] Exactly when Dodge learned of the fate that had befallen the Eighth Infantry in Texas is uncertain, for confident knowledge of events deep in enemy territory was difficult to secure. All that stood clear was the inevitability of violence to come.

During May, Dodge remained in garrison with his company at Fort Wood, awaiting orders. Restless, in midmonth he requested a leave of absence for an indefinite term, intending to take part in the consolidation of volunteer forces then under way without sacrificing his commission as a regular army officer.[6] He hoped to command a regiment of volunteers, probably from the state of New York, where he had influential friends who would support his appointment. But the principle of permitting officers to set aside their duties in this manner had not yet been embraced at army headquarters,[7] and no action was taken in the matter.

President Lincoln's call for ninety-day volunteers yielded a response well in excess of the 75,000 men he had asked for. Bodies of state militia streamed toward Washington, encamped there, and in the absence of other duties, engaged in daily drills, awaited supplies, and took in the sights of the capital. Their morale ran high, but their military preparedness was almost nonexistent. Meanwhile, when the state of Virginia allied itself with the Confederacy, on April 25, it became enemy territory. Military prudence dictated that Union troops should occupy the south side of the Potomac River, opposite the national capital, as a buffer against Confederate assault. Accordingly, a military Department of Northeastern Virginia was created, and most of the volunteer units went into camp across the river. Observers likened the plains and slopes around Arlington and Alexandria to nomadic tent cities. Meanwhile, to the south, Confederate units gathered. Lincoln, fearing that a contest between armies of this size would extend beyond the ninety-day enlistment of his initial wave of volunteers, issued a second call, for 42,034 more troops, this time for three years—or if less, for the duration of the war.[8]

How to shape the new volunteer units into effective combat forces was a vexing problem for the president and his advisers. Not only did the troops require rations, clothing, equipment, and transportation, but they must have knowledgeable leadership. The enlisted men among them were private citizens who valued their personal freedom; they must somehow be taught a habit of obedience and imbued with respect for their military superiors. From his long experience, General Scott held volunteer troops in low estimation, and to meet the present contingency he favored enlarging the regular army, training all recruits up to a professional level of soldiership before sending them into battle.[9] Given the exigent needs of the times, however, his views were not practicable. Lincoln was convinced that the union of the several states must be defended primarily by the states themselves, under federal guidance. If the quality of the soldiery they supplied needed improvement, efforts would be made to achieve that aim. At any rate, the loyal citizenry must be encouraged to express its will by participating in the war effort. Units of army regulars were dispersed from coast to coast at present, and in any case their number was inadequate to deal with the already evident might of the Confederacy.

Public opinion in the northern states favored a campaign to put down the Confederate rebellion at an early date. Moreover, since the "ninety-day men"—as those volunteers who enlisted for ninety days were called—would complete their terms of service by late summer, they wished to take part in some offensive action before returning to their homes. Unfortunately, contingency plans for military action in the event of a crisis of this kind had never been drawn up, nor had the overall organization of a largely volunteer federal army been given more than token consideration until recently.[10] Equipment remained scarce, and facilities for the housing and training of incoming volunteers were few. Recognizing these and other impediments, Lincoln and his advisers moved ahead with a plan for summer operations that would at least manifest the Union's resolve. After all, within a few miles of Washington some 35,000 rebel troops were making vigorous preparations of their own. Brigadier General P. G. T. Beauregard of the Confederate army would soon assume command of a large force approximately forty miles to the east, at the junction of two railroads near Manassas, Virginia. Further in that direction, at the northern end of the Shenandoah Valley, Major General Joseph E. Johnston commanded another army that had captured the federal arsenal town of Harpers Ferry, Virginia.[11] Successful engagements against these two generals would have considerable strategic value, perhaps opening the way for a movement to threaten the Confederate capital at Richmond, Virginia.

As part of Union operations in the region, Dodge and his company moved from place to place, attached first to a corps under Major General Robert Patterson, then to a second force under Major General Irvin McDowell, the commander of the Army of Northeastern Virginia. Company G, Eighth Infantry, formed part of an eight-company brigade that was joined in July by a battalion of marines, a detachment of dragoons, and six batteries of artillery. This ill-assorted accumulation of regulars numbered about 800 men, a tiny fraction of the 35,000 that comprised the federal strength in the area.[12] On June 6 Dodge reported with his men to Colonel George A. Thomas, Second Cavalry, who then commanded the First Brigade of Patterson's army. Patterson was responsible for establishing federal control over territory immediately south of the Potomac River and at least as far west as Harpers Ferry. Thus on June 15, marching south from Chambersburg, Pennsylvania, Dodge reached Williamsport, Maryland, crossed the river, and proceeded two miles into Virginia before going into camp, all without incident. On the following morning he received orders to end the occupation of the vicinity. An anticipated attack by Johnston along this line had not materialized, and it soon developed that the Confederate general had withdrawn all his forces near the river. Harpers Ferry was now in Union possession, to be guarded by Patterson. It was believed that Patterson might also be able to move south toward Winchester, Virginia, where Johnston was expected to remain for a time.

Meanwhile, the concentration of other Confederate forces nearer Washington demanded an early response. General Scott believed that the presence of regular army troops would have a settling effect upon the motley aggregation of militia units and volunteer regiments under McDowell then in camp at Arlington. Dodge and his company therefore recrossed the Potomac, marched to Hagerstown, Maryland, and boarded a train for the capital, where they arrived early on the morning of June 20. During the next two weeks they remained in the city as a provost guard, helping keep order in the days leading up to an emergency session of Congress scheduled to meet on July 4. Beginning on July 5 they encamped near McDowell's headquarters at the Custis-Lee mansion, Arlington Heights, Virginia.[13]

The major federal campaign of the summer was about to begin.[14] In consultation with General Scott, McDowell had developed a plan to strike a decisive blow at the Confederate force under Beauregard at Manassas, little more than two days' march away from Arlington. Provided only that Patterson could deny Johnston the opportunity to join Beauregard, the prospect for success looked bright. Although as yet untested, McDowell's army was a large one, approximately 40,000 men in five divisions. Its cavalry was weak, numbering only 400, but its artillery would be all he could reasonably hope for. McDowell understood that his wagon transportation would encounter difficulty along the rutted paths that led to the anticipated field of battle, but at least the maps in his possession made clear where those troubles were most likely to occur. Unfortunately, owing to delay the rebels were already apprized of his general intention. He hoped to seize the Manassas Gap Railroad at a point south of the Confederate army and so cut off Beauregard's chief supply line from Richmond, forcing him to retreat in whatever direction he could. To deny him this result, the rebels had dug earthworks, prepared gun emplacements, and secured reinforcements, but the initiative was still his.

Confident assurance of success in the coming action lent a holiday atmosphere to Washington, D.C., as McDowell's army prepared for its march westward. The force was actually impeded in its movement by women who lined the roads to offer bouquets and sweets. Citizens accompanied the troops, intending, as they said, to "watch the fun." On July 17 Dodge's company reached Fairfax Court House, seventeen miles from Arlington, and after a hot and dusty march on the next day it bivouacked adjacent to a road known as the Warrenton Pike, one mile east of the village of Centreville. The battalion of regulars was commanded by Major George Sykes, Fourteenth Infantry, an 1842 graduate of West Point and an experienced campaigner.[15] Sykes's battalion formed part of a brigade, one of two that comprised McDowell's second division. The brigade was under the command of Colonel Andrew Porter, Sixteenth Infantry, and the division was commanded by Brigadier General David Hunter.

An incident on the night of July 19 revealed the tension in camp as the battle drew near. By accident, perhaps while assembling his gun, someone fired a shot. Immediately a fusillade of answering rifle reports rang out, all from friendly forces but all potentially lethal. An officer later recalled this outburst as one of the hottest storms of gunfire he had ever witnessed. Weirdly, amidst the melee one of the officers' strikers walked across an open space in leisurely fashion, as if nothing unusual were occurring. Others had rushed to shelter, understanding the danger of friendly fire. "Lie down, you damned fool!" Dodge shouted, and he was instantly obeyed.[16]

The march to Centreville had already revealed the rawness and want of conditioning of these volunteer troops. Being ignorant of the numberless precautions they should take to ensure their comfort and safety, they were not yet soldiers. Later, outside the village, the battalion was drawn up into a square to witness the flogging of two deserters. The scene was sobering to all, but when one of the volunteers inquired of an officer whether he would be treated in the same fashion if he were to desert during battle, he was answered, "No, you would be shot!"[17]

At 8:00 P.M. on July 20 General McDowell met with his division and brigade commanders to review the battle plan for the next day. Information obtained two days earlier had led him to abandon one part of his scheme—namely, to cross a watercourse known as Bull Run at a point south of the Warrenton Pike, which ran roughly east and west, and advance from there to turn the right wing of the enemy. If successful, the move would have left open the approach to Manassas Junction, three miles further distant. But it was now clear that Beauregard's forces had concentrated around the points McDowell had planned for the stream crossing; besides, reconnaissance had revealed that the rolling, wooded terrain west of the stream did not permit the rapid advance that had been hoped for. McDowell's revised strategy would entail a longer march by his attacking forces but should make possible an assault at points where the enemy was vulnerable. At 2:00 A.M. the first division, under Brigadier General Daniel Tyler, would lead an advancing column along the Warrenton Pike toward a stone bridge that crossed Bull Run, making demonstrations to convince the enemy of his intention to cross it. Hunter's second division would follow Tyler until it reached a county road that ran north toward another ford, at Sudley Church. At that point it would cross the stream and, moving south, attack the Confederates' left flank. Once Hunter had reached an intervening ford, the third division, under Brigadier General Samuel P. Heintzelman, would cross it and join him. Meanwhile the fifth division, under Colonel Dixon S. Miles, Second Infantry, would make a diversionary show of force south of the Warrenton road, where an inconclusive battle had been fought two days earlier. The fourth division, commanded by Brigadier General Theodore Runyon and consisting almost entirely of volunteer troops, would remain at Centreville as a reserve, to be itself reinforced as necessary by Miles.[18] McDowell anticipated a forced march by Johnston to join the battle, but he hoped to capture the town of Gainesville, on the Manassas Gap Railroad, before the rebel reinforcements could arrive.

Final preparations for the action began at 10:00 P.M. that night, as the brigades under Tyler formed just west of the village. At 3:00 A.M. the column moved out, but slowly, delayed by efforts to maneuver heavy artillery pieces across a suspension bridge over a stream known as Cub Run. The first division did not pass that point until 6:30 A.M., well after the battle had been planned to begin. However, Hunter's division reached the road to Sudley Ford by that time and moved along it at a more rapid pace. The first brigade, under Brigadier General Ambrose E. Burnside, took the lead, followed by Porter and his men, including Dodge and his company. The side road proved to be little more than a cart path, requiring hard labor with shovels and axes to fell trees and clear underbrush. The day was already oppressively hot. At a fork in the road, Hunter's guide further complicated matters by leading the column onto the right fork, which followed a longer and more circuitous route to Sudley Ford than the left.

At 9:15 A.M. the two regiments of Rhode Island volunteers, under Burnside, reached the ford and began crossing it despite the withering fire directed against them by Confederate Colonel Nathan Evans. The rebel officer had recognized the movements of Tyler at the Warrenton Pike bridge as a feint and double-quicked his men north to meet Hunter's advance. Nevertheless, the Union general managed to cross Bull Run with his entire force. He ordered a Rhode Island regiment and a battery of artillery forward to meet the Confederates, forming the remainder of Burnside's brigade in a battle line behind them as an intimidatingly visible reserve. Captain Charles Griffin, Fifth U.S. Artillery, boldly advanced his guns to within 1,000 yards of the enemy and opened fire. However, the advance by Burnside was slowed by fierce opposing fire, and the momentum of attack was slowed when General Hunter was wounded in the neck and left cheek. Being carried from the field, he assured Burnside that the Rhode Island regiment "went in bravely" and that the federals still held the advantage.[19] Burnside quickly brought the remainder of his brigade into action, directing it at Evans's left. At the same time, the brigade under Porter took up a new advance position on Burnside's right.

As the senior brigade commander, Colonel Porter now assumed command of the second division. Receiving an urgent request from Burnside for protection of an exposed artillery battery, he ordered Major Sykes to bring his battalion forward. It was a critical moment, for a rebel artillery battery to the far right of Burnside was pouring destruction into his ranks, and enemy reinforcements must be expected soon. A man of few and well-chosen words, Sykes observed to his men that, as one recalled, "there would probably be some work for us to do."[20] He led his force at double-time southward across an open space, through a belt of timber, and to a point opposite a masked Confederate battery near a house close to the junction of the Warrenton and Sudley roads. It was about 11:00 A.M., and units of Heintzelman's third division had crossed Bull Run. They were hotly engaged, but they moved aside to permit the companies under Sykes to spearhead this part of the action.

Sykes now divided his command into two. He deployed his three left companies, under Dodge, as skirmishers against the masked battery and the infantry force that protected it. The remainder of his force he led toward Burnside's endangered battery position. "For more than an hour," he wrote in his official report, his portion of the command "was here exposed to a concentrated fire from the batteries and regiments of the enemy, which seemed doubled when the guns of the Rhode Islanders opened" again. At the same time, he continued, "the companies under Captain Dodge, Eighth Infantry, did great execution" against the Confederates.[21] The battle now took on a seesaw character as regiment after regiment attempted to force the rallying rebels to retreat, only to be driven back themselves. From the east, brigades under Heintzelman led by Colonel William T. Sherman, Thirteenth Infantry, and Colonel Erasmus D. Keyes, Eleventh Infantry, made repeated assaults. As the day wore on, Major Sykes moved to his right, encouraging crowds of retiring troops as reinforcements moved into position. Dodge's three companies remained in place, holding the forward position while Sykes took one slightly to the rear of the Union army's extreme right flank. More than twenty years afterward, General Beauregard paid tribute to these men as "a small but incomparable body of regular infantry."[22]

By mid-afternoon both the Union and the Confederate armies were depleted, but the federal forces appeared poised to gain the day. Just at that time, however, reinforcements from General Johnston's army reached the field and turned the tide. Union men had earlier advanced onto a plain to the southwest, only to be driven back from it, but their strong flanking position on the right held the promise that a renewed charge over this disputed space would be successful. They were rallying for the advance when, to the south, a brigade of Confederates under Colonel William Kirby Smith reached the field and attacked them vigorously. Amid the noise, dust, and smoke, the effect of this latest development along a lengthy line of battle was not immediately evident. But like an exhausted fighter battered once too often, the federal right slowly began to give way. Distraught officers encouraged, then threatened their men, but to no avail. The afternoon was insufferably hot. The rumor passed from soldier to soldier that the rebels had been reinforced. Where were the Union reserves that had been placed at the ready at Centreville?[23] Now, at approximately 3:30 P.M., began what Colonel Sherman described in his official report as "the scene of confusion and disorder that characterized the remainder of the day. Up to that time all had kept their places, and seemed perfectly cool and used to the shells and shot that fell comparatively harmless all around us; but the short exposure to an intense fire of small-arms at close range had killed many, wounded more, and had produced disorder in all the battalions that had attempted to destroy it. Men fell away talking and in great confusion."[24]

The swelling of the Confederate force by a large body of men that General Patterson had failed to hold in check proved decisive. The Union army had lost the initiative, then the battle, and it now faced the challenge of retiring from the field in the best order possible. After a vain effort to rally his troops, General McDowell ordered Sykes to advance and cover the retreat of other units in his section of the field. Supported by a battalion of cavalry regulars that had been positioned behind Dodge, Sykes therefore moved south. Amid heavy fire, with his entire battalion he occupied a small plateau west of a hill, known as the Henry Hill, that had been the scene of the most intense fighting. From this elevation he could observe the retreat of units toward the fords they had crossed that morning. When threatened by a troop of rebel cavalry, Sykes "formed square"—a classic defensive posture designed to discourage an advancing antagonist by presenting a broad front against him on all avenues of approach. Here was textbook infantry tactics put into practice at a moment of crisis. The battalion "nobly executed the task assigned it," an officer recalled years afterward, "marching in line of battle, with colors flying, and ranks aligned as if on parade."[25] The visual effect of a defensive square in process of formation can be dramatic, resembling an angry bird spreading its wings in menace. One of the enemy, a tall, gangly man who wore a shako that had slipped to the back of his head, leapt into the air and shouted frantically, "They're trying to flank us! They're trying to flank us!" In that panicked moment, the dire and the ridiculous thus expressed themselves simultaneously, for in fact Sykes had himself been flanked, on his right. But having held his position until the federal troops had moved past him toward Bull Run, he was able to retreat in battle formation toward the bridge. After crossing the stream, he was again threatened by a cavalry force, but the order and regularity of his maneuvers rendered an attack impracticable.

Moving toward Centreville, the battalion under Sykes was an island of discipline in a sea of panicked movement wherein it seemed every man looked out for himself alone. First Lieutenant Daingerfield Parker, Third Infantry, nervously inquired of his commander what he made of it all. "Looks very much like a rout, lieutenant!"[26] Sykes replied laconically. Sykes and his men reached their camp at 8:00 P.M. but remained on duty for fourteen more hours, on guard against further attack and helping restore order in the defeated army.[27]

Upon learning the outcome of the battle, General Scott gamely responded in a telegram, "We are not discouraged." But President Lincoln admitted in private that the news from McDowell was "damned bad."[28] Beyond question, through their hard-won victory the armies under Beauregard and Johnston had conferred military legitimacy on the Confederacy. If the government in Washington was to make good Lincoln's assurance that the rebellion would be put down by force, much work needed to be done, including the mobilization, organization, and training of immense armies. But wise heads on both sides realized that further operations on a large scale had better be delayed for the present. Neither Washington nor Richmond was in danger of attack, and both armies were depleted, exhausted, and more or less in disarray.

In the immediate aftermath of the Bull Run battle, various reasons were advanced to explain the Union defeat. Prominent among these was the lack of subordination exhibited by McDowell's volunteer troops, whom one regular officer characterized as "sovereigns in uniform, not soldiers."[29] However, other analysts considered that the ninety-day men had fought about as well as anyone could expect. Until their retreat degenerated into an ignominious rout, they had done their duty bravely and to the point of exhaustion, and almost with success. The Union had sustained serious casualties; according to official reports, 460 were killed, 1,124 wounded, and 1,312 missing and presumed killed or captured, for a total of 2,896.[30] Of that number, the battalion of regulars accounted for only a small fraction, consisting of 13 killed, 20 wounded, and 44 missing, for a total of 77.[31] Indeed, the one bright spot that shone even in the face of defeat was the stalwart performance of the regular soldiers. Contrary to the panicked rumor on the battlefield that "the regulars had run," they had displayed gritty steadiness under fire, a fact noted by McDowell in his official report. A few days after the battalion had returned to Arlington, President Lincoln came over from Washington to review it. "Mr. President," McDowell spoke in a loud voice as they faced the assembled troops, "these are the men who saved your army at Bull Run." Lincoln looked attentively up and down the line and then replied, "I've heard of them."[32]

Captain Dodge and his men had fought bravely in the battle of Bull Run, earning mention in official reports for their gallant performance. Yet in the aftermath, Dodge was deeply troubled at the part he had played in this first major action of the war. Not only had he faced as enemies former regimental comrades like Theophilus Holmes and James Longstreet, but he had fought against volunteer officers and men from his home state.[33] The prospect of going into battle against his friends and kinsmen was abhorrent to him, no matter how strongly he opposed the cause they were willing to die for, and he did not wish to do it again. On July 27 he addressed a letter to the adjutant general, asking that it be laid before General Scott. "I am a North Carolinian," he began in a forthright statement of his case:

> A large proportion of my relations and friends reside in that state, and many of them including a brother in law, Uncle, and several more distant relatives are now serving in the Rebel Armies.
>
> I have no sympathy with Rebels, as I have attempted to show in the recent battle, but I cannot take part in a contest, when I am afraid to look at a heap of slain enemies, because I may there see the body of near and dear Friends. I have no heart for the fight. If I have done my duty, it has been from no desire to injure my opponents, but simply because it was duty. It was necessary to go into a battle, or my enemies would have said "He is a rebel or a Coward." I have fought one battle. I have proved I am neither the one or the other, and now I feel that I have done enough for honor and for principle, and that I have a right now somewhat to consult feeling.

Dodge asked to be withdrawn from his present assignment as a combatant. "I care not what or where the other duty is or may be," he concluded, "so that it relieves me from the horrid necessity of fighting my own brothers."[34]

The battle at Bull Run had forced upon this able officer a choice between divided loyalties he could not reconcile. He knew well that distinguishing himself in battles to come would hasten his advancement through the army ranks, but since such a quest for military renown would entail the risk of slaying men connected to him by ties of blood or friendship, he was unwilling to pursue it further. Under current circumstances no course of action available to him was altogether satisfactory. To resign his commission and play no part whatever in the conflict might argue a kind of moral purity, but from a professional point of view it would be an evasion, suggesting want of resolution, perhaps even cowardice. To continue supporting the Union from within the army, even if not by bearing arms in battle, would indeed distance him from "fighting [his] own brothers," but it would not make him any less their sworn enemy, nor would it absolve him from a sense of responsibility should they come to harm. All Dodge knew for certain was that at Bull Run, he had acted out a role he did not wish to play again.

His letter was received at army headquarters on the day he wrote it, but General Scott took no action on it, and it was placed on file in the Adjutant General's Office. Meanwhile, as proposals for all kinds of emergency initiatives swirled around Washington, Dodge formulated one of his own. On August 7 he addressed a second letter to the adjutant general, suggesting a productive use of his military knowledge and experience. While at Arlington, he reported, he had been providing practical instruction to several regiments in camp there, and with success. As a result, "I have been encouraged to hope that I can be of vastly more service to the Country, in my capacity as Instructor of officers in the 'Art of War' than in any other position I am likely to be called upon to fill." Men he had spoken with applauded the idea, he added, as addressing "a very evident and immediate need." He therefore requested a twelve-month leave of absence from his regular duties that would enable him to establish in New York City "a School of Instruction for Officers of Volunteers and Militia."[35]

If acted upon, Dodge's proposal offered obvious benefits. The need for facilities to instruct volunteer enlisted men in their duties had been widely noted, and his variation on this theme addressed a similar shortcoming. Tutelage of the sort he had in mind would help provide badly needed leadership to the Union armies, many of whose officers comprehended only too well their lack of preparation. His letter moved quickly through the chain of command to Major General George B. McClellan at headquarters of the Division of the Potomac, and from him to General Scott, who forwarded it to the secretary of war on August 9 for his decision.

Meanwhile, Dodge administered intensive courses of instruction at Arlington to regiments whose officers expressed interest in that training. On August 10 he was granted a seven-day leave of absence for travel to provide instruction in New York City to the rank and file of volunteer regiments being formed there, but he accepted it with an understanding that neither he nor the army wished to act upon: Officially he remained attached to Company G, the unit he had trained for combat, but he now found that position intolerable. Whatever duty was to be found for him, it must be something else. And thus, should his application for a year's leave to establish a school of instruction not be granted within that seven days, he intended to resign his commission.[36]

As events unfolded, Dodge's application proved unsuccessful.[37] However, being as yet unaware of the action, he went ahead with his work as military instructor to the 65th New York Infantry, commanded by Colonel John C. Cochrane. Delighted with his success, he planned to meet with another regiment on Monday of the following week and yet another soon after. He was convinced that he had before him as much productive labor as he could perform, and on Friday, August 16 he telegraphed an application to be placed on duty as instructor or assistant instructor at a camp of instruction that, he had just learned, was to be established near New York City.[38] He made clear that the new initiative was a viable alternative in case the leave of absence should not be granted him.

By August 17, the day agreed upon for him to submit his resignation if no satisfactory action had been taken, Dodge had received no notification from army headquarters in regard to either of his initiatives. He therefore addressed a letter, marked "Private," to Colonel Edward G. Townsend, the assistant adjutant general. Reminding Townsend of the events that had transpired in his case thus far, he informed him that he had duly forwarded his resignation earlier that day. "Now," he continued, "as my attachment to the Army is very strong, I write to beg you will if necessary detain my Resignation in your office until the success or failure of my [first] application is assured."[39] Evidently Townsend did as he was asked, for although Dodge's letter to him survives in the files of the Adjutant General's Office, it was not docketed in the register of letters officially received by that organization. Instead, it was filed as an enclosure to the letter of July 27 requesting reassignment. The letter of resignation, also not docketed, is no longer to be found among surviving records. Probably Townsend retained it, as requested, until the problem of Dodge's placement in a suitable new position had been successfully dealt with. Then, acting as a fellow officer and friend, he quietly destroyed it.

On Monday, August 19, Townsend presented Dodge's case to General Scott and secured from him the recommendation that he be detailed as an instructor in one of several rendezvous camps for volunteers that had been designated in a General Order of four days before.[40] Presently another staff officer pointed out that a volunteer, Brigadier General Egbert L. Viele, had already been assigned to command the camp of instruction near New York City. Dodge, this official suggested, might be assigned to command at a camp about to be established, near Elmira in south central New York. On the same day, Special Order 223 was issued from the Adjutant General's Office, directing Dodge to repair to that place.[41]

Belatedly but effectively, Captain Dodge's personal crisis was resolved by this official action. His career as a direct combatant in the Civil War was now behind him, and years of essential if inglorious service behind the lines lay ahead. Ironically, his early experiences on the western frontier had gone far toward defining his sense of himself as an army man, but the years in Texas now seemed of less immediate usefulness than his more recent work in recruitment and formal instruction. At any rate, a sphere of duty in which he could take pride had been found for him. On September 7 he reported himself at Geneva, New York,[42] not far from the as yet unlocated camp of instruction at Elmira, awaiting further orders.

4

Behind the Lines

Elmira, New York, took on several military functions during the Civil War, being situated at a railroad junction that connected it on the east to New York City and on the south to other population centers. The post commanded for a time by Dodge, Camp Rathbun, was the first of four established in the vicinity of Elmira. These served variously as a rendezvous for individual volunteers, an assembly point for volunteer regiments, a facility for units in training, and barracks for convalescent soldiers and Confederate prisoners of war.[1]

Dodge's service in the camp of instruction at Elmira lasted only two months because the War Department elected to focus more attention on organizing, equipping, and transporting men to the front lines than to training them in the niceties of battle by the book. As a result, in October 1861 Dodge was transferred to Harrisburg, Pennsylvania, 120 miles south of Elmira, where he took up a different form of duty.[2] With brief interruptions, he remained there almost until the war's end.

Harrisburg, the state capital, never became the scene of battle between the opposing forces, but it was exposed more than once to the threat of military action in its streets.[3] Confederate forces invaded Pennsylvania in 1862, 1863, and 1864, forcing a hasty redeployment of federal units and obliging the state governor, Andrew G. Curtin, to call out the state militia as home guards. The crucial battle of Gettysburg, on July 1–3, 1863, was fought only thirty-five miles from Harrisburg. Chambersburg, forty miles distant, was occupied by Confederate troops in that year and also in 1864. Dodge was thus behind the lines while stationed at Harrisburg, but not far.

The city was a key dispatching point for troops and supplies, situated approximately eighty-five miles by railroad from both Philadelphia, Pennsylvania, and Baltimore, Maryland. Its peacetime population of 30,000 rose to twice that number during the war. An air of tense energy pervaded the place as a steady stream of men and materiel passed through. Governor Curtin, a Republican and a staunch ally of President Lincoln, exerted himself to ensure that the commonwealth of Pennsylvania contributed its full measure of wealth and manpower to the Union cause. Curtin had regular correspondence with Lincoln and also the secretaries of war—Simon Cameron, a fellow Pennsylvanian who occupied the position through January 1862, and thereafter Edwin M. Stanton. Under Curtin's leadership, Pennsylvania supplied a total of 337,936 men to the federal armies, second among the loyal states only to New York, whose population of men eligible for military service was much larger.[4]

The conflict and the tasks it imposed were constant realities at Harrisburg. From the time of Dodge's arrival in the city, he worked closely with Pennsylvania state officials, especially Curtin, with whom he early formed friendly relations. The two men worked well together, both having energetic, sociable dispositions and a faculty for devising systems and procedures to bring about results they desired. Owing in part to the satisfaction he gave this influential state governor, Dodge occupied progressively more responsible positions while at Harrisburg. Through December 31, 1861, he was the federal government's mustering and disbursing officer in the city, in charge of formally receiving volunteers into federal service and of paying the expenses of recruitment and other government undertakings. From January 1 to September 30, 1862, his authority in this area was expanded; he became chief mustering and disbursing officer and also superintendent of volunteer recruiting for the entire state of Pennsylvania. Thereafter, following four months performing these same duties in the neighboring state of Maryland and subsequently as assistant inspector general for the Fourth Army Corps, in February 1863 he accepted an offer to return to Harrisburg. From March 1, 1863, to July 31, 1864, his assignment included an additional component—namely, command over the federal troops stationed in the state capital. Finally, on August 1, 1864, he was appointed acting assistant provost marshal general for the western division of the state of Pennsylvania.[5] By that time, the printed letterhead for correspondence from his office displayed a lengthy list of abbreviated titles. Dodge's activities behind the lines thus afforded him ample opportunity to demonstrate his ability to wear several hats at once. From another point of view, they exemplified the War Department's need to stretch its administrative resources to the limit.

Captain Dodge was frequently called upon to conduct himself with a combination of decisiveness and diplomacy while stationed at Harrisburg. Because he was a federal officer at work in a state capital, questions of jurisdiction, precedence, and privilege between federal and state powers inevitably cropped up, especially in the early months of the crisis. For example, it was understood that the governors of states had power to designate the officers of volunteer regiments being organized under their authority. The political value of this function was evident even to the most patriotic state executives, but in December 1861 Governor Curtin complained to the secretary of war that Dodge was seemingly denying him his right. "Captain Dodge refuses to muster in officers of regiments as I indicate," he telegraphed, "and I understand him to say that he will be the judge of when consolidation [of companies into regiments] is made. Is he not mistaken in the character of his instructions?" Secretary Cameron made clear in his reply that the captain was performing his duty as directed. For the sake of efficiency and economy, he was not to receive any volunteer officers into service until the commands to be placed in their charge had been recruited to the full.[6]

Of course, war conditions necessitated close cooperation between federal officials such as Dodge and representatives of the State of Pennsylvania. Secretary Stanton, Cameron's successor, once observed that superintendents of volunteer recruiting in the loyal states seemed to consider their chief function as "to baffle and thwart the government" by creating obstructions,[7] but Dodge was not one of these. In fact, in May 1862 Governor Curtin inquired of Stanton whether Dodge could be authorized to act as his agent in detailing volunteer officers. Shortly afterward, Curtin asked that Dodge be directed "to place himself under my orders and assist me" in raising volunteers.[8] Temporarily at least, during these weeks when troops were being rushed to the front for engagements in Virginia, the governor's request was complied with.

Later in that difficult year for the Union, the combined toll of losses in the field, expired terms of enlistment, and desertions led President Lincoln to issue a call for additional volunteers.[9] Federal reverses at Second Bull Run and elsewhere had sapped morale in the northern states, reducing the inflow of fresh recruits. In accordance with government policy, thus far Dodge had refused to muster in volunteers who were minors between eighteen and twenty years of age unless they could supply written statements of consent from their parents. But Governor Curtin raised the question why these willing boys, who had made their way to Harrisburg and other rendezvous points, should then be sent home, quite possibly to be drafted soon afterward. He submitted that the public good dictated some adjustment of the regulations being enforced by federal mustering and disbursing officers, and within a few days his suggestion was acted upon. Dodge was directed to receive such minors upon affidavit from the captains of their companies that the necessary consent had been given.[10]

Another instance of accommodation between the federal government and Pennsylvania authorities occurred one month later, this time in regard to a call by Governor Curtin for 50,000 Pennsylvania men to serve for three months or less as a militia force to protect the state against Confederate incursion. The ordinary term of enlistment for volunteers from within Pennsylvania at this time was three years, and neither Lincoln nor Major General Henry W. Halleck, commander in chief of the Union's land forces, favored the recruitment of militia for shorter terms. The military value of these men was local only, and rather limited; moreover, supplying and paying them would be disproportionately expensive. Federal authorities believed that state militias could be best utilized in defense of the beleaguered Union generally. But at the same time, Governor Curtin was pulling his weight as a supplier of three-year volunteers and could hardly be denied the president's sanction of his call for short-term troops. Thus on September 17 Dodge received from the War Department a directive to muster Pennsylvania volunteers into the service of the United States for a period of three months, it being understood that the federal Quartermaster Department would pay for their transportation; and the Subsistence Department, their rations.[11]

This accommodation seemed satisfactory to all, but when Dodge called on the governor to show him the telegraphic order authorizing the short-term enlistment, he was taken aback at Curtin's response. "It cannot be done," he exclaimed. "The men will not come out for three months, and are not prepared for that term. They will not submit to it." The governor now desired a term of enlistment shorter than three months—specifically, whatever brief period might prove necessary to drive Confederate forces away from Pennsylvania soil. Dodge, as the unwitting bearer of ill tidings, left the order with Curtin to deal with as he chose but reported the interview to his superiors.[12]

Not many days afterward, the Adjutant General's Office clarified the directive that had so distressed Curtin. The three-month enlistment, Dodge was now informed, had been specified "not with the intention of holding the said troops for three months if the exigency making them necessary should sooner pass, but to guard against complications as to pay, &c., which always arise when troops are not regularly received." In short, the War Department was backing away from its earlier instructions. In the meantime the immediate need for militia troops in Pennsylvania had passed, Confederate troops having retreated, and the men were free to go home. Of course, Dodge was told, a muster into and out of the federal service would be required for them all before they could receive pay from the general government.[13] He was learning that the coordination of effort even between organizations eager to cooperate, as in this instance, could be maddeningly difficult, testing tempers and imposing much dreary deskwork.

The initial surge of patriotic zeal in the northern states yielded such a flood of Union volunteers that for a time the federal government actually suspended its recruiting program. However, by the spring of 1862 regiments in the field required a supply of new men. In May, therefore, the official effort to maintain the strength of the armies was resumed.[14] By early August a total of 634,320 volunteers had been mustered into the Union service, 80,626 of them from Pennsylvania,[15] but General Halleck wanted more. He ordered two experienced troubleshooters, Major General John E. Wool and Brigadier General of Volunteers William S. Ketcham, to Harrisburg on an errand to help speed up the process. Halleck authorized Ketcham to adopt "the most summary measures . . . to push forward the troops. The railroad must give them the preference, and, if necessary, exclude all other passengers."[16]

On August 4, 1862, President Lincoln issued a proclamation calling for 300,000 militia volunteers to serve for a period of nine months, with any shortfall to be made up by a draft from the militias of the several states.[17] But Governor Curtin hoped to reach the quota assigned his state, 45,321 men, without resort to a draft. Any compulsory enlistment, he warned, would need to be treated "delicately" in Pennsylvania.[18] His concerns were well founded, for American citizens had never yet been subjected to conscription in wartime, and they were not likely to welcome its introduction. They associated forced military service with the tyrannical practices of European nations, where it had long been imposed, and they disliked the notion of its use in a nation that professed devotion to individual liberty. That the Confederate government had instituted a stern conscription act in the spring of 1862[19] did not alter the matter. Rather, to many persons it made more clear that forced recruitment was a betrayal of first principles on which the United States had been founded. Others, however, viewed a draft law as a practical necessity. They understood that opposition to a draft would necessarily occur, but they held that a system for conscription must be put in place just the same.

As superintendent of volunteer recruiting for the state of Pennsylvania, Dodge bore responsibility for directing the effort to muster in a sufficient number of recruits to render a draft unnecessary. He assured his subordinates in counties across the state that enlistments recorded in their offices would be credited against the quotas assigned them until the last practicable moment. However, when appeals to patriotic sentiment and local pride had failed to produce a sufficient response, the militia draft commenced in Pennsylvania. In some regions the process moved ahead without hindrance, but in many others it met opposition. Some residents, informed of its approach, fled the state. Others who remained, and whose names had been drawn from the lottery boxes, refused to serve. They were arrested and jailed, but sympathetic state judges invoked habeas corpus to secure their release from custody. The judicial resistance prompted President Lincoln to order habeas corpus suspended as a war measure,[20] but even that bold stroke produced limited results. In November the adjutant general, Brigadier General Lorenzo Thomas, informed Secretary Stanton that one-quarter of the draftees in Pennsylvania had not reported for duty, and that the state authorities were "powerless to deliver them."[21]

The federal draft of 1862 had been placed in the hands of loyal states to enforce, but events had demonstrated that the states were unable or unwilling to bear that responsibility. Meanwhile, the Union armies were in acute need of more manpower. When Governor Curtin and others urged Secretary Stanton to supply federal troops to enforce the draft where resistance was threatened, the secretary reacted angrily. The very necessity of resorting to a draft proclaimed that he had no troops to spare. "If a State cannot enforce its own laws without U.S. soldiers," he wrote Curtin, "we may as well give up at once."[22]

The winter of 1862–1863 was thus a comfortless time for supporters of the Union cause. The year just past had brought few military victories, and continued operations against a resolute and resourceful foe such as the Confederacy did not appeal to some persons who under more propitious circumstances would have supported them eagerly. Lincoln's Emancipation Proclamation of September 22, 1862, did add fervor to those in the North who favored the abolition of slavery. Moreover, it opened up new possibilities of internal discord in the South and of eventual service to the Union by large numbers of black men who fled to freedom. But future prospects remained clouded. The campaigns of the coming year might prove decisive, and some effective means must be devised to swell the federal armies to a level that ensured their overwhelming force.

On March 3, 1863, following a four-month interval of service elsewhere, Dodge resumed his duties at Harrisburg.[23] Coincidentally, this same date witnessed a turning point in the Civil War. Narrative histories of the contest, with their emphasis on campaigns, strategies, battles, and leaders, tend to undervalue the event, which did not take place on the battlefield. Instead, it was a victory in the legislative sphere—the approval by Congress of an "act for enrolling and calling out the national forces, and for other purposes," commonly known as the Enrollment Act.[24] By this legislation, Congress laid the basis for ensuring an adequate supply of men to the Union armies for the duration of the war. The insufficiency of the previous systems for volunteer recruitment, and subsequently for drafting, was undeniable. The federal government now assumed control of the recruiting and conscription efforts that had earlier been administered by the loyal states and territories. Whereas formerly the quotas announced to these entities had been apportioned by their governors to the counties that comprised them, henceforward all quotas would be set by authorities at Washington and the quotas assigned to congressional districts, not counties. Each district would be governed by its own provost marshal, who would ensure compliance with federal statutes and would submit to Washington regular reports of the operations under his authority. This official would be assisted by a physician and a three-man Board of Enrollment, the latter consisting of responsible citizens who resided in the district.[25]

The federal government's provisions for marshaling military force as needed were to be administered by a newly established bureau within the Department of War, that of the Office of the Provost Marshal General. Formerly the business of recruitment had been one of many operations supervised by the Adjutant General's Office; now, as befitted its importance, it would be transacted by a separate organization under the direction of the secretary of war. The Enrollment Act was so named because it mandated a full enrollment, under authority of the provost marshal general, of men between twenty and forty-five years of age who were not then serving in the armed forces and were therefore eligible for selection to perform military service. The records of prior enlistments, often fragmentary and maintained in differing fashion by various offices, afforded no reliable basis for estimating the number of persons who comprised the pool of potential soldiers. But a completed enrollment compiled by officers serving under the provost marshal general would provide such a basis. As a single set of records whose entries were available for inspection by all, in future calls for troops it would ensure an equitable calculation of quotas throughout the Union. Those close to the matter hoped that the very prospect of a draft might stimulate volunteering. Under the new system, men who freely offered themselves could still be granted inducements such as premiums and bounties by the grateful citizens of their districts.

Before the immense task of enrollment could begin, the organizational framework mandated by Congress must be put in place, and therefore on March 17 Colonel James B. Fry was appointed to the position of provost marshal general.[26] Fry, an 1847 graduate of West Point, was a career soldier who had served with honor in the war thus far—performing ably, for example, as General McDowell's adjutant at the first

James B. Fry. Courtesy U.S. Army Military History Institute.

Bull Run battle. Fry was well known in Washington and well acquainted with staff duties, and he possessed remarkable organizational and diplomatic skills. A clear thinker, a lucid communicator, and a man of discretion, he was without ambition other than for recognition as having done his duty fairly and fully.[27] General Ulysses S. Grant later declared him "the officer best fitted" for the office.[28] At this critical stage of the Civil War, Fry joined other men who combined administrative ability with energy and strong will and who were devoted to advancing the Union's war effort. Among these leaders were Brigadier General Montgomery C. Meigs, the quartermaster general; Edwin M. Stanton, who for all his headstrong excesses as secretary of war was a decisive leader, utterly committed to the cause; and after April 1864, General Halleck, who served with greater effectiveness as chief of staff to the new commander of the army, General Grant, than when he had occupied that position himself. Meanwhile, proven field commanders like Grant and William T. Sherman played their more dramatic parts in subduing the Confederate foe.

In the weeks that followed his appointment, Colonel Fry addressed a series of letters to Stanton with suggestions for the operation of the Provost Marshal General's Office. With few exceptions, these won prompt acceptance. One of Fry's ideas was for the creation of an Invalid Corps, subsequently renamed the Veteran's Reserve Corps, to be staffed by officers and men no longer capable of active service in the field but still able to perform other useful duties. The existence of the Invalid Corps would enable field commanders to replace those accepted into it by men better prepared to withstand the rigors of protracted campaigns, and it would also provide corps members an honorable means of continuing to serve the cause. Depending on their level of physical ability, members might perform guard duty, serve as hospital attendants, escort prisoners of war to the camps designated for them, and help protect against civil discord—for example, in locations where the draft was being resisted.[29] The Invalid Corps was an experiment that, as Fry later wrote, proved successful "to an extent not at first even hoped for."[30]

Secretary Stanton approved another of Fry's proposals, for the appointment of officials to be stationed in state capitals and other major cities, serving there as his immediate assistants. The duties of these men would be supervisory, and in a sense diplomatic as well, for the federal and state powers must continue to work together harmoniously. Fry suggested that appointees at the state level should be officers of the regular army, ranking as majors or higher, who from age or physical condition were less than fully qualified for field service. Additionally, he recommended that they must have demonstrated good judgment and the social skills necessary to represent the government creditably in state capitals.[31] These men would be designated by a lengthy official title, acting assistant provost marshal general—"acting" because properly they were commissioned army officers, "assistant" because they would report directly to Fry, and "provost marshal general" because while on duty they would wield the authority of his office.

At the time acting assistant provost marshals general were first appointed, in April 1863, Captain Richard I. Dodge, Eighth Infantry, would have been a natural selection for service in Pennsylvania on account of his successful experience in working with Governor Curtin and supervising volunteer recruiting efforts in the state. Inasmuch as he had declared a wish not to take the field in battle, his good physical condition was no detriment. However, he was a captain, not yet a major, and so fell short by that criterion. Nevertheless, since the recruitment of volunteers would henceforward proceed under supervision of the Office of the Provost Marshal General, in the months to come Dodge would work closely with Colonel Fry's appointees, Lieutenant Colonel Charles F. Ruff, Third Cavalry, and after May 25, 1863, Lieutenant Colonel James V. Bomford, Sixteenth Infantry.[32] Through this cooperative effort he would become acquainted with the duties of his superior officers in Harrisburg.

The task of enrollment having been carried out in Pennsylvania, in July 1863 an initial draft was conducted under the new system, but not without resistance. In the southwestern part of the state, near Waynesburg, where pro-Confederate sentiment was strong, members of the Board of Enrollment, traveling together to compile a roster of eligible citizens, were shown a coiled rope, suitable for hanging. They were warned to depart at once, which they did. In the coal mining districts of the state's north-eastern section, laborers rioted in protest, and Lieutenant Colonel Bomford called upon the commander of the District of the Susquehanna, Major General Darius N. Couch, for detachments of troops to put down the uprising.[33] Subsequently he stationed units of the Veteran's Reserve Corps as provost guards at places where the work of conscription was going forward. Colonel Fry had instructed him and other acting assistant provost marshals general to demonstrate, tactfully but firmly, that the will of the federal government was not to be trifled with. Once the draft had been announced as to begin in a congressional district on a particular date, it was to be conducted on schedule. However, for caution's sake, Bomford was given the authority to schedule drafts on a different day in each district so as to permit the movement of troops from one place to another.[34]

Violence in protest of the federal draft continued for days at a time in New York City and some other places during the summer of 1863.[35] Nevertheless, by August a satisfactory response to the president's latest call for troops had been achieved. Organized to operate in tandem with the continued effort to attract volunteer recruits, the arrangements set in place by Colonel Fry to enforce conscription were a practical success. On September 5 the recently established *Army and Navy Journal*, a semiofficial weekly devoted to military matters, praised this result. Not only was the draft "a vital, practical necessity," the editors wrote, but it was proper on principle, "fair and just and equitable. . . . The duty of bearing arms, when called upon in defense of the Government and the laws is obligatory upon all able-bodied citizens. This is a sovereign right which the State must be able to demand."[36] Military leaders expressed similar views. When another draft went forward in September 1864, Major General Sherman welcomed the nation's resolute enforcement of its own laws. "Our Government," he wrote, "though a democracy, should, in times of trouble and danger, be able to wield the most despotic power of a great nation." Lieutenant General Grant saw the matter in more practical terms. He predicted to Secretary Stanton that "enforcement of the draft and prompt filling up of our armies will save the shedding of blood to an immense degree."[37]

Meanwhile, Dodge's supervision of clerical duties at Harrisburg during 1863 placed him in an anomalous position, as a preserver of orderly procedures amidst continuously stressful events. Thus in June, as Confederate forces marched menacingly into Pennsylvania, he received direction from army headquarters to continue observing all the established regulations for mustering in new troops,[38] almost as if a military emergency did not exist. By August the immediate threat posed by Confederate forces was reduced as the army under General Robert E. Lee retreated following the battle at Gettysburg, but the air remained charged with excitement. The veneer of civil order was thin, for emotions were brittle and tempers volatile. These were the conditions under which, on one occasion, Dodge lost his soldierly discipline and provoked an altercation with a fellow Union officer.

On the morning of August 10 a draft drawing was in progress in the county court house in Harrisburg. A detachment of the Veteran's Reserve Corps stood at the entrance with their muskets crossed, and when Dodge was about to walk past them into the building he was challenged. In angered response to the question where he wished to go, he answered that he would go "wherever he damned please," shoved the weapons out of his way, and brusquely pushed past. Moments later, apparently in reference to the military display outside and also to the challenge directed at him, he declared that the officer in command of the guard, Captain Isaac J. Neall, was "making a damned fool of himself."[39] Naturally this remark gave offense to Neall, for Dodge made it in the presence of the Enrollment Board and other persons. Both officers felt themselves aggrieved, and the result was charges and countercharges filed with Bomford and reluctantly forwarded by him to Colonel Fry at Washington.

The incident was hardly momentous, but once it had led to legal action, the questions of guilt or innocence it posed had to be dealt with. Court-martial proceedings initiated by Dodge against Neall resulted in an acquittal, and in reviewing the written proceedings of that court, General Couch was obliged to consider the question whether Dodge should be subjected to trial in his turn. Couch explained to the adjutant general that he had deferred making that decision as long as he could. The delay, he believed, was "due to the War Department, and to the Captain [i.e., Dodge] who must have the confidence of the Department by its retaining him in this responsible position."[40] Subsequently, Fry suggested that Dodge ought not to be tried for his "misbehavior" but should instead receive a reprimand from the general in chief. General Halleck approved this course and delegated the duty to the adjutant general, ordering him to "reprimand Capt Dodge as he thinks he deserves."[41] In comparison to other matters that occupied the attention of Halleck—such as the doubtful results of the recent Battle of Chickamauga in Georgia and Tennessee—this dustup between two officers behind the lines was hardly worth his time. A letter reproving Dodge went out on October 20,[42] and there the matter ended.

In the following spring Dodge's impatience with the performance of activities under his supervision burst out again, this time with results more satisfactory to himself. Responding to his complaint over the slow rate at which volunteers reporting at nearby Carlisle Barracks were being paid the bounties due them, Captain Charles C. Churchill, on duty as mustering and disbursing officer at that post, bitterly criticized the office arrangements there. The facilities were inadequate, the clerks were obliged to perform tasks that should have been completed elsewhere, and efforts to rectify matters were stymied by "the entire want of any preparation of the accounts and necessary papers." In Churchill's view, responsibility for the slipshod procedures rested with the post commander at Carlisle Barracks, Major David H. Hastings, Fifth Cavalry, and Dodge agreed. Forwarding Churchill's letter to Washington, he contrasted the alleged office practices with those under his own supervision. "If the Comdr of the Rendezvous will cause the receipt Rolls to be made out properly and signed, the enlistment papers and Forms 'B' assorted and arranged, in proper order, I [as Hastings's commanding officer] will guarantee to pay one thousand men per day." At Harrisburg, he continued, "I have no difficulty in paying one hundred men per hour. . . . It can be done at Carlisle only when the same or as good system is observed by the officers in charge." This stinging assertion had its desired effect. General Thomas directed that a letter be sent to Hastings with information of the complaints that had been made and a direction to correct without delay the problems that had led to them.[43]

Though burdened with multiple duties and sometimes frustrated by conditions he could not control, Dodge actually found much to enjoy in Harrisburg, even in wartime. He and Julia lived there frugally, economy being a necessity in view of inflated prices and the inadequate living allowances he received.[44] They attended social engagements at the homes of persons wealthier than themselves, and Dodge's regular contact with Governor Curtin and other persons of responsibility resulted in invitations to official functions. Colonel Fry and Dodge had been acquaintances at West Point, and the visits of the provost marshal general to Harrisburg sometimes included calls upon Dodge and his family.[45] Julia, who loved company, formed a social circle of her own. A photograph preserved among Dodge's papers shows a well-turned-out group of five young ladies and gentlemen at Lewisburg, not far distant, captioned "Our Quintette."[46]

Lieutenant Colonel Bomford, a former Eighth Infantry comrade of Dodge's, served with energy and intelligence as acting assistant provost marshal general, earning the regard of Governor Curtin and fully satisfying Colonel Fry. Of course, as a representative of the War Department and the federal government's self-imputed power over free citizens, Bomford was subjected to criticism despite his best efforts. The approach of Pennsylvania's gubernatorial election of November 1863 also made him the target of politically motivated abuse at the state level. As the working colleague of Curtin, who was a candidate for re-election, he became fair game for attacks by the governor's political foes. Criticism of him even appeared in the Harrisburg *Republican*, a newspaper co-owned by Curtin's fellow Republican and former secretary of war Simon Cameron. Nevertheless, when Curtin had won re-election and was asked by Fry whether he would prefer to see Bomford replaced, he declined the offer. Bomford was "an honest man and a true soldier," he wrote in response, and should not be held to account for the accusations that had been leveled against him. Yet, tacitly granting that the incumbent acting assistant provost marshal general might not be able to serve effectively much longer, Curtin asked for an interview with Fry in the event of Bomford's removal. "[A]lthough I do not ask to name his successor," he wrote, "I hope you will hear me on the subject."[47]

In July 1864 the newspaper attacks on Bomford resumed, and in addition, Cameron complained of him directly to President Lincoln.[48] As a result, Fry dispatched a trusted deputy, Assistant Adjutant General George D. Ruggles, to Harrisburg to assess the situation. Through interviews with General Couch, Adjutant General Russell of the Pennsylvania militia, Curtin, Bomford, Dodge, Cameron, and others, Ruggles elicited some material facts about the campaign of vilification against Bomford. Cameron had alleged that Bomford refused to muster in certain one-hundred-day men—that is, militia enlisted for that period—as directed by Curtin, and moreover that he had failed to provide these men subsistence while they remained at the nearby volunteer camp, Camp Curtin, awaiting his action. After making his inquiries, Ruggles was satisfied that both accusations were false. The newspaper attacks had begun when Bomford ceased to employ the proprietor of the paper to print public advertising and other notices. The prices demanded by this individual, Cameron's business partner, were twice those of other local printers. Once the proprietor had lost Bomford's business, he became his bitter enemy and did all he could to have him removed from office.

All this was sorry behavior by men in positions of influence, but apparently the tide had turned against Bomford. Curtin now appeared impatient with his practice of conducting his official activities according to all the prescribed forms. On a similar note, Cameron insisted that the federal government must replace Bomford at once "by some officer, such as Captain Dodge, who would exercise discretion and common sense, and not hold himself tied down by the rules and regulations of the War Department." Cameron announced his intention to travel to Washington and take up the matter with the president. Ruggles witnessed an exchange between Dodge, Bomford, and Russell in which the adjutant general complimented Dodge but claimed that Bomford was too much tied down by rules and regulations. Evidently a united front had formed in opposition to the incumbent acting assistant provost marshal general.

Bomford told Ruggles that he had sought faithfully to discharge his duty to the government and believed he had done so. He and Dodge were on excellent terms, deploring the efforts that had been made to bring them into conflict. Ruggles, too, regretted having to submit "this report of personalities" in describing the situation to Fry.[49] Nevertheless, unseemly as the state of affairs in Harrisburg might be, the days of Lieutenant Colonel Bomford as acting assistant provost marshal general were numbered. Moreover, the preference of some interested parties for the individual to succeed him was clear.

Dodge was now a field officer, having been promoted in June to major, Twelfth Infantry.[50] He was qualified by rank as well as by experience and ability to take the place of his unjustly maligned comrade. On July 22, three days after Ruggles submitted to Fry a detailed report of his investigation, Bomford was relieved from duty as acting assistant provost marshal general for the western division of the state of Pennsylvania, and Dodge was named as his successor.[51] Thus, after almost three years of yeoman's duty behind the lines, Major Dodge was appointed to a position that reflected official recognition at the highest levels of his contributions to the war effort thus far. On August 1 he assumed responsibility for helping bring the conflict to an end by supplying troops from Pennsylvania to the rallying Union armies.

5

Acting Assistant Provost Marshal General

Dodge took up his duties as acting assistant provost marshal general (AAPMG) in a time of discontent, war weariness, and uncertainty. Hopes for an end to hostilities in this fourth summer of the conflict had been dashed, and the opposing armies continued locked in a desperate embrace. Union armies were gaining the advantage, with General Sheridan moving south through the Shenandoah Valley, General Grant fighting battles of attrition nearer Richmond, and General Sherman overcoming determined resistance as he approached Atlanta, Georgia. But the Confederate armies, unbowed, were mounting attacks of their own. On July 30 they invaded Pennsylvania once more. Their political leaders understood that the protracted military campaigns could turn to their advantage the growing antiwar sentiment in the northern states.

The approaching presidential election provided a convenient platform for those who opposed President Lincoln's war policy. Spokesmen for the rival Democratic party fanned citizens' discontent so effectively that during the summer of 1864 the re-election of the president appeared unlikely.[1] Most Democratic leaders advocated some form of accommodation with the Confederacy, but their views failed to sway Lincoln. On July 18 he had issued a call for 500,000 more volunteers, with deficiencies in the quotas to be made up by a draft that would begin on September 5. The proclamation became a lightning rod for persons who opposed Lincoln or objected to conscription. Nevertheless, if the Union armies were to prevail, the men must be had. Along with other AAPMGs, Dodge was being called upon to help satisfy a politically unpopular military need.

At Harrisburg

On the day he took office, Dodge learned of a renewed outbreak in Pennsylvania of armed resistance to federal authority. A small official party, including two former officers of the Pennsylvania Reserves, had entered the township of Sugarloaf, in Columbia County, intending to arrest two members of a family named Smith. One of these men was a deserter from the Eighth U.S. Infantry, the other a draftee who had fled before being mustered in. The search for the fugitives was a dangerous errand, for the region was a hotbed of Copperheads, persons hostile to the Union cause within the otherwise loyal states. When the wife of the fugitive draftee caught sight of the arresting party, she blew a horn, and at once a group of men took position in the road a few rods from the intruders. Shouting defiances and threats, some members of the outlaw group, including the draftee, leveled their guns and, despite calls to desist, shot and wounded the leader of the arresting party, Lieutenant James Robinson. The resisters had so intimidated loyal residents of the community that no person could be found who would admit the wounded man into his home, and as a result he died.

Upon learning of the seditious events, Dodge forwarded documents describing them to Washington, adding his "urgent request" for troops to put down the opposition.[2] In the days that followed, deputations from other known trouble spots, Cambria and Greene counties, appeared in his office asking for help in response to similar incidents of violence. Small detachments of troops had already been posted in all the disaffected districts, but their presence was only aggravating the malcontents. In Columbia County the outlaw parties were organized and numbered five hundred men; in Cambria County they were thought to be even more numerous. Faced with opposition from armed groups of that size, provost marshals in the districts were powerless to perform their duties. It was suspected that political enemies of President Lincoln were fomenting the uprisings in order to weaken his resolution to continue prosecuting the war.

On August 10 Dodge renewed his request for troops. Not only had many Union sympathizers been overawed by the resisters, he wrote General Fry, but others, formerly supporters of the Lincoln administration, were wavering in their commitment, "preferring their comfort to their principles." He asked that a full regiment be placed under his authority, and on August 16 Fry complied, informing him that the Sixteenth Regiment of the Veteran's Reserve Corps had been ordered to report to Harrisburg at once. Fry expressed hope that Dodge would "so use this force as to secure a thorough administration of the law without unnecessary collision."[3]

Dodge planned to move deliberately, directing the units to enter the districts known to harbor disloyal elements one by one. By this means, he hoped, the large body of uniformed soldiers would put a damper on whatever resistance had been declared in the area and give second thoughts to other persons similarly inclined. He instructed the Sixteenth Regiment to work expeditiously but to remain in a district "until every deserter, delinquent drafted man, and abettor of rebellion be arrested or run out of the country. When that is done, proceed to another."[4] It was a comprehensive plan of operations that resembled a military campaign behind the lines, as indeed it almost was.

In several loyal states, the September draft aroused anxious concern among the officials responsible for its operation. As a result, it was postponed two weeks in order to provide time for last-minute volunteer enlistments that might render it unnecessary. Maine Congressman James G. Blaine was one of the few persons of influence who could view the imminent proceedings with a measure of good humor. He likened "the dreaded draft" to an old ladies' tea party—something everyone concerned would be glad to get over with.[5]

According to plan, Dodge dispatched companies of his Veteran's Reserve Corps regiment to the northeastern mining districts, where more trouble was anticipated, and also to places where volunteering had fallen far short of the quotas. He held a few companies in reserve at Harrisburg in case unexpected needs should arise, as they soon did. In the Twenty-fourth Congressional District, in the southwestern part of the state, it proved necessary to draft 432 persons, the greater number from Greene County. However, various townships in that region greeted the officers sent to deliver draft notices with open hostility. In Whitley township the delegation was unable to serve its notices, and the ears, manes, and tails of its horses were cut off. In Dunkard and Rich Hill townships the results were little better, leading the district provost marshal, John Cuthbertson, to telegraph Dodge on September 26 requesting a force of fifty men. On the following night a company of the Veteran's Reserve Corps and, for good measure, a company of cavalry arrived on the scene with orders to arrest the resisters and remain there until the draft was completed. The arrival of these units led to the desired result: the draft notices were served, several deserters were arrested, and the quota was filled.[6]

Shortly after the re-election of President Lincoln, in his annual report to the secretary of war, General Fry pointed with satisfaction to the success of his organization in enforcing the recent draft. "In several places," he wrote, "parties of men were bivouacked in the woods, partially organized, and armed with pistols and shotguns, for the avowed purpose of preventing the execution of the law. [Nevertheless,] The draft has been made without resort to military force on the part of the Government."[7] Of course, this statement was accurate only insofar as the troops made available to Dodge and other AAPMGs had not been required literally to fire their weapons. The successful result had been achieved in part through an intimidating demonstration of military might, ready at hand should its use be called for. Still, Fry praised his assistants in the states for manifesting an "unflinching determination" to carry out the orders of the government without compromise. Through their good judgment, he wrote, the AAPMGs had enforced the law "fully and fairly."

Characteristically, Dodge addressed himself with enthusiasm to the challenges presented by his responsibility as an AAPMG. Having discovered an especially able officer, Captain Simon Snyder, who was then serving in the General Recruiting Service at Harrisburg, he appealed for this man's reassignment as his immediate subordinate, to be placed in charge of volunteer recruiting. He drew attention to the irregularity with which some regimental recruiting officers submitted to his office reports of their activities and accomplishments.[8] He had crossed swords with a few district provost marshals who, he informed Fry, seemed to regard his office "merely a vehicle for the transmittal of their correspondence to the Provost-Marshal-General."[9] On the whole, however, he found provost marshals around the state capable and well intentioned, if not always well organized.

With approval from Washington, Dodge rented a three-story building, with attic, where almost all the business under his immediate supervision could be transacted. On the ground floor, the U.S. mustering office occupied the front of the building; the post adjutant and provost marshal had offices in the rear. The work of the adjutant for the Volunteer Recruiting Service went forward on the second floor, Dodge retaining for his own use a room in the rear. The business office of the AAPMG occupied the third floor and a part of the attic, the rest of which housed the quartermaster of the Volunteer Recruiting Service. Because no space was available for the disbursing officer, who transacted a great deal of business, Dodge assigned him to a nearby building that had been rented for another purpose. Thirty-six civilian employees, including a physician, occupied the main building as clerks, messengers, and in other capacities. On weekdays from 9:00 A.M. to 5:30 P.M., or later at the discretion of the persons in charge, the place buzzed with activity.[10]

In the intervals between his other duties during his first few months as AAPMG, Dodge studied the manner in which the work of the several offices under his charge was being conducted and coordinated. In common with several other AAPMGs, he was not satisfied with what he saw. For example, the district provost marshals did not adhere to a uniform system of record keeping, and consequently the reports they submitted were difficult to use together. On muster reports, for example, volunteers were sometimes credited against quotas to the district of their residence, sometimes to the districts where they had enlisted, sometimes to both, and sometimes not at all. The records on hand for the period before enactment of the Enrollment Act were fragmentary and imperfect, if they existed at all. For employees of his office to navigate with confidence through this administrative Sargasso was all but impossible.

In a report to General Fry of December 12, 1864, Dodge announced his intention to "systematize" the work being done under his supervision. He recommended that each provost marshal in his division be directed to compile record books, as follows: "One letter book, letters received; one letter book, letters sent; one indorsement book; one account book, dr. and cr. [debit and credit] for each creditor; one roll book of drafted men entered by sub-districts; one muster and descriptive book of drafted men mustered in; one muster and descriptive book of drafted substitutes mustered in; one muster and descriptive book of drafted volunteers mustered in; one book of credits by Nos. from A, one book of credits by names from B, one book of quotas or credits from C forwarded to Provost-Marshal-General December 8, 1864; one book of exemptions; one record of deserters after muster; one record of delinquent drafted men; and the books now prescribed for surgeons."[11]

Physically, any one of the books Dodge enumerated was a formidable affair, folio or quarto volumes being then in use for the kind of record keeping he described. However, taken together, the compilations he proposed made possible an unwieldy but complete system of mutual reference that would exhibit at a few glances the status of every enrolled person, together with the response to various draft calls made by every district and subdistrict.

To some provost marshals, dispensing with procedures that had become comfortable because habitual was an unwelcome change, but to most others, the benefits of the reformed practices imposed by Dodge quickly became apparent. The provost marshal for the Sixteenth District, at Chambersburg, later recalled with satisfaction his receipt of a fresh set of blank books, with instructions, from Harrisburg. The directions "inaugurated an admirable and intelligible method for the classification and preservation of credits," he wrote, regretting that the plan had not been put in place sooner.[12]

By the time Dodge forwarded to Fry his description of this change of system, he could take satisfaction in the tangible results of his efforts as AAPMG. Being confident of support from Fry, he expected to continue in his current position for the duration of the conflict. On December 19, when President Lincoln issued another call, this time for 300,000 volunteers with a draft on February 15 to make up unfilled quotas, he was in a stronger position to enforce the law than he had been in September. On the day of the president's proclamation, the Adjutant General's Office issued a statement to all officers and men that "[e]very effort must be put forth to fill up the ranks, strengthen the armies, and aid the patriotic and gallant troops now smiting the reeling enemy with victorious blows."[13] Union successes in the field and the re-election of Lincoln had brought an end of the war into view.

In his December report to Fry, Dodge described, with good humor, some of the special difficulties that beset the AAPMG for the state of Pennsylvania. The chief of these was not geographical, despite the difficulty of communicating with some remote regions, nor was it administrative, despite a bookkeeping system that required correction. The challenge he found most vexing was political, visited upon him by interest groups in Harrisburg and persons from distant communities who were on errands to the state capital. The "political cliques and cabals of the State" all centered in the city, he wrote, and each of them "thinks the acting assistant provost-marshal-general should be its creature and obey its behests." Any action he took was bound to antagonize one group or another. He had sought determinedly to steer clear of political entanglements, but he was satisfied that "no man on the face of the earth can come here and do my duties for three months without making bitter enemies of some one of the cliques."

Hardly less irritating were the little great men from outside Harrisburg who supposed themselves influential enough to bully the AAPMG into deciding all questions in the manner they prescribed. Only the day before, a lawyer from some small village had left his office in high dudgeon, declaring that he would have Dodge put out of his position in short order. Dodge had declined to amend certain orders in a manner to suit the special needs of this man's clients. "I do not mention these things in the way of complaint," he noted; "I am, I think, entirely competent to deal with these people—but to show the Provost-Marshal-General the obstacles thrown in the way of prompt and consistent execution of my duty. . . . If they cannot use us, they abuse us."[14] Dodge's comical tone reflected his assurance that those who disliked him or his policies stood little chance of undermining his authority or interfering seriously with his work. But the weeks ahead would disabuse him.

On February 6, 1865, still confident but by now embattled, Dodge reported to Fry that two high officials, Governor Curtin and Secretary of the Commonwealth Eli Slifer, "are after me again, this time through the House of Representatives, State Legislature." Designating these state leaders with irony as "my friends," he enclosed for Fry's perusal two documents from a campaign of verbal attacks that had begun against him. One was a letter written by Slifer to the Speaker of the Pennsylvania House of Representatives; the other, an extract from the journal of that body's deliberations on the following day. The latter document, he observed, should "amuse" Fry, especially the remarks of William Searight, a representative who had earlier drawn up a resolution censuring Dodge's conduct. That statement had not been approved, but now Searight, "as a citizen of the glorious old Commonwealth of Pennsylvania," spoke in support of another member who had introduced a motion to censure Dodge for willful disregard of his official duty. Searight informed his fellow legislators that he had himself been treated in "a very ungentlemanly manner by this man, Major Dodge." Recently he had attempted, informally and without official authorization, to collect from Dodge a bounty from the federal government that was owed to a constituent of his. He branded as "a monstrous outrage" Dodge's refusal to bend the rules to satisfy him, and with the memory of that "intolerable treatment" in his mind, he declared his willingness to vote "cheerfully and heartily" for the censure resolution.

That resolution, introduced by Henry C. Alleman of Dauphin County, included a request to President Lincoln that an inquiry be made into the official conduct of Dodge, who "persists in a disregard of his official duty to the people of the Commonwealth, whose interests are affected by the draft of 1862." Alleman proposed that Dodge should either be directed to discharge his duty properly or else be relieved from his position so as to enable "some competent and faithful officer" to serve in his place.

The alleged dereliction was Dodge's refusal to perform a task that Secretary Slifer had himself been unwilling to take up. Inasmuch as the Militia Draft of 1862 antedated creation of the Office of the Provost Marshal General, Dodge had returned to Slifer's office a number of papers relating to the Militia Draft that had been sent in bulk to the office of the AAPMG, declining to have anything to do with them. Slifer's angry description of this refusal in a letter to the Speaker was the proximate cause of Alleman's resolution, and the letter was one of the documents Dodge now forwarded to Fry. Alleman admitted to the legislature that Dodge was "a perfect gentleman" but asserted that "if he disregards his official duty I have a right, as the representative of a constituency who have been injured by his acts, to have them investigated."

At one level, the issue being raised by these vindictive state officials and legislators was the precise nature of Dodge's official portfolio as AAPMG. Still, notwithstanding their professions of patriotic feeling and devotion to their own duties, they were addressing other issues as well. They resented the presence in Harrisburg of this powerful representative of the federal government, and they wished to do him official harm. Additionally, Dodge recognized a personal animus in the statements of his detractors and informed Fry that Alleman did have some cause for indignation. The legislator's brother had applied for a clerkship in the office of the AAPMG but had been passed over on the ground of incompetence. "For three years in Pennsylvania," Dodge wrote, "I have been fighting the same sort of cabals and rascally influences which you have now to fight in New York"—referring to a group of citizens who were attempting to discredit Fry. He assured the provost marshal general that he had no fear of his enemies in the current imbroglio. His only concern was that the persistent attacks by Alleman, Slifer, Searight, and their sort might induce Secretary Stanton to remove him from office for the sake of peace. "I don't want to be relieved," he wrote Fry, "simply because I am most decidedly indisposed to give my enemies a triumph, and if Mr. Stanton will not remove me until I do something to warrant it I shall triumph over them in the end, I think." Meanwhile, he asked Fry to assure Stanton that the allegations against him were utterly without foundation, and that he was ready to vindicate himself whenever called upon to do so. "I should like to have a good talk with you," he added.[15]

Dodge now sensed the possibility that, irrespective of his own defensible conduct, he might be outflanked by the Pennsylvania politicians and ordered to retire from the field. Comrades in arms, Fry and he were well entrenched against their civilian foes and defending themselves dexterously. The doubtful point was the political judgment of their superiors. In view of conditions elsewhere on the field of struggle, Secretary Stanton and President Lincoln might judge it prudent to order a tactical retreat at Harrisburg.

Under cover of a new set of concerns, the campaign against Dodge intensified. Lincoln's recent call for troops was in one sense without precedent, being issued in midwinter. Given the bitter weather that prevailed, the question arose whether incoming soldiers could be housed comfortably at rendezvous camps. On February 8, two days after Dodge had informed Fry of the efforts to discredit him, Governor Curtin joined the hue and cry. In a letter to Secretary Stanton, he pointed out that recruits currently at Camp Curtin were not being given adequate accommodations. Federal authorities knew that men would be arriving in the city, he insisted, and could have made due preparation for them, but they had not; as a result, many volunteers had been without shelter or blankets. "I very earnestly entreat you," Curtin continued, "to peremptorily order that provision be made at once for the citizens of the State who volunteer for military service." He named no names in thus alleging a lax performance of duty by federal officials, but his telegraphed remonstrance caught the attention of the busy secretary of war. Stanton directed Colonel James Hardie, the inspector general, to assure Curtin that every effort would be made to house the recruits as they deserved. "Peremptory orders have been issued to the officers at Harrisburg," Hardie telegraphed Curtin. "In case of their failure or neglect of duty, he [Stanton] requests you to make proper provision and report the officers in default, that they may be promptly punished."[16]

On the day after this exchange, the clerk of the Pennsylvania House of Representatives, A. W. Benedict, forwarded to Stanton a resolution adopted by that body requesting official inquiry into the conduct of Dodge as AAPMG.[17] On the same day, Dodge received from Stanton a telegraphic order to move recruits from Camp Curtin to other rendezvous, at Pittsburgh and Philadelphia, in case the accommodations at Harrisburg were less than satisfactory. This prompt attention in Washington to the conditions Governor Curtin had complained of might have been expected to mollify the state leader, but upon being informed of the order by Dodge, he objected to it strongly. He was satisfied, he declared, that the men were as comfortable as could be expected in the tents that had been provided for them, and he did not wish them removed. Accordingly, nothing was done, and the winter nights continued cold.

On the afternoon of February 14 the problem of alleged suffering among the men temporarily housed at Camp Curtin resurfaced when the adjutant general of Pennsylvania state troops, A. L. Russell, called upon Dodge to ask whether he could do nothing more to improve conditions at the camp. At least four recruits had been frostbitten, he said. Dodge therefore undertook to ascertain the extent of the difficulties and do what he could to correct them. He established that men at Camp Curtin who wished to spend nights at the "Soldier's Rest," an adequately heated building in the city, were welcome to do so. Next, he directed the post commander at the camp, Captain Abraham Cottrell of the Veteran's Reserve Corps, to inform the recruits of this opportunity. However, of the three hundred men then housed at the camp, not one elected to stay at the Soldier's Rest. Thinking that the offer might have been misunderstood, Dodge sent a lieutenant out to the camp the following day to renew it. Still, despite many comments about the bad weather, only twelve persons elected to leave Camp Curtin for a night's sleep elsewhere. Later that day Dodge informed the adjutant general of the conclusion he had reached in regard to the alleged sufferings of men at the camp. Despite "all of the complaints and exaggerated statements which have been made," he wrote, "I cannot ascertain that a single one has originated with the recruits themselves."[18] He refrained from stating what he understood perfectly, that the clamor had been raised by persons who were determined to discredit him.

The governor now professed himself satisfied with conditions at the camp, but the state legislature continued to abuse Dodge for neglect of duty. Inasmuch as Pennsylvania officials evidently disagreed in their evaluation of his official conduct, that conduct remained in question. Earlier he had declared to Fry his intention to ride out the campaign of vilification against him "in a soldierlike way,"[19] keeping silence until directed to give an account of himself. However, the intervening events had altered his resolution. A definitive examination of the facilities made available to recruits at Camp Curtin must be made, he now believed, and with it an evaluation of his own performance. Dodge therefore requested that an inspector be sent from Washington to look into both these matters. "I ask this in justice to my own reputation," he explained, "as whatever may be the ulterior object of the Legislature in its abuse of me, the repeated assertions of neglect on my part by members of that body may injure me with those [in] whose esteem it is my desire and honor to stand well."

Dodge's continued tenure as AAPMG at Harrisburg now hung in the balance. The fate of his predecessor, Lieutenant Colonel Bomford, must have crossed his mind as he wrote out his request for an official review, for certainly the campaign being waged against him resembled that of the previous summer. On February 21 General Fry laid Dodge's case before Stanton, and the secretary directed that the request of the beleaguered AAPMG be honored. Brigadier General Gustavus Adolphus De Russy was detailed to perform the inspection Dodge had asked for.[20] Not surprisingly, he was vindicated, and yet for political reasons his continued presence in Harrisburg was judged inadvisable. As it happened, Stanton and Fry had an even more challenging position to assign him, in a larger and yet more contentious area of responsibility, the Southern Division of the State of New York. When Fry suggested that Dodge switch places with Brigadier General Edward W. Hinks, recently installed and already embattled as AAPMG in New York City, Stanton approved the recommendation. Accordingly, on February 27, 1865, the two officers were directed to exchange assignments without delay.[21] As AAPMG at Harrisburg, Dodge had lost the battle for official survival but had won what he valued more highly, the confidence of his superiors in Washington.

At New York City

Dodge's new region of authority as AAPMG, the Southern Division of New York, presented special challenges to the Office of the Provost Marshal General. Comprising the first ten congressional districts in the state, the region encompassed New York City and some outlying areas, including Westchester County.[22] The wartime importance of that financial and mercantile center had given it considerable leverage in its relations with the Union government. Thus, instead of recruiting and drafting men through the offices of provost marshals, as General Fry had directed, a group of citizens had formed a Supervisory Committee to direct the process. This influential body of men effectively removed the marshaling of manpower from federal administration and, so far as possible without open defiance, from federal oversight. In general, their endeavor was motivated by determination to conserve political influence at the regional level. Strident claims from the Southern Division that inaccurate enrollment by the provost marshal general had resulted in disproportionately high draft quotas there had more than once resulted in abatements, agreed to by Washington to preserve the peace.[23] The Supervisory Committee professed a spirit of cooperation, but it devoted much of its activity to resisting federal mandates. It challenged quotas for volunteers, created delays, and made excuses for its failures.

In early February 1865 a deputation from New York City visited Washington in an effort to bully the federal government into reducing the quota that had been assigned the Southern Division in connection with President Lincoln's latest call for troops. However, this time they were unsuccessful. In interviews over several days, committee members called upon Fry to demonstrate to them once more, from detailed reference to the records in his office, the accuracy of calculations that had yielded the quotas for their congressional districts. At last, his patience tried to the limit, Fry took his case directly to the president. Lincoln, confident of Fry's ability and good faith and determined to make the best possible use of him at this critical stage of the war, supported him without qualification. When the committee urged the president to order Fry to give them four more hours of his time to satisfy their doubts, the provost marshal general assured him that he would be unable to do so without injury to the service. And "therefore," Lincoln wrote in a summary note, "he is excused from doing it."[24]

However unpatriotic and disruptive the actions of the Supervisory Committee might seem, its members justified their effort as supportive of the local citizenry, who were being treated unfairly. Whether or not the Southern Division had been saddled with an unfair quota, the threatened draft itself continued to be regarded as an imposition. Efforts to circumvent it or delay its action were acts of enlightened patriotism in the view of some Union supporters. Thus, while the citizen committee had been bested by Fry in its latest attempt to interfere with the work of his office, it kept up its stalling tactics on other fronts. Notable among them was the issuance of rosy progress reports followed by the circulation of petitions recommending that, in view of the success in recruitment being realized thus far, the draft should be deferred, at least in the Southern Division.

Brigadier General Hinks had succeeded to the position of AAPMG in New York on January 31, 1865, and in the few weeks since, he had held his own against the Supervisory Committee and its allies. However, owing to his exchange of assignments with Dodge, he remained in office in New York for little more than one month. His final public statement to the committee was a letter of March 3 to its chairman, Orison Blunt. There, noting the "elaborate array of statistics" that had been spun out to demonstrate alleged progress in recruiting, he insisted that the actual level of success was far below what was required, and that the draft would therefore go forward on the appointed date, March 15.[25] It remained for Major Dodge to make good that assertion.

To complicate matters, the government's effort to enlist new volunteers was also being impeded by a large number of persons who had no connection with the Supervisory Committee. These were lawless individuals who saw opportunities for profit in the generous bounties being offered to volunteers. Representatives of provost marshal districts throughout the state of New York converged on New York City to secure the men they were being called upon to supply, and as a result the traffic in volunteers became a seller's market. Eligible individuals sold their induction into military service to the highest bidder, ignoring the claims upon them of the congressional district where they were enrolled—if indeed they had been enrolled. Some "volunteers" enlisted under assumed names and then, upon being mustered in, found means to escape and enlist elsewhere under other names. A class of men called "bounty brokers" drove a prosperous trade, supplying men to representatives of outlying districts in return for a share of the funds authorized by local, state, or other authorities as payment to the enlistees. In collusion with unscrupulous printers or with clerks at the provost marshal offices, the bounty brokers hawked false enlistment papers that certified the mustering-in of nonexistent "volunteers." Unwary citizens were drugged and held prisoner, then delivered to the highest bidder; corrupt police were induced to empty jail cells in their care; forgeries of all kinds were available to order.[26] Despite efforts to bring this carnival of crime under control, in the absence of sufficient manpower it ran on virtually unchecked during the winter of 1864–1865.

However, on March 10, one day after Dodge began his duties as AAPMG for the Southern Division, a skillfully executed sting operation shut down much of this illegal activity. Lafayette C. Baker, a special inspector in the employ of the Office of the Provost Marshal General, baited a trap that netted him and his assistants hundreds of absconded volunteers and also a goodly collection of bounty brokers. Upon being informed of Baker's coup, Fry at first approved his suggestion that the malefactors be paraded in chains through the city streets as a deterrent to others, but then he decided against the idea.[27] Criminals these men certainly were, but simply removing them from circulation would better serve the aims of the government. At this stage of the war the men being mustered in could reasonably anticipate only a short period of military service, but hostility toward conscription remained strong enough to warrant continued caution. The best course was to carry on as in the past, promoting legitimate efforts to secure volunteers but scheduling the draft as a recourse.

By what means, then, could Dodge stimulate recruitment in the districts that had been placed under his charge? His first official action was to assert the exclusive role of his own office in enforcing provisions of the Enrollment Act. Previously the Supervisory Committee had fashioned rules of its own for crediting volunteers against the quotas of various districts. Henceforward, he announced, each man would be credited against the quota of the district in which he had enrolled. This system complied with the published rules for governance of the Office of the Provost Marshal General,[28] but initially it caused consternation among committee members. Fortunately for Dodge, he had already made acquaintance with several of these persons, including Chairman Blunt, and was able to effect the change without causing an undue clamor. The committee retained other functions it had arrogated to itself, including the safekeeping of funds received from various sources for the payment of bounties. Under a veneer of friendly cooperation, it continued to operate behind the scenes in efforts to retard Dodge's efforts.[29] Nevertheless, with the Supervisory

Committee thus far curtailed, he was in a position to test a new approach he had devised.

This was a decentralized, grassroots program to enlist the support of leading citizens in wards of the several congressional districts. By encouraging the people themselves to assume responsibility for fulfilling their quotas, he hoped to dispel the indifference that had prevailed at the local level thus far. Citizens' committees, actuated by community self-interest as well as by patriotic duty, would organize the procedures in their wards to attract volunteers. Working in cooperation with the district provost marshals, they should be able to secure a larger number of reliable men than previously, since all volunteers would now represent their own communities. Dodge threw himself into the organizational effort, and the result was a rash of newspaper announcements of public meetings to be held in the wards.[30] Their immediate goal, it was made clear, would be to secure a sufficient number of volunteers to render a recourse to the draft unnecessary.

On March 14, one day before the draft was to go forward, Dodge traveled to Washington for consultation with General Fry, having instructed the district provost marshals under his authority not to begin until he returned.[31] The results he had looked for had not been realized as yet, but he knew that stirring up more antidraft agitation could prove counterproductive. Certainly to conduct operations on March 17, Saint Patrick's Day, would not sit well with the unruly Irish. Fry prudently issued an order suspending the draft on that day throughout the Union states, and upon returning to New York City, Dodge brought with him another, confidential directive. He was to announce a suspension of the draft for as long as the citizens' committees in the provost marshals' offices were kept "fully occupied" in examining and enrolling volunteer recruits. Under the guise of humane forbearance, Dodge would thus place responsibility for delaying the draft squarely upon the populace of the districts.[32]

The seeming reasonableness of this policy ended resistance to conscription in the Southern Division of New York, and new bounty funds flowed in to attract prospective recruits. Concurrent events also played a positive role, as local newspapers reported mass demonstrations of thanksgiving at a succession of victories against the retreating Confederates. Meanwhile, Dodge kept up the official fiction of an immediate recourse to the draft in case the rate of enlistment should fall below an acceptable level. When the chairman of the Draft Relief Association of the Twenty-second Ward announced that potential draftees need not concern themselves with the possibility of their ever being called up, Dodge corrected him in a letter published in city newspapers on April 9: "I have no reason to think that New-York City will not be required to fill her quota under the last call," he wrote. "Unless ordered to the contrary by the War Department, I shall exact of New-York City every man of her quota, and the sooner the people make up their minds that the men must be furnished, the better it will be for all concerned."[33] But in recent days he had modified his published requirement for the level of activity by the Enrollment Boards, from "fully occupied" to "reasonably busy."[34]

Striking the first note in a weird cacophony of events, on the evening of Thursday, April 13, Secretary Stanton issued a directive "To stop all drafting and recruiting in the loyal States." On the next morning, the *New York Times* printed this statement together with a detailed account of the surrender, at Appomattox Court House, Virginia, of Confederate General Robert E. Lee and his Army of Northern Virginia.[35] But on April 15, in counterpoint to the demonstrations of joy unleashed by this news, the front page of the *Times* was edged in black, its headline declaring "Awful Event. President Lincoln Shot by an Assassin."

Elsewhere in that issue, placed inconspicuously, were a report that one hundred guns had been fired at City Hall Park, Brooklyn, to celebrate the raising of the Union flag at Fort Sumter, and also a circular issued the day before by Brevet Lieutenant Colonel R. I. Dodge, the AAPMG, announcing that "the business of recruiting and drafting will be discontinued in this division until further orders."[36] The latter statement surely relieved some city residents, while the news from Fort Sumter offered them the satisfaction of a symbolic closure. But like a dark cloud, the news from Washington blanketed all in an atmosphere of stunned grief. As elsewhere in the Union states, in New York City these were disorienting days, of affirmation, sorrow, shock, and emotional exhaustion, all experienced as one. Poignantly, April 16 was Easter Sunday, celebrating renewal.

For Dodge and other officials of the Office of the Provost Marshal General, the months to come would bring duties of a different character. For the present, Dodge remained on duty in his office but participated in local observances that celebrated the war's end and mourned the fallen president. As a Union man and a southerner, he was mindful of his countrymen on both sides of the conflict who had lost their lives and loved ones in the past four years.

From War to Peace

On May 1, 1865, a total of 1,034,064 officers and men awaited mustering-out of the Union's volunteer armies.[37] Facilitating the prompt return of these citizen soldiers to their homes and peacetime pursuits was now the primary goal of Dodge and his fellow AAPMGs and mustering officers. Speedy accomplishment of the task was simple justice to the men who had swelled the ranks of the Union armies in time of need. However, the nation was not much better prepared to muster out its fighting men at the end of the war than it had been to muster them in at the beginning. New York City was a focal point for the War Department's effort to speed the transition, and as AAPMG for the city, Dodge naturally encountered logistical, jurisdictional, and organizational difficulties of all kinds. Where, for example, were regiments that had arrived for disbandment to be put in camp? In what order were they to be dealt with, and were the necessary supporting documents for their men all available? The colonels and lieutenant colonels of the volunteer regiments were little disposed to accept without question the directions they received from Dodge and his subordinates. After all, despite his official position as AAPMG and his commission as a regular army officer, he was only a major. The delays and disruptions created by these questions of precedence were compounded by confusion as to the nature of Dodge's authority as acting assistant provost marshal general. The first two words of the title suggested that the office he held did not amount to much. Then again, the words "provost marshal" led many persons to inform him of lapses from army discipline and other situations calling for action by a military police force.[38] But the police power of the Office of the Provost Marshal General was limited to enforcement of the Enrollment Act and the specific terms of the late president's several calls for troops. Apprehending deserters fell within this charge, but the bureau lacked the manpower to pursue even that aim vigorously.[39]

The most serious impediment to Dodge and his fellow officers as they sought to muster men out was the fragmentary and inconsistent records they had to work with. Here the interlocking system of credits and registers he had put in place at Harrisburg and later at New York was of some use, but cross-referencing could not supply information that did not exist, nor could it obviate the frequent need to consult multiple records among those that had been preserved, searching for some elusive entry that might still be in existence.[40] The returning soldiers were impatient, their officers imperious, but the necessary forms had to be filled out for each man, and the information was not always at hand. Mustering-out was tedious, thankless labor, frustrating to some degree for all concerned.

By August, however, Dodge was able to recommend that three of the seven commissioned officers then serving under him should be assigned to duty elsewhere.[41] The flood of returning soldiers had crested, and the work of the mustering and disbursing office was taking on a steady regularity. Much of the labor now focused on the processing of applications for pensions, the payment of bounties, and the ascertainment of doubtful or disputed facts. Dodge was thus able to begin drafting his response to an order issued by General Fry in late April, that each provost marshal and AAPMG should submit an historical report on the work of his office, with commentary thereon and with suggestions for the future conduct of the Office of the Provost Marshal General. As part of the preparation for writing his own report, Dodge reviewed and annotated those that had been submitted by the ten provost marshals in his division. His own discussion, received at Washington on August 21, 1865, was thorough—fifty-eight legal-sized pages in length.

In accordance with Fry's instructions, the report focused on the work of the office Dodge occupied at the end of the war, namely the Southern Division. However, it also alluded to his tours of duty at Harrisburg, and many of his comments brought together ideas he had been developing during the whole course of the war. The Southern Division of New York, he wrote in his introduction, "has caused more trouble to the Government and furnished, from its citizens, fewer men in proportion to its population than any other in the loyal states." The Draft Riots of 1863 were "a foul blot on the fair escutcheon of New York City," but they were only a part of the resistance to federal initiatives that was kept up in the area. The real source of the difficulty was the acknowledged position of New York City as an indispensable source of financing for the Union war effort. Because President Lincoln's administration was reluctant to risk alienating those who held the purse strings, city politicians developed an unmistakable sense of entitlement. Dodge wrote that during his tenure as AAPMG, the more loyal districts under his charge complained to him "with great justice, of the exceptional favor shown to the most disloyal Division of the North."[42]

He believed that the scheme for recruitment he devised at the end of the war would have corrected this inequity had it operated longer than it did. Most citizens, he had found, were loyal and willing to do their part, and what he called his "divide and conquer" campaign against the Supervisory Committee would have transferred power to the several provost marshal offices and the wards they served. For the future, he was satisfied that asserting federal authority at the local level was the key to success. More generally, however, the system that had evolved during the war to secure volunteers for military service was in Dodge's opinion deeply flawed, especially as it had been administered in New York City. It engendered in volunteers a false perception that they were rendering "a special favor" to their country. Not only did the practice of offering bounties transform a citizen's honorable performance of a patriotic duty into a sordid quid pro quo transaction, but it cast a false light on the essential fairness of the conscription system. The local boards organized to help administer the Enrollment Act and the draft tended to "forget the wants and necessities of the country in sympathy for the individual man, and this overplus of tenderness has resulted in bringing the drafted man to look upon himself as a martyr to the tyranny of the Government."[43]

Dodge had come to believe that military conscription should be a permanent fact of life in the United States. Contrary to prevailing public sentiment, in his view it was "without doubt the fairest, most just, and equal to the citizen, and best for the country that can be adopted." In order to continue enforcing provisions of the Enrollment Act and future draft laws, he thought the Office of the Provost Marshal General ought also to be made permanent. Even though its creation was an outgrowth of urgent needs during the war, its continuance in peacetime remained a practical necessity. After all, most northern states still maintained militias of their own, and in the event of another national emergency, a centralized authority must be ready to coordinate their response. Dodge proposed that the Office of the Provost Marshal General should remain an organization within the War Department, but that to distinguish its functions from the operations traditionally associated with provost marshals, it should be renamed the Census and Conscript Bureau.

As at present, a corps of AAPMGs would mediate between congressional districts and the central office at Washington. AAPMGs would also serve as superintendents of the Volunteer Recruiting Service and as mustering and disbursing officers within the regions of their responsibility. They "should be independent of control of any one except the Provost Marshal General and Adjutant General U.S.A. and should have supreme control of every person and thing connected with the Draft or Drafted Men in his Division."[44] In view of their considerable authority, they should all hold "at least the local rank of Colonel of the Regular Army." But at whatever rank, a working AAPMG should be "an Officer of experience, and selected for his knowledge of and attention to details, and for the promptness and correctness of his decisions."[45] It seems clear from this latter profile that while serving as AAPMG at Harrisburg and New York City, Dodge regarded himself as occupying positions that drew upon his talents and warranted his best efforts.

On March 17, 1866, General Fry submitted to the secretary of war his own detailed report on the operations of the Office of the Provost Marshal General. In lucid style and drawing upon tables of statistics that bespoke painstaking care in its preparation, he described the unprecedented effort by his organization to help maintain the Union's fighting forces at victorious strength. He submitted that his subordinates had performed their unpopular and often misunderstood duties with scrupulous fairness that reflected great credit on them as public servants.[46] Soon after submitting his report, however, Fry found himself subjected to gross misrepresentation in Congress. Roscoe Conkling, a bitterly partisan congressman from central New York,[47] had earlier failed to extract special favors from Fry and in retribution had sought repeatedly to discredit him with his superiors, always without success. Conkling now carried his campaign into the public forum, accusing the provost marshal general of favoritism, suggesting that he had failed to disclose all the benefits he had enjoyed, and for good measure denouncing the organization he led as an instrument of tyranny over a suffering people.[48] Conkling's claims were outrageous at a glance, but having been uttered on the floor of Congress, they became part of the public record, and they called for a response.

On April 27 Fry therefore addressed a letter to Congressman James G. Blaine, who had repelled the slanders by Conkling at the time they were uttered.[49] After setting forth the causes of the animus held against him by Conkling, in sober, straightforward fashion Fry went on to render ridiculous the charges the congressman had made. Shortly thereafter, Blaine secured the permission of the House of Representatives to have its clerk read Fry's response into the record, resulting in the appointment of a committee to investigate the statements by both Conkling and Fry. The eventual report of that committee was not edifying, however. Representative Conkling's claims underwent no examination—possibly, it was averred, because some committee members were his close associates. As for Fry, the mere reading of his letter into the record was declared a breach of privilege, and on that account alone his statements were found to be without foundation. Thus ended the adjudication in Congress of the claims and counterclaims by Conkling and Fry. More than two decades would elapse before the latter was able to place in their true light the slurs that had been leveled against him.[50]

As the Conkling incident suggests, for a time Congress did not treat Fry with the consideration he deserved. Indeed, as the chief representative of the Office of the Provost

Marshal General he remained a target of popular resentment. Most congressmen agreed that creation of the bureau had been the regrettable necessity of a past time, and that its discontinuation would be an enlightened act of a nation determined to put that time behind it. This was a theme Conkling had developed as part of his attack on Fry. Commenting on a bill before the House to reorganize the regular army, he moved to strike from it a provision for continued operation of the bureau. That section of the bill, he declared, "fastens as an incubus upon the country a hateful instrument of war, which deserves no place in a free government in time of peace."[51] In due course the Army Reorganization Bill was passed, but with the amendment Conkling sought. The secretary of war was directed to continue the bureau in existence only so long as was necessary to conclude its business, and in any case no longer than one month from the date of passage, July 28, 1866.[52]

Congress eventually did acknowledge the wartime services of Fry and several of his subordinate officers by awarding them brevet commissions. For a time these valued recognitions were bestowed less freely upon men who had performed staff duty or served behind the lines than upon those who had risked their lives in battle.[53] Thus, Fry was first breveted colonel and brigadier general for his gallantry in actions, respectively, at First Bull Run and at Shiloh, Tennessee, and Perryville, Kentucky. Ultimately, however, his work as provost marshal general won him the brevet of major general[54]—a high tribute, even if devalued somewhat by his being one of 138 men who were accorded the same distinction. In Dodge's view, Fry richly merited all the recognition he received. Years afterward he declared his friend and former commander "a most admirable man—as clear headed & upright as there is in the Army."[55] Dodge himself was one of the 2,000 officers who were also awarded brevets. He was breveted lieutenant colonel as of March 30, 1865, for "meritorious and faithful service in the recruitment of the armies of the United States." As of the same date he was commissioned a brevet colonel "for faithful and meritorious service connected with the volunteer armies of the United States."[56] Thenceforward to the close of his career, he would be known familiarly as Colonel Dodge.

While the postwar Congress debated the future of the regular army, Dodge kept the Adjutant General's Office informed of his whereabouts but did not join his regiment, the Twelfth Infantry.[57] Instead, on January 12, 1866, he was named mustering and disbursing officer for the entire state of New York, at Albany.[58] In this position he brought to bear the managerial skills he had developed at Harrisburg and in New York City. At the state capital he oversaw a cadre of clerks, mostly civilian employees, who dealt with applications for bounties, pensions, and other considerations from discharged soldiers and their representatives. It was an unexciting but comfortable posting that permitted him an extended period of home life with Julia and their son, Freddie, now seven years of age. Julia kept in touch with members of her family in New York City and its vicinity, and Dodge was now in regular contact with his own close relations as well. At the war's end his parents had come north, and James Dodge had secured employment as a storekeeper in the New York City customs office.[59]

Richard and Julia were enjoying an interlude of domestic comfort that was unusual for a military family. He understood that before many more months, the needs of the army would probably take him away from this urban assignment in an eastern state. But unlike some fellow officers who had resigned their commissions to become volunteer officers at higher rank, at least he still had a place in the postwar army. With the fratricidal conflict now behind him, he was ready to resume his career as a commander of troops in the field.

In the foreseeable future, the U.S. Army would bear two primary responsibilities besides garrisoning the forts and fortifications already in existence. First, it would preserve order in the recently rebellious states and ensure compliance with federal Reconstruction policies. Second, it would provide a measure of security to the citizens who joined the nation's expansion westward. Estimates of the approximate numerical force that would be required to fulfill these mandates varied widely. Reporting on the strength of the army in October 1865, General Grant informed Secretary Stanton that the combined force of regular and volunteer troops stood at 210,000 men and was being further reduced. "In view of the vast extent of our country," he continued, "the recent hostile condition of a portion of it, with the possibility of future local disturbances arising from ill-feeling left by the war or the unsettled questions between the white and black races of the South, I am of the opinion that a Regular Army of 80,000 men is needed."[60] That figure was almost twice the strength of the regular regiments then authorized. Stanton, in his annual report submitted later that year, offered a more economical estimate. "Unless war be actually raging," he wrote, "the military force can be brought within very narrow limits."[61] But the *Army and Navy Journal*, now becoming recognized as an unofficial vehicle for the army's point of view, warned against false economy. It reminded its readers of a consensus that had prevailed in the early months of the Civil War: that the standing army must never again reach the feeble state it had exhibited in that time of crisis. To those who urged that it should now be reduced to 50,000 or even 25,000 men, the editors cautioned "Not so fast." In their opinion, to settle for fewer than 100,000 men would be imprudent.[62]

As finally adopted, the Army Reorganization Bill of 1866 inclined to the economical views of Secretary Stanton. Many legislators remained unsympathetic, on principle, to calls for a large standing army; others were simply not persuaded that the nation required a large defense force any longer. The maximum authorized number of officers and enlisted men was fixed at 54,661.[63] This fell short of what General Grant had wished, but at least Congress had not reverted to its niggardly prewar appropriations. Thanks in part to the influence of politically powerful fighting men, the War Department had at its disposal a reasonable level of manpower to meet its anticipated responsibilities.

The task remained for Grant, as general in chief, to reshape the regular army as it then existed into the somewhat larger force that had been authorized by Congress. One part of the problem affected Dodge: by what formula or other means were the nineteen current infantry regiments to be transmogrified into forty-five? The solution decided upon was to dice up the current units and impose on some of them a new organization. Prior to enactment of the Army Reorganization Bill, the Eleventh through Nineteenth Infantry, each commanded by a colonel with the assistance of a lieutenant colonel, had all consisted of three battalions, each under the authority of a major. Thereafter the three-battalion system would be abolished, with a single major being assigned to each regiment. The first ten "old" regiments had included only one major apiece and would retain their organization. The other nine would be divided into twenty-seven, with their first battalions becoming the new Eleventh through Nineteenth, their second battalions the Twentieth through Twenty-eighth, and their third battalions the Twenty-ninth through Thirty-seventh. Major Dodge, who was then on detached service from the third battalion, Twelfth Infantry, thus became major of the new Thirtieth Infantry, stationed at Washington, D.C. Four regiments to be composed of "colored" enlisted men were the Thirty-eighth through Forty-first Infantry, and four to be officered by wounded men were the Forty-second through Forty-fifth.[64]

General Order 1, issued from the office of the adjutant general on January 2, 1867, directed the transfer of the Thirtieth Infantry to the Department of the Platte, with headquarters at Omaha, Nebraska. On the same day, Dodge received a telegram informing him that another officer, Brevet Major N. R. Pease, had been ordered to relieve him at Albany. "The public interest imperatively demanding field officers with your regiment," Dodge was to complete the necessary transfer of records and public property to Pease as soon as possible and depart for the West.[65] The end of his duties in the aftermath of the Civil War was at hand.

A few days afterward Dodge was presented a farewell gift, a cap and a pair of gloves, by the employees in his office at Albany. In a witty note of thanks he acknowledged their "most acceptable present":

> To one just starting on a Winter Campaign against Indians, your present while most comfortable, is singularly inappropriate. You want me to be hot-headed, when I should be most cool. You give me gloves when it is my desire to handle the Indians without gloves.
>
> Be assured that warm as your present will keep me, it will not make my heart one whit warmer than before, towards those with whom I have had for so long, the most pleasant relations.
>
> You have all done your whole duty to me, and to the Country we delight to serve, and so long as I live I shall cherish the warmest sentiments of respect and regard for each and all of you.[66]

On this happy note Dodge rounded out over five years of army service behind the lines. Leaving Julia and Fred behind him, he made his way to Omaha, where, in accordance with orders issued on February 2, he continued across the winter prairie toward his regiment. On the first stage of that journey he conducted a group of recruits 292 miles, to the western terminus of the Union Pacific Railroad, at North Platte, Nebraska. Then, at the end of a 102-mile march further west, eight days later he reached Fort Sedgwick, at the eastern edge of Colorado Territory. On February 14, in a tent camp on the north bank of the Platte River adjacent to the post, Dodge reported for duty to Lieutenant Colonel Joseph Haydn Potter, in command at headquarters, Thirtieth Regiment of Infantry.[67] Thus began the second stage of his career as an army officer on the western frontier.

Part Three

Frontier Service, 1867–1873

Dodge's unwillingness to go into battle more than once against his southern friends and relations had denied him rapid elevation in rank, but he could take just pride in his service to the Union in the Civil War years. During his second tour of duty on the western frontier, his value to the postwar army steadily became even more evident. A seasoned plainsman in his physical prime, he was well prepared for hard service afield. Moreover, he had acquired a familiarity with staff duties that was unusual for an infantryman, and his dealings with civilian leaders had enhanced his poise, self-confidence, and personal force. This combination of attributes greatly increased his usefulness, and as a result he was selected for two special assignments in the eastern states. But prior to his promotion to a lieutenant colonelcy in 1873, Dodge passed the greater part of his time amid the rapidly changing conditions on the western plains. These had been the scenes of his apprenticeship, and these would also be the setting for his coming of age as a senior army officer. In his later career Dodge would be best known for his association with the region, beginning in this period.

6

The Course of Empire

Omaha, Nebraska, was in 1867 a burgeoning city, a gateway to development in the western states and territories. Like Saint Louis, Missouri, in earlier years, its status as a commercial center at the edge of the plains frontier lent it a hybrid character. A newspaper correspondent visiting Omaha from Cincinnati, Ohio, seven hundred miles east, took note of its mongrel character. He planned to travel farther west as a passenger on the Union Pacific Railroad, then under construction, but he observed that stagecoach lines from the city were still numerous, "their names suggestive of Indians, grizzly bears, and gold mines." The human scene was equally diverse. "Railway directors, speculators and visitors from the eastern cities, with eastern fashions and manners, jostle against bronzed miners and hunters from the plains. At the table you will see ladies whose dresses trail the required number of yards, and women who inspect them with wonder, as they sweep by."[1]

The industrial heart of Omaha was the offices and yards of the Union Pacific, on the west bank of the Missouri River not far from the business district. The corporation was busily pursuing its part of an initiative, authorized by Congress in the Pacific Railway Act of 1862, to span the western portion of the American continent by a railroad line. Construction crews had set to work not long after the Civil War ended, laying forty miles of track during 1865. In the following year 254 more miles were added along the valley of the Platte River, to a point ten miles beyond the confluence of its north and south branches.[2] Bad weather forced an early suspension of construction that November, but under the leadership of its chief engineer, Grenville Mellen Dodge, and a corps of high-pressure businessmen, the enterprise was poised to resume operations in the spring.

Quite aside from the logistical difficulties involved, the construction of a railroad across hundreds of miles of territory almost devoid of permanent inhabitants, except Indians, was a remarkably intrepid undertaking. Having served as a senior army officer during the war, Grenville Dodge easily convinced military leaders of the importance to the nation of an early completion of the railroad. As a result, Generals Grant and Sherman both pledged him military protection for surveyors, graders, construction crews, and company property.[3] It was understood, of course, that providing absolute security was an impossibility. The railroad would pass through traditional hunting grounds of the Sioux and Cheyenne Indians, and its intrusion there would surely be contested. The directors of the Union Pacific were anxious to foster a public perception that the regions to be traversed by the road were safe and secure,[4] but the army men knew better. As commander of the broad range of territory known as the Military Division of the Missouri, Sherman understood that the military demands would be considerable in the section of his command that included the Union Pacific route—the Department of the Platte. When the veteran commander of that department, Brigadier General Philip St. George Cooke, was replaced in February 1867 by a younger man, Colonel Christopher C. Augur, Twelfth Infantry, Sherman was pleased.[5] Augur was an efficient administrator and a field general of proven ability; he would not shrink from active campaigning on the plains.

The army was accustomed to providing security to plains travelers, having done so for many years. Its resources had always been limited, however, and before the Civil War, merchants and emigrants had prudently formed wagon trains for mutual protection as they passed over commercial and emigrant routes such as the Santa Fe Trail, which led to New Mexico, and the Smoky Hill Trail, toward settlements in Colorado. Increased wagon traffic after the war led the army to play a more active role as a protector of American citizens and their property. Beginning in February 1867, travelers intending to follow these trails were required to assemble beforehand at one of three military posts in Kansas—Forts Larned, Riley, and Harker—so as to form companies of sufficient size to discourage Indian marauders.[6] Many travelers refused to comply with this policy, but in going their independent way they pursued a dangerous course. West of the forts, Indians ranged freely across virtually the entire breadth of the plains.

Undaunted, increasing numbers of citizens passed through this territory in pursuit of their own aims. Driven by gold fever, beginning in 1865, thousands of would-be miners and enterprising merchants traveled to Montana Territory, most of them along the Bozeman Trail leading north from Fort Laramie, Dakota Territory. The presence of these interlopers in the Indians' ancestral hunting grounds provoked them to violence, and to secure the region the army established three posts along the trail, Forts Reno, C. F. Smith, and Phil Kearny. But the presence of the military only confirmed the Indians' determination to repel the intrusion. The Oglala Sioux, under Red Cloud, furiously contested the presence of the forts. The most dramatic result of this Indian offensive occurred on December 21, 1866, when, lured outside Fort Phil Kearny by a feint, the entire pursuing army force was ambushed and killed by the Sioux. Separated from each other by scores of miles, the army posts could supply only minimal protection against Indians. Often they were themselves on the defensive, being effectively besieged.[7]

General Sherman was mortified at the ascendancy "a few bands of roving Indians"[8] had gained over American troops. Yet he was not without sympathy for the tribes, for he understood the concerns that prompted their murderous behavior. They were being invaded by a powerful force, the tide of emigration and enterprise, that threatened their way of life. The "poor devils" would "wriggle" to escape the fate that awaited them,[9] but ultimately they would fail to stem the course of American empire, which in Sherman's view embodied historical progress. As a military commander, he hankered after an opportunity to strike a resounding blow that would end their opposition. However, as a servant of the national interest he stopped short of that purpose.

In his 1866 report to the secretary of war, Sherman set forth some general ideas that in future years became the effective basis for a portion of U.S. policy toward Indian tribes of the northern and southern plains. Earlier in the year he had made an inspection tour over much of the Military Division of the Missouri. That experience led him to comprehend anew that the army could never guarantee security throughout the region so long as Indians remained there. The only way to achieve stability in the western plains and mountains was to remove these native peoples from the path of progress. To achieve that aim, Sherman proposed creating two great reservations of public land that would thereafter become the protected homes of the plains tribes. In the north, the Sioux would occupy territory west of the Missouri River, north of the Platte, and east of the Bozeman Trail. In the south, tribes including the Arapaho, Cheyenne, Kiowa, Apache, and Navaho would find homes in a range of country south of the Arkansas River and east of Fort Union, New Mexico.[10]

Sherman believed removal of the Indians to those reservations of land would create conditions that fostered their development toward a civilized mode of life. He urged that responsibility for the tribes' welfare be vested in the U.S. Army rather than with civilian agents, arguing that the Indian could be induced to exchange his nomadic ways for the benefits of civilization only through awareness of responsibility to a controlling force. Meanwhile, while residing on their reservations the Indians would no longer pose a challenge to American development westward. The arrangement "would leave for our people exclusively the use of the wide belt, east and west, between the Platte and the Arkansas, in which lie the two great railroads, and over which passes the bulk of travel to the mountain territories."[11]

During the Civil War, Sherman had won a reputation as a stern combatant, a man of intense nervous energy and at times brusque vehemence,[12] but other facets of his character were not well known as yet. He was also a master of detail and something of a theoretician. William Swinton of the *New York Times* described him as possessing "a rare and felicitous union of method and originality."[13] Although Sherman's plan for the coexistence of Indians and others on the western plains was never realized exactly as he described, it did address with elegant simplicity the military problem he faced. Protecting the Union Pacific Railroad as it was extended along the Platte River and further west was a major component of that plan. As early as August 1865 he had assured the president of the Pacific Railroad, as it was then named, of his intention to "work for the security and prosperity of the Great West, where my heart has always been."[14]

By 1867 tentative surveys of the Union Pacific's route were completed as far west as the Wasatch Mountains of Utah Territory,[15] and with one exception the entire length of the projected road lay within the Department of the Platte. A few miles of track not far from Fort Sedgwick would run near northeast Colorado Territory, which formed part of the more southerly Department of the Missouri. For administrative purposes, this post was therefore temporarily assigned to the Department of the Platte.[16] As yet, of eleven posts quartering troops in the latter department, only five were in locations that afforded easy access to the Union Pacific line. Passing westward from Omaha, the first two were Fort Kearny and Fort McPherson, both established on the south side of the Platte River to protect the old wagon roads, but both now somewhat cut off from the railroad, which followed the north bank. The third post, Fort Sedgwick, was eighty-six miles west of Fort McPherson. It was also on the south side of the river but was more advantageously located for military purposes, the South Platte being fordable at that point almost the entire year. More importantly, the fort was only three miles distant from a settlement, Julesburg, where a railroad station was planned. Further west, two posts that had been established for other purposes would soon support railroad construction as well. These were Fort Sanders, near present-day Laramie, Wyoming, and Fort Bridger, in the southwest corner of Dakota Territory.[17] Additional posts would be constructed in response to evolving military needs, but in the winter of 1866–1867 Fort Sedgwick occupied the crucial position for the coming year. The end of track was then eighty miles east of it, and with resolute optimism Grenville Mellen Dodge hoped to lay track during 1867 as far as Fort Sanders, two hundred miles to its west.[18] Indian resistance, changeable weather, possible shortages of supplies, and other variables, including conditions in neighboring military departments, would determine how fully that aim could be realized. For all those concerned, it would be a busy year.

"Our Crisis on the Plains"

At the time Dodge assumed command at Fort Sedgwick, on February 14, 1867, its garrison included only three companies, two of infantry and one of cavalry, with a total of 172 officers and men available for duty.[19] As spring approached, the force posted there was rapidly enlarged, filling the available barrack space and obliging new arrivals to go into camp nearby. By May, five companies of infantry and four of cavalry were stationed at the post or adjacent to it. In addition, the regimental headquarters of the Fourth and the Thirtieth Infantry occupied tents a short distance away.[20] By that time the scene resembled a bivouac just prior to some grand campaign. However, in February the year's active operations had not yet begun, for construction crews could not lay track across the still frozen ground.[21]

An emergency within a week of Dodge's arrival exemplified dramatically the perils of winter service on the plains. A party of Indians had stolen stock from a rancher not far west, along the wagon road to Denver, and on February 21 Dodge ordered a company under Captain John Mix, Second Cavalry, to pursue them. A few days afterward a fierce snowstorm developed, with high winds, arousing fears for the men's safety. To send out a rescue party would be folly, for the exact course Mix had followed was unknown, and rescuers could hope to make little progress in any direction across the winter waste; all that could be done was to wait. When the cavalrymen arrived back at the post on March 5, several were severely frostbitten, but all were glad to have escaped with their lives. Struck by the storm while on the march due north, Mix had ordered his men to dismount and form a single file so as to keep together. Abandoning two of his wagons, he directed the first man in line to continue northward, breaking through the snow that accumulated before him for as long as he could, and then hand the compass to the man behind him and move to the rear. Eventually some troops were overcome by exhaustion and cold and lay down, refusing to go further. Orders, appeals, and even the threat of a cocked pistol failed to bestir them. At last, Mix drew his saber and belabored the fallen men with its flat side, forcing them to stand and ultimately saving their lives.[22]

The party under Mix failed to accomplish its purpose, for the stolen horses were never found. But a few weeks earlier Mix's subordinate, Second Lieutenant George A. Armes, Second Cavalry, had returned successful from a similar errand. Pursuing Indian depredators for seventy miles, he and his detachment attacked them, recovered most of the pilfered stock, and returned through the leaden cold, all with the loss of only one man.[23] Most expeditions on the winter plains were routine, such as escorting teamsters and their wagons on the road to Denver, but experienced troops such as these knew that none were without danger.

Anticipating a "state of quasi war" for the remainder of 1867, which he declared the year of "our crisis on the Plains,"[24] General Sherman required officers who possessed the hardy courage of such men as Mix and Armes. He cautioned Colonel Augur to assign only his best officers to important posts in the Department of the Platte, for their best efforts would be called for.[25] One man stricken from the list of preferred candidates was Captain James P. W. Neill, Thirty-sixth Infantry, who had commanded Fort Sedgwick for a time but was under arrest when Dodge reached there. Not long afterward, the department commander directed that the charges pending against Neill be withdrawn, sparing him a trial by court-martial "in the hope that his subsequent conduct would justify the act." However, within days the captain made trouble for himself again. Upon receiving an order from Dodge to report for duty at the post commander's residence, he failed to do so. Required to account for the lapse, he offered no explanation other than that he was then on duty as officer of the day[26] and would not comply with Dodge's order unless it was delivered to him in writing. The consequence was charges of insubordination, a trial by court-martial, and a light sentence—to be reprimanded in general orders by the department commander. Augur took the occasion to insist on due discipline among all officers in his command. "To establish that a commanding officer must select his office or his quarters agreeably to the likes or dislikes of his subordinates, before they obey his orders, is certainly a novel idea," he wrote. "It is unfortunate for Captain Neill that he is possessed of such delicate sensibilities, for, if he finds it so very painful to report to his commanding officer because in joint occupation of public quarters with an officer personally inimical to him, his military career does not promise to be either a very pleasant or a very useful one."[27] It was not, at any rate, a long one; Neill was mustered out of service on January 1, 1871.[28]

The year's military operations in support of the Union Pacific Railroad began well before the end of winter. In late February a westbound surveying party was assigned an escort of troops from Fort Sedgwick, and two weeks later a party of civil engineers was assigned another. Dodge sent out detachments from the post to patrol the projected path of the railroad and for a variety of other purposes—to escort mail stages, paymasters, and wagon trains, to investigate reports of violence, and to pursue troublesome parties of Indians.[29] As the end of track approached the fort, the pace of activity accelerated, and ominously, rumors of Indian mischief were heard more often. Plans were developed to fan out a considerable body of troops along the railroad from Fort Sedgwick, providing some degree of security along the entire line of construction. Two subposts would be established, one to the east at North Platte, the other sixty-seven miles west along the projected route, to be named Sidney Barracks.[30]

As part of these initiatives, Dodge's tenure as post commander ended on May 17, when he was replaced by his immediate superior, Lieutenant Colonel Joseph Haydn Potter. Two weeks later Dodge was assigned the duty that would occupy him in the coming summer and fall, to command a four-company battalion of his regiment, headquartered at North Platte. He would have responsibility for protecting government property at the depot there, providing security for trains and stations to the east and west, and responding to calls for troops in case of emergency. Telegraph communication existed between Omaha and the settlement at North Platte and would soon be established to Fort Sedgwick and points further west. Dodge's force should thus be able to reach points anywhere along the railroad with a minimum of delay. On June 9, accompanied by Companies A, F, H, and I, he set out along the wagon road, bound east.[31] About twenty miles from the post, the battalion caught sight of the railroad construction crew on the other side of the river, laying track in the opposite direction.

The town of North Platte was strung out along the tracks at the west end of a 3,000-foot railroad bridge across the North Platte River. It was a company town, but in addition to Union Pacific offices its thirty-seven business establishments included a respectable hotel, general stores, and buildings that housed a gaudy carnival of vice and violence. Warehouses and yards overflowed with supplies and implements of all kinds. North Platte was the first of the ephemeral communities that sprang into existence at the western terminus of the tracks—Grenville Dodge called them "terminal towns"[32]—and then in most cases simply disappeared as construction moved further west. It catered to the unruly tastes of railroad crews and others who had business along the road, legitimate or otherwise. Henry Morton Stanley, the English traveler, visited North Platte and observed that "[e]very gambler in the Union seems to have steered his course here. Every house is a saloon, and every saloon is a gambling den. Revolvers are in great requisition."[33]

For a time, the allurements of North Platte impaired the efficiency of the military force stationed nearby. The records of Dodge's command include frequent references to drunkenness on duty, reduction of noncommissioned officers to the ranks, and desertion. To distance his command from the town, he presently directed that the post be moved to the opposite side of the railroad tracks. Some time afterward he took a further step, forbidding any soldier to visit North Platte after the daily retreat call, except on duty.[34] He joined Grenville Mellen Dodge and other army officers in informing the secretary of war of the dangers created by the sale of alcohol along the railroad, but no action was taken in the matter.[35]

During the summer of 1867 the village of Julesburg, ninety miles west, took on new life as a boisterous railroad town. Grenville Mellen Dodge considered Julesburg "a much harder place than North Platte,"[36] and his namesake Major Dodge agreed. He described it as the supreme example of its kind, remarkable for "jolly recklessness of life, for utter indifference as to who 'went under,' [and] for careless abandon and entire disregard of all the ordinary rules of self-preservation." He described an incident that took place later in the summer while he was playing a game of billiards there, at the east end of the main street. Hearing yells and laughter and then pistol shots, he hurried outside to see what was causing the ruckus. "A spare but powerfully built frontiersman, two thirds drunk . . . mounted bare backed on a fine Indian pony, went flying past. Reining up at the end of the street, he turned his horse and with a whoop of defiance yelled out, 'You can't shoot worth a d——. I'll give you another show. Fair play, now. Don't shoot till I get started.' Bending low on the neck of his horse, he plunged in his spurs, dashed down the street through a perfect Balaclava of fire and noise, and to the astonishment of every spectator escaped without a scratch, though at least fifty shots were fired at him." On another day Dodge watched an uproarious crowd in the street encouraging a drunken man in his efforts to stand on his head.[37]

In June, General Sherman took a brief inspection tour of the area. On June 11, when he was almost to Julesburg, he addressed a letter to General Grant summarizing the military problems posed by construction of the Union Pacific Railroad: the extent of territory to be secured, the limited number of troops made available to him by Washington, the wily tactics of the Indians, the inferiority of cavalry horses to Indian ponies, and, finally, the determination of some westerners to do away with the Indians entirely. The "only course" for the army, he believed, was "to destroy the hostile, and to segregate the peaceful" Indians on reservations, where they could be maintained permanently.[38] Having visited Fort Sedgwick, on June 12 he departed from General Augur's camp at the end of track, returning to his headquarters at Saint Louis.

A few days afterward, Sherman and Major Dodge were caught up together in a scandal that, although based on imperfect information, threatened to besmirch the reputations of both. Correspondents of the *Cincinnati Gazette*, the *New York Times*, and the *New York Tribune* all reported one or another of four incidents that had occurred at Fort Sedgwick between June 12 and 15. The accounts differed among themselves as to dates and other details, but they agreed that the events had begun only one hour after Sherman had left the fort. As subsequently set in order by the *Army and Navy Journal*, the allegations were, first, that on June 12 a soldier of the Thirtieth Infantry received twenty-five lashes with a plaited thong as punishment for his theft of a gun. Second, on June 13 another enlisted man was bucked and gagged for an hour, and on the same day yet another was laid out "'spread-eagle' fashion on the ground for two hours, under a hot sun, the buffalo gnats covering his face and hands, and putting him in horrible torment." Finally, on June 15, one hundred lashes were administered to an unlucky civilian for selling a bottle of whisky to two soldiers. All these barbarous punishments, it was alleged, were meted out under the auspices of a certain "Lieutenant Lautz," but according to the *New York Times* the last one was ordered "in a very summary manner" by "Colonel Dodge."[39]

In its July 6 issue, the *Army and Navy Journal* gave top billing to these reported incidents but warned that "Justice to Colonel Dodge, and justice to all the officers and men of our Army" required an early investigation of the newspaper reports. After all, flogging had been abolished in the U.S. Army in 1861,[40] summary punishment of civilians by army officers was contrary to law, and any punishment whatever without due process contravened army regulations and was itself an offense warranting trial by court-martial. The published accusations against these officers may have been motivated by a desire to portray the military as incapable of wielding its power in a humane fashion. However that might be, they challenged all army officers' conception of themselves as an honorable corps of men. As to Dodge, the editors of the *Army and Navy Journal* regretted his "unenviable fame," registering their opinion of him as "entirely worthy of respect, a good soldier, and an estimable man."[41]

Remarkably, but in the manner of many apocryphal events reported from the western territories, the attention of eastern newspapers to the floggings at Fort Sedgwick ended as soon as these alleged acts had been breathlessly made public. Official records confirm that one instance of flogging did occur, however. In the absence of his two senior company officers, Second Lieutenant Peter A. Lantz (not Lautz), Thirtieth Infantry, authorized a punishment of twenty-four lashes for Private Isaac Rogers of Company I. Lantz, a recent appointee with little prior experience, had arrived at the fort only a few days before and was evidently asserting his authority with an iron hand.[42] Even so, no evidence has come to light to corroborate the bizarre accounts of his directing other punishments. Dodge was of course innocent of directing that an aged civilian, a former volunteer soldier, should be publicly humiliated and lashed until flesh hung in shreds at his sides. On June 15, the date he supposedly ordered the flogging, he was nowhere near Fort Sedgwick, having left the post with his battalion six days earlier. Weeks afterward, following a complaint from Private Rogers, he was instructed to investigate the circumstances surrounding the punishment that Second Lieutenant Lantz had authorized. However, when the soldier requested in writing that the charges be withdrawn, Dodge recommended that no further attention be given the matter, and there it ended.[43]

During that same summer of 1867, both rumored and real incidents of Indian violence engaged the full attention of military and railroad officials alike. Bands of raiders, usually of unknown tribe, attacked parties of workers at locations ranging from Fort Kearny all the way west to the Colorado line, and as a result trenches were dug at Fort McPherson and Fort Sedgwick in case of a concerted attack. Detachments were kept in the field continuously, either in pursuit of war parties or as a show of deterrent force. Approximately one hundred miles south, another railroad under construction, later known as the Kansas Pacific, was also under siege. Much of the territory that General Sherman had envisioned as a safe zone for American travelers and settlers was in fact a no-man's-land.[44]

At North Platte, Dodge complained that he had too few men to perform adequately the several duties being required of him.[45] On one hand, demands for escorts to one wagon party or another reduced the force available to protect government property and help secure the railroad. On the other, scouts over wide ranges of country were usually uneventful and yielded little useful information, while they further reduced the force available to answer emergency calls for assistance. During July, Company H marched 182 miles through the oppressive heat, without incident; Company I, 180 miles.[46] It was difficult duty, with units of the battalion widely dispersed and in sporadic mutual contact. The army was struggling to counter the guerilla tactics of the Indians, who possessed greater familiarity with the land and who, mounted on their swift ponies, could strike without warning. In mid-July Second Lieutenant Lyman Kidder, Second Cavalry, was dispatched south from Fort Sedgwick into Kansas, bearing messages for Lieutenant Colonel George A. Custer, who was operating there with a large force. Kidder and his small detachment were waylaid by Sioux Indians under a chief known as Pawnee Killer and perished to a man.[47] The news of this and similar incidents led eastern newspapers to denominate the summer conflicts "the Indian War of 1867."[48] Little wonder that Colonel Augur chose to direct operations within the Department of the Platte from a headquarters in the field, moving his encampment further west as the progress of railroad construction warranted.

Dodge also took the field this summer, ordinarily on scouts along the railroad and often accompanied by auxiliary soldiers from among 150 Pawnee Indians who were assisting the army under the general supervision of Frank J. North. The Pawnees had made their peace with the U.S. government several years earlier, and they welcomed this opportunity for military service in their ancestral homeland. Not only were they issued uniforms and equipment, fed rations and regularly paid, but they had the satisfaction of helping wage war against their deadly enemies the Sioux. With their encyclopedic knowledge of the country, they were valuable, if sometimes unruly, allies.[49] Dodge established friendly contact with a Pawnee named Li-Heris-oo-La-Shar, or Leading Chief, who was known by the English name Frank White. More than once the two men found themselves alone and in mortal danger, being surrounded by Sioux warriors who attempted without success to steal a march on them.[50] Such experiences formed a bond of mutual respect between the Indian and the army officer, a bond that held despite an ignorance of each other's culture that might otherwise have doomed the relationship. For example, as a compliment Frank White once brought to Dodge the raw, granulated liver of an elk he had just killed. Wrapped in a rag and with gall sprinkled over it to impart a spicy taste, to the Pawnee this bonne bouche from the fresh kill was a special treat. As politely as he could, Dodge declined the gift; whereupon, no doubt bemused by his comrade's lack of discriminating taste, Frank White buried his face in the rag and dispatched its contents on the spot.[51]

On August 11 a body of Cheyenne Indians sabotaged a Union Pacific train near Plum Creek Station, eighty miles east of North Platte, in a section of track being guarded by one of the companies under Dodge's command. The attackers derailed and set fire to the train, murdered the employees who had survived the initial incident, and then caused more mayhem when a second train collided with the wreck of the first.[52] Informed that the telegraph signal from Plum Creek had failed, Dodge dispatched fifty Pawnees, under Captain James Murie, to find out what was the matter. One hour later, learning that hostile Indians had taken possession of the stage station on the south side of the river, he commandeered a locomotive and hurried there with every man he had. Murie had been ordered to cross the Platte and engage the enemy on the south bank. Dodge, arriving at the railroad station close to the north bank, climbed to a lookout ledge on the roof and saw the end of what he described as "one of the prettiest and most successful fights that I have ever known among Indians." He recounted it as a triumph of cooperation between regular army forces and their Indian auxiliaries:

> As soon as he had crossed the river, Captain Murie discovered the position of the enemy, which was a most admirable one. Plum Creek is a deep bed, generally dry, some sixty feet wide, with high, almost perpendicular banks. The stage road crossed by a bridge. The Cheyenne line was drawn up about one hundred yards from the eastern end of this bridge, directly facing it. The right flank, which might be turned, was protected by eight or ten dismounted Indians posted in the loop-holed stable of the stage station. The Pawnees wore the uniform and used the tactics of the United States Army, and the Cheyenne leader evidently believed that the advancing force was United States cavalry. His plan was to permit them to partially cross the bridge, and then by a vigorous onslaught, accompanied by the usual yells and shaking of buffalo robes to frighten the restive and half-broken cavalry horses, render them

> unmanageable, and thus throw the whole force into confusion in a most difficult and dangerous position.
>
> Noting that the Indian pickets retired rapidly, and without hostile demonstration, Captain Murie suspected some trap, and on closer examination of the Cheyenne position he divined the stratagem of his enemy. Being greatly inferior in force (the Cheyennes numbering one hundred and fifty-four warriors), he resorted to a counter-stratagem. Dismounting his men under cover of the tall grass of the river bottom, he caused them to strip to Indian fighting costume (breech-cloth alone); then he made each put on his uniform hat, throw over his shoulders his uniform overcoat, buttoning only the top button. Then mounted and formed, he moved slowly to the attack, at the head of what to all appearance was a company of United States cavalry, too much encumbered with clothing to make a good fight.
>
> The Pawnees advanced by flank left in front. As soon as the leading files passed the bridge they inclined rapidly to the left, to enable those in rear to come up promptly into line. When nearly half the company had passed, the Cheyennes charged with furious yells. When they had arrived within probably fifty yards, the Pawnees threw off hats and overcoats, and with a true Indian yell dashed at their enemy. The latter, entirely surprised and utterly stampeded, wheeled their horses, and fled in confusion and dismay. The Pawnees took sixteen scalps, two prisoners, and a number of animals without a man or horse being even scratched.[53]

Experiences like this confirmed Dodge as a staunch advocate of using Indians against other Indians to achieve the army's strategic objectives.

While at North Platte, Dodge came to respect another Indian leader—one who, though not inclined to adopt the ways of Americans, chose not to oppose their presence provided they paid due regard to his people and recognized their prior claim to the lands now being occupied. This was Spotted Tail, chief of the Brulé band of Sioux, who encamped near North Platte beginning in the fall.[54] The Brulé chief stood apart from other leading men of his nation who refused to reconcile themselves to American encroachment. He accepted food, guns, and ammunition from the federal government, but he insisted upon being a party to any of its decisions that might concern the Brulés. Some persons doubted his good faith, but Dodge, who encountered him on many occasions, considered him an "an able and judicious ruler."[55]

With statesmanlike Indian leaders like Spotted Tail in the minority, and with approximately 3,000 hostile tribesmen ranging between the Arkansas and Platte Rivers, the military challenge faced by the army in that region was substantial. Indeed, General Sherman wrote that even if only fifty Indians were to remain, army detachments would still need "to guard every stage station, every [wagon] train, and all railroad working parties. In other words, fifty hostile Indians will checkmate three thousand soldiers."[56] Colonel Augur estimated the cost of neutralizing the Indian threat by military means alone at $10 million weekly for a period of two years,[57] an obviously prohibitive amount. Meanwhile, advocates of the Indians and their rights pressed for a peaceful solution to the problem of coexistence on the plains. In the summer of 1867 Congress therefore authorized a commission, the Indian Peace Commission, to explore the possibilities of an equitable accommodation between American interests and those of the Indian tribes. The seven-member body included three military officers and four other citizens, all well qualified to undertake their shared task but representing various approaches to the Indian Question—or as it was also known, the Indian Problem.[58]

After convening in Saint Louis, the commissioners first ascended the Missouri River by steamboat for discussions with representatives of northern tribes. Next, returning to Omaha, they boarded a train for North Platte, hoping to confer with the Brulé and Oglala Sioux and the Cheyennes. General Sherman, who was serving as a commissioner,[59] at once placed the railroad town under martial law, with guards from Dodge's battalion posted outside the saloons. A contingent of newspaper reporters and other interested persons swelled the audience at the conference, which began on September 19. The Oglalas had sent a message that they were too busy to make the journey to North Platte just then, but the commissioners found before them prominent chiefs from several other tribes. Dodge, who was present as a facilitator, thought the meeting "probably the most important council of late years, between whites and Indians."[60] Pawnee Killer, whose warriors had murdered Lieutenant Kidder, was in attendance, as were other more or less fearsome Sioux and Cheyenne leaders including Turkey Leg, Whistler, Swift Bear, and also Spotted Tail.

A warm conviviality prevailed in informal gatherings before the speechmaking began, but at the formal sessions Indians and commissioners alike comported themselves as befitted the gravity of the occasion. The ill-assorted costume of the Cheyenne chief Turkey Leg attracted Dodge's attention, however. He had on a tall stovepipe hat, and a green veil covered his face, but despite the hot weather he kept a buffalo robe folded tightly around him. When he rose to speak, Turkey Leg removed the robe, disclosing as the rest of his attire only a calico shirt and a pair of moccasins. According to Dodge, the auditors had some difficulty concentrating on his translated message.[61]

On the first day of the conference nearly all the Indians expressed dissatisfaction with the steady traffic of Americans along the Smoky Hill Trail and the routes to Montana that had been scenes of violence the year before. They had little to say in opposition to the Union Pacific and Kansas Pacific Railroads, which they seemed to regard as posing no serious threat to their hunting grounds. All expressed hope that, on account of their peaceable disposition, at the end of the meeting they would receive gifts of supplies, including guns and ammunition.

The conference resumed at noon the next day. N. G. Taylor, the commissioner of Indian Affairs, began by announcing that General Sherman would speak for the peace commissioners as a body. Sherman then rose, and with his customary nervous fluency he delivered a statement that made a visible impact on the Indians. After reminding them of agreements some of them had made at Fort Laramie the year before and had then, apparently, forgotten, he assured them that neither one of the two emigrant trails they had objected to would be abandoned. Then he offered them some advice. They could see for themselves, he said, that white men were growing more numerous in all directions. This inflow would continue, so if Indians hoped to secure permanent homes for themselves on good land, they had better do so at once. Sherman now outlined a version of his plan for segregating American citizens from the plains Indian tribes: "We therefore propose to let the whole Sioux Nation select their country on the Missouri River, embracing the White Earth and Cheyenne Rivers; to have their land like the white people forever, and we propose to keep all white men away, except such agents and traders as you may choose." The Cheyennes and other, more southerly tribes would inhabit a homeland south of the Arkansas River, but if the Sioux preferred to remove to that place as well, they were free to do so. They would enjoy the same privileges accorded the other tribes.

Sherman described the advancing railroads as virtually a natural force, not to be resisted. Americans "build iron roads," he said, "and you cannot stop the locomotives any more than you can stop the sun or moon, and you must submit and do the best you can." Lest some of his hearers should be tempted to continue hostilities, he reminded them that he and his colleagues were "not only a Peace Commission but a War Commission also." He assured them that those who chose to fight the American presence were doomed, for they would encounter a military force directed against them beyond anything they had yet seen. Soldiers "will come out here as thick as a herd of buffalo, and if you continue fighting you will all be killed." As to the Indians' expressed hope for special gifts at the close of the meeting, "[w]e will give you some presents because you have come up here to see us, but we will not give you much till we come to a satisfactory agreement."

The Indians listened to Sherman's speech without comment, but a short time later Pawnee Killer left the council in evident disgust. Hurrying to his tipi, he painted his face deep red, mounted his pony, and galloped away across the sand bluffs. This was no favorable omen. Still, when the rest of the chiefs insisted that they had no desire to harm the white man, the commissioners yielded to their appeal for ammunition to hunt the buffalo, and the conference ended on a positive note.[62] More meetings between the commission and representatives of Indian tribes were planned for coming weeks, but the gathering at North Platte helped shape their positive outcome.[63] Sherman had successfully promoted his vision of Indian reservations to the north and south of a wide space that would ensure security for the transcontinental railroads. Meanwhile, during the two-day meeting at North Platte the terminus of the Union Pacific Railroad had advanced westward approximately four miles toward the new town that would spring up at the close of the year's construction—Cheyenne, Dakota Territory.[64]

By the time of the Peace Commission's visit to North Platte, the activities of the battalion commanded by Dodge had become routine. Each company patrolled a section of track, and detachments of that unit were inspected daily by one or more of its officers, who passed from station to station as escorts on the passenger and construction trains. Two companies of the original battalion had been transferred, one to Fort Sedgwick, the other to the railroad station at Julesburg, but they had been replaced by Captain Murie's company of Pawnee scouts.[65] The headquarters at North Platte had been given an official name, Camp Sargent. As the weather began to change in mid-September, Dodge made requisition to the department quartermaster for a supply of lumber to help his men endure the coming winter. "My Camp is necessarily in a very exposed situation," he wrote. "The winds are very high, blowing down the Tents, Tearing out ropes, &c." He realized that it would be impossible to erect barracks given the constraints of time and expense, but he insisted that at a minimum the tents should all be reinforced by a frame of timber.[66]

The departure of the peace commissioners began a period of reduced responsibility for Dodge, and on the day afterward he granted himself a seven-day leave of absence.[67] This was a perquisite of post commanders, to be used at their discretion when conditions warranted. During his subsequent years of service on the plains he regularly availed himself of the privilege during the fall hunting season. Additionally, on some occasions he remained officially on duty but performed a scout, accompanied by a suitable escort, that took him into territory likely to yield good sport with rifle or shotgun. This year he took with him twenty enlisted men, seven Pawnees, and six visiting civilians on an elk hunt in country south of the post. Despite the possibility of interference by the Sioux, the party hunted successfully, bagging sufficient game to supply all its members with an abundance of meat.

For Dodge the high point of the trip came on the second day out. After the weary pursuit of a magnificent bull elk, he found himself out of the race, but, reaching a hilltop, he managed to witness the finish. Though winded, the wily animal had eluded all but two Indians, one mounted on a poor pony, the other on a mule, and the final chase did credit to the hunted and the hunters alike. The elk would dodge out of his pursuers' sight, double his track, and then turn to one side and hide in a clump of sagebrush or run down a ravine. The Indians would dismount, follow the trail, and at last jump the game, which would bolt out again in a renewed effort to save itself. This happened again and again until, exhausted, the beast squatted silent in some grass, and one of the Indians walked up and finished him off with a pistol shot.[68]

The Pawnees were indeed resourceful hunters, but on that night Dodge witnessed another remarkable phenomenon, their ability to consume what seemed to him inordinate quantities of food. He supervised the division of the huge elk carcass, which he estimated at seven hundred pounds, for distribution to various groups back at camp. Cutting the midsection in two behind the ribs, he gave the entrails to the Pawnees, who ate them at once. He then distributed one forequarter to the soldiers and the other to the Indians, reserving the hindquarters for his own mess. That night he and his companions ate a few pounds of the supply he had brought, and the twenty soldiers consumed about one-third of their liberal allotment. But the seven Indians feasted and danced all night, gorging themselves on what Dodge estimated at fifteen pounds per man, and the next morning came to him for more.[69] As in this incident, the friendly relations between the Pawnees and the rest of the party were accompanied by a sense of wonder on both sides.

Following another leave of absence, on December 25, 1867, Dodge was directed to remain on duty at North Platte until further orders.[70] Besides guarding government property, his chief responsibility during the winter would be to keep discreet watch over Spotted Tail and his band, who were encamped a few miles to the north. In the intervals between storms that precluded activities other than ensuring one's survival, he passed these quiet months pleasantly. Islands in the river downstream were dotted with scrub forests that harbored red deer.[71] The billiard tables at North Platte provided opportunity for him to sharpen his considerable skill at the game. The mail service from Omaha was regular, enabling him to indulge a habit of frequent letter-writing. And the proximity of Fort McPherson, only seventeen miles distant,[72] made possible some contact with fellow officers—and indeed, with Spotted Tail, who occasionally visited there.

Indians also appeared in North Platte, most often to offer goods for barter or sale. Sioux men regularly traded the sexual favors of their wives for bottles of whisky, a commerce that, however deplorable to Dodge and others, nevertheless thrived. Sexual attitudes and practices were one more area of mutual incomprehension between the Indians and the whites, as evidenced by an interchange between Spotted Tail and the citizen physician who was stationed at Fort McPherson. In the Brulé band it was customary for a man of consequence to furnish a wife to any guest whom he wished especially to honor during his stay. But while on a visit to Fort McPherson, Spotted Tail found himself being made an object of amusement by the medical man, who mocked several Indian customs, including polygamy. The doctor, a devoted admirer of the ladies, had a charming wife who was, however, utterly without his disposition to flirt. One evening, after enduring his raillery for some time in the presence of several army officers, Spotted Tail evidently decided he had taken enough and rebuked him for his discourtesy. "Doctor," he said through an interpreter, "you come to my camp, I give you plenty to eat, good bed and wife to sleep with. I have been in your camp three days, and you no say wife to me once." This quickly chilled the wit of the physician, who soon after made an excuse to leave the room.[73]

No one who came into contact with Spotted Tail could doubt his intelligence. Several years after giving the physician his comeuppance, he engaged a friend of Dodge, Captain George M. Randall, Twenty-third Infantry, in a conversation about religion. He recalled the efforts of various men—a Methodist, a Baptist, a Presbyterian, and recently an Episcopalian—to talk him out of his ancestral faith and into theirs. What was he, an ignorant Indian, supposed to believe? Randall told him that in his opinion religious belief was a matter of individual conscience and not of membership in one sect or another, and Spotted Tail agreed. Taking the proselytizers all together, he had decided "either [that] they all lie, or that they don't know any more about it than I did at first."[74] By the time of this conversation Spotted Tail had

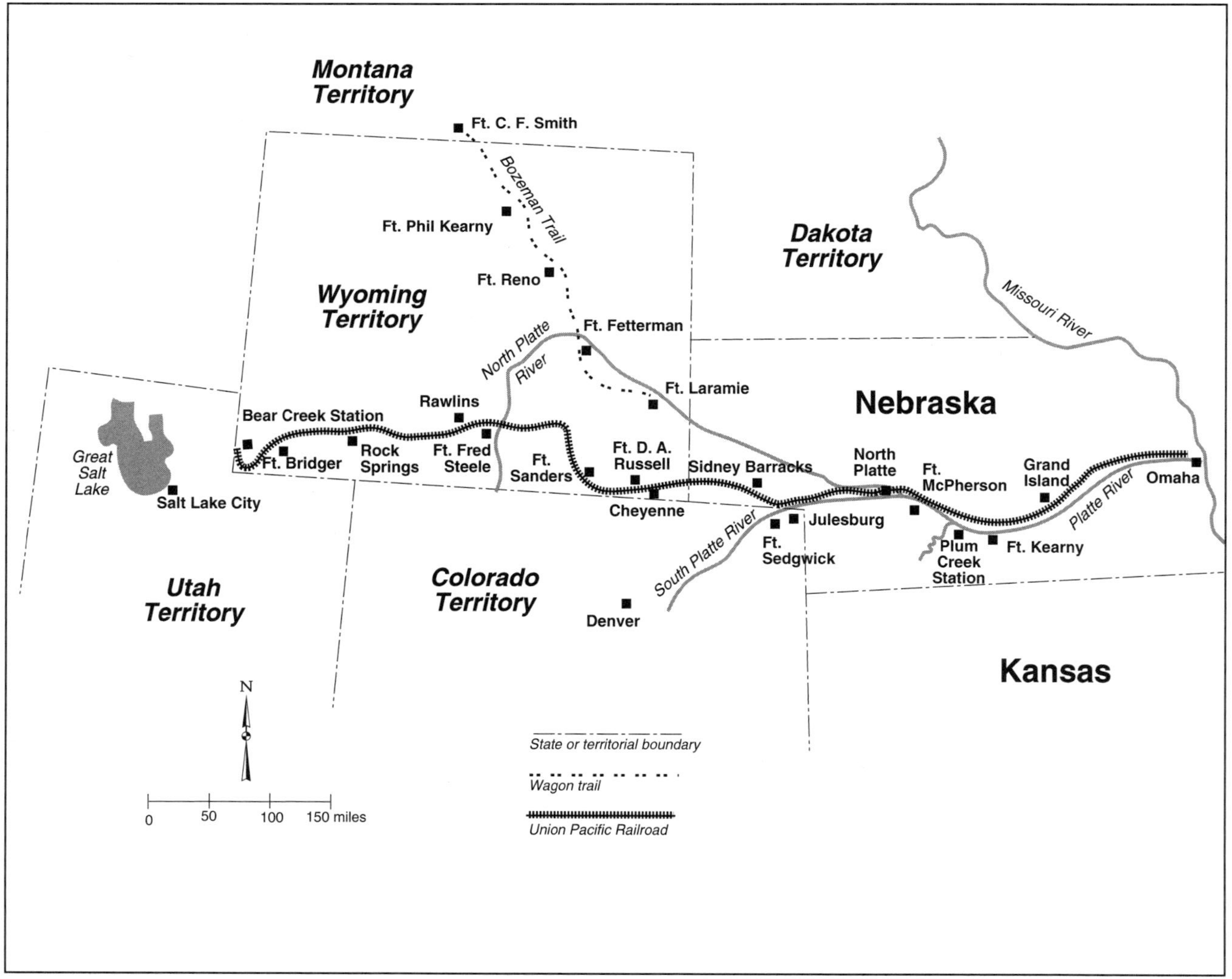

Region of Dodge's service, 1867–1868

visited eastern cities more than once and understood the undeniable power of American civilization, but he had given up neither his independent point of view nor his sense of the ridiculous. During the winter of 1867–1868 he proved a reliable neighbor.

The Rocky Mountain District

In April 1868 Spotted Tail joined other Indian leaders, including Red Cloud of the truculent Oglala Sioux, at a treaty conference with American authorities at Fort Laramie, approximately ninety miles north of Cheyenne. The purpose of the meeting was to hammer out terms of an agreement by which in return for annuities and other considerations, the tribes represented would inhabit reservations of land set aside for their exclusive use north of the Platte River.[75] Though the Union Pacific Railroad was as yet far from complete, it was already an accomplished fact that would forever alter their nomadic mode of existence. The question remained whether and under what circumstances the Indians would retain the right to hunt buffalo south of the Platte, but prospects seemed good for relatively peaceful relations with them in the coming months. Colonel Augur, who attended the conference, expressed this view in a letter to Grenville Mellen Dodge even as he ordered the bulk of his troops to move westward and provide security for the year's work along the railroad line.[76]

By April, Union Pacific crews were getting out the wood for crossties near Fort Sanders, approximately fifty miles west of Cheyenne, near the site of a town to be named Laramie. This section of track would present the severest engineering challenges of the coming construction season. In the first thirty-one miles from Cheyenne, the roadbed would rise 2,180 feet in elevation, to 8,242 feet above sea level, the highest point yet reached by any railroad in the world. Four miles beyond, a vertiginous bridge 700 feet in length would be required to pass Dale Creek, an otherwise inconsiderable stream. In view of these difficulties, for the first 150 miles of track west of Cheyenne, the Union Pacific corporation stood to receive $48,000 per mile from the federal government once the road had been officially inspected and approved.[77] This was three times the rate that had been granted for the 517 miles from Omaha to Cheyenne. Once the railroad had passed the Laramie Mountains, the laying of track was expected to proceed more expeditiously. Another lengthy bridge would have to be constructed across the North Platte River in central Wyoming Territory, but thereafter the railroad directors expected smooth sailing all the way to Utah, which they hoped to reach by fall. For that section of completed track they would receive $32,000 per mile, on account of the difficulties created by its remoteness.[78]

The headquarters of Dodge's regiment was now located at Fort D. A. Russell, a storage and shipping depot three miles west of Cheyenne.[79] Early in March Dodge was directed to report there,[80] and on April 19 he led a four-company battalion of regular troops marching west from that post along the railroad route.[81] The road was without tracks as yet but had been graded for a considerable distance, and accordingly they moved rapidly up-country, camping near Fort Sanders on the night of April 21. Established in July 1866, this post was also the regimental headquarters of the Thirty-sixth Infantry. Its commander, Colonel John Gibbon, had been assigned responsibility for protecting the railroad to the west of the post, and the battalion under Dodge formed part of the force he was deploying to do so. Approximately 1,000 laborers would be working at the end of track, comprising a formidable force by themselves, even though they were not officially equipped for defense. But hundreds more men would fan out in small groups for miles ahead, and these would be vulnerable to attack.

After conferring with Colonel Gibbon, Dodge continued toward his destination, the point 135 miles distant where the railroad was to cross the North Platte River. Small groups of Indians had already begun harassing the railroad crews. Four members of a grading party were wounded on April 23, one day before Dodge's battalion arrived at the scene of the incident.[82] A few days later Dodge left three of his companies in camp at Rock Creek while, supported by Company B, Second Cavalry, he unsuccessfully pursued another party of hostile Indians. In accordance with instructions, he now began posting one after another of his companies at points along the road. Breaking camp in the morning of April 28, he left the cavalry company at Rock Creek and pushed ahead with three units of his own regiment. After a seventeen-mile march to Medicine Bow, he left behind him Company G. On the following morning, April 30, he posted Company H at Summit, twenty miles farther on. Later that day he reached the North Platte River and went into camp there. The troops under his command were thus positioned at points extending one-half the distance back to Fort Sanders.[83]

Despite the attenuation of this military presence, instances of Indian violence along the Union Pacific line were few during the spring and early summer of 1868. Ordinarily the attacks were made by boys and young men, more for the thrill of the thing than from genuine hostility. In western Kansas, eastern Colorado, and regions further south, troops saw more serious action, but the forces under Gibbon were conspicuously successful in keeping the peace. By July 15 a bridge across the North Platte River was ready for traffic, and a locomotive pulling a specialized construction train crossed it on that day. Two months later the tracklayers reached Green River, 150 miles further; and by early November, as projected, the road extended to Bear River City, 890 miles from Omaha and just east of the Utah line.

Shortly after Dodge arrived at the crossing of the North Platte, he received an order from departmental headquarters to establish a permanent post at that point.[84] This installation, the only one between Fort Sanders and Fort Bridger 180 miles further west, would protect the railroad at the strategic river crossing. Additionally, it would supply barrack space for troops from the three posts that had guarded the Bozeman Trail but were being abandoned in accordance with the recent agreement at Fort Laramie. Working with the few men he had, Dodge laid out the post and began construction using what little wood could be found in the vicinity.[85] The fort's location, on a high, level plot of land at the west end of the planned railroad bridge, was healthful and strategically perfect. Perhaps as a legacy of his years in Texas, he welcomed the challenge of improvising to construct buildings of approved design. The post was still more a conception than a reality when, on June 30, he first referred to it by its official title, Fort Fred Steele; but when the railroad arrived two weeks later it was ready for occupancy.[86] Access to rail transportation facilitated further construction, and within a few more weeks the site was capable of housing eight companies of troops. The railroad also spawned a new town near the post, named Benton, but Dodge quickly distanced his command from it. He proclaimed a three-mile military reservation in all directions from the fort, forbade citizens from residing anywhere else within that space except at the townsite already occupied, and placed the settlement under military authority. The gamblers and whisky sellers soon decamped to a more accommodating location fifteen miles west, the new town of Rawlins.[87] On July 23 Fort Fred Steele became the headquarters of the Thirtieth Infantry.[88]

Dodge's service along the Union Pacific Railroad during the summer and fall of 1868 was divided into two segments of time. The first, through July, ended with his establishment of Fort Fred Steele. Thereafter he was a staff officer with responsibility for ensuring the adequacy of all military operations and facilities along the railroad west of Fort Sanders. An administrative unit called the Rocky Mountain District, under Colonel Gibbon, had been created within the Department of the Platte, and Dodge was named its acting assistant inspector general.[89] The assignment was a sensitive one, requiring discretion and discriminating judgment, but he was well prepared to undertake its duties, having performed them for a time during the Civil War and also while at North Platte the year before. Gibbon, six years his senior, was a good man to work for. A North Carolinian like himself and an able military leader, he was also a lively conversationalist with a wide range of interests, many of which tallied with his own.[90] Fort Sanders, headquarters of the Rocky Mountain District, was a comfortable posting, and Dodge's immediate superior and friend Lieutenant Colonel Potter now commanded there.[91] In all, the late summer appointment was everything Dodge could have wished for.

His movements up and down the railroad and into uncompleted sections beyond the railhead proved continuously interesting to him. Railroad construction naturally brought with it situations that required special attention, but not often, and meanwhile he found Wyoming without peer in the western territories as a place to hunt game. Once, near Fort Fred Steele, he caught sight of an elk herd that numbered no fewer than five hundred animals. Cougar, deer, and antelope were all to be found, and also game birds, including several varieties of grouse. He led a group of thirty visitors on a two-day grouse hunt from Fort Sanders, bagging a quantity sufficient to feed all the guests in princely style and also bring a supply back to the post.[92]

By the end of the summer, railway passenger service was available to Fort Bridger, but Fort Sanders remained a preferred stopping-place for officials and groups of dignitaries. Accompanied by General Sherman, in late July General Grant visited there as part of his campaign tour for the presidency of the United States. The two generals conferred at the fort with Grenville Mellen Dodge and other directors of the Union Pacific, lending decisive assistance to their former comrade in a dispute that pitted him against the vice president of the road, Thomas C. Durant.[93] On another occasion a famous savant from Harvard, the comparative zoologist Louis Agassiz, dazzled his hosts with insights into the character of fossil specimens that had been collected in the vicinity and brought to him for analysis. Agassiz listened with interest to Dodge's accounts of phenomena he had witnessed in recent weeks, including miles-long rows of serrated ridges south of the Laramie plains, a dry lakebed that now sat atop a high plateau, and a petrified tree trunk, perfectly preserved, with petrified chips beside it that resembled fragments left by some prehistoric axe. The scientist wished to see some of these curiosities, but he was prevented from doing so by his poor physical condition and also the constraints of his schedule.[94] Nevertheless, Dodge's conversations with the Swiss American researcher left a lasting impression on him. His interest in observing and speculating upon geological phenomena of the western plains and mountains dated from this eventful summer.

In September Dodge made the acquaintance of another visitor to Fort Sanders who was destined to play a role in his life history. This was William Blackmore, a forty-one-year-old English lawyer and venture capitalist who had been invited to accompany the official inspection party to certify the satisfactory progress of the Union Pacific Railroad during 1868. Probably Blackmore had earned this consideration through his activities in England raising funds for construction of the railroad. However, he was already well known as an influential friend of western development and of the United States generally. On his first visit to America, in 1863 and 1864, he had attempted to arrange a loan of $500 million to the cash-hungry federal government, secured by lands in the public domain.[95] Though ultimately unsuccessful, this commercial initiative brought him into contact with Salmon Chase, the secretary of the treasury, with William H. Seward, Edwin M. Stanton, and even President Lincoln. A gregarious personality and a firm supporter of the Union cause, Blackmore was also granted the privilege of interviewing high army officials in the field. He made the friendly acquaintance of Generals Sherman, Sheridan, Gibbon, George G. Meade, and others before returning to England to inform prospective investors there of what he had learned.[96]

Prior to his departure from the United States, this wealthy man of affairs purchased for $10,000 a national treasure that had failed to excite sufficient interest among Americans to ensure its finding a permanent repository at home. The unexampled Davis-Squier collection, artifacts obtained from the great Indian mounds of Ohio, was a compendium of early North American material culture. It became the core of the Blackmore Museum, lavishly endowed by the collector and founded in 1867 near his home in Salisbury, Wiltshire.[97] Philanthropist, antiquary, explorer, capitalist, land developer, sportsman—Blackmore's interests and pursuits all interpenetrated, expressing together his energy, grand ideas, and enthusiasm for new undertakings. His second visit to the United States, in 1868, introduced him to the nation's newly accessible western territories, where he discovered sources of keen personal interest, including seemingly numberless financial opportunities.

Accompanied by an English colleague, Colonel Edward Bridges of the Grenadier Guards, on September 21 Blackmore boarded a Union Pacific train at Omaha on the first leg of his western tour. Following a brief buffalo hunt at Fort Sedgwick, the visitors proceeded to Laramie, arriving there on September 25, one day before the official party was fully assembled. At Fort Sanders they visited Colonel Gibbon and met Lieutenant Colonel Potter, Major Dodge, and other officers. Blackmore recorded in his diary the suggestions made by these men for a hunting expedition in the nearby hills and canyons. Dr. Charles B. White, the post surgeon, suggested Elk Mountain. Dodge spoke up for the North Platte River near Fort Fred Steele, but he must have intimated the possibility of trouble with Indians, for Blackmore wrote "Scalp trap" beside his notation of the area. Potter recommended using Fort Bridger as a base camp and foraging about in that vicinity, and his was the plan eventually decided upon.[98]

On the following morning the inspection party set out from Laramie across what Blackmore described as a "Desolate scene — sage brush and snow." However, the travelers had been provided a luxurious sleeping car, and they were kept comfortable as the scenery improved. Officers and officials boarded the train or left it at station stops, but in his capacity as acting assistant inspector general, Dodge remained aboard to the end of track, then near Green River in far western Wyoming. During part of this railroad journey, he and Blackmore passed time together, and the interests they shared made their different personal histories all the more engaging to each other. Both loved the outdoors, were ardent sportsmen and more than casual students of primitive culture, and both were fascinated by the natural curiosities of the country they were passing through. Dodge's duties precluded his accompanying Blackmore and Bridges on their four-day outing from Fort Bridger,[99] but the party was complete again on October 4, when they set out by wagon for Salt Lake City.

During the ten days that followed, several party members pursued their own interests, on their own schedule. Railroad officials wished to discuss with leaders of the Mormon church the labor being performed under contract by Mormon workmen who were grading and blasting tunnels in Weber Canyon, north of the city. Blackmore investigated opportunities for mining, and possibly for the establishment of agricultural settlements in the region. He contacted John Willard Young, first counselor to President Brigham Young, and later he discussed economic matters with the president himself. Following his interviews with church officials, Blackmore returned to the railroad terminus at Green River. Still on the alert for business opportunities, on his way there he purchased a one-half interest in a mining concern, the Coalville Coal Company. On October 12 he rejoined the rest of the inspection party at Echo City, Utah.[100]

During the wagon journey back to the railhead, Blackmore exchanged stories with Major Dodge and the wagon driver. Dodge regaled his new acquaintance with anecdotes of Indian cruelty ("Dutchman flayed near Denver"), sometimes with an ironic twist ("Man tied to wagon wheel and skinned and then left with his friends – on Platte. Had boasted that he would kill the first Indian he saw").[101] While at Omaha, Blackmore had recorded in his diary some details of Major George Alexander "Sandy" Forsyth's dramatic standoff against a horde of Sioux, Cheyenne, and Arapaho attackers, expressing curiosity about the strategy that had preserved the lives of the wounded officer and some of his men.[102] On the stage ride with Dodge, he set down an entry on the "Best troops to fight Indians," evidently reflecting the experience of his companion: "5 or 6 troops of Pawnees With 2 of the Cavalry."[103]

Early on the morning of October 18 the eastbound train reached Laramie and the inspection party broke up, some members continuing their homeward journey at once. Blackmore elected instead to pass a few hours at Fort Sanders and take another train departing that afternoon. The trip to Utah had proved propitious for him, opening up far more possibilities for investment, exploration, and adventure than he could hope to realize at present. His energies were already being taxed by enterprises in Europe, Africa, and India, but the American West was peculiarly to his taste. He planned to return, in part for business purposes, in part also as an inspiriting getaway. While on the tour he had made friends with Ferdinand V. Hayden, a geologist who had recently begun an ambitious series of explorations and surveys of the western territories. Blackmore discussed with Hayden the possibility of producing a handsome volume of photographs as an adjunct to these explorations, documenting the characteristic features of certain Indian tribes. He was interested in providing financial support for Hayden's scientific inquiries, and he looked forward to accompanying him in some future expedition.[104] Another of Blackmore's valued new friends was Dodge, whose congenial personality and skill as a plainsman would make him a splendid future hunting companion. Exactly when and where they would find time to take the field together remained in doubt, but a spark of good feeling had been lit between them that suggested its eventual likelihood. Having passed the day pleasantly with his "friends at Fort,"[105] Blackmore set out on his return to England, probably leaving behind him a strange quiet, as from the removal of an abundant fountain of energy.

Dodge's tour of duty as acting assistant inspector general ended on November 27, one week before the Rocky Mountain District was discontinued as being no longer required. For the time being, the protection of the railroad, telegraph line, and other public interests between Fort McPherson, Nebraska, and Fort Douglas at Salt Lake City became the responsibility of post commanders in their respective regions along the way.[106] With the 1868 construction season at an end, the Union Pacific and, passing east from California, the Central Pacific Railroad were within a few score miles of each other and would surely meet in the coming year. Dodge's contribution to the work of supporting this effort was completed.

Throughout December he presided at general court-martial sessions at Fort Sanders—dreary but essential duty. Probably one case was of particular interest to him, as recalling a debated point from his days in Texas: Could the period of confinement of a convicted enlisted man be extended beyond the term of his enlistment? The court's ruling, that it indeed could, was eventually sustained and helped clarify army policy on the matter.[107] This was a useful development, and yet, surveying the frigid plains that surrounded the post, not altogether satisfying. Dodge was lonely for his wife and son, whom he had not seen since his most recent leave of absence, in October 1867.[108] Of course, in the ordinary course of affairs he could expect to be granted another leave before spring. He had no inkling that within days he would be ordered east on a special assignment entrusted to him by the secretary of war.

7

The Wheels of Government

In October 1868 the quartermaster general, Brigadier General Montgomery C. Meigs, forwarded to the secretary of war a report by Captain David Parkinson, formerly regimental quartermaster of the Twenty-fifth Infantry. Parkinson, then stationed at Memphis, Tennessee, had alleged persuasively that gross frauds were being perpetrated on the federal government by pension and bounty claim agents in that city, and Meigs recommended that the charges be brought to the attention of other army bureaus and also the commissioner of pensions.[1] That course was approved by the secretary of war, John M. Schofield, who took a summary measure of his own. He directed that a claim for $7,741 on the Freedman's Bureau by Moyers and Dedrick, a Memphis law firm that Parkinson had named in his allegations, should be held in abeyance, and also that the firm's privilege of doing business with his department should be suspended pending further inquiry.[2]

Misrepresentation and price-gouging by persons acting as middlemen for soldiers or their family members who wished to apply for bounties and pensions was hardly new. It had been rampant during the Civil War, owing chiefly to the proliferation of bounties offered to volunteer recruits by various entities. The varieties of abuse were legion, but those most publicized included demanding fees for unnecessary services, selling forged documents, underpaying funds that had been disbursed to agents on behalf of pensioners, and submitting applications under false pretenses—for example, in the names of individuals no longer living. Persons ignorant of government procedures were easily imposed upon, and in many cases residents of rural locations were unable to gather and complete the necessary paperwork without the help of some practiced hand. Many claim agents who advertised their services in city newspapers were scrupulously honest and charged modest fees,[3] but not all. In an effort to increase efficiency and combat the problem, in July 1866 the War Department issued a set of regulations for the payment of federal bounties.[4] However, this action only swelled the bureaucracy for processing bounty and pension claims. Illegal activities by pension agents were particularly troublesome to the Freedman's Bureau, an organization established at the end of the Civil War to ensure that former slaves were accorded their full due as American citizens.[5] The bureau, which operated primarily in the formerly rebellious states, was heartily resented there as a part of the Reconstruction policy being imposed upon the South. In the minds of many persons, it was an instrument of Yankee oppression and a fitting target for subversive attack.

Secretary Schofield was well acquainted with the tensions that still smoldered in southern states. Owing to their recalcitrance, not all had been granted renewed representation in Congress even yet.[6] Himself a career military man, Schofield had served the Union cause with distinction during the war. As a participant in General Sherman's southern campaign, in November 1864 he defeated Confederate General John B. Hood at the battle of Franklin, Tennessee. A short time later, in cooperation with General George H. Thomas, he defeated Hood again at the battle of Nashville. In February 1865, when the state of North Carolina was constituted a Union military department, Schofield was named its commander, cooperating with General Sherman as that leader moved northward along the Atlantic coast following his March to the Sea from Atlanta. Early in 1867 Schofield was named to another challenging post, as military governor of the state of Virginia. His record of providing steady leadership in times of roiling crisis qualified him well for his next appointment; in April 1868, he became secretary of war amid the furor that led to the impeachment of President Andrew Johnson.[7] Although a military man, Schofield was judged capable of acting judiciously in that civilian office despite the threats of renewed violence that echoed from all sides.

On December 30, 1868, Secretary Schofield directed the office of the adjutant general to supply the name of a suitable army officer to perform a further investigation of the allegations brought to light thus far against the firm of Moyers and Dedrick. Major Richard I. Dodge, Thirtieth Infantry, was duly nominated, and on January 5 a telegram went out to General Sherman at Saint Louis requesting—not directing—that he order Dodge to Memphis.[8] Schofield was sensitive to niceties of this sort, and his deviation from the imperative voice usual in army orders and directives was no doubt intentional. Schofield was Sherman's former subordinate and, now holding the lineal rank of brigadier general, was still outranked by him. For the present he was the lieutenant general's civilian superior, but only until a new secretary of war could be installed following the inauguration of President-elect Grant. The message to Sherman gave no inkling of the duty in prospect for Major Dodge, other than that it would be temporary and that he would be sent instructions once he reached Memphis.[9]

With his extensive experience in recruiting, disbursement, record keeping, and the payment of bounties and pensions, Dodge was clearly qualified to perform this sensitive assignment. Not only was he a southern man whose good faith and loyalty could be relied upon, but, especially through his experiences in New York City, he was versed in the wiles of those who victimized others while appropriating government largesse to themselves. Cool in the face of conflict with aggressive business types, quite willing to take a principled stand, a friend to black Americans and an enemy to chicanery, he could be expected to perform his task with a relish. His directions were not to assume the role of judge and jury but instead to interview persons connected with the alleged misconduct of the law firm, take depositions from them, and summarize the results *ex parte*, in the manner of a prosecutor laying evidence before a grand jury for its review. Schofield wished to know whether the evidence against Moyers and Dedrick, taken together, warranted a civil trial. The letter of instructions to Dodge went out on January 23, and within a few weeks he had completed his work at Memphis and was in Washington, D.C., at work on a report summarizing his findings.[10]

In conference with the secretary of war, Dodge outlined some of the "outrageous frauds" he had confirmed. Schofield was sympathetic to the strong position he took: that in view of the evidence he had uncovered, the work of all claim agents in the southern states ought to be suspended until Congress could devise some effective means to guard the processing of pension cases from corrupt influence.[11] At the same time, the secretary was statesman enough to comprehend that a sweeping remedy such as this would be politically explosive. Something must certainly be done, and soon. Still, he decided that for the present, continuing to bar Moyers and Dedrick from doing official business with the War Department would have to suffice. With Grant about to be inaugurated and himself about to return to military duty, this was not the time to stir up more southern hostility. Meanwhile, Dodge was reviewing information that supplemented the depositions he had gathered, and he had yet to submit a comprehensive report.[12] Perhaps something decisive might be done once the new presidential administration was in place.

On March 5, the day after taking the oath of office, President Grant transmitted to the Senate three nominations that would significantly influence the character of the U.S. Army for a generation to come. He proposed Lieutenant General William T. Sherman as his successor as General of the Army; Major General Philip H. Sheridan for promotion to lieutenant general, to occupy the position vacated by Sherman; and Brigadier General John M. Schofield for promotion to major general. A fourth nomination, well deserved, proved less momentous for the army but was probably of equal interest to Dodge at the time. This was for the promotion of his departmental commander, Colonel Augur, to brigadier general.[13] Quickly confirmed by the Senate, all these were auspicious appointments. Also considered noteworthy was the appointment of John A. Rawlins, who on March 11 became secretary of war. Rawlins, formerly Grant's chief of staff, would continue as the president's trusted confidant and supporter in this civilian capacity. On March 13 Dodge joined other army officers then in Washington at a reception where they paid their respects to the new president and congratulated Secretary Rawlins on his appointment.[14]

Observers were aware that Grant's appointment of Rawlins to the cabinet-level office was an act more of friendship than of executive prudence. Weakened by tuberculosis, the new secretary of war was in no condition to shoulder the responsibilities that had now become his.[15] Nevertheless, he was attracted by the opportunity to serve in so high an office and had declined another appointment, in Arizona Territory, that might have proved physically beneficial to him. As a result, a second postwar reorganization of the army that had been mandated by Congress would be his to oversee.[16] Coming as it did at the very beginning of his tenure, when he had much to learn about the routine work of the War Department, this burden exacted a heavy toll on Rawlins. Meanwhile, working under his putative supervision, Dodge completed his report alleging against Moyers and Dedrick "outrageous frauds committed in connection with pension cases."[17] After he had submitted his findings, they were reviewed in the Adjutant General's Office and on June 15 were returned to the War Department,[18] but nothing further was done. Under ordinary circumstances, Dodge's special assignment would now be ended and he would be directed to return to his regiment, but instead he remained at the national capital under the earlier orders.[19] He was on duty under the direct authority of the secretary of war, but the new incumbent was indisposed or unable to exercise it.

Anxious to clear their names and resume business with the War Department, the principals of Moyers and Dedrick naturally sought to defend themselves. On May 11 they requested that before any action was taken on Dodge's report, they be furnished the names of parties who had testified against them and copies of the evidence that had been collected. Three days later, noting that they had been granted no fair hearing as yet, they asked to be heard, and that their case be acted upon immediately. Receiving no reply, on June 30 they requested that two Washington lawyers, Richard McAllister and Louis Dent, be recognized as their attorneys in the case.[20] Interestingly, the latter was well known to the War Department, being a relation of Colonel Frederick T. Dent, formerly an aide-de-camp to General Grant and now serving in the same capacity under General Sherman. At the end of July, Moyers and Dedrick continued their campaign for exoneration by submitting a detailed statement in their defense.[21] Having by this time discovered the role of Captain Parkinson in bringing on their corporate difficulties, they filed suit against him, forcing him to request authority to use federal funds to defray his legal costs.[22] Shrewdly, they enlisted support from a prominent northerner, J. M. Howard, senator from Michigan and chairman of the Ordnance Committee, who urged that they be given the right to defend themselves.[23]

Dodge was aware of all this activity, but being satisfied that Moyers and Dedrick were guilty as he had reported, he had no sympathy with them. Early in August he restated to the adjutant general his opinion that the activities of all southern claim agents, including the Memphis firm, should be suspended. Since at this point he could do nothing more in the matter, he requested permission to visit his wife and was promptly granted it.[24] Happily for him, the protracted inaction of Secretary

Rawlins had brought about an impromptu second honeymoon for the Dodges, at a fashionable watering place on the New Jersey shore. In due form, upon his arrival there he reported his address to the Adjutant General's Office. Upon receipt of the letter, his friend Major Thomas M. Vincent wrote a discreet note below its text: "Col Dodge has not yet been relieved from the S[pecial]. O[rder]. ordering him to this City for certain duty."[25]

Eight months after Secretary Schofield had directed an investigation of Moyers and Dedrick, the case that Dodge had developed against the firm showed no sign of an early resolution. As a result, on August 28 the adjutant general, Brigadier General Edwin D. Townsend, took the initiative, issuing the following summary recommendation to Secretary Rawlins:

> 1st. That the firms of *Moyers & Dedrick*, *Dailey & Stryker*, and *W. Combs Jr. & Co.* and *B. D. Hyam* be suspended from practice in the War Department.
>
> 2d. That the papers be referred to the Attorney General for his opinion and action as to prosecution in civil court.
>
> 3d. That the Treasury and Interior Departments cease payment of claims to colored soldiers or their legal representatives until Congress shall have taken cognizance of the entire subject.[26]

One week later the Attorney General's Office returned for filing in the Adjutant General's Office the papers and reports relating to the claim agents named in the recommendation and also several other firms.[27] The matter seemed ready for final review and action when once again fate, or human frailty, intervened. Rawlins, who had been visibly failing in recent weeks, died on the day after the file of papers reached his office. For lack of leadership in the War Department, the case against the claim agents seemed lost in limbo.

What followed was an odd shift in policy that manifested the confused state of affairs in the early months of Grant's presidency. The late Secretary Rawlins was replaced *pro tem* not by an assistant secretary but by General Sherman, who only a few months earlier had suffered a demoralizing abridgement of his authority at the hands of Rawlins and Grant. Prior to his inauguration, Grant had promised to direct that, unlike previous secretaries of war such as Jefferson Davis and Edwin M. Stanton, in his administration the holder of the office would not be permitted to exercise day-to-day control over the army. He was firm on this point, and was in agreement with Secretary Schofield and other military leaders, including Sherman, who understood the army's need for undivided military authority. Of course, by constitutional provision the president was commander in chief over the army, and as his designated official the secretary of war oversaw the administrative affairs of the War Department. Still, it remained the president's prerogative to direct that the General of the Army be entrusted with authority over the army itself. With that arrangement in mind, on March 5, 1869, Grant issued an executive order that the General of the Army should participate fully in official business directed to or from the secretary of war. Moreover, "chiefs of staff corps, department bureaus will report to and act under the immediate orders of the general commanding the army."[28]

Grant's directive gratified Sherman and other senior officers of the line, but it distressed the heads of army staff departments such as the quartermaster general, the commissary general, and the chief of ordnance. Previously these officials had reported directly to the secretary of war, bypassing the commanding general and therefore enjoying effective parity with him and immunity from his oversight. Situated as they were in the national capital, the staff corps had lobbied successfully to preserve the status quo until Grant's action changed the rules of the game. The *Army and Navy Journal* praised the president's initiative as a stroke for efficiency and morale in army matters, which, as it observed, Grant "so thoroughly understands."[29]

But within days of John Rawlins's installment as secretary of war, the rules were changed again. Rawlins was displeased that Sherman's direct authority over the staff departments would deprive him, Sherman's civilian superior, of power that had formerly been vested in his own office. He expressed his concerns on the matter to the president, intimating that Sherman, a volatile personality, had perhaps been granted too free a hand. Then, in a move that augured ill for Grant's decisiveness as chief executive in the eight years to come, the president relented. Sherman, stunned at the news that Rawlins might henceforward exercise all the powers that had been arrogated by his predecessors, wrote Grant at once, imploring him to hold firm. He pointed out that to rescind the order of March 5 would cause "the Army and country [to] infer your lack of confidence"—certainly in Sherman, but perhaps also in his own executive judgment. To better argue the matter with his war comrade and friend, he hurried to the White House, where he put a pointed question to Grant. Should not Rawlins acquiesce from the beginning in "a public measure he has known you have advocated for years, and which he has known you were determined upon?" But Grant had begun the conversation by explaining that "Rawlins feels bad" about the new arrangement, that "it worries him, and he is not well." In answer to Sherman's query about the secretary's willingness to comply with the president's known wishes, Grant managed only the lame observation that "it would ordinary [*sic*] be so, but I don't like to give him pain now; so, Sherman, you'll have to publish the rescinding order."[30]

Thus on March 26, "By command of General Sherman" and over the signature of Rawlins, the official record of Grant's about-face was issued to the public. Sherman believed himself betrayed—his command restricted and his authority as a military leader compromised. In his view, Grant had made his latest decision for the wrong reasons, bowing to political pressure and harming the army in the process. In the tradition of his profession, he resolved to obey future orders, but the incident strained the friendship and severed the bond of implicit confidence between him and the president.

These events in March formed the background of Grant's request, upon the death of Rawlins in September, that until a permanent successor could be named Sherman would serve simultaneously as secretary of war and General of the Army. The offer was a mark of confidence, and perhaps also a tacit indication of regret at the shadow that had fallen over their relationship. Sherman accepted the temporary position, even though he was not entirely familiar with the workings of the War Department and knew he would have much to learn in a short space of time. He disliked politics intensely, but at least he had the satisfaction of certainty that his tenure in the secretary's office would be brief. The politicians would not tolerate for long the presence in a civilian office of a take-charge military man like himself.

The beginning of Sherman's incumbency as secretary of war quickly brought to an end the special assignment Major Dodge had received from General Schofield. On his first day in office, Sherman was shown the adjutant's general's report of August 28, with recommendations. Satisfied with what he saw, in his flowing hand he wrote "Approved," and below it his name and a double title, "W. T. Sherman [/] General & Sec of War."[31] Later that day a circular was issued, embodying as orders the terms of the recommendations, and the matter seemed resolved at last.[32] Two days later Major Vincent wrote a memorandum recommending that since the secretary had now taken action on the report of Major Dodge concerning pension and bounty funds, that officer should be ordered to rejoin his regiment. Thus on September 15 an order was issued to that effect, bringing to a close Dodge's rustication at the seashore.[33] As a measure of the events that had passed him by during his eight-month tour of duty in the east, he was now an officer of a new regiment, the Third Infantry, with headquarters not in the Department of the Platte but in the Department of the Missouri. Coincidentally, the latter department was under command of the man whose order had brought him to Memphis and thence to Washington, Major General John M. Schofield.[34]

But even as Dodge made ready to report to his new departmental headquarters in Saint Louis, like some bureaucratic phoenix the saga of Moyers and Dedrick came back to life. The firm protested the circular Sherman had authorized, professing themselves "grievously wronged," having "never been heard in their own defense." At a loss for a proper course of action on a matter he had thought closed, Sherman therefore addressed a letter to the attorney general, asking his assistance. The report of "Major Richard J. [*sic*] Dodge" lay before him, he wrote, having been reviewed by the judge advocate general of the army and "finally summed up" in the recommendation of the adjutant general. The latter official had told him "that the course of cutting off the practice of Attorneys involved in fraudulent claims was usual & common." However, inasmuch as the debarred parties "allege their entire innocence," he was unsure that he had acted with due deliberation. "I fear," he confessed, "I may have as an act of official routine, done them [Moyers and Dedrick] an injury." The accuracy of Dodge's ex parte report was not itself at issue, but Sherman asked the attorney general to cause the Department of Justice staff to review all the documents, give the affected parties a hearing, and report back to him whether the accumulated record justified the course he had taken. He reminded his fellow cabinet member that while he wished to be just, he did not feel bound to comply with all the protocols of a court of law. "I take it for granted," he observed, "that access is a privilege not a right, and that though harsh, a Secretary may withhold the privilege on testimony of a less degree, than would be expected in case the party were indicted and prosecuted criminally."[35]

Despite the predisposition suggested by Sherman's concluding disclaimer, the prospects for Moyers and Dedrick were brightening. After all, the secretary of war was seeking counsel from trained attorneys who would give them an opportunity to frame their own defense. During October two officials of the Judge Advocate General's Office, Lieutenant Colonel William McKee Dunn and Captain Wager Swayne, addressed inquiries to several government departments, soliciting their impressions of the firms whose conduct was under renewed review.[36] In the case of Moyers and Dedrick, evidently the responses they received were satisfactory to some degree, for on October 26 they recommended that the Memphis firm be permitted to collect from the Freedman's Bureau the $7,741 that had been withheld from it.[37] Thus as one of his final acts as secretary of war, General Sherman approved that course. Technically he had already been replaced in office by a permanent appointee, William W. Belknap, who had been named the new secretary on October 25 but had not yet taken up his duties.

If Sherman was mortified at being obliged to reverse his own order, he gave no sign of it. Justice may or may not have been done; but however that might be, he had authorized a proceeding to ensure due process, and it had run its course. He breathed a happy farewell to his brief term of participation in the day-to-day affairs of state. In later years he came to believe that involvement in politics "ruined" Grant.[38] For himself, from this time forward he affirmed a wish to be remembered as a soldier alone.[39]

Ponderously, belatedly, but at last successfully, the Forty-first Congress of the United States took notice in its second session of the fraudulent practices Secretary Schofield had directed Major Dodge to investigate. On December 13, 1869, John H. Benjamin of Missouri, chairman of the Committee on Invalid Pensions, introduced before the House of Representatives "a bill to define the duties of pension agents and prescribe the manner of paying pensions."[40] Shortly afterward the bill was referred to Benjamin's committee, then reported and discussed on the House floor before being sent back to the committee for revision. Members from several states spoke of abuses that had been reported to them by constituents, describing ways in which would-be pensioners and bounty claimants had been imposed upon. For example, James B. Beck of Kentucky reported that he and fellow members of the Committee on Appropriations had learned of "most enormous frauds . . . being perpetrated by false personations and in everything connected with these pensions."[41] It was agreed that limits should be placed on the amounts to be charged by attorneys and pension agents, that fines should be instituted for violations, and that the processes for application and payment should be simplified as much as prudently possible. As revised in committee, the Benjamin motion was reconsidered, tabled, and finally taken up again and voted upon. "An Act to define the Duties of Pension Agents, to prescribe the manner of paying Pensions, and for other purposes," approved on July 7, 1870, became Chapter CCXXV of the laws of the United States enacted by that session of Congress.[42]

Thus, in a small but significant way, the investigation and report by Major Dodge helped turn the slow wheels of government. The political process lacked crisp military efficiency, but eventually it brought forth the legislation he had urged. In the one area of abuse this army officer had helped lay bare, the era of open season to bilk the federal government through its system of entitlements was coming to a close.

8

An Officer Alone

The reorganization of the army in 1869, the second in three years, resulted in more major changes, including consolidation of the forty-five infantry regiments into twenty-five. Advocates of the measure insisted that it was a reorganization, not merely a reduction in force, but the distinction was semantic at best. Many commissioned officers who were no longer attached to a regiment were ordered to their homes to await further directives. Eventually positions were found for some of these; others were directed to appear before boards charged with assessing their fitness for active service; still others simply resigned. Meanwhile, promotions were suspended and new appointments kept to a minimum.[1] Those officers, including Dodge, who had been assigned positions within the new regimental structure could take comfort in what seemed secure places, but in little else. The maximum authorized number of enlisted men now stood at 35,036; of officers, 2,277.[2]

Prior to Major General Schofield's assumption of command in the Department of the Missouri, it had been under the authority of then major general Sheridan. During 1868 and 1869 Indian resistance to the American presence in Kansas, eastern Colorado, and points as far south as the Red River country of Texas had made the Department of the Missouri the theater of frequent military conflict. That winter Sheridan led a campaign south from Fort Hays, Kansas, into the heart of the country occupied by the hostiles, dealing them severe blows but failing to break their spirit. Chiefly Kiowa, Comanche, Arapaho, Cheyenne, and Apache Indians, these people were unwilling to comply with the terms of the Medicine Lodge Treaties of 1867.[3] They refused to confine themselves to the reservations of land south of the Arkansas River that had been set aside for their use, but Sheridan intended to keep up the pressure against them. In his annual report for 1869, he emphasized that the government was extending to the Indians all the benefits its representatives had promised in the treaty sessions. The Indian "cannot now plead bad faith," he wrote; "and if he does not now give up his cruel and destructive habits, I see no other way to save the lives and property of our people, than to punish him until peace becomes a desirable object."[4]

Schofield was less bellicose than Sheridan, but as department commander he adhered to the general policy of his predecessor. In a conference with Major Dodge at Saint Louis, he explained the role the latter would play in furthering this policy.[5] He would command Fort Lyon, Colorado Territory, a post of importance from several points of view but not yet ready to meet the demands that might be placed on it. Located on the north bank of the Arkansas River approximately two hundred miles west of Fort Dodge, Kansas, Fort Lyon was the western anchor of the army's presence on the plains at that latitude.[6] Approximately 190 miles to its southwest, near the Santa Fe Trail, was Fort Union, New Mexico; 150 miles northwest of it lay Denver, Colorado Territory. In a mountain valley 125 miles west and out of strategic reach was Fort Garland, established in 1858 to control mountain tribes of Indians in that vicinity. Around Fort Lyon, Indians had rarely been seen since the infamous Sand Creek massacre of 1864, when a column of Colorado volunteers under Colonel John M. Chivington had treacherously assaulted a peaceable band of Cheyennes.[7] Nevertheless, its vicinity was well known to several plains tribes, for it lay not far west of a route regularly followed by groups of Cheyennes passing on visits to their people in lands to the north or south. In the event of renewed hostilities or of harassment against the Kansas Pacific Railroad as its terminus approached the Kansas-Colorado line, troops at Fort Lyon would take the field. In any event, scouting parties east and south of the fort would continue affording protection to wagon trains along the Santa Fe Trail.[8] Eventually another railroad was expected to follow the roughly east-west course of the Arkansas River as the Union Pacific did the Platte, rendering the old trail a relic. However, at present a third railroad crossing the plains remained only a fond hope.

Fort Lyon was still a relatively isolated place, in contrast to military posts to the east and north of it that had supported advancing settlement and in some instances had already been passed by. The nearest community was Las Animas, a sleepy Mexican village a mile upriver, and the only other permanent residents were farmers who had settled in the bottomlands of the Purgatory River a few miles distant. Not long after his arrival at the fort in October, Dodge wrote without irony of his "neighbor," Lieutenant Colonel Charles R. Woods, Fifth Infantry, at Fort Wallace, Kansas, 130 miles away.[9]

Because Fort Lyon was likely to remain of military importance for years to come, General Schofield wished Dodge to move ahead with the task of constructing permanent buildings, a project that had languished under his predecessor, captain and brevet brigadier general William H. Penrose, Third Infantry. Penrose had commanded the post since its re-establishment at its present location in January 1867.[10] Shortly after his arrival, Dodge divined the cause of the slow progress thus far. "I don't wonder that Schofield was anxious to supercede Penrose," he wrote his wife. "The latter is so very military that he dont want to do anything but drill, have reviews, dress parades

&c &c. I've done more work in six weeks of short days than he had done in six months of spring & summer." Penrose had become accustomed to holding sway at the post and for a time ventured to question Dodge on certain points, but the new commanding officer promptly discouraged liberties of that sort from a subordinate, no matter what brevet rank he held. Describing his own character in phrenological terms, he admitted to Julia that "I have something of a bump of obstinacy, & a *suspicion* of vanity." The latter trait led him to assert his belief that "I can run a post as well as any man who has not been [an Army officer] half as long – nor a third as long as I have been."[11] Once brought to heel, Penrose proved an able company commander and a reliable substitute when Dodge was absent from the post.

Dodge threw himself with enthusiasm into designing and directing the construction of several new buildings at Fort Lyon. The post commander's residence, almost complete when he arrived, was a handsome sandstone structure, with four high-ceilinged rooms in each of its two stories and a large kitchen on the ground level at the back. Three sets of barracks and two warehouses had also been completed. High on Dodge's priority list were six new buildings, each containing two sets of officers' quarters, that would replace the temporary makeshifts then in use. He hoped to have two of these complete by Christmas, as also a large icehouse, built of logs and poles set into the side of the bluff overlooking the river. When suitably insulated, the icehouse was expected to hold a three-years' supply. Other projects Dodge had in view included a powder magazine, a new hospital building, cavalry stables, and a thorough remodeling of the old hospital for service as the post headquarters.[12] These were ambitious plans, especially in the absence of quartermaster's funds to pay civilian workmen. "It's awful slow work," he admitted in December, "since soldiers dont know how and dont like to work." Nevertheless, his interest in the ongoing projects caused time to pass "with such wonderful rapidity that I hardly realize it." He was especially satisfied with work on the icehouse, which seemed "to respond to the pride & pleasure I take in its progress."[13]

"A *Home* as Well as a *House*"

In letter after letter to Julia, Dodge expatiated on the satisfactions of life at Fort Lyon. In October he assured her jocosely that to arrive there after the wagon journey from the westernmost station on the Kansas Pacific Railroad, at Sheridan, Kansas, "is like getting to Heaven after a sojourn in the other locality." The valley of the Arkansas River was covered with luxuriant grass, and the groves of trees along its banks were then changing color. "There is nothing romantic or wild," he added. "It is all simply very beautiful." The climate on the high plains of southern Colorado was excellent, he wrote: "The dry warm day, the delicious evenings, & the cool sound-sleeping nights are perfection. We sit out until dark, when the cold drives us in to a nice wood fire. The Ladies sit out in the dark without head covering or wrapping & never think of taking cold."[14]

As winter approached he descanted on "the *comfort* of Army life" as he now experienced it. "Twenty & more years of service ought to be compensated by something nice," he observed, "& I have got it here." While stationed at Fort Sanders, he recalled, he had been attended to by the best servant he ever had. Still, "this is a far better house, & better still, *I am in command*."[15] He informed Julia that the six officers' wives then in residence ranged from the "stilish" to the "quiet and ladylike." Excepting Penrose, the officers were "all young, & apparently a very good set." He boasted that, as usual, "I bear off the palm in Billiards & dancing."[16] The chief social event, a formal dance with refreshments—known in Army circles as a "hop"—went off weekly. Social activities also included ceremonial visits, receptions, picnics, performances at the post theater, and functions organized to entertain visitors.

Unquestionably Dodge was sincere in his praise of life at the post, but in his letters to Julia he had another motive: he wished, ardently, for her to join him. He understood her reluctance to make the experiment, accustomed as she was to city conveniences. "I know," he once wrote her, "how every old woman (who expects to go to N.Y. as her heaven after death) will roll up her eyes & hold up her hands in horror at the mere idea of anybody's coming to the frontier."[17] He understood too that young Fred's condition—he was sickly and subject to convulsions—and her own delicate health stood in the way of a decision to leave New York. To counter these concerns, he informed her that Mrs. Penrose's younger sister had also suffered frequent convulsions but since her arrival at Fort Lyon had experienced much relief. One of Penrose's two sons, a boy one year younger than Fred, was a healthy "specimen": "He has a donkey, & rides all about. He told me he was very sorry I did not bring my boy, as it was very lonesome to have to play alone."[18]

Some army officers of the era preferred to spare their wives and children from the deprivations and dangers of frontier life,[19] but Dodge was taking a different view. "If I only had my dear little wife here," he wrote her shortly after his arrival, "I would be happy as the day is long."[20] He told her frankly that he considered the recent weeks at the seashore, "when I had you all to myself[,] as the foundation of our present and future happiness." His letters to her now were filled with fond ardor, sprinkled with epithets of endearment. "I believe darling that I love you better & with a worthier love than ever before," he wrote in November, "& for that very reason – knowing love to be reciprocal – I believe that you love me better than you did before."[21]

Apparently Julia was considering the possibility of joining him, for Dodge often described the improvements being made to his residence in preparation for her arrival. His head was full of plans for her comfort. Their bedroom, he reported, was "the envy & admiration of the whole post." A sideboard for the dining room was being constructed, together with a "huge wardrobe" upstairs. "I can imagine I can even sometimes almost see you bustling about, full of importance, & busy as a little bee, setting your house in order," he wrote just before Christmas. In case she intended to send him a gift, he suggested a few chromolithographs that he could have framed and hung on the parlor walls.[22] A few weeks later he included with his weekly letter two sketches showing floor plans. One was captioned "Our house on a small scale—ground floor"; the other, "Tootie's Bed Room."[23] (Tootie, or Tooty, was his nickname for her.)

The letters Julia wrote Dodge during this period have not survived, but the husband's side of the correspondence makes clear that she wrote less frequently to him than he did to her. That he craved assurance of her affection for him is also clear. Early in 1870 he urged her to write more often, describing the effect on him of her silence. "Be a darling little girl," he wrote cajolingly, "& write more frequently, not long letters for I know writing is irksome & painful to you, but 'wee' little letters just to tell me that my loved ones are all well & that you love me. If I could only make you comprehend how much a few lines are from you. How happy they make me. I feel like a new being. All the world is bright & pleasant & joyful. But when day after day & week after week pass without a line, I get all out of sorts. I become unhappy, then angry, then doubtful of your love, & I worry & torment myself, until a sweet loving letter comes, to fill my heart with happiness & make me ashamed of my former anger."[24]

Hoping that in the spring Julia would elect to make her first visit to the West, Dodge kept before her his belief that the journey would bring fulfillment to them both. He now granted that the post had little to offer her in itself, even though "I am interested as it all belonged to me." Still, he held fast to the idea that domestic life as the wife of an army field officer would suit her well.[25] "I believe that you will find your greatest happiness here, in your household, & in the love & constant tenderness of your husband," he wrote.[26] In April he learned from her that, had he only continued on to New York following a journey he had recently made to Saint Louis as a witness before a court-martial proceeding, she might have returned to the post with him then. "I shall never get over my disappointment," he replied, even as he explained that travel to New York while on duty was not a privilege he enjoyed without special authorization. "You don't know how I have hoped to get every thing nice & as you would like it, & have spent every cent of my money . . . in buying furniture Carpets, cooking & table utensils," he added. Expressing hope that she would be able to find a good boarding house in New York City, he betrayed self-pity. "I have never loved any other woman nor ever will," he assured her. "If I have loved you all these years so devotedly, & when I knew you did not so clearly love me, you can or should have no fear of change so long as I have a hope that you return to me a true love."[27]

Like the fortunes of some young lover in a perfervid romance, those of forty-two-year-old Major Dodge as he wooed his wife of twelve years swung dizzyingly between sorrow, joy, and equally intense feelings between. When he learned in late May that she planned to make the trip to Fort Lyon, he was ecstatic. He filled a letter with instructions, cautions, and promises, declaring his intention to meet her at Saint Louis and accompany her the rest of the way, including the fifty-five-mile wagon ride from the settlement of Kit Carson, Colorado, the new terminus of the Kansas Pacific. Once she arrived at the post he would not, he promised, go out on long hunts and leave her alone. "Sometimes," he explained, "I get stuffed up for want of exercise, & require to go out, but home will be too attractive to me, to want to go for long." Nor would he ever take Freddy anywhere she did not wish him to go. Recently he had secured excellent servants, a young black man and wife from Leavenworth, Kansas, who attended to all the housekeeping chores. Julia should consider herself his guest for a stay of at least four months, at the end of which he could obtain a thirty-day leave that would permit his returning east with her for a visit. Perhaps in the coming year they could repeat the arrangement, but for a total of six months rather than five. "My own darling Dearie, it seems almost too good to be possible, after as it were giving you up entirely, to have the hope of folding you in my arms, in my own home, in happiness unspeakable. My eyes fill with tears of happiness at the prospect."[28]

But then came a suspenseful delay, and after that a reversal in the marital romance. In mid-June, having heard nothing from Julia since her announcement of the intended visit three weeks before, Dodge wrote her in anxious concern about a multitude of misfortunes that could have kept her from writing. He would attempt to remain philosophical, he added, and would continue hoping for a letter every day until it came.[29] But when one did come, a full month later, it brought the news that she would not be traveling west. She had decided to spend the summer at Cold Spring, New York, a resort overlooking the Hudson River opposite West Point.

In the latter pages of his reply, dated July 17, Dodge kept up a brave air of acquiescence in the choice she had made and almost of relief that she had not come, the weather at Fort Lyon being "terribly, insufferably hot" just then. He discoursed on this subject, apologizing for the length of his letter with the observation that "when once I get to talking to my dear little wife I don't know when to stop." But at the outset of his "talk" he had expressed clearly enough the disappointment, frustration, and anxious jealousy he felt. He began on a well-worn theme, a complaint about the infrequency of her letters, but now in a tone of self-pitying reproach: "I wish I could induce you to give me a little more of your time," he wrote, "but I suppose I must bear my lot. It does seem hard to love a woman devotedly, & then not only to be separated from her, but to hear from her at such rare intervals, that [it] is truly a wonder to myself how my love survives."

Dodge now turned to a yet more painful theme, one he had not broached earlier in his surviving letters to her. He was both glad and sorry, he wrote, that she had gone back to West Point: "Glad, because I know that you will enjoy yourself most there – & sorry because knowing your disposition as well as I do, I am & shall be constantly fearful of being tormented again with reports, such as flew about the Army in reference to you three years ago." The exact character of these rumors about Julia during the summer of 1867, a few months after he had joined his regiment in the West, is unknown, but their general tenor is evident. "Though I do honestly & sincerely believe you now to be incapable of a modern flirtation," he continued, "you are so fond of attention & so impressing in your manner that you will certainly get credit for flirting, & the pain & unhappiness comes to me." Besides, he wrote, Julia's very presence at West Point proclaimed to the army, "whose opinion I value most," that their separation was voluntary on her part. After all, "going to all the parties as I know you will & taking part in all the gaieties & festivities, no one will or can believe that your plea of ill health is a true one."

Possibly Dodge was not fully aware of his words' corrosive force. At any rate, the spurned husband-lover seemingly could not stop writing. He confessed that the society at West Point was not at all to his taste, however attractive it might be to her. "The tone of sentiment & of morals is about as low as it can get, & the woman who makes a practice of going to West Point, soon gets the reputation of at least wanting advances." He only hoped, he added, that she would not do anything there that would bring him unhappiness. The bubble of delusive hope that she would become a contented army wife, the center of a domestic circle that accompanied him as he moved from post to post, had burst. "I never expect to live with you again," he declared, "at least until Gracie & Fred are married – but I love you as devotedly, as the day when you gave me yourself, and my honor & my standing are bound up in your actions."[30]

The effect upon Julia of Dodge's passionate statements can only be guessed, though no record exists that she ever again brought on him the embarrassment he complained of. In future years the two did live together on occasion when his postings could boast access to the amenities and city attractions she was accustomed to. However, the task of raising Fred and his cousin Grace remained primarily hers. Dodge was grateful to her for this devotion and provided her what financial support he could, but their continuing relationship was strained by deep differences in tastes and habits as well as by Dodge's professional commitments as an army officer. As he later wrote, "domestic felicities and domestic duties are sadly at variance with the active duties of a soldier."[31] His flawed relationship with Julia proved a source of continuing pain and misfortune to him and was the chief disappointment of his lifetime.

After venting his regret that she would not join him at Fort Lyon, Dodge went on to confess what was already obvious enough, that "my heart yearns for some present affection." As a commanding officer he could not associate too freely with his subordinates, lest favoritism be imputed to him or someone be tempted to shirk his duty under the immunity of friendship. Nevertheless, he wrote, "I am like a schoolgirl in always wanting a confidential companion, some one to whom I can talk with perfect freedom, & to whom I am first (for my jealous temperament extends not only to love but to friendship)."[32] For a time his need for companionship had been supplied by a former acquaintance who had recently reported for duty at the post. This was Captain Jacob F. Kent, Third Infantry, like himself a former instructor of infantry tactics at West Point and a combatant at First Bull Run.[33] However, the arrival of another officer, Captain William A. Elderkin, had weakened that bond; Kent and Elderkin were West Point classmates and naturally took up their old comradeship.

A new candidate as Dodge's familiar companion was George P. Fountain, his former chief clerk at Albany, whom he had invited for a visit later in the summer. Dodge intended to put Fountain in the way of financial opportunities that might free him from life as "a mere clerk, with the hopelessness of a clerk's future forever hanging over him."[34] He could occupy a spare room in the outsized post commander's residence while he was looking around him for a suitable investment. When Dodge learned that his father might be turned out of his position in the New York City custom house, he was almost pleased, for he could also offer his parents comfortable quarters at Fort Lyon.[35] "It would be delightful to have them here," he wrote Julia. "I can make them happy as princes – & if George comes as I hope, we will have a family reunion. I would again have a *home* as well as a *house*."[36]

As it happened, James Dodge was spared the loss of employment, but George Fountain did resign his clerkship and make plans to arrive at the fort early in September. Dodge would meet him at Fort Leavenworth, where he had been ordered for a consultation. He was aware that, like Julia, George harbored certain negative prejudices about life on the frontier. "I expect to have to bullyrag him hugely on homesickness," he wrote his wife, "or rather on a desire to return to the sweets of civilization. Poor Kent makes himself quite a nuisance some times, by getting so homesick for Eastern life, Operas & Turtle soups, that he is quite unbearable, but if I can only take him out with me on a hunt or fish, he is quite happy & willing to admit that Eastern life has no charms to equal ours."[37]

On the first day after Fountain's arrival at the post, a powerful thunderstorm raged past it, hurling down hailstones that broke the glass in all the exposed windows and caused much other damage. This storm was less destructive than another a few weeks before that had killed almost all Dodge's brood of chickens,[38] but the demonstration badly discomposed the newcomer. A stiff drink helped restore George's equilibrium, but he assured Dodge of his intention to dispel any beliefs Julia might harbor about the supposedly mild climate of Colorado. George admitted his surprise at Dodge's comfortable residence and mode of life, but in the days that followed he demonstrated himself an inveterate easterner. If his response to frontier life was any measure of what Julia's might have been, Dodge wrote her, "I thank my lucky stars that you did not get out." George, he now realized, was "less fitted for life on the frontier than any man I have ever seen. Cares nothing for hunting or fishing. No billiards – not even the most innocent & simple games of cards. Cares not for riding driving or walking & doesn't talk." Dodge believed that only George's pride kept him from taking a stagecoach back to his "beloved civilization." However, he continued hopeful that his guest would "get over his homesickness – or whatever you may call it – in his own way."[39]

Troubles with Indians on the southern plains were few this year, and several visitors therefore stopped at the post, most of them traveling to or from the South Park in the Rocky Mountains of Colorado, then winning fame as a tourist attraction. An incident of Indian violence against a surveying crew along the Kansas Pacific Railroad east of Kit Carson Station dampened the enthusiasm of travelers for a time,[40] but Dodge was a busy host nevertheless. One of his guests was William J. Palmer, an official of the Kansas Pacific who in the previous fall had included Dodge in a celebrity tour to Denver and the mountains west of it. Palmer's party included his intended wife, "full of fun & very sensible," and her father. "Palmer is especially pleasing to me," Dodge wrote his wife, "so I enjoyed their visit immensely."[41] Another visitor, returning east from California, was a Mr. Barney, of Irvington, New York, a friend of Captain Kent and the owner of a house that had once been occupied by one of Dodge's aunts. Shortly after his departure, Barney sent his hosts some select vines for planting and a supply of Brahma chicken eggs.[42] A third guest was an esteemed friend, Thomas Tasker Gantt, whom Dodge had met in Saint Louis. Presiding judge of the court of appeals in that city, Gantt was a former army man, an avid outdoorsman, and an active correspondent. Dodge, himself a strong performer in the latter category, later expressed the opinion that "I write to him better than anyone else."[43] Early in September he and Judge Gantt, accompanied by a small escort, left the post on a ten-day hunt in the canyons to the west in pursuit of black-tailed deer.[44]

Telegraph communication had not yet reached Fort Lyon, but through contact with visitors like these, correspondence with friends and relations, and newspapers and magazines—Dodge subscribed to the *Army and Navy Journal* and the *New York Herald*—officers and men at the post eventually learned of national and international developments. Contact with officers at other posts on court-martial duty or other errands kept them abreast of rumors and initiatives within the army. Captain Penrose, for example, was promoting a set of implements he had devised for use by soldiers in the field.[45] For his part, Dodge corresponded with a board of officers that was meeting at Saint Louis under General Schofield to draft a new set of army tactics, one that would be applicable to all three arms of the field service—infantry, cavalry, and artillery. He understood the importance of this effort, for he could recall the confusion at First Bull Run, when orders shouted to men of one arm sometimes proved unintelligible or misleading to those of another. On one occasion, after spending an entire day responding to a query from the Saint Louis board, he showed the result to Kent, who endorsed it fully. Dodge himself thought it "a tip top letter."[46]

The construction projects at the post moved ahead reasonably well during 1870. Kent was installed in a new house whose waxed floors were a great source of pride. The icehouse, which skeptics had predicted would fail, served its purpose admirably, and in short, Dodge boasted to Julia, "every thing I have done here so far is a success." Recent Indian attacks in the vicinity of Fort Wallace had necessitated the transfer there of two companies, severely reducing the number of men available for construction duty.[47] Nevertheless, in a summary report on the facilities at the post, Assistant Surgeon H. R. Tilton was complimentary. He noted that the ovens in the post bakery, formerly unusable, had been rebuilt of burned brick rather than, as previously, of sandstone and adobes and were in "fine condition." The present hospital building, its interior brightened by transom windows and with plastered, hard-finished walls, was almost ready for occupation, and the new hospital was expected to be complete by winter.[48]

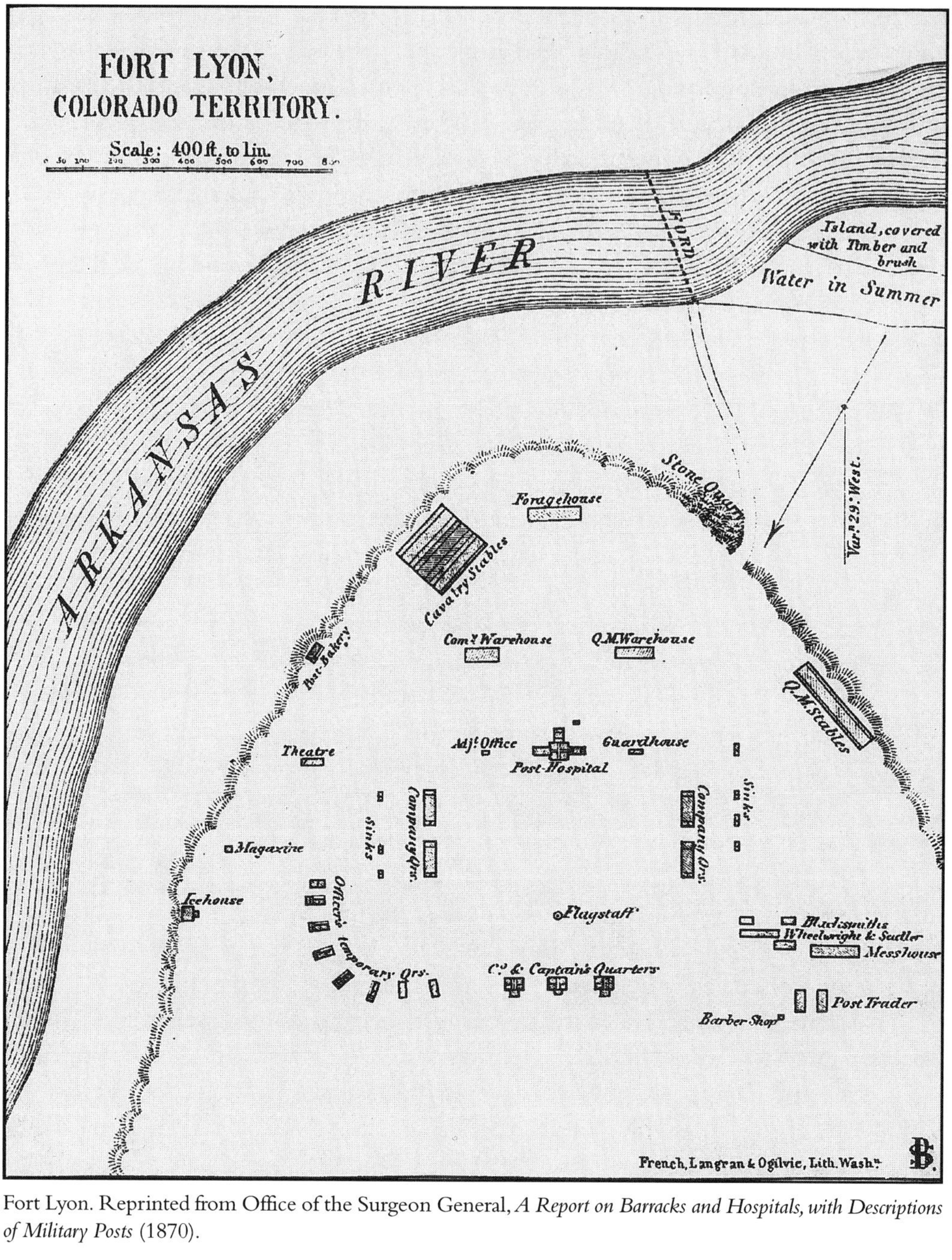

Fort Lyon. Reprinted from Office of the Surgeon General, *A Report on Barracks and Hospitals, with Descriptions of Military Posts* (1870).

"Real Military Work"

Dodge's second major undertaking as post commander was a stint of what he termed "real military work"[49]—that is, an excursion south to Fort Union to determine the path of a new wagon road between the two installations. In 1870 the cost of transporting supplies from Fort Leavenworth to Fort Union was high, five cents per pound.[50]

Yet the expense had to be incurred, for Fort Union was the primary depot for goods shipped from the east to New Mexico and also to Fort Garland. Should Dodge succeed in laying out a road from Fort Lyon that was shorter and less demanding than the one that had been in use for several years past, he would save the government thousands of dollars annually.

The road currently in use, known as the Raton route, was actually the less traveled of two trails. The one better known, the Cimarron route, followed the Arkansas River west from Fort Dodge, Kansas, to a point called the Cimarron Crossing, where it crossed the river and passed to the southwest over a sixty-mile desert, followed by crossings of other watercourses before reaching Fort Union.[51] Except that it was a target of Indian marauders and other desperadoes, the Cimarron route had in the past been preferable. However, the completion of the Kansas Pacific Railroad to Kit Carson, Colorado, altered the calculation. If goods could be shipped to that point, transported by wagon to Fort Lyon, and moved south along a successor to the roundabout Raton route, they would reach Fort Union more rapidly, safely, and inexpensively than by the Cimarron.[52]

Accompanied by three officers and a working party of enlisted men, Dodge left his post on May 5 and arrived at Fort Union eleven days later, "ragged & dirty & looking . . . like 'beggars of the plains.'" It had been a hard but delightful trip, he wrote his wife. "For most of the distance there is no road now, & we came through the praries & mountains, enjoying to the utmost the wild & beautiful scenery, & drinking in the bracing air."[53] On the third day out the snow-covered Rocky Mountains came into view, and thereafter the great upheavals that had formed them over the eons stood all around, like illustrations in a geology book. A portion of that country was a region of extinct volcanoes, some with perfectly symmetrical cones, as if they had been poured in place there the day before. One of these Dodge named Mount Tilton, after the post surgeon, an enthusiastic student of natural history.[54] Significantly, Dodge's travel attire on leaving Fort Lyon had been his "hunting toggery." He, Kent, and the other officers bagged sufficient game for the entire command to dine sumptuously every day. There were "plenty of wagons, tents &c, plenty to eat, plenty to drink, & a most interesting country to travel through."[55]

At Fort Union, Dodge was glad to encounter Colonel William N. Grier, Third Cavalry, a former colleague of his at Harrisburg, Pennsylvania.[56] Now within a few months of his retirement, "Old Billy" was about to depart with his command for Cheyenne, Wyoming Territory, where they would board a westbound train on their way to taking post in northern California.[57] However taxing the journey might prove to the older man, Dodge speculated that Grier looked forward to it as a way of putting distance between himself and his preternaturally jealous wife. As for himself, "I have splendid health," he wrote Julia on May 17, two days before his birthday, "and feel like a young man, tho' long before you receive this I shall have passed the 43d milestone on my journey of life."

Fort Union was considered a desirable posting, but he could not help comparing it unfavorably to his own.[58] The road-hunting expedition was proceeding according to plan, and on the return trip Dodge expected to lay out a route thirty miles shorter than the one he had taken south. His party left the post the next day and made the return trip without incident, arriving at Fort Lyon on May 27, two days ahead of schedule. Reporting his arrival, he observed that "I dont think I ever had a more pleasant [trip], in my life, of the kind."[59]

Affairs at the post had gone on smoothly during his absence, but the transfer of two companies shortly afterward, followed by a rash of discharges among the men that remained, seriously depleted the garrison. At one point Dodge had only thirty enlisted men under his command—approximately, he calculated, one man per building should he be attacked by Indians.[60] Uneasy at this situation, he remonstrated with departmental headquarters, and late in July sixty recruits reached the post. Fifty more arrived in October, and drawing upon that manpower he saw the year's construction program finished on schedule.[61]

The peaceful tenor of life at Fort Lyon was disturbed during 1870 by the arrest, trial, and conviction of two officers in the garrison, both of whom subsequently lost their commissions. One of these, First Lieutenant John R. Bothwell, Fifth Infantry, was the post quartermaster and also a relation by marriage to a close friend of General Schofield.[62] With regret, Dodge preferred the charges against Bothwell, and after interviews with members of the judge advocate's staff who came to the post to gather further information, he was ordered to Fort Leavenworth for a consultation. From that point the case followed a steady course to its termination.[63]

In May, when Schofield left department headquarters to take command of the Military Division of the Pacific, at San Francisco, California, Dodge regretted his departure. Still, he expected that his successor, Brigadier General John Pope, would give general satisfaction, as he had in an earlier tour of duty in the Department of the Missouri. "If he will only sustain me as Schofield does," he wrote, "I shall be well content."[64] Happily, that proved the case in the several years of his service under Pope.

Early in the summer, before he had given up hope of Julia's joining him, Dodge described to her a spot eight miles from the post where they might enjoy a picnic together. In company with three other officers, he happened onto this place in the course of a day's hunting and fishing that yielded three hundred fish, two antelope, and a live antelope fawn that he brought home as a pet. "There has been no such days sport known in the history of this post," he exulted.[65] Other excursions included scouts as far as sixty miles southeast, to the country around Two Butte Creek or else west to the foothills of the Rockies. Species seen or bagged within a day's travel from Fort Lyon included buffalo, antelope, elk, black-tailed deer, panther, wild cat, wolf, coyote, cinnamon bear, fox, weasel, mink, otter, and many others—not to mention the prairie dogs whose dens dotted the earth's surface along virtually the entire length of the road to Kit Carson. Birds, no less abundant, included golden eagle, bald eagle, pigeon, hawk, prairie falcon, great horned owl, woodpecker, kingfisher, wild turkey, plover, prairie chicken, several varieties of duck, and others.[66] On the journey to Fort

Union, Dodge reported that he had never heard so many singing birds. "The Mocking Bird made night vocal with their songs, & the Bobolink twittered & flirted his very life away on the high Praries."[67] Indians did not molest him on any of these journeys, but unpredictable weather sometimes did. On two occasions his party was almost blinded by sudden snowstorms, and the men were forced to hurry from their exposed position to find what shelter they could.[68]

The region of Fort Lyon was also a rich repository of physical features that stimulated Dodge's interest in geology and natural history. An outcropping of limestone a few miles from the post was dense with fossils. Elsewhere, in a ravine formed by a tributary of Two Butte Creek, he chanced upon what seemed to be an obstruction of logs. "As it is a perfectly treeless country," he later wrote, "I was led to a closer examination, and to my surprise found that the logs were stone. Never elsewhere have I seen petrifications so large or so perfect. One huge trunk of a pine tree was about six feet in diameter and ten or twelve feet long. It was hollow, and a portion of the hollow part had been burned away. The bark, the wood, the hollow, the marks of fire were all perfectly natural, yet the 'log' was solid stone."[69] North of the post, on a rocky cliff along the Purgatory River, he discovered another object of wonder, the outline of a bear, "rudely drawn and a little larger than life size." Who or what had created this image? Not Indians, for the yellowish gray stone was blackened to the depth of about two inches. "One Savant," he reported, identified it as "a photograph of a bear taken by lightning on the rock." Dodge could offer no better explanation and contented himself with the observation that "it certainly is a remarkable freak of nature." Near the site of old Fort Lyon, twenty miles west, he found limestone that came from a quarry in perfect cubes or parallelopipeds. Without cutting them, one could lay them together on a wall, like bricks.[70] However monotonous and undifferentiated the high plains might seem to persons who knew it less well than he, Dodge was finding it literally a region of wonders.

On December 11, 1870, he departed from Fort Lyon on a thirty-day leave of absence that would include a long-awaited reunion with his wife and family in New York City.[71] By that time the Kansas Pacific Railroad had reached Denver, a new railroad passing south from that city was under active discussion, and a third railroad across the plains, the Atchison, Topeka and Santa Fe, was poised for a season of construction in the coming year. Dodge's experience at Fort Lyon had occurred just beyond the reach of these tentacles of progress.[72] History was closing in on a mode of existence he found more satisfying than anything the more sophisticated eastern states could offer, and yet his mission as an army officer was to facilitate the course of that history. The disjunction between his personal tastes and his professional duties cannot have escaped him as he rode east to Kansas City, Saint Louis, Chicago, Buffalo, Albany, and New York City, but he was not bitter. He would return to the western frontier, and for the next few weeks he would not be alone.

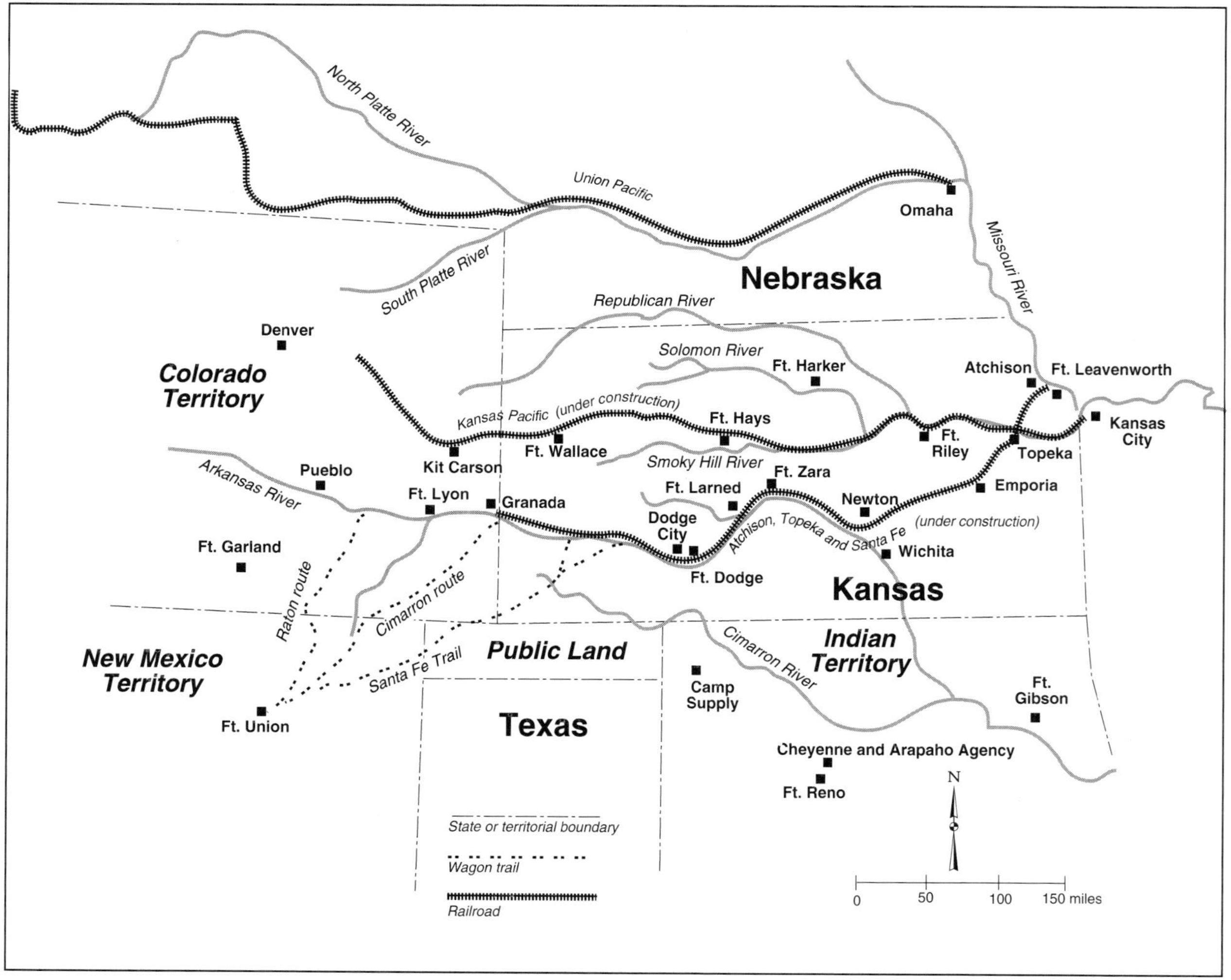

Region of Dodge's service, 1869–1873

AT FORT LARNED

Shortly after his return to Fort Lyon, in February 1871, Dodge was relieved of command there by his immediate superior, Lieutenant Colonel John R. Brooke. He was being transferred to Fort Larned, on the Pawnee fork of the Arkansas River, 260 miles due east from Fort Lyon. Established in 1859 to protect emigrants and wagon trains along the Santa Fe Trail and also as a depot for distribution of treaty goods to Indian tribes in its region, Fort Larned was nearing the end of its colorful history.[73] Parties of Indians bent on trouble remained a threat in the area, and the old wagon road was still the chief east-west thoroughfare along the Arkansas River, but in the spring of 1871 the Atchison, Topeka and Santa Fe Railroad would begin construction west of Emporia, Kansas, transforming the region.[74] Dodge's regiment was being deployed to support the work of the new railroad in much the same manner as the Thirtieth Infantry and other units had done for the Union Pacific a few years before. Fort Larned, approximately 150 miles west of the end of track at the time Dodge assumed command there, was in a location analogous to that of Fort Fred Steele in the summer of 1868. At present it was an outpost at a river crossing along the already surveyed route, but it would soon be the base from which detachments of soldiers were sent to protect grading and tracklaying parties. Like the Union Pacific, the Atchison, Topeka and Santa Fe was laying track under a deadline that carried with it a financial incentive. In order for the company to receive from the federal government a grant of property that paralleled its course, the railway must be operational by March 3, 1873, to the Kansas-Colorado line, a distance of 408 miles from Emporia.[75]

With the help of his domestic servants, John and Julia, who would accompany him on his wagon journey to the new posting, Dodge packed his household possessions and set out overland on February 26. The volume of furniture and other items he had acquired in the hope of attracting Julia to Fort Lyon now complicated his move. Transporting it all to Kit Carson, thence by rail to Fort Hays, Kansas, and from that point sixty more miles southeast along a wagon road to Fort Larned was not an attractive option. Not only would repeated repacking be required, but the expenses involved were beyond his means. Out of his $2,500 annual salary[76] Dodge helped support his wife and son, his parents, and a sister, "Sis Molly," who was blind. He had few funds to spare and was glad, for example, to accept complimentary tickets for passage along the railroad whenever they were offered him. Thus the task at hand would be cumbersome and far from expeditious, but with the use of a few army wagons the overland journey eastward could be accomplished easily enough. Accompanied by a small infantry escort, Dodge therefore set out into the uncertain weather of late winter, hoping to do some hunting along the way.

The two-week passage along the north bank of the Arkansas River proved a good deal more eventful than he had anticipated. If ever he seriously credited the idea that in passing east from remote country near the slopes of the Rocky Mountains he was leaving behind him the wilderness, with all its satisfactions and perils, he was corrected by two incidents of grave danger. Both demanded a cool presence of mind and confident knowledge of the appropriate behavior under the varieties of stress they presented. Only a plainsman such as Dodge could have met them with the resourcefulness he did.

About thirty miles west of Fort Dodge, on a section of high prairie known as the "nine-mile ridge," he found himself in a predicament he had been obliged to deal with more than once before—namely, he was discovered by a superior party of potentially hostile Indians. The worst possible behavior in such situations, he knew, was to run away. The safest was to keep constantly on the watch for a good defensive position, exposed and on level ground, that was beyond rifle range from nearby timber, ravines, holes, large rocks, or other possible cover for an enemy. If a small party was ever surprised by Indians, it should move quickly but without panic to the nearest such place, and there prepare itself against possible assault.[77] On this foggy morning, Dodge and his servant John were looking into the little ravines along the river, hoping to find antelope. Julia and the cook wagon, along with two of Dodge's men, were a short distance away, and the rest of the escort was farther off. He had been out for about two hours when the fog lifted a little and he caught sight of two men on horseback about two hundred yards away. Because they were wearing overcoats, for a moment he took them to be soldiers from Fort Dodge. Some years afterward he recounted what followed:

> As soon as they saw me however one of them rode the signal "danger," "collect together," and I began to think of my escort. Looking round I was greatly annoyed to find the spring-wagon, in which was my colored cook about six hundred yards from me opposite the Indians, while the wagons and escort could not be seen.
>
> Making the best of the situation I galloped back to the spring-wagon, had it driven well out into the plain, the mules unhitched and well secured. The driver got out his rifle and everything was satisfactory except the presence of the cook. I not only feared that she might be hit, but I knew the Indians would be more dangerous if a woman was likely to be a prize. Making her lie down in the bottom of the wagon, I packed around her lunch and other boxes, blankets, cushions, seats, everything that might stop a bullet, and gave her positive orders to remain perfectly quiet and concealed, no matter what took place. I then took position with my two men, some paces on one side of the wagon to spare it from shots. During all this time the Indians had been collecting and soon after I was ready, a line of about thirty moved slowly toward me. At about eight hundred yards they broke into a sharp canter. Expecting the charge to come in a moment I went toward the wagon to be sure that the animals were tied safely, when to my great indignation I found Julia (the cook) revolver in hand, and her head thrust out of the front of the wagon. "Get back there" I angrily ordered. "Do you want to be shot?"—"Lord[,] Colonel" she answered, "let me alone. I'll never have another chance to see an Indian fight."

The earnestness of this, under the circumstances, most unexpected answer set all to laughing, and John, the husband, who a moment before was almost white with apprehension, regained, with good humor, his natural black.

Every moment of delay being most important to us, I, when the Indians had got within about four hundred yards, stepped forward, made the Indian signal "Halt" and displayed a white handkerchief. To my great gratification they halted, and in a moment one came forward, with what had once been a white flannel shirt fastened to the pole of a lance. We met half way, I very friendly, he very gruff, I disposed to talk, he to be saucy. I asked the name of the Tribe. He answered by demanding something to eat. I asked where they came from. He answered "powder, lead, sugar." We could not understand each other well, which I was rather thankful for as it prolonged the talk. He wanted everything and asked not as a beggar, but demanded as one having right. I am compelled to admit a certain duplicity on this occasion, having to gain time promised things which I had no intention of performing.

The Indians had not seen the wagons which were crossing one of the long depressions below the level of the plain on which we were. They were sure of us, but preferred getting what we had, without a fight if possible, especially as we had a good position. While we continued to talk, I heard most welcome sounds, and looking in that direction, saw the wagons coming at full speed of the mules, with a line of "the boys in blue," rifle in hand, stretched at a run towards the spring wagon. I pointed them out to the Indian and told him to go. He needed no second bidding, but rushed back to his party which was in the greatest turmoil and confusion. I went back to the wagons, hitched up and started, the Indians holding a consultation. As I got on the road the Chief came to me with the flag. He was very much aggrieved. "I had deceived them. They could have killed us and taken everything before the Troops came up. They did not kill us because I promised to give them what they wanted, therefore I must give them all I promised. He was hungry and tired. He wanted to go with his young men and sleep in my camp that night, that I might give them plenty to eat and powder, lead and other things I promised." I told him that he and his party were robbers and murderers, that he must go away and that if he or any of them came near my march or my camp I would kill them.

He left me and rode back to his men, the most disgusted looking Indian I ever saw. We went our way, leaving the band sitting in a circle on the ground, evidently discussing in no amiable frame of mind the outrage that had been perpetrated on them.[78]

Dodge recounts this tense confrontation with a light touch, but in fact his party's predicament was quite dangerous. He had met the Indians in a no-man's-land, where whoever could make the most of the resources available to him would have the best of the encounter. Delay was on his side, and by prolonging the charade of a peaceful interchange, he managed to rescue his party and its goods from the Indian pirates who had thought to appropriate them, if not to do worse harm.

Once his party reached Fort Dodge, Dodge was within sixty miles of his new posting. Pushing on from there, he followed the north bank of the river until one blustery, cold night he camped along Big Coon Creek, a major tributary of the Arkansas. He knew the danger of flash floods in times of inclement weather, but to escape the wind he made camp almost in the bed of the creek, sheltered by steep hillocks on either side. His tents and wagons were cramped together, but the arrangements seemed satisfactory as the travelers composed themselves for a night's rest. Nevertheless, that night brought with it what Dodge later described as "as close a shave as I ever made to 'passing in my checks.'" The threat, altogether unexpected yet unmistakable, was not from flood but from another overwhelming natural force, a stampeded herd of buffalo. Dodge portrayed the party's close encounter with the crazed beasts:

> It was late at night and I was in bed. The camp, except one sentinel was buried in sleep, the fires were all out, darkness and silence reigned supreme. A faint and very distant sound struck upon my ear. Thinking of water, I rushed out at once, and running up the side of the hill, peered up the stream into the darkness to discover an approaching line of foam, precursor of the flood.
>
> Just then the wind brought the sound more distinctly. It came from the prairie, not from the stream, and was approaching. I sent the sentinel to wake up the corporal and other two men of the guard, who soon made their appearance with their arms.
>
> Explaining to the men in a few words the nature of the danger, I warned them to keep perfectly cool and to obey orders. By this time the black line of the moving mass of buffalo was distinctly visible. It was bearing directly down upon us with tremendous speed and irresistible force. We were in an excellent position for the protection of the camp, being directly between it and the buffalo and about fifty yards from it. My only chance was to split the herd. If this could be done we and the herd would be saved, if not, all would go to destruction together. Waiting until the advance line of buffalo was within thirty yards the muskets were fired in rapid and continuous succession, and we in unison let out one of the most unearthly yells that ever split the throats of five badly frightened men. A few of the leading animals fell dead, the others swerved from the line of fire and noise, the herd was split, and tumbling in fright and confusion down the bank on each side of the camp went thundering and roaring into the darkness.
>
> In all my life I have never seen so badly frightened a lot of people as those in camp nor do I blame, or disparage them in the least. Waked from sound sleep by the rapid firing and hideous yells, they rushed out of their tents to find themselves in the very midst of a plunging, struggling mass of buffalo.
>
> The edge of one portion of the split herd passed within thirty feet of one flank of the camp, while the nearest of the other portion was about seventy feet from the other flank. The members of my little party had the living stream within fifteen or twenty feet on each side.

I consider this the most imminent danger that I have ever encountered on the plains. Had I and the sentinel been asleep, nothing could have saved my whole party from a horrible death[,] for the banks under which we were camped were so steep, that even had they seen and been sensible enough to try to avoid the camp, the buffalo in front would have been driven upon and over us by the pressure of those in rear. There must have been four or five thousand animals—and "stampeded."[79]

In comparison to the onslaught of panicked buffalo, the threat posed by the Indian marauders who had waylaid Dodge was of a distinctly lesser order. More than once during this period of his career, he witnessed stampeded herds of buffalo racing to cross railroads in front of oncoming locomotives, or else to outpace a train moving along the tracks alongside it, so as to cross to the other side. Railroad men had learned to stop their trains when stampeded herds were in sight, for to do otherwise was to court disaster.[80] Dodge believed that the stampeded buffalo was "as dangerous a beast collectively as can be found in the world."[81]

Arriving at Fort Larned after his eventful journey, Dodge assumed command there on March 13, 1871. In the two years to come he would work closely with the troops stationed at this post as he deployed troops along the railroad, but his present tour of duty was brief, lasting less than four months.[82] Its most noteworthy event was another encounter with a buffalo herd. This experience also contained a measure of suspenseful drama, as in the crisis at Big Coon Creek, but his published portrayal of it conveyed a somewhat different impression—that is, of the seemingly numberless buffalo that then covered the plains.

One day in May, Dodge drove a light wagon on some official errand thirty-four miles east to Fort Zara, not far from Walnut Creek near its confluence with the Arkansas River. Abandoned by the army in 1869, the military reservation of Fort Zara had been turned over to the Interior Department only a few weeks before. As he drove back toward his post along the broad, level valley of the river, Dodge found himself surrounded almost continuously by buffalo. He described the scene, and also the measures he was forced to adopt to make his way through it.

At least twenty five miles . . . was through one immense herd, composed of countless smaller herds, of buffaloes, then on their journey North. . . .

Some few miles from Zara a low line of hills rises from the plain on the right gradually increasing in height and approaching the road and river until they culminate in Pawnee Rock, when they again recede. The whole country appeared one mass of buffalo, moving slowly to the northward, and it was only when actually among them, that it could be ascertained that the apparently solid mass, was an agglomeration of innumerable small herds, of from fifty to two hundred animals, separated from the surrounding herds by greater or less space, but separated. The herds in the valley sullenly got out of my way, and turning, stared stupidly at me, sometimes at only a few yards' distance. When I had reached a point where the hills were no longer more than a mile from

The buffalo plains. Reprinted from War Department, *Reports of Explorations and Surveys, to Ascertain the Most Practicable and Economical Route for a Railroad from the Mississippi River to the Pacific Ocean* (1855–1860).

> the road, the buffalo on the hills, seeing an unknown and unusual object in their rear, turned, stared an instant then started at full speed directly toward me, stampeding and bringing with them the numberless herds through which they passed, and pouring down upon me all the herds, no longer separated, but one immense compact mass of plunging animals, mad with fright, irresistible as an avalanche. The situation was by no means pleasant. Reining up my horse (which was fortunately a quiet old beast, that had been in at the death of so many buffalo, that their wildest, maddest rush, only caused him to cock his ears in wonder at their unnecessary excitement) I waited until the front of the mass was within fifty yards, when a few well directed shots from my rifle split the herd and sent it pouring off in two streams to my front and rear. When all had passed on, they stopped apparently perfectly satisfied, though thousands were yet within reach of my rifle, and many within less than one hundred yards. Disdaining to fire again I sent my servant to cut out the tongues of the fallen. This occurred so frequently within the next ten miles, that when I arrived at Fort Larned, I had twenty six tongues in my wagon, representing the greatest number of buffalo that my conscience can reproach me for having murdered on any single day. I was not hunting, wanted no meat, and would not voluntarily have fired at these herds. I killed only in self preservation and fired almost every shot from the wagon.[83]

As he implied in this passage, Dodge took little interest in the buffalo as a game animal. However exciting the pursuit of buffalo might be to eastern visitors who were less familiar with the habits of the beast than he, in his opinion a buffalo hunt was hardly a test of a sportsman's skill. In the present instance, the "murders" he committed were acts of self-preservation.

Subsequently Dodge's published account of his journey from Fort Zara to Fort Larned became the basis for attempts to calculate the number of buffalo that ranged the plains just prior to the wholesale slaughter of the 1870s that eventually threatened them with extinction. In correspondence with William T. Hornaday, then at work on his classic study *The Extermination of the American Bison*, in 1887 Dodge estimated the size of the herd he had passed through at more than 4 million animals. "From the top of Pawnee Rock I could see from 6 to 10 miles in almost every direction," he wrote. "This whole vast space was covered with buffalo, looking at distance like one compact mass, the visual angle not permitting the ground to be seen." In his published work, Hornaday described Dodge's account of his dangerous journey as "Perhaps the most vivid picture ever afforded of the former abundance of buffalo." For himself, later in life Dodge took a melancholy satisfaction in recalling that he and his servant had been two men alone among "the last of the great herds."[84]

9

Toward Army Reform

When President Grant reneged on his commitment to invest General Sherman with authority over both the staff and line of the army, the latter was dismayed but accepted the result with soldierly fortitude. He still hoped to implement reforms that would help ensure the army's ability to meet its postwar mandates, but he recognized that carrying out his plans would not be easy. As he anticipated, Secretary of War John A. Rawlins and later William W. Belknap were determined to impose civilian control over the military, and their influence weakened what limited authority remained to him. Congress was relatively indifferent, if not hostile, to army needs. Some lawmakers were determined to reduce annual appropriations merely for economy's sake, while others, including Representative John A. Logan of Illinois, were actuated by vindictive resentment of perceived slights they had suffered during the war.[1] Still, Sherman was determined to push ahead. "I will help keep in mind the End," he wrote General Sheridan, "and try gradually to effect in time [that] which we all want to do and should have done by a single step" had Grant not gone back on his promise.[2]

The creation of a tactics board under General Schofield in August 1869 was one of the initiatives Sherman had in mind. Similar boards had met in recent years, one under Grant in 1867 and another in the previous winter under Colonel William F. Barry, Second Artillery, but neither had produced what Sherman considered satisfactory results.[3] In his view, the *Infantry Tactics* that had been prepared by Lieutenant Colonel Emory Upton, Twenty-fifth Infantry, and recommended for adoption by the Grant board was well enough in itself. The next step was to devise a system that reconciled those tactics currently in use by the infantry, cavalry, and artillery and could therefore be adopted by all arms. An innovation such as this might not be appreciated by ordinary citizens, but a common set of commands and maneuvers intelligible to all combatants would help form a practical basis for operations in the field. When, in January 1871, the Schofield board submitted its three-volume report, Sherman was pleased with the accomplishment. He submitted it, with his official statement of approval, to the secretary of war for final action.[4]

In the same month, Sherman supported Secretary Belknap's call for other army reforms. In a wide-ranging general order, the two leaders urged commissioned officers at all levels and in all branches of the service "to address themselves with renewed energy to the task of raising the military establishment to the highest degree of discipline, efficiency, and economy." The order published rules governing travel when on duty and set forth procedures for obtaining sick leaves and transfers. It directed regular meetings of Retiring Boards, charged with examining and reporting on officers who were possibly no longer capable of active service. It discontinued the policy of awarding advance pay and mileage allowances. And it discouraged the pervasive practice of seeking political or other influence to secure preferential treatment such as special assignments and desirable postings. "Officers must not apply to the Secretary of War or General of the Army for leaves of absence, or other personal favors, or address them on official matters in any other manner than as prescribed by Regulations and military usage," it warned. "Applications in any other mode will not be entertained, but will be construed as a breach of discipline."[5] At least in theory, this prohibition was definitive; but in practice it remained far less so.

In 1871, shortly after his return to Washington from an inspection tour of army posts in the southwest, General Sherman took another step toward setting the military on a firm practical footing. This was to order the drafting of a new code of army regulations that, when officially approved, would supersede the outdated code, promulgated in 1860 and revised in some of its details in 1861 and 1863, that remained in force. Recognizing the need for a set of regulations that would govern the army as it was reorganized in 1866, in that year Congress had directed the secretary of war to have prepared for its review a document "which shall embrace all necessary forms and orders of a general character, for the performance of all duties incumbent on officers and men in the military service, including rules for the government of Courts-Martial." A board of officers under Sherman thus prepared a set of regulations that was approved by General Grant in February 1868 and submitted to the secretary of war later that month.[6] However, amidst the turmoil of President Andrew Johnson's administration, Congress took no action to ratify the proposed new regulations and Articles of War. Following the army reorganization of 1869, the need for an updated code became yet more apparent, and in the following year Congress directed that a set of proposed new regulations be laid before it during its next session.[7] Thus on July 3, 1871, an order was issued from the War Department creating a board of five officers under Sherman's trusted inspector general, Colonel Randolph B. Marcy. This group would convene on July 15 at the army building in New York City to begin preparing "'a system of General Regulations for the Administration of the affairs of the Army,' under the special instructions of the Secretary of War."[8]

Sherman's detailed familiarity with the careers and personal characteristics of his subordinate officers became legendary in later years. How fully he had developed this capacity thus far during his tenure as General of the Army is uncertain, but the four other men named to the Marcy board were all well known to him. They included Colonel John H. King, Ninth Infantry; Colonel Henry J. Hunt, Fifth Artillery; Major Richard I. Dodge, Third Infantry; and Major Andrew J. Alexander, Eighth Cavalry. Dodge accepted his appointment at once. Not only did it signify his commander's good opinion, but the duty it entailed was of particular interest to him. Besides, it would enable him to pass several months in close contact with his family.

One nominee, Colonel King, was reluctant to leave his present posting for an assignment in New York City that was likely to be a long one. The search for a suitable replacement brought into play the exact sort of jockeying for favors that Belknap and Sherman had forbidden earlier in the year. Taking the initiative, on July 8 Belknap telegraphed the adjutant general from Keokuk, Iowa, that, unless Sherman objected, the officer named would be Colonel William B. Hazen, Sixth Infantry. However, Sherman did express a reservation about the proposed appointment. Hazen, a tireless self-promoter, was the favorite of an influential congressman from Ohio, James A. Garfield, and had benefitted from his sponsorship more than once.[9] Sherman wrote to the adjutant general that while Hazen was "perfectly satisfactory . . . he has had *so many favors* that I would telegraph to Belknap that either Wood [sic] or Hazen would be acceptable to me—but that Wood [sic] has more claims to the present detail, or at least to be offered it."[10] Belknap acquiesced, and when Dodge's colleague Lieutenant Colonel Charles R. Woods, Fifth Infantry, was offered the appointment, he promptly accepted it. The board thus included representatives of all three arms of the field service, with the infantry predominating, as befitted Sherman's estimate of its tactical importance. Army interest in the regulations board and the work before it was considerable. The *Army and Navy Journal* pronounced the board "a good one" and volunteered its pages as a forum for discussion of topics that should receive attention.[11]

For Dodge the appointment to the Marcy board was timely, since in recent months he had been considering questions that would surely be addressed as the deliberations moved ahead. When, where, and how freely should a junior officer comment publicly on the policies and personality of his commander? What was the proper demeanor of a post commander toward the officers and men serving under him? When an officer was placed "in arrest" as a preliminary to possible judicial action against him, what rights and privileges did he and his family members retain? While at Fort Lyon he had discussed these and related questions in letters to his wife. However little his commentaries may have interested her, they addressed problems that he was dealing with from day to day and that needed to be resolved. The *Regulations* of 1863 sometimes touched upon them and sometimes did not, or in too little detail. The potential value to the army of the regulations board was thus clear to him. Probably he was also aware that his own articulateness and flair for organization would make him a useful contributor to its labors.

Dodge would soon discover an additional source of satisfaction in the close working relationship with Colonel Marcy that the assignment offered him. He shared tastes, abilities, experiences, and acquaintances with this respected senior officer. Both were gregarious, and in the intervals between working sessions they would have a great deal to talk about. For example, in an 1848–1849 reconnaissance mission from Fort Smith, Arkansas, to Santa Fe, New Mexico, then captain Marcy had become acquainted with Black Beaver, the Delaware Indian who a few years later impressed the young Dodge with his wide travels and encyclopedic memory of the country he had passed through. Other shared Indian acquaintances from these early days included the Comanche leaders Sa-na-co and Issikeep.[12] Marcy, as the father-in-law of former General George B. McClellan, was probably familiar with the name of Dodge's Saint Louis friend Thomas Tasker Gantt, who had been judge advocate of McClellan's Army of the Potomac.[13] And like Dodge, Marcy loved the outdoors and was a dedicated sportsman.

A distinctive feature of Colonel Marcy's career was his status as the author of books that drew upon his army experiences on the western frontier. In 1859 he had published a practical guide, *The Prairie Traveler*, and in 1866 he brought out an enter–taining collection of sketches, *Thirty Years of Army Life on the Border*. At the time the regulations board began its work, he was completing a sequel, issued in 1872 as *Border Reminiscences*.[14] Military memoirs of the Civil War years were being issued in steadily increasing numbers, but books by army officers recounting their western experiences remained few. In fact, Marcy was among those who opened up this fertile field. In later years, when Dodge elected to test his own ability as a soldier-author, he remained respectfully aware of Marcy and his literary accomplishment.[15]

The offer of the *Army and Navy Journal* to print the communications of army men for consideration by the regulations board yielded a rich and varied response. Lack of space obliged the editors to include only those communications they considered of the greatest general interest. It soon became apparent that some readers harbored deep resentment against certain policies and procedures, and also against certain departments within the army. "Infantry," whose five lengthy statements appeared in the newspaper between July 22 and September 2, seems to have had little else to occupy him during that period except writing. In one of his letters he urged that both the paymaster's and the inspector general's departments be abolished at once as perpetrators of an intolerable abuse—namely, that "our handful of an Army is done to death with bureaus, papers, reports, and returns."[16] His vituperative manner did not commend his views to Marcy, who had served ably as inspector general for several years, but it did register the intensity of his belief that reform was necessary. All were aware, of course, that the regulations board was not empowered to recommend major administrative changes. It might be true that, as "Infantry" alleged in another letter, the Quartermaster General's Department was "the stronghold of red tape," and that an unbiased observer would react to its methods of operation "as the feeling may alternately seize him, either with amazement, chagrin, or uncontrollable laughter."[17] Still, more specific complaints and suggestions would be of greater use to Marcy and his colleagues.

Most of the statements published aired grievances and perceived inequities. Civilian physicians serving under contract, known as "acting assistant surgeons," received smaller salaries and were accorded less respect than their professional colleagues the assistant surgeons, who had status as commissioned officers within the Medical Department.[18] Bathing facilities for enlisted men were inadequate.[19] Noncommissioned officers were underpaid.[20] Post commanders in remote locations, beyond the reach of controlling superior authority, were petty tyrants.[21] The regulations board could not make right all these alleged wrongs, but its members did have authority to travel wherever necessary to pursue inquiries that might assist them in their work. Winnowing legitimate concerns from the rhetoric was not difficult; the guiding criterion was the good of the service.

While the Marcy board was still engaged in gathering information, it was assigned an additional responsibility, that of recommending to the secretary of war a new style of uniform for adoption by the army.[22] News of this initiative opened up another flood of queries, reminders, and remonstrations. Meanwhile, the board continued its work in response to the original charge. To ensure harmony between it and the Schofield board, it reviewed the papers accumulated by that body and also its final report.[23] By December 1871 the regulations board had made sufficient progress at New York City that it requested and was granted permission to remove to Washington, where its members could confer with Secretary Belknap and other officials whom he might call upon for counsel.[24] General Sherman would not be a party to these final deliberations. He had sailed for Europe in November, intending to familiarize himself with developments in military practices there and so consider further innovations for the U.S. Army. During Sherman's absence, the day-to-day operations of the military would be under the direct supervision of the secretary of war.

While in Washington, Dodge renewed acquaintance with another visitor in the city, William Blackmore, the English lawyer-entrepreneur whom he had met in 1868 at Fort Sanders, Wyoming. Since that time Blackmore had committed himself to further exploration of western lands as opportunities for investment. During his third visit to the United States, in 1871, he purchased two large tracts of land, in Colorado and New Mexico, which he hoped to develop through stock raising and mining. Additionally, he became involved in the financing of a new railroad, the Denver and Rio Grande, whose projected route south from Denver would carry it within convenient distance of the lands he had purchased.[25] Following a brief return to his homeland, Blackmore would spend the greater part of 1872 in the United States, pursuing one or another of his philanthropic, scientific, and financial enterprises. When Dodge chanced to meet him in the national capital, he was busy consulting members of Congress and other officials about pending legislation that might affect his investments. Genial, munificent, self-assured, and overflowing with ideas, Blackmore was a highly visible presence in Washington, where he seems to have impressed almost everyone he met. He spent an evening with President Grant and his family at the presidential mansion. He sponsored a daylong boat ride on the Potomac River for a group of visiting Sioux Indians and various high officials, including Grant.[26] And after conversations with Dodge, he hit upon a plan that might further his investment aims while also making possible a renewal of the outdoors companionship the two men had enjoyed four years before.

Although in 1871 Blackmore had visited the tracts of western land he now owned, he had not yet examined the extensive properties closely enough to form a confident estimate of their resources and possible future use. However, because the territory was frequented by not-always-peaceable Ute Indians, the onsite assessment would require that he be accompanied by an armed party. Thus, "in the interests of science, and with the object of obtaining information relative to the resources of one of the most interesting and least known portions of the United States," on April 16 he applied to Secretary Belknap for a military escort on that proposed expedition. He was less than forthcoming about the financial motives that underlay his request, but on the following day Joseph Henry, director of the Smithsonian Institution, wrote Belknap in his support, characterizing him as "a generous patron of science, both in his own and in our country." Blackmore, expressing himself in the best genteel style, indicated to the secretary of war that he hoped to depart from Fort Garland, Colorado, around the end of August and that he expected to be in the field for between six weeks and two months. "If I might also so far venture to take so great a liberty," he continued, "I would suggest, if practicable and convenient, that Colonel Richard J. [sic] Dodge should take the command of the escort, as I have previously travelled with him in the West, and he understands my intentions and views."[27]

That Dodge fully comprehended Blackmore's plans and their ramifications is doubtful, but the possibility of taking part in his proposed expedition was certainly attractive to him. The journey would take him into country he had not yet visited, and during the height of the hunting season. Blackmore was full of praise for the San Luis Valley and the mountains that surrounded it as a haven for sportsmen. During the previous fall he had enjoyed himself "on the rampage after Mountain buffalo" in the Tarryall range of mountains just to the north.[28]

Requests such as Blackmore's were not uncommon, and several had been granted in recent years. During 1871 Sheridan and Blackmore had made plans for a buffalo hunt together, accompanied by an army escort,[29] and earlier in the current year the general had organized a lavish expedition for the entertainment of a distinguished foreign visitor, the Grand Duke Alexis of Russia.[30] Secretary Belknap therefore directed the adjutant general to ask Sheridan to extend to Blackmore "every facility and courtesy in your power."[31] Sheridan's response, indicating that he would be pleased to do so, reached Washington on April 24, and on the next evening Blackmore dined with Dodge, a colleague of his on the regulations board, and three other gentlemen.[32] The conversation at that gathering surely included anticipations of the hunting adventures to come.

Unfortunately, through a remarkable miscalculation Blackmore deprived himself of the expense-free military support he had succeeded in arranging. In a chatty letter to Sheridan he described his plans for the fall expedition at some length, noting again that he hoped Dodge would be permitted to command the army escort out of Fort Garland. "I have traveled with Col. Dodge before in the Rocky Mountains," he wrote, "and know and appreciate his good qualities as a pleasant companion, and practised hunter." He went on to explain that he intended to bring with him several wagons "to take out provisions, forage and other necessaries, and to bring back whatever I may find of interest to science." To ensure the security of these wagons he hoped to be allotted from twenty-five to thirty "Infintary" soldiers; and to ensure the safety of his party when away from the wagons, he asked for approximately fifty cavalry.[33] Had Blackmore consulted Dodge or any other informed person, he would surely have trimmed this estimate—an outrageous one in view of the army's chronic lack of manpower. Excepting commissioned officers, the entire garrison of Fort Garland numbered only twenty-five infantry and thirty-nine cavalry soldiers.[34] Familiar in manner, plausible in content, and respectful in tone as it might be, his call for almost two companies of troops was doomed to failure.

Without further consultation with Belknap, upon receipt of Blackmore's letter General Sheridan retracted his offer of an escort. Demonstrating his own capacity as a framer of highfalutin phrases, he declared himself "very sorry to disappoint so enthusiastic a lover of nature as you are" and begged leave to assure Blackmore "that my personal feelings of friendship make this course very unpleasant to me."[35] But in a letter to Belknap explaining the course he had taken, Sheridan adopted a quite different tone. The "real object" of the explorations the Englishman had in mind, he wrote, "is the discovery perhaps of gold and silver mines believed to exist in that section." He went on to characterize Blackmore in unflattering terms, relating his activities to those of other foreigners whose interests did not coincide with those of the United States:

> Even independently [of the "real object"] I consider Mr. Blackmore's request as irreconcilable and immodest. He has no claims on this country, which should place him at the head of a large exploring party. His alleged benefits in developing, heretofore, certain sections in the west were in the interest of railroads and other parties, who paid him well. He is not a citizen of the United States, is not likely to be one, and to fill his escort would require troops to be drawn from Fort Union, many miles away. . . .
>
> We are harassed to death to meet the legitimate wants of our own people on the frontier, and I hope you will coincide with me in declining to give escorts to foreigners for their pecuniary interests or scientific fame.[36]

Sheridan's distrust of Blackmore was no less manifest in this statement than was his frustration as a military commander saddled with responsibilities beyond his means of fulfilling them. Perhaps also he betrayed a reservation about the priorities, good judgment, and good faith of the secretary of war.

Dodge went unmentioned in Sheridan's letter and seems to have been spared his censure. To him the denial of Blackmore's request was not a serious disappointment. It meant the loss of an enjoyable fall hunt, but some other excursion in company with his English friend remained a possibility. Meanwhile, he and the other regulations board members were busy completing their assigned tasks, while Blackmore had pursuits of his own. Wishing to establish a firm legal title to Mexican land grants that he had purchased, on May 10 he appeared before the Senate Committee on Public Lands.[37] He was determined to examine more closely his land purchases in the West by some means.[38]

The proposed new body of army regulations submitted by the Marcy board to Secretary Belknap in May 1872 was a significant updating and expansion of the 1863 code. In general, its organization followed that of the earlier version, but many of its sixty-five numbered articles were without precedent. Among these were the first four—Theory of the Military Establishment; War Department; The General-in-Chief; and Military Geographical Divisions, Departments, and Posts—all dealing with broad organization and delimitations of authority. Two new main headings elsewhere in the work elaborated this theme: General Staff, detailing the operations and departments under the general in chief; and The Administrative Services, describing the staff departments. Other new articles reflected the changed conditions under which the army now operated,[39] and still others were much expanded from corresponding sections in the earlier version.[40] The articles numbered XLVIII–L, entitled respectively Organization of an Army in the Field, Marches, and Prisoners of War, were expanded from material that had previously appeared under a single heading, Troops in Campaign. In short, the Marcy report was a thorough, searching description of the current organization and operations of the army. It proposed no major recommendations for change, but it was nonetheless potentially an instrument for significant reform. If officially adopted, it set the terms for service-wide consistency in a great many matters that had earlier been left to the discretion of individuals.

Having submitted its report, together with a set of recommendations for a new army uniform, on May 17, 1872, the Marcy board was dissolved and its members ordered to return to their posts.[41] Colonel Marcy would remain in Washington and deal by himself with the objections and requests for clarification, reconsideration, modification, and justification that the report would yield,[42] at least until the return of General Sherman. The other members of the board naturally felt a continuing interest in the document they had labored together to prepare. As Dodge took up his new assignment as post commander at Fort Dodge, Kansas, he carried in his consciousness a detailed familiarity with the proposed new regulations that in future years would redound to his benefit as a soldier's soldier. Whatever the ultimate fate of the document he had helped create, formulating its articles had brought into sharp focus the working institution that gave him his professional identity. Whether he agreed with some provisions, such as the limitation of official powers granted the general in chief (he did not), was one matter; whether he comprehended those provisions in all their implications was another. He had shared in defining the duties and proper official behavior of a U.S. Army officer as these were understood in 1872.

Unfortunately, the efforts to promote army reform that General Sherman had set in motion three years before and in which Dodge had thus played a part were less successful than the commanding general had hoped. Well before Sherman's departure for Europe, Secretary Belknap had begun to usurp authority in areas the general considered his own. Leaves of absence, changes of station, and assignments to the U.S. Military Academy were regularly authorized by the secretary, or else by the chiefs of army departments, without Sherman's knowledge until, perhaps, he read of them in a newspaper on some subsequent day.[43] Forthrightly, in August 1870 Sherman wrote Secretary Belknap requesting a definite statement of exactly what authority he still retained, but he received no reply. When he took up the matter with Grant, he was given answers that came to little more.[44] Sherman had a short fuse and was little disposed to receive slights without rejoinder, but by an effort of will he swallowed the humiliation and pushed ahead.

In January 1871, when Sherman forwarded the report of the Schofield tactics board to Secretary Belknap, he noted that he and the members of that board spoke as one. He had reviewed the entire document, he wrote, but his recommendation for its adoption was based chiefly on "the confidence I repose in the ability of the Board and the great labor" they had manifestly devoted to their work. Wishing to ensure that the new tactics be made available to officers in a form for convenient reference, he proposed that each of its three parts be issued separately as a small volume, "about the size of Upton's Tactics," one each for infantry, cavalry, and artillery. Sherman was aware that the secretary might balk at the cost to the government of producing such a work, but he expressed confidence that Harper & Brothers of New York or another reputable publisher would undertake the project and offer it for distribution to the army at a moderate price.[45]

Seven months after receiving the Schofield report, the secretary of war had not yet taken action on it. At that time Sherman received for his endorsement a request from Lieutenant Colonel Upton that the War Department give its "informal consent" to his issuing a revised and corrected edition of his *Infantry Tactics*. Sherman took the occasion to draft a statement to Belknap in which he placed the Upton request in the context of the army's present needs. Any changes Upton might wish to make to his original *Tactics* need not be approved or disapproved by the secretary of war, he wrote, for those changes did not form part of the work that had already been approved; they were Upton's private property, to be done with as he pleased. Moreover, whatever the merits of the revisions, they concerned infantry only and so failed to address the needs of the army at large: "[T]he Army needs something now, applicable to all arms of Service; and a Board of Experienced officers assembled by the order of Secretary of War Rawlins, has prepared after great labor, Tactics for the *Three* Arms of Service [—] Infantry, Artillery and Cavalry—with full instructions for all the forms for Parade,

Guard Mounting &c, which Consolidated Tactics were long since submitted to the Secretary of War, bearing my official approval and from which I have not yet had an answer."

Sherman noted that from time to time he had sent along other material for the approval of the secretary, but he affirmed the importance of taking action on the Schofield report before anything else. Returning to Upton's request, he concluded that "until officially advised that the Secretary of War rejects the labor of the Board," he could not advise even considering the changes proposed by that officer.[46]

More than one year after writing these comments, upon his return from Europe in September 1872 Sherman learned with consternation that the report of the Schofield board had still not been officially approved. Once the Marcy board had studied it as part of their inquiries, they had returned it to the Adjutant General's Office, where it remained on file. Nor was the General of the Army alone in his frustration at Secretary Belknap's seeming indifference to matters others considered crucial. In September 1872 Lieutenant Colonel James Van Voast, Sixteenth Infantry, informed the adjutant general that since serving on the Schofield board he had been asked by several officers for copies of those sections of the final report that applied to their arms of the service. Van Voast expressed a strong desire to place the work in the hands of persons who could benefit from it and even expressed willingness to pay the cost of printing a few copies for private distribution, but he did not feel at liberty to do so without the sanction of the War Department. It was common knowledge, he wrote, that in drilling their troops, company commanders often adopted whatever practices they thought best, irrespective whether authority for them existed in print. Van Voast wished to help dispel some of the confusion. Nevertheless, in endorsing the letter of this conscientious officer, Sherman could only write that "without the distinct approval of the War Department, I doubt the wisdom of increased confusion by the publication of these Tactics." In a note written over the text of Sherman's endorsement, the chief clerk of the War Department recorded that Secretary Belknap "concurred in" it.[47] However, he gave no indication that the official approval Sherman and others wished for would ever be forthcoming.

In December 1872 another member of the tactics board, Lieutenant Colonel Wesley Merritt, Ninth Cavalry, made a request similar to that of Van Voast. In the absence of any other code that had been authorized, he suggested that a system of cavalry tactics prepared by Brigadier General Philip St. George Cooke be approved for use by his regiment. The Cooke tactics had formed the nucleus of the Schofield board's recommendations for that arm of the service. But once more, and for the last time, General Sherman asserted his conviction that "the true and only solution" to the problem of need for a controlling authority to describe tactical maneuvers was to adopt the Schofield report. "I again invite the attention of the Secretary of War to the importance of the subject," he wrote in frustration, "and beg his early consideration of the Record [*sic*] which has been in his hands more than two years."[48] At last, by direction of Secretary Belknap, the manuscript report of the Schofield board was placed in the hands of Colonel Upton for final revision, and in January 1873 Sherman wrote to him expressing his particular wishes.[49]

The initiative to revise the outdated army regulations, Sherman's second major project for army reform during this period, met a fate hardly less frustrating to him. Although Secretary Belknap had received the report of the Marcy board in May 1872, he delayed submitting it to the House of Representatives for its consideration until February 17, 1873. His reasons for this inaction are unknown, but the effect of the report's not being transmitted until late in the final session of the Forty-second Congress was not surprising. Presented with a lengthy and detailed document for its review, the Committee on Military Affairs was unable to act upon it. Moreover, in forwarding the report, Belknap had drawn attention to a practical difficulty likely to cause further delay. The Army Reorganization Act of 1866 specified that the regulations then in force—those of 1863—would remain so until Congress acted upon a new code to be prepared and submitted to it by the secretary of war. The consequence of this legislation, Belknap noted, was that the executive power had no authority to alter any feature of the 1863 regulations except by an act of Congress. "The length of a letter on a knapsack, for example, being prescribed therein, the Executive has no power to alter its size until Congress shall authorize it, and the regulations now presented will be subject to precisely the same objection." Some persons suspected that Belknap was drawing attention to this interference of the legislative branch with the executive as an excuse for his department's inaction. At any rate, he recommended that if Congress approved the Marcy report, it should do so with a proviso that returned the proper prerogatives to the executive branch. The new regulations should be adopted "subject to *such alterations as the President may from time to time adopt*."[50]

The Marcy report was ordered to be printed and thus became part of the published record of Congress's activity during that session, but no further action was ever taken on it. Until it was drawn upon amid preparations for a new code of regulations that was adopted and promulgated in 1881, it remained consigned to the same administrative limbo as the report of the Schofield tactics board. In the interim, the anachronistic regulations of 1863 continued to govern the army. The reports of both boards were significant accomplishments on paper, but they were denied their intended impact on the work of the service. Like Gulliver in Lilliput, Sherman found himself caught in a web of political constraints that rendered him all but helpless to bring forward the reforms he wished in the early years of his tenure as General of the Army. Both the secretary of war and Congress appeared to interpret the phrase "army reform" more narrowly than he, as synonymous with reduced appropriations and reductions in force. Thus in 1874 Sherman stoutly resisted a proposal to reduce the authorized strength of the army to 25,000 enlisted men. He testified eloquently on the issue before the Committee on Military Affairs,[51] but his effort was unsuccessful, as he knew it would be. The current operations of the army in remote western territories did not impress most congressmen as sufficiently important to the national welfare to justify large expenditures.

Paradoxically, Sherman's very lack of success as an advocate for the military force he nominally led produced a positive result, firming the morale of the officer corps and molding the regiments of the line into a more cohesive body. Through the *Army and Navy Journal* and other newspapers, the fates of innovations he sponsored became well known to his subordinate officers and men across the country. His frustration as a commanding general granted only limited authority was appreciated by others who viewed their performance of duty as ignored, underestimated, or even resented by the majority of citizens. Public opinion might not rate their contribution to the national welfare at a high value, but they understood themselves as an elite corps—as Dodge later expressed it, a "bulwark of civilization" that was "rendering possible an immigration unequalled in the history of the world."[52] General Sherman's words and actions on their behalf resonated among his fellow soldiers as affirming the honor of their profession and the value to the nation of its dedicated service.

10

At Fort Dodge, Kansas

Another epoch in Dodge's career began on June 3, 1872, when, after reporting at Fort Leavenworth for orders, he assumed command at his military namesake, Fort Dodge. Initially his chief mandate as post commander was the same as during his brief posting at Fort Larned, to support construction of the Atchison, Topeka and Santa Fe Railroad line. At the time of his arrival, the end of track was approaching the town of Larned, sixty miles distant, and Fort Dodge was still relatively isolated, without telegraph communication and with no large communities nearby. The weekly mail reached it over a road from Hays City, a stop on the Kansas Pacific Railroad eighty miles north. But during the summer of 1872 the vicinity of the post experienced the influx of an unruly population that followed the railroad. Fort Dodge became an oasis of order and the rule of law amid conditions that verged on chaos.

The problems Major Dodge dealt with as post commander far outnumbered those he had encountered along the Union Pacific a few years earlier. Working with limited facilities and supplies, and with at best sketchy information concerning developments that concerned him as a public official, through wise deployment of the military force allotted him he more than once averted violence in confrontations that approached a flash point. In the published code of proposed army regulations submitted by the Marcy board, the description of a post commander's duties filled four densely packed pages.[1] As thus formulated in the ideal, those responsibilities constituted a workload manifestly beyond the powers of one frail mortal. However, Dodge was winning a reputation as a "very wide-awake commander,"[2] and his performance at this duty station justified the epithet. That he accomplished as much as he did while at Fort Dodge was a notable testimony to his judgment, administrative ability, and diplomatic skill.

Named after Grenville Mellen Dodge, who had directed its establishment in 1864, the post was situated on the north bank of the Arkansas River between two Indian trails that crossed the stream, twenty miles to the east and to the west.[3] A visitor described it in 1865 as a thoroughly unprepossessing facility, "a few huts made of poles set endwise in the ground and covered with dirt and tents, inclosed by a ditch and dirt embankment."[4] During General Sheridan's military campaign of 1868–1869, the fort was a staging depot for supplies, serving the troops bound south into Texas. Its position near a camping ground for wagon trains along the "dry route" of the Santa Fe Trail gave it continuing usefulness as a deterrent to tribes of Indians that frequented the vicinity—particularly Kiowa, Cheyenne, and Arapaho. By 1872 several stone buildings had been erected at the fort, including two large warehouses, barracks for three companies of troops, and a large stable for cavalry mounts. Vigilance remained necessary against parties of thieving Indians who sought to stampede the stock herd and make other mischief. Nevertheless, despite the poor defensive position it occupied between the river and a range of low bluffs immediately to its north, the fort itself was secure.

Protecting the railroad as it approached the large military reservation of Fort Dodge and then passed beyond it on the 163-mile distance to the western border of Kansas was strenuous but in other respects not particularly difficult. To the east, Dodge made use of both infantry and cavalry. Detachments of infantry from Fort Dodge and Fort Larned were posted at railroad stations as far east as Newton, Kansas. These troops, led by Captain Henry Brevoort Bristol, Fifth Infantry, guarded supplies and provided a visible peacekeeping presence.[5] Cavalry moved between Fort Dodge and the vicinity of Fort Larned and back again, following the south bank of the river. This kept them between the railroad, on the north side, and a range of sand hills further south that could afford protection to parties of Indians or other persons bent on trouble.[6] In case of an emergency, General Pope gave Dodge authority to call upon another company of the cavalry troops stationed at Fort Hays.[7]

Once the railhead passed beyond Fort Dodge into the sparsely inhabited country to the west, the military situation was altered. This region was often traversed by Indians, and the need for an infantry presence to protect the newly constructed railroad stations was more obvious. Detachments of cavalry continued to patrol the railroad line, but now on the north side of the tracks as well as the south bank of the river. The mounted troops to the north had orders to follow a zigzag course in search of Indians or bands of outlaws that hid in ravines opening onto the railroad.[8] Installation of a telegraph line concurrently with the advance of the tracks greatly facilitated the troops' capacity for a rapid response. Incidents of violence did occur along the line, but none that resulted in the injury or death of more than two men. Thanks to the energetic measures adopted for its security, construction of the Atchison, Topeka and Santa Fe Railroad moved ahead on schedule.[9]

Scouts to the South

Protection of the railroad was a straightforward task; it entailed securing known distances within a narrow strip of land, over which persons passed in a small but steady stream. More challenging was to preserve order in the 7,500-square-mile area to the south and east of Fort Dodge. The post stood 54 miles north of the border separating the state of Kansas from Indian Territory, and approximately 140 miles west of the new town of Wichita.[10] Despite its location at the northwest corner of this region, Fort Dodge bore responsibility for monitoring developments and responding to situations that required military intervention throughout the area. At the time of Dodge's arrival at the post, the most feared cause of such incidents was attack by hostile Indians.

Not all the tribespeople who formerly ranged this area as their own were disposed to take up permanent residence in Indian Territory. Responsibility for the welfare and the conduct of Indians within that territory rested with agents of the Bureau of Indian Affairs, commonly known as the "Indian Bureau," a division of the Department of the Interior. By law, the army had no authority to conduct operations there unless called upon for a specific purpose by a representative of the Indian Bureau.[11] On the other hand, should reservation Indians leave Indian Territory, with or without permission from their agents, and enter public lands such as those in Kansas, the army was charged with controlling them. But should they commit thefts or other unlawful acts, the tribesmen needed only to return to Indian Territory to elude pursuit by the army.

To Dodge and other military men this allocation of responsibility was farcical.[12] Nevertheless, his duty was to preserve the peace within the severe constraints it imposed. To forestall trouble with reservation Indians, he therefore ordered a series of scouts from Fort Dodge into regions of southern Kansas where the native tribespeople were known to congregate to make medicine, hunt buffalo, or engage in other pursuits. Except during the winter months, detachments of cavalry were kept in the field almost continuously. The scouts ranged in duration from one week to a full month, and in distance from 150 to 500 miles. Dodge granted the officers in command discretionary powers in case of special conditions such as the lack of water or unusual weather, but he specified with care the routes to be followed. Additionally, his written orders included directions for conduct in case Indians should be met with. For example, in April 1873 he ordered Captain Tullius C. Tupper, Sixth Cavalry, to lead a scout through country the soldiers had passed through often—first south from the post, then east to Medicine Lodge Creek, and finally up that stream to "Griffith's ranch," from which point Tupper was to decide for himself the best return route. "The object of the Scouting party," the order continued, "is by a display of force to prevent any Indian outbreak. Captain Tupper will therefore while affording protection to the settlers, carefully avoid anything which would probably exasperate the Indians. He will be very careful in his intercourse with them, treating them kindly but firmly, and on no account allow more than one or two to enter his camp at once. Force is not to be used except as a last necessity and only in case of outrage."[13] Often the scouting parties returned without seeing any sign of Indians, but on some occasions they fell in with bodies of Southern Cheyennes. More than rudimentary communication with the leaders of these parties was not always possible until the spring of 1873, when Dodge succeeded in obtaining a full-time interpreter. Before then he relied on interpreters made available to him for short periods by the post commander at Camp Supply, Lieutenant Colonel John R. Brooke, Third Infantry.

During 1872 the constant military presence proved an effective deterrent to Indian violence in the country southeast of Fort Dodge. In 1873, recognizing the need for similar patrols in the yet larger area west of the post to the New Mexico line, Dodge obtained authorization to order scouts in that country as well.[14] These covered a range of land extending north from the Kansas border to a point approximately halfway between the Atchison, Topeka and Santa Fe and the Kansas Pacific Railroads. In both 1872 and 1873, Dodge commanded several such missions, being absent from the post sometimes for weeks.

Incidents of Indian violence occurred, but not often. On one occasion a party of Cheyennes was en route to New Mexico to take blood vengeance against white settlers for losses they had suffered there, but happening onto a group of railroad surveyors they attacked them instead and then returned to their reservation.[15] Rumors of outrages perpetrated by Indians were rife but rarely accurate. More often the wrongdoers were gangs of outlaws who either disguised themselves as Indians or else attributed their own misdeeds to Indians who, they alleged, had been seen in the vicinity.[16] Crimes of all kinds were committed by these renegades. One band of horse thieves had the temerity to rob the infantry escort to a railroad surveying party west of the post. Acting on orders from Dodge, Sergeant P. L. Beatty and thirteen men of Troop G, Sixth Cavalry, pursued these men over three hundred miles, to the head of the Dry Cimarron River. In a surprise attack they killed two of the fugitives, routed the rest, and recovered almost all the stolen property, earning a commendation from Dodge, who reported their exploit to department headquarters.[17]

Those thieves had betrayed themselves by lack of caution, but other wrongdoers were more circumspect. Dodge reported that they were "difficult to manage, as they either go along the [railroad] grade ostensibly in search of work, or roam about the country in the guise of Buffalo hunters." Nevertheless, he continued, "I propose to keep out scouts almost continuously, and hope to make this horse stealing a dangerous pastime."[18] Only recently a scouting party to the east had arrested a known ne'er-do-well, Nathan Hudson, who had stolen the greater part of a cattle herd and was driving it toward Leavenworth, or so he claimed. But Dodge knew his man and described him to the U.S. marshal at Topeka, Kansas, as "one of the gang of cattle thieves that makes its headquarters at Boyles Ranch near Fort Larned."[19]

Life at the Post

With many of his troops on assignment elsewhere, Dodge was without sufficient manpower to complete needed repairs and renovations at the post, for as usual his quartermaster's budget included few funds to hire civilian laborers. He did direct the construction of a properly designed powder magazine, a smaller version of the one at Fort Lyon,[20] and his increasingly urgent appeals at last yielded authorization to repair the cavalry stables. Some of them had fallen in, causing injury to the horses.[21] Too often, his efforts to preserve government property necessitated tedious correspondence with representatives of the staff departments at Fort Leavenworth, officers who seemed oblivious to the conditions that complicated his daily existence. For example, despite a succession of failed efforts to operate a ferry across the Arkansas River—wrecks lay mired in quicksand, mute witnesses to the futility of the enterprise—the Quartermaster's Department seemed determined to push ahead with this project.[22] When Dodge asked for authorization to employ six teamsters at a depot to be constructed on the edge of the Fort Dodge military reservation, where it met the Atchison, Topeka and Santa Fe tracks, the departmental quartermaster responded that his idea seemed to be a good one; but he neglected to make available the necessary funds.[23] Amid bitter winter weather, when cases of frostbite were common and the post surgeon, Captain William Tremaine, was kept busy amputating limbs of soldiers and citizens who required emergency care,[24] Dodge appealed to the Quartermaster's Department for the issue of a horse-powered saw to cut firewood. Noting that twenty men were sometimes needed to cut sufficient wood to keep buildings warm, he observed that he could name "so many more important things that soldiers may be employed at than cutting wood."[25]

In the spring of 1873 Dodge appealed once more, this time to departmental headquarters, for attention to the basic needs of his men. If scouts were to proceed as planned in the coming months, then the cavalry troops attached to the post must be supplied a portable forge to protect the hooves of their mounts. The Ordnance Department was not yet ready to issue these implements, and the Quartermaster Department was unwilling to send any of those it had on hand because, according to usual practice, they should be issued by the ordnance staff. "Between these two obstructive Departments," he complained, "no forges can be had," with the result that scouts would soon become impossible for the lack of sound horses.[26] Later in the year the department quartermaster disapproved Dodge's request for an issue of fire fenders to protect the post's wood buildings from sparks that flew from the hard wood in the stoves. Dodge remonstrated that "the expense is small and the saving to the U. S. may be very great," noting that he understood a surplus of the fenders existed at another post, Fort Riley.[27] After repeated appeals and lengthy delays, several of the items he requested eventually reached the post, but at the cost of severely tried patience on his part. "[S]ome of our Staff Officers," he wrote a few years later, "are as complete fossils, as can be found in the tertiary deposits of the Bad Lands. . . . Their occupation becomes a matter of routine, in which the correctness of a form is of more importance than the establishment of a fact."[28]

Living conditions at Fort Dodge were plain but adequate according to army standards, and the morale of the enlisted soldiers was as high as could be expected. However, there was too much work, with too few men to perform it. Ordinarily Dodge supplied a small detachment of infantry as an escort to wagon trains carrying goods to Camp Supply and points further south, but in June 1873 he discontinued the practice. The contractors could take their own precautions or else abide the result; he had no men to spare.[29] Thanks to the extent of the military reservation that surrounded the post, such men as he had were at least removed from the temptations of the nascent railroad town five miles away, Dodge City. However, dispensers of illicit amusement made their appearance on the south side of the river, directly opposite the post. Dodge urged that the reservation be enlarged to include the lands occupied by these operators of "rum shops and disreputable resorts,"[30] but without success. The post trader, Robert M. Wright, complied with his order to dispense liquor by the drink only, and never in a quantity sufficient to make a man drunk,[31] but the problem of liquor smuggled onto the post was all but unsolvable.

A dramatic instance of the damage one drunken man could cause to military discipline and morale was the case of a commissioned officer, Second Lieutenant Edward P. Turner, Tenth Cavalry. In July 1872 Turner, then stationed at Camp Supply, was ordered with some of his men to escort an officer of the Quartermaster Department, Captain Ezra B. Kirk, on his ninety-mile journey north to Fort Dodge. Formerly a private soldier,[32] the lieutenant was on companionable terms with his men. Evidently he was drunk by the time he reached the vicinity of the post, for after miring his wagons and mules in the Arkansas River, he simply left them there and proceeded with some of his men to the post trader's store. By the time Dodge was informed of his arrival, Turner had fired a shot in the store, ridden his horse into the soldiers' billiard room, and also tried to ride it into Bob Wright's private residence. Hurrying to the scene, Dodge found him in the barroom, obviously roaring drunk, and ordered him arrested. But Turner, armed and potentially dangerous, defied him. "It would take an armed party to arrest me," he boasted.

Dodge, wishing to avoid serious injury to anyone, approached him and by some means managed to get his arms around him while the officer of the day, Captain Edward Moale, Third Infantry, took away his pistol. Stepping back, the post commander urged Turner to behave sensibly and obey the arrest. But the drunken officer called out to his men for assistance and lunging forward, began striking him with his fists. Dodge, a large man of considerable strength, seems to have retained his composure amid the melee. "When I thought I had taken as many blows as I ought to be called upon to bear," he wrote in a report, "I knocked him down with a billiard cue, and had him taken to the guard-house."[33] Shortly afterward, without securing permission to depart from the post, the soldiers who had accompanied Turner set out for Camp Supply. But the next day Dodge directed Second Lieutenant Sebree Smith, Sixth Cavalry, to overtake them and keep them under strict discipline for the rest of their journey.[34] Second Lieutenant Turner, in chains and under guard by Smith, would reach his post together with his men, to face charges that led to a trial by court-martial.[35]

In June 1873 a citizen of Hays City notified General Pope of derelictions by the post commanders at Forts Hays and Dodge, who, he claimed, "should get cashiered immediately for doing more harm than good to the public service." It was no wonder that desertion was becoming a problem, he wrote. Enlisted men under Major Dodge "get treated like dogs, have to work from 8 to 10 hours, have to drill, have Dress-parade, &c. &c." When Pope directed that the letter be forwarded to Dodge for his information, the latter reacted angrily. "If the Dept Comdr has the slightest doubt of the propriety and justice of my rule," he wrote in an endorsement, "I respectfully recommend that he send an Inspector to this post, or what is greatly better that he will come out and see for himself."[36] Dodge was sensitive to allegations that his "rule" was tyrannical, being an officer particularly attuned to the needs of the enlisted men under his charge. He was himself concerned about the increasing prevalence of desertion and had recently addressed a letter on the subject to departmental headquarters. "Large numbers of men," he wrote, "boatmen &c, enlist regularly every winter, and desert as regularly as soon as the rivers are open in the spring. The Govt. is put to immense expense and the Army is getting to be a sort of Pauper Asylum for men not at work. The moral[e] of the Army is being constantly lowered, & desertion, the most serious Military Crime, is looked upon as rather a good joke." As a way to combat the evil he proposed a change in policy—that is, to pay citizens the $30 reward for apprehension of a deserter immediately upon their delivering him to proper military authority. Under current practice, months might elapse before vigilant citizens were reimbursed for their trouble, an inconvenience that discouraged them from helping the army enforce discipline in its own ranks.[37]

A bright spot in Dodge's working relationship with representatives of the staff departments at Fort Leavenworth was the close cooperation between him and the departmental engineer officer, First Lieutenant Ernest H. Ruffner. Among his other duties, Ruffner was responsible for compiling and reconciling data forwarded to him for use in preparing maps and itineraries. Dodge took particular interest in mapmaking and understood that the issuance of more accurate maps would be an important byproduct of the plains campaigning his men were regularly engaged in. Intending to gather topographical data about the country surrounding Fort Dodge, he obtained from Ruffner odometers, prismatic compasses, and a supply of volumes designed to enable travelers conveniently to record their observations of the terrain. After some delay owing to the shortage of staff members in his office, Ruffner also made available to Dodge the temporary services of a sergeant and a private soldier, both trained in mapmaking.[38] During the spring and summer of 1873 these men proved valuable to Dodge and Ruffner alike, for one or the other accompanied all the scouting parties that left Fort Dodge.[39] The noncommissioned officer, Sergeant R. N. Harper, provided instruction in mapmaking to younger officers in the garrison, and with Private A. C. Kelley he also offered hints to the enlisted men who were assisting them in the field. The result of this cooperative effort was the accumulation of detailed topographical knowledge, with accompanying maps, unexampled in the Department of the Missouri for its extent and exactness. In a circular dated November 5, 1873, General Pope expressed thanks to Dodge and other named officers and enlisted men "for the admirable manner in which the maps have been made and the various journals, etc., kept, pertaining to the scouts made from Fort Dodge, Kans., during the last season," commending their example to other men serving in the department.[40]

The numerous scouts from Fort Dodge in 1872 and 1873 thus accomplished a variety of purposes. They increased knowledge of the region's topographical features, discouraged Indian misbehavior, denied sanctuary to outlaws, enabled Dodge to monitor the rapid progress of settlement, and also afforded a prime opportunity for him and likeminded officers to bag game. A further advantage that accrued to Dodge was his contact with Indians, in Kansas or in Indian Territory. In light of developments later in his lifetime, these meetings were perhaps the most beneficial to him personally.

Encounters with Indians

At the post, Dodge was sometimes called upon to assist John D. Miles, the Indian Bureau's hardworking representative at the distant Cheyenne and Arapaho Agency, in his effort to protect his charges and the land they occupied from victimization and despoilment. Whisky-sellers drove their wagons onto reservation lands to make sales, an activity forbidden by federal statutes, or else skirted the law by ensconcing themselves just north of the Kansas state line and dispensing their product to whoever might appear. Buffalo hunters and other unauthorized persons regularly entered Indian Territory, again flouting federal regulations. However, virtually no effective force was available to enforce the laws except for the scouting parties sent out from Fort Dodge, and these were ill-prepared to provide strict police action. Criminals fled with impunity to hideouts in Indian Territory, where state authorities had no jurisdiction. On those occasions when Agent Miles managed to arrest criminal intruders on Indian lands, he sent them first to Camp Supply and thence to Dodge City in a lengthy, danger-filled journey toward arraignment. But the populace of Dodge City had little sympathy for Miles and others who sought to enforce the laws. To protect persons connected with the legal processes, including witnesses and Indians, Dodge provided them sleeping space at the post and an escort on their short journey to the railroad station.[41]

At the heart of Dodge's disagreement with the Peace Policy that had been instituted under President Grant in 1869 was his perception that its intended beneficiaries, the Indians, were being victimized by it. Men like Miles, however well-intentioned, were unable or unwilling to exert the forcible sway necessary to create conditions for the cultural transformation that had been envisioned for the Indians. Meanwhile, less principled persons took advantage of the Indians' effective incarceration by obtaining lucrative contracts to supply them food and annuity goods, usually of inferior quality. Dodge's observations and experiences moved him to write anonymous articles on these subjects, probably for publication in newspapers.[42] Like General Sherman, he believed that the army was the arm of federal authority best prepared to foster among the Indians the capacity to assume the responsibilities of U.S. citizenship.

At various times when on scout, Dodge encountered bands of Indians and took the opportunity to observe their behavior and customs. Of course, their presence in Kansas was not lawful, but he chose not to press the matter provided they seemed to be engaged in peaceable pursuits. Ordinarily they were, but in one interview with an Arapaho chief, probably Little Raven, he was informed that the band intended to steal some property in order to help make ends meet. "They wanted to remain at peace," Dodge later wrote, "but were too poor to live in peace, and they relied upon the stealings of the summer and the gifts they would receive for making peace, for means to start again in a condition of comfortable independence."[43] Interviews with other Indian leaders including Big Mouth, Stone Calf, White Head, One Eyed Bull, and Whirlwind of the Southern Cheyennes and Left Hand, Little White Wolf, and We-Sesh of the Arapahos gave him further insight into the predicament they faced.[44] Despite the language barrier, he sensed the seasoned leadership of these men, who were seeking to preserve the nomadic way of life that was their heritage. Formerly lords of the land, they were now strangers in most of it. He was not one of them, but evidently he impressed them as well. During the summer of 1872 he was permitted to witness, at a respectful distance, a Cheyenne Sun Dance. The protracted observance, in which men were tethered to a central lodgepole by long ropes of leather secured by incisions through their chest muscles, aroused his keen curiosity. In an act of ritual self-torture they danced, sometimes for days, until released from suffering by the rope's tearing through their flesh. The Sun Dance was not only a rite of passage for young adults but evidently for others a mode of divination through which the disposition of the Indians' deity was revealed.[45]

Beginning that summer, Dodge's inquiries into the culture of the Plains Indians took on new importance for him. His interest in their religious beliefs led him to set down his impressions of the Sun Dance and related topics in another series of anonymously published articles.[46] Although neither a professional student of primitive culture nor a delegated policymaker, at this time he began his development toward status as an authority on two closely related subjects concerning Indians of the plains: their traditional cultures, and the ordeal they were enduring as those cultures decayed during their confinement on reservations.

In October 1872 a scout southwest of Fort Dodge doubled as an entertainment for Dodge's friend William Blackmore, who was then concluding a seven-month visit to the United States. Since his stay in New York City and Washington in the spring, the Englishman had kept up his activities as explorer, investor, and bon vivant at a punishing pace. Traveling west, he had conferred in Denver and Colorado Springs with officials of the newly organized Denver and Rio Grande Railway, crossed the Rocky Mountains to Salt Lake City to inspect mining properties, and then joined the geologist Ferdinand V. Hayden as an honorary member of his official party while it performed a geological survey of the Yellowstone basin in Wyoming Territory. After parting with Hayden in the recently established Yellowstone National Park, Blackmore returned to Salt Lake City, boarded a train to San Francisco, California, and journeyed thence to Nevada County, California, to inspect the gold and silver workings there. Returning to San Francisco to hobnob with its wealthy residents, including William C. Ralston, president of the Bank of California, he and two friends began a journey east toward New York City, intending to depart for England in late October.[47] They arrived at Fort Dodge on October 6.

Blackmore looked forward eagerly to the hunting expedition Dodge had promised him, for it would be at once strenuous and free of the multifarious business considerations that ordinarily preoccupied him. Two days after his arrival, a combined scouting and hunting party set out southward into country Dodge and his men knew well, chiefly the waterways and ravines of tributaries along the Cimarron River, then eastward toward Medicine Lodge Creek. The military escort, under Captain Tupper, included a civilian scout and an interpreter.[48] The visitors had come at an ideal time for a miscellaneous hunt, for the fall weather was mild and the game varied and abundant. This was just the sort of hunting Dodge liked best, unhurried and "of the vagabond order," without pressure to bag large quantities or prize specimens but taking advantage of whatever opportunities his skill and good fortune might present him. Dodge later averred that the hunt he organized for Blackmore and his companions was the most delightful experience of this sort he ever enjoyed. The meals prepared for the party from the successive days' bag must have been gargantuan, for in addition to buffalo and antelope the hunters took turkeys and game birds, two badgers, seven raccoons, and eleven rattlesnakes, among other species, for a total kill of 1,262 head.[49]

Since the final day of travel would be through country devoid of game, at lunch-time on their last day in hunting country Dodge decided to give his guests one more exciting experience of plains life while at the same time securing a quantity of meat that could be taken in to Fort Dodge. On preceding days the party had passed through throngs of buffalo, but no one had cared to take a shot at them. Now, as a display of what could be done by experienced hands, Dodge directed a few men of the cavalry escort to dash into a nearby herd. The men were to give the rest of the party a good view of their handiwork as they killed as many calves as possible without making a long run in pursuit, and the ambush went off brilliantly. Delighted, and fired with determination to emulate what they had witnessed, the Englishmen all set out in pursuit of the herds that surrounded them. They were soon out of sight, and after seeing the just-killed buffalo meat loaded onto the wagons, Dodge moved on slowly toward his post.

At this point the exciting climax to a memorable hunt swerved out of control. Messrs. Tyndall and Cook, Blackmore's friends, returned from the impromptu chase, covered with dust but exhilarated and bearing trophies of their success. Blackmore, however, had disappeared. Thus far he had acquitted himself well as a novice plainsman, but killing a fleeing buffalo from horseback could be dangerous sport, and fears for his safety were expressed. That evening the main party camped at the place that had been agreed upon, fired guns, made smokes, and when night fell built fires on surrounding high places, all without result. Distressed, on the next morning Dodge sent out search parties and hurried back to the post to send out more. He arrived and went to his residence shortly before noon, and there on the porch, "as clean, rotund, and smiling as if he had never crossed a horse, or given a moment's uneasiness in his life," stood his lost friend Blackmore!

When last seen on the day before, the Englishman was shooting at a gigantic buffalo bull he had brought to bay. However, the animal broke away and gave him a sharp chase of two or three miles before being dispatched, and on looking around him, the successful hunter found that he had lost his reckoning and could not even be sure of what course he had followed in the pursuit. To his credit, Blackmore did not panic. He took out a map and compass, set out for the Arkansas River, crossed it, and then followed the north bank back to the fort, where he arrived at 6:30 P.M. after a journey of some thirty miles. "While we were lighting fires and bemoaning his fate," Dodge wrote in an account of the adventure, "he was passing the bottle after a good dinner, and having a jolly time relating his exploits."[50] The discovery of his guest safe at the post was for Dodge a happy conclusion to the week of hunting together. This excursion, they agreed, would be the first of others no less satisfying. On the following day Blackmore and his companions boarded a train of the Atchison, Topeka and Santa Fe Railroad, which had begun service to Dodge City two months earlier, and rode east, back to the civilized world.

The Buffalo Hunters

Beyond question, Dodge City was at this period of its existence not yet a part of that world. The railroad's arrival accelerated a process Dodge had witnessed in other places, opening the territory to what he called "swarms of ruffians." Law-abiding citizens had lived there from the first, but they could not combat the "cold-blooded ruffianism" that prevailed. The agenda of the town's "vigilance committee" was not to enforce the law, for effectively there was no law. According to Dodge, this self-constituted body was "an organization simply for plunder and murder, composed of individuals of wolf-like nature, too cowardly to attack even the most defenseless, except in gangs. The number of most atrocious and cold-blooded assassinations committed by this gang of ruffians almost exceeds belief, and though eighty-two graves were filled by the pistol there was but a single instance of a fair stand-up fight between the parties."[51]

Unlike some settlements along the two great east-west railroads to its north, Dodge City did not yet boast great commercial advantages. Plans existed to link the plains of southern Kansas and points further west to markets in the eastern states, but they would be years in the fulfillment. Neither had the function of Dodge City as a shipping point for herds of cattle driven north from Texas been developed.[52] Yet in the fall of 1872 the town burgeoned into a minor metropolis, and for one reason only: its location in the heart of country under occupation by professional buffalo hunters. Dodge attributed the worst excesses of the frontier city to the presence of these ruthless individuals. "Thousands of city and village loafers," he wrote, "eagerly seized the opportunity for a hunt that would pay expenses," and hurrying to Dodge City they brought with them "the vices and the cowardice in which they were brought up."[53] The Atchison, Topeka and Santa Fe was in dire need of funds and welcomed the business of these men and their intermediaries. Great heaps of stinking uncured buffalo hides stood in warehouses or exposed to the air outside them, stacked like chips in some outsized game of chance.

In recent months the excesses of the hunting parties and the possible consequences of the grisly trade they pursued had received some official attention. Writing from Fort Hays, Colonel William B. Hazen had informed the Society for the Prevention of Cruelty to Animals of wanton slaughters he had witnessed.[54] Working in groups of from three to twelve, he reported, the hunters shot as many animals as they could, ripping the hides from the carcasses in the most expeditious way possible and leaving what remained, except possibly the tongues, to rot or be consumed as carrion. They loaded the hides onto wagons, transported them to a station along the railroad, and sold them to purchasers there, usually for $2.50 apiece, then drove back onto the prairie for more slaughter. Writing from the same post in June, Dodge's regimental commander Colonel De Lancey Floyd-Jones estimated that 25,000 hides had been shipped over the Kansas Pacific Railroad from Hays City in the last thirty days. He informed General Sheridan that "a continuous line of fire" on the buffalo was said to exist as far south from his post as to the Arkansas River. But Sheridan was unimpressed; he suspected that Floyd-Jones was exaggerating.[55]

One week after assuming command at Fort Dodge, Major Dodge described to his department commander the killing south of his post, drawing attention to the danger of conflict between buffalo hunters and Indians. The hunters, he wrote Pope, "are killing countless numbers of Buffalo, simply for their hides, Exasperating the Indians by this wanton and wholesale destruction of game, and tempting them by the smallness and carelessness of the hunting parties. To let them go on as at present is to invite depredation and outrage by the Indians." From what he had witnessed, the Indians had been "singularly forbearing" thus far. Yet, he continued, for him to interfere with the hunters was to invite difficulties of a different kind. The buffalo parties claimed to be residents of Kansas and asserted their right to go where they pleased and be protected by the army wherever they went. "To bring them in by force will cause an outcry from all the newspapers and politicians of Kansas."[56] Faced with this dilemma, Dodge stood in need of direction from higher authority.

The official responses to his letter as it moved up the chain of command and back to him help explain events that occurred in southern Kansas in the year to come. Forwarded from the Department of the Missouri to the Military Division of the Missouri to army headquarters, and then from the Adjutant General's Office to that of the secretary of war, Dodge's letter prompted a letter by Secretary Belknap on June 22, authorizing General Sheridan to "correct the evil." Sheridan's headquarters staff forwarded this response to General Pope "for such action as he may deem best," and on July 15 Pope's adjutant directed Dodge to "take such steps in this matter as may be authorized by the laws of Kansas and of the U. S. which govern it."[57] Yet, decisive as this statement might seem, it referred to laws that either did not exist or were of little use to him. The buffalo hunters had a perfect right to slaughter animals on lands not owned by someone who objected to it; and should they be attacked by Indians while in Kansas, it was the duty of the army to come to their aid. All Dodge could do was to warn them of the reprisals they were inviting, refuse to grant them military escorts, and arrest them if they entered Indian Territory. However, even in the latter case he was empowered only to remove them from the territory; once they were back in Kansas, he must set them free. The provisions in the *Revised Statutes* that might help protect the buffalo were weak and all but unenforceable.[58] As Dodge later wrote, "it was the duty of no special person to put a stop to" the killing of millions of buffalo,[59] and so the slaughter went on.

When William Blackmore returned to Fort Dodge, in October 1873, he found a scene changed ruinously from what he had witnessed one year before. East of Dodge City, putrescent buffalo carcasses lay along the north bank of the Arkansas River for thirty or forty miles, and the air was "pestilential and offensive to the last degree." Hunters had encamped along the river and shot the buffalo at all hours of the day as they came down to drink. In one area of not more than four acres, Blackmore counted sixty-seven carcasses.[60] This year's hunt organized by Dodge lasted for two weeks and was almost as successful as the last, but what captured the attention of Blackmore was the buffalo hunters and the evidence everywhere of their activity. He estimated that south of the river, five hundred parties remained out, even that late in the season, and that in 1873, one million hides had been shipped east, and that only from Kansas and Nebraska. One sociable hunter, "Old Jones" of Clinton, Missouri, bragged to him of slaying 450 buffalo in August alone. A resident of Sun City, a settlement of about three hundred inhabitants, reported witnessing 87 buffalo killed at a single stand. This man assured Blackmore that he was attempting with other Kansans to secure legislation that would protect the buffalo that remained. "The real bona fide settlers," Blackmore wrote in his diary, "who would only kill a few for meat are the real sufferers – Buffalo hunters a lawless reckless set – not settlers – no real interest in country."[61] Herds of buffalo were scarce now. The animals were to be found in numbers only further south, away from the railroad. Approaching Fort Dodge near the end of this year's 204-mile hunting journey, Blackmore "met hunter driving wagon piled up with Buffalo hides – gray horse behind – Caught his sleepy eye."[62]

By the time he reached the post, Blackmore was recovered from bouts of lumbago and sunstroke that had rendered him immobile for a day or two during the hunt. He and Dodge agreed that an excursion in the fall of next year was an absolute necessity, wherever the latter might then be stationed. Amusing himself at the post, Blackmore was impressed with the good feeling that prevailed between the officers and men. He had witnessed a game of baseball that pitted the John R. Brooke club of Camp Supply against the Dolly Varden team of Fort Dodge, reputedly for the championship of

The Slaughter of the Buffalo, drawn from a photograph. Reprinted from *Scribner's Magazine*, September 1887, p. 293.

Kansas.[63] But the overriding impression he carried with him on October 20, as he boarded a train bound further west, was the rapid change all around the post, much of it wasteful.[64]

Dodge had himself assessed some of these developments just prior to the arrival of Blackmore, on a scout east of the Camp Supply road along the Kansas state line as far as Medicine Lodge Creek. He saw parties of buffalo hunters, but because none had been molested by Indians he anticipated no trouble in that vicinity for the rest of the fall. However, in the area to the west of the Camp Supply road, the prospect was more ominous. Acting on his instructions, Captain Joseph Kerin, Sixth Cavalry, had made a thorough scout in "the long tongue of Indian Territory between Ka[nsa]s and Texas." Now known as the Oklahoma Panhandle, in Dodge's time this was actually public land that belonged to neither of the two states nor to Indian Territory. Kerin reported that the region was being used as a base of operations by the buffalo hunters. Cheyenne Indians whom he met alleged that the hunting parties had slaughtered buffalo almost in their very camps and were committing other outrages. In an endorsement to Kerin's report, Dodge noted that the Indians were showing "very great forbearance" toward the despoilers. Nevertheless, they complained justly "that as they are not allowed to go off their reservations to hunt Buffalo, the White hunters should not be allowed to go on the reservation for that purpose." Denominating the intruders "the lowest class of border ruffians: men who combine the pursuit of Buffalo hunting with horse stealing, and whiskey selling," Dodge expressed his opinion that "they should be kept out of the Territory." In a response to his endorsement, the departmental adjutant assured him that south of the state line, "particularly in the Indian territory," he had full power to expel the intruders.[65] But in view of the considerable distances involved and the few men available to him, this official counsel was more true than useful.

Shortly after the departure of Blackmore, Dodge made a final attempt to influence federal policy in regard to the buffalo hunters. In a letter to departmental headquarters, he described the hunters and their activities, noting that they now roamed freely in Indian Territory, "slaughtering the Buffalo . . . immediately in the presence, and almost in the very camps of the Indians." Whirlwind, a prominent Cheyenne, had encamped with his band to hunt buffalo on a tributary of Beaver Creek about thirty miles south of the state line, but parties of hunters took a position nearby and killed or drove off the animals grazing there, forcing him to move. Dodge warned that the same kind of intrusion was likely to be repeated, and that if the hunters were not stopped, "one of two things must occur. Either the Indians becoming exasperated will drive out the hunters, probably with bloodshed – which will inaugurate a war, or they will fail to obtain their winter's supply of meat and skins, which means to them starvation, or extreme suffering." Dodge mentioned that his warnings to the offenders had produced only token and temporary compliance with the laws prohibiting trespass and hunting in Indian Territory. He predicted that "serious consequences will result unless immediate steps are taken" against the interlopers.[66]

Like Dodge, General Pope had neither the men nor the mandate to deal decisively with these problems. In an endorsement of Dodge's letter forwarded to General Sheridan, he admitted that while the present state of affairs was likely to lead to violence, it was hard to say what should be done about it. "No doubt the destruction of all the Buffalo on the Plains, which now seems in a fair way to be accomplished, will force the Indians to depend for subsistence entirely on the Indian Department, and thus keep them quiet[;] but whether it is best to do this, is a question on which it is not necessary for me to express an opinion."[67] On an earlier occasion General Sherman had expressed himself quizzically on just that point, suggesting that the most expeditious way to compel the Indians to settle down to civilized life was to kill all the buffalo and so render their way of life impossible.[68] In the present instance he simply forwarded the communication to Secretary Belknap, "asking for instructions." In response, Belknap sent him a copy of the covering letter he had addressed to the secretary of the interior in forwarding Dodge's letter with its endorsements. Eventually another copy of the secretary's letter made its way back to Dodge.[69] Once more, the federal government had not seriously addressed the problems presented by the destruction of the great buffalo herds and the illegal, rapacious entry by American citizens into Indian Territory. As Dodge later wrote, the provisions of the *Revised Statutes* ensuring the rights of Indians on reservations and enjoining citizens from infringing upon them were all but dead letters.[70]

Imminent Promotion

At the time Dodge summarized to General Pope the dangerous conditions in the region south of his post, he was aware that his statement might prove his last major initiative as post commander at Fort Dodge. After twenty-five years of service, he now stood first in the adjutant general's lineal list of infantry majors.[71] His promotion to lieutenant colonel should come shortly, for a vacancy at that rank in any infantry regiment would result in his succession to the position. Meanwhile, the season for active field service being almost concluded, he applied to departmental headquarters for a thirty-day leave of absence, a request routinely granted. But this year he also requested an unusual privilege—namely, permission to apply to army headquarters for a twelve-month extension of the first leave.[72] In conversation with Blackmore, he had formed the plan of traveling abroad with his friend, who had business interests in Africa and family connections in India, and of joining him in hunting expeditions on both continents. Thus on November 5, having been granted permission to do so, he asked the adjutant general that his annual leave "be extended for twelve (12) months, and that I be permitted to go beyond seas."[73]

Dodge's fantasy of world travel in company with his cosmopolitan friend was short-lived, however. On October 29 Secretary Belknap created a place for him as lieutenant colonel of the Twenty-third Regiment of Infantry by nominating the incumbent officer, George Crook, for immediate promotion to brigadier general.[74]

President Grant's formal approval of this unusual action was a foregone conclusion, since the secretary of war had been acting on his instructions in nominating Crook. The promotion would be controversial, for it would propel Crook past four lieutenant colonels and twenty-five colonels of infantry, many of them highly deserving an elevation in rank. General Sherman disliked the move, which smacked of favoritism and set aside seniority as the criterion for promotion of field officers, but he was powerless to oppose it.[75] Of course, he could understand the rationale that had led to it. As commander of the Department of Arizona,[76] in the past two years Crook had achieved signal successes against the Apache Indians, who were shrewd tacticians and fearsome mountain fighters. Employing innovative tactics to pursue his foes in their fastnesses, he had won a reputation for ability to fight Indians by turning their own strategies against them. "Oh, Indian hunting is Crook's specialty," an unnamed officer was quoted as saying in 1871. "The fact is, Crook is nothing but an Indian anyway. . . . Perfectly self-reliant for any venture, delighted with lonely travel and personal hazard, carrying nothing but his arms, he will walk after a trail all day, and when night comes, no matter how cold, he wraps himself in an Indian blanket, humped up Indian fashion, and pitches himself into a heap of sage-brush, there to be perfectly easy till morning." If a bit eccentric, according to this source Crook was the ideal Indian fighter, "utterly ignorant of fear, and yet stealthy as a cat."[77]

Secretary Belknap and others considered that such a man as Crook deserved a high place in the army, whose sole combat function in the foreseeable future was against Indians. The nominee's promotion being all but certain, on November 1 the Adjutant General's Office issued an order directing Lieutenant Colonel Richard I. Dodge, Twenty-third Infantry, to proceed "without delay" to join his new regiment in Arizona Territory.[78] But owing to the poor interoffice communication that still afflicted the army at this period, Dodge did not learn of this order for several more days. On November 3 he was granted a thirty-day leave of absence by his department commander,[79] but his request of November 5 for a twelve-month extension was not acted upon in Washington until November 11, when he learned by telegram from the War Department that it had been disapproved, "General Sherman deciding your services needed with new regiment."[80] He had received a letter informing him of his promotion and transfer to the Twenty-third Infantry only two days before,[81] and by then a rumor was circulating that General Pope wished him to displace Lieutenant Colonel Charles R. Woods, Fifth Infantry—presumably to ensure his continuing service within the Department of the Missouri.[82] At last it was made clear that, following a period of annual leave, he was to report for duty at Fort Whipple, Arizona. Thus upon the arrival of the newly designated post commander, Major Charles E. Compton, Sixth Cavalry, Dodge relinquished command of Fort Dodge on November 14, 1873.[83]

In almost seven years of postwar service on the western plains, Dodge had become a well-known figure in that rapidly developing region. The open country had fascinated him anew with its "freaks of nature," its native inhabitants, its opportunities for hunting and exploration in regions still little known, and its very emptiness. However, the unfolding fates of the buffalo herds and the plains Indians were stark reminders that to live there in the early 1870s was also to witness sometimes cataclysmic change. He lacked the power to direct the course of history by himself, but he had done what he could for both the victimized populations. He took satisfaction in the knowledge that his efforts had won him respect among superior officers, including generals Schofield, Pope, and Sherman. Army service suited him well, and he welcomed his promotion, looking forward with eager interest to more years of frontier duty.

Part Four

A Soldier-Author, 1873–1877

Dodge was not driven by ambition to win a general's star, but he was confident of his abilities and valued the good opinion of other military men. In the early years of his lieutenant colonelcy he was gratified to receive assignments that tested his professional skill, for he understood that successes in the field remained the high road to official recognition. On more than one occasion during these years, his military missions sparked national interest and, for the first time, won him brief celebrity. However, in the intervals between these high-profile duties he began another career that, almost from the outset, earned him a wider reputation. Drawing on his years of experience in the western territories and on his natural aptitude for expression, he wrote for publication on the topics he knew best—the plains environment, and the animals and Indian tribes indigenous to it.

In particular, Dodge's commentaries on Plains Indians won praise, in part for the combination of unsparing honesty yet discriminating sympathy that informed them. In his criticism of federal Indian policy, he forcefully advanced the view that the army was the arm of government best equipped to preserve the native tribes from extinction and guide them toward amalgamation with the rest of American society. Mark Twain, for one, was impressed by what he wrote. "There's a man," he told William Dean Howells in 1877, "who knows all about Indians, & yet has some humanity in him – (knowledge of Indians, & humanity, are seldom found in the same individual)."[1] The humorist's favorable judgment echoed that of book reviewers on both sides of the Atlantic and marked one facet of Dodge's success as a soldier-author.

11

New Scenes, New Initiatives

Dodge's promotion to lieutenant colonel late in 1873 denied him a tour "beyond seas," but the land journey to his new posting in Arizona Territory would prove more time-consuming and certainly more arduous than any transatlantic voyage. The headquarters of the Twenty-third Infantry were at Fort Whipple, which doubled as headquarters for the Department of Arizona, one of the most remote and least known regions then occupied by army forces.[1] Telegraph communication had just been established between San Diego, California, and Prescott, Arizona, adjacent to the fort,[2] but the military department commanded by Brigadier General Crook remained difficult of access, subject to extremes of wind and heat, and extremely dangerous. Supplies reached the ten posts in the department by wagon train, from either the Gulf of California or the Pacific coast. Veterans of service in Arizona, especially the sun-baked desert regions near the Mexican border, likened it to the Sahara Desert or else to hell. Though diversified by uplands and mountain ranges, the territory bore everywhere the centuries-old imprint of Mexican culture and Indian occupation. Once he arrived there, Dodge would be reminded of his early years in Texas.

Circumstances modified considerably the at first peremptory directive that he join his regiment at Fort Whipple. Technically, he could not be issued orders in his new rank until Crook had been confirmed as a brigadier general, a process that would involve some delay. Moreover, during midwinter no urgent reason presented itself for either Crook or Dodge to change station. As a result, intervention on Dodge's behalf by Simon Cameron, the former secretary of war, effectively extended his thirty-day leave of absence. He was directed to remain in New York City until further orders and did not set out for northern Arizona until early March 1874.[3]

His itinerary differed from those ordinarily followed by officers en route from the eastern states to the Department of Arizona. Except for men traveling from Texas, who could move along the mail route west from El Paso, the usual course was to travel by railroad to San Francisco, take ship for San Diego or the Gulf of California, and proceed thence to one's destination by wagon. The wagon ride from San Diego to Fort Whipple was eleven days in duration. Instead, Dodge journeyed directly overland into Colorado country he knew well, next into territory in New Mexico he had seen once before, and finally through a region altogether new to him. He traveled south from Fort Lyon, skirting the Mogollon Rim along the wagon road he had laid out four years before, to Fort Union. From that point he wrote to his friend Major Vincent at the Adjutant General's Office that he had "had a good time considering the season – & anticipate a better, as I get further west." On March 31 he left the post for Fort Wingate, approximately two hundred miles due west.[4] The final leg of the overland trek took him approximately 250 miles further in that direction to Fort Whipple, where he arrived on May 20. Travel between the latter two posts was infrequent, as evidenced by another military party's use later in the year of the itinerary he compiled describing that segment of the journey.[5] After passing through Navaho and Zuni country that displayed a whole class of geological curiosities previously unknown to him, at Fort Whipple he found a familiar military setting amidst scenes interestingly new. That he would occupy the same position General Crook had held since the formation of the Twenty-third Infantry in 1866 was surely auspicious.[6] On May 21 he assumed command of Fort Whipple and of his new regiment.[7]

The Twenty-third Regiment of Infantry

Companies of the Twenty-third Infantry were dispersed within the Department of Arizona, being stationed at eight different places, several of them temporary camps.[8] Months would pass before Dodge encountered them all, but in common with other army officers he already knew of the regiment, which had served in the far western territories since its establishment. During almost that entire period its official commander, Colonel Jefferson C. Davis, had not served with it, being assigned other duties according to his brevet rank of major general. However, Davis had also spent the greater part of that time in the far West, as commander of the District of Alaska and later of the Department of the Columbia. In 1873 he led the army in avenging against Modoc Indians the murder of Brigadier General Edward R. S. Canby.[9] A weak constitution frustrated Davis's wish to continue active operations in the field, but he remained a mettlesome officer, with a healthy sense of his own capacity. He was an appropriate leader of the regiment that was under his authority, at least officially.

But in practice, the leader of the Twenty-third Infantry for the past seven years had been Davis's second-in-command, Lieutenant Colonel Crook.[10] The commonplace that a regiment is the chief school of an army[11] was preeminently true for the Twenty-third, which had taken its tone from Crook's example. Like him, its company officers and men employed tactics against Indians that were rarely in use elsewhere. When called upon, the regiment pursued the hostiles at all times of the year in spite of distance, forbidding terrain, and adverse weather conditions. Crook's pursuit parties gained maneuverability and range by leaving their supply wagons behind them, carrying into battle minimal supplies other than ammunition and rations. As a result, the Indians' secluded rancherías no longer provided them the security they once had. Assisted by Indian scouts, Crooks's men were gradually wearing down the Apaches, who had preyed upon inhabitants of the region for centuries. Skeptics, including General Sheridan, deplored his reliance on Indians in campaigns against other Indians, but thus far the results spoke strongly in favor of the practice.[12] Crook's annual report to the secretary of war for 1874 conveyed an unmistakable note of finality, as if he were summarizing a mission near completion.[13]

Like Crook, most officers in the Department of Arizona did not harbor vindictiveness toward the hostile tribes, once those peoples had subjected themselves to federal authority. Arizona Territory was a sufficiently distant and forbidding place that the Indian Bureau was hard pressed to enlist as agents men willing to brave the dangers and discomforts awaiting them there. As a result, army men often wore two hats, as soldiers whose controlling force had asserted itself, and also as de facto agents.[14] Such an officer was Captain George M. Randall, Twenty-third Infantry, who had participated in mountain operations against some of the most renowned Apache leaders and who now commanded Camp Apache, a three-company post in the eastern part of the territory. Known among the Indians as "Black Beard," Randall had won their respectful regard, in part owing to the respect he showed them.[15] He was one of several officers in the regiment who took more than ordinary interest in the languages and customs of the Indians. All this was just as Crook wished it. Another of his officers, First Lieutenant William C. Manning, had photographed the ruins of "strange cities" once inhabited by Indians of Arizona.[16] Both his aides-de-camp, Captain Azor H. Nickerson, Twenty-third Infantry, and Second Lieutenant John G. Bourke, Third Cavalry, were students of Indian culture. In later years Bourke would earn lasting scientific reputation for his published studies of Indian rituals.

Even though it did not enjoy the relative comfort of postings further east, the Twenty-third Infantry maintained a healthy level of morale. Citizens back in "the States" might be oblivious to its accomplishments, but within the army its name stood high. When, in January 1874, General Sherman described to Congress the activities of regiments under his command, his comments on the Twenty-third showed the respect he felt for its services in "an immense, miserable country full of Apache Indians."[17] Shortly after the publication of Sherman's testimony, "Cum Tux," an anonymous correspondent of the *Army and Navy Journal* expressed the regiment's gratitude to him and also its hope for an early transfer. "Whether we move or not," he wrote, "or as a regiment cease to exist, we all of us feel more buoyant by remembering the noble advocate at Washington."[18]

Unlike Dodge, General Crook was of a quiet disposition, impatient of large social gatherings and little disposed to make conversation for the mere pleasure of it. At social gatherings he confined himself to chatting with his particular friends or else playing whist. Still, he and Dodge shared some personal characteristics and complemented each other in others, auguring a good working relationship. Dodge had long since won a measure of trust from Crook, and not only because his years of army service outnumbered those of his commander. Crook had not forgotten some good advice Dodge gave him at New York City in August 1861, when he thought of resigning his regular army commission to accept an appointment at higher rank in the volunteers.[19] In a real sense, that counsel at a crossroads in his career had helped lay the basis for successes that came after for Crook. Both officers were West Point graduates, infantrymen, experienced outdoorsmen, and avid sportsmen. Both were enemies to the Indians if necessary but friends if possible, and both subscribed wholeheartedly to the view that the army, not the corrupt Indian Bureau, offered the Indians their best hope of survival. Crook greatly preferred expeditions afield to desk duty at headquarters; Dodge could do either and had a taste for both. Crook was a delegator and not a detail man, which suited Dodge perfectly. Not surprisingly, the arrival of the latter was eagerly anticipated at Fort Whipple.

Crook's accomplishments in Arizona had suggested the possibility of utilizing his abilities in some other military department where his talents might be even better employed. Moreover, the Twenty-third Infantry had performed a full stint of hard frontier duty and was entitled to a change of station. Only three weeks after Dodge's arrival at Fort Whipple, the latter of these considerations led to an order from army headquarters for the regiment to proceed, "as soon as practicable, and as the season favors," to new postings in the Department of the Platte.[20] General Crook would remain in Arizona for the time being, but wise heads foresaw his eventual transfer to headquarters at Omaha as well.[21] Once the necessary arrangements had been completed between Crook and Brigadier General E. O. C. Ord, the current commander of the Department of the Platte, it would be Dodge's task to help coordinate the transfer. The prospect of his working closely with Crook in the Department of Arizona was therefore at an end almost before it began. From a military point of view his long journey west, however satisfying to him personally, must have seemed to him somewhat anticlimactic at this point. Still, the return to country he knew well in the Department of the Platte would have its own benefits. Omaha Barracks was a comfortable post, just north of the city, and quite possibly Julia and Fred would join him there.

The month of July can be a searingly uncomfortable season for travel in some parts of Arizona. Nevertheless, in that month all ten companies of the Twenty-third Infantry left their postings for the transfer. They traveled in groups, first west to the Gulf of California, then on a roundabout sea journey to San Francisco, and finally east by railroad to their respective new stations. The largest body of troops that traveled together was commanded by Dodge and left Fort Whipple on July 9. Comprised of Companies A, B, and K, the regimental band, and the headquarters staff, it marched 164 miles southwest to Hardeyville, on the Colorado River, where it boarded a sternwheel steamer, the *Gila*. At Fort Yuma, California, the command disembarked and was joined by Company C, under Captain Otis W. Pollock, which had marched 235 miles from Camp McDowell, Arizona. The *Gila* now carried the troops to a point near the river's embouchure in the Gulf of California, where they awaited an oceangoing steamer, the *Montana*. On August 11 that ship began a slow voyage to San Francisco, making stops at Guaymas, La Paz, Mazatlán, Cabo San Lucas, and Magdalena Bay in Mexico and arriving at its final destination on August 29. Later that day, at the wharf of Oakland, California, the men boarded a special train for Omaha, where they arrived on September 4, ending a wearisome two-month passage of some 3,200 miles.[22] Two more months would elapse before all the rest of the companies had reached their new posts, chiefly at points along the railroad east of Cheyenne, Wyoming. Meanwhile, on September 8 Dodge assumed command of Omaha Barracks[23] and, still in command of his widely dispersed regiment, turned his attention to directing its change of stations.

In recent months Indian unrest within the Department of the Platte had been minimal, with one important exception that boded trouble. The cause of alarm was an organized U.S. military incursion from the north onto the great Sioux Reservation, an action that contravened a provision of the federal government's 1868 treaty with the tribe. Although the expedition had ostensibly been organized for peaceful purposes, to the Indians it evinced the government's lack of good faith and suggested the possibility of an attempt by American citizens to seize the little known Black Hills country. Under command of Lieutenant Colonel George A. Custer, Seventh Cavalry, the Black Hills Expedition marched from Fort Lincoln, in the Department of Dakota, entering the northwest section of the region and performing a wide-ranging reconnaissance.[24] Accompanied by a small corps of naturalists, geologists, and practical miners, Custer was gathering information about the value and possible future use of territory within the Black Hills. On August 2 he sent to the telegraph operator at Fort Laramie a progress report that, as he well understood, would prove fateful. He praised the region generally as splendid grazing land, potentially the site of prosperous future settlements, but he also included in his letter a more specific incitement to enterprise. The prospectors in his party, he wrote, had panned gold in several mountain streams. In a second dispatch a few days later, Custer mentioned that gold was in evidence not only along the watercourses but "among the roots of the grass."[25]

Newspapers across the nation seized upon these phrases as the herald of a new bonanza, a northern El Dorado that offered gold for the picking. Thus, by the time Dodge and his men reached Omaha in early September, miners, suppliers, and speculators were swelling frontier towns like Sioux City, Iowa, and Cheyenne, Wyoming. Access to the Black Hills from these jumping-off points would be difficult and dangerous, but the newcomers were willing to brave Indian resistance, winter weather, and the threat of arrest by federal officials for a chance to strike it rich. Clearly, the army must anticipate playing some part in the events that were poised to ensue. So long as the Black Hills territory remained reserved by solemn treaty for sole occupation and use by Indians, the military might be called upon to enforce federal law against its fellow citizens. Conversely, should the presence of trespassers on Sioux lands lead to violence against them from the Indians, army intervention against the

Sioux would be required. What possible combination of these scenarios would develop was unforeseeable, but it was certain that the Custer reconnaissance had initiated a sequence of events that would eventually involve troops stationed in the Department of the Platte.

For the present, in the absence of a military emergency Dodge obtained leave to keep a promised rendezvous at Sidney Barracks, approximately 150 miles south of the Black Hills, with his hunting companion William Blackmore. The Englishman's traveling companions on his sixth visit to the United States were an Irish couple, Mr. and Mrs. John Adair, who hoped to share with him the excitement of another buffalo hunt.[26] In his now customary fashion, upon reaching Omaha the entrepreneur laid in a supply of foodstuffs and liquor for consumption during the excursion. His purchases in the latter department included two cases of fine sherry, one of cognac, one half-case apiece of "Fish Gin," "V.P. Cognac, 1868," and "Overholt's," with one large bottle of Angostura bitters.[27] At Sidney Barracks the post commander, Major Albert P. Morrow, Ninth Cavalry, greeted the Blackmore party with gracious hospitality, and arrangements were made for a hunt south of the post toward the South Platte River. The military escort would be under command of Captain Alexander Sutorious, Third Cavalry, and Blackmore hired an experienced civilian scout, Leo Palliday, at the generous rate of five dollars per day. Anticipating a strenuous adventure on the plains, he made a note of the three principals' weight "Before Buffalo Hunt": Adair, 160 pounds, Dodge, 204 pounds, Blackmore, 173 pounds.[28]

On October 7 the group traveled twenty miles down the river valley. They saw no buffalo, but after making camp, Blackmore and Palliday rode a few miles farther and were surprised to come within sight of a large Indian camp. Approaching, they were greeted and entertained by the chief, a Sioux named Two Lance, whose women were busy cutting up the carcasses of 150 buffalo the hunters had killed in a "surround." In the two days that followed, members of the party continued their visit with the accommodating Sioux.[29] The Indians were amazed at the sight of Mrs. Adair riding sidesaddle, a style previously unknown to them. Two Lance, speaking through Palliday as interpreter, informed Dodge that he knew his people were hunting off their reservation without authority. He intended no harm, he said, but the rations supplied at his agency were so poor that to feed his people he had to go where game was to be found. He was hoping to cross the river back onto to the reservation before being discovered and attacked by his tribes' hereditary enemies, the Utes.[30] Blackmore busied himself recording "Indian habits" in his diary and collecting curiosities, including a bag of scrapings from buffalo hide by the wife of Two Lance.[31] Following a council in which Blackmore addressed the Indians, on the evening of October 8 the Dog Soldiers of the band hosted a feast in honor of the visitors. On the following morning Blackmore distributed gifts to his hosts, who were about to break camp, and the social exchanges ended on a friendly note.

Later in the hunt, small groups of buffalo were seen, but the bag of this year did not compare with those of the previous two. One day Blackmore did join Adair in a "splendid run" at a herd of eighty to one hundred buffalo they had cautiously approached. Blackmore was within thirty yards of a fleeing animal when the excited Adair, riding near him, discharged his gun and accidentally shot his own horse through the head, killing it instantly. Extricating him from under the dead animal proved difficult, and meanwhile Dillon, Mrs. Adair's orderly, injured himself while lifting her into her saddle. Somewhat the worse for wear but still in good spirits, the party returned to Sidney Barracks on October 14. That evening Dodge, Blackmore, and a few officers had a long, comfortable conversation in which Dodge promised a better hunt in the coming fall from Fort Hartsuff, a post just established on the North Loup River. Blackmore confessed in a diary entry his "unwillingness to say good by," for he had come to value his hunting adventures with Dodge.[32] However, on the next morning he resumed his multifarious enterprises, departing for meetings with business associates in Denver and for another visit to his properties in southern Colorado.

An Experiment in Authorship

Bad weather had plagued this year's hunt, necessitating more days spent in camp than anyone desired. Dodge made up for the inconvenience by entertaining his guests with stories of plains life—adventures with Indians, narrow escapes, strange individuals he had met, game animals he had bagged, glimpsed, or heard about.[33] His stories inspired in the listeners some of the same pleased interest they felt when in the presence of Two Lance and his band. This year Blackmore was even more impressed by his friend's talent as a raconteur than he had been on earlier expeditions. He urged him again, and more insistently, to gather some of his stories into a book. He knew from experience that it would be a simple matter, for he had written and edited several volumes for publication, chiefly related to his speculations in land.[34] If Dodge would only write out the sort of work he was surely capable of, Blackmore assured him that he would be quite willing to edit the manuscript for publication. Once in print, he declared, the book was assured of popular success, for despite its great interest there existed nothing else like it.[35]

Not long after his return to Omaha Barracks, Dodge was relieved as post and regimental commander by his superior officer, Colonel Davis, who had been transferred there after a period of service in New York City.[36] The regular garrison duty that remained to him provided no lack of occupation, but in his hours of leisure Dodge considered more seriously the flattering suggestion of his worldly-wise friend Blackmore. He knew that a few army men had published volumes describing their experiences in the western territories. Prominent among these were the recently retired Brigadier General Philip St. George Cooke,[37] Dodge's regulations board colleague Colonel Marcy, and Lieutenant Colonel Custer, whose *My Life on the Plains* had appeared earlier in 1874. Even so, a book he wrote would be quite different from any of those three. Cooke and Marcy were self-consciously literary, modeling their works on Dickens and the local color sketches published in popular magazines, while

Custer had evidently conceived his as an exercise in self-glorification. Dodge, if he were to become a bookmaker, would simply tell what he knew and had seen in plains life—entertainingly one hoped, but without specific literary models. Nor would he direct attention to himself, except as the recounter of first-hand observations and experiences.

As Dodge thought over the idea, its possibilities were certainly appealing. He knew he was capable of writing respectably for publication—witness his official reports and anonymous pieces on Indian rituals and the Indian Question. True, he knew next to nothing about composing, printing, and marketing a popular volume, but Blackmore's assistance could help solve that problem. A further inducement was that authorship ran in his family. His father had won local reputation as the writer of comic pieces,[38] while his uncle, Washington Irving, was among the nation's best known prose writers. Dodge never once made written reference to his family relationship with the distinguished author of *The Sketch-Book* and of works about the West including *A Tour on the Prairies* (1835), *Astoria* (1836), and *The Adventures of Captain Bonneville, U.S.A.* (1837)—but the connection must have occurred to him as he considered trying his own hand at authorship. He liked to keep busy, and certainly he could use some extra money. Living in comfortable quarters but as yet without Julia and Fred, he had the free time to try setting down some of what he knew. He did have plenty to say, and some of it might possibly sway public opinion about the Indian Question. These were the considerations that led him to begin drafting a popular account of the western plains and their inhabitants, and so to begin his career as a soldier-author.

Always an organizer, as a first step Dodge divided his prospective material into five general categories: The Plains, Indians, The Army, Frontiersmen, and Hunting.[39] All these were subjects he could claim to know well, but they encompassed a great range of subject matter. Whether he would ever have time to explore them in a manner satisfactory to himself was doubtful, but the preliminary list at least enabled him to consider the possibilities. Blackmore had referred to the book as "The Plains," the first of Dodge's main divisions, but the novice author elected to pass over that topic for a time and begin with an account of Plains Indians. Possibly the recent encounter with Two Lance had played a part in this decision, for his recollection of that meeting made its way into his commentary at more than one point.[40] Besides, he had already developed ideas about the subject in his anonymous pieces. While retracing some of this familiar ground, he could work his way into a more comprehensive treatment.

In an introductory chapter, Dodge described his overall intention in the commentary: he would set forth information to correct false notions of Indian character cherished by persons in both the eastern states and the western states and territories. On one hand, the novels of James Fenimore Cooper, accounts by "enthusiastic Missionaries," and self-serving statements by Indian agents and "professional Humanitarians" had confirmed in many minds "a romantic admiration for the 'Red Man.'" On the other hand, inhabitants of the western frontier who had suffered at the hands of the Indian "have no words to express their detestation of his duplicity, cruelty and barbarism."[41] Without attempting to reconcile these mutually exclusive views, he would describe the Indian's mode of life, with its system of values that characterized as virtues the very qualities that detractors considered marks of his irredeemable savagery. At the same time, he would offer instances of that savagery as a means of dispelling another false conception, of the Indian as a natural nobleman.

In a summary account of an Indian boy's development into manhood and status as a warrior, Dodge indicated that he intended to draw upon material that related to various tribes. However, he added, his sketches would relate chiefly to the Cheyennes, whom he considered "the best specimens of Indian man and womanhood on the plains."[42] He proceeded to draft a series of five chapters, averaging 2,500 words in length, describing tribal government and, in fuller detail, Indian ceremonies and religious beliefs. In each of these he first discussed in general terms the topic designated by the chapter title ("Medicine Dance," "Happy Hunting Grounds," and so on) and next introduced anecdotes that elucidated aspects of the material. But beginning with a sixth chapter, on Indian social life, his discussions became less structured. Probably this easy discursiveness reflected his growing confidence. The chapter entitled "Social Life" swelled to 8,000 words and included sundry stories and character sketches—of Romeo, the interpreter at Fort Dodge in 1873; of Powder Face, an Arapaho man who doted on his wife; of Black Beaver, who refused to credit the existence of a "talking wire"—that is, a telegraph line. Dodge's good nature, abundance of material, and enjoyment of writing shone forth in these passages. Subsequent chapter titles no longer controlled so firmly the subjects they dealt with, and he allowed himself freer rein introducing examples, indulging in digressions, and occasionally setting down wry observations.[43]

In a chapter entitled "Employment," Dodge introduced a new theme, the failure of the U.S. government's Indian policy. Earlier chapters had portrayed a people who, though strange and perhaps "savage," were not without admirable qualities, and who shared much in common with others of the human species. A later series of chapters would detail Indian practices in predation and war, presenting a much less appealing facet of native life. However, before moving into that area he observed that the U.S. government actually encouraged the Indians' habits of violence:

> The Indians are half starved on reservations, and exposed to the amiable attention of whiskey sellers, until too poor to stand it longer. Then they break out. Sending their families to the staked plains [in northern Texas], or some other almost inaccessible refuge, they make dashes and raids on the exposed frontier settlements, killing people and carrying off all the stock they can lay their hands on.
>
> When they have stolen enough to restart them comfortably, or when too closely pursued by the Troops, they either send a messenger to their agent, or avoiding the Troops, slip back into the reservation, and declare their willingness

> to make peace. The proposition is not only eagerly accepted by the Department, but the new Treaty entered into is celebrated by many and valuable presents to the Indians.[44]

Dodge held that the Indian Bureau, by supporting the cycle of escape, violence, and negotiations for renewed peace, failed to foster the Indians' progress toward maintaining themselves independently and with dignity. Many victims of Indian atrocities owed their sufferings to the temporizing of the Indian Bureau, he wrote. Here he yoked the mistreatment of white female captives by Indians with the Indian Bureau's inability or unwillingness to hold the native tribes responsible for their actions. "At the very moment of this writing," he insisted, "several unfortunate white women are prisoners in the hands of the Indians, undergoing all the hardships and outrages, which those words imply, scarcely an effort for their relief being made by a Bureau, which finds it more to its convenience and profit to preach humanity in the East than to do right in the West."[45] Dodge would develop these themes in later chapters.

On January 31, 1875, he wrote William Blackmore, then in England, asking for his advice and support on the book project. He had been "amusing" himself, he began, by "writing up my knowledge of Indians – of plains life generally," and had accumulated a goodly pile of manuscript. "I have the vanity," he continued, "to believe [it] is worth printing – at least (as the Indian matter is treated, as far out of the common line of such writing as possible – & contains much that has not been published before –) that it will pay to print." His idea was to publish the completed work first in England rather than in the United States. "If published here," he reasoned, "few Englishmen would ever see it. If published there Englishmen would read it, & many people here, would buy it simply because it was published there." In order to satisfy English tastes he thought of adding to the "Indian matter" a sufficient number of "hunting stories" to make the work "pleasurable to sportsmen." He solicited Blackmore's reaction to these ideas, especially "what *kind* of matter" would be most attractive to the British.[46]

The latter chapters of Dodge's section on Indians constituted a colorful but not pleasant review of warfare as a way of life among Plains Indians. But here the Cheyenne tribe received little mention; Dodge featured instead the Sioux, "the meanest, most treacherous, and most cowardly of plains Indians," and also the Comanches, Lipans, Tonkaways, Pawnees, Crows, Arapahos, and Utes. He attested to the courage and tactical skill of the Indians at war, but he emphasized that "the higher qualities of courage" were absent from their fighting spirit. If actuated by desire to win reputation, to obtain scalps, or to steal ponies, an Indian was unquestionably resolute and brave. Even so, a native warrior lacked "the firmness of soul which enables a man to take his chances of wounds and death, for the sake of principle or duty, without hope or expectation of reward."[47] Unlike the initial chapters, the tone of these passages was predominantly sober, even grim, as for the revelation of harsh truths. Lest any readers should question his veracity, Dodge observed that he was recounting only representative examples of the Indians' savage behavior, including scalping, rape, and protracted torture. The chapter entitled "Stealing" consisted almost entirely of examples, but as he neared its conclusion he remarked that "hundreds" of additional instances could readily be cited.[48]

Two chapters, dealing with the Indians' treatment of captives and with the practice of cruelty as an art, stood apart from others in this group for the harrowing revelations they contained. Concluding the former, Dodge assured readers that he could provide examples of brutal treatment "far worse than any here described" but preferred not to. "I have told enough for elucidation, and I am glad to leave the sickening, horrible subject." In that discussion he had described the treatment of male captives, who ordinarily were dispatched "in the most convenient way consistent with a proper amount of suffering," and of boys and girls, who often were treated kindly and adopted into the captors' tribe; but the bulk of the commentary dealt with the abuses visited upon women, Indian or otherwise. With the observation that "Cooper and some other Novelists knew nothing of Indians" when they portrayed their heroines safe in the hands of savages, he stated what he knew to be true:

> I believe I am perfectly safe in the assertion, that there is not a single "wild" Tribe of Indians in all the wide Territory of the United States which does not regard the person of the female captive as the inherent right of the Captor, and I venture to assert further that in the last twenty five years, no woman has been taken prisoner by any party of Plains Indians, who did not as soon after as practicable, become a victim to the lusts of every one of her captors.
>
> The rule is this. When a woman is captured by a party she belongs equally to each and all, so long as that party is out. When it returns to the home encampment, she may be abandoned for a few days to the gratification of any of the Tribe who wish her, after which she becomes the exclusive property of the individual who captured her, and thenceforward has protection as his wife.

Before recounting a series of incidents wherein this "rule" was imposed upon women he had met, Dodge tasked his descriptive ability to portray it in operation:

> No words can express the horror of the situation of that most unhappy woman, who falls into the hands of these savage fiends. The husband, or other male protectors, killed or dispersed, she is borne off in triumph to where the Indians make their first camp. Here if she makes no resistance she is laid upon a buffalo robe, and each in turn violates her person, the others dancing, singing and yelling around her. If she resists at all her clothing is torn off from her person, four pegs are driven into the ground and her arms and legs stretched to the utmost, are tied fast to them by thongs. Here with the howling band dancing and singing around her, she is subjected to violation after violation, outrage after outrage, to every abuse and indignity, until not infrequently death releases her from suffering. The Indian woman knowing this inevitable consequence of capture, makes no resistance and gets off comparatively easy. The white woman naturally and instinctively resists, is "staked out" and subjected

> to the fury of passions four fold increased by the fact of her being white and a novelty. Neither the unconsciousness, nor even the death of the victim stops this horrible orgie, and it is only when the fury of their passions has been glutted to satiety, that she is released if alive, or scalped and mutilated if dead. If she lives, it is to go through the same horrible ordeal in every camp until the party gets back to the home encampment. Should the Indians not wish to be burdened with a captive, they may, after surfeit of their passions tie her to a tree and leave her, as I have known in two instances, or butcher her in cold blood of which there are numberless instances.[49]

More than any other chapter Dodge had written thus far, "Captives" challenged those who cherished the primitivist axiom that the savage state was one of simple virtue.

The chapter entitled "Cruelty" was hardly less troubling in its details than the one on captives, but perhaps wishing not to administer too large a dose of unpalatable matter, Dodge presented it in a less melodramatic fashion, even occasionally with a touch of humor. As examples multiply, the impression that builds is of wonder, perhaps awe, and even amusement in some cases. The chapter closes with a story about an unnamed army officer, a companion of Dodge. This man was being visited by a party of Indians who professed sincere friendship. Evidently impressed with the handsome auburn beard he wore, one of the visitors reached out as if to stroke it. Dodge's comrade, being vain of his appearance, was flattered by this attention. Good feelings prevailed all round until "the Indian unfortunately let out that he so admired the beard, because it would be such fun to hang the officer by it to a tree and shoot at him with arrows."[50]

Dodge insisted that the cruelty exhibited by Indians, sometimes in ingenious fashion, was not unique to them, being rather "a normal trait of humanity."[51] Still, the impulse to inflict suffering for mere sport was not to be encouraged. How, then, was it to be restrained? Dodge answered this question in his concluding chapter. The Indian of the present day was indeed savage, he wrote, but at some earlier period the ancestors of present-day American citizens were no less brutal than he. "That the Indian at this day is the cruel inhuman savage that he is, is partially the fault of the Government which has never done its duty by him."[52] Had federal authorities dealt with Indian tribes in a more enlightened manner over the years, the ongoing Indian Question would be all but answered. Dodge attributed the sorry current state of affairs to three causes. First, the nation had failed to honor its treaty obligations to the several tribes. Second, it dealt with the Indians through two different administrative systems, one of which, the Indian Bureau, was corrupt and ineffective, while the other, the army, lacked authority to regulate Indians while they were on their reservations. Third, its decision makers gave credence to the fantastic views of "sentimental humanitarians" who thought the Indian an impossibly noble being.[53]

To solve the problems created by these three errors, Dodge proposed three innovations. First, he advocated setting aside the fiction that Indian tribes were sovereign nations, like Russia or Spain, capable of forming relationships with the United States by treaty. He proposed rigid adherence to agreements already made, but he also urged governing Indian reservations through a code of civil law. Second, he held that the army should be entrusted with effective control over the Indians, both on reservations and off. Third, he submitted that the views of "these good sentimental, hobby-riding people" who cherished an untenable belief in Indian virtue must be set aside "as amiable, but fallacious; their pleas for constant forgiveness of Indian outrages should be kindly entertained and quietly ignored." Dodge's wide-ranging, sometimes troubling account of Plains Indians thus led to a summary statement, measured but firm, on their behalf. Some features of their present condition were clearly repellent, and yet they were capable of rapid and significant development as a people. "The Indians should be put on reservations, under the control of practical men. . . . They should be well treated, fed, clothed and induced, not forced, to work. They should be taught by precept and by experience that an Indian is no better than a white man, that comfort and plenty will be the reward of good behavior and industry and that crime of any kind will be followed by sure and immediate punishment."[54]

When Dodge wrote again to William Blackmore, on March 21, he had just completed his chapters on Indians. He had received no response to his earlier letter, but he was no longer concerned about what subject matter the completed work ought to contain. Ideas on that issue had taken shape in his mind, and he now wrote confidently that "I believe you will like what I have written." What now concerned him was the question whether his opportunities for profit were indeed greater by publishing the book first in England or in America. The manuscript had grown to 55,000 words in length, and he continued to write fluently. If no interruption occurred, he expected to complete the section on the plains environment by mid-May, yielding a two-part volume of fair size.

However, he had recently learned that an important military assignment might take him away from his desk at Omaha Barracks, possibly for the entire summer. A second army expedition into the Black Hills of Dakota Territory was to be organized, and a possibility existed that he would be named its commander. Whether the coveted assignment would be his depended, he believed, on what duty would be found for Colonel Davis. If Davis remained in command of the post and regiment at Omaha, his lieutenant colonel would be free to assume command of the expedition. Major George A. "Sandy" Forsyth, Ninth Cavalry, had written Dodge recently, praising the Black Hills country enthusiastically. Forsyth, formerly an aide-de-camp to General Sheridan, had commanded a battalion on Custer's expedition to the Black Hills and had much to say of its scenery and game animals. Dodge thus awaited developments with interest, but for the present he kept himself fully occupied. His wife and son had joined him, Julia seeming well content with her army home,[55] and work on the book occupied all his spare time and energy.

The six extended chapters dealing with the plains country evidenced the confidence Dodge now felt in his capacity as a writer. Like the chapters in "Indians," each bore a simple title designating its general content, but on average the chapter texts were more than three times the length of those in the other series and more varied in content. For instance, to illustrate the proper method of traveling across "divides," networks of ravines in deeply eroded "badlands" territory, he drew upon his experience as a mapmaker, fashioning two sketches to complement his verbal descriptions. To document the danger posed by flash floods along plains watercourses, he copied from an official report submitted not long since by an officer at Fort McPherson, Nebraska.[56] More frequently than in the section on Indians, he included sketches of his own experiences, especially from the years in Texas, when he had learned the most about conditions on the plains.

Following a "General Description" that contained geological speculations, the chapters in this section dealt almost exclusively with the precautions and skills required to ensure safety and comfort when crossing the plains. Dodge described the proverbial fickleness of the weather and the conditions most suitable for travel; the criteria for a good camping place; the ease of becoming lost or turned around and the consequent necessity of reliance upon a compass and, if possible, a map; the limited value of professional guides; and related topics. He conveyed his enthusiasm for both the challenges and the rewards of plains travel. Adopting a familiar comparison, he likened the seemingly limitless plains scene to an ocean, not only in its visual effect but "in its romance, in its opportunities for heroism, and in the fascination it exerts on all who come fairly within its influence." Life on the empty plains, he continued, offered a unique field for self-realization. "At no time, and under no circumstances can a man feel so acutely the responsibility of his life, the true grandeur of his manhood, the elation of which his nature is capable, as when his and other lives depend on the quickness of his eye, the firmness of his hand and the accuracy of his judgement."[57]

Concluding the section on the plains, he mixed his exalted conception of that environment with a regretful description of the transformation it was undergoing. He recalled that when he was a schoolboy, the entire region was a mere open space on maps, marked "The Great American Desert—Unexplored." Only a few years since, a journey across its full extent remained the work of an entire summer. Yet, notwithstanding the dangers and difficulties of travel in those times, the compensations were even greater. "To the fascination of a life of perfect freedom from all conventional restraints, of constant adventure, was added that other fascination, far stronger to many natures, the desire to penetrate the unknown." More recently, thriving populations had established themselves at many points, ending the existence of the plains in its pristine state. The railroads had laid open the remote mysteries of the region "to the inspection of every shop-boy."[58]

Dodge's completed chapters on the plains, approximately 30,000 words in length, ended the second stage of his five-part experiment in authorship. Well satisfied with his progress, he was certain that what he had written merited publication, but at the same time he was content to set aside the project for a time in favor of another undertaking. As he had hoped, an order issued from headquarters of the Department of the Platte on May 1, 1875, designated him commander of the Black Hills Expedition then in process of organization and directed him to report without delay to Lieutenant Colonel Luther P. Bradley, Ninth Infantry, commanding officer of the District of the Black Hills, at Fort Laramie.[59] Fortuitously, the summer to come offered him an extended experience of plains and mountain travel of the exact sort he had celebrated in his just-completed account. Marching with the army escort assigned to protect a group of scientists, he would pass several months in little-known regions of the great Sioux Reservation. As he had written concerning plains travel in earlier years, his party would be in a measure "lost to the world," existing "only in and for itself," with "no mails, no news, no communication of any kind with civilization."[60] To Dodge as a soldier, the assignment was a rare opportunity for field duty of unquestionable importance. At the same time, the experiences of the summer could not fail to provide him new material for his writing. From both points of view, the appointment as commander of the Black Hills Expedition was tailor-made for him as a soldier-author.

12

The Black Hills Expedition

The report by Custer that men of his command had discovered gold "among the roots of the grass" along Black Hills streams sparked an intense debate over the probable value of that country. The Reverend Samuel D. Hinman, a missionary to the Sioux Indians and an advocate of their cause, passed through the region three weeks after Custer and reported finding no gold there. But some persons cast doubt on Hinman's testimony, ascribing it to his wish to protect the tribe from opportunistic prospectors and contractors.[1] Doubts about the alleged gold deposits were also expressed from within the party that had accompanied Custer. Newton H. Winchell, the official geologist of the army reconnaissance, declared publicly that he had seen no evidence of gold in the Black Hills and indeed rather doubted its presence there. Widely reported, this professional opinion raised the question whether Custer had lied, or perhaps "salted" the diggings. In his annual report for 1874, Commissioner of Indian Affairs Edward P. Smith deplored the "exaggerated statements of rich mines and agricultural lands" made by the army officer. He pointed out that, even though not reliable, the reports had encouraged many citizens to take possession of the Black Hills country.

Stung by these slurs against his veracity, Custer responded to them in a spirited letter to the *New York World*. If Professor Winchell had failed to see gold, he contended, the reason was simply "that he neglected to look for it." As to Commissioner Smith, "sitting in his comfortable chair in Washington," Custer had some pointed comments of his own. "If, instead of assailing representatives of other departments of the Government upon false grounds . . . the same time and attention were devoted to his own department, which, by the way, is a glass house of huge dimensions, great benefit might result to the Indians."[2]

Newspaper editors entered the fray, and nefarious motives were ascribed to those on both sides of the gold question. Discussion of the issue opened out into debate over federal Indian policy and the future of the Black Hills generally. Meanwhile, groups of miners made their way to the eastern slopes of the hills and began operations there. They were flouting the nation's solemn obligations to the Sioux tribe, and the government was obliged to have them expelled. The army, which in recent years had served in a police capacity chiefly to control the Indians, was thus called upon to operate against delinquent citizens. On December 26, 1874, a detachment of the Third Cavalry, under Captain Guy Henry, marched north into the Black Hills in search of miners. Two weeks later they returned to Camp Robinson, having suffered terribly from severe winter conditions but not having seen even one of the interlopers.[3] A second command, sent out from Fort Laramie in March, was more successful. Entering the hills from the west, Captain John Mix, Second Cavalry, came upon the settlement and defensive stockade along French Creek of twenty-eight persons, who became known as the Gordon party. "As a class," Mix wrote in his official report, these adventurers "bore the appearance of hardy, intellectual, and enterprising men."[4] Mix remained at the stockade for a few days to enable members of the arrested group to gather their effects, then escorted them back to the fort, where they were released. Grateful for this humane treatment, the ejected miners distributed to soldiers in his command specimens of the ore they had unearthed.

Despite the official efforts at deterrence, miners remained at work in the Black Hills, and many of those who had been removed vowed to return there as often as they were expelled.[5] But the federal government made known its own resolve. On March 17 General Sherman informed General Sheridan of a presidential proclamation that so long as the present treaty with the Sioux continued in force, all expeditions into the Black Hills country must be prevented. Efforts to arrange with the Indians for the extinguishment of their legal title had begun, but should those fail, all unauthorized persons were to be kept out. Sheridan therefore notified Brigadier Generals Alfred H. Terry and E. O. C. Ord, commanders respectively of the Department of Dakota and the Department of the Platte, that forces under their command were to move against all intruders. Specifically, they were to burn the wagon trains, destroy the outfits, and arrest the leaders of quasi-military "expeditions" then being organized in Yankton, Dakota Territory, and Sioux City, Iowa, once those bodies entered onto the Sioux Reservation. Moreover, if any trespassers should succeed in reaching the interior, cavalry forces were to be sent out in pursuit.[6] Leaders of the citizen organizations were undeterred by these directives. One of them, "Captain" Charles C. Carpenter, boasted to the *St. Louis Daily Globe* that no military force would be able to resist the march of his "troops." The men with him had adopted the motto "Black Hills, or bust."[7]

The approaching confrontation between the army and the miners threatened violence, while on the Sioux Reservation resentment against the U.S. government festered. Already aggrieved by what they considered systematic mistreatment at their agencies, the Indians continued to view the Custer expedition as a hostile intrusion. One of their leaders spoke of the trail left by his ten companies of troops as "that thieves' road."[8] Spotted Tail, Dodge's acquaintance from his days at North Platte, informed

Columbus Delano, the secretary of the interior, that the Great Spirit had told him never to steal anyone's country without paying for it. "If you had the same sense of right," he added, "we might get along well enough."[9]

Against this complicated background of disputed facts, conflicting interests, and mutual suspicion, in March 1875 President Grant directed Secretary Delano to organize a scientific study of the Black Hills, especially with regard to their reputed mineral wealth.[10] The results of the examination would provide a basis for evaluating the potential of the region and its fair value in trade to the Indians, should extinguishment of the Sioux title be called for. Under the direction of Delano's subordinate the Commissioner of Indian Affairs, in the weeks that followed the composition of the scientific expedition was decided upon. Professor Walter P. Jenney, of the Columbia School of Mines, New York, was named the geologist in chief,[11] and the party under his direction would include sixteen other persons: an assistant geologist, topographer, astronomer, naturalist, photographer, head miner, and ten laborers. Early in April, General Sherman was directed by Secretary Belknap to organize a suitable military escort for the scientists, who were expected to remain in the Black Hills throughout the summer. Commissioner Smith thought it unlikely that the Sioux would offer resistance to this second organized entry into their country, once its purpose had been explained to them, but Sherman was more wary. He telegraphed Belknap that the "true point of departure" for the expedition was a military post, Fort Laramie, not an Indian agency, as Smith had proposed. Moreover, he considered that if the scientists were to be assured of safety, an army force of at least eight companies, six cavalry and two infantry, would be required.[12]

The War Department and the Bureau of Indian Affairs were often bitterly at odds during these years, as evidenced by the vitriolic exchange between Custer and Commissioner Smith. However, in the present instance the two organizations worked together without ill will. Each stood to gain from cooperation with the other, and perhaps the shared purpose of facilitating the labors of the civilian scientists served as a buffer. It was agreed that the Black Hills Expedition would move northward from Fort Laramie, escorted as Sherman had advised, as soon as arrangements were complete and the advancing season ensured an adequate supply of forage for the cavalry mounts and pack animals.

Army officials interested themselves in the question whether gold existed in the Black Hills only so far as the results of the inquiry might influence their military mission. When asked by Sherman what he knew of the region, General Sheridan recounted an "Indian romance" he had heard years before from Pierre-Jean De Smet, the Jesuit missionary, that a great mountain of gold existed somewhere in the hills. He was satisfied, he added, that the fable had no objective basis, even though the hills might well prove to be gold-bearing. What had impressed him in recent years was the strategic importance of the territory, which the Sioux could employ as a rallying area for attacks on settlements in Nebraska. His "purely military" motivation in ordering the Custer reconnaissance had been his belief that an army post must be established to counter that threat. Of course, the alleged discovery of gold altered circumstances considerably. For the present, he agreed with Sherman that the army had "no alternative" but to direct its energies against trespassers in the Indians' domain.[13]

The publicity given the forthcoming Black Hills Expedition included a rumor that the commander of the military escort would be Lieutenant Colonel Custer himself. As late as May 15, the usually reliable *Army and Navy Journal* reported that the new Custer expedition, numbering about 1,000 persons, would depart early in July from Fort Abraham Lincoln, Dakota Territory.[14] Secretary Belknap's office was besieged by persons requesting permission to accompany the colorful colonel, obviously confident that participating in the mission would work to their advantage in some way.[15] Upon inquiry, it was determined that the misapprehension was being perpetuated by General Terry. He had intended to send out cavalry from posts along the Missouri River, under Custer, to intercept adventurers en route to the Black Hills but not to enter the hills themselves.[16] However, command over the cavalry force from the Department of Dakota to deter trespassers was eventually assigned to another officer, Captain Frederick W. Benteen, Seventh Cavalry.

In the Department of the Platte, organization of the military escort to the Jenney party began in early April. Probably the delay in naming an officer to command the escort was a courtesy extended by the outgoing department commander, General Ord, to his successor, General Crook. Ord assumed command at his new posting, the Department of Texas, on April 11, but until Crook reached Omaha and took command of the Department of the Platte, on April 27, military affairs at the latter place awaited his direction.[17] Crook's journey from Fort Whipple was lengthened by the necessity of his appearing at civic functions, first in Arizona and later at San Francisco, where he was praised as a miracle of military prowess. Arriving at Omaha Barracks, he was welcomed first by the six-company garrison of the post, all units of the Twenty-third Infantry, and two days later at another public function. On the latter occasion, a reception at the Omaha Merchant's Club, he heard speeches by Captain Azor Nickerson, his senior aide-de-camp, and Lieutenant Colonel Dodge before offering a few remarks of his own.[18]

The formalities ended, Crook set to work as department commander. His first major order, promulgated on May 1, probably made official a personnel action already decided upon. He assigned "Lieutenant Colonel *Richard I. Dodge*, 23d Infantry . . . to the command of the escort of six companies of cavalry and two of infantry for the Black Hills Geological Surveying Party."[19] Five days later, after conferring with Crook and making some last-minute arrangements, Dodge boarded a train for Cheyenne, Wyoming, and began compiling the first of six journals he would fill with notes and observations as the summer passed.[20] Officers traveling in little known country were expected to describe for future reference the physical features of the regions they passed through,[21] and in the present instance that information would form part of his official report.

Except for Mr. and Mrs. Adair, his hunting companions of the previous fall, no one clamored to accompany Dodge on the coming expedition, as they had Custer. He declined the Adairs' request but urged Blackmore, by letter and by telegram, to come from England at once and accompany the command if he possibly could. "I expect a glorious time," he wrote, "& especially in the fall when we go to the Big Horn country, the finest game and fishing region on the continent."[22] He was taking with him his son, Fred, now sixteen years of age, hoping to fix in him a love of the outdoors that might lead to comradeship in years to come. Except that he planned to take stringent security precautions, he seems to have felt no concern about the possibility of attack by the Sioux. General Crook, after discussions with General Sheridan in Chicago, would proceed to Fort Laramie and help make final arrangements for the military escort. That visit would form part of an inspection tour of the posts now under his authority, but he planned to make an excursion of his own into the Black Hills and join Dodge there later in the summer.

In May 1875 the town of Cheyenne swirled with activity, much of it connected with the Black Hills. Outfitters and would-be miners were everywhere, and Dodge noted strong sentiment in favor of the federal government's taking possession of the hills by whatever means necessary. At nearby Fort D. A. Russell he secured some necessary equipment and made social calls on brother officers, and in Cheyenne he met Professor Jenney, who was busy making his own preparations. His initial opinion of the young geologist was positive but qualified by the observation that he seemed "rather timid and fearful of his knowledge of things."[23] Jenney, perhaps burdened by the weight of his responsibility, was anxious to meet all expectations despite his lack of experience in undertakings of this kind. He was in regular contact with officials in Washington concerning minor matters that hardly warranted the effort.[24]

On May 9 Dodge left Cheyenne on the ninety-two-mile journey to Fort Laramie, riding in a mule-drawn spring wagon. That afternoon he met a group of Sioux leaders, with their agents and interpreters, who were traveling to Washington for negotiations over the possible sale of the Black Hills. They assured him that he would meet with resistance from northern bands of the tribe, who intended to lay waste to Harney City, the settlement and stockade of the Gordon party, whom Captain Mix had arrested a few weeks before.[25] Arriving at the fort on the afternoon of May 10, Dodge reported to Lieutenant Colonel Luther Bradley and began a routine that, while pleasant enough, merely passed the time until the general made his appearance. He paid more social calls, many of them on old acquaintances such as Mix and Colonel William B. Bullock, formerly the post sutler and a "47th cousin" of his from Virginia. He played billiards, "gassed" with local residents including John Collins, the post trader, wrote letters, sent telegrams, and at mealtimes often accepted the hospitality of Bradley and his agreeable family. His selection for quartermaster of the army escort, First Lieutenant John F. Trout, Twenty-third Infantry, had not yet reached the post, and Dodge chafed at the delay.[26]

Crook and his two aides-de-camp made their appearance on May 16, and preparations entered a new phase. Crook's aide Second Lieutenant John G. Bourke, Third Cavalry, had been named engineer officer of Dodge's command and was present at the initial conference, in which the two senior officers discussed problems of transportation and supply. To Dodge's satisfaction, the general consented to an allotment of seventy wagons for use by the command instead of the fifty that had earlier been thought necessary, and also to the employment of a local guide and interpreter. In his notes of the meeting, Bourke summarized one feature of Dodge's necessarily tentative plan: "Some where near *Harney's Peak* of the *Black Hills*, in *S. W. Dacotah, Colonel Dodge* intends forming a dépôt, surrounded by a stockade, and guarded by one company of Infantry, the others being employed in escorting the wagon train to and from *Laramie*."[27] The rather formal style exemplified here was characteristic of Bourke, who planned to draw upon his journal entries for articles as a correspondent for the *San Francisco Alta California*, the *Cincinnati Gazette*, and probably other newspapers. Evidently he was impressed with Dodge, for in his notes of the interview he characterized him as "experienced in Indian warfare and of great natural sagacity in matters military and otherwise."[28]

Following the arrival of First Lieutenant Trout on May 18, the pace of preparations quickened. On the next day, Dodge's forty-eighth birthday, he learned that his command would consist of Companies C and I, Second Cavalry; A, H, I, and K, Third Cavalry; and C and H, Ninth Infantry. As guide and interpreter he hired Joe Merivale, a longtime resident of the vicinity who claimed to be familiar with the topography between the post and the Black Hills. As a packer he hired "California Joe" Milner, whom Custer had praised in *My Life on the Plains* for his serviceable qualities as a frontier man-of-all-work.[29] This eccentric veteran mountain man and backwoods philosopher was eager to see the gold diggings in the hills—one of the few territories, he said, that he had not yet explored. While still at the post Joe got riotously drunk, and Dodge dismissed him, declaring him "a worthless vagabond." Nevertheless, as events unfolded, Joe found means to rejoin the command and would eventually play a key role in its work.[30]

On May 21 Dodge issued a general order assuming command of the expedition.[31] Trout supervised the ferrying of commissary supplies to the north bank of the North Platte River, opposite the fort, and with considerable difficulty the beef herd was made to swim across the river. Three days later the army companies and then the scientific party crossed by ferry, and for the first time the entire command went into camp, ready for departure the next morning. A supply train of 71 wagons, a herd of 134 cattle, a military contingent of 452 men and 376 horses, with a proportionate number of civilian employees—not to mention the scientists with their gear—were for a few hours all together, with everything in order or close to it. Bourke wrote an evocative sketch of the scene:

> Those officers of the post who were not to form part of the Expedition, now presented themselves to say goodbye to their comrades and receive parting messages of the description usual upon such occasions. Old and almost forgotten war times were vividly recalled by the long streets of white canvass sheltering officers and soldiers, by the long train of 75 wagons laden with a three months supply of provisions, by the thousands of rounds of extra ammunition supplied in case of need against hostile Sioux. In the cavalry companies and in the Q. M. train, long lines of animals were groomed and rubbed preparatory to the long march of the morrow; our efficient Quartermaster, Trout, ran from point to point, inspecting and examining to see that every essential had been supplied and jotting down at intervals memoranda of mistakes to be rectified and omissions to be made good. The Infantry soldiers were drilled in the school of the skirmisher and exercised in the evolutions of the company formation; bustle prevailed on all sides, indicative of the earnestness with which all concerned regarded the duty to which they were assigned, and which they felt the country required should be done thoroughly and well.[32]

Unfortunately the official photographer of the scientific party, A. Guerin, was ill in Saint Louis and did not record this scene.[33]

The March into the Hills

At 6:00 A.M. on May 25 the command broke camp and set out northward through undulating terrain, some of it sandy and made muddy by a recent rain. "Most delightful day for marching," Dodge wrote that night after traveling seventeen miles to Rawhide Creek, but "Heavy hauling for animals."[34] He was concerned about the toll the journey ahead would take on the pack animals and cavalry horses. The marching orders he had issued provided that the cavalry companies and their mounts would incur an equal share of more difficult duty. Each day one of the cavalry units would be the pioneer party, moving at the head of the command, and would also serve as the picket and camp guard, with its commander the officer of the day. On the next day that company would take up a much less demanding position, in the rear of the column, and then gradually work its way forward. On a day's march, the pioneer company would be followed by the headquarters and scientists' ambulances, four cavalry companies, the infantry companies, the artillery pieces, an ordered succession of wagons, and finally the rear guard of cavalry.[35] In proper military fashion, these arrangements strictly regulated Dodge's force as it moved through conditions of weather and topography that were less amenable to discipline.

Segments of a day were marked off by familiar bugle calls. "Reveille" was at 4:45 A.M., for the summer sun rose early in that high latitude. Following roll call, stable duty, and breakfast, the "General" signaled the time to strike tents. "Boots and Saddles" was the command to saddle and bridle the cavalry horses, and at "Assembly," the companies fell into line under arms.[36] The pioneer company then moved forward, bringing with it the pioneer wagon, which carried axes, hatchets, spades, shovels, nails, rope, timber, and other necessities for excavating, embanking, and setting in place corduroy roads. As the engineer officer, Bourke paid close attention to the work of the road-making parties, particularly as they approached watercourses, for here the wagons might be caught in the muddy bottoms and the horses and mules risked injury. He was well pleased with the work he saw at the streams: "Arrived at a point where it is needful to guard against the miring of trains or horses, detailed men move out with axes, fell suitable cottonwood trees, which another party strip of their branches and cut into lengths suitable for stretchers and cross-pieces. Stretchers are disposed across the stream, two feet apart, while the cross pieces cover these closely at right angles. Smaller branches fill in any gaps that may occur while a uniform hard-packed covering of earth makes the road-bed. The Bluffs, edging the stream are now cut down to make a convenient ramp and wagons and horse are crossing almost before the written description is completed."[37] On one day's march, uncertainty about the route to be followed necessitated crossing the Cheyenne River in this fashion three times.[38]

The difficulty of identifying a viable route was evident almost from the beginning of the expedition; whatever other services the affable Joe Merivale might render, Dodge soon learned that as a guide he was all but useless. One day Joe assured him that a cutoff he knew would save miles of travel, but after the command had slogged two and one-half miles through deep sand, he admitted his error, forcing a weary return. Passing a landmark known as Rawhide Butte on the next day, Dodge struck due north by compass even though Joe declared the territory ahead impassable. Acting as his own pathfinder and working closely with Trout, who directed the wagons past difficult spots, he located what he termed "a splendid route."[39] Maps of the area by earlier military explorers, notably Captain Gouverneur K. Warren in 1856 and Captain William F. Raynolds in 1859, proved of little value. Dodge was informed that Raynolds had never even passed through the country; he had drawn this section of his map from a description given him by a guide at Fort Laramie.[40]

From time to time the command met tracks that had been left by other large groups of travelers. On the afternoon of May 28 Dodge and his men passed the camp, probably three days old, of an Indian war party bound west. Dodge estimated its strength at one hundred men and was unusually cautious about his stock that night. On succeeding days he found three other trails passing roughly south to north. One had been made by Indians, another by Captain Warren, and the third by a party of emigrants to Montana under one James A. Sawyer. The latter road, identified by an old packer, was in remarkably good condition given its age of about ten years. "I prefer it greatly," Dodge wrote, "to the guidance of Joe Merivale, who knows nothing of this country, nothing of distance, nothing of road hunting for wagons."[41]

A more serious impediment than Merivale to the progress of the expedition as it sought a practicable entrance to the Black Hills from their western slope was the imperious will of Professor Jenney. Dodge had established friendly working relations with the young scientist but was not overly impressed with him. "He is undoubtedly a man of some ability," he wrote, "but very weak, very jealous, and very much disappointed that he has not Military Com[man]d of the Expedition."[42] For reasons of his own, Jenney wished to locate the 104th degree of longitude, the western boundary of Dakota Territory, and then move northward along it, apparently without regard to the possible difficulties for travel. More than once Dodge lost time by acquiescing in this determination, even though he knew Jenney's instructions made no reference to any line of longitude. However, when he learned from other members of the scientific corps that they lacked the instruments to locate the line, he acted.

In an interview with the geologist in chief, Dodge discussed the determination of a route north as a practical problem to be worked out by Jenney himself; however, to assist him he described what seemed some relevant considerations. Although geological study would require work in mountain country, following the 104th degree of longitude would take the command some distance west of the Black Hills. The health of the men demanded access to good water; the strength of the animals, good grass; and the comfort of all, a plentiful supply of wood. Jenney must therefore choose between following the 104th degree of longitude or else pursuing his work in the mountains, which offered wood, water, and grass. After much indecision, which Dodge privately attributed to "the boyish hope of getting everything just as he desires," Jenney gave over his search for the Dakota-Wyoming line.[43] Shortly afterward, Dodge issued orders to return as far east as Beaver Creek, which flowed from north to south, and go into camp there.

As Bourke delicately expressed the matter, Jenney "has not apparently succeeded in making a striking impression on any who have been thrown in contact with him."[44] However, the other professional members of the scientific party worked well together and won general regard. Dodge liked the assistant geologist, Henry Newton, whom he later described as an accomplished student, "so patient and indefatigable that . . . there is scarcely a rock in the whole length and breadth of the 'Hills' which does not bear the mark of his hammer."[45] Horace P. Tuttle, of the Harvard Observatory, he thought "a Gentleman of culture refinement & sense." Valentine T. McGillycuddy, the topographer, was in his opinion the next of these accomplished persons in "rank and merit." As it happened, the Black Hills Expedition included two topographers—Bourke in the military escort and McGillycuddy in Jenney's party. Being himself adept at mapmaking on the unadorned military model, Dodge perhaps discounted somewhat the products of McGillycuddy's expertise. He thought him "smart and bright, well up in his business as a professional map maker, but [running] too much to fancy, & pretty."[46] At several times during the summer, Dodge reflected to himself that the work of the scientists would proceed more smoothly if any of Newton, Tuttle, or McGillycuddy were in charge of the investigations, rather than Jenney.

Relations between Jenney and the two civilian newspaper correspondents who accompanied the command were rocky from the outset. At Cheyenne, the geologist had objected to their being permitted to accompany the military escort,[47] and presently Reuben B. Davenport, correspondent of the *New York Herald*, returned the compliment. He described Jenney sarcastically as, "like all great minds," glibly setting forth "his intentions, conclusions, and the contents of the text books which he committed to memory as an undergraduate on the slightest provocation."[48] Thomas C. MacMillan of the *Chicago Inter-Ocean* was only a bit more charitable. In their dispatches both newspapermen persisted in misspelling the scientist's surname as "Jenny," "Janney," or "Janny."

For his part, Dodge maintained pleasant social relations with both the civilian journalists, but he declined to admit them to his mess, offering as excuse the wish to speak freely and without worry that some ill-considered words of his would be blazoned to thousands of metropolitan readers.[49] Davenport wrote well, he thought, "& has the regular reporter knack of pumping people – but he is as green as a gourd, as credulous as a ninny." The young easterner was new to the Indian country, somewhat naive, and not courageous. As a result, some officers amused themselves by telling him outrageous stories of dire events, raising him to a high pitch of apprehension. He lost sleep one night after being warned by these jokers that the distant hooting of an owl was in fact the chant of Indian women, inciting their men to show courage in a fight that would surely take place the next day. Dodge warned Davenport that he was being imposed upon and urged him to beware of publishing anything he gleaned from the gamesome lieutenants.[50] MacMillan, a slender, twenty-four-year-old Scotsman, was also new to the western country, but Dodge considered him "of an entirely different stamp – very gentlemanly, hard to stuff & with excellent good sense." He won the good will of everyone and was given the pleasant nickname "Little Mac."[51] The national interest in the findings of the expedition resulted in the presence of three newspaper correspondents within Dodge's own command. These were Bourke; Captain Andrew S. Burt, Ninth Infantry, for the *New York Tribune*; and Acting Assistant Surgeon J. R. Lane, for the *Chicago Tribune*.

A number of colorful personalities among the military and scientific contingents gave added interest to the work of the Black Hills Expedition. One of these was Jane Dalton, alias Jane or Martha Canary, better known as Calamity Jane. During the first few days out, she rode with a cavalry company, disguised as an army private. Though her identity was known to many, her presence was not officially acknowledged until, sixty miles out from Fort Laramie, she was discovered and reported to Dodge by an irate sergeant. According to an observer, the commanding officer "tried to look impressive" as he ordered this unauthorized woman from camp, but "a smile hovered about his lips" as he did so.[52] Having pronounced sentence, Dodge let the matter rest. On the next morning Jane surreptitiously hitched a ride with the wagon train and continued on the journey. Thereafter she was allowed to remain, helping around the camps and proving a useful member of the civilian party. According to MacMillan, she gained a reputation as "a better horseback rider, mule and bull whacker (driver) and a more unctious [*sic*] coiner of English, and not the Queen's-pure, either, than any (other) man in the command."[53]

Other noteworthy individuals included "Old Joe" Bratton, a resourceful pack train employee whose abilities caught Dodge's attention. A miner all his adult life, Bratton had several times been worth $100,000 but was now glad to have steady work. Dodge thought him "a very intelligent man" and a "True American" who had experienced a "true miners fortune."[54] John Brown, Jr., Jenney's general assistant, was indeed a son of the abolitionist firebrand. Being of an independent disposition, in midsummer he resigned his position and returned to his home.[55] Probably the best remembered individual in the command was California Joe, who changed his ways after being dismissed by Dodge and began a discreet effort to secure renewed employment. Contrite, the wiry veteran followed the northbound body of men, gradually insinuating himself with the rear guard. Before many days, Jenney hired him as a laborer and messenger, and from that time he became a fixture. He received a good deal of attention from the newspapermen and favored them with a steady stream of stories and droll observations.[56]

On a few occasions Dodge ruffled the feathers of some officers by peremptorily ordering them to cease activities that had tried him beyond patience, but on the whole he enjoyed a good reputation among all parties. The two citizen journalists were liberal in their praise of him. "The government is fortunate as having selected for the command of this expedition an officer of the ripe experience and thorough knowledge of the Indians and their country possessed by Colonel Richard J. [*sic*] Dodge," Davenport wrote. "A character combining enterprise, discretion, fearlessness, judgment, mildness and tolerance, if it is not rare is certainly valuable. Without incurring undue risks, Colonel Dodge would shrink from no necessary responsibility which duty might impose, and the qualities required by the exigencies of a position such as he now occupies are as various as those which I have mentioned."[57] MacMillan was again more restrained, dwelling on Dodge's years of service on the frontier. Interestingly, in an early dispatch from Fort Laramie he included an erroneous statement in his summary of Dodge's qualifications, describing him as "the author of several valuable and interesting works on themes of a western and border nature."[58] Evidently Dodge was making no attempt to keep secret his recent activities as a writer.

The most detailed sketch of Dodge published during this eventful summer formed part of a dispatch to the *Chicago Tribune* by Dr. Lane, the citizen physician. As an employee of the army, Lane was a member of the commander's mess, and his description probably derives some of its content from this familiar relationship:

> The commanding officer of the Black Hills expedition, Col. R. I. Dodge, was born in North Carolina, of a good old stock, that bequeathed to him a powerful physique, a large brain, and an active mind. Standing full six feet in his stockings, his powerful frame surmounted by a fine Grecian profile, graced by a pair of intensely human blue eyes, and bearded like a pard, with the heavy growth slightly streaked with gray, he is a fine type of the rapidly-passing-away Southern gentleman and soldier. He is a close student, a keen observer, and a fine conversationalist, and of course loves to talk; but, when a man can talk well, he is pardonable in any little display of vanity. Col. Dodge's greatest weakness

> is map-making and shooting, and he excels in these two accomplishments to a wonderful degree.[59]

At some point during the summer the younger officers coined a nickname for their military lord and master, "Richard the First," a typographical pun on his given name and middle initial.[60] Yet if he did play the tyrant on occasion, Dodge was approachable, sensible, task-oriented, and fair. He praised those who performed their duties well, and often at the end of a day's march a session of sociable "gassing" occurred around his campfire.

On June 3, 140 miles from Fort Laramie and with the tree-covered slopes of the Black Hills now in view, Dodge selected that day's campsite as his first permanent base for supplies, Camp Jenney. "If I had had the making the spot," he wrote with satisfaction, "I could not have suited better all my ideas of what we want in our permanent camp."[61] Here, under the direction of Bourke, a palisade work would be constructed on an elevated stretch of ground that commanded the campsite. From this point, Bourke wrote, "our artillery [a twelve-pound howitzer and a Gatling gun] can be enabled to play with deadly effect upon any party of Indians that may have the temerity to attack us."[62] Additionally, timber would be cut and trimmed for construction of a storehouse and stockade. The work would require remaining in camp for a few days before the command moved on; meanwhile, the scientists were free to begin their inquiries, escorted by small detachments of cavalry.

Some officers and men obtained permission to hunt, fish, and explore the vicinity during this short period of delay. Dr. Lane and Second Lieutenant Charles Morton, Third Cavalry, left camp to attempt an ascent of Harney Peak, said to be the highest point in the hills. Captain Burt described his own adventures in a dispatch to the *New York Tribune*: "I killed an elk, climbed the first range of the hills, nearly fell into a deep cañon, skinned my hands and knees scaling a cliff after an eagle's nest, and ended . . . by nearly drowning a horse—and that in a stream not three feet wide, one of those alkali ditches which have no bottom to speak of, and water so brackish, though clear, that quinine or epsom salts is delicious in comparison."[63] The hunters of First Lieutenant Christopher T. Hall's company killed four elk that afternoon, and those of Burt's company bagged a cinnamon bear. Strolling the vicinity, one man picked up a curiosity that he gave to Dodge. Bourke described it as a piece of "silicified wood, or rather half petrified wood, one half being stone, the other still retaining its ligneous fibre and condition."[64] On the night of June 4 some men of Jenney's party caught a beaver and brought it back to camp almost unharmed. The next morning Dodge took Fred over to see it, and later he recorded the scene: "He was very quiet, and allowed himself to be handled & felt of by us all. I felt sorry for the poor beast, especially as his fur was of no account at this season and persuaded them to turn it loose. We then drove it quietly to the water and when he had got where it was deep enough he gave us a fine specimen of his skill in diving & soon disappeared."[65]

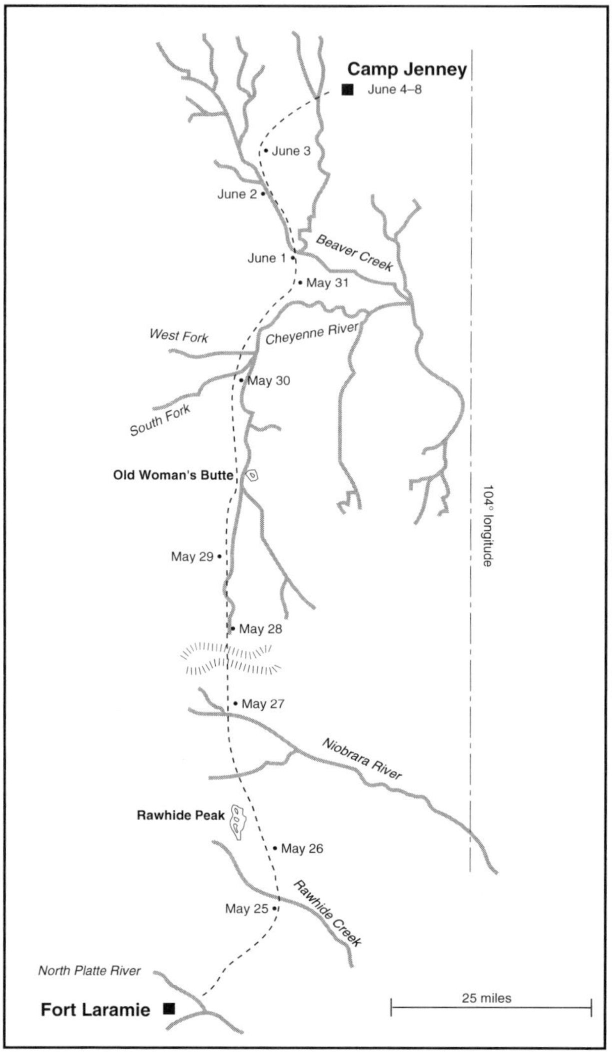

Itinerary, Fort Laramie to Camp Jenney, May 25–June 8, 1875

According to plan, on June 4 Dodge issued an order for the two infantry companies, under Captain Burt, to return to Fort Laramie with the unloaded wagons and obtain there a shipment of fresh supplies. Burt had been aware of this intention, but nevertheless he felt victimized. He expressed this and other grievances to Dodge, resulting in a grating of personalities. In a journal entry Dodge recorded his private impression of Burt, drawing upon Proverbs for one telling phrase: "He is a turbulent, ill-contrived fellow, wise in his own conceit, and gives me great exercise in my virtue of patience. He is the only officer along who I have a contempt for. He is visionary & so full of vanity that it requires tact to manage him, & so disposed to say ill-natured & impertinent things that I have hard work not to 'go back on him,' – I wish I could get rid of him."[66] Burt's errand to Fort Laramie would serve that purpose temporarily.

Another officer who required careful handling, but whose stellar performance of duty justified the effort, was First Lieutenant Trout. Dodge regarded Trout as "a most invaluable man[,] not only possessing wonderful energy but great practical ability." Still, the quartermaster-commissary could be arbitrary and "just a little disposed to make the most of his work"—that is, to take credit for more than he had done. One night the cattle herd was stampeded by thunder, and Trout and his assistant hurried from camp to head them off. After an absence of perhaps twenty-five minutes he returned, reporting that the animals had been recovered after a three-mile chase. Dodge "couldn't quite swallow it," but despite his doubts about the distance he gave Trout credit for a worthy accomplishment. "He may have thought it full three miles," he wrote before going to sleep, "and twould likely have been a dozen to me, but he could not have gone a mile."[67]

During these days of consolidation and planning at Camp Jenney, Dodge and Bourke separately addressed their thoughts to the purpose and probable results of the Black Hills Expedition. As to the scientific party and its eventual report, Dodge was convinced that the appointment of a young man such as Jenney to head up a major geological study such as this indicated "a job of some kind" among decision makers in the east. "My opinion is that the report to be made in regard to Gold has been decided upon already at Washington, & that the sending him out is the merest blind."[68] Bourke considered the expedition within the wider perspective of the federal government's ongoing relationship with the Indian tribes. Naturally, too, he viewed events in terms of the role his commander, General Crook, would be called upon to play in them. In a long diary entry he worked through the problem:

> Upon the confines and within the limits of the Black Hills Reserve, the reflection arises what good does the present expedition do except to witness to the world that our Government is not desirous of depriving the Sioux of any treaty rights until after careful consideration of the subject involved, and maybe a feeble scientific light thrown upon the topography of the country and the true astronomical position of a few insignificant peaks and streams? Professor Janney [*sic*] has a great responsibility to bear and an unenviable position to occupy. Granting his report admits the existence of gold; has that not been known already? Or, supposing no auriferous indications meet his eye, will a non-committal or a flat denial avail to stay the influx of adventurous men now congregated at Cheyenne, Sioux City and other points, fully satisfied of the existence of valuable treasures in the Sioux country, which they are all the more determined to seize because on forbidden ground? One phase of the business, do what the Govt. can to prevent it, will be a Sioux and Cheyenne war in which those tribes will be doomed to receive the castigation so long merited. The probable method of procedure will be the establishment of a few large depots of supplies in the heart of the enemy's country, from which as foci can radiate forth columns of cavalry and Infantry, carrying supplies by pack-trains, to the most hidden recesses of the Indian territory. A winter campaign may become a necessity, but in such a case the troops by *following* up the *streams*,

> can effect two objects: one, the avoiding of much rigorous cold; the other, the assault of the enemy's villages near the streams and their expulsion to the frigid plains where they will soon freeze to death if they do not promptly submit. A change to this policy from the poor and vascillating one prevailing before General Crook's arrival may bring to light the worthlessness of many officers who have no desire to serve the Army and country except at Sybaritic stations or in soft places. But, under General Crook, the subjection of all hostile Indians within the limits of the department may be accepted as a foregone conclusion.[69]

This assessment, the rumination of an officer not only intelligent but privy to some of Crook's private counsels, was farsighted and in some respects prophetic. Bourke believed that whatever results the scientific study might yield, powerful forces among citizens, Indians, and the federal government were impelling events inexorably toward conflict.

On June 7 two exploring parties, one under Dodge and one under Jenney, left camp in search of a practicable route for travel into the central Black Hills. Dodge's strenuous efforts on that day did not lead to the success he had hoped for. He lacked good maps, and the lay of the land proved difficult to read. His party labored up ridge after ridge, hoping in each case to reach a level space at the top. "The affair became seriously monotonous," he wrote that night. "There seemed no end to the ridges."[70] As he had written in his manuscript chapter on travel, in order to bring on the wagons, he would need to locate and scale the "divide" that connected all the ridges he had crossed, as a spine connects ribs.[71] Fortunately, Jenney's exploration offered some promise of success. Following the bed of Beaver Creek, he had come upon a road that led toward what appeared in the distance as an elevated plain. That night Dodge lay awake in his tent studying the problem. He decided to move forward with three companies, establish a second permanent camp, and from that point send back for the three others that remained at Camp Jenney. The plan would involve dividing the military contingent into three segments, separated by perhaps scores of miles, but he saw no other option.

At 6:45 A.M. on June 9, Dodge, three companies of cavalry, and the scientific party set out along the creek bed that Jenney had passed over. Beaver dams created bogs at many points, and steep banks along the watercourse made wagon travel impossible except by bridging. Dodge was disgusted with the performance of that day's pioneer company, which took its tone from an officer "with no snap to him," Captain Henry W. Wessells, Jr., Third Cavalry. Fortunately, the deficiencies of the men under Wessells were made up by those under Trout, who worked "like a beaver."[72] Early in the afternoon the command passed the last bog and followed a wide Indian trail along the left bank until they reached the creek's headspring, about ten miles from Camp Jenney. Crossing the sandy bed to the right side, four miles further on they made camp. Dodge had hoped to reach a point several miles farther ahead, but the time lost in the morning frustrated his plan. Thunderstorms that night threatened more delay, but the still visible Indian trail held out hope.

Early the next morning the command moved out through open pine woods that covered the long, rounded mountain slopes. The day was bright and clear, and while laboring up a steady grade they admired the country around them. To their right was the deep canyon of Beaver Creek, "inaccessible to any thing but bird or bear." Beyond it, a range of mountains rose 1,000 feet above them, while directly ahead lay a wide plain, bare of timber. The trail led across this open space, but nine miles from camp it dived into a canyon in a manner impossible for wagons. While the command stopped to rest, Dodge searched for a way forward. Believing he might have found one, he led the party two miles eastward along the edge of the chasm. Then, to his delight, the way ahead moved up a divide that separated the Beaver Creek canyon from another on the left. After an ascent of perhaps a mile, to a point whose elevation he estimated at 7,850 feet, he and his men were rewarded by a magnificent panorama that displayed almost the entire eastern watershed of the Black Hills.[73] The whole country, he later wrote in his official report, was "spread out like a map at our feet. The Black Hills were open to us."[74]

From this place a series of steep hills that challenged the capacity of Trout and his teamsters brought the party into a deep valley, its sides covered with quaking aspen. After two more miles, they reached a larger valley and came upon a trail, unmistakably the one Custer and his men had made the previous summer. Because a storm was upon them, they found a sheltered site and went into camp after a twelve and one-half mile march. That night Dodge studied the map of the Custer expedition, prepared under direction of Captain William Ludlow of the Engineers, and also the published diary of Sandy Forsyth. He ascertained that he had reached Custer's camp of July 25, 1874, and that, using the map as guide, he could expect unimpeded travel in the coming days.[75] Several officers stopped to congratulate him on this day's march, which had been a tour de force of mountaineering and plainscraft. As Burt commented in a dispatch, "The difficulty of traversing with wagons such a country as this can hardly be conceived by those who have never had the good or ill fortune to experience it."[76]

Dodge's camp lay in what Custer had named Floral Valley for its display of wildflowers, but he was here earlier in the season than Custer. The streams were full with the spring runoff, and at some points the route before him, to the south and east, was through a continuous bog. On June 12 the mules labored at a hard pull but managed to move only four and one-half miles; at many points the wagons could progress only after a corduroy road had been laid down. Despite these troubles, Dodge gave Custer much credit for the course he had taken through this country. The cavalryman "must have had a corps of guides more reliable than usual," he thought, "for they certainly struck about the only route at all practicable for wagons."[77] Reaching what the Ludlow map showed as the headwaters of Spring Creek, on June 13 he left the Jenney party to pursue their researches there, with the laggard Wessells company as escort. Jenney, he knew, was eager to test the sand deposits along the creek for gold; but being secretive, he was determined to do so privately. Meanwhile, Dodge moved ahead in search of a permanent camping place, traveling ten and one-half miles on that day and over sixteen miles on the next. On the afternoon of June 14 he reached French Creek and the stockade of the expelled Gordon party. Well satisfied with that position, he decided to make it the site of Camp Harney, his base of operations for the next several weeks. "The camp is lovely," he wrote in his journal, "a level sward, thick turf, surrounded by low hills, & masses of rock the hills covered with pine. In front is the pretty little creek. Plenty of wood, splendid water and fine grass!! What more can the most fastidious 'Camper' desire[?]"[78] Unlike at Camp Jenney, sixty-eight miles behind him, the need for construction here would be minimal. Trout could use the stockade as a storehouse and also as a corral for the beef herd.

Gold in the Black Hills

Shortly after the party's arrival at the Gordon stockade, a meeting occurred that forced on Dodge a decision in regard to his duty as a representative of the U.S. government. While riding in search of the best position to make camp, he caught sight of some domestic animals and then glimpsed a man dashing amongst them into a narrow gorge. It was, he knew, "the inevitable miner." The army was operating under orders to arrest and expel all citizens found trespassing on the Sioux Reservation. As commander of the military escort to the Jenney survey, what course was he to follow?

Once the command was in camp, Dodge's adjutant, First Lieutenant Morris Cooper Foote, Ninth Infantry, asked permission to visit some of the mining parties that were sure to be found, and Dodge let him go. Thus far he had avoided contact with any of these men himself, even when, as at Camp Jenney, some had camped not far away from him. However, when Foote failed to return in a reasonable time, he mounted his horse and went out to investigate. Coming upon him in a little ravine, in the company of six miners, he rode up to the group. "How do you do, Colonel?" one of the strangers called out. Dodge did not recognize this man, named Harrison, who assured him they had made acquaintance three years before, at Fort Larned. After a few more exchanges, Dodge asked the group whether they understood they had no business where they were.

"We do," a spokesman promptly replied.

"Do you know that the military have orders to arrest you?"

"We do."

"Well," Dodge declared after a pause, "I don't intend to arrest you."

"Thank you," the man returned. "I am very glad to hear it." Now more at ease together, the miners and the army officers walked over to the men's claim for a look at the gold they had taken out. They hoped to complete a flume in one more week and estimated they would then realize from twenty to fifty dollars worth daily per man. After the interview, Dodge brought off a bit of gold to send General Crook.

In a journal entry that night he wrote out his rationale for adopting the course he had taken, adding some thoughts about the future ownership and use of the Black Hills. He was assuming that his specific assignment to escort the scientists freed him

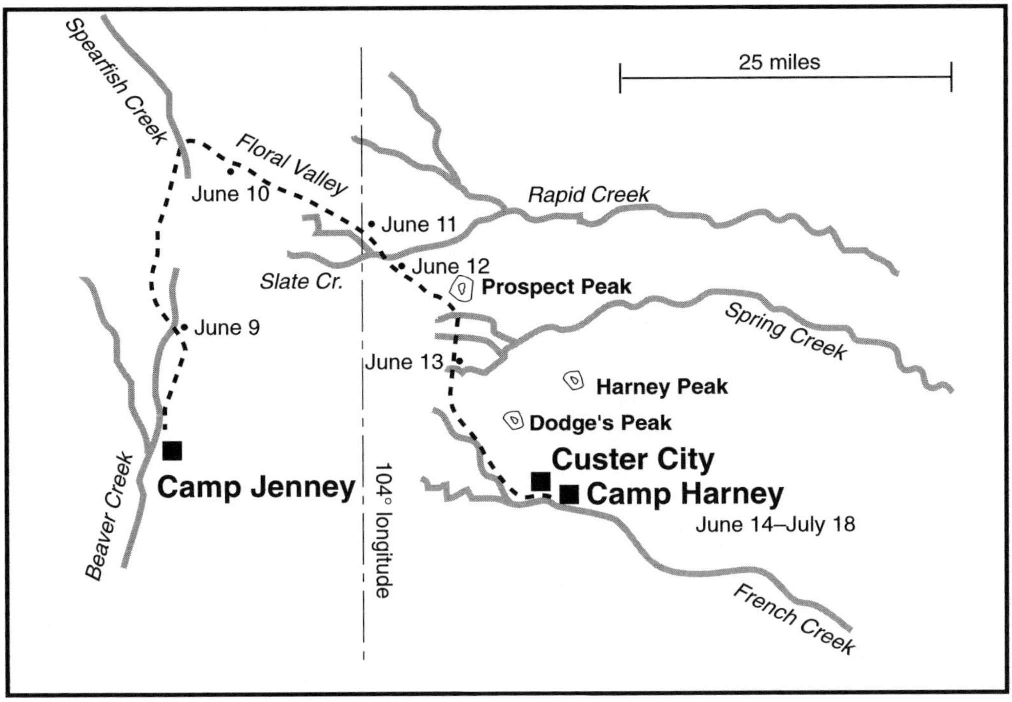

Itinerary, Camp Jenney to Camp Harney, June 9–28, 1875

from obligation to arrest miners, "for if I have to race round the country looking for miners, I must neglect the true object of my trip here." Besides, he lacked the men and resources to send in all the trespassers he was likely to find, unless he was to leave the command shorthanded for the tasks that had brought it here. He would need to report to Crook the determination he had made, but he felt himself on reasonably safe ground. As to the Black Hills themselves, so far as he could tell, the Indians had no use for them, other than occasionally to fell trees for lodgepoles. Yet the country was "rich in gold, in timber and tho' the season may be too short for agriculture, it is a most glorious grazing country, & will furnish cattle butter & cheese for a nation." He intended to "arrest no man if I can help it."[79]

On the following day Dodge wrote a long letter to General Crook elaborating these views, and on the day after that, as one of several communications to army comrades and family members, he wrote out a terse message to be telegraphed to the general from Fort Laramie:

> Harney's Peak, June 17.—Gold has been found in paying quantities on French Creek. Custer's report is confirmed in every particular. The command is well and in fine condition.[80]

When released to the public and printed in newspapers across the land, this announcement would strengthen public sentiment in favor of permitting U.S. citizens to help themselves to the gold deposits in the Black Hills. Four weeks later, when "Captain"

Carpenter arrived at the stockade with a body of men, he declared with his usual hyperbole that thousands more miners were on the road behind him.

Dodge now took steps to bring together the widely dispersed detachments of his command. On June 15 he sent Trout, with wagons, back to Spring Creek to bring up Wessells and the scientists. On the following day he sent the quartermaster-commissary on a second mission, this time with another stalwart, Captain Edward J. Spaulding, Second Cavalry. Taking with them twenty-five men and a wagon train, they were to travel by "the best possible route"—a route not yet determined—to the Beaver Creek bridge, which the command had built about fifteen miles south of Camp Jenney. Trout would proceed from that point to the fortified permanent camp, collect the troops and supplies there, and return to Spaulding. The latter would dispatch a sergeant and ten men from the bridge to Fort Laramie with the mail, but he was to remain there, awaiting the arrival of Burt and his pack train from the fort. Once Burt and the Camp Jenney contingent had both reached the bridge, Trout would assume responsibility for conducting the entire train back to Camp Harney. Dodge's instructions included reference to some rather serious imponderables, including the possibility that Spaulding and Trout would fail to discover a pass through the mountains and that Burt and Trout would therefore need to use the difficult route the command had taken from Camp Jenney.[81] Like the dispersal of troops he had ordered from that camp, his plan of operations was a necessary makeshift; but also like the earlier arrangement, it worked out well. By the evening of June 23 Burt, Spaulding, Trout, and the wagon train were all back in camp, having brought with them a valued bag of mail. That night Dodge wrote, "Burt & other officers owled me . . . so that I did not get to bed until very late."[82] The Black Hills Expedition had passed a second severe test with flying colors.

On the day of his interview with the affable miners, Dodge had observed in his journal that Jenney would "go wild when he arrives here, to find that the soldiers have panned out fifty times more gold today than he has found in all the trip."[83] This was a safe prediction, for Jenney was jealous, sometimes pettish, and determined to make the first discovery of gold and also to announce his feat to the public. On the evening he reached Camp Harney the mortified young geologist paid Dodge a visit. "Jenney is 'scooped,'" the latter wrote after the interview. "I felt sorry for him, & did not pitch into or crow over him as I might. But he is a 'royal' ass – Trout informs me that one of Jenneys men, in a moment of confidence told him that the scientific party had found gold some days ago, but that Jenney had bound them to secresy, & they were not to tell the military." When Trout had informed the savants of the discovery at French Creek and showed them samples, they threw off their professional reserve. "Each abused the other and if you believe all, every man is a d——d fool, for each says that of the other." By attempting to arrogate to himself the credit for confirming Custer's announcement, Jenney had doomed his own effort. "The ass! ass! ass!" Dodge exclaimed. "There are private soldiers in this Com[man]d who know more about gold hunting than he can ever hope to learn. I am very glad that we found the gold, tho' we are entitled to no credit for it as the miners really found it."[84]

A few weeks afterward, still at Camp Harney, Dodge had a long talk with Jenney. When the geologist remarked that he was grateful for the help he had received from men of the army escort and would like to continue utilizing their labor, Dodge had a response ready at hand. He had often wondered, he said, at Jenney's not having thought of the possibility before. He urged him to consider the military his willing collaborators, recalling the eager interest Professor Agassiz had inspired among soldiers, including himself, at Fort Sanders in 1868. Jenney "had it in his power," he continued, "by showing interest & sympathy in the work of the men, to convert every soul of this command into his active & valuable assistant. That he could only see with one pair of eyes, while they could see with 400 pairs & that the exertions of all properly directed, would teach him more of the country in a week, than he unassisted could find out in 3 months."[85] Jenney was impressed by these ideas and said he would do all he could to interest the men in his work. Dodge was finding him a curious compound. He could be headstrong, petulant, even dishonest, but at times like this he was ingenuous, grateful for attention, and really likable.

The mail brought in by Spaulding was the first that had reached the command since its departure from Fort Laramie one month before. Dodge's share was small but satisfactory; Julia and the rest of his loved ones were all well. One unwelcome item of news came from a former army officer, William McE. Dye, who was now a colonel in the Egyptian army. Dye offered Bourke a position as major in the army of the khedive, and with his letter came one from Captain Nickerson, Crook's senior aide-de-camp, advising Bourke to accept the appointment. Dodge regretted Bourke's prompt decision—subsequently retracted—to leave the U.S. service. Two days later, when the lieutenant left the command and returned to Fort Laramie with a mail party, Dodge characterized him as "an intelligent energetic ambitious officer [who] will make his mark in the world yet."[86] Fortunately, the Black Hills Expedition included a good supply of able young men. As the new engineer officer, Dodge appointed Second Lieutenant Charles Morton, directing him to join a party under Dr. McGillycuddy that was to leave camp the following day.[87]

Newspapers from Chicago and New York, weeks old, brought information quite possibly of importance to the immediate future of the Black Hills. The Sioux leaders Dodge had met near Cheyenne had reached Washington, but the discussions between them and officials there were not productive. After airing many complaints and refusing to sign a treaty that had been prepared, the Indians left the city on June 6. Secretary Smith did manage to elicit from them a promise to call together the Sioux bands for discussion of a pact that would provide for their abandonment of the Black Hills in return for a compensation. According to the *New York Herald*, informed persons from the frontier believed that "nothing can be done with the Sioux until they have had a sound thrashing."[88] A related story was the examination of charges leveled against the Indian Bureau by Othniel C. Marsh, a professor of paleontology of Yale College who had visited the Red Cloud Agency in 1874. In recent months Marsh had issued strongly worded reports, supported by corroborating testimony from military officers, alleging fraud and corruption at the agency. According to Marsh, the "Indian Ring" of business interests that profited from this state of affairs was seeking to perpetuate it, regardless of consequences.[89]

These two news stories moved Dodge to set down an angry journal entry in which, taking as his point of departure the alleged behind-the-scenes influence of the Indian Ring, he registered outrage at the solid citizens who comprised its membership: "The Indian Ring is in danger. Nothing but a war can save it, & a war we will have. Their ill-gotten gains have been cemented in the blood of many a good man before now, & many another good man will go down before their rapacity. Blood is nothing to them, so it is the blood of other men, & so long as they can sit in the seat of power, & pocket the money that ought to go to the Indian. They care not a fig for war & rapine – for ravished women & depopulated settlements. They go to church regularly, are immaculate in dress, & conversation, & with the mass are 'honorable men' – That such a country should be ruled by such men, is enough to shake our faith in republican institutions, in human nature, & almost in God himself–"[90] Having delivered himself of the philippic, only the latter portion of which appears here, he condensed it into a single paragraph under the heading "Item for my Book – Conclusion on Indians."[91]

The condensed passage did not make its way into Dodge's already completed chapters on the Plains Indians, but drafting it turned his attention to resuming work on the book manuscript. The intense pressure of his activity in recent weeks had left him no time or energy for composition, beyond writing his journal entries. He hoped soon to take up the book project and begin a third section, which would deal with hunting. Certainly his experiences in the Black Hills thus far merited mention at some point in the work, possibly in the section on topography. In an undated note he enjoined himself to "develop the ideas" that the hills could be likened to an oasis in the desert: "Approaches through alkaline deserts, sage brush – horrible water. Describe Hills – if possible."[92]

The same mail that brought newspaper reports of events elsewhere also brought the rumor that Indians were in the Black Hills, their intentions not known. Dodge reacted to this apocryphal report with prudent caution, issuing an order for increased vigilance over the stock herd and distributing a circular on the subject to the officers who rotated as officers of the day. He reminded the entire command "that the only danger to be apprehended is the loss of our animals, that for a stampede two or three Indians are as effective as a hundred and that our only security from loss is untiring watchfulness while the animals are out grazing."[93] Privately he wrote in his journal that if a general conflict with Indians should break out this summer and fall, he had no objection. "It had just as well come now, & as far as I am concerned, it is the very best time. I have a good command, & unless Mr. Lo is too smart for me & gets my stock, I am in a fine condition for whatever may transpire."[94]

A few weeks later the failure of a mail party to reach the command on schedule gave Dodge some concern. A pencilled note from his topographical officer, Second Lieutenant James E. H. Foster, Third Cavalry, informed him that signs of Indians were everywhere in the vicinity he was then surveying, and that the prairie all along the Cheyenne River to the south had been set afire. Miners voiced a rumor that General Crook had ordered all the Cheyenne Indians out of his department and had directed troops to kill them wherever found.[95] But, as in this latter instance, information received at Camp Harney was spotty, delayed, and often unreliable.

On July 10 Dodge sent out another valuable officer, Captain Gerald Russell, Third Cavalry, with his company to bring in the missing mail party and find out what he could of the rumored Indian trouble. Six days later Russell returned with the mail but with no more information about the Indians. None were seen in the vicinity of Camp Harney until July 18, when two were reported sitting near a miner, watching him pan gold. Dodge went over to investigate and found them very civil, even though conversation was not possible in the absence of an interpreter. He noted that they seemed to be members of a party that included whites and persons of mixed race. They were "just harmless enough," he decided, "to bear watching all the time."[96]

Authorship, Amusements, and an Indian Council

When Dodge resumed work on his book manuscript, he found it "terribly hard to get started again."[97] His mental energy was depleted, and the free-flowing compositional mode eluded him. When on his third attempt he managed to write a few pages, he was encouraged. "The buffalo is my subject now," he wrote, "& anyone ought to make that interesting at least to sportsmen."[98] A reduced level of physical activity and perhaps also the reading of old favorites, including novels by Charles Dickens and Captain Frederick Marryat's *Mister Midshipman Easy*, stimulated his creative powers. He spent the entire evening of June 26 "story telling" at the campfire of Assistant Surgeon George P. Jaquette, and one week later he completed a lengthy chapter on the buffalo.[99] He read parts of it to MacMillan of the *Chicago Inter-Ocean* and to Captain Samuel Munson, Ninth Infantry, and both were complimentary. MacMillan asked permission to copy the text for printing in his newspaper as an extract "from a forthcoming work by Col Dodge." The author was glad to comply, for as he wrote in his journal, "I can take no harm from having a little eulogium & puffing in advance."[100] He now began a chapter on wild cattle that drew upon his experiences in Texas, and thereafter he made steady progress on the section devoted to game animals. In each chapter, he described the habitat, behavior, and best methods for bagging a particular species. He completed the chapter on wild cattle on July 8, the chapter on elk on July 13, and so on through the summer, occasionally returning to a completed discussion to add an anecdote or two. Encouraged by Burt, on July 22 he read him a few passages. Burt admitted that he envied him the profit he would earn from the published book, but even more the mere authorship of it.[101]

Periods of leisure at Camp Harney, while Jenney and his men were at work in the field, enabled Dodge to pursue his book project and also to pass the time pleasantly in other ways. Shortly after arriving at the camp, he rode twenty miles to the south

"Saw Teeth" of granite, near Harney Peak. Reprinted from Newton and Jenney, *Report on the Geology and Resources of the Black Hills of Dakota* (1880).

and west, in company with two young officers and old Colonel Bullock, who had accompanied the expedition as the guest of Captain Spaulding.[102] On the following day he joined a small party on an excursion to scale Harney Peak. Davenport and First Lieutenant Foote reached the tip of the crag, but Dodge "got high enough & quit" about three hundred feet below them. Three weeks later he accompanied another group of climbers and this time completed the ascent. However, on reaching the highest point he was disgusted to see before him another, higher peak that was "undoubtedly the true *Harney*."[103] As a result of climbs like these, the names Dodge's Peak and Fred's Peak were assigned to bare-granite spires in the vicinity of Camp Harney. On July 19, the day after he had climbed Fred's Peak, Dodge recalled the elation he had felt. "There is something fascinating," he wrote, "in the idea that one steps where no foot of white man ever trod before." The journal statement virtually duplicated one he had written at Omaha in his chapter celebrating the unspoiled plains environment.[104]

Young Fred Dodge, a city boy, was adapting to a new mode of life. Dodge attributed his son's timidity to an upbringing by women but found that he showed some promise of developing into an outdoorsman like his father. On the challenging journey from Camp Jenney, Fred's ability to ride a horse had improved markedly. Dodge now gave him a shooting lesson, directing him to fire eight rifle shots at as many pieces of paper set thirty yards away. Fred was nervous with the gun, but to his father's satisfaction he hit all the marks. At once the boy began to talk of going squirrel hunting, and the next day, out on his own, he shot his first birds. Dodge calculated that if Fred killed one or two squirrels within the next week he would henceforth be a sportsman.[105]

H. "Deacon" Willard, an employee of the sutler at Fort Laramie, dispensed miscellaneous goods from a wagon that had accompanied the command, traveling just in front of the rear guard. His exchange rate to miners who offered gold as payment was eighteen dollars per ounce.[106] Incidents of drunkenness among soldiers who patronized the sutler's wagon were few, owing to the high prices charged by Willard and also to Dodge's requirement that whisky be sold to the military by the glass only. Horace P. Tuttle, the astronomer, was of course free to purchase whatever quantity he wished, and did so, celebrating his arrival at Camp Harney by a monumental drunk. One or two days later Dodge remarked that Tuttle was suffering "an attack of the Jimjams & is as invisible as Venus"—a reference to the scientist's as yet unsuccessful efforts to deduce the exact position of elevated points by occultations on certain heavenly bodies.[107]

A form of mental aberration even more potent than inebriation by alcohol prevailed among many persons in the vicinity. This was gold fever, a malady virulent even among members of the Black Hills Expedition. James, Dodge's "no-account" manservant, decided to try his fortune as a miner and asked for a settlement of the wages due him.[108] Burt, a versatile man who loved to throw his energy into some new project, commenced a mining operation downstream on French Creek. He built a dam, causing the backwater to flow over a spring that Dodge's headquarters was then using and also spoiling the conditions for all those at work downstream from him. Dodge ordered him to cease his operations forthwith, but when a few days later Jenney decided to make more use of army assistance, Burt was "wild" to go with him. Between attending to his regular duties, writing newspaper articles, playing prospector, and looking after his eleven-year-old son, Burt was a busy man.

Dodge's dislike of him had abated considerably, but he still thought him "a very Singular animal."[109]

Dodge maintained good relations with the citizen miners, whose number he estimated at five or six hundred. Harrison, his former acquaintance at Fort Larned, was doing reasonably well; he and his comrades had put in a sluice box and were averaging about thirty dollars apiece in gold per day. Another man, Trainor, worked with only a cradle at what he declared was the best claim on French Creek; he was averaging ten cents to the pan.[110] But other prospectors had left the creek in search of richer diggings, and still others were leaving the hills altogether. Gold was here, but whether it existed in quantities that justified the trouble and expense of mining was not yet clear. Jenney inclined to believe it did not. In a letter of July 31 to Commissioner Smith, he amended the usual interpretation of Custer's declaration one year before: "It is truly said of this region that there was gold in the very roots of the grass; but it is not the gold of the gravel bars or quartz ledges; not the gold of the miner or the geologist, but the future solid worth of the Black Hills is to be sought in the luxuriant growth of the grasses that everywhere spread over the beautiful country."[111] Notwithstanding this expert opinion, miners were everywhere. Dodge remarked that they seemed to have sprung up as from a seed sown by Cadmus.[112]

While amusing himself with Dodge's rifle on the first day of travel from Camp Jenney, James, the manservant, had broken the weapon's double hair trigger. Dodge feared that he would have to send the rifle back to Fort Laramie for repair, but fortunately Trout's blacksmith was able to perform the delicate task at Camp Harney. On July 6, even though "off in shooting for want of practice," Dodge bagged a white-tailed (or red) deer, his first in many years. Trout and he tested his suspicion that the rifle was shooting to the right, but they concluded that the sights were true; he was aiming a little too high. Within a few days he was satisfied that his skill as a marksman had returned to what it should be. A red squirrel showed itself high up in a pine tree and quickly paid the penalty.[113]

On July 2 Dodge wrote a second letter report to General Crook, describing in detail his observations and the activities of the scientists. He made no effort to interrelate the several developments that were centering upon the Black Hills—the Indians' anger and intransigence, the multiplication of miners, and the uncertainty as to the extent of the gold deposits. Rather, he sketched a pleasant picture of life at Camp Harney, with all eight companies gathered there. "The Com[man]d is in excellent health & fine condition," he wrote. "I have no trouble at all. Every one seems anxious to do his best when on duty, & the whole affair is so far a delightful pic nic (without the ladies)."[114]

On July 15 Newton and McGillycuddy returned to camp following a survey of country to the south. The topographer reported that his military counterpart, Second Lieutenant Morton, had prepared a good map of the country they had passed through, and the next day Dodge pronounced as more than acceptable another map, by Second Lieutenant Foster, of a scout he had just completed. This was encouraging, for Dodge had himself mapped the immediate vicinity.[115] Building on the preliminary work of Bourke, he and his two subalterns were on course to produce a visualization of the Black Hills topography that he thought would equal in merit any similar map extant.

After a full month at Camp Harney, the scientists' researches in that vicinity were complete, and the time was at hand to begin another cycle of investigation. Jenney had found gold along Rapid Creek, twenty-two miles north, and wished to explore that region further. Accordingly, on July 19 Dodge left camp with two companies of cavalry and the headquarters wagon, in search of a route that could take the rest of the command there. On the first day out he encountered California Joe, with whom he had earlier talked over the problem of moving wagons to Rapid and Spring creeks. Whatever his faults and eccentricities, Joe had a good eye for the lay of the land, and upon his indicating a wish to accompany the command, Dodge hired him as a guide and packer.[116] Miners were seen often that day, but Dodge was not much impressed by their industry. "Evidently the large mass of them are loafers at home – & came out here expecting to pick up gold without work – The usual picture is one man leisurely digging in a hole, while a dozen others are sitting around looking on, & commenting."[117]

On the afternoon of July 20 Dodge established a third permanent camp, Camp Crook, on Rapid Creek. Two days later he greeted a party of official visitors whose proximity he had been unaware of until almost the last moment. These were the Reverend Samuel D. Hinman, Abraham Comingo, and W. H. Ashby, members of a commission that had been appointed to negotiate for purchase of the Black Hills. Accompanying them were two other citizens, Dr. J. W. Daniels and John S. Collins, and twelve Sioux Indians. The group was en route to various Indian agencies to confer with bands that, it was hoped, would send representatives to a conference proposed for September.[118] Dodge was gracious to all his guests, but he was suspicious of Hinman, who had charge of the preliminary arrangements for the conference. At best, this advocate of the Sioux was a man who "has either lied most wofully, or been most wofully belied"; at worst, he was a friend of the Indian Ring, "one of those Preacher Scoundrels who cloak their stealings with their religion." Judging from Hinman's appearance, he inclined to the latter view, for the missionary's face was "secret and crafty – never looks square."

Red Dog, a member of the Sioux party, insisted on engaging Dodge in a formal talk. The latter had little confidence in speechmaking as a vehicle for genuine interchange of views with Indians, but he made the necessary preparations. It soon developed that Red Dog did have something definite to say, and to Dodge in particular. While at Washington, he stated at the council, he had been assured by the Great Father that white men would be kept out of the Black Hills until the country was properly purchased. He understood that the soldiers would guard the hills against intruders, yet he now saw miners and soldiers on good terms together. He demanded that Dodge remove the miners until it was determined whether this was to be white or Indian territory.

According to Dodge's detailed notes of the interview, he responded forthrightly, but not in a manner that gave satisfaction to Red Dog. "The white man's country surrounds the Black Hills on every side but one," Dodge began.

> Heretofore the posts of the soldiers have been located solely with a view to the citizens. There are only a few posts & the troops at these cannot prevent the miners from coming in. They sneak in through the mountains or by the valleys – & the soldiers however they may work, can only secure a portion of them. It is said that troops have within a few days been ordered from the posts to come into the Blk Hills, & take in all the miners that can be found. This is a matter for the chiefs above me –
>
> The U. S. wants to buy this country, but before doing so they want to see what kind of a country it is & whether it will do for homes for white men. They therefore have selected some good men who are to make a careful examination of the whole country. I am sent with my command to see that these men are not injured or molested by bad people either white or Red men. I cannot arrest miners, for I have no troops to spare to hunt them up, no rations to feed them when captured, and no companies to send into the posts with the arrested miners – I have not therefore, nor do I intend to arrest or interfere with the miners. I am here for a particular purpose – & shall not do anything to interfere with it.

This was a lucid statement of the case, but as Dodge later observed, "There were no violent demonstrations of applause when I got through."[119]

Shortly afterward the commissioners, their entourage, and their military escort left camp, taking with them Joe Merivale, whom they wished to employ as a guide and interpreter.[120] Later Dodge also dispensed with the services of James, whose gold fever had left him but who was "more than unusually worthless today (which is saying a great deal)." Then, after a thundershower, he went fishing with Trout, who was to leave for Camp Harney the next morning to bring up the rest of the command. Even though Trout did not comprehend "the delicacies of fishing," he landed nine, while Dodge caught thirty. That evening Dodge and Burt chatted far into the night. In a modest, miscellaneous way, it had been a successful day's activity.

While the rest of the command made its way to Camp Crook, Dodge took out his book manuscript and in a stint of about eight hours wrote twenty-one pages on the black-tailed deer. The text was "quite equal to my average" in quality, he thought, and as to quantity it was the best day's work he had ever done. Writing now with freedom, two days later he completed that chapter, removed two pages from the one on buffalo, and made those the germ of a chapter entitled "Game: How to Get It," which would begin the section on game animals. Pleased with his progress, on July 27 he noted that he had written 175 manuscript pages while in the Black Hills, about one third of them within the last week.[121] This success reconciled him to the interruption that would be caused by a development he had just learned of, a visit from General Crook.

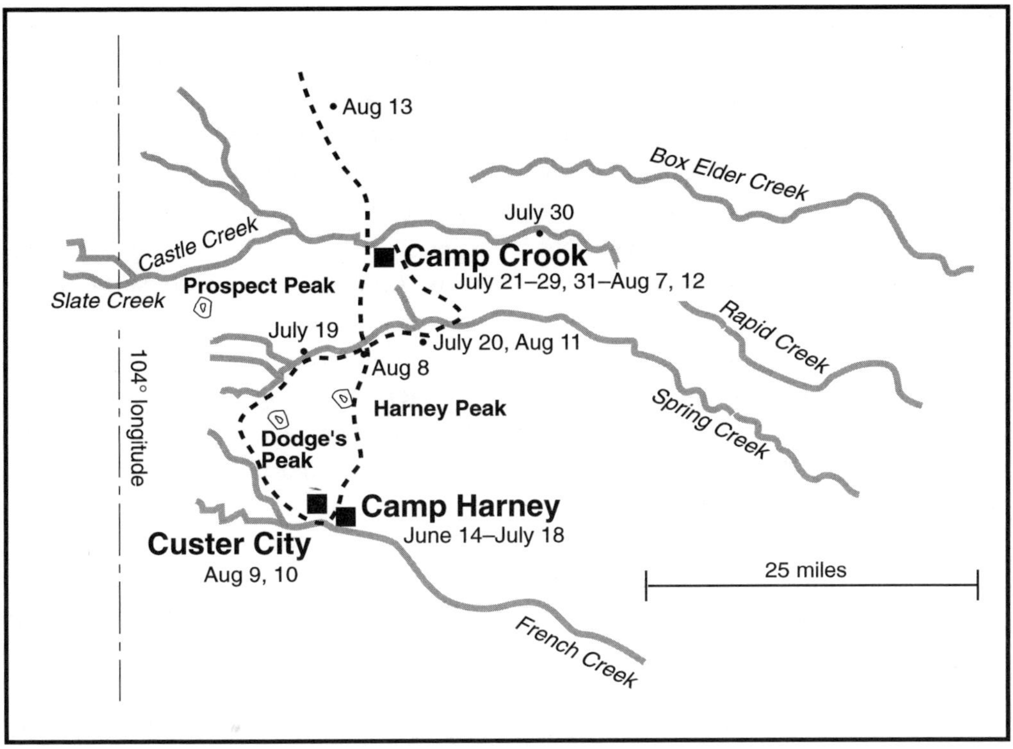

Itinerary, Camp Harney to Camp Crook, June 29–August 13, 1875

General Crook and the Miners

The department commander was due in camp shortly, accompanied by the paymaster and a group of friends. Crook had wished to assess for himself the military conditions prevailing in this contested territory, but he was now also on an additional errand. On direction from President Grant, he had been ordered to expel miners from the Black Hills and to arrest those who refused to go. The "chiefs above" Dodge were determined that the treaty obligations of the United States should be observed pending the outcome of the September negotiations.

Crook arrived on the afternoon of July 28, one day ahead of the paymaster and the citizens, whom he proposed to take out on a hunt. That night he brought Dodge up to date on his other plans. The order to remove the miners by August 15 was absolute, but he wished to obey it without working undue injury or even indignity to the men. He intended to issue a proclamation to all citizens then in the hills without authority, informing them of the order to depart but also recommending that on August 10 they assemble at the stockade adjacent to Camp Harney. There, he would suggest, they could pass whatever resolutions they thought necessary to secure to each man his rights of discovery and occupancy once the hills were opened.

To ensure compliance with the expulsion order, Crook had at first intended to establish a three-company post at the stockade under command of Captain Edwin

Pollock, Ninth Infantry, who had been recommended to him as an appropriate man for the position.[122] However, on the journey into the Black Hills he had seen enough of the blustering, self-important Pollock to realize that he was ill-suited for any duty that required diplomacy and tact. To mend matters somewhat, he was directing Pollock to obey orders from Dodge until August 10. He wished Dodge to attend the miners' meeting on that date, accompanied by whatever force he thought necessary, and speak a few words to the assembly.[123]

The day that followed this policy session was "very busy" for Lieutenant Colonel Dodge. The camp buzzed with activity, everyone impatient to pursue some project of his own. Meanwhile, just after breakfast Crook gave Dodge a pencil and paper and asked him to write out a proclamation to the miners. Working together they did so, and copies were made to ensure a wide distribution.[124] There was trouble about mess arrangements for the citizens, and one delay followed another until the hunting party set out at 1:00 P.M. toward a new, temporary camp. The task of determining a location for that camp fell to Dodge and required a ten-mile search that kept him from joining a brief hunt. However, his hours of intense activity ended on a pleasant note. Several deer were bagged, including one by the general; and after a fine dinner by candlelight, the party went to bed late.

The next morning Crook and his guests were off in several directions before Dodge woke up, for he was to move the camp again so that the general could give the visitors "a show." That day's bag was sixteen, Crook taking four deer and former major general William Sooy Smith one deer and one elk. Dodge's duties had again kept him from sharing the excitement, but on the third and final day of the hunt he was up at daylight. Moving through the same country some of the visitors had worked the day before, he shot and killed four deer, three bucks and a doe, the best result of the day. When Spaulding returned to camp having taken only one deer, Dodge rallied him about it, whereupon the captain challenged him to a contest of shooting at a mark. Spaulding was a good fellow and a good shot, but the result of this match was not what he expected. A distance of sixty yards was agreed upon, and as Dodge later wrote, "I walloped him."[125] Dr. Lane witnessed the contest and summarized it pleasantly in a letter to the *Chicago Tribune*. "Capt. Spaulding," he wrote, ". . . thought he would cool down his commanding officer a little; but after a good and fair trial, he now says that his own thermometrical conceit has fallen several degrees."[126]

General Crook wished to pass a few hours among the miners at Spring Creek on his way back to Fort Laramie, so on the morning of August 1 he left camp, escorted by Captain Mix and his company. While Dodge's men sought ways to rid themselves of the two-months' pay they had received from Major T. H. Stanton, the paymaster, he stayed close to camp, recovering from the consequences of his recent activity. He was ill for a day or two, but he broke the fever by dosing himself regularly with aconite.[127] While on the mend he added a few pages to the book manuscript.

The scientists were out exploring in various directions, but after a few more days of relative peace in camp they would return and it would be time for a move into the northernmost section of the hills and then over to their western edge. In preparation for that adventure in "hunting road," Dodge issued an order for Burt, with the two infantry companies and the artillery detail, to return with the wagon train to Fort Laramie and load a final shipment of supplies. In a variation of the arrangement for Burt's journey to the fort from Camp Jenney, Dodge designated a place of rendezvous, on September 2, between the returning infantry companies and a detachment of his own command. This was Indian Springs, near Floral Valley at the head of Beaver Creek.[128] How to transport his wagons to a point within convenient distance of the appointed place was a problem yet to be solved.

Dodge planned to depart for the miners' meeting at French Creek on August 8, accompanied by two companies of cavalry as a safeguard against trouble. Before he did so, however, he was called upon to quell a disturbance in his own camp. The source of difficulty was Professor Jenney, whose inattention to the needs of his men had caused them much inconvenience. After going forty hours without food, Tuttle was said to have refused to work any longer. McGillycuddy and Foster had lost their outfit and had to sleep without bedding on their way back to Camp Crook, and Newton was not to be found. According to Dodge, all the scientists were "mad as March hares at Jenney" and his "tom fool arrangements." He was himself aggrieved, for despite being aware of General Crook's proclamation, the geologist had hired "some of his special miner friends" as his employees, an obvious injustice to all the others. Dodge broke up this arrangement and, sensing a possible insurrection, sent Jenney a letter directing him to return to camp.

Having thus far managed Jenney by reasoning with him, offering him advice, and other indirect means, Dodge was now satisfied that to preserve the peace he must pre-empt some of the young man's authority and take over the management of the pack trains. Accordingly, "quietly & without flourish," on August 8 he assumed command of the entire outfit, assigning one train to Second Lieutenant Morton and the other to Second Lieutenant Foster. Naturally, he expected that Jenney would be miffed; however, when he ushered the geologist into his tent for a confidential review of the steps he had taken, he received a surprise. "Instead of a dignified protest, or a passionate tirade against my interference (one or other of which I entirely expected) he siezed my hand, thanked me for what I had done & said that he would rather I should direct, than direct himself."[129] Jenney was glad to set aside the duties he had failed to perform adequately and appreciated Dodge's offer to supply all the soldiers he needed in place of the miners he had hired. What Dodge had termed a "coup d etat" improved his relations with Jenney markedly, and moreover, it mollified the scientists. Jenney, assigned a sergeant and six privates as his personal escort, could now address himself to the scientific study he was best qualified to pursue.

On the afternoon of August 9 Dodge arrived at the stockade on French Creek, where the miners' meeting was to be held the next day. He learned that the place had been given a new name by the miners, and by majority vote. Those from southern states had favored "Stonewall," but they were outnumbered by northerners, who united on "Custer City." Many of the adventurers had already left the Black Hills, but as many as 250 were encamped here, intending to depart once the proceedings were over. Also on the scene were two other groups whom Dodge had not expected: several Brulé Sioux, accompanied by their agent, E. O. Howard, and a company of cavalry under command of Captain Frederick W. Benteen. Acting on orders from General Terry, Benteen had traveled 280 miles to this place from Fort Randall, on the Missouri River. Fortunately, he had chanced to meet General Crook and his party, for his instructions from Terry had been to arrest all the miners he found and bring them with him on his return to the post.

Agent Howard, with Spotted Tail and ten men of his band, were here to inspect the gold diggings and ensure that the interests of the Sioux were protected. In interviews with three newspaper correspondents, Spotted Tail insisted that his people should be paid for the gold that had already been removed by the miners.[130] "Old Spot" was an accomplished politician, accustomed to the ways of the white man, and he gave as good as he got. After witnessing a demonstration of mining methods that yielded no color of gold, he shrugged his shoulders and declared it a ruse, designed to persuade him that the hills contained less gold than they actually did.[131] On the night before Dodge's arrival he had addressed a meeting of miners, scolding them for trespassing in Indian country. When someone laughed at his demand for damages, he stood his ground, indifferent to the danger of standing before an unfriendly audience, many of whose members were armed. "White men laugh when I talk," he said; "if a squaw did that while a white man were talking in my camp she would be whipped."[132]

On August 10 the miner's meeting was convened in the open air at 10:00 A.M., with C. L. Craig in the chair. Dr. Lane thought this "one of the most striking scenes ever witnessed in the Western country": "There were 250 miners, in all imaginable costumes, all heavily bearded, with their bronzed faces set in a determined, self-reliant manner, and all heavily armed. They offered a striking contrast to the trimly built and well-dressed army officers mixed up with them, holding friendly conversation, and giving friendly advice; while Spotted Tail and his braves sat on their horses at the edge of the circle, with feathered heads, and well painted, looking over the throng, awaiting the result of their deliberation. On either side, the pine-clad hills made a dark relief against the high rocky wall beyond." Dodge spoke a few words at the morning session, which was devoted to the formal establishment of Custer City, distribution of town lots within it, and provision for its future government. Later in the day, resolutions of thanks were offered to General Crook, to Jenney, and last "to Col. R. Dodge and other officers of the Agency [*sic*], for their courteous and gentlemanly treatment of the miners of the Black Hills."[133] The adoption of this resolution sparked an outburst of genial enthusiasm, three hearty cheers for Dodge followed by three cheers and a "tiger" for Crook.

The general's endeavor to perform his duty in a humane manner had earned him the good will of the very men whom he ordered out of the hills. In his official report on the Black Hills Expedition, Dodge minimized his own contribution but characterized the miners' meeting as a "most interesting and instructive day, illustrating the power of words[.] By manifesting a kindly interest in the men, and by a few well chosen words, General Crook peacibly and at once, cleared the Hills of a body of men, the forcible removal of whom, would have caused much bitter feeling, propably [sic] some bloodshed and an immense sum of money."[134]

By late afternoon long lines of wagons crowded the trails south of the stockade. Agent Howard and his Indians had departed, and it remained for Dodge only to write out letters of instruction to Captain Pollock and his second-in-command, First Lieutenant Hall,[135] and return to Camp Crook.

A Route through the Mountains

The scientific examination of the southern and central Black Hills was now completed, and upon arriving back at camp, Dodge issued orders for part of his command to begin the move into new territory on the following day, August 13. The journey northward had a double purpose. First, a new camp must be established to serve as a base of operations for the scientists, who with their escorts had already departed in that direction. Second, a route to the west must be found to enable the command to keep the rendezvous with Burt at Indian Springs. Travel was facilitated for the first few miles by following the trail Custer forged as he exited the hills. However, on the second day out California Joe and Morton agreed that the only practicable route in the right general direction was "the crookedest thing on earth."[136] A still greater difficulty was clearing away fallen timber and felling trees to create a lane for the wagons. Here Trout and his twenty-man pioneer party worked every foot of the way. After progressing thirty-three miles in four days of hard travel, on August 16 Dodge stopped at a spot he named Camp Terry and sent Trout to bring forward the three companies that had remained at Camp Crook.

The movement from Camp Terry to the rendezvous point proved yet more challenging; indeed, it was the severest test in the entire expedition of Dodge's ability to "hunt road." Here he was without maps and prior trails and must rely on his compass, his developing sense of Black Hills topography, and persevering effort. What had been gentle declivities in the southern sections were now yawning, thousand-foot canyons. The divides separating these were steep, and the ridge that connected them all was not to be found. Trout and his men were exemplars of efficient effort, but on more than one day Dodge confessed himself foiled and returned with them to camp having made no real progress.[137] To complicate matters, Jenney and his men were at work in this same forbidding country, and sometimes they became stranded or got lost. The command was in a predicament, but no one seems to have doubted the eventual discovery of a way out of it. Dodge and other officers combined their search for a route west with outdoor sport, bagging black-tailed deer, elk, and antelope. In the evenings Dodge worked on his book, often introducing anecdotes of the day's adventures.

On August 22 a passage through the mountains was found at last, by California Joe. Once they had descended a deep canyon which they named Morton's, they had only to make their way up its length to come upon an elevated highland that offered free travel in several directions. "Our route today has been a marvel of engineering," Dodge wrote happily that night, "& Joe deserves great credit for working it out so well."[138] On the following day they reached the mouth of Floral Valley, which had burst into bloom, and August 24 brought them to Indian Springs well ahead of schedule. The water there being alkaline, Dodge decided to make camp in a region to the north that would give the Jenney party a fresh field for study. Thus, on the afternoon of August 25, twelve days after leaving Camp Crook and exactly three months after leaving Fort Laramie, he established Camp Bradley a few miles north of a mountain landmark named by the Indians Inyan Kara ("the peak that makes the mountain").

Although the passage through the mountains was generally acknowledged as the summer's premier feat of mountain travel, it also witnessed the expedition's most severe casualty. While supervising the clearing of a road through a dense pine forest, Trout was struck on the head, shoulder, and leg by a falling tree and knocked unconscious. Presently he revived, and the contusions to his head and body were judged not serious, but his leg was badly broken at the ankle. Placed in an ambulance, the injured man was driven back to camp for care by Dr. Jaquette. When Dodge arrived a short time afterward, he found Trout in good spirits, but the appearance of the mangled foot and leg sickened him and forced him to leave the hospital tent. His regret for the quartermaster-commissary was deep. "It seems selfish to think of my loss of him, when he has such loss himself," he wrote that night, "but I had rather lost any six of my Officers than him. . . . He is the best officer in his place I ever knew."[139]

Dr. Jaquette set Trout's leg and devised a box to minimize the effects of jolting as the ambulance moved through rugged country. Remarkably, Trout stood up well on the next day's travel, up Morton's Canyon, and remained cheerful. At Camp Bradley he expressed a wish to remain with the command, and after consultation with the physician, Dodge assented. He wrote to General Crook that the mountain air seemed to benefit Trout. "To a man of his disposition nothing would be so trying as inaction, & I think he has the best chance for a prompt recovery in the fine climate & occupation of mind that his daily duties give him."[140] By then Trout was up and about on crutches, hard at work. Happily for both men, Dodge and Trout would serve together for several years to come.

The same was true of another member of the Black Hills Expedition, Private Charles E. Cook, Dodge's orderly. At present Cook was assigned to Company I, Third Cavalry, but he could not do hard service on horseback, being "ruptured." As a result, in 1876 he would be transferred to the Twenty-third Infantry, Dodge's regiment, to resume his duties as orderly. Dodge appreciated Cook's faithful service and considered him "a character. . . . He has not the slightest idea of politeness – no bump of reverence – never thinks of saying 'Sir' to anybody. . . . But he is perfectly invaluable – a splendid hostler, a fair cook an eye like a hawk for game[,] is thoroughly honest – that is he would only steal for me, if I needed anything. He never forgets or loses anything – is always rough & always ready for anything."[141] Dodge's success as a field officer owed much to his capacity as a judge of men and his ability to earn their regard. His confidence in officers like Trout and soldiers like Cook inspired their loyalty. For the same reason, a few civilian employees followed him from assignment to assignment, obtaining what employment they could with the quartermaster's department.[142]

Upon his arrival at Camp Bradley, Dodge sent a wagon train back to Camp Terry to bring up the men and supplies that had been left there, and for the next few days he devoted himself to work on his book or else to hunting. August 27 being cold and rainy, he passed the day in an unusually productive stint of composition. At its end, he had written all he intended about the four-legged game animals of the plains, leaving only what he might add about game birds and fish. Two days later he added a few pages to the introductory chapter. He was not satisfied with its connection to what he had already written, but he consoled himself with the reflection that it was impossible to "do all artistically when am in camp."[143] When the weather permitted, he left his tent and rode out in search of the game animals themselves. He was delighted with his rifle, which had enabled him to make some remarkable shots. Recently he had bagged a handsome buck at 350 yards, sighting just as he would at one-tenth the distance. Foote, who was with him, confessed to a superstition about the gun. "I think if you only pull the trigger," he said, "it will kill the game whatever the distance & whether pointed at it or not."[144] Accompanied by Foote and Dr. Jaquette, on August 30 Dodge leapt from his horse and bagged another buck, which was running from him full speed at a distance of about 130 yards. All declared it a superior shot, and at the campfire that night Dodge added to the fun by boasting about his prowess. On the next day a package of mail included a letter from William Blackmore, dated at London and expressing an intention to arrive at Fort Laramie by August 20—already ten days past. Nevertheless, Dodge still hoped his friend would join him in a few days. "If so," he wrote, "I will take him back to Rapid [Creek], &"—imitating Blackmore's pronunciation—"have a *geloorious* hunt."[145]

At Camp Transfer—that is, Indian Springs, renamed for the transfer of supplies that would occur there—Burt and his infantry companies arrived exactly on schedule. Trout took to his crutches, hunched over to an ambulance, and had himself driven to the place, where he could take account of the incoming supplies. Shortly after Burt's arrival the two companies from Camp Terry made their appearance, and later, Foote and California Joe, who had been out on a survey—making the rendezvous a general reunion. Burt brought with him vegetables, dairy products, and delicacies, long untasted, that made supper that night something of a feast. "One does not know how he misses these things," Dodge observed, "until he gets them again

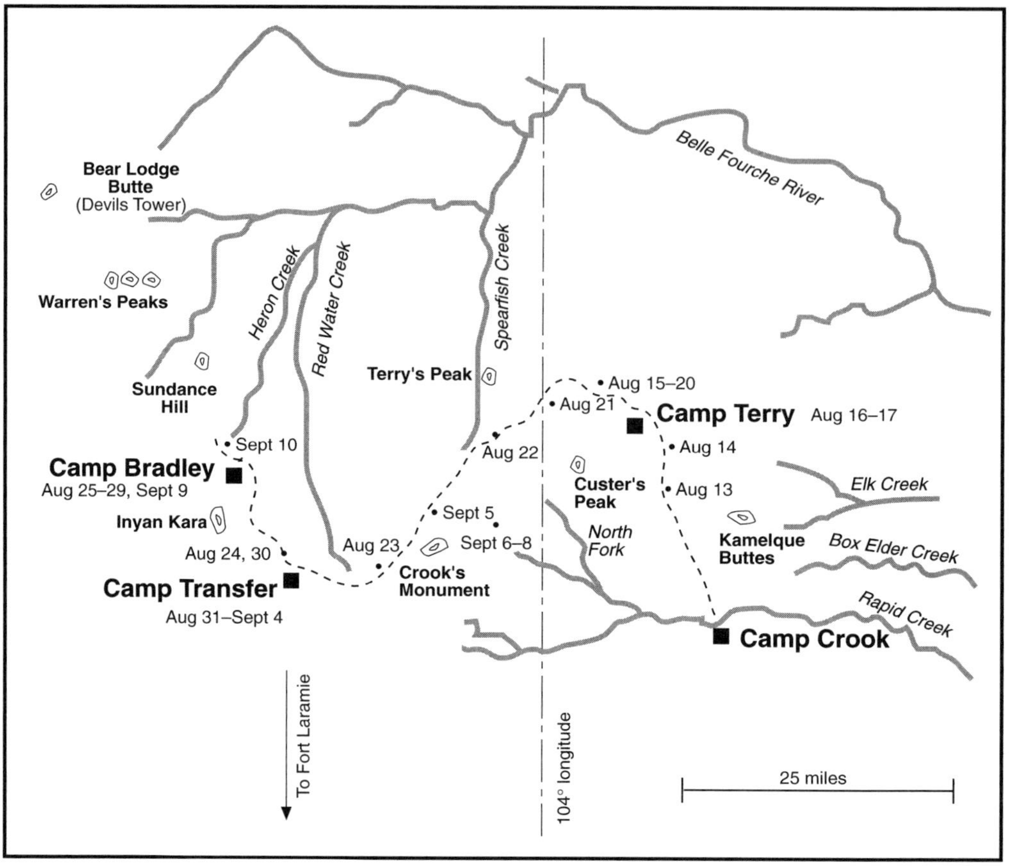

Itinerary, Camp Crook to Camp Bradley, August 13–September 10, 1875

after a deprivation."[146] Conversation at the campfire had a gala air, for by now the Black Hills Expedition had accomplished the greater part of its work.

The Return to Fort Laramie

From Camp Bradley the expedition would pass further north to the Belle Fourche of the Cheyenne River, follow that stream east, then turn southward to enable the scientists to explore the canyons on the eastern slope of the Black Hills. After passing through the weirdly eroded "Badlands" southeast of the hills, the company would obtain supplies at Camp Sheridan, adjacent to Spotted Tail Agency, then proceed south and west back to its starting point, rounding out an elongated loop. Much of this latter movement would be plains travel, less demanding than in recent weeks. The threat of assault or predation by Indians was no longer a major consideration, and members of the command anticipated a routine month's journey.

The future fate of the Black Hills continued to attract national attention, but the expedition under Jenney and Dodge was no longer its focus. The presence of gold on the Sioux Reservation being a confirmed fact, the questions now asked were what amount, if any, the Sioux would accept from the U.S. government in return for legal title to the Black Hills country, and how much the government was willing to pay. These were among the topics to be discussed at the forthcoming council near the Red Cloud Agency, adjacent to Camp Robinson, and naturally the civilian newspaper correspondents who had accompanied Dodge were determined to be there. On September 5 Davenport, MacMillan, and also Burt set out for the conference, the latter having obtained special permission from Dodge. The command was "nearly out of reporters," the latter noted.[147] On the same day he relieved the infantry companies from duty with the expedition and ordered them back to Fort Laramie under command of Captain Munson, carrying with them the artillery pieces and surplus ammunition.[148] Deacon Willard accompanied Munson, prompting another quip by Dodge, that the command was "so sober, he is nearly broke."[149] One company of cavalry had been sent back to help garrison Captain Pollock's camp on French Creek, so the command now included only five companies, all cavalry.

On September 10 the expedition moved through still mountainous country in quest of the Belle Fourche. Five days later, while following a stream that flowed in the proper direction but might not be the one they sought, individuals disputed its identity and at last placed bets on the matter. Second Lieutenant Foster, the topographical officer, was positive that the watercourse was not the Belle Fourche, but eventually he was proved wrong. An anonymous limerick memorialized his discomfiture:

> There was a young topog named Foster,
> Who found La Belle Fourche and then lost her
> Getting mad, bet his pile
> Which Sam took with a smile
> And scooped this young topog named Foster.[150]

When not out hunting road, Dodge amused himself with hunting game birds and writing about them back in camp. On September 28 he revised and rearranged the chapters he had written since July 4 and after eight hours of steady effort, declared himself satisfied with the result. The section on game included 340 manuscript pages; the entire three-part work, 1,100. "Of course I shall have to go over it all this winter at Omaha," he wrote, "revise correct punctuate & prepare it for the press."[151]

During this portion of the journey, two camps were established as bases for the scientists, Camp Raynolds and Camp Warren, both named after military explorers of the Black Hills. Near the latter of these places, California Joe happened onto the skeleton of a bull elk, with its humped shoulders, and seeking out Professor Jenney, played on his credulity. Joe identified the remains as those of a "camelk," which he explained had originated through crossbreeding between elk and camels brought into the territory by the War Department. No such importation had occurred, of course, but Joe managed to convince the young man of science that the Black Hills actually harbored such a curiosity.[152] The Kamelque Buttes, a geological formation near the scene of California Joe's discovery, took its name from this bit of mischief.

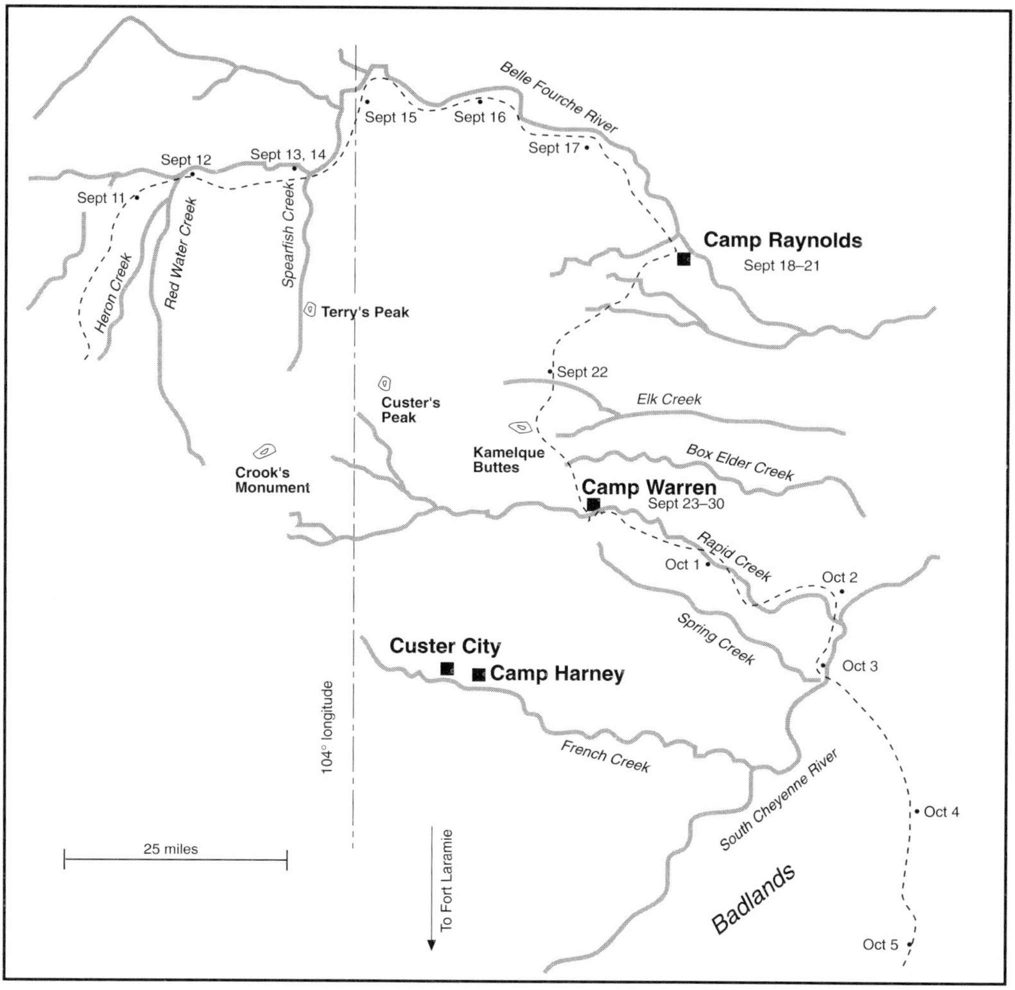

Itinerary, September 11–October 5, 1875

On September 27 Dodge ordered First Lieutenant John H. Coale, Second Cavalry, to proceed with his company from Camp Warren to Camp Sheridan, and on his arrival there to arrange for a wagon train to bring forage and incidental supplies back to the command.[153] Two days later the remaining companies broke camp and followed Coale's trail. On the afternoon of October 2 they fell in with Jenney and his men, who had completed their field work in the southeastern Black Hills. But to Dodge's surprise, a clash of wills ensued that threatened to sour the cordial relations he had managed to preserve with Jenney. The young scientist declared himself not yet ready to continue on toward Fort Laramie. His wish to remain out somewhat longer posed no serious problem in itself, but what complicated matters was his refusal to say how much more time he required or even what work he intended to perform. At Camp Warren Dodge had asked him to detail his plans, so as to make possible an appropriate requisition of supplies from Camp Sheridan, and at that time he had given no hint of this intention. His new project, whatever it was, placed the commander of his military escort in an awkward position. The Black Hills Expedition was rationed and supplied through October 15, which Dodge thought the probable date of its reaching Fort Laramie, but now Jenney was set on delaying progress for an undeterminable time.

Dodge suspected that the scientist's intention was to explore for fossil remains in the "bone fields" to the south, hoping to make some momentous discovery. Should he now remain in this vicinity as escort to Jenney, whose researches in the Black Hills were evidently complete, or should he continue on to Fort Laramie? The question of sufficient supplies was only part of the matter for debate. A rupture between him and the geologist would have political consequences, affecting relations between the War Department and the Indian Bureau at a time when harmony should be preserved if at all possible. That evening Dodge wrote out for review the options before him. He could refuse Jenney a military escort and pack mules, forcing him to abandon his plans, but that would produce ill feeling. Second, he could send in to Camp Sheridan for more supplies. However, he no longer had with him a wagon train, no provision had been made for supplying him further from that post, and Jenney still would not provide him the information he needed as the basis for a requisition. Third, he could leave Jenney with some men and supplies, allow him to go his way, and continue on with his own command. "This is really the only course that seems to be open to me," he decided. "I am truly sorry that this so harmonious & successful expedition, should have had this faux pas at the end of it – but it is not of my seeking or making. I am doing the best I can so far as my judgment goes, & if any mishap occurs I shall not be able to blame myself, tho' I may be blamed by others." Upon learning of Dodge's plan, Jenney left the campfire that night "very happy, – in avoiding explanation & getting rid of me."[154]

The two parties separated on the morning of October 3, Dodge moving due south toward Camp Sheridan while the scientists lingered somewhere behind. Arriving in the Badlands on the following day, the army companies examined thousands of fossils, many of which young Fred took with him as mementos of his summer adventure. Two days later the command was overtaken by Jenney, who had run out of rations and now announced himself "done." Good spirits prevailed in the reunited command, and Dodge was relieved that his course of action had proved "right tho' somewhat risky."[155] Indians returning to their home country from the now adjourned treaty council ruined the prospects for hunting, but the fishing was excellent on the White and Niobrara Rivers not far from Camp Sheridan. The command reached that post on October 7 and two days later passed Camp Robinson, forty miles west. "But how horribly monotonous these plains are," Dodge exclaimed while traveling from one to the other, "after the beauty & variety of the Hills." A temporary diversion as he passed the Red Cloud Agency was the sight, "picturesque in the extreme," of hundreds of Indians gathered there in all their finery on ration day.[156] Parting at Camp Robinson with Captain Gerald Russell, Third Cavalry, Dodge now had with him only three companies.[157]

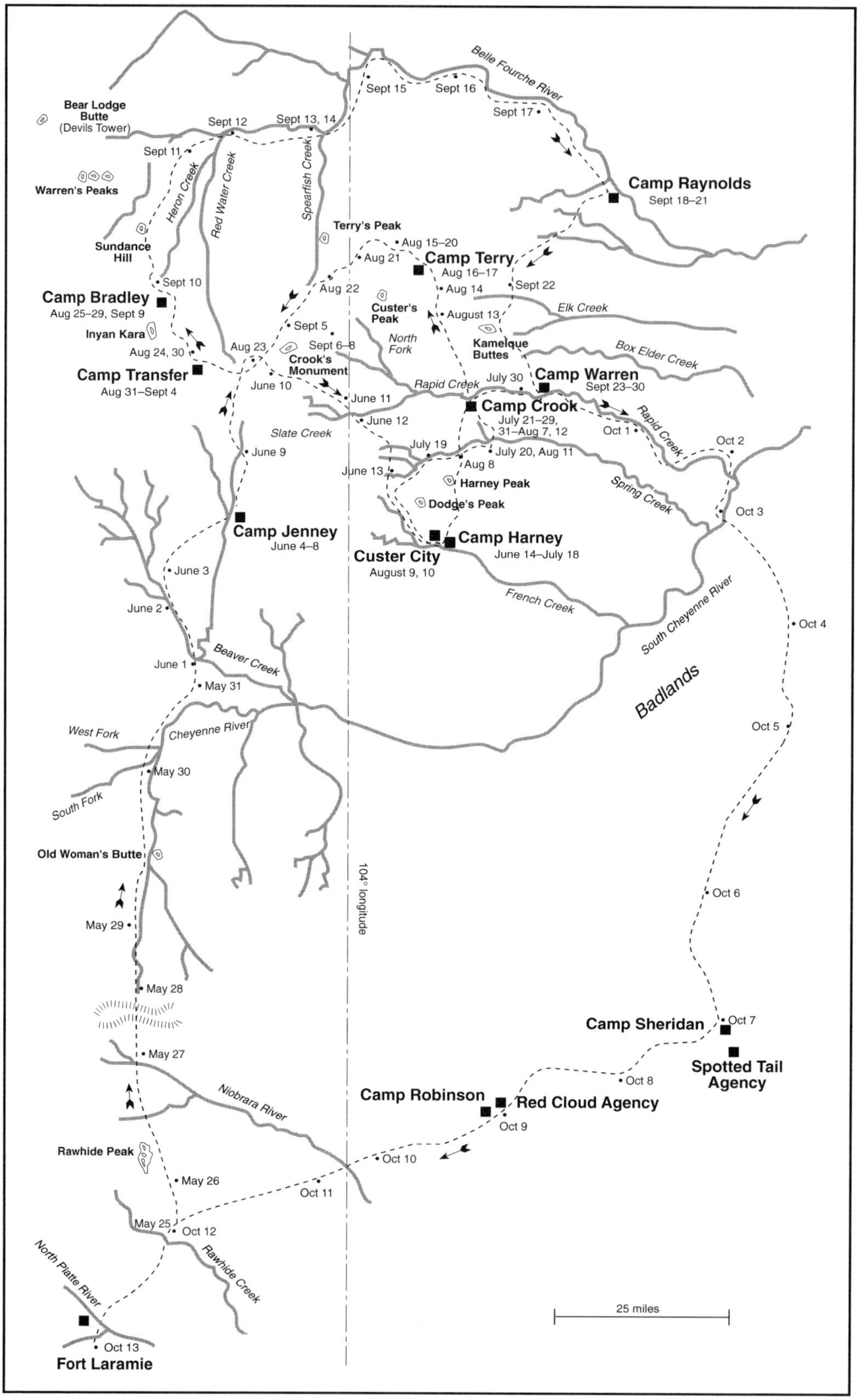

Itinerary, the Black Hills Expedition, 1875

On the morning of October 13 the command reached the point where it had crossed Rawhide Creek on its first day out from Fort Laramie. "What a long succession of pleasurable incidents & emotions in that 140 days!" Dodge exclaimed to himself.[158] Twelve miles after recrossing that stream, he reached the North Platte, crossed it, and went into camp on the west bank of the Laramie River about one-half mile below the post. After officially reporting his arrival to Lieutenant Colonel Bradley, he telegraphed messages to General Crook, returned to camp and read his mail, and relaxed, indifferent to the wind that blew all afternoon. He would not issue an order formally breaking up the command for two more days, but the summer's work was all but done, and well done. He ended his journal entry for this day with a declaration in miner's vernacular: "The Black Hills Expedition is Busted ——"[159]

Since May 25 the headquarters wagon had passed over 795 miles, Dodge's men had opened up more than 1,500 miles of wagon road, and the scientists and surveying parties had followed more than 6,000 miles of horse trail.[160] As the result of the geologists' exhaustive study, the physical structure of a region that had been all but unknown was now determined. Information was at hand to produce an excellent map of the Black Hills, which Dodge planned to prepare as part of his official report. What impact the map and report, and separately the reports of Jenney and his men,[161] might have on the course of continuing events was not his to say. As he had told the disgusted Red Dog at their impromptu conference in July, federal policy was for "the chiefs above him" to decide upon. The commission to treat with the Sioux for purchase of the Black Hills had been unsuccessful, for the Indians had made exorbitant demands and were unwilling to negotiate.[162] Captain Pollock and his men now occupied Camp Collins, in the heart of the Black Hills, but his force was inadequate to offer more than token resistance to incoming miners who were determined to take events into their own hands. Dodge's expedition had passed through the Hills without a single incident of violence, but the months of uninterrupted travel and study it had performed seemed in retrospect the calm before a storm.

Whatever the future might bring, Dodge had served ably as commander of the army escort to the Black Hills Geological Surveying Party. He had worked smoothly with his department commander, General Crook, and in five months of highly publicized field service had gained new prominence within the army and also outside it. From a personal point of view, the summer of 1875 was hardly less successful. Blackmore had not made his appearance to participate in the "*geloorious*" hunt in store for him, but young Fred had begun an outdoors relationship with his father that promised summer comradeship in years to come. Dodge had completed a draft of his book, hunted and fished amid magnificent scenery, and acquitted himself ably as a plainsman, mapmaker, administrator, diplomat, judge of men, rifle shot, raconteur, and all around good fellow. If the labors he and his men had performed were not exactly the "delightful pic nic" he described to General Crook, they warranted his later characterization of the Black Hills Expedition as comprising "the most delightful summer of my life."[163]

13

The Plains of North America and Their Inhabitants

On October 19, 1875, Dodge was met at Omaha by his regimental quartermaster, First Lieutenant William F. Rice, who accompanied him on the three-mile wagon ride to Omaha Barracks. Julia was in New York City, but Dodge's residence was spotless and ready for occupancy under the care of Joe and Laura, a married couple he employed as live-in domestic servants. The homecoming was, he wrote in the final entry of his Black Hills journals, "a splendid wind up to a splendid trip."[1] On the following day he assumed command of the regiment and post, Colonel Davis being on an extended leave of absence,[2] and for the rest of the year and throughout 1876 his energies were fully engaged by military duties, family responsibilities, and multiple projects of authorship.

Except one week in November when he attended court proceedings in Topeka, Kansas, through January Dodge remained at the post and, when possible, devoted himself to writing. The first of his undertakings was official—drafting a report on the Black Hills Expedition. This extended discussion, forwarded to the Adjutant General's Office on December 22, followed the approved pattern for such documents. It began by identifying the personnel who constituted his headquarters staff, the companies in his command, and the orders that had mandated the expedition. Next, it gave a day-to-day account of the command's progress into and through the Black Hills, with observations on conditions for travel, alternate routes, and noteworthy events, such as the fortuitous meeting between General Crook and Captain Benteen. In this section Dodge drew extensively from his field journals, and the same was true of the section that followed, a series of ten discussions under subject headings such as "Soil," "Climate," "Gold," and "Indians and the Indian Question." None of Dodge's reflections in his Black Hills journals on the character and motives of Walter P. Jenney were included in the official report. Rather, he paid tribute to "the tireless ardor and indefatigable perseverance of Mr Jenney and his small corps of most able assistants.

No mountain was too high or chasm too profound for their exploration." At the close of the 25,000-word report, he noted that a map of the Black Hills country would be forwarded as soon as possible.[3]

Dodge had informed General Crook of his wish to have the Black Hills map prepared under his own supervision rather than, as was customary, by personnel of the elite Engineers. "The Engineer Dept may make (or would if they knew of it) some objection to this," he admitted, "but as I am responsible I ought to have the making of my own maps."[4] Crook was amenable, and the three men who had served under Dodge as engineer and topographical officers were therefore assigned temporarily to duty at Omaha Barracks.[5] Additionally, a soldier from Captain Gerald Russell's Company K, Third Cavalry, Private William Schwerdtfeger, was transferred from Camp Robinson to assist in the work and draw the final version. After two months of painstaking labor, a map was completed that showed the routes followed, permanent camps, elevations, place names, and the topography of the Black Hills in rich detail. A recopied version, with notes designating sections of the plat for which each of Dodge's junior officers had served as primary authority, was completed by Private Schwerdtfeger and forwarded to departmental headquarters on February 17, 1876.[6] As Dodge had foreseen, the Engineer Bureau was not pleased to have been circumvented in this manner, but its staff found no fault with the product.[7] From Dodge's point of view, the mapmaking effort was an unqualified success.

Early in January he was granted a one-month leave of absence, with permission to apply twice for one-month extensions. On January 10, upon the return of Colonel Davis to Omaha Barracks, he left the post for New York City,[8] where he would see Julia and also consult with publishers about two book manuscripts he had in hand. The first of these was a spin-off from the just-completed report. Since public interest in the Black Hills still ran high and his association with the region was still known in some quarters, he hoped to capitalize by bringing out a slim volume entitled *The Black Hills. A Minute Description of the Routes, Scenery, Soil, Climate, Timber, Gold, Geology, Zoölogy, etc.* As the list of headings in the subtitle suggests, much of *The Black Hills* was little revised from what he had written for official purposes. He intimated as much in the preface, where he described the work as "thrown together in the intervals of public and private duties of much graver importance." Still, he added, "while asserting no claim to literary merit, it may be relied on as in strict and impartial accordance with facts."[9]

The text that followed omitted some material in the official report that was uniquely of interest to the army, such as a section on the best location for a future post in the Black Hills. On the other hand, it included new commentary on topics such as the character of the gold-bearing streams in the hills and the probable future use of the region. Dodge began his "Conclusion" by developing a stray thought in an undated journal entry: that the Black Hills was "a true oasis in a wide and dreary desert."[10] In the final lines of the book manuscript, he looked beyond the current rage for gold to a time when adventurous miners "will settle down into valuable citizens of a country destined in a few years to be an important and wealthy part of the great American Republic."[11]

During the summer Henry Newton, the assistant geologist, had agreed to supply Dodge a brief description of the hills' geological structure, with appropriate tables and sketches. These now formed part of the package Dodge offered for sale in New York City.[12] Additionally, he had with him photographic prints of scenes captured by Jenney's official photographer and one other item, perhaps the most valuable of them all—namely, a copy of the detailed map. It was an attractive gathering of material and was quickly snapped up on "very favorable terms"[13] by James Miller, a publisher of miscellaneous works who undertook to issue it without delay. Miller was as good as his word, for by early March *The Black Hills* was available for purchase, a handsomely lithographed copy of the map sewn into its endpapers as a foldout.[14] That Dodge was making private use of his official report, both text and map, was perhaps irregular, but it did not contravene the army's regulation against divulging material likely to be of strategic value.[15] The title page announced the work's authorship as "by Richard Irving Dodge, Lieut.-Colonel, U.S. Army."

Dodge's negotiations with James Miller were simplicity itself in comparison to the discussions with publishers that now began in regard to his more substantial book manuscript, which he had given a rough title, "The Plains." While at Omaha he had reviewed and revised the three-part manuscript, and he now had with him two identically paged copies.[16] What he did not possess was sufficient knowledge of the book trade to enable him confidently to make financial arrangements, in New York and possibly also in London, that would yield him the greatest possible return. He needed expert guidance, and the man to provide it was William Blackmore, if only he could be reached. Dodge had written asking his assistance in November and again early in January, but as yet he had received no reply. On January 20, now with some urgency, he wrote once more.

He would have no difficulty publishing the work in New York City, he reported, but friends had urged him to secure British copyright, and British royalties, by getting it out first in England. These same advisers informed him, accurately, that since he was not himself a British subject, he was powerless to obtain a copyright even if he traveled to London for that specific purpose. However, if the work was edited by a Briton, such as Blackmore, who publicly declared his role in the production, the legal protection was assured.[17] Reminding him of his earlier offer to edit the book, Dodge asked Blackmore's help.

As a related practical matter, he described certain publishing arrangements that had been urged on him. These were to have the stereotype plates for an English edition sent to the United States for reuse, or else to have the American edition printed at London and the sheets sent to New York to be folded, cut, and bound there. "I know nothing of these things," he confessed. "You are really the Father of the book, as it was only on your persistent demands that I ever commenced it, & if you are not too much occupied I wish you to Father it in England. It is dedicated to you." Dodge noted that the cooperation he had in mind might well prove impracticable for Blackmore, and should that prove the case he would place the work in the hands of a New York publisher at once. On the other hand, if Blackmore did feel able to take on the project, he would send him a copy of the manuscript without delay. "Of course all the details, in fact everything will be left to your judgement & friendship," he wrote.[18] Blackmore no doubt understood better than his American friend what "all the details" of the publication process would be. Even so, Dodge knew that he was asking a great deal. After two suspenseful weeks, a telegraphed response reached him on February 3: "Will edit book. Have arranged with publisher. Send manuscript. I write."[19] From this point the eventual publication of the book in both sides of the Atlantic was all but assured, for Dodge had a staunch friend in England.

Of course, Blackmore had reasons of his own for joining Dodge in the project of bookmaking. As editor he would share some of the credit for the work's success. His status as a knowledgeable commentator on the Indian and more generally the American West would benefit, and thereby his reputation as an agent for English investors in the region should be enhanced. Ultimately he would further some of his own interests, for his investments in Colorado and New Mexico required an infusion of funds. Yet Blackmore also had more generous motives. He liked Dodge, thought him talented, and was convinced that a market existed for the kind of book he could write. His willingness to oblige his American friend was actually not prudent in view of his already overcrowded schedule, but he at once began negotiations with publishers, and upon receiving a copy of the manuscript, he went through it for an initial review, pen in hand.

Meanwhile, Blackmore and Dodge exchanged ideas on several topics connected with the book's character, design, and prospects for sale. Fortunately for Dodge, his leave of absence was extended twice, giving him until April 10 to devote himself to matters that concerned him.[20] In addition to his forthcoming books, these concerns included making provision for his parents, who had returned to North Carolina following James Dodge's loss of employment at the custom house. Accidents of the Civil War had taken from them their family home along the Yadkin River, and they now resided in a nearby village with Dodge's sister, Annie, whose husband had died in the war.[21] Because both Annie and the elder Dodges were in reduced circumstances, "Rich" bore much of the financial burden of supporting them. As he explained to Blackmore, these responsibilities caused him to be "miserly just now." To conserve funds, he would bring Julia and Fred back to Omaha with him on the expiration of his leave.

Lest Blackmore should fear that he had "swallowed a hog" in agreeing to associate himself with a book he had not yet seen, in forwarding the manuscript, Dodge informed him that several publishers had reviewed the work and all were complimentary. Harper & Brothers were "enthusiastic," and G. P. Putnam's Sons declared the book "fresh," "important," and destined to become an "authority."[22] Reading through the manuscript, Blackmore formed an equally favorable opinion. He judged

This photograph of Dodge, over his signature from a letter to William Blackmore, served as frontispiece to *The Hunting Grounds of the Great West* (1876), the English edition of his book describing the plains and their inhabitants.

it "infinitely more interesting and . . . better written" than Lord Dunraven's *The Great Divide* (1876), whose success he had promoted by supplying photographs from his collection for use as illustrations. In his view, Dodge's book should rank in popularity with such classic treatments of its general subject as George Catlin's

Manners and Customs of the North American Indians (1841) and George Frederick Ruxton's *Adventures in Mexico and the Rocky Mountains* (1847).[23]

Acting on the suggestion that a duplicate copy of stereotype plates might be prepared in England and forwarded for use in printing the American edition, Blackmore negotiated on the author's behalf with two publishers—Sampson Low & Co., which had issued his own *Colorado: Its Resources, Parks, and Prospects* (1869), and Chatto & Windus, which had just published Lord Dunraven's book. Following a disagreement about terms with Sampson Low, he closed with Chatto & Windus, a house that regularly issued writings by American authors and was accustomed to helping coordinate more or less simultaneous editions in England and the United States.[24] Dodge had by this time selected G. P. Putnam's Sons as his American publisher, provided that the plates could be imported from England. The head of the firm, George Haven Putnam, visited London in June, and at that time a definitive understanding was worked out between him, Blackmore, and Chatto & Windus. The two publishers would share the cost of typesetting and preparing the illustrations; Dodge would pay through Putnam for a set of plates to be sent to New York as soon as possible; G. P. Putnam's Sons would pay Dodge a royalty of twenty percent on the price of each copy sold; and Chatto & Windus, five shillings.[25] Dodge was "much pleased" with the arrangement and expressed gratitude to Blackmore for the services he was rendering without direct financial benefit to himself.[26]

Blackmore had indeed been exerting himself generously and resourcefully throughout the spring, performing tasks crucial to the success of the book yet beyond the author's immediate ability to perform. At the time Dodge sent his manuscript to England, several basic questions remained unanswered. What would be the book's title? In what order should its three main sections be arranged? Should the three parts already written be issued as one volume or two? Should Dodge write out his proposed series of chapters on the army and on frontiersmen, to appear with the others? Clearly, most of these issues needed to be resolved before definite arrangements could be made and production begin. It was agreed that the two unwritten sections would needlessly complicate the situation and should be set aside for the time being, and Dodge repeatedly professed willingness to accept whatever determinations were made in regard to the other matters. Still, he found it impossible not to register his opinions on questions that remained undecided, so far as he knew. He offered suggestions, forwarded bits of text he had neglected to send earlier, and made available other material for Blackmore to use—or not—as he thought best.[27] One item he thought especially valuable was a printed map of the western states and territories that he had obtained from the Department of the Interior. Using pencil, he marked on this sheet the limits of the buffalo range as it existed in 1830 and, reduced in extent and divided into two, in 1876.[28]

Because Dodge believed the English reading public would be most interested in his section on game, he thought it best to place these chapters last. Blackmore agreed about the book's likely appeal to sportsmen, but he favored ending it with the lengthier section on Indians. Eventually Dodge came over to this view. Somewhat lengthier discussion was necessary to decide whether the work should be issued as one volume or two. Dodge was inclined to two volumes, and Chatto & Windus and Blackmore were in agreement that English readers would pay a high price for a two-volume edition brought out in a sumptuous format. On the other hand, the number of potential book buyers in England was relatively small in comparison with that in the United States, and George H. Putnam spoke up strongly for a single volume, reminding Dodge that American readers resisted high prices. On this matter Putnam's view carried the day.[29]

Curiously, the most vexing problem dealt with together by author, editor, and publishers was selecting a title. Dodge had written "The Plains" on the cover page of the manuscript, but soon after sending a copy to Blackmore, he informed him that something so "bare" and inexpressive now seemed inadequate. As an improvement he proposed "The Plains of North America," to be followed by a descriptive subtitle, but he urged his friend to respond with suggestions of his own. Three days later he offered another possibility, "The Great American Desert."[30] Blackmore, wishing to highlight the work's appeal to sportsmen yet also to emphasize the Indian component, suggested as a solution "The Happy Hunting Grounds of the Great West. Being a Description of the Plains, Game, and Indians of the Great North American Desert." But Dodge and Putnam agreed on this title's ludicrous unsuitability. The phrase "happy hunting grounds" would be misleading, referring as it did to the afterlife of Indians, whereas the manuscript portrayed their present state of existence. Putnam suggested simply dropping "Happy," but Dodge held that the result would be no improvement since the plains, the book's encompassing subject, were not in fact the finest "hunting grounds" of North America. Yet he still could not come up with a title he thought clearly superior. With rueful humor, he admitted that "I find it more difficult to name the baby than to get it."[31]

At last, just before returning to Omaha, Dodge hit upon the solution: "The Plains of North America and Their Inhabitants." Putnam concurred, and on April 13 the publisher wrote Blackmore to inform him of this determination.[32] But by that time the editor had worked out another title that satisfied him, and he elected to retain it. The English edition of the book would thus be issued as *The Hunting Grounds of the Great West: A Description of the Plains, Game, and Indians of the Great North American Desert*.

One other decision Blackmore made at about this time requires mention in light of later developments. Dodge suggested repeatedly that Blackmore consider whether to delete from the book five passages, totaling approximately 3,500 words, which it was feared might offend some readers. On February 15 the author wrote Blackmore that Harper & Brothers had judged as "too broad" certain statements "detailing the domestic affairs and treating of the general unchastity of the Indians." Dodge added, however, that he personally considered the material important and did not wish to sacrifice it unless absolutely necessary. "If not too broad for the English market," he wrote of the passages in question, "I can trust them here."[33] A month later he reported, more anxiously, that Putnam disagreed with him, considering the statements "too '*free*' for popular sale. The expressions are not criticised, but some of the ideas are." At the suggestion of the American publisher, he had relegated the possibly objectionable comments to an appendix in the New York manuscript copy.[34] A few weeks later he forwarded to Blackmore a list of the passages Putnam thought should be relocated. "If you think [these shiftings of material] desirable, you can adopt them (or not[)] as you think best," he wrote.[35] Alerted to the need for editorial tact, Blackmore marked the mooted discussions for placement in an appendix, but after further thought he elected not to be swayed by the apprehensions of the American publisher. He restored the passages to their original positions and added a few sentences, writing as if he were the author. While deploring, he wrote, the "sickening and horrible" subjects these paragraphs dealt with, he asserted their value "in the interest of truth" to account for the "antipathy" that existed between frontiersmen and Indians.[36]

Dodge remained unaware of the decisions Blackmore had made about the passages in question and also about the title of the book. Following his return to Omaha Barracks, he fell out of touch with both Blackmore and Putnam, but he was unconcerned, for he knew the work was in good hands. He assumed that it would be published in the fall, as planned, and that he and his English benefactor would enjoy a splendid celebratory hunt together at that time.[37] Meanwhile, he was optimistic about its reception, for the year's events were conspiring to make it timely. Early in August he wrote Blackmore that the "sad fate of Custer," who had lost his life in action on June 25, "and the splendid fighting of Sitting Bull will add a zest to my story of the Red Man, & ought wonderfully to increase the sale of it."[38]

Given the impossibility of close collaboration across the Atlantic, Dodge's ignorance of some decisions being made by Blackmore was inevitable, and if in some instances the Englishman took steps that ran counter to the author's preferences, that was part of the bargain. Blackmore had been sincere when he assured Dodge in April that "I will do more for you than I would for myself,"[39] and according to his lights he was shaping and polishing Dodge's rough-edged production in the best manner possible. Of course, some of his tastes differed materially from those of Dodge, and his editorial handling did result in many changes that the author would not have authorized had he been in a position to review them.

While reading through the manuscript for the first time, Blackmore marked places where illustrations could be introduced and also wrote marginal notes and queries about topics that interested him, either because he had information about them or because he wished to know more. He planned to place his personal imprint on the work by adding to it short notes and interpolations and also three extended passages—a general introduction and two chapters for the section on Indians, on sign language and Indian chronology. However, the small, blue-tinted manuscript pages left too little free space for his markings and would not be convenient for use by a printer. Accordingly, while he was negotiating with the London publishers, he directed his assistant to recopy the entire manuscript onto legal-size lined paper for further use.[40]

At this point Blackmore had already revised Dodge's text here and there, usually to clarify a meaning or "improve" minor points of style. For example, he preferred "whilst" to Dodge's "while," "plentiful" to Dodge's more colloquial "plenty."[41]

The labors of Blackmore's assistant, Andrew Chinn, also led to word changes at many points. Perhaps working under generalized directions from his employer, Chinn corrected misspellings and various slips but also made revisions, indulging his own tastes. For example, within a few lines Dodge's "facts" became "fact," "may be" became "may truly be," and "eager" became "ardent."[42] When Chinn saw no need for an entire sentence, he simply omitted it. Once, impatient with Dodge's predilection for the word "very," he inserted a sentence that included the locution "varies very," followed by a sentence with two more "very"s.[43] Blackmore's secretary thus interpreted his function as a copyist liberally, trimming and revising with a free hand.[44]

Following a review of the recopied manuscript by a copyeditor for Chatto & Windus, Blackmore responded to the copyeditor's queries, regrouped certain of Dodge's short chapters into longer ones, and made other revisions. Throughout, he rephrased Dodge's statements to bring them closer into line with his own British notions of proper literary usage. He still intended to draft an introduction and two supplementary chapters of his own, but for the present he confined himself to tinkering. At points where he wished to insert comments from personal knowledge, he added footnotes, some signed "W. B." and some not. Drawing upon memory and upon notes he had taken of Dodge's campfire stories, he added savory bits to these same tales in their written form.[45] In these ways he added an overlay of his own to the work.[46]

Dodge's inability to participate in the later stages of his book's production shielded him from the frustration felt by persons closer to the process as they encountered repeated delays. George H. Putnam had made clear to Blackmore that in order to reap the benefits of the fall book-buying season in the United States, the work would have to be stereotyped by August.[47] But the editor did not return the manuscript to Chatto & Windus for typesetting until early July, and even then it lacked the supplementary material he planned to write. Blackmore was busy marketing shares in his companies for the development of western lands in the United States; pressed for funds, he needed to attract new capital in order to stave off ruin. The financial stresses brought on him a physical breakdown so severe that for a time it was feared he might not live.[48] By mid-August he had recovered sufficiently to correct proofs, but he did not manage to submit copy for the introduction until October 5. The unwritten chapters had to be set aside, necessitating last-minute shiftings of text to fill in pages the typesetters had left blank. Correction of faulty illustrations occasioned further delay, and as a result *The Hunting Grounds of the Great West* was not published until November 23, 1876, months behind schedule.[49]

Eventually Dodge had some inkling of these difficulties through contact with George H. Putnam. On August 5, three days after he had written Blackmore urging him to cross the Atlantic for a hunt in the fall, the death at Omaha Barracks of his mother-in-law, Maria Paulding, brought on him a new family responsibility.[50] He had been named the executor of her will, and in order to transact business connected with the estate, his presence in New York City was imperative. He therefore appealed for some official arrangement that would enable him to perform these duties—assignment to a special board, a short leave of absence, whatever might be available. However, he was in command of the regiment and post at this time, and the army's active operations in the Department of the Platte made his presence at Omaha necessary until September 3, when he was granted a fifteen-day leave, subsequently extended for fifteen more days.[51] The return to New York allowed him to initiate legal proceedings in favor of Julia, her mother's chief heir, and, incidentally, to look in at G. P. Putnam's Sons.

By September 23 Putnam had received from England stereotype plates and proof sheets for about one-half the book, but he was powerless to move ahead because he lacked the printed table of contents, list of illustrations, and electrotype plates for the illustrations. All he could do was inform Chatto & Windus about the material he still required and consult with Dodge about possible adjustments to the material on hand. Glancing over the proofs, Dodge was not satisfied with Blackmore's title, and he and Putnam agreed that the English and American editions must be recognizable as the same book. They settled on *The Plains of the Great West and Their Inhabitants*, to be followed by a subtitle almost identical with Blackmore's.[52]

On November 1 Dodge forwarded to Putnam from Omaha Barracks a list of the persons to whom he wanted copies of *The Plains of the Great West* sent with his compliments.[53] Six weeks later, on December 11, he recorded in his journal that he had received two letters that day from Blackmore, "noble friend – who . . . tells me that [the book] is out . . . and that I will be proud of it."[54] Yet he did not see a copy of either the English or the American edition for almost two more months.

Had William Blackmore been able to oversee preparation of the English edition more closely, the coordination of effort between Chatto & Windus and G. P. Putnam's Sons would surely have been smoother. As it was, the working relationship could hardly have been less satisfactory, at least to Putnam. Hopeful of the book's popular appeal, he advertised it in *Publisher's Weekly* at the head of his fall list, designating an October publication date.[55] By the end of October he had in hand most of the material he required, but he still lacked plates for the table of contents and so was uncertain what was yet to come. As the fall publishing season ran its course, Putnam gamely purchased a full-page advertisement for *The Plains of the Great West and Their Inhabitants* in the "Christmas Number" of *Publisher's Weekly*, featuring it as the centerpiece of his holiday offerings.[56] Unfortunately, the final shipment of plates from England arrived so late that to print, bind, and distribute an American edition in time for the Christmas season was impossible. The book was offered for sale on January 10, 1877, at the beginning of the winter lull in the book trade and in the midst of a nationwide financial depression.[57]

Meanwhile, as Putnam watched the prospects for near-term sales success of *The Plains* fade away, in England William Blackmore had regained his vigor and was exerting himself to promote awareness of *The Hunting Grounds of the Great West*. The English edition was handsome, bound in rich red cloth and densely embellished with black tooling and gold foil on its covers and spine. The names "DODGE AND BLACKMORE" stood one above the other on the spine, imprinted in capital letters of equal height. On November 18 Dodge's collaborator began sending advance copies to persons he judged might have a particular interest in the book.[58] An inveterate accumulator of published clippings and a storer-away of personal papers on matters large and small, Blackmore kept a file of the acknowledgments from recipients of the complimentary volumes. Most were mere politeness, but a few included discerning observations that promised a favorable reception for the work. Dr. George H. Kingsley, who had accompanied the Earl of Dunraven on his visit to the Yellowstone region in 1874, pronounced it "the best [book] on the West which I have yet seen." Kingsley added that he had offered to review *Hunting Grounds* for the *Field*, a newspaper for country gentlemen, but presumed the task had already been assigned.[59] In fact, a few days earlier Blackmore had received a request for biographical information about Colonel Dodge from a reviewer for the *Field*, Francis Lawley, who declared *Hunting Grounds* "the best that I have read (& I think I have read everything on cognate subjects) since Ruxton's little volume." It was "much fuller and more graphic," Lawley went on, than recent books like Custer's *My Life on the Plains* and Dunraven's *The Great Divide*.[60]

Within days of its publication, *Hunting Grounds* began to be noticed in English newspapers and magazines,[61] and the reviews were solidly positive, even enthusiastic. One of the earliest, in the *Nonconformist* for November 29, proclaimed the book "one of the most able and most interesting works which has ever proceeded from an American pen." On December 23 the *Field* published the anonymous judgment of Lawley that Dodge's volume was without peer in its subject area. The *Saturday Review* characterized it on January 13 as "a most miscellaneous treasury of instruction and amusement." And the *Times* of London, which delayed its notice until April 9, estimated it as "by many degrees the best that we have met with" on its subject. From British publications little disposed to generosity in judging the productions of American talent, this was high praise.

Many of the reviewers of *Hunting Grounds* touched on the same few themes. Several gave prominence to their countryman William Blackmore, pointing out the roles he had played, first in encouraging Dodge to write the book and later as its editor. They dwelt uncritically upon his rambling and derivative introduction, expatiating on a topic only touched on there—the pronounced contrast between British success in keeping the peace with the Indian tribes of Canada and the U.S. government's failure to devise a workable approach of its own. In a representative statement, the *London Daily News* observed that the Americans "seem to have essayed every possible means of putting an end to the horrors of Indian warfare except the simple and obvious remedy commended by the practice and experience of their neighbours" to the north.

In their criticism of the U.S. government, the English reviewers never implicated Dodge himself, who as a working soldier bore no blame for policies beyond his control. Rather, as an American military man he received sympathetic, if mildly patronizing, treatment. And as author he won resounding praise for his book's authoritativeness, intrinsic interest, and literary merit. "From the swamps of the Mississippi to the cañons of the Rocky Mountains," marveled the *Pall Mall Gazette*, "he has been almost everywhere, seen almost everything, and killed every variety of game." Opinion was almost unanimous that Dodge's rare opportunities for observation had increased the value of his reportage. The fresh originality of his material was mentioned often, and the personal anecdotes he included were quoted at length. *Land and Water Illustrated*, a magazine for outdoorsmen, noted with approval the "sportsmanlike style" of these hunting stories, and *Nature* agreed, characterizing them as "told well in barrack-room fashion." The imperial *Times* of London commented graciously that despite the length of his book, "the author writes with so much animation that it is seldom indeed we tire of him."

Most English reviewers singled out the section on Indians as the most important in *Hunting Grounds*. They were impressed by the evidence Dodge provided against the conception of the Indian as noble savage. However, despite their confidence in his accuracy and their sense that what he had to say was significant, several commentators registered revulsion at the facts he made known. At issue here were the passages concerning sexual license and brutality that Blackmore had elected not to omit from the work or to place in an appendix. In a typical statement, the *Nonconformist* objected that the "picture is revolting to all our senses": "It is so because the author is unsparing in detail, giving information almost too disgusting to be given, and of a character which, in other works, is generally half concealed in classical language. So plain and unadorned, in fact, are some portions of the text, that few persons, notwithstanding the handsomeness of the book and its splendid illustrations, would care to leave it for general inspection on their drawing-room tables. It is not coarse, but it is not delicate. The author's justification, no doubt, would be that it could not be both delicate and truthful. We are sorry, for our human nature, to believe this to be the case." Reviewers like this one manifestly considered that Dodge, however well-meaning, was in poor taste. *Hunting Grounds* was therefore out of the question as a gift book, or for a general audience.

By early January the critical reaction to *Hunting Grounds* was well defined. Some arbiters of opinion had disliked the descriptions of Indian licentiousness, but overall the book was receiving a hearty welcome for its appearance, authoritativeness, originality, interest, and breezy felicity of style. Justly pleased, Blackmore wrote to George H. Putnam enclosing copies of reviews he had collected, together with three specially bound copies of the English edition to be forwarded to Colonel Dodge. He suggested that the next edition might be a less expensive abridged version, divested of the indelicate matter and otherwise adapted for popular sale. On January 31 Putnam replied, expressing interest in the idea but noting that orders for the initial

American edition were not yet brisk. He continued hopeful that the book "will come to be considered the authority on the subjects of which it treats, and will remain in permanent demand."[62]

Judging from reviews of *The Plains of the Great West and Their Inhabitants* that began to appear at this time, the long-suffering Putnam had reason for optimism.[63] The general assessments of the work in U.S. newspapers and magazines were even more positive than those registered by the British. The *Galaxy* praised it as "a rare combination of acute observation, long experience, and the spirit of good fellowship." The *Atlantic Monthly* recommended it as "an excellent book," one that "must long serve as the most trustworthy compendium of an evanescent phase of our nation's history." The *Eclectic Magazine* declared it the "most animated, most picturesque, and most vivid account of the physical structure, climate, inhabitants, and modes of life of the vast region lying between the Missouri and the Rocky Mountains that has yet been written."

American reviewers did approach some topics from points of view different from those of their English counterparts. Simmering resentment against the mother country was observable on occasion. The writer for the *Nation*, observing that *The Plains* gave evidence of having been printed in England, remarked snidely that its foreign origin "may explain numerous blunders in proper names but ought not to excuse certain other blunders in proofreading." American commentators did not ignore William Blackmore, but they paid him less attention than the British had. And besides reaching their own near-consensus as to the accuracy and authoritativeness of Dodge's book, several American writers pointed out its practical value not merely to sportsmen, as the English had done, but to what the *Army and Navy Journal* termed "the rough, untutored frontiersman" as well. Interestingly, the contrast between English relations with Indians in Canada and United States policy toward the native tribes often received comment. However, the emphasis was actually not comparative but self-critical, focused on the United States. In this light *Scribner's Monthly Magazine* acknowledged the service Dodge had performed in making known "the cruel wrongs that the Indians suffer . . . from a partly mistaken, partly corrupt policy of successive governments."

The opinions of American reviewers about the literary qualities of *The Plains* were virtually identical with those of the British about *Hunting Grounds*. The originality and lively energy of the book regularly compelled attention, its overlay of British usages going unmentioned. According to *Popular Science Monthly*, Dodge demonstrated "a happy faculty of seizing the most striking and significant features in description, and embodying them in vivid and forcible language." The straightforwardness and ease of his style received perhaps the highest praise. The *Atlantic Monthly* likened reading the book to hearing intelligent conversation, "the talk of a man who has a good deal to say and knows how to say it." The *Nation* found in the author's personal anecdotes "all the charm of oral narrative." The *New York Tribune* considered Dodge the possessor of a natural gift, "which though not betraying a high degree of literary training, is equal to the production of an exciting and effective narrative."

Most American reviewers commented favorably on the initial two sections of *The Plains*, but they were unanimous in judging the section on Indians the most significant. Almost all accepted without question Dodge's analysis of the Plains Indian's moral nature and approved his assertion that the threat of military force was the most effective means of keeping Indian savagery in check. The *New York Times* represented this predominating view, praising the book as "indispensable to a correct understanding of the Indian and the Indian problem." On the other hand, a few publications objected to Dodge's unconcealed disrespect for those whose view of the Indian was more benign than his and who therefore advocated a more pacific federal stance. Thus, *Harper's New Monthly Magazine* chided the author for his lack of "faith in humane and philanthropic influences." Such influences, the *Harper's* reviewer believed, were surely effective in bringing to bear "the real power of the higher motives on even the lowest nature."

As Dodge had foreseen, reviewers in the United States showed less distress at his account of the sexual brutalities perpetrated by Plains Indians than had the English. Several reviewers pointed out the novelty of Dodge's Indian material—according to the *Chicago Inter-Ocean*, it enabled readers "to know [the Indian] better than we have ever known him before"—but not one suggested that the statements about sexual license broke new ground. Among U.S. publications the *Galaxy* came closest to faulting the author for the unpleasantness of the information he recounted. Dodge had written with such plainness, its reviewer observed, that his book was likely to "be objected to in just those quarters where its revelations are most likely to do good."

Dodge did not see reviews of *The Plains* until some time after he reached Fort Riley, Kansas, following a winter campaign in Wyoming Territory under General Crook. On January 31, 1877, he received there a letter from Blackmore enclosing a selection of the English notices, and that same day he replied, declaring himself "greatly flattered & much better satisfied with my work than before I knew what 'other people' think."The *Nonconformist*'s elevation of *Hunting Grounds* to among the very finest American books had sent "a cold chill of gratified vanity" down his spine, he admitted. As to that journal's distaste for the commentary on Indian sexual behavior, he was unrepentant. After all, "readers want *facts*," and if the facts he had given were worth knowing, he was justified. He agreed with Blackmore that an abridged edition might easily be fashioned that, as he expressed it, "could be put in the hands of a young Lady, or made a holiday present to the boys."[64]

At the time he responded to Blackmore, Dodge had not yet seen *Hunting Grounds* but had just received a copy of *The Plains*. Three days later, having looked through the American edition, he wrote again with a personal reaction to the finished product. He was "more than delighted" at the appearance of the Putnam edition, in its sober green cloth. The printing was crisp and the illustrations fine, and if the text did include some errors, "principally verbal," such slips were inevitable since he had not been able to proofread. He now understood far better than a year before how heavy a burden he had placed upon Blackmore's time and energy. He could not find words, he wrote, to thank him for the "kindness & friendship" he had shown:

> But for your partiality & amiable bullying I should never have attempted to write – & your offer to edit the book for me, while it was scarce a germ of my brain . . . is something which I cannot yet understand. You did not know whether I could write or not, & I have often wondered that so astute a man as yourself should have allowed his friendship to get him into such a scrape as you would have been in, had my book been a foolish or stupid one –
>
> I assure you that your confidence in me has been the mainspring of my action – & in all my writing I have had you as my audience – (if I may so express it) constantly asking myself "how would Blackmore like that?" & it is one of the most delightful, of the many delightful emotions that come of success, that you like & approve my work.[65]

As a visible fruition of his comradeship with Blackmore and also as a work of generally acknowledged merit, the book was a triumph in Dodge's eyes no matter what royalties it might yield. That Blackmore had failed to write the additional chapters he had intended was unfortunate but not without remedy. "We must 'do' this," Dodge wrote, "for a future edition."[66]

Beyond question, *The Plains* did merit further attention, not only to correct the errors and infelicities it contained but also to build upon its manifest strengths. Dodge's ambitious experiment in authorship had proved a decided success. As the enthusiastic reviews attested, his contemporaries on both sides of the Atlantic regarded the book as superior to other titles in the field. "It would be hard to name a book, or collection of books," the *Atlantic Monthly* affirmed, "in which could be obtained anything like the light on the subject that is thrown by this modest volume."[67] Better than any other author of his time, Dodge satisfied his contemporaries' appetite for reliable information about the plains of North America. The *Eclectic Magazine* intended solid praise when it characterized *The Plains* as possessing "much of the value of evidence in a court of law."[68] The book was a clear, unpretending yet comprehensive arrangement of observations, anecdotes, and opinions about a region its author knew intimately. It was popular literature at its best—"a lively, entertaining, and withal a very instructive volume," as *Popular Science Monthly* described it.[69] *The Plains* was a work of precisely the sort that Thoreau wrote in *Walden* he required of every author: a "simple and sincere account" such as he "would send to his kindred from a distant land."[70]

14

The Powder River Expedition

In October 1876 Dodge traveled on court-martial duty to Fort Fetterman, on the North Platte River ninety-five miles northwest of Fort Laramie. Returning to Omaha Barracks, he encountered on the eastbound train two other army officers, Colonel Wesley Merritt, Fifth Cavalry, and Lieutenant Colonel William B. Royall, Third Cavalry. Both men had participated in General Crook's recently completed summer campaign against the Sioux and Northern Cheyennes. To his surprise, they informed him that in all probability he would be detailed to command the infantry in Crook's coming winter expedition, then being organized.[1] Other informed sources confirmed the rumor, leaving him both elated and anxious. The assignment would be a stroke of professional good fortune, but he still needed to transact business in New York City as executor of his mother-in-law's will. Arriving at Omaha, he at once telegraphed to Crook, then at Fort Laramie, explaining his predicament and requesting ten days' leave if indeed he was to go with the expedition. That afternoon the general replied through his senior aide-de-camp, Captain Nickerson. Command of the infantry and artillery battalions, numbering fifteen companies, was his if he wished it, but in that case the leave of absence would not be possible.[2] Confronted once more with a necessity to choose between his professional and private lives, he dispatched a message accepting the assignment and began making arrangements for a trip back to Fort Fetterman, the starting point of the Powder River Expedition.

Slow but Sure: Infantry against Indians

Dodge exulted that at last he was being offered a chance to demonstrate what he and his foot soldiers could accomplish in a major operation against Indians. As yet he had played no direct part in the Sioux War, which had broken out not many months after his return from the Black Hills Expedition. The stalemated efforts to induce the Sioux to give over a part of their reservation had led to an edict by the Indian Bureau that they must all report to their agencies by January 31, 1876. Most of them refused to do so, and as a result the army was authorized to compel them, and thus the conflict began.[3] On March 1, when General Crook led a 900-man expedition north from Fort Fetterman into the Bighorn country, Dodge was not available to participate, being then on leave. An engagement against a Cheyenne village on March 17, fought in hilly territory near the Wyoming-Montana border, was the decisive incident of that brief campaign. In Crook's view, decisions made on the field by Colonel Joseph J. Reynolds, Third Cavalry, squandered what advantage the troops had managed to gain over the Indians. Moreover, Reynolds ordered his men to burn food and supplies he had captured, denying Crook the use of them and thereby forfeiting the possibility of a lengthened campaign. Upon his return to Fort Fetterman, Crook filed charges against Reynolds and two other cavalry officers that eventually led to general court-martial proceedings.[4]

Later in the spring, as Crook prepared at Omaha for a second campaign, Dodge offered him his services. "Gen[era]l," he said, "I wish you would take me & 6 or 8 Co[mpanie]s of the Reg[imen]t with you," referring to the Twenty-third Infantry.

"Why what could I do with Infantry against Indians?" Crook asked.

"Everything that you can do with cavalry," Dodge replied, "except perhaps dash in & capture stock – but that inability will be more than compensated by the better & steadier fighting they will do."

Even though Crook was a career-long infantry officer, he did not take seriously this challenge to his settled opinion. He would take along a couple of infantry companies as an escort to the wagon train, he said, but he seemed to consider them of little value as combatants against Indians. Dodge stood his ground: "Well Gen[era]l, you will of course do as you please, but the very best campaigns against Indians, in this country, were made by Infantry. Let me have the management of the men for the first three weeks, & after that I will guaranté to march just as far & as long as the Cav[alr]y &"—indulging in a bit of hyperbole—"to run down the Indian stock, provided only that you keep me supplied with rations."[5]

Crook's second campaign, officially designated the Big Horn and Yellowstone Expedition, included fifteen companies of cavalry, under Lieutenant Colonel Royall, and five of infantry, under Major Alexander Chambers, Fourth Infantry. This force was intended to execute part of a three-pronged pincer movement authorized by General Sheridan to seek out and subjugate the hostile Indian bands.[6] Crook's was a substantial assemblage of military might, and moving northward from Fort Fetterman on May 29, it made an impressive show. However, amid the challenges and disappointments he encountered in the weeks that followed, he recalled more than once his conversation with Dodge. In the Battle of the Rosebud, waged on June 17 against 1,000 warriors of several tribes, the line of engagement stretched out almost five miles. The cavalry units could not maneuver well in the broken terrain and had difficulty communicating. Some of them narrowly averted disaster before two infantry companies arrived and enabled them to regroup and leave the field. That night Crook camped on the battlefield and claimed victory, but in fact he had been outmaneuvered. His opponents retreated to their village near the Little Bighorn River, where eight days later, a southbound command under Lieutenant Colonel Custer met its fate.[7]

To Crook's evident surprise, some time afterward Dodge asked him whether he had recalled their earlier conversation during the six-hour affair on the Rosebud. "Well Dodge," he laughed, "when my Cavalry got scattered all over creation, & I could not get it together, or to obey orders, I did wish for a few companies of the Old Reg[imen]t." Recalling this latest exchange, Dodge observed to himself that Crook had never abandoned his idea that the Battle of the Rosebud was lost through the poor performance of certain cavalry officers, "while I, though not there, know that it was lost for lack of Infantry."[8]

Early in August, after weeks of inaction as he awaited reinforcements and further orders, Crook moved down Rosebud Creek, uniting with forces under Brigadier General Terry on August 10. After marching together for two weeks, the commands separated, Terry and Colonel John Gibbon, Seventh Infantry, leaving the field and Crook moving east toward the Black Hills, where he believed warriors returning to their agencies posed a threat to the mining settlements.[9] The privations endured by his command in the three weeks that followed must have reminded Crook again of Dodge and his stoutly held views. He was low on rations, and his cavalry mounts were starving as they struggled through country made boggy by unseasonable rain. Horses had to be shot and butchered for food, earning for this desperate trek the name Horsemeat March. Good men grew so exhausted that, reduced to tears, they refused to move forward; they were carried on the few good mules until they had recovered sufficiently to resume the march on their own. Prior to reaching the village of Deadwood, Dakota Territory, on September 15, many of Crook's men were denouncing him among themselves for bringing on them this suffering.[10] But no one found fault with the hardened infantry soldiers in the column, who as Cuthbert Mills of the *New York Times* wrote, "walked down the cavalry." Mills continued, "I think there will be no more sneering at infantry in Indian campaigns, at least if they are like the infantry we have with us. They have won the admiration of every body, both in marching and fighting."[11]

The Walk-a-Heaps, as the Indians were said to call foot soldiers, were slow but sure, and the balance of preference between them and cavalry as the more effective opponents to Indians was shifting somewhat. Crook said nothing definite on the matter, but the infantry and artillery force that would come under Dodge's command in the next expedition was three times the size of the one under Chambers. On November 1 an anonymous correspondent of the *Philadelphia Press*, possibly First Lieutenant John G. Bourke, wrote from Fort Fetterman that in a skirmish with Indians "the foot-soldier with his long gun and no clumsy horse to bother with, is worth six cavalrymen."[12] Shortly after Dodge's arrival at the fort nine days later, he had a long talk with Crook one evening. "He is very liberal in his allowances," Dodge wrote in his journal, "& says laughingly that he wishes he had taken my advice last year as to his Indian campaigns."[13] The stage was set, it appeared, for him and his men to do something decisive and so end the debate.

In fact, however, Crook was only hedging his bets by including such a large contingent of foot troops in his late fall expedition. He did not intend to deviate materially from a strategy for operations against Indians that he had adopted while serving along the Pacific Coast in the 1850s and refined in Arizona.[14] Once again he would rely upon a well-conditioned wagon train, supplemented by pack mule transportation, as the guarantor of his force's maneuverability and range. Profiting from lessons learned in the summer, he had arranged for readier access to ampler supplies and was assembling a much larger complement of Indian scouts than before. The hardy foot troops would help prolong his presence in the field when winter struck, and in case of an engagement, they should be a steadying influence and a reliable reserve force. But his primary arm for attack would be cavalry. Under the command of Colonel Ranald S. Mackenzie, Fourth Cavalry,[15] a vigorous campaigner who had recently been transferred from Texas, that body would include eleven companies, six selected from the colonel's own regiment and the rest from units familiar with conditions in the Department of the Platte. What Crook hoped for most was the chance of a surprise raid against the enemy, preferably just at dawn.

The army's operations against Indians this year had been arduous, costly, and thus far at least, strategically inconclusive. Nevertheless, in a conference at Fort Laramie, Crook, Mackenzie, and Sheridan agreed that pressure ought to be kept up against the roving bands.[16] The effort might not succeed in crippling the fighting force of the Sioux and Cheyennes through direct engagement. Still, its unremitting presence in their hunting grounds ought to impose on them a sense of vulnerability. Eventually it should convince them that submission to federal authority and removal to a reservation was their wisest course. Shortly after this conference, Crook explained to a newspaper reporter another facet of his strategy: "The best time to strike Indians is in the winter. They cannot remain together in large bodies at that season. The necessities of subsistence compel them to separate, and then is the time to throw a large force on each band and crush them all in detail."[17] By his direction, the men of the Powder River Expedition were to be well protected against winter conditions. Sealskin caps, gloves, fur leggings, and felt boots were ready for issue,[18] and thanks to a steady flow of matériel into Cheyenne Depot, Medicine Bow, and other distribution points, Crook could anticipate a steady supply of rations, forage, and other necessities. The task of transporting these by wagon across the snow-covered country of northern Wyoming remained forbidding, however. To cite only one example, the horses and mules would require as much as 30,000 pounds of forage per day.[19] Cantonment Reno, approximately ninety miles north of Fort Fetterman, would serve as Crook's primary base for supply while in the field.

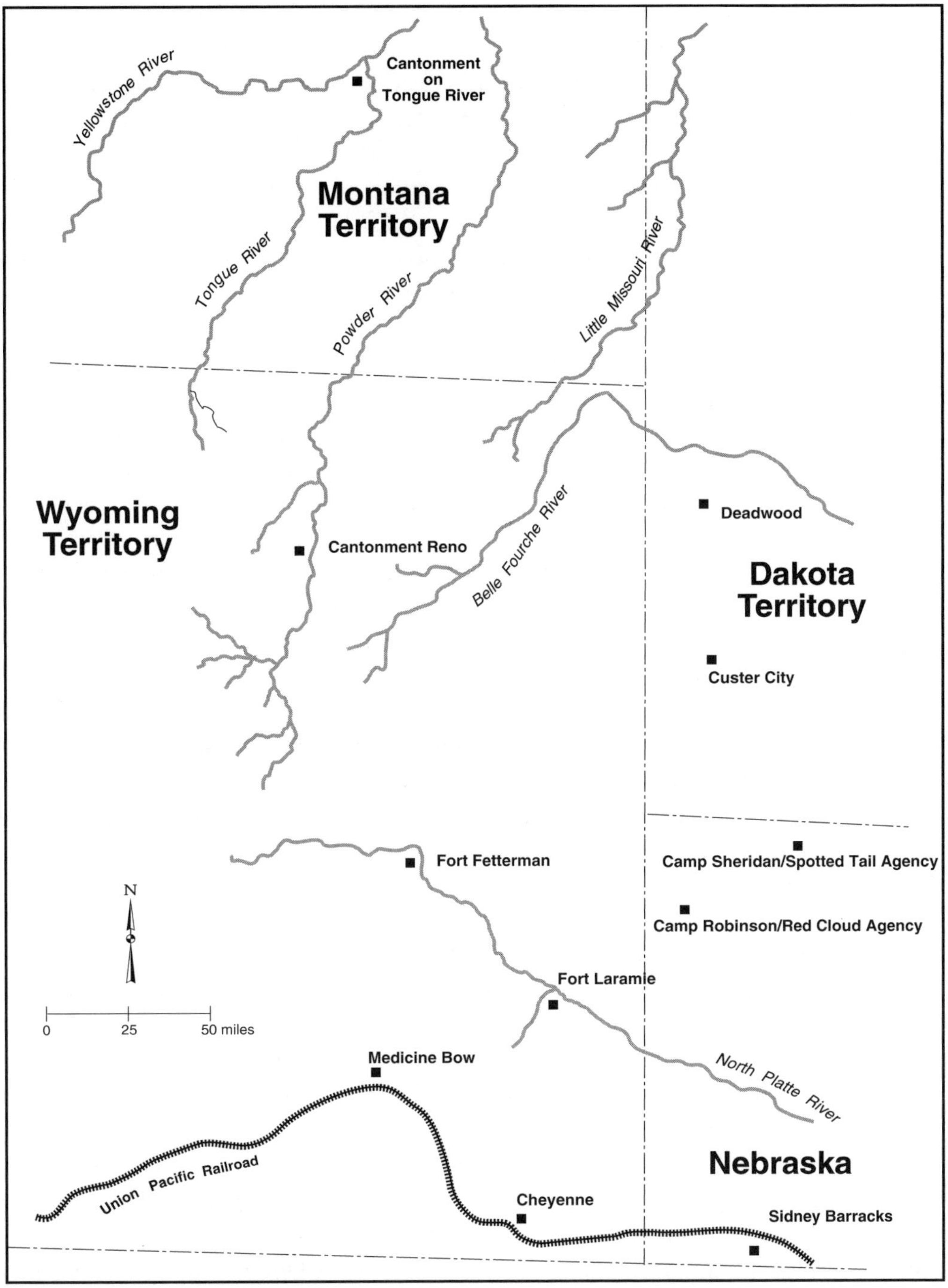

Region of projected military activity, fall 1876

General Sheridan again ordered a pincer-like movement to close in on the Indian antagonists from north and south, this time consisting of two commands rather than three. From the south, Crook would move along the Powder River toward the headwaters of the Little Missouri, where the Oglala Sioux chieftain Crazy Horse and his followers were expected to encamp for the winter. From the north, troops under the energetic Colonel Nelson A. Miles, Fifth Infantry, would conduct a search-and-destroy mission, using as their supply base a cantonment on the Yellowstone River near its confluence with the Tongue.[20] Miles and Crook both had pressing professional reasons to hope that the Indian scouts accompanying them would discover villages of the hostiles, making possible a major confrontation. Miles was in determined pursuit of a general's star, and Crook had yet to prove through results the wisdom of his being awarded one.

For himself, Dodge was proud of his plucky "Doboys" and also pleased that in the expedition's command structure he would be "playing Brig[adier] Gen[era]l"—that is, the companies under his authority would comprise two battalions, each with a commander. The role of brigadier under Crook, the field commander, certainly had its compensations, for Dodge would designate a headquarters staff of his own. But the arrangement sacrificed the direct mode of command he was accustomed to,[21] and unlike Mackenzie, who had been given independent authority over a portion of the wagon train, Dodge had not. For transportation of his men's supplies he would need to rely on the good offices of Crook's quartermaster, Captain John V. Furey. But at least Furey, a veteran of the Big Horn and Yellowstone campaign, was an experienced hand whose desire to satisfy him could be relied upon.

On November 14, the expedition headed north to Cantonment Reno. Stretching out for three miles across the valley of the icy cold North Platte, the Powder River Expedition was an impressive sight as it began its march. The largest military assemblage since the Civil War, it numbered more than 2,000 men, including some 300 civilian teamsters and packers, 818 cavalrymen, 679 foot soldiers, and 363 Indian auxiliaries—Pawnees, Sioux, Shoshones, Bannocks, Arapahos, and Cheyennes. Bourke, the adjutant of the expedition, declared the force the best equipped and best officered he had ever seen.[22] Dodge agreed, confiding to his journal that if Crook failed to accomplish something decisive with an outfit like this one, "he is a very unlucky, or incapable man."[23]

Dodge described the scene as "a beautiful and exhilerating sight." The road quickly grew muddy from the passage of so many men, animals, and wagons, but within the command spirits ran high. Three days later, marching into a windy snowstorm that blew hard, frozen pellets into the eyes, one of Dodge's men began singing the old war favorite, "Marching through Georgia." At once a chorus of other voices chimed in. Riding beside his men, Dodge was tempted to strike up the tune but restrained himself, having "no more voice than a crow, & moreover . . . the dignity of Acting Brigadier General to support." That night he expressed some of his lingering satisfaction in a journal entry. "It is a glorious life this soldiering," he wrote. "However

The Powder River Expedition crossing the North Platte River. Reprinted from *Harper's Weekly*, December 16, 1876, p. 1017.

great the trials discomforts or suffering[,] there is pluck endurance & patience to counterbalance all – We are going on a campaign fraught with not only the natural dangers from the enemy, but with a thousand unnamed dangers from the elements. Yet not a man flinches – not one but would rather suffer all than turn back."[24] Events in the weeks to come would test this upbeat assessment.

A source of interest to Dodge and other officers was the large body of Indian scouts. These were organized by tribe, each group under the authority of an army officer except the Pawnees, under Frank North, Dodge's comrade of a decade before. Riding past the Pawnees while on the march, Dodge several times noticed that they looked up at him intently and pleasantly.[25] He supposed they were simply showing deference to his rank, but on arrival on Cantonment Reno he learned the real reason. That night Crook organized a meeting of the Indians in which he urged them to set aside old enmities among themselves, accept his assurance of concern for their long-term welfare, and consider his advice to abandon their doomed way of life. He urged them to adopt a mode of living similar to the one followed by American citizens in rural areas, supporting themselves by farming and raising livestock. Next, representatives of the various tribes all made statements, and Dodge was delighted to find that a spokesman for the Pawnees was Frank White (Li-Heris-oo-La-Shar), his comrade in many a tight situation in 1867.[26] After the meeting Frank came over to Dodge's tent, and they had a talk about old times. Dodge learned that the Pawnee had told his fellow tribesmen all about their exploits together, and that the glances cast upon him by the Indians had signified friendly recognition.

Dodge was somewhat mystified by the power of persuasion Crook exerted over the Indians in the few words he spoke to them. As if indifferent to the traditional Indian emphasis on eloquence and a dignified demeanor, the general expressed himself in a low tone, with his eyes downcast and his hands in his pants pockets. It was "the worst manner I ever saw," Dodge wrote, "more like a schoolboy trying to fabricate an excuse for a delinquency than a general com[man]d[in]g an army." Yet Crook possessed remarkable influence over these people, beyond that of anyone Dodge had met. He attributed it to Crook's "most wonderful knowledge of Indian character."[27]

Early in the campaign Mackenzie and Dodge exchanged courtesies and established a friendly working relationship, and they were both bemused by the behavior of Crook, who did not act like a general. Noting that "I cant state what I see except in this private journal,"[28] Dodge began setting down his sometimes conflicting reactions to his commanding officer. For a time he was inclined to credit Reuben B. Davenport's slanderous characterization of Crook that had recently appeared in the *New York Herald*. In an article entitled "General Crook's Sham Simplicity of Life," Davenport alleged that Crook had played a double game on the Big Horn and Yellowstone Expedition, affecting a life of spartan self-denial when in public view but behaving quite differently when attended in private by his "familiars and toadies."[29] Dodge soon dismissed this notion, but the mere fact that he entertained it reveals the depth of his confusion.

Some of what he saw he could not approve. For example, the general was more attentive to locating good camping positions for the packers and the Indians than for the troops. Moreover, his preference for these favored populations was evidently social and well as military. "He scarcely treats McKenzie & I decently," Dodge complained to himself, "but he will spend hours chatting pleasantly with an Indian, or a dirty scout." He struggled to reconcile his reactions to the general. Crook was "warm-hearted," but he estimated men according to their potential usefulness to himself. He was ill-mannered, but possibly more through ignorance than intention.[30] As many officers had done before him, Dodge was finding Crook an enigma.[31]

At Cantonment Reno the expedition made ready for a movement further north, after which the troops would cut loose from the wagon train. On November 21 Dodge drilled his men the entire day. The next day, at the end of a twenty-eight-mile march to a camp on Crazy Woman Creek, he issued a circular directing each company commander to reduce his unit to thirty men, those most able to bear "the hardships of a pack mule campaign," leaving the rest in camp.[32] Crook intended to strike out in search of Crazy Horse, who was then believed near the site of the Rosebud battle. Ten days' rations were packed on the mules, one hundred rounds of ammunition were issued to each man, and all preparations for departure were complete when, at dawn on November 23, a new development abruptly changed the expedition's objective. Sitting Bear, a Cheyenne scout, brought into camp information that included two important points. First, Crazy Horse would soon be alerted to the existence and location of the command, and the hope of taking him by surprise must be abandoned. Second, a large village of Cheyennes was said to be encamped in the mountains to the southwest, near the sources of Crazy Woman Creek.[33]

This was exactly the kind of opportunity Crook had hoped for. He ordered Mackenzie to set out at once for the Cheyenne village and if possible attack it, taking with him all but one of the cavalry companies and almost all the Indian scouts. By noon Mackenzie had left camp with approximately 1,100 men, preceded by a cadre of scouts specially qualified for a reconnoitering mission in this rugged country. The striking force was expected to be gone five or six days, and in their absence the troops that remained would await further news, with possibly a call to join them. Crook had not yet abandoned his plan eventually to move north, but for the present the infantry and artillery battalions could expect no duty more daunting than a few additional hours of skirmish drill. Upon receiving Dodge's order to pitch their tents again, his men yelled with delight. His own thoughts were with the Mackenzie contingent. "I hope with all my heart they may be successful," he wrote that night.[34]

What proved the central incident of the Powder River Expedition began shortly after dawn on November 25, when Mackenzie raided the village of the Northern Cheyenne chief Dull Knife.[35] The encampment consisted of 173 lodges situated on either side of the Red Fork of the Powder River, which there passed through a rugged canyon lined by steep sandstone cliffs. In the first hours of the battle that ensued, Mackenzie captured more than seven hundred of the Indians' horses and forced the

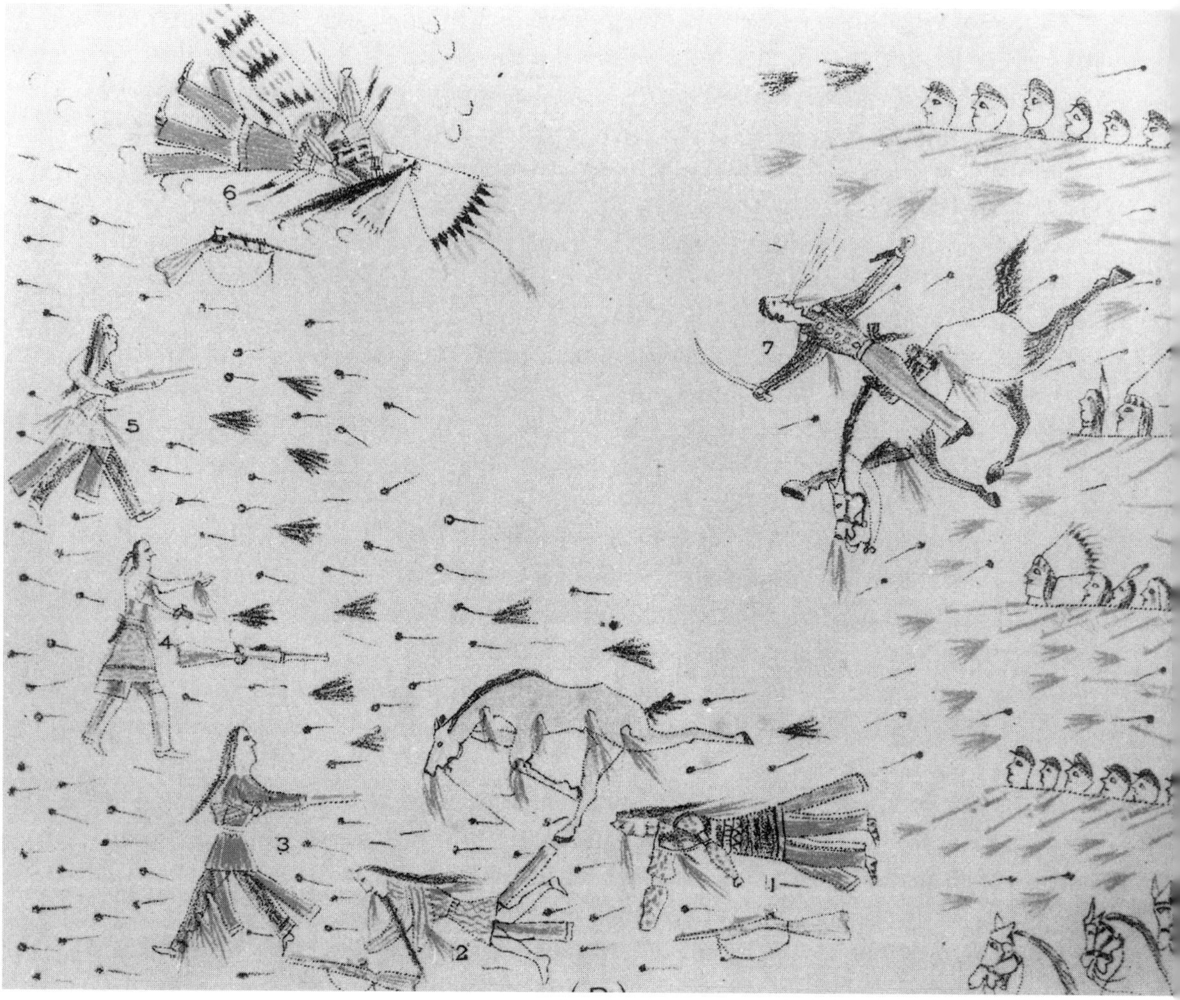

Sketch with colored pencils of the Dull Knife battle, by Big Back, a Northern Cheyennne Indian. "Only prominent chiefs who were killed at this fight are represented on the Indian side. . . . The names of the chiefs thus shown are: (1) High Bull; (2) Walking Calf; (3) Whirlwind; (4) White Face Bull; (5) Bull Hump; (6) Old Bull. The bullet passing through Lieut. McKinney's body (7) indicates the manner of his death." Reprinted from Dodge, *Our Wild Indians* (1882), p. 412.

250 fighting men of the village to take defensive positions in the outcroppings of the canyon. The Cheyennes had suffered severe casualties in the surprise attack, but they now set up a withering fire from their all-but-impregnable positions.[36] One officer and five enlisted men had been killed and twenty-six more soldiers wounded when Mackenzie dispatched runners to Crook, calling for reinforcement by the infantry. Meanwhile, he ravaged the abandoned village, burning the tipis and all they contained, including tons of food, a large store of military supplies, and almost all their occupants' personal possessions.[37]

Before dawn on November 26 General Crook entered Dodge's tent, bringing the news he had just received. Crook planned to depart at once, taking with him the one remaining company of cavalry and the rest of the Indians. Dodge and his men were to make their preparations and follow, reaching the battleground as quickly as they could. Allotted three wagon mules per company for blankets, and with each man carrying two days' rations and one hundred rounds of ammunition, the foot soldiers left camp at 11:40 A.M. If in truth one infantryman was worth six cavalry soldiers in a fight with Indians, an opportunity to drive home that point was almost at hand. In an army career that extended over twenty-eight years, Dodge had never come within such close reach of military glory, and he knew it. Three inches of snow had fallen the night before, but he and his men marched as they never had, covering twenty-five miles over treacherous terrain until, at about 11:00 P.M., they reached Crook and his headquarters guard bivouacked in a little valley. There, energized but exhausted, they spread out their blankets and buffalo skins for rest.

Dodge's account of the march, written while still in the field, conveys its challenges and its excitement:

> The men were in good spirits. For 18 miles they did well, but after that we struck the mountain, & came for 6 or 7 miles over one of the worst trails I ever saw – Up & down long & tremendously steep places – over rocks & through bogs – & all covered with snow. . . . Many men straggled, indeed it was simply impossible not to straggle. The trail was so narrow that the Com[man]d had to move in single file. Sometimes it ran diagonally around a steep slope, when if a man slipped, he was out of ranks at once, & had to get in where he could. In going down one almost precipice one fellow slipped fell on his bottom & gliding swiftly forward was set upon by at least thirty men. A whole Co[mpany] was down in an indiscriminate heap & the swearing was something terrific.
>
> We were blessed with about a ten days old moon – but its light was fitful in the extreme. Clouds were constantly passed over it, & always (it seemed) just when we were in the worst places. The scene was weird & picturesque in the extreme. Far as the eye could reach to the south & east & north only the unbroken snow, wreathed in all uncouth & fantastic shapes by the broken crags & yawning ravines it covered. To the west the huge pile of the Big Horn Mts, here bare & white, there black with its forests of pine. Bad as it all was, everybody (almost) was in good spirits. I felt first rate, & except that I had to walk down all the steep ravines (my horse being smooth shod) & lead my horse at the risk of having him slide on top of me, I got along first rate. I dont like walking at any time, & I took some promenades on that night that I shall remember all my life –[38]

Captain James (Teddy) Egan, Second Cavalry, who commanded the headquarters guard, assured Dodge afterward that the infantry in Crook's summer campaign never made a march that compared with what he and his men accomplished that night.[39] Filled with anticipation, Dodge fell into a "splendid sleep." At 3:00 A.M. he was awakened by snow falling on his face, but he pulled up the buffalo skin and dozed until dawn.

Following a breakfast of frozen bacon and bread made edible by toasting on hand-held sticks, Dodge's column moved down Willow Creek for two miles, crossed, and coming upon Mackenzie's trail, pushed ahead through a country of upturned ledges and little valleys that reminded him of the territory around Fort Fred Steele. About one mile farther on, they met a sergeant from Egan's company who brought instructions from Crook—namely, to countermarch the column, return to the last night's camp, and await him there. Mackenzie, ascertaining on the morning of November 26 that the Cheyennes had retreated upstream to a point beyond practicable pursuit, had decided to return to Crazy Woman Creek, where his injured men could be properly attended to. All parties thus set course back to the main camp, Crook reaching it the evening of November 27, Dodge at about noon the next day.

Mackenzie had not yet arrived, but that evening the two other senior officers met in Dodge's tent and exchanged views on the events of the past days and nights. Naturally, Crook was gratified. Only a little too optimistically, he believed this stroke against the formidable Northern Cheyennes would end the fighting—that Crazy Horse would either surrender or else retreat to the Badlands north of him. He was "well pleased," he told Dodge, with the work the foot soldiers had done. "I doubt if any men made a more difficult march in better time than mine did on 26th," Dodge wrote in closing his journal entry for that day.[40] But he knew that the day belonged to Mackenzie and his cavalry.

Jerry Roche, a correspondent of the *New York Herald*, had been present at the Dull Knife fight and wrote enthusiastic accounts of the battle.[41] Newspapers across the country blazoned Mackenzie's victory over the Indians as a counterstroke to the disaster suffered by Custer exactly five months before. However, for several days after his return to camp on November 29, the protagonist of Roche's narratives was despondent. Betraying the onset of a mental illness that would cut short his career, the young colonel bitterly reproached himself for what he considered a clumsy failure. In an intense interview following the funeral of the five enlisted men whom Mackenzie had lost, Dodge listened with alarm as his fellow officer "opened his heart to me." Later that day he described the meeting:

> He talked more like a Crazy man, than the sane Comdr of a splendid body of Cavalry. He said to an officer that if he had courage enough he would blow his brains out. . . . He is excessively sensitive – He said he had often done better with a third of the force at his comd here – that he believed he degenerated as a soldier as he got older – that he was a fool, & ought to have captured every Indian – that he regarded the whole thing as an utter failure. He even stated that he was sensitive that some one might attribute cowardice to him – & much more of the same kind. He was so worked up that he could hardly talk, & had often to stop & collect himself. I bullied him & encouraged him all I could, told that he was foolish & absurd to talk so, that we all regarded the affair as a grand success, and that his record was too well known for anyone to attribute cowardice to him[.] I left him feeling much

> better, but he was in such a state that I thought it right to tell Genl Crook about it.[42]

Crook, concerned at Mackenzie's distress, sought him out and tried to divert him by proposing a game of whist.

Drawing upon eyewitness accounts, on the next day Dodge wrote in his journal a detailed narrative of the Dull Knife battle. Eventually he planned to make use of this material in his still unwritten series of chapters on the work of the frontier army. "Altogether," he wrote afterward, "it has been a very successful affair. . . . [that] stamps our campaign as a success even if nothing more is accomplished – I only regret that my portion of the Com[man]d had no share or lot in the affair. All say that had the Doboys been there not an Indian would have escaped. If I had been allowed to go we would have had a more complete story to tell."[43]

On December 1, still at Crazy Woman Creek, Dodge was just starting toward Crook's headquarters when he met Mackenzie walking toward his tent. Both men had heard something of an intended move, but neither was certain of its direction or the end Crook now had in view. Discussing the possibilities, they were verging toward an exchange on Crook's unnecessary reticence when, to their surprise, the general entered. Asked to sit down, he said "I've only a moment to stay. You will march tomo[rro]w & should make arrangements tonight for crossing the river." "What river?" Dodge asked. "This," Crook answered. "I have heard we are to march back to Reno," Dodge ventured. "Is it so?" "Yes," Crook answered, then ducked out of the tent just as Mackenzie moved to ask a question of his own. It could hardly be called an interview, but Dodge and Mackenzie took comfort in at least that much interaction.[44] Scouts, packers, and Crook's quartermaster and aides all seemed to know more than they.

In the eighteen days since he had marched from Fort Fetterman, Dodge had almost filled a pocket notebook with journal entries, many of them recording the eccentricities of the sometimes clubbable, sometimes tight-mouthed general. "Orders given & all ready for an early start tomorw," he concluded this day's record, "and with this book ends the first chapter of the great Winter Campaign of 1876."[45]

The Expedition Continues

The second chapter was longer and less eventful than the first, but it provided Dodge ample opportunity to write a detailed account of the winter campaign. Additionally, his notes recorded a determined and finally successful effort to bring his blurred mental impression of General Crook into focus. He gained some insight into the general's plans from Frank Grouard, the chief scout, whom he met at the post trader's store at Cantonment Reno. According to Grouard, the next stage of the expedition would be to pass eastward to the Belle Fourche and move along it toward the Little Missouri, where scouts radiating in all directions might discover another Indian village vulnerable to attack.

On December 3 the command moved fifteen miles east of south to a staging area called Buffalo Springs, where orders for a further move were issued and countermanded twice in the next two days. Dodge and Mackenzie were at a loss to account for these abrupt reversals. Dodge suspected that Crook had no real plan, intending only "to go a certain distance in a certain direction hoping like Mr Macawber [Wilkins Micawber, in Dickens's *David Copperfield*] that something may turn up." On the morning of December 5 Crook and Mackenzie came into Dodge's tent together, both in high spirits. They had just received copies of telegraphed congratulations on the Dull Knife battle from Generals Sherman and Sheridan.[46] The time seemed right for an attempt to draw out Crook, so immediately upon Mackenzie's exit Dodge "boxed" the general. He was not asking out of mere curiosity, he said, but if there was no reason for secrecy, he would like to know of Crook's plans for the next thirty days. To his pleased surprise, Crook answered that there was no secrecy whatever. They spread out Dodge's maps before them, and he proceeded to explain himself. The command was en route to the junction of the Little Powder and Big Powder rivers, approximately 115 miles north. If they learned of an Indian village in that area, they would attempt to reach it by pack mules; if not, they would return to Fort Fetterman. Perhaps presumptuously but evidently quite to Crook's satisfaction, Dodge quizzed him about the long distances and limited supplies involved. Crook had questions of his own about the sixty-mile stretch of land west of the Black Hills, between Camp Jenney and the Belle Fourche. It was a productive exchange that led Dodge to dismiss his idea of Crook as a commander without a plan. "I feel a great deal better since Crook unburdened himself," he wrote.[47]

The winter march across country severely tested the skill of the wagon masters and the strength of the mules. On the second day out from Buffalo Springs, the command reached the Belle Fourche, thirty miles distant. However, in the two weeks that followed it moved only thirty-four more miles downstream, a far shorter distance than Crook had hoped. Rugged terrain, worsening weather, and weakening animals combined to render the general's projected journey northward all but impossible. Even so, in an interview on December 9 with an anonymous correspondent of the *New York Tribune*, Crook asserted that he did not consider the continued expedition a waste of effort. "I do not anticipate obtaining any great success for the balance of this campaign, measured by tangible results," he said. "But I do expect to so annoy and worry the hostiles as to make it evident to them that they are having the hot end of the poker. . . . The country I am going to is the winter quarters of the hostiles, and has hitherto been exempt from attack during that season. When they see that it makes no difference to us, and that we will be after them in all seasons, they will begin to appreciate their status. The campaign will be necessarily short. Our animals cannot get along without forage, and the supply is limited, with no means of replacing it. We are too far from a railroad."[48] Bourke, who kept track of the forage on hand and scheduled for delivery, bore out Crook's assessment. According to the original plan, 300,000 pounds of forage were to move out from Fort Fetterman every two weeks. However, on December 10 a message arrived from the post commander, Major Caleb H. Carlton, Third Cavalry, that winter storms had blocked the Union Pacific Railroad and made wagon travel from Medicine Bow Station extremely difficult.[49] Despite all efforts, the supply of forage reaching Crook was insufficient.

Dodge understood this, but he was less disposed than either Crook or Bourke to ascribe the command's poor progress to weakened animals. On December 7, he arrived in camp at 3:00 P.M. and after waiting six more hours discovered that some company wagons had still not arrived. He walked over to headquarters to discuss with Crook the bad management of the wagon trains. The general had gone to bed, so Dodge scolded Furey, but only a little, for the quartermaster promised an improvement. Besides, Dodge could not gainsay that the mules were played out. "They are kept in harness from daylight till dark," he noted, "then tied to a wagon pole until daylight again. Not one has been curried or any other care taken of him since we started, & they are expected to do all the work on half forage of grain."[50]

The next day Dodge sought out Crook and, as he expressed it, "talked to him quite freely on the mule question." This was a delicate subject, for the general was renowned for his reliance on pack mule transportation.[51] In response to Dodge's report of the teamsters' lax attention to the mules, Crook remarked that he knew the condition of the animals, that he had a certain problem to work out, and that he was doing the best he could with his materials.[52] Dissatisfaction with this exchange of views simmered in Dodge's mind for several days. He counseled himself that responsibility for the wagon transportation was not his, and that nothing was to be gained by more complaints. But eventually his frustration would break out in an angry scene.

The expedition moved downriver only three more times, stopping at successive points for the nights of December 9–11, December 12–19, and December 20–21. Crook was awaiting a wagon train from Fort Fetterman, subsistence supplies from Buffalo Springs, returning Indian scouts, and another group of Indians who were to bring a report of conditions at Red Cloud Agency. Meanwhile, the command attempted to divert itself as the weather grew worse and the temperature colder. Dodge passed more time than he wished as president of a general court-martial, the irascible Mackenzie having brought charges against a young lieutenant who had given him offense in a minor matter. He wrote a long journal entry about frontiersmen, adding to his budget of material for use in a future publication.[53] On most days he chatted amiably with General Crook, learning from him on December 15 that Captain George M. Randall, chief of scouts in the Department of the Platte, had arrived safely at Cantonment Reno with a group of Crow Indian auxiliaries after a thirty-one-day march from the Crow Agency in Montana. This was happy news, for fears were widespread that Randall had perished in a winter storm, and indeed he and his fellow travelers had had a narrow escape.[54] On the same day Dodge walked to the sutler's wagon and had his flask filled with whisky, a welcome accompaniment to conversation in the evenings. "We are all satisfied that nothing further can be done," he wrote, "& therefore are all anxious to go back as soon as possible. Were there any hope of striking the hostiles I would say 'go on' particularly as we poor Doboys have so far had no show, but if we can't strike there is no sort of use in our staying out here – losing horses & mules, & suffering ourselves without necessity."[55]

On December 20 Dodge received a visit and a tribute from Frank White, who had fought bravely in the battle against the Northern Cheyennes. Frank had informed him earlier of his intention to give him one quarter of a scalp taken from a Cheyenne enemy; Major North would receive another. This was a high compliment, for in the Indian's view the ceremony of bestowal would seal him and Dodge as brothers. Although Dodge understood the significance of the gift, originally he discounted it. "I dont want the thing at all," he wrote then, "but it would be an insult not to accept it."[56] Yet the observances that attended Frank's sharing of his trophy impressed him beyond his expectation. Eventually he sent the scalp fragment to William Blackmore as a contribution to the collection at the Blackmore Museum.[57]

On the day of the ceremony uniting Frank White and Dodge as brothers, General Crook was in a bad humor, having just learned of events at Red Cloud Agency that ran directly counter to his instructions. Acting on instructions from General Sheridan, the post commander at Camp Robinson, Major Julius W. Mason, Third Cavalry, had collected the ponies and guns of all Indians at the agency. Crook had wished to disarm only those Indians who remained hostile, permitting those who submitted to authority to retain their arms and mounts. His reputation for good faith was being swept away, for he had declared his policy to the Indians. Crook told Dodge that the oversetting of his arrangements had so agitated him that he had not slept the night before, and Dodge sympathized. He believed Crook "knows more about the management of Indians than Sheridan will ever know, & it is very hard after working so long & indefatigably to get things in shape, to have all overturned in a moment."[58] The next morning Dodge strolled over to headquarters and saw the general for a short time, but Crook seemed so preoccupied and troubled that he left. He was walking back to his tent when he met Mackenzie, just then on his way to see Crook. Dodge informed the cavalry commander of the general's distracted state and suggested they leave him alone, but Mackenzie demurred. "That is the more reason for our going to see him," he urged. "Lets go & give him some consolation & propose a game of whist."[59] Dodge suppressed a smile, for these were almost the same words Crook had used when he learned of Mackenzie's anguish after the Dull Knife fight.

At Crook's tent they made their greetings and suggested the game, but in response they received a revelation. He could not play, Crook said; it was almost time for him to attend an Indian council. "The fact is," he continued after a pause, "I have made up my mind to turn back tomor[ro]w & want to give the Indians a good talk & let them go direct to the Res[ervatio]n[s]." He explained the considerations that had led him to this choice, and his senior subordinates indicated respectful assent. Mackenzie said that he knew the matter was not his responsibility, but for the past week he had thought it best to return to Fort Fetterman. Dodge observed that he would probably gain more from a successful continuation of the campaign than either of the two others.

He was willing to stay out as long as the chance of another engagement existed, but he thought the wisest course was to put the men and animals back into good quarters as soon as it could be done.

After an hour's conversation the meeting broke up, Crook spoke to the Indians, and Dodge ordered his battalions to prepare for a move to the rear. "I don't believe there is a man in the Com[man]d," he wrote that night, "who is not happier for the order." The Indians danced, sang, and disported themselves all that day. Despite snow in the daytime and cold at night, the mood in camp was celebratory. After the evening meal Mackenzie appeared at Dodge's tent, and they had a good talk. Mackenzie was still chagrined that he had not done more with the chance he had; still, he was pleased with what he did accomplish and gratified at the praise he had received. Later that night one of Dodge's battalion commanders, Captain Joseph B. Campbell, Fourth Artillery, also paid him a visit "& we had an 'Old Army' talk – scandal reminiscence anecdote & stories of all kinds very badly mixed with sundry drinks of whiskey."[60]

On the day after Crook's decision to conclude the second stage of the Powder River Expedition, Dodge completed the second of his journals recording its progress. "I have been summing up today," he wrote, "some of the causes of Crook's failure." The initial section of this analysis was a set of calculations that revealed a striking disproportion. The citizen employees of the Quartermaster Department were carrying for their exclusive use a weight of impedimenta—cast iron cooking stoves, wall tents, and the like—that would ordinarily be required for a body of troops nearly twice the size of the present one. Moreover, the teamsters were "held in no sort of discipline & do just as they please," neglecting the mules under their care without the slightest objection from Furey. Yet General Crook regarded Furey as an excellent officer, a really indispensable quartermaster. How could this be?

In answer to the question, Dodge shifted his focus to Crook. A series of parallel formulations registered his now confident assessment of the general as a military commander: "Crooks great lack is organization. He knows nothing about it & is obliged to trust to others. He asks no questions & believes what is said to him. He give no orders – examines into no details. He is told he can carry only certain stores & does his best on that. He thinks his mules break down from hard work when they are neglected & starved. His successes must always be accidents as was this last – & he must fail – because he cannot himself organize, & has not the judgment to select men who can. He is brave tenacious & the best judge of Indian character in the Army, but he lacks ——"[61] Two weeks before, Dodge had set down in a journal entry the words he left unwritten here: "However good a soldier Crook may be, he has no administrative ability whatever."[62]

Midwinter on the Northern Plains

As if to confirm the timeliness of Crook's decision to turn back, weather conditions rapidly deteriorated and made travel yet more difficult. On the march east, the ground had been relatively soft and covered with a thin coat of snow, enabling the mules to make steady progress. Now, with the animals weakened and smooth shod, the earth was hard frozen and covered with ice slippery as glass. The mules could not secure a footing, and movement up even a small incline required digging with picks to enable their hooves to gain a purchase. For several hours a sun dog appeared, strangely beautiful but portending deeper cold. The experience of Captain Guy Henry and his men on their march into the Black Hills two years before was in the minds of many. In a day of unremitting effort the command marched eleven miles west. "It is fine weather for campaigning & tent life is a romance," Dodge growled in his journal that night.[63] Throughout the expedition, he had been alert for symptoms of the pneumonia that had threatened to cut short his career two decades before. He wore a sealskin cap over his face, a thick padded hood, and a cashmere handkerchief tied to keep the hood in place. His midsection was swathed in "a perfect bundle of clothing – two flannel & 1 buckskin shirt, a vest, a cardigan & an overcoat." Underneath standard-issue trousers he wore two pair of drawers, one of flannel and the other of buckskin, and to keep his feet warm he had on two pair of woollen socks, a pair of "soldier boots," and buffalo overshoes. Two pairs of gloves shielded his hands from the cold, one of silk, the other of wool.[64] That night, lacking wood, he went to bed early to keep warm.

On December 24 the command made only seven more miles, but there was cause for celebration in the arrival of Captain Randall, in company with the eighty Crow Indians from Montana. After an initial chat in Dodge's tent, he and Dodge walked over to Crook's, where they had been invited along with Mackenzie and Townsend. The officers addressed themselves to a Christmas Eve bowl of hot brandy punch, toasting the occasion and their absent loved ones. Afterward, hurrying toward his tent through the cold, Dodge chanced upon Teddy Egan and invited him for a nightcap, which Egan gratefully accepted. As they passed that officer's woodpile, Dodge mentioned that he had no wood himself and could use a log. Egan obliged, Dodge poured him a drink from his private supply, and both were well satisfied.[65] The night was windless, and there was hope of better conditions on Christmas Day.

That hope proved vain, however, for at 7:00 the next morning the mercury was frozen in the bulb of Dodge's thermometer. He and Assistant Surgeon Curtis E. Price estimated the temperature at minus fifty degrees Fahrenheit, achingly cold. Before breakfast could be set on the mess table, the heated food was frozen stiff. But when the wagons were loaded and the men ready to march, they had to stand and wait, for it was found that the teamsters had not yet reported. Then someone discovered that mules had been allowed to wander away and would have to be hunted up. The command did not move out until late morning on a day Bourke remembered as "one of the most disagreeable" of his lifetime: "We were pushing across the Pumpkin Buttes, doing our best to get into bivouac and escape the fury of the elements, which seemed eager to devour us. Beards, moustaches, eye-lashes and eye-brows were frozen masses of ice. The keen air was filled with minute crystals, each cutting the tender skin like a razor, while feet and hands ached as if beaten with clubs. Horses and mules shivered while they stood in column, their flanks white with crystals of perspiration congealed on their bodies, and their nostrils bristling with icicles."[66]

Dodge had gone ahead at 9:00 A.M. in search of a good road, leaving his part of the command to follow. After twenty miles of hard travel, he went into camp at 2:00 P.M. and joined Crook and his staff at a campfire. As the wagons began to arrive two hours later, he watched their slow progress with rising anger. They straggled in for four more hours, well into the night, so that after a punishing march the men were still without food. Unable to keep down his frustration any longer, Dodge "ventilated . . . very openly" to Crook his opinion of the packers, "princes in disguise" who apparently rated their own comfort and convenience above the needs of everyone else. "I told him," he wrote later that day, "it was an outrage on my men – on human nature, & demanded that some steps be taken to remedy the evil." The general heard him out, then turned and walked away without a word.

Dodge now directed his ire at Crook's staff, who held their peace. At last, attempting to rescue the situation, Furey's chief clerk spoke up. "It can't be helped, Colonel. The teamsters have a ring, & if we were to discharge one, a hundred would go." But Dodge was not to be reasoned with. "Well, let them go," he roared out. "I will give you a better man in place of every scoundrel who leaves. Put them off in the pra[i]rie here & let them go!"[67] A tense silence settled over the group. Dodge was intemperate, but it was hard to argue against his premises. He was a professional soldier who respected the men under his authority and was solicitous about their welfare. Moreover, he subscribed to the view that, as he later expressed it, the "foundation-stone of an army is obedience, its key-stone discipline."[68] The civilian teamsters were here to serve the army, not the reverse.

Hooking his arm into Dodge's, Mackenzie led him away from the campfire and over to his tent, where he offered him a drink. "I think you are too hard on Furey," he ventured after a few moments. "He does the best he can." "Admitted," Dodge returned, "but that best leads to suffering of my men, & it is time somebody was put in his place who can do better than Furey's best." Dodge must have sensed his own absurdity. Abruptly replacing Furey was no more a possibility than casting the packers out to fend for themselves in the winter waste. "You have your own Q[uarte]r M[aste]r," he reminded Mackenzie, "& your train is under your own control. The Gen[era]l will not allow me to have Control of mine. My men suffer[,] yours dont, & there is all the difference."[69] Mackenzie had succeeded in cutting short an uncomfortable scene, but he could hardly debate this last point. As it happened, on the very next evening Dodge found him administering a tongue-lashing to Furey that made his own seem mild. Afterward Mackenzie apologized—oddly, to Dodge rather than Furey—for abusing the quartermaster in the way he had.

After his outburst on Christmas night Dodge had difficulty calming himself. Writing out his account of the day, he described Furey as charitably as he could, as "a willing, energetic, hard working man, & one of the best regular Qr Mrs I know."

Nevertheless, he judged Furey "utterly unfit to have charge of such a train as this," deficient in the personal authority and snap to ensure the smooth operation of a large expeditionary force. Among other officers who were equal to the task but not regularly assigned to the Quartermaster Department, he thought of two, Mackenzie's regimental quartermaster, First Lieutenant Henry W. Lawton, and his own First Lieutenant John F. Trout. "Trout would have the whole thing run as smoothly as a Sewing Machine," he assured himself, but of course Trout was not at hand. Further protests were useless, and he resolved to keep silence on the matter. "I congratulate myself that the expedition is over," he wrote, "& I most sincerely hope I will never go on another under Crook."[70]

On December 26 the general saved travel time by striking out a new road to the south that shortened the distance to Fort Fetterman. Despite the uncertainty involved it was a wise course of action, for it was obvious that the men and animals were suffering. The cast iron feed troughs of the mules were covered with blood and pieces of flesh where the animals had touched the frozen metal while eating. Iron tent pins had to be left in the ground where they had been driven in. Dodge saw one man who, failing to observe this practice, picked up a number of the pins and, throwing them into a bag where they were kept, lost the skin off his palm.[71] Bourke described a soldier who wore an Arctic cap that covered his entire face, leaving only peepholes for his eyes. He had his eyelids frozen, and a ring of purple skin encircled each orbit. Horses fell down and died. Cavalry officers and men dismounted and walked most of the morning, to keep themselves from freezing.[72]

Strangely, Mackenzie had remarked at mess the night before that the command was returning from the campaign "without any suffering at all." He was referring to the expedition's overall success, but Dodge nevertheless took him up at once:

> "Well" I said, "while I agree with you generally on the good effect of our winter['] s work, I can not agree that we have done it without suffering. We have not suffered permanent ill, nor lost our lives or our limbs, but when a man lies in his bed under a weight of clothing actually uncomfortable, & yet shakes & trembles with cold – when he was to work with his nose & his fingers for three or four hours without intermission to prevent their freezing, he suffers, & he suffers acutely. It is nothing to boast of, when a man has a good heart, & accepts what fate sends him, – but did he give up, he would suffer permanently. One additional step, would have made our suffering permanent for some of us. So while we congratulate ourselves in getting through without permanent disability, we cannot say truly that we have done so without suffering."[73]

Mackenzie took this response in good part, observing only that men in similar circumstances had sometimes suffered worse. Happily, when the command made camp on December 26 a wagon train loaded with forage was awaiting them, and the animals received an extra measure of grain.

The train brought with it a large shipment of mail, including a letter to Dodge from his parents, who were at once anxious for his safety and ambitious for his distinction.

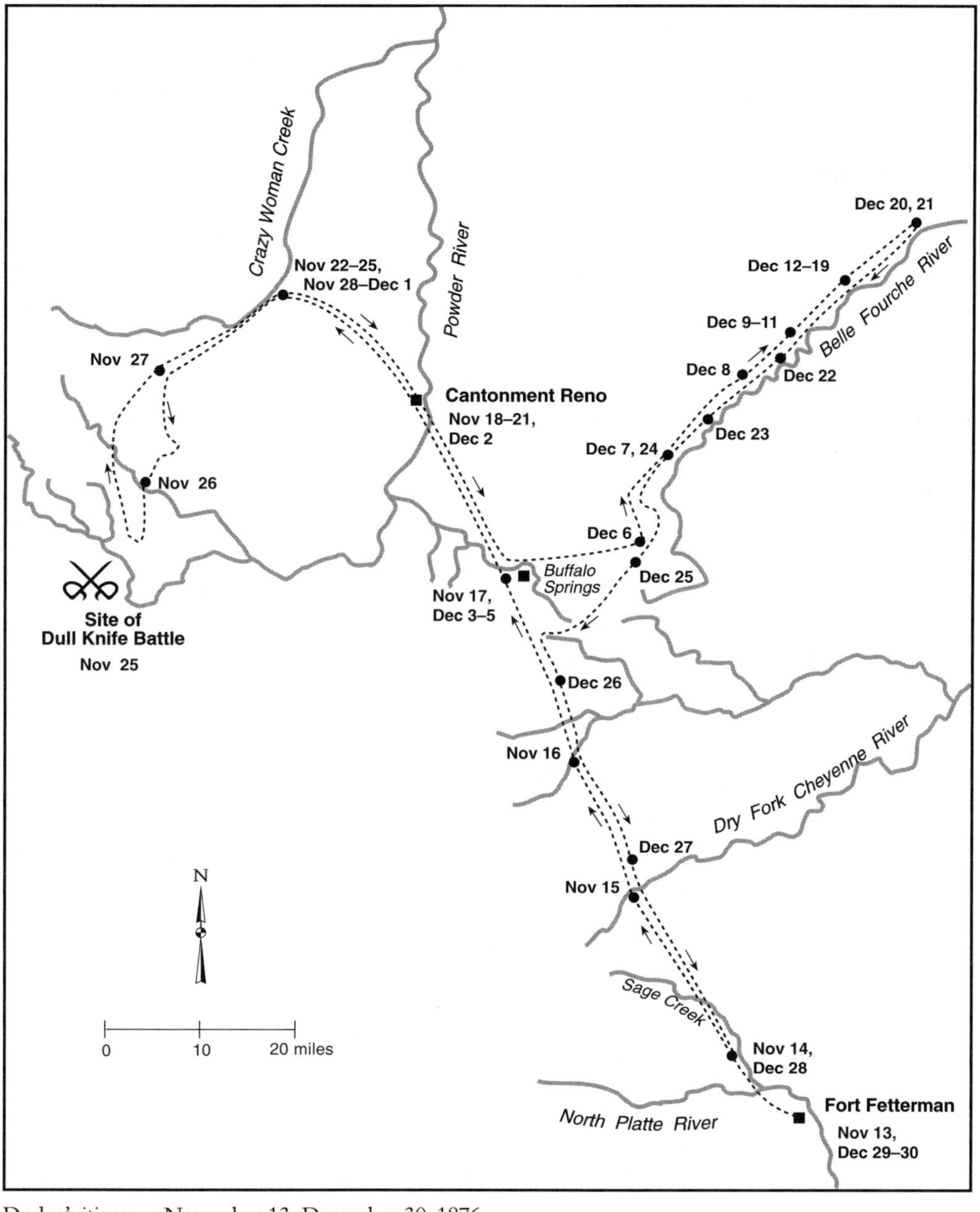

Dodge's itinerary, November 13–December 30, 1876

Musing fondly on that paradox, he admitted to himself that the letter "did me a world of good, & reconciled me somewhat to going home without any special glory." He reflected on the part he and his Doboys had played in the Powder River Expedition, now almost ended: "The world applauds success, while success is an accident that may come to the stupid & unenergetic, as well as to the brightest & hardest worker. The world applauds the success, but conscience approves him, who does his work to the best of his ability whether he be successful or not. Neither myself nor my com[man]d have done anything brilliant but we have done our very best, & had our luck put us in a fight, we would have made a name for ourselves – or I am mightily mistaken. Thats all!"[74]

On the morning of December 28 General Crook left the command and rode the thirty miles to Fort Fetterman to transact business there before going on to Cheyenne. The long- delayed court-martial of Colonel Reynolds and one of the two other officers was to begin in that city on January 5.[75] Meanwhile, spirits rose as the army moved toward the fort. While awaiting the wagons that afternoon, Dodge and his staff lay in the snow, chatting around a sagebrush fire. A young lieutenant was describing the satisfactions of picnics in the leafy summer when, deadpan, Dodge broke in: "Why should there be anything in the color, Green, to give it a preference over other colors? You eulogize green grass, green leaves & all things green. Is not the mantle, that Mother Earth now wears as becoming to the eye – as soft to the touch. Why should pic-nics be identified only with verdancy?" The youngster stared with surprise at this flight of rhetoric, while veterans grinned.[76] About the only green design on Mother Earth's mantle that day was the water at Sage Creek, which Bourke described as "black & greenish like writing ink, and putrid with Sulphuratted [*sic*] Hydrogen."[77]

After marching steadily for eight days, on December 29 the command reached the fort, where a "Jamboree" of visits, exchanges of news and recollections, and bouts of billiards, whist, and cribbage ensued. Dodge was amused that his fellow officer Captain Otis W. Pollock, Twenty-third Infantry, received two invitations to dine, at 3:00 and 5:00 P.M., and accepted both. On December 30 Mackenzie left the post on his way east, first to report to General Sheridan at Chicago and then to continue on to Washington, D.C. President Grant wished him to take command of troops in the national capital in the event of an emergency growing out of the still hotly disputed election of Rutherford B. Hayes as president, over Samuel Tilden.[78] On December 31 Dodge and his men began their march to Fort Laramie, where he was to break up his command before proceeding to Cheyenne and thence back to Omaha.

Arrived at his first destination, on January 3 Dodge issued General Order 13, Headquarters Infantry and Artillery Battalions, dissolving the brigade and ordering its companies to their respective stations. In orders of this kind it was customary for the commanding officer to include a farewell statement to the men who had served under him, but what Dodge wrote was more than a formality: "In parting with his command the Lieutenant Colonel takes pleasure in commending the discipline and excellent spirit of the officers and enlisted men of each and every company under very trying circumstances, and he only regrets that the fortunes of war gave them no opportunity of showing as good conduct in battle as they have displayed endurance and fortitude in all the hardships privations and suffering incident to a winter campaign in this terrible country, on their safe return from which he is happy to congratulate them."[79] Dodge had not succeeded in demonstrating the superiority of infantry over cavalry in engagements with Indians, but this result was for lack of opportunity, not lack

General Crook's Headquarters, Fort Fetterman. Reprinted from *Harper's Weekly*, December 16, 1876.

of effort. In camp on the last night of the campaign, he wrote a concluding exclamation: "Thank Heaven!!"[80]

Arrived at Cheyenne, he witnessed more rank in one place than he had since the Civil War. More than one hundred officers were there, connected in various ways with the Reynolds court-martial. General Pope, who was presiding, was now also Dodge's department commander, for the Twenty-third Infantry had recently been transferred to the Department of the Missouri.[81] When the two men met on the afternoon of January 6, Pope told Dodge to take his time reporting to his new post, Fort Riley, Kansas,[82] and he therefore availed himself of the chance to mix with old comrades and catch up on army news. That evening he chatted with Pope, his regimental commander Colonel Davis, and Crook in Pope's hotel room, noting in his journal that Crook "was more cordial than he ever was before." Court was not in session the next morning, it being a Sunday, so Dodge had time for some more socializing. "I find myself quite a hero & an authority," he wrote later, "(though I knew as much before I went on this Expedition as I do on my return) except in the matter of managing Indians, and Crook is the best teacher in that branch of knowledge I ever saw."[83] Under the influence of Crook's good will and perhaps also the deference he received at Cheyenne, Dodge was disposed to give the general his full due as the Powder River Expedition began to fade from memory.

The third volume of his journal of the expedition ended with the entry for January 8, 1877, the date of his arrival at Omaha. Riding toward Omaha Barracks in company with Randall, he was about to cross a bridge over a ravine opposite the post when the ambulance went out of control and almost tumbled down a steep incline. Fortunately, as the unhitched mules bolted for the stables, the front of the carriage ran diagonally into the end of a bridge railing, bringing it to a dead halt and averting disaster. The irony of the incident was not lost on Dodge. "So the greatest danger I encountered on my great winter expedition, was at my own post, & at the very last moment of the expedition."[84] He and Randall walked the rest of the way to his quarters and were welcomed by Joe and Laura, who prepared a cot for the guest. Good nights were said, and the expedition was over.

A Résumé of the Campaign

Dodge's two months in the field had been such eventful ones that he was moved to bring together his scattered impressions in a single statement, entitled "Resumé," that comprised the fourth volume of his journal record. Drawing upon the entries that preceded it and on experiences he had not set down in writing, he addressed himself primarily to the character, views, and abilities of General Crook. He began with an enumeration of whatever positive could be said about the general and the campaign he had led, then turned to criticism. In his published writing of later years, Dodge portrayed Crook favorably,[85] never expressing in print the serious reservations that comprised the greater part of the 2,500-word "Resumé."

Although he was convinced that the operation had dealt a powerful blow to Indian resistance and would probably help end the conflict, he believed it "has not been so eminently successful as it might have been." Acknowledging Crook's unique power over Indians, he described him as "a good strategist," a man possessed of "wonderful tenacity of purpose, will & pluck," and—contrary to the falsehoods published by Davenport—a military leader "entirely careless of personal discomfort." Crook lacked only one characteristic of a great general, "Administrative ability":

> He can decide how many & what troops to take into the field with him, but there his power ends. How to fit them out, & care for them afterwards is a problem, which to him has no solution. His ignorance of such things is remarkable & painful. It is even ludicrous, for he carries it to such an extent, as to regard with the most profound admiration any man who evinces even a moderate ability in this direction. He must be fully aware of his own deficiency in this respect, for having selected Officers to do this work for him, he never interferes in any way, by order or suggestion, & when he gets hold of a man who does tolerably well, he can never admire him sufficiently or praise him enough. This would be admirable did he only get hold of first class men, but though a fair judge of human nature, he yet in the nature of things sometimes gets a man unequal to his work. The success of an expedition depends more on the administrative ability of the Staff, than the genius of the General – & this is more true in Indian, than in Civilized Warfare – for in the former, each army, or active force must depend on itself for everything.

Humanly, Dodge was faulting Crook for lack of competence in an area where he himself excelled.

Briefly turning his attention to Crook's much maligned quartermaster, he also gave Furey his full due before insisting on his inadequacy. Furey was "an industrious energetic hard working man – a gentleman in manners & education, & with the disposition to be a good officer. He did the very best he could, but he did not know how to do." Recalling his angry confrontations with Crook and Furey over the packers' slack performance of duty, he admitted that "I felt like a common scold & was ashamed of myself." Still, the conditions that had so aroused him were "a most infernal outrage, & would not have been tolerated an instant, by any Comdg Officer that I know of except Genl Crook." Had the mules been properly attended to, and had rations and forage been carried with the command instead of the packers' burdensome conveniences, the force would have been much more mobile. No doubt with some exaggeration, Dodge estimated that it might have marched three times the four hundred miles it did, "& probably struck Crazy Horse."[86]

The "Resumé" clearly grew out of Dodge's experiences and observations, and in writing it, he evidently still felt some of the frustration he had amid the events themselves. He was hardly dispassionate, and he lacked a full appreciation of the uncertainties and other challenges Crook faced from day to day. Unlike Bourke, who kept current with virtually all incoming information, Dodge enjoyed less access to

George Crook. Reprinted from Dodge, *Our Wild Indians* (1882), p. 492.

Crook's plans and considerations. On the other hand, his years of army experience gave weight to his observations, and his frequent agreement with another senior officer like Mackenzie was an added endorsement. Dodge had come to know Crook reasonably well prior to the Powder River Expedition, but the truth that a soldier's essential qualities evince themselves most fully in campaign, or on the field of battle, applied in this instance. During weeks of contact on the winter expedition he witnessed not only Crook's admirable virtues as a field commander but also a besetting deficiency—his inadequate attention to the practical details of his command's progress into hostile territory.

Because Dodge possessed a wise awareness of his own finitude and also a sense of irony, he would likely smile at the idea that his most memorable accomplishment as an officer in the Powder River Expedition should be his written record of it rather than his participation in it. Yet the four-volume journal record, set down in the intervals of the campaign and after its conclusion, remains his chief claim to remembrance from this episode in his military career. After all, the Dull Knife battle, the centerpiece of the expedition, was "Mackenzie's Last Fight against the Cheyennes," as Bourke titled his published narrative—not Dodge's. Owing to Crook's strategy and the whims of fortune, Dodge had occupied an almost paradoxical position as both a brigade commander and also something of an onlooker. That double point of view manifests itself often in the journals, some of whose entries reflect his intense engagement with the matters they treat, while others are more detached, discursive, even playful. The sometimes trenchant commentary on Crook and the unfolding campaign is diversified by descriptions of day-to-day events, atmospheric phenomena, anecdotes, characterizations, personal reflections, recollections, and speculations on many topics. Dodge had developed a taste for expressing himself in writing, and setting down his observations in all their variety was clearly a source of satisfaction to him. His private record of "this most disagreeable winter campaign" is thus a revealing personal document as well as an historical resource. Even as the Powder River Expedition unfolded, he was winning an international reputation as an author through the publication of *The Plains*. His private journals of the campaign remained unpublished during his lifetime, but they also possess virtues that assure him of lasting memory as a soldier-author. They are the fullest, the most thoughtful, the most personally revealing, and the most entertaining firsthand account we have of an important U.S. military campaign, the Powder River Expedition of 1876.

Part Five

Duty Officer, 1877–1880

Dodge's service in the Department of the Missouri between 1877 and 1880 warranted the later characterization of him in the *Army and Navy Journal* as "a duty officer second to none."[1] His broad range of experience, varied talents, and still-vigorous physical condition made him exceptionally valuable to his departmental commander, General Pope. The personal interest he took in the duties assigned him ensured their being performed with energy and judicious intelligence. He was forthright and self-reliant yet faithful, respectful, and utterly devoted to the army. As a result, Pope called on him repeatedly in situations that demanded a combination of military competence and tact. Dodge had succeeded in two major assignments to duty under General Crook, but a series of less visible services under General Pope demonstrated convincingly his versatile merit as a senior duty officer. Dodge served well under Pope, earning his regard; and at an opportune time Pope served him in return by helping advance his career.

Administrative ability, which Dodge had identified as Crook's besetting weakness, was one of Pope's pre-eminent strengths. Pope combined orderly habits of mind with an acute sense of the shifting balance between the limited forces at his disposal and the duties they might be called upon to perform. He was accustomed to playing the odds, deploying what troops he could at potential trouble spots while repeatedly calling the attention of his superiors to the acute need for reinforcements. However well justified, those appeals usually came to little, for the army lacked the resources to supply him and other departmental commanders what they required. Pope was left to make do with what he had, and these were the circumstances that demonstrated to him the value of Lieutenant Colonel Dodge. Dodge's multiple missions beginning in 1877 reflect a neat conjunction between the demands being made upon the Department of the Missouri at that time and his varied abilities. He was just the kind of adaptable senior officer Pope could make full use of.

15

Multiple Missions

Upon his arrival at Fort Riley in January 1877, Dodge took up pursuits he had left in abeyance during the Powder River Expedition. While still in the field with General Crook, he had read one prepublication notice of *The Plains*,[1] but a collection of newspaper clippings sent him by William Blackmore was the first indication he had of reviewers' response to the published work. Wisely, in expressing gratitude to Blackmore for helping bring out the book, he made no mention of infelicities such as the verbal Anglicization his text had undergone.[2] Privately, however, he planned in the next printing of the work to correct as many errors and imperfections as he could without undue expense.

Between February 28 and April 30 Dodge was on leave of absence, attending to business in New York City.[3] He called at G. P. Putnam's Sons to pick up the three copies of *Hunting Grounds* that Blackmore had sent him and also to inquire about sales thus far of the American edition. The report he received was indifferent: demand was steady but slow, and given the work's high price of four dollars, a sudden inrush of orders from booksellers could not be expected. The controversial portions of the section on Indians did not appear to be inhibiting sales as Putnam had feared; the problem was simply one of economics and poor timing. Meanwhile, the stereotype plates were on hand for reuse, and the two men agreed that a second impression would be warranted before long. Accordingly, Dodge directed ninety-eight word changes to the plates, limiting himself to alterations that could be made with a minimum of resetting and recasting.[4] In this way he brought the American text somewhat more closely into line with his wishes as he had embodied them in his manuscript.[5]

The second impression of *The Plains*, issued later in 1877, was its last, and the sales history of *Hunting Grounds* ran a similar course. Once Blackmore had completed his campaign to ensure that the book was widely reviewed, he played almost no further part in advancing its fortunes. He did send out a few more complimentary copies, including one in March to the Empress of Austria and another in June to former President Grant,[6] but his waning energies were necessarily directed elsewhere. His efforts to hold together an overextended network of investments brought on an exhaustion that, aggravated by excessive drinking, precipitated a second physical collapse. Blackmore consented to a summer convalescence at Torquay, on the southern coast of England, but there he suffered a sunstroke that prostrated him anew. Months passed, and in the absence of close supervision his financial crisis deepened. By July, Chatto & Windus had sold out the seven hundred copies of their first edition of *Hunting Grounds*,[7] but Blackmore was unavailable to help prepare a new issue. He did regain sufficient strength to plan a trip to the United States in the winter of 1877–1878, but he did not make the journey. Grown thin and pale and wanting his old mental vigor, Dodge's friend and benefactor sought vainly to shore up his crumbling financial empire until, on the morning of April 12, 1878, he shot himself.[8]

Despite its somewhat disappointing sales, *The Plains* established Dodge among his fellow citizens as an authoritative source of information about the subjects treated in it. Among his military colleagues, his status as an author was enhanced by the generous publicity given the book in the *Army and Navy Journal*. The weekly newspaper's anonymous reviewer concluded his notice, in the issue for January 20, 1877, by confessing that he had tried hard to identify some feature that merited less than strong praise. However, "we are disarmed by the entire simplicity of the style, the soldierly candor of the writer, and the irresistibly attractive material which he has crammed into a work which must take the lead as the best authority on the three main topics treated therein."[9] Each of the next three issues included an excerpt from the chapters on the plains environment, and the issue for February 10 also included a paragraph commending Dodge's remarks about camp life to the attention of "young officers, or . . . civilian travellers."[10] Eventually one young officer, Second Lieutenant Edward S. Farrow, Twenty-first Infantry, paid Dodge the compliment of minimally revising, without attribution, chapters in *The Plains* for inclusion in his volume entitled *Mountain Scouting: A Hand-Book for Officers and Soldiers on the Frontier* (1881).[11]

Dodge's book brought him into correspondence with researchers on topics within the broad fields of inquiry he had surveyed. With Garrick Mallery, of the fledgling Bureau of American Ethnology at the Smithsonian Institution, he exchanged letters about the sign language in use among Plains Indians.[12] With Joel Asaph Allen, author of a *History of the American Bison* (1877), he discussed the original size of the disappearing herds and the possible existence of a subspecies, the "Mountain Buffalo."[13] With Spencer F. Baird, director of the Smithsonian Institution, he exchanged a variety of information, forwarding to Washington animal and mineral specimens and Indian artifacts.[14] To these eastern savants Dodge was an obliging source of reliable information and opinion about the plains.

Julia Dodge now possessed a substantial portion of her late mother's bequest to her, and she urged her husband to accompany her and Fred on a visit to England in the summer of 1877.[15] For eighteen-year-old Fred, the journey would be more than a simple pleasure excursion. While at Omaha Barracks he had participated in activities of the Officers' Dramatic Association and had shown such aptitude as an actor that he was considering a professional stage career.[16] Eager to foster his development, his mother wished him to witness productions at the great theaters of London, even perhaps to receive some formal training. In recent years Henry Irving, a distant relation of the American Irvings, had won acclaim for his performances in London in the great Shakespearian roles of Hamlet, Macbeth, and Othello; it was possible that Fred might study with him.[17] Dodge liked these ideas and was glad to see his wife and son set off on their adventures, but he could not accompany them. Even if he secured the necessary permission from army authorities, he lacked the money.[18]

The exact nature of an emotional gulf that opened up between the Dodges at about this time cannot be specified, but probably Julia's inheritance and the changed lifestyle it made possible for her were among the root causes. Dodge economized for himself while assisting members of his family out of his limited means. More free in her spending habits, Julia perhaps resented his warnings against squandering her inheritance. At any rate, a clash of wills occurred between husband and wife, leading to settled hostility on Julia's part. She had the means to go to her own way without advice from him, and she intended to do so. Dodge, helpless to mend matters, could only hope for a reconciliation.

The Fort Riley Bridge

Ironically, Dodge had welcomed his assignment as post commander at Fort Riley because he believed the style of life there would suit Julia.[19] One of the oldest and most attractive posts in the Department of the Missouri, it no longer served its original purpose, as a protector to wagon trains and a deterrent to Indians in the vicinity. Its formerly strategic location at the confluence of two rivers, the Republican and the Smoky Hill, had since given it new importance, for it now stood at the intersection of two railroads, the Kansas Pacific passing east to west and the Missouri, Kansas, and Texas passing north to south. Located near Junction City, 136 miles east of Kansas City, it served chiefly as a depot for supplies bound elsewhere in the department. Its garrison included only three companies.[20]

The chief issue that arose during Dodge's brief tenure as post commander at Fort Riley grew out of its location at a transportation hub. A railroad bridge that had been erected in 1867 by a corporation called the Republican River Bridge Company was in danger of collapse, and shortly after his arrival at the post, Dodge informed the War Department of the legal legerdemain that had brought about this state of affairs. Representatives of the company had first convinced Congress to grant the State of Kansas some 4,000 acres of land, lying between the two rivers, which then formed part of the Fort Riley military reservation. In return, the State of Kansas guaranteed that once a "good and permanent" bridge spanned the Republican, the structure would be maintained in proper condition and its use granted free of charge to the government of the United States. Friends of the Republican River Bridge Company next introduced a bill in the Kansas state senate granting it title to the 4,000 acres of land once it had completed construction of the bridge. This bill was passed and became law, and by the end of 1867 the bridge was ready for use, as promised. A transfer of title was made in the following year, and thereafter the Republican River Bridge Company began pursuing its real object, selling off the valuable land it had obtained. Dodge observed to Secretary of War George W. McCrary that "the whole thing is a swindle, and I think it very likely that it was intended to be so when so very absurd an action was urged on Congress."[21]

The Republican River Bridge Company failed to maintain the bridge it had built, and having sold off its land for approximately $200,000, the company eventually ceased to exist. Meanwhile, use of the deteriorating bridge remained necessary at Fort Riley, but who was to pay for its repair and maintenance? Upon inquiry, Dodge discovered that neither the county commissioners nor the state government would have anything to do with the matter. Nevertheless, he was satisfied that legal responsibility rested with the State of Kansas, and he therefore urged the secretary of war to call upon the state to make the proper repairs at once. Should that effort prove unavailing, he suggested that the whole matter be reported to Congress so that the act of 1867 could be repealed.[22]

In response to a demand from Secretary McCrary, Governor George T. Anthony of Kansas eventually declared his intention to hold the bridge company to its obligation. In the meantime, he suggested, the federal government should repair the bridge and submit to him a claim for the costs. By this time Dodge had already received a telegram from McCrary directing him to use all measures he could to save the bridge. He responded that his officers and men had done what they could, but that he had no money and no lumber to attempt further repairs. Four hundred or five hundred dollars made available to him now "will save as many thousands in six months or a year," he warned, for the bridge was "rapidly going to pieces."[23]

The race between deterioration of the bridge and the delay occasioned by governmental inertia and legal wrangling was close, and Dodge was not on hand to witness the finish. On June 13, ten days after writing his appeal to the secretary of war for funds, he relinquished command at Fort Riley in order to take post at Fort Leavenworth.[24] Undoubtedly he would learn that generals Pope and Sheridan became involved in the effort to save the bridge, and that on July 30 the quartermaster general at last issued orders to begin repairs. Probably he also heard the news when, three weeks later, the structure fell into the river. The quartermaster general's annual report for 1877 included the text of a resolution by the commissioners of Davis County, Kansas, asking for help from the state and federal governments in building a new bridge, "that the general travel may not be longer interrupted."[25]

Visions of the New Army

Fort Leavenworth, on an elevated plain overlooking the right bank of the Missouri River twenty-three miles upstream from Kansas City, was the largest military post in the Department of the Missouri and the seat of General Pope's headquarters. Its access to several railroads made it a convenient distribution point, and it was garrisoned by a full regiment of troops.[26] Owing to the steady influx of settlers into country formerly unoccupied except by Indians, smaller forts that had been established to help maintain the peace in the eastern sections of the department were obsolescent. The time had not yet arrived when more westerly facilities such as Forts Larned, Dodge, and even Lyon could be dispensed with, but events were moving in that direction.[27] Meanwhile, the network of railroads traversing much of the department made practicable the speedy movement of troops to depots within relatively short distances from places where their presence was required. At the time of Dodge's transfer to Fort Leavenworth, nine of the Twenty-third Infantry's ten companies were stationed there. The regiment would thus help put into practice the army's policy of consolidating troops at a few strategic locations.

During the summer of 1877 General Pope and other army commanders were called upon to help quell a civil uprising that posed a practical test of the consolidation policy. During July a strike in West Virginia against the Baltimore and Ohio Railroad Company set in motion a wave of labor violence that threatened extensive destruction of property and serious interference with the nation's rail transportation system. A proclamation by President Hayes proved unavailing, and the efforts of state militias, notably Pennsylvania's, to bring the rioters under control were embarrassingly unsuccessful. Mob rule prevailed along routes connecting major cities, and the army was therefore called in.[28] On July 23, following a dispatch to Pope from the secretary of war, Colonel Jefferson C. Davis was ordered to proceed with six companies of the Twenty-third Infantry from Fort Leavenworth to Saint Louis, Missouri, a major railroad junction point. On the following day eight more companies were ordered to the same place by rail, including two from distant Fort Lyon.

Davis was provided four Gatling guns in case of need, but his instructions were to avoid provoking violence. It was hoped that the presence of troops would give moral support to the citizens' organizations that were being thrown together to deal with threats to life and property. Davis occupied the cavalry recruiting depot in Saint Louis as a base of operations, and from that point he dispatched troops to protect public property in the city. The men were housed in barracks placed under Dodge's authority. Soldiers secured the Illinois and Missouri bridge across the Mississippi River and so ensured free movement along that major artery, but they played no other direct part in ending the disturbance. "They neither did too much nor too little," Pope later wrote with satisfaction.[29] Once volunteer organizations were in place, the federal forces were withdrawn. Dodge and the men of his regiment arrived back at Fort Leavenworth on August 10, having set an example to convince skeptics

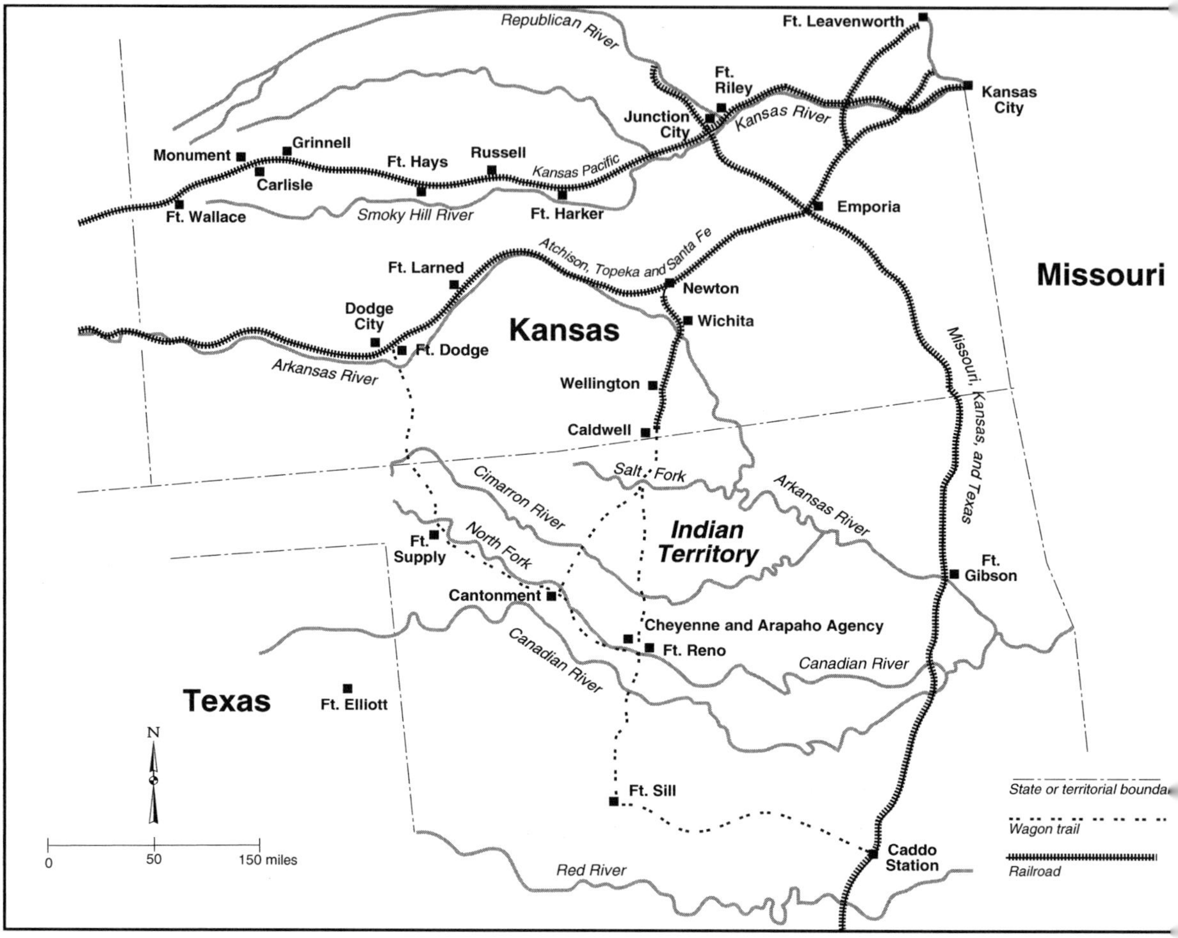

Region of Dodge's service, 1877–1880

of the continuing need for a credible U.S. military force. The usefulness of railroads to speed troops to points of possible conflict had also been demonstrated.

The emergency call to Saint Louis interrupted a program just begun at Fort Leavenworth, a course of drill and instruction being administered to the entire Twenty-third Infantry. With the support of Generals Sherman and Sheridan, Pope was giving literal application to the adage that a regiment is the chief school of an army. Whereas the dispersal of a regiment's companies at several posts reduced the sense of its elaborated military order, concentration at a post like Fort Leavenworth engendered that awareness and made possible a protracted period of training for the regiment as a whole. Thus, pending the success of an experiment with the Twenty-third Infantry in the coming year, General Pope was considering the establishment at Fort Leavenworth of a permanent "regimental school."[30]

Almost exactly at the time Dodge reported for duty there, Pope issued a general order setting forth his ideas for the subjects to be covered in the program. "Relying upon the zeal and energy of the officers of the regiment," he wrote, "the Department

Commander will not prescribe in detail the course of instruction, or the time to be devoted to each branch, but calls attention to the following as matters in which it is expected that instruction will be given and decided improvement be made." The list that ensued suggested an ambitious effort: "The performance of guard duty by officers and enlisted men; drill of company and battalion; target practice; instruction of officers and enlisted men in military signalling; study of tactics by officers and non-commissioned officers; school for enlisted men, where the elementary branches of studies will be taught; study by officers of military law and practice of courts-martial; instruction of officers in military administration; the keeping of company records, and the manner of doing business and keeping accounts in the quartermaster's and subsistence departments." Pope noted, correctly, that the Twenty-third Infantry was being afforded an opportunity to develop its soldierly competence that was unique in the army. He named Colonel Davis as the officer who bore chief responsibility for carrying out the spirit of the order.[31]

Of course, inasmuch as Davis already commanded Fort Leavenworth as well as his regiment, limitations of time and energy dictated that he delegate some duties to Dodge, his second-in-command. Whatever part Dodge may have played in determining the organization and content of the course of instruction, once the program was initiated he became its instructor in chief. As the officer charged with giving literal form to the ideas of Pope and Davis, he was pre-eminently the man whose "zeal and energy" would be called upon to make the experimental program a success. "I'd almost as lief be in prison," he wrote Blackmore in September. "No hunting, no getting away for anything. It is the most unsatisfactory fall I have passed in years – & I see no present prospect of change." That he was helping lay the basis for a course of studies in the military art that thrived for the rest of his lifetime and continues to exist at Fort Leavenworth today was no consolation. "Oh," he exclaimed to Blackmore, "for the old times at Ft Dodge!"[32]

Of course, it was natural that he should fondly recall another time in his career, and not only because he was cooped up at the post during hunting season. Owing to congressional inaction, just then he was performing his duties without even being paid. Congress persisted in viewing support of the military as an expense of doubtful value, even though General Sherman was gradually making headway arguing the opposite side of the question.

In 1874 a frustrated Sherman had actually exiled his headquarters to Saint Louis on the ground that his presence in the national capital was unnecessary, he being an administrative cipher. But the impeachment and resignation of William W. Belknap two years later had been a stroke for the army. Inducements by President Grant and Belknap's successor, Alphonso Taft, brought Sherman back to Washington,[33] and the election to the presidency of Rutherford B. Hayes was another hopeful development. Hayes, a moderate Republican, was a friend to the service, and his secretary of war, George W. McCrary, was a man whom Sherman could work with. The general in chief still lacked control over the whole army, but his status was markedly improved.

Opposition to the regular army remained a powerful force in Congress, however. Late in the Grant administration a commission was formed to consider possibilities for a further "reorganization," the real intention of some legislators being to reduce the army's size and expense. Ironically, in February 1877 the commission submitted a report explaining that its members, having important business to transact elsewhere in government, had not had time to develop any recommendations.[34] This was a reprieve, but in the next session of Congress the House Committee on Military Affairs took up the task again. Through a subcommittee, it distributed for comment a circular containing nine questions relating to the proper aggregate strength of the army, the number of general and staff officers, the organization of staff departments, and other issues.[35] Among the officers whose responses were included in the published report of the subcommittee were Generals Schofield and Pope, Colonel Davis, and Lieutenant Colonel Dodge. The two generals, both experienced politicians, wrote lengthy statements that ranged outside the limits implied by the subcommittee's questions. Their views on two topics, the organizational status of the staff corps and the duties of the General of the Army, were virtually identical. They agreed that the staff corps should no longer be independent of direction by the general in chief and that the latter should be free to express his views about army administration to his civilian superior, the secretary of war, rather than being denied that privilege as at present.[36]

The circular with its questions arrived at Fort Leavenworth during a quiet period, and being then in command of the post, Dodge wrote out his responses without delay. Unlike his superior officers, he confined himself to brief answers to the numbered questions. However, what his statements lacked in subtlety of disquisition they gained in force. In response to the fifth question, "How should the staff departments of such army be organized? Should they be an independent corps; and, if not, how should they be formed?" he wrote: "The staff departments should be for the benefit of the line, or fighting portion of the Army, and should therefore be under the direct control of the General-in-chief. Those serving in departments should be under control of the department commander." Here, as on several other points, his views essentially duplicated those of Schofield, Pope, and Davis. All agreed that the staff corps employed more officers than their functions warranted; in Dodge's words, they were "hugely preponderant."[37]

The subcommittee's final question was "What changes, if any, in the regulations and discipline of the Army can be made to improve the morale of the non-commissioned officers and men, and prevent desertion?" The first of Dodge's several suggestions, that "The pay of non-commissioned officers should be largely increased," is of particular interest here, since it reiterated an opinion that had attracted considerable attention when he and others expressed it two years earlier. In November 1875, then in command at Omaha Barracks, Dodge received a communication from Captain Otis W. Pollock to be forwarded through official channels. Making use of the regimental press, Pollock had printed a proposal for adjustments in the pay of enlisted men, especially noncommissioned officers. Men at the ranks above private were then paid monthly salaries as follows: corporal, fifteen dollars; sergeant, seventeen dollars; first sergeant, twenty-two dollars. Observing that noncommissioned officers earned little more than the thirteen dollars per month being paid private soldiers, as a company commander Pollock pointed out that competent corporals and sergeants were hard to find. Owing to the small pay differential, "when suitable men are found, the position is not of sufficient importance for them to take it." To attract the best men possible as the connecting link between private soldiers and commissioned officers, he proposed increasing the monthly pay of corporals to twenty dollars, sergeants to thirty dollars, and first sergeants to forty dollars. Taken together with economies that he suggested, these increases would, he wrote, "incalculably" enhance the efficiency of the army at less cost than at present.

Impressed by Pollock's statement, Dodge added to it an endorsement that the changes it suggested "would be beneficial to the Army, and the subject is worthy the highest consideration." General Crook also "earnestly recommended" the letter, but General Sheridan forwarded it "disapproved," as did General Sherman, so that by the time it reached the secretary of war, the initiative was all but doomed. Pollock had requested that the secretary place his letter before Congress to "urge . . . the necessity for the required legislation," and it was therefore duly forwarded, but without support,[38] and there the matter ended, at least officially. However, as the lead article in the issue for February 5, 1876, the *Army and Navy Journal* featured a 2,500-word commentary on Pollock's ideas. Noting the endorsements of officers who had reviewed it, the newspaper urged that the plan be so modified as to obviate all objections to it.[39] Except to stimulate some correspondence on the issues involved, this public support was unavailing; nevertheless, Pollock held to his views. Aware that army reorganization was in the wind, he contributed to the *Army and Navy Journal* for December 1, 1877, an article developing his argument that "the efficiency of the service could be enhanced, at least one-half, by a substantial improvement in the condition of the non-commissioned officers."[40]

Pollock's as yet unsuccessful proposal was surely in Dodge's mind as he drafted his response to the congressional subcommittee. Colonel Davis was also aware of the proposal when, on January 17, 1878, he wrote out his own answers to the questions in the circular. He invited the committee members' particular attention to it, enclosing a copy of the 1875 statement as well as the more recent one. "The distribution of the pay of the enlisted men as suggested would have a great influence in inducing good men to enlist," he wrote, "and would have a wonderfully good effect in stimulating zeal and energy in seeking promotion &c."[41] The unanimously expressed opinion on this matter by Davis, Dodge, and Pollock suggested a high degree of consensus on military matters among officers of the Twenty-third Infantry, but it failed to produce the result they advocated. The rates of pay for enlisted men that had been established in 1872 remained unchanged for two more decades, until 1898.[42]

Like Schofield, Pope, and Sherman, these regimental officers publicly expressed their views when asked, swimming upstream against the current of resistance to their conception of a national defense force as it ought to exist. A bill introduced in January 1878 by Congressman H. C. Banning of Ohio would have further reduced the authorized number of enlisted soldiers in the army to 20,000, but it was defeated.[43] This negative victory was a cause for rejoicing among army men. It preserved an inadequate status quo, but it was a victory nonetheless.

Soldier-Author at Fort Leavenworth

During his year of service at Fort Leavenworth, Dodge saw much of General Pope, and a relationship of friendly regard grew up between them. Pope, a West Point graduate six years his senior, shared Dodge's active curiosity, sense of humor, capacity for hard work, and pride in his profession. Since the embarrassment of his defeat at Second Bull Run in 1862, Pope had gone far toward restoring his damaged reputation, at least within the army. Whatever his shortcomings as a field commander may have been on that one occasion, he was now generally acknowledged to be a resourceful leader and a thoughtful man.[44] Since 1870 he had commanded the Department of the Missouri with deft skill.

Like Dodge, Pope took pleasure in conversation as a pastime.[45] An exchange between these loquacious individuals in the spring of 1878 exemplifies the good feeling that existed between them despite their difference in rank. The building that housed the post commander's office, which Dodge then occupied, was only about five hundred feet away from another where the affairs of the military department were transacted.[46] In conducting official business Dodge ordinarily wrote out whatever communications he intended to reach Pope, but one day the general chided him for this practice. "Dodge," he said, "I wish you would quit writing letters. If you want anything or anything goes wrong, come over here and we will talk about it." "No you don't," Dodge returned. "You can beat me talking hollow, & I'd have no show to get anything that way, but I can beat you writing." Disrespectful as it may have seemed, his boast went off well. Later, in recording the exchange, Dodge admitted that it was "an awful piece of vanity on my part, for Pope is one of the clearest, most logical & most forcible writers I know."[47] It was an accurate assessment, for Pope did write fluently, even if his prose lacked the economy and colloquial vigor of Dodge's. In fact, the flow of the general's letters and discursive endorsements sometimes nettled his superiors. Sheridan, who did not possess the same gift of expression and did not value it highly, implied to Sherman that Pope seemed more interested in conducting discussions than in getting things done.[48]

No doubt Dodge's boast of his ability as a writer was prompted by his known success as a published author. Coincidentally, at the time of his exchange with Pope he was making plans for another writing project. He intended to gather material for an account of the army in its years of presence on the plains, and in the *Army and Navy Journal* for February 13, 1878, he addressed a letter to officers and former officers, calling upon them for assistance. Explaining that a discussion of the army was one

John Pope. Courtesy Massachusetts Commandery, Military Order of the Loyal Legion of the United States, U.S. Army Military History Institute.

of five sections he had wished to include in *The Plains*, he added that the work's favorable reception and the encouragement of friends had induced him to carry on with his project. He could easily compose one unwritten section, "The Frontiersman," but such an account would necessarily be based almost entirely on his own experience and observation; and the same was true for the other, "The Army." Without access to official files at Washington that could provide him additional material, in the latter discussion he could write only "a chapter of my own life." If he was to fashion "an epitome of frontier and army life" generally, as he wished to do, he needed input from others. He therefore sought to generate interest in the project among potential collaborators.

Dodge pointed out the disparity between the army's many services on the plains during the past thirty years and the small number of works yet published to describe them. Before the "now ubiquitous reporter" had become an institution, he wrote, the work of the frontier army had gone on virtually unnoticed. "The experience of such men as Harney, Cooke, Heintzelman, Kendrick, Graham, Shepherd, Sykes, Sully, and many others I could name, are now confined to their own breasts, and in the nature of things will soon pass beyond the reach of any historian. It is not right nor just," he continued, "that the Army should lose the record of the experiences of the men of those days, and as the old leaven of distaste to authorship still lingers in most of their breasts, I offer my services as compiler."

Turning to military activities in more recent times, Dodge identified some of the memorable narratives yet to be given the shape they deserved, adding that the story of the advancing western frontier continued to unfold: "The great Sully campaign against the Sioux, the operations culminating in the Phil. Kearney massacre, the almost constant and desperate warfare waged by almost all the plains tribes from 1867 to 1872, the conflicts in Oregon and Arizona, the Modoc war, the three years of unrelenting contest of the Northern Sioux, and, latest of all, the magnificent effort of Joseph and his little band of daring spirits; each and all furnish material for the most thrillingly interesting narrative of the labors and exploits of the 'New Army.'" Dodge's enumeration of topics for development made an impressive display of his project's potential. "There is scarcely an officer or lady, soldier or civilian, who has lived at a frontier post or on a military reservation," he assured *Army and Navy Journal* readers, "but can give interesting illustrations of frontier life and its surroundings." He invited contributions from them all, promising that any material they sent would be acknowledged, and used if suitable, and that the names of contributors would not be divulged except with their permission. He would shape the facts presented him to suit his own fancy but would strictly adhere to the recounted facts themselves.[49]

Assuredly, the sequel to *The Plains* Dodge had in mind was rich with possibilities. He had cast his nets wide, but for the present he could only await responses to his appeal, and he recognized that they might be slow in coming. "Officers of the Army," he wrote William C. Church of the *Army and Navy Journal*, "are afflicted with two virtues (run to seed). They are very modest, & very much indisposed to put 'pen to paper' – & it requires a violent stimulant to get anything from them. I have many promises but so far very few contributions." He was confident of eventual success, however, and he assured Church of his intention to send him "many valuable & interesting sketches. No people on earth have more thrilling romantic & dramatic adventures than officers of the Army, & if I can only get them to permit me to be the reservoir into which they will pour their contributions, it will be to the advantage of myself & of the Army at large."[50]

Meanwhile, Dodge's celebrity as a popular authority on Indians led him to pursue further inquiries in that area. Whereas in writing *The Plains* he had relied almost entirely upon his own observations, to test the validity of what he had written he obtained copies of standard works by earlier writers, including Henry Rowe Schoolcraft and George Catlin. During the Powder River Expedition he had informally interviewed Frank North on the subject of Indian religious beliefs,[51] and in the spring of 1878 he turned for information to Captain George M. Randall, who possessed extensive first-hand knowledge of Indians and their ways.

For a time after the transfer of his regiment to the Department of the Missouri, Randall had remained on duty in the Department of the Platte as commander of

George M. Randall. Courtesy Roger D. Hunt Collection, U.S. Army Military History Institute.

Indian scouts. However, in November 1877 he was given a new assignment, as supervisor of 431 Nez Perce prisoners of war.[52] These were the people who, accompanying their Chief Joseph in a desperate flight east from their ancestral homes in Oregon, had surrendered on October 5 of that year to a pursuing force under Colonel Nelson A. Miles.[53] Accompanied by Randall and a military escort, the Nez Perces were later transported by boat down the Missouri River to Fort Leavenworth, where during the winter and spring they were confined on an island in the river. Since Dodge was the post commander during the greater part of this period, he had ample opportunity to observe the captive Indians as they went on with their lives during their enforced exile. In company with Randall, he observed their customs and heard much about that officer's experience in contact with the Sioux, Cheyennes, Crows, and other tribes.[54]

One anecdote about Indian beliefs told him by Randall seemed to Dodge worth making public at once, no matter what the future fate of a sequel to *The Plains* might be. In the form of a letter to the editor of the *Army and Navy Journal* from "D.," this was the pleasant account of an interchange between Randall and the Brulé chieftain Spotted Tail on the subject of religious belief. "White men have education and books and ought to know exactly what to believe and what to say," the wise old Indian was quoted as observing, "but hardly any two of them agree on anything."[55] As a story exemplifying the shortcomings of white men, especially those associated with the

Indian Bureau, this was delectable fare for army readers. The same was true of a statement by Chief Joseph that formed part of an interview published not long afterward in the *North American Review.* Frustrated by wrangling among government organizations about the disposition to be made of him and his captured people, he declared, "The white men have too many chiefs. They do not understand each other."[56]

The Southern Utes and Jicarilla Apaches

During the spring of 1878 a protracted official correspondence, eventually centering upon Dodge and his command, exemplified the dictum of Chief Joseph. What initiated the intragovernmental exchange was the perceived need to relocate two bands of Indians, 310 Southern Utes and 440 Jicarilla Apaches, from their current homes in northeast New Mexico to new ones where it was hoped they would be less likely to steal and destroy the property of American citizens.[57] The Utes were henceforth to be issued their rations at the Southern Ute Agency, in southwest Colorado, and the Apaches would receive theirs at the Mescalero Agency near Fort Stanton, in east central New Mexico. A request to that effect by Senator Stephen W. Dorsey of Arkansas began a correspondence among and between representatives of the War Department and the Department of the Interior concerning the arrangements needed to effect the changes.[58] From the beginning, these statements evinced mutual mistrust. Early in March General Sherman emphasized that costs of the removal would have to be borne by the Indian Bureau. He suspected that the Indian agents at the affected sites would not have the money or the wagons for transportation, "trusting to throw the whole expense on the War Department" as on earlier occasions.[59] Later in the month he insisted to the secretary of war not only that the Indian Bureau pay for the removal but that its agents accept responsibility for it and perform their share of the work. He was ready to act, but he wanted an understanding that "all the War Department should do is to afford the agents the necessary aid, by furnishing escort whilst the Indians are en route."[60] Carl Schurz, secretary of the interior, was nettled by the general's unflattering reflections on the department he led, but he assured the secretary of war that the necessary funds would be made available.[61]

Because the requested military action would take place within the Department of the Missouri, General Pope was receiving official copies of the correspondence between bureau heads. Early in April, having just been issued orders in the matter, he informed General Sheridan that he had no troops available to effect the removal. Lieutenant Colonel Edward Hatch, Ninth Cavalry, commander of the District of New Mexico, was doing all he could, but widely separated emergencies in southern Colorado and the vicinity of El Paso, Texas, left him no men to spare.[62] Men were needed, however, for Hatch presently informed Pope that the Indians in question had expressed a will to fight if an effort was made to remove them forcibly.[63] Sensing a determination to displace them from country they considered their home, they were encamped near the Texas Panhandle, where they could easily subsist on game for the rest of the summer. A campaign to take them into military custody would therefore be necessary. Hatch thought a body of 250 cavalrymen and 150 infantry soldiers would suffice to control them, but from within his district he could spare at most only one hundred cavalry.[64]

Possessed of this definite information, Pope explained to Sheridan that the current threat of an outbreak by disaffected bands in Indian Territory made redeployment of the cavalry companies currently stationed there unthinkable. No other cavalry units were stationed in the Department of the Missouri, so the best he could do was to send a body of infantry equipped as cavalry, trusting that they would quickly become adept enough in their new role to complete this temporary assignment. Sheridan concurred, and Pope therefore requested that 150 sets of cavalry equipment be forwarded to Fort Leavenworth from the arsenal at Rock Island, Illinois.[65] Meanwhile, as the generals attempted to cobble together a workable plan, the Commissioner of Indian Affairs complained to Secretary Schurz that "as yet there is no co-operation on the part of the War Department as promised."[66]

While accusations and misrepresentations echoed back and forth in the offices of his superiors, Dodge was on temporary duty in Saint Louis, serving on a board of officers to examine several intrenching tools for possible adoption by the army. However, on April 20 another officer was named to replace him, and he was ordered to return at once to Fort Leavenworth.[67] Arriving there, he received a letter from Pope's adjutant informing him in vague terms of a "special and temporary" duty he would shortly be called upon to perform. He was to select three companies, filled up to an average of fifty men each, and equip and mount them as cavalry in preparation for a field assignment that would probably require two or three months. "Orders will be issued in due time for the movement," he was told, "which it is expected will take place about the 20th proximo, and in the mean time it is desirable that the men and officers be familiarized as much as possible with the care and use of their horses and equipment."[68]

This directive gave no hint of the circumstances and considerations that had prompted the assignment, but irony abounded on its face. Dodge, a staunch advocate of foot soldiers as a force superior to mounted troops in engagements with Indians, was to command a faux "cavalry" battalion. The term in use to describe this variety of troop deployment was oxymoronic: "mounted infantry." Another irony became evident once Dodge learned the background of his prospective field duty: urgently requested two months earlier, the removal of the Indians would not go forward for at least another month. However, what was being designated "the Ute Expedition" would at least take place in territory he knew well from his years at Fort Lyon. To accompany him he selected companies B, G, and K of his regiment, and the men so designated responded enthusiastically. Anticipating the torrid summer conditions they would encounter, with his permission some soldiers purchased wide-brimmed felt hats to wear against the heat and glare.[69]

The order for Dodge and his men to depart was duly issued on May 8—none too soon, for only a few days earlier the agent for the Southern Utes had reported unrest and insubordination among the Indians in his charge and requested army troops to help restore order.[70] Dodge and his men were at the point of departing by rail for Fort Lyon when, by direction of the secretary of war, their mission was suspended until further notice.[71] It had been learned from F. H. Weaver, the Indian agent, that the bad conduct he reported earlier was caused by the presence of a few soldiers in the vicinity, "just enough . . to excite the Indians, and make them impudent."[72] Army troops, the remedy to the fears Weaver had expressed only a few days before, were now considered their cause, and the Department of the Interior thought it best that the army should stay away. Nevertheless, on May 28 the Department of the Interior renewed its request that the War Department cause the transfer of the Indians as soon as practicable. General Sherman pointed out the whimsical illogic of this latest policy shift. "I do not comprehend the arguments," he wrote, "that because these Indians are . . . better behaved now than when irritated by the small squad of soldiers, and therefore should be moved. While they are well behaved why again disturb them by a removal for which we are not prepared with the force needed to compel them? If they are willing to go, no soldiers seems [*sic*] to be necessary."[73]

On June 20 Congress took action in this matter that representatives of the War and Interior departments had debated, delayed, planned, and prepared for in recent months, then put off indefinitely; it approved a special appropriation to pay expenses for the removal of the Southern Utes and Jicarilla Apaches.[74] Late in July Lieutenant Colonel Hatch telegraphed General Pope that the two Indian bands were then making their way peaceably to their new agencies and that no military involvement would be required. "I presume," he wrote, "the Indians have promised to move upon receiving the amount of appropriation five thousand dollars in presents."[75] What the grudging gestures toward cooperation between the executive bureaus had failed to accomplish, Congress had achieved expeditiously through an infusion of funds.

Dodge's reaction to this resolution of the problem that had almost resulted in the Ute Expedition of 1878 and transformed him into a cavalry officer may be inferred from his reference to recent events in a letter of August 5 to William C. Church. He had been "very busy" of late, he wrote, "first organizing the so-called Ute expedition (which was stopped after we had been partly loaded on the cars –)."[76] Of course, it was not his part to criticize the lawful actions of his superiors, no matter how dilatory or dithering they might seem. Still, the lame conclusion of this long-drawn-out affair must have reminded him somehow of his experience with the bridge at Fort Riley.

At Fort Hays, Kansas

The aborted mission to escort the Indians to their new agencies was the last major incident of Dodge's posting at Fort Leavenworth. On July 13 he and the three companies he had designated to comprise the Ute Expedition received orders to take post at Fort Hays, on the Kansas Pacific Railroad approximately 240 miles west, and eight days later he assumed command there.[77] At the time of Dodge's posting at Fort

Dodge, seventy-seven miles distant, Fort Hays had been a relatively important facility, a distribution point for posts to its south, including some in Texas and the Indian Territory.[78] It no longer exercised that function, and since the era of need for a deterrent against Indians in central Kansas was all but over, regular patrols of the surrounding country were no longer made from the post. Its current value lay in its location adjacent to the railroad. Like Fort Wallace, farther west along the Kansas Pacific, it had already been named by General Sheridan as a facility that could safely be dispensed with before many more years.[79] Dodge's mandate at Fort Hays was to oversee repair of its somewhat dilapidated buildings to ensure its adequacy for service as a four-company post in the remainder of its useful life.

In army parlance this was "ordinary garrison duty," necessary if unexciting, yet it afforded Dodge an opportunity to exert himself in a variety of activity he understood well. Assisted by First Lieutenant Trout, his post quartermaster and commissary of subsistence, he set to work, testing what could be accomplished with a minimum expenditure of funds. He arranged for the upper portions of the collapsed post bakehouse to be rebuilt by a master mason, this time with the proper materials. He began discussion with officials of the Kansas Pacific about construction of a railroad loop that would connect the quartermaster's shed with the main line running through Hays City, less than one mile north.[80] Upon learning that the authorized post trader, Hill P. Wilson, had advertised his position as for sale, he informed Wilson that he had no legal right to do so.[81] As part of an effort to identify candidates for membership on an army rifle team, he arranged for a trial of target shooting among certain enlisted men.[82] "For some months to come," he wrote William C. Church early in August, work at the post would keep him too busy to permit his devoting much attention to "my book of Army adventures." The response to his published appeal for material included only a few communications thus far, a result he attributed to laziness and selfishness among his fellow officers. "Those who have no disposition or ability to write, will do nothing to give another the advantage of their experiences, while those that can write, hold onto anything good that comes in their way, with the expectation at some time of themselves writing up their own experiences in book form." However, he still hoped to secure sufficient matter to move ahead with the project in the fall and winter.[83]

Dodge was turning his attention to repairs of the cavalry stables at Fort Hays when, on September 11, the bubble of normalcy burst. Telegrams received that day notified him of a military emergency 250 miles distant and directed him to make preparations to meet it, should it possibly spread so far as to reach his vicinity. A large body of Northern Cheyenne Indians had departed without authorization from their agency, near Fort Reno in Indian Territory, and were apparently bound for their ancestral homeland in the northern plains and mountains. Their present whereabouts were unknown, but their passage would probably take them through Kansas, and they must be kept from accomplishing it. Once the fugitive Indians showed themselves, they were to be attacked unless they surrendered at once.[84]

Almost two years before, Dodge and his Doboys under General Crook had narrowly missed joining a decisive engagement with a village of the Northern Cheyennes. The events in Indian Territory now reawakened his ambition for distinction as a commander of troops in the field against these Indians. If the army forces south of him failed to halt their progress, he might soon be offered a second chance to come upon them and, should they choose to fight, help make history.

16

The Northern Cheyennes

In the aftermath of Mackenzie's attack on their village in November 1876,[1] the Northern Cheyennes under Dull Knife made their way north through the mountains to Crazy Horse, who gave them what limited assistance he could before the two bands parted. Reduced in number and impoverished, Dull Knife and his people wandered east and south for a time, but having no other recourse, they came in to the Red Cloud Agency and surrendered in the spring of 1877. In conference with General Crook and others, they agreed to occupy reservation lands in Indian Territory that had been set aside for them by treaty. As a result, in late May almost 1,000 tribespeople began a journey south to their new home, under supervision of a military escort under the command of First Lieutenant Henry W. Lawton, Fourth Cavalry. More than two months later they arrived at Fort Reno, Indian Territory, and were transferred to the care of John D. Miles, the Indian Bureau's agent at the adjacent Cheyenne and Arapaho Agency.

Unfortunately, this relocation opened a new chapter in the ordeal of Dull Knife's people.[2] They were disappointed with their new home and soon became dissatisfied with the treatment they received there. They balked at the rationing system imposed upon them by the agent, which deprived headmen of authority to distribute goods to members of their bands. They did not mix well with the Southern Cheyennes already enrolled at the agency. They felt betrayed, for they had understood from senior military officers like Crook that they would be free to return north if they wished,[3] but now that option was denied them and they were effectively imprisoned. Unaccustomed to the southern climate, they grew ill with malaria and other diseases, and in the absence of adequate medical treatment many died. They were homesick, and gravest of all their afflictions, they were hungry.

The potential for all these causes of discontent had been recognized and reported on within weeks of the Northern Cheyennes' arrival in Indian Territory. Under orders from Colonel Mackenzie, on September 30, 1877, First Lieutenant Lawton revisited the Cheyenne and Arapaho Agency and Fort Reno to ascertain the condition of all the Indians enrolled there. In an interview with the post commander, Major John K. Mizner, Fourth Cavalry, he was informed that Agent Miles seemed to be doing all he could, faithfully issuing to the Indians their rations from the supplies made available to him by the Indian Bureau. However, the quantities for distribution were in Mizner's view "entirely insufficient and inadequate to their wants." On the next day Lawton observed a weekly issue of rations. The sugar was of inferior quality, he later reported, and the beef "not . . . merchantable for any use." In all, the food allotted the Indians amounted to no more than two-thirds the legally authorized provision, evidently owing to the failure of the Indian Bureau to make available sufficient supplies. Lawton sensed the frustration of the Indians but regarded them as peaceably disposed unless driven to violence "as the alternative to starvation." His report received strong endorsement from Mackenzie, who warned that any future outbreak by the Northern Cheyennes would be the fault of the federal government and would be caused by starvation. In forwarding the document to army headquarters, General Pope observed that its contents warranted serious consideration by officials of the Indian Bureau.[4]

The Lawton report, which became known within the Department of the Interior as the "Lawton charges," had little practical effect except to intensify hostility between the army and the Indian Bureau. Accusations of dishonesty were leveled against Lawton as the federal agency under criticism rallied to protect its good name. On October 20, 1877, Secretary Schurz reported to the secretary of war that the official who oversaw operations in the Indian Territory had assured him there was "no scarcity of supplies at that agency," though the Indians would need to supplement their rations by hunting or farming. His informant had suggested that as a precaution, additional army troops should be transferred to Fort Reno from Fort Sill, approximately seventy-five miles south. The small number of troops at Fort Reno tended to embolden the already warlike Indians and could bode trouble.[5]

In November 1877 Indians attached to the Cheyenne and Arapaho Agency were permitted to leave their reservation in order to hunt buffalo, as they had done with success in recent years. However, this year the hunt was an abject failure, for the seriously depleted buffalo herds were not to be found. Destitute and in danger of starving, the hunting party was issued emergency rations at Camp Supply, on the North Fork of the Canadian River 130 miles upstream from the agency, to enable it to return home.[6] Meanwhile, General Pope and other concerned officials warned of an imminent outbreak. Earlier in the year Pope had expressed dismay at the duty imposed on the army, of forcing the Indians to remain on their reservations and "starve peaceably." General Sherman agreed, writing that it was "simply useless for the Army to capture and compel Indians to live on a reservation if they must starve by remaining thereon."[7] Army officers in Indian Territory found it distasteful to bear responsibility for sufferings they had no legal power to alleviate. Thus Colonel Mackenzie directed

Dull Knife, Northern Cheyenne. Courtesy Western History Collections, University of Oklahoma Libraries.

Mizner to use no force whatever against Indians at the Cheyenne and Arapaho Agency unless in extreme situations, lest the army "be placed in a position of assisting in a great wrong."[8]

The Flight and Pursuit

Against this background of disputed facts and jurisdictional jealousy, the Northern Cheyennes continued to suffer and grew desperate. Dull Knife had earlier expressed to Lawton his will to remain on the reservation and follow a course of gradual adjustment to American ways, according to the wishes of the Indian Bureau. Yet as more of his tribesmen fell ill during the oppressive summer of 1878, the chief's resolve lost strength. Some of his young men were restless and inclined to violence. In a statement often heard, they expressed their own resolution: "We are sickly and dying here and no one will speak our names when we are gone. We will go north at all hazards and if we die in battle, our names will be remembered and cherished by all our people."[9]

Acting on a report that some Northern Cheyennes had left the reservation, on September 6, 1878, Mizner ordered his cavalry force, companies G and H, Fourth Cavalry, under Captain Joseph Rendlebrock, to encamp within sight of the Indians' village, which they had moved to a location several miles from the agency. Rendlebrock's orders were not to interfere with them unless they moved still farther from the agency offices, where Agent Miles wished to re-enroll them all in order to ascertain whether in fact any were absent. Ordered to return, the Indians delayed for two days, offering one excuse or another, but it was understood that on the morning of September 10 they would comply with the agent's demand.[10] However, with Rendlebrock's pickets in distant view, Dull Knife and his followers slipped away unnoticed the night before, leaving their campfires burning and their tipis standing, outlined against the dark sky. Their flight was discovered early the next morning, and Rendlebrock set out on their trail with orders to overtake them and return them to the agency. If at all possible he was to accomplish this object without resorting to force, for Mizner feared violence among Indians still on the reservation who felt sympathy with their fellow tribespeople.[11]

Moving with difficulty through rough country north and west of the agency, Rendlebrock and his men pushed hard, traveling sixty miles on their first day out. That afternoon he sent a courier to Camp Supply with a request for reinforcement, and by noon the next day Company I, Fourth Cavalry, under Captain William Hemphill was moving north on the ninety-mile wagon road between that post and Fort Dodge, Kansas. Rendlebrock continued to march rapidly on September 11 and 12, and midmorning of the following day he met the Northern Cheyennes. They had doubled back on their own trail and fortified a position at Turkey Springs, Indian Territory, thirty-five miles east of the Dodge-Supply road and a few miles north of the Cimarron River. In response to a demand to surrender and return to the agency, their spokesman Little Wolf refused, indicating their willingness to fight.[12] Skirmishing began at once and continued for most of the next day. At the end of that period, after thirty-six hours without water, the soldiers were suffering from thirst; and after managing to break the Indians' position and put them to flight, Rendlebrock retreated to find fresh water and sent his wounded soldiers under escort to Camp Supply. Three of his men had been killed and three wounded.[13]

News of the Northern Cheyenne outbreak reached General Pope on September 11.[14] He at once began marshalling forces to intercept the Indians, ranging troops along the Atchison, Topeka and Santa Fe Railroad and the Kansas Pacific Railroad from seventy-five to one hundred miles north. One infantry company from Fort Dodge began patrolling the region west of that post and south of the Atchison, Topeka and

Santa Fe. Troops at Fort Lyon were alerted to watch the country east of them and move at once along the railroad once the route of the Indians was determined. Should the Northern Cheyennes reach the vicinity of Fort Dodge, Lieutenant Colonel William H. Lewis, Nineteenth Infantry, would assume command of the combined pursuit force. To ensure stability at Fort Reno in the absence of troops ordinarily posted there, Pope ordered one company of cavalry from Fort Sill to reinforce the garrison. To the north, along the Kansas Pacific he ordered one hundred mounted infantry troops to Fort Wallace. Two other infantry companies from Dodge's garrison at Fort Hays took station at points between that post and Fort Wallace, 131 miles west by rail. Pope was taking what precautions he could, but the resources available to him were quite limited in proportion to the large tracts of country involved. On September 12 he suggested to General Sheridan that preparations for action should also be made in the Department of the Platte.[15]

The Northern Cheyennes easily held their own against the troops under Rendlebrock, proving themselves both elusive and formidable. They seemed in no hurry to make their way north into Kansas. On September 18 Captain Hemphill with his troop of cavalry managed to locate them along Sand Creek, south of the state line, but he was badly outnumbered and after a brief engagement withdrew to Fort Dodge. Three days later, acting on information that the Indians were still in that area, Hemphill's company and an infantry unit under Captain Charles E. Morse, Sixteenth Infantry, joined the cavalry under Rendlebrock and, commanded by Rendlebrock as senior officer, fought the Indians inconclusively that afternoon and all the next day.[16] On the morning of September 23 the troops marched northwest in pursuit of the fugitives toward the Arkansas River, approximately fifty miles distant.

By this time the outbreak had received nationwide publicity, and the army's obvious inability to control the Northern Cheyennes was giving concern to military authorities. Pope reported to Sheridan on September 18 that he had reinforced the troops available to Lewis, who should soon have three companies of cavalry and five of infantry. If Lewis did not stop the renegade band at the Arkansas River, he would pursue them toward the Kansas Pacific. "The want of cavalry is severely felt," he concluded, "but I will do all possible with the force I have."[17] Sensing Pope's fragile confidence, Sheridan urged General Crook to do everything possible to cut off the fugitives. Should Dull Knife and his band succeed in returning to their homeland, he feared their accomplishment would threaten the fragile peace then prevailing with Indians of the entire northwest. Moreover, it would surely destabilize the reservation system in Indian Territory, encouraging disaffected bands there to make more trouble. On September 19 Sheridan assured General Sherman that "every effort will be made" to capture Dull Knife and so help preserve the peace.[18]

At Fort Hays a steady stream of information and speculation reached Dodge by telegraph. Citizens in the area were alarmed, and dire rumors and calls for special assistance multiplied. Dodge received reports from soldiers and civilian scouts in the field, and to make provisional arrangements he was in frequent communication with his counterpart at Fort Wallace, Lieutenant Colonel James Van Voast, Sixteenth Infantry. On September 18 he received a telegraphic order from Pope to proceed to Monument Station, 101 miles west of Fort Hays by railroad, and assume command of all troops east of that point along the Kansas Pacific line.[19] Pope believed that, should the Northern Cheyennes succeed in moving this far north, they would attempt to cross the railroad at some point where one of the old Indian trails intersected it. Those were at or near Monument and the two railroad stations immediately east of it, Grinnell and Buffalo. Dodge was thus being positioned where his department commander thought troops were most likely to see action, and on that day he began a journal describing his experiences in the campaign to come.[20] The notebook would serve him in writing an official report at the end of the action, but it might also become a repository of material for future literary use. His chapters recounting the exploits of the army on the western plains remained to be written, and it was just possible that the pursuit of the Northern Cheyennes would take an honorable place among those stories.

Arrived at Monument Station, Dodge sent and received several telegrams daily, making preparations for a move from the railroad. He secured an order for First Lieutenant Trout to be sent to Fort Wallace to organize pack trains. He requisitioned wagons, hired civilian scouts, ordered packsaddles and ammunition, and received three companies of reinforcements, one from Fort Riley and two from Fort Leavenworth. Major Alexander J. Dallas, Twenty-third Infantry, was sent from Fort Leavenworth with three companies of the regiment that would serve as mounted infantry. By September 22 nine companies of infantry occupied points along the railroad, but Dodge and Van Voast were still without information about the location of the Indians. A misunderstanding between the two officers on that day revealed the intensity of Dodge's desire to direct the pursuit force. Interpreting an ambiguous message from Van Voast to mean that he wished to turn over to him the entire command in the event of a pursuit, Dodge at once telegraphed back a message urging him to make the fact known to General Pope. But Van Voast had meant the entire pack train, then being organized under Trout, not the entire pursuit force.[21]

On September 25 the news reached Dodge that the Northern Cheyennes had crossed the Arkansas River, just south of the Atchison, Topeka and Santa Fe line. Anticipating that they might reach the Kansas Pacific on the following day, he awaited the coming developments eagerly. "The pursuing Comd. will be first rate," he wrote, "& if the Comdr. is the right sort of man he will capture [the Indians], unless something very unforeseen occurs."[22] All depended on where the Indians crossed the railroad. Once the call came, he could be on the march within two hours.

On September 26 there was no more news nor even a rumor of the fugitives. Other information received that day made Dodge uneasy, however—namely, that Colonel Davis would arrive at Fort Wallace with the regimental staff the next morning. Dodge feared that after he and Van Voast had completed all preparations for the campaign, Davis would preempt the command of it at the last moment. Of course, as the ranking officer the colonel was entitled to that privilege if he wished it, and a telegram on the morning of September 27 confirmed that he did. "I am very sure that Pope did not aim this blow at me," Dodge counseled himself amid his disappointment. "Pope would be foolish to put me aside for Davis if he could help it. I know all this country, the Indian trails & where they are likely to go. Davis knows nothing but what he learns from day to day from guides &c. I am vain enough to believe I am a better Comdr. here than Davis, & I am very sure I would have it did my rank warrant it."[23] That Dodge knew the region better than Davis was undeniable. His scouts while stationed at Fort Dodge had prepared him well to direct an effort to intercept Indians moving north from there. In contrast, prior to December 1876 Davis had never served in the Department of the Missouri, and since that time his sole posting had been at Fort Leavenworth.

On the night of September 27 Trout arrived, bringing Dodge an order from Davis to concentrate at Monument all his troops posted east of that station. According to Trout, Davis did not intend to pursue the strategy of watchful waiting that Pope had laid out. Rather, he planned to seize the initiative by ordering Dodge and his force to move south from the railroad in search of the fugitives. Dodge thought this unwise, especially since the whereabouts of the Indians remained unknown. "Our only chance is to watch the R. R. all ready for a move," he wrote. "As soon as the Indians cross, the whole Comd. should be taken by Rail to that point & put on the Trail. We ought to be on trail within 6 or 8 hours of their crossing. If Jeff sends his Comd away from the R. R. he will, when he hears they have crossed have to send out for the Comd. & it will have to march to R. R. losing two or three or more days – entirely too much to be made up on a stern chase."[24]

Moments after he had written this analysis, another telegram arrived. He was ordered to march rapidly south, with four companies, to a point on Poison Creek approximately forty-five miles from Monument, searching for signs of the Indians. Thus at 4:00 P.M. that day Dodge left the station with three companies, leaving directions for the fourth to follow him as soon as it arrived by train. When darkness fell he continued traveling by the North Star, but his guide lost the trail and a dispersal occurred, causing a delay. At 11:30 P.M. the command reached the Smoky Hill River and went into camp, having marched sixteen miles. The fourth company, under Captain James Henton, Twenty-third Infantry, arrived later.

Shortly after dawn the force was about to move out again when a citizen arrived at a gallop from Monument, bearing a telegraphed message from Davis with a new set of orders. On the afternoon of September 27, about thirty-six hours before, a pursuit force under Lieutenant Colonel Lewis had overtaken the Northern Cheyennes on the Punished Woman's Fork of the Smoky Hill, south and west of Dodge's present location. Lewis was severely wounded in the engagement that followed, and Captain Clarence Mauck, Fourth Cavalry, assumed command, sending a lieutenant, a surgeon, and twenty-five men to Fort Wallace as escort to Lewis and two other wounded men. The party arrived at the fort at 1:00 A.M. on September 29, Lewis having died of blood loss during the journey. Meanwhile, on the night of the battle, the Indians had resumed their march. Wishing to head them off, Davis now directed Dodge to move west along the Smoky Hill. If he failed to discover the Indians, he was to proceed at once to Sheridan Station, the first railroad stop west of Monument. Davis was confident that he now knew the approximate location of the Indians and could act decisively. "Prospects good for capturing the Indians," he telegraphed to Pope. "Dodge's command must be in close proximity to them. He will move at daylight for them."[25]

Dodge marched as ordered but saw no evidence of the fugitives, and on his arrival at Sheridan, to his "very intense disgust," he learned the reason why. They had crossed the railroad the night before, twelve miles east of Monument. Mauck with his cavalry was now in pursuit of them, and that fact was just as galling. "Had it not been for Jeff's foolish order sending me away from the R. R. I would now be at least 20 miles North of the R. R. on the track of the Redskins & if Pope had not sent Davis to command, I would have been there with 6 Cos Infy & 3 Cos M[oun]t[e]d Infy. – better for a fight than any Cavalry." Reporting by telegraph to Davis, Dodge requested permission to move north from Sheridan, toward a point where Indians traditionally crossed a watercourse known as Sappa Creek. Evidently aware of the tactical error he had committed, in his response Davis was unusually familiar. "I was afraid that you were left out in the cold in the pursuit," he wrote, "but now I think you are fully abreast of the other commands. . . . Mauck starting from Carlyle tomorrow morning, trailing the Indians will be on your right [to the east]. You will not delay in order to communicate with him, but push. I wish you and your command had the fabled seven-league boots."[26]

Four bodies of troops were to move north from the railroad from east to west: those led by Mauck, by Dodge, by Dallas, and a column of seventy-five infantry and twenty-five cavalry under Captain Duncan M. Vance, Sixteenth Infantry. For a time Davis had intended to direct their operations from the field, but he elected to remain at Fort Wallace and rely upon couriers for communication. To ensure a rapid march, Dodge sent nine sick men back to Fort Wallace and issued strict orders limiting the amount of baggage to be taken. At 10:00 A.M. on Monday, September 30, he crossed the railroad. Some of his troops were already footsore, and the near absence of water on the seemingly interminable prairie ahead threatened danger to both men and animals, but the battalion nevertheless marched twenty-two miles that day. Keeping up the pace, on the afternoon of October 2 Dodge caught sight of a farmer's house that had been gutted by a small party of the Northern Cheyennes. "The Indians are not far ahead of me," he assured himself; "in fact we ought to have them pretty well cornered if all the Comds. have marched as fast as I have."[27] Thus far he had received no messages from them, but he had seen fresh wagon tracks that he took to be Mauck's. He expected that his Walk-a-Heaps would overtake the cavalry within a day or two.

About seven miles into the march of October 3, Dodge reached a pretty, cultivated valley and rode up to a ranch to ask a man there whether he had heard anything of the Indians. "Yes," this person replied, "we have seen & felt them. Our whole valley is in mourning & we are not yet through burying the dead."[28] Thus began a succession of interviews whose details were so painful that Dodge recorded only a few. On the morning of September 30, before he had even left Sheridan, this little community had been devastated by a small group of Cheyenne men. "Every house has been sacked, every female over 10 years of age captured was ravished. . . . I have never seen such a horrid picture of devastation," he wrote. "A lovely valley laid waste, horses, food, bedding, clothing all gone." Dodge's visit to this scene of sorrow lent new urgency to his pursuit of the Indians, but the anger he felt was not directed toward them alone. "I can write no more," he confessed in closing this day's journal entry. "I am disappointed – & stricken with horror that in a civilized country such things as I have seen & heard today are fostered & encouraged by people who think themselves Christian & humane." For himself, "I would wipe every Indian off the face of the earth, sooner than allow it."[29]

Dodge's interviews with the grieving settlers occasioned some delay, but his command marched twenty-four miles on that day. He had received no communication from Colonel Davis since leaving Sheridan, and he still knew nothing of the positions either of the other pursuit forces or of the Indians, except that the latter were probably at least two days ahead of him. However, on October 4 he obtained some of the information he wished from a group of citizens who were traveling south with abandoned Indian ponies. They reported that Mauck was two if not three days ahead of him; Dallas and Vance were both better than one day ahead, probably thirty miles, and moving rapidly, Dallas's men being mounted and Vance's infantry riding on his wagons. Dodge continued on for a time after this meeting, but during the break for lunch he held "long and anxious communication" with himself about what he had just learned. How was he to overtake the other commands, and if he did, what difference would it make now? He had heard rumors that the Indians had already crossed the Platte River, into territory patrolled by troops under General Crook. After much thought, he decided that continued pursuit of the fugitive Indians by his command had no practical value. On the other hand, his timely return to the disordered country south of him might still prove useful. Reluctantly, therefore, he determined to reverse course.[30]

That night Dodge made camp on Beaver Creek at the same site he had occupied the night before. Shortly after setting out again on October 5 he was overtaken by a courier from Vance's column. This man carried with him the recopied text of an order Vance had received from Davis, directing Dodge to take command of Dallas's column and push on to the Union Pacific Railroad, reporting from there to Generals Pope and Crook. Vance, not knowing Dodge's location, had copied the order, retaining the original, and sent the messenger in search of the proper recipient.[31] Of course, by the time Dodge received the communication from Davis he knew that compliance with it was impossible, even if he had owned a pair of seven-league boots. He therefore resumed his southward course and that night wrote out a report to

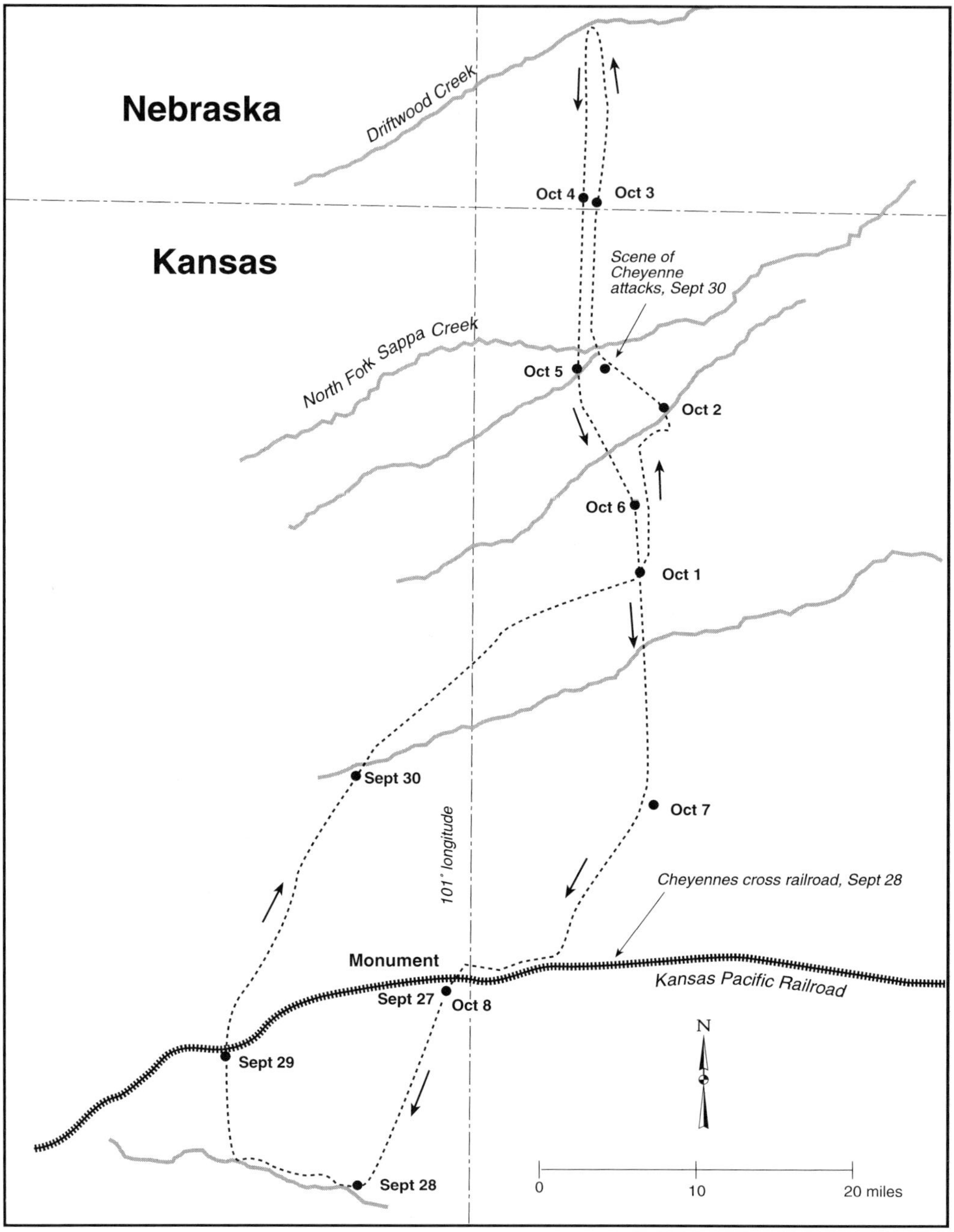

Dodge's itinerary, September 27–October 8, 1878

Davis, recounting his movements in recent days and stating his reasons for abandoning the pursuit. With the three other commands well in advance of him and all equipped to increase the distance, he was "hopelessly out of the race," he wrote. Even so, his men had "marched admirably . . . and have endured with soldierly constancy the privations incident to a rapid pursuit on the most limited allowance of transportation."[32]

On the afternoon of October 8 Dodge reached Monument Station and telegraphed to General Pope the news of his safe arrival. Pope relayed this information to Sheridan, noting that "why he returned instead of pushing on to U. P. R. R. is not explained." He asked whether Dodge and his men should be sent by rail to the Department of the Platte to rejoin the pursuit,[33] but Sheridan already had fifteen companies of troops in the field north of the Union Pacific Railroad. He was concerned that posts further south might be undermanned if outbreaks occurred in Texas or the Indian Territory, and Pope shared his unease.[34] Dodge had been directed to remain at Monument until further orders, prompting speculation within his command about what new adventure was in store, but on October 10 he was ordered to return to Fort Hays.

Analyses and Accusations

Shortly after his arrival at the post, at 3:30 A.M. on October 11, Dodge learned with interest that the Northern Cheyennes had crossed the Union Pacific Railroad line at 1:00 P.M. on October 4, almost exactly the time when he had abandoned the chase, one hundred miles distant from them. By now the determined band of Indians had been absent from their reservation for more than a month, and excepting Mauck's column, troops stationed in the Department of the Missouri were no longer participating in the effort to capture them. Within Pope's department nothing further was to be done except to identify the causes of the failed pursuit and, if possible, take steps to prevent its recurrence.

Drawing on the information he had obtained thus far, Dodge wrote out a private assessment of the campaign. From what he had learned of the Indians' rapid movements after the battle with Lewis, he believed nothing could have altered the unsuccessful result. The Northern Cheyennes had traveled more than twenty-four hours at a single stretch, baffling all anticipations of their likely progress. Moreover, when crossing the railroad, they had dispersed, leaving numberless trails that extended for eight miles along the tracks. For a time that strategy had confused the Indian scouts who accompanied Mauck, and Dodge's guide Boon Tomlinson acknowledged that he would have been completely at a loss. By the time some of the Indian men began their brutality along Prairie Dog and Sappa creeks, the band was already a full day's march ahead of Mauck; moreover, they could easily outdistance him by exchanging worn-out ponies for fresh stock in the settlements. "I still believe," Dodge wrote, "that my plan, to sit on the R. R. every thing in readiness & when the Indians cross concentrate & pursue with vigor /was\ best – but Jeff [Davis] thought differently & he was in a position to decide."

If outbreaks from Indian Territory should occur in the future—and Dodge believed they would—he envisioned three means of cutting them short. Cavalry troops must be stationed along the railroad line; pack trains must be maintained at the ready; and each post in the region must be furnished with one good Indian guide. He still agreed with General Crook that the army's Indian troubles "will never be settled until we learn to use Indian against Indian." With Generals Pope, Sheridan, and Sherman he agreed that once in a fight "the Army will almost always beat the Indians . . . [but] you can't make people fight who don't want to fight & can outrun you."[35]

That seemed definitive, but on the day after Dodge had written his analysis he learned from departmental headquarters that other persons still saw the matter quite differently, and that his own conduct was about to be reviewed. "Sir," the letter from Pope's adjutant read in full, "the Department Commander directs that as soon as possible, you make such explanation as you may have to offer for your failure to obey the orders which Col. Jeff. C. Davis reports he had sent you to follow up the hostile Indians as far as the Union Pacific Railroad, unless they were sooner captured."[36] Dodge was excitable and had a temper, and the demeaning tone of this directive stirred him. Nevertheless, in responding at once to the adjutant, he kept his composure and confined himself almost entirely to facts. As preparation for writing an official report he had already made copies of all orders and other messages he had sent and received during his absence from Fort Hays, together with extracts from his daily journal. He now enclosed these with his self-exoneration, as constituting its documentary basis. "From these papers," he wrote, "it will be seen by the Dept. Comdr. that I and my Command did all that men could possibly do, and that no shadow of blame for the non-capture of the Indians can fairly be attributed to us." Noting that at the time he received the order from Davis he was "fully two days march from Dallas," he submitted that the order was "impossible of fulfillment and therefore of no effect."[37]

In fact, General Pope had no intention to lay blame on Dodge unless his explanation of the noncompliance with Davis's order should prove unsatisfactory. The stern tone of his adjutant's message was probably in response to input from Davis. Since October 5 Pope had been gathering material for his own report, and in that document he made no mention of Dodge. He had hoped, he informed General Sheridan, that the cavalry under Lewis would be able to delay the Indians long enough to permit infantry to reach the scene of action. However, the Northern Cheyennes were armed with long-range rifles, and the cavalry with their short-range carbines were no match for them. In order to place cavalry soldiers on an equal footing with Indians, Pope recommended that henceforward they be armed with long-range Springfield rifles. As he had urged before, he proposed again "that Cavalry should be sent here in view of the actual and prospective necessities of the frontier. There is at present no appearance of further trouble at the Cheyenne Agency, but the quiet is likely to be broken unless the Indians are sufficiently and regularly fed"—a condition not likely to be satisfied.[38]

Pope thus laid the blame for his troops' failure to capture the Northern Cheyennes on inadequate equipment and an insufficient number of cavalry troops. To be sure, he was aware that some officers engaged in the pursuit had performed less well than others. Three officers of the Fourth Cavalry were subsequently tried by court-martial on charges that grew out of their conduct in the campaign.[39] But Pope had ample information to comprehend that whatever the exact circumstances, Dodge's failure to obey an order from Davis was not a cause of the Indians' success in eluding pursuit. Even so, army discipline required that the lapse be looked into, for by the Articles of War, Dodge's action was a punishable offense unless clearly warranted by the circumstances.

Dodge, having sent off the explanation demanded of him, remained defiant. He welcomed a searching inquiry into the course he had taken, for "if they force me on a defence, I will very easily show that the only mistakes made were by Pope & Davis – Pope in sending Davis to command, & Davis in sending the troops away from the R. R." He blamed the latter officer for the embarrassment he was being subjected to. "There is no doubt that Davis feels badly," he wrote in his journal.

> He took Command with his usual good opinion of himself. He knew it all, & would take advice from no one. His egotism & desire *to do*, led him to make the only real mistake of the Campaign – not that he would likely have done better in any event – but our only hope was in sticking to the R. R.
>
> He felt his mistake, when he found the Indians had crossed, while his Comd. was in advance of the R. R. . . . He did what he could & failed, with no blame to fairly attached to him – as after all, it was a mere difference of opinion, & at the very worst an error of judgment.
>
> But the Great *I*, which solely composes the man prevents him from accepting the situation. He was necessarily right, & somebody else must be wrong. He looks around for a scape-goat, some one on whom he can thrown some suspicion of blame, which he absurdly hopes may cover up his own fault, & rushes off to Pope & reports me for disobedience of his orders. . . . Of all /the\ Commanders to pitch on me – who had a foot command solely, who was already far behind in the race – (although I marched tremendously, sending one poor fellow to his grave)
>
> He is a huge Ass – worse than an Ass, or he would have had sense enough to keep quiet.[40]

Although harsh, Dodge's characterization of Colonel Davis was based on more than a year of close official contact and on knowledge of his regimental commander's checkered career. Colonel James B. Fry, the former provost marshal general, later wrote an extended sketch of Davis, whom he had known from youth. According to Fry, his comrade considered himself a "born military chieftain." In 1852, then only twenty-four years of age, he had expressed perfect confidence in his ability to direct an invasion and capture of Cuba. Summarizing the diverse elements that coexisted in the character of Davis, Fry described him as "brave, quiet, obliging, humorous in disposition, and full of ambition, daring, endurance, and self-confidence." Fry wrote a riveting account of the incident on September 29, 1862, wherein Davis, then a brigadier general of volunteers, shot and killed his commanding officer, General William Nelson, after an argument.[41] Davis was never tried by court-martial for the homicide, and civil charges against him were dropped, but his act of violence against a fellow officer made him the object of quiet but unresolved controversy thereafter.

During the remainder of the Civil War Davis served with credit, and at its close he was rewarded with the brevet rank of major general and the colonelcy of the Twenty-third Infantry. Nevertheless, he was bitter that he had not attained the rank of brigadier general in the regular army, to which he felt himself entitled. He sought duty that would bring him renewed glory in combat and perhaps amend matters. For example, in 1873 he attempted without success to displace then Lieutenant Colonel Crook as commander of operations against the Apaches.[42] By 1878 he was no longer in good health, and probably that fact influenced his decision not to take the field in pursuit of the Northern Cheyennes. Nevertheless, directing the efforts of Dodge and the other officers from headquarters at Fort Wallace was a rare opportunity to demonstrate his skill as the commander of four bodies of troops.

Dodge's explanation of his failure to comply with the order from Davis reached departmental headquarters on October 14,[43] and Davis incorporated a response to it in his official report, submitted three days later. This document comprised a summary review of the campaign from the Kansas Pacific Railroad. Taking no blame to himself for its unsuccessful outcome, Davis briefly praised the performances of Dallas and Vance, then condemned those of Mauck and Dodge bitterly and at length. Mauck came in for the harshest criticism. Davis ridiculed his "utter failure" to keep pace with the Indians as they passed north. In his view, the cavalry officer was "satisfying himself with merely herding the Indians . . . and was not intent on pushing and bringing them to an engagement as he should have done." Mauck had failed to send timely notice to Fort Wallace of the engagement in which Lieutenant Colonel Lewis was mortally wounded. Had he communicated sooner, reinforcements from the post might have intercepted the band. Instead, he permitted the Indians to outdistance him and then "murder citizens, and steal stock at pleasure in his front." Davis pronounced Mauck's allegedly lax performance of duty "highly censurable,—so much so, as to demand a thorough investigation."

Turning to Dodge, he shifted his tone from censure to contempt. Commenting on Dodge's report from the field, he quoted the phrase "thrown utterly out of the race" and followed it by three exclamation marks to register amazement at its frivolity. He faulted Dodge for failure to stay in contact with field headquarters at Fort Wallace, for want of energy in not marching further, and for want of purpose in marching with no particular object in view. "He was out nine days, marched 25 miles a day, and accomplished nothing so far as I can see." Davis did not address Dodge's rationale for not attempting to comply with the order to take command of Dallas's column, but he implied that a more able and energetic officer could have done so.

The report by Davis was received at the office of Pope's adjutant on October 18, entered in the official register of letters received, assigned a file number, marked "file" with a cross-reference to Dodge's letter exonerating himself, and quietly buried.[44] Like Davis, Dodge had not achieved all he had hoped for during the pursuit of the Northern Cheyennes, but that he should be criticized for lack of energy in the effort was absurd. Far from lowering Pope's estimate of him, his performance as a battalion commander under Davis produced exactly the opposite effect.

Within days of his return to Fort Hays, Dodge briefly returned to authorship, drafting a 2,500-word history of the Northern Cheyennes from the time of the Dull Knife battle up to their odyssey northward from the Cheyenne and Arapaho Agency. Making no mention of the part he had played in the recent pursuit, he based his account on telegraphed dispatches, comments heard in the field, his own journal, a letter he had received from Mauck, and possibly newspaper reports. At the time he wrote this account, the Indians had not yet been captured, and he assumed they were all "well on their way to the Brittish Possessions [i.e., Canada]."

Despite what proved to be errors of fact such as this one, Dodge's narrative brought together his deeply divided responses to the events of recent weeks and to the Northern Cheyennes generally. He expressed horror at the cruelties some of them had visited upon the settlers at Sappa Creek, characterizing the acts as "not to be voluntarily thought of, much less described." Still, he expressed sympathy for the attackers as well as for their victims. Desperate to keep alive their former way of life, the Cheyennes were "revenging on the innocent and unarmed settlers, the miseries they themselves have suffered at the hands of the whiteman." He detailed their sufferings in the weeks that followed the Dull Knife fight and especially later, when they were transferred to Indian Territory. He made clear his belief that derelictions by the Indian Bureau were the root cause of their eventual outbreak and the suffering it occasioned to all. However, he also allocated a share of blame to the U.S. government at large for saddling the army with an impossible task. Noting that the garrison at Fort Reno included only four companies of troops, for a total of perhaps 150 men capable of field service, he asserted the ridiculous inadequacy of such a force to control the Indians enrolled at the Cheyenne and Arapaho Agency. By "some grand fiction of the elastic Governmental brain," he wrote, the commanding officer of that post was expected to maintain control over "four thousand of the best fighting men in this or any country."

As he had in *The Plains*, Dodge expressed admiration for the military prowess of the Northern Cheyennes and also for their "gallant spirit" under duress, their bravery, and their indomitable will to survive as a people. He likened their journey northward to the arduous return home of the Greeks under Xenophon after the death of their former leader, the younger Cyrus. That comparison helped register his belief that the Northern Cheyennes were "a tribe of men as brave as ever trod the soil of Greece,"[45] and that, unlike the frontier army in its hapless pursuit of them, they merited a place in the annals of military glory.

17

A Convergence of Events

While the drama of official explanation and recrimination played itself out in the Department of the Missouri, the Northern Cheyennes roamed at large in the Department of the Platte. Troops under Major Thomas T. Thornburgh, Fourth Infantry, and Major Caleb H. Carlton, Third Cavalry, continued the search for them, but a successful outcome remained far from certain. Posts further north were placed on alert.

Not long after crossing the Union Pacific Railroad, the Indians separated into two groups—the larger, under Little Wolf, moving toward the Powder River country and the smaller, under Dull Knife, toward the former site of the Red Cloud Agency near Fort Robinson. Little Wolf and his people managed to elude the authorities for several more months, camping through the winter in the sand hills of western Nebraska and points north. In the spring of 1879 they were persuaded to surrender at Fort Keogh, Montana Territory,[1] where many went on to serve with credit as scouts under Colonel Nelson A. Miles. The band under Dull Knife, numbering about 150, were less fortunate. Being discovered in the sand hills seventy miles southeast of Fort Robinson, they at first prepared to fight, but after tense negotiations and the arrival of cavalry reinforcements they agreed to surrender. Disarmed and dismounted, on the evening of October 24, 1878, they reached Fort Robinson with their military escort.[2] What should be done with them next became a matter for debate. Dull Knife's people vowed to die rather than return to the reservation in Indian Territory, and General Crook favored permitting them to remain in the north; but General Sheridan regarded such a course as a sign of weakness and a threat to the reservation system. The "ringleaders," he thought, should be sent to Florida for training in civilized customs, as had been done in 1875 at the close of the Red River War in Texas. For the present the Indian Bureau took no position on the issue.[3]

All parties agreed that a third body of Northern Cheyennes, designated the "friendly Cheyenne prisoners," should be transferred to the Cheyenne and Arapaho

Agency in accordance with a previous plan. Many of these Indians had previously served under Colonel Miles in various capacities. They did not wish to relocate, but they acceded to the will of the authorities upon being promised that they could retain the guns and ponies they had captured during their military service. During the summer of 1878 this group, numbering 186 persons, had begun a long trek south, and at the time of the Dull Knife outbreak they had come as far as Sidney Barracks, Nebraska. As a precaution, their arms and ponies were temporarily taken from them while at that post, and an effort was made to keep them ignorant of the action of their tribespeople. Eventually they did learn of the events in Indian Territory, but they made no attempt to break away from their military escort. On October 14 Captain Mauck, still in command of troops from the Department of the Missouri, received orders to take charge of the friendly Cheyennes and conduct them to Fort Wallace, Kansas, where further orders would await him. He did so, and on November 17 he began the next stage of his journey, to Camp Supply, Indian Territory.[4]

Before many more weeks a convergence would take place in Indian Territory between three disparate sequences of events: Mauck's mission, the consequences of an official debate over responsibility for the Dull Knife outbreak, and a hunting expedition by Dodge. For Dodge, and ultimately also for the Northern Cheyennes under escort by Mauck, that fortuitous convergence would prove fateful.

Reports and Rebuttals

Within days of Dull Knife's flight from the Cheyenne and Arapaho Agency, a war of words over the causes of the outbreak broke out between adherents of the army and those of the Indian Bureau, each side seeking to denigrate the other. On September 19, 1878, Major Mizner at Fort Reno had forwarded to General Pope a report, based upon information supplied him by Agent Miles, demonstrating that the food and supplies furnished to the agency in the current fiscal year amounted to only two-thirds what the Indians needed. Recent events, he warned, made clear the importance of the government's living up to its treaty obligations. Indians continued to suffer from hunger and were forced to eat dogs, coyotes, and horseflesh in order to survive.[5] Five days later Agent Miles reported a fuller set of reasons for the outbreak to his own superior, Commissioner of Indian Affairs Ezra A. Hayt, noting, however, that the government's failure to observe treaty stipulations was one of the problems.[6]

What might have been a dispassionate argument over the details rapidly changed character when a third report, by Lieutenant Colonel Lewis at Fort Dodge, reached Washington and was made public. While Captain Hemphill's company of cavalry was detained at his post awaiting further action, Lewis had discussed the fugitive Northern Cheyennes with Amos Chapman, the interpreter at Camp Supply, who was then accompanying the troops as a scout. Chapman was married to a Cheyenne woman and said he had visited the agency a short time before the breakout. From what he had been told by Indians and also from his own observation, he knew the Northern

Cheyennes were suffering from lack of food, for they were driven to eat flesh cut from horses that had died of disease or natural causes. In his view, they had fled in order to seek out a place where they could feed themselves and their families. Lewis's report of this interview made its way through the army's chain of command, then from the secretary of war to the secretary of the interior, and finally back through that organization to Agent Miles, who received it on October 2.[7]

Miles at once denounced the Lewis report as "false in every particular," and the more offensive as originating with an individual like Amos Chapman, "known throughout the country as a squaw man."[8] The matter received wide circulation on October 15 when the *New York Times*, drawing upon Lewis's report, accused Miles of failure to issue full rations to the Northern Cheyennes and therefore of responsibility for their outbreak. Likening the Indians to Oliver Twist and Miles to the niggardly Mr. Bumble, it held up the image of famished Indians devouring diseased horseflesh as proof that the agent was wrong in contending that the Indians had plenty to eat.[9] The imputation of dishonesty stung Miles to a heated rebuttal, obviously intended for publication, in a letter of November 1 to Commissioner Hayt. While he spared the late Lieutenant Colonel Lewis from rebuke, Miles did point out that an officer at a post like Fort Dodge, many miles distant, could have no direct knowledge of conditions at the Cheyenne and Arapaho Agency. The real problem was the unreliability of Chapman, who according to Miles had visited the agency for only one day and spent that time "carousing at Fort Reno" and bargaining with Indian women "for purposes of prostitution." On the horseflesh question, Miles denied that any Indian had been "*compelled* to eat decayed or any other kind of horse meat."[10]

Presently Commissioner Hayt entered the fray, lending it a tone of greater dignity while suavely putting the army on the defensive. Transmitting to the secretary of the interior another document from Agent Miles on the causes of the outbreak, Hayt disputed statements in the report of September 19 by Mizner, who "by his want of familiarity with the subject, is led into a serious error" in regard to the supplies called for by the treaty of 1876 between the United States and the Cheyenne Indians. Hayt suggested that Mizner was meddling in matters not his proper concern, and also that he and other "military authorities" were themselves to blame for the damage wrought by the outbreak. Had the Indians been properly disarmed and dismounted, the rifles they used so effectively during the rampage that followed would not have occurred.[11]

The patronizing treatment by Commissioner Hayt goaded Mizner to a rejoinder, published in the *New York Herald* for December 8. That letter provoked Agent Miles to write a further statement of his own, citing a "determined effort" by the army to attribute the escape of the Northern Cheyennes to their near-starvation. Yet, he observed, they had not traveled like starved men, nor was hunger the reason their army pursuers were outwitted and ambushed. Perhaps further inquiry would fix responsibility for the escape on the laxity of "certain officers" whose duty had been to prevent it. The habitual drunkenness of army men was surely a contributing factor.[12]

The controversy that raged in December 1878 over events three months earlier had taken on a life of its own.[13] On December 17 Amos Chapman made affidavit confirming the accuracy of his statements to Lewis.[14] Later in that month Mizner wrote angrily to the adjutant general in response to yet another attack on him by Hayt. He wished his new statement to be published in the New York City papers, but to discourage further hostilities this was not permitted to occur.[15] The breach between the two federal agencies that shared responsibility for conditions in Indian Territory already seemed absolute. George W. Manypenny, a longtime proponent of staffing Indian agencies with representatives of religious denominations, regarded the imbroglio as a "hungry raid" by the army to gain control of the Indian Bureau.[16] On January 2, 1879, General Sherman wrote a terse memorandum on a document that was to be copied in the Adjutant General's Office and forwarded: "I doubt the wisdom of sending so many of these communications to the Secretary of the Interior. It seems labor absolutely wasted."[17]

The passage of the Northern Cheyennes through western Kansas had brought fear and panic to rural settlers, exposing the still fragile veneer of civil order in that region. As the extent of the depredations became known, Kansas citizens expressed outrage and demanded protection from future attacks. Governor George T. Anthony asked General Sheridan to post additional troops at Forts Reno and Sill in order to restore public confidence and ensure safety,[18] but Sheridan could offer him no immediate satisfaction. Presently he did suggest to General Sherman that Colonel Mackenzie with six companies of his regiment be moved from the Rio Grande in Texas to Indian Territory, and that perhaps also the Eighteenth Infantry be transferred from its station at Atlanta, Georgia. The general in chief demurred, however, arguing that the recent surrender of Dull Knife ought to deter other Indians from rash efforts to break away, and meanwhile the troops in Indian Territory would need to rely on "vigilance and increased activity."[19] General Pope was thus left to deal with the tense state of affairs as best he could.

As debates and discussions between generals, governors, and heads of government agencies moved forward, their subordinates sought to restore conditions that approximated those prior to the outbreak. At Fort Hays, Dodge took up the routine activities he had set aside upon taking the field in September. He made arrangements for the installation of a telegraph office at the post to save the trouble and delay of travel to use the one in town. He began work on an icehouse, ordered ceilings and partitions installed in the men's quarters, planned the construction of stables and cowsheds for the officers' houses, and directed that the post hospital be painted inside and out. With the assistance of First Lieutenant Trout, he expected to have "the prettiest cleanest & best arranged post in this Dept" before many more weeks.[20] Trout's injured leg and ankle made field duty a severe hardship for him, but for work of this kind his abilities were unimpaired.

A Trip through Indian Territory

A few days after drafting his narrative of the Northern Cheyennes' recent history, Dodge added a message to his journal record of the unsuccessful Army pursuit before putting it in the mail to his parents:

> *November 3*
>
> Keep this book until I come, then give it back to me. You may read such portions as you like to any person who will not publish it.
>
> I shall keep a diary on my Fort Sill trip & expect to beat the hunting record at the end of this book hollow. Will send it to you when I finish it.
>
> Have got all my work done & am nearly ready to start.
>
> Lovingly
>
> Rich.[21]

This notation marked a departure from Dodge's earlier use of his journals, for until that time he had compiled them for his own eyes alone. By forwarding the journal through the mail, he was giving it a larger audience and a new function. Anticipating that family members would read his entries, from this point on he modified his purpose in writing them. He kept in mind the special interests of his small audience—as, for example, his father's love of hunting and his mother's interest in family matters. Probably he restrained somewhat his earlier inclination to set down whatever thought crossed his mind. At the same time, he continued to employ the journals for his own use much as before, jotting down in them notes to support official reports, reminders for later development in his writing, and entries made simply for the satisfaction of recording his impressions.

The Fort Sill trip mentioned in the November 3 entry was to be a lengthy journey, first by railroad and then by military ambulance, to that post deep in Indian Territory, where a general court-martial was scheduled to convene on November 15.[22] Once his duty as a member of the court was finished, Dodge had orders to return to Fort Hays by a different route, one that would afford him opportunity to indulge his enthusiasm for hunting and fishing. From Fort Sill he and his escort would pass northward along the military road to Fort Reno, and from there he would travel upstream along the North Fork of the Canadian River to Camp Supply, passing through country little known except as a prime habitat for the wild turkey. The last leg of the return trip would be along the wagon road north to Fort Dodge, and thence to Fort Hays.[23] Dodge expected to be absent from his post for about a month.

This period of detached service yielded a variety of experiences that together made the journey a memorable one for him. On November 5, aboard the train to Junction City, Kansas, he met army officers including Lieutenant Colonel James Van Voast, a fellow court member, and also Lieutenant Colonel Absalom Baird, assistant inspector general for the Military Division of the Missouri. While awaiting a southbound connection on the Missouri, Kansas, and Texas ("Katy") Railroad, these three called on the post commander at Fort Riley, Colonel Galusha Pennypacker,

Sixteenth Infantry, and met another court member of the same regiment, Captain Thomas E. Rose. What Dodge and Van Voast may have discussed in regard to the pursuit of the Northern Cheyennes can only be guessed at, but on the journey south they passed time pleasantly with Preston B. Plumb, a senator from Kansas and a member of the Committee on Military Affairs. Plumb was a talker, and he held forth all the way to Emporia, Kansas, where another court member, Captain Philip H. Remington, Nineteenth Infantry, boarded for the trip to Caddo Station, in Indian Territory. Like Dodge and Rose, once the court proceedings had adjourned Remington planned to return to his post, Fort Dodge, by the wagon route that would enable him to hunt and fish along the way.

As the train moved through southeast Kansas, Dodge was impressed by the agricultural prosperity he saw, describing the Neosho Valley as a "garden spot."[24] However, upon entering Indian Territory he was no less struck by the contrast between Kansas and the "scarcely inhabited solitude" that now surrounded him. Except during his years at Fort Dodge, he had never been in Indian Territory before—a curious fact, given his reputation as an expert on Plains Indians.

Members of the military court had been informed that wagon transportation for the 160-mile journey to Fort Sill would be on hand to meet them at Caddo Station, but when they arrived, it had not yet made its appearance. By the time the westbound party set out on the morning of November 8, it numbered sixteen persons—eleven officers, three women, and two other individuals, one of them a black man named George whom Dodge hired as a manservant. Dodge, Rose, and Remington occupied an ambulance together, and during the first three days of the journey the weather was clear and the travel pleasant despite a road made muddy by rains. The travelers went into camp together early each afternoon, permitting some of the men to divert themselves in pursuit of fish and game for that night's supper. On Rock Creek, a beautiful stream whose bottom was clearly visible through at least six feet of water, Dodge sought without success to catch some of the bass that lurked there. In his journal entry he jocosely assured his readers that "the disgust I have this day contracted for the Bass family, I hope will be avenged on it by my family to its latest Generation."[25] Personification of animals and the use of vaguely biblical language were features of his comic parlance in letters to family members.

The wagon journey to Fort Sill took three more days and part of a fourth, during most of which time Dodge was ill with dysentery. However, after arriving at the fort, he made himself comfortable in a room he had reserved in the post trader's building. He, Van Voast, Remington, and Rose agreed to mess together, availing themselves of facilities placed at their disposal by the post commander, Lieutenant Colonel John W. Davidson, Tenth Cavalry. The court proceedings were to begin on the following day. Probably anticipating some tedious sessions, that evening Dodge and Remington walked together to the saloon and played a few games of billiards before going to bed early.

The case to come before the court was a subject of general concern at Fort Sill, for the defendant, Captain Philip L. Lee, Tenth Cavalry, was known to be waging a campaign to discredit Lieutenant Colonel Davidson, an officer with a long and honorable record of service. Lee's activities had by this time come before the General of the Army and were to continue doing so—so often, indeed, that Sherman at last determined to make an example of him.[26] Despite Dodge's impatience with extended court proceedings,[27] the case of Lee was also of professional interest to him. It involved issues of due discipline and subordination, topics essential to his understanding of himself as a career officer and about which he would eventually write for publication.[28]

The campaign against Davidson by Lee and his fellow officer at Fort Sill, Captain Theodore A. Baldwin, Tenth Cavalry, began in May 1878, when Lee was ordered to appear before a general court-martial at Fort Concho, Texas. After initial meetings, this court was reconstituted and reconvened at Fort Sill in July.[29] Amidst continuing controversy Lee was acquitted, but he began preparing a set of countercharges to secure revenge against Davidson for preferring the charges that had resulted in his trial.[30] Meanwhile Baldwin, smarting from a written rebuke by Davidson for wearing unmilitary costume and for disrespectful conduct, transmitted early in August a request for official redress, followed in September by a set of his own formal charges.[31] The two men were collaborating in a vendetta through official channels against Davidson and a group of officers whom they considered his favorites and toadies. Their efforts suffered a reversal on September 14. In an argument with Davidson's adjutant, First Lieutenant S. R. Whitall, Sixteenth Infantry, Lee struck the man repeatedly over the head with a cane and challenged him to a duel. As a result, Lee was placed under arrest and charges were filed against him of conduct unbecoming an officer and gentleman. This was the matter to be considered by the general court-martial at Fort Sill.[32]

After two days of sessions, largely attended by post residents, the court held a recess on November 17, a Sunday. For Dodge that day of release from confinement was the most pleasant of his stay at the post. In the morning he walked to the parade ground to watch guard mounting, then spent an hour chatting in Davidson's office before riding out to the Kiowa, Comanche, and Kiowa-Apache Indian Agency for a look at the Indian farm and school. On that excursion he enjoyed "a drink or two of very fine brandy" offered him by John S. Evans, the authorized Indian trader. Later, he and his messmates dined on a young wild turkey Davidson had sent them, and in the evening he had "Visitors & plenty of gass."[33]

Following its public proceedings, the court met for private discussion and voting on the charges and specifications against the defendant. On the first of two charges, violation of the Twenty-sixth Article of War in challenging First Lieutenant Whitall to a duel, it found Lee guilty. On the second, conduct unbecoming an officer and gentleman as instanced in the attack on Whitall, it judged him not guilty of the charge but guilty of the specification. It recommended as punishment that Lee be reduced to the lowest level of seniority among cavalry captains and that he forfeit five hundred dollars in pay at the rate of fifty dollars per month. Considering the seriousness of the offenses he was charged with, this was a relatively fortunate outcome for Lee.[34] However, since the determinations of the court were confidential until reviewed by superior authority and published, suspense about the fate of the accused officer continued to taint the social atmosphere at Fort Sill. At a "hop" on the evening when Dodge completed his court-martial duty, only three women were present.[35] An entertainment for court members on the next evening proved more satisfactory. Arranged by Mrs. Davidson, this gathering featured a supper with champagne, cards, and dancing. Van Voast confided at one point that he was "just properly gentlemanly drunk," and Dodge estimated himself at "about 40 pr ct. behind him."[36]

In the morning of November 21, Dodge, Remington, and Rose left Fort Sill together on the wagon road to Fort Reno. While comfortable enough for travel, their route was not particularly well adapted for hunting, as residences and Indian villages were scattered along the way. At the first night's camp, sixteen miles out, a courier from Davidson brought disquieting news—that another body of Cheyennes had broken away from their reservation. However, the situation that had prompted the report was later found to be less serious than appeared on its face. On November 1 Little Robe, a Southern Cheyenne, had been given permission to go with many of his people to his farm, about sixty miles from the Cheyenne and Arapaho Agency, in order to hunt there. Three weeks later, with three hundred men organized as a war party, he was ranging far south of his authorized destination. He had found buffalo and killed many, but at the end of the hunt he showed no inclination to return. Lieutenant Colonel John P. Hatch, Fourth Cavalry, believed Little Robe was demonstrating to all concerned that he was not to be kept from hunting or otherwise treated lightly.[37] The army kept discreet watch over his activity, and eventually he returned to the agency.

On November 22, while preparing to cross the Washita River, the travelers caught sight of some geese and tumbled out of their ambulance to shoot at them. Dodge bagged one bird but Rose was unsuccessful, which made him so aggravated that later in the day he borrowed a horse from the escort and rode back for another try. At 8:00 P.M. he returned to camp, still unsuccessful and very much put out. Relations between Remington and Dodge had been uniformly friendly thus far, but the braggadocio of the now disappointed Rose was setting him apart from them. In his journal entry that night, Dodge characterized Rose as "oddity itself, & the hugest 'blower' I have ever met."[38]

Rose was known in army circles for his exploits as a volunteer officer in the Civil War. His best-remembered accomplishment was an escape from the infamous Libby Prison in Richmond, Virginia; in February 1864 he led the group of forty-nine Union soldiers who dug a lengthy tunnel to freedom.[39] Awarded brevets in both the volunteer service and the regular army, in 1866 Rose was commissioned a captain of infantry, the rank he had held since.[40] That Dodge and Remington did not take him at his own value as an outdoorsman rankled him. Probably none of the three men anticipated that personal antagonism would break out among them, but a parting of the ways came on the afternoon that followed Rose's failed efforts to bag a goose.

Just as Dodge was about to lie down for a nap on that day, Rose fired his shotgun at a tree nearby. Shortly afterward, as he and Remington entered the tent, Dodge said to them, "Now Rose if you go popping off your gun any more, I'll fill your bottom with No 4 shot, & Remington, if you go making any noise around the camp I'll put that foot on you" (holding up one foot). This was characteristic humor from Dodge, who often accompanied playful threats by allusions to his physical stature. All seemed pleasant enough, but while Dodge slept, Rose packed his bedding and baggage and sat outside the tent, evidently deep in thought. When awakened by the call to supper, Dodge called Rose to come and sit down with him, but Rose answered that he was not hungry. Upon rising from the table, Dodge met Rose, who stood before him wearing his overcoat, his gun in one hand and his India rubber boots in the other. "Colonel," he said, "I think I will walk into Reno tonight."

Astonished, and aware that the post was still twelve miles distant, Dodge asked him why. "You don't seem to like my popping my gun around & I think I'd better go," Rose answered. "Why Rose," Dodge said as he turned to retrieve a pipe from his tent, "you are acting very foolishly, my remarks about your popping were only in fun, & its very absurd in you to act in this way." To this point Dodge had kept within himself, but what followed roused him to anger. "I am used to have people speak out when they dont like what I do," Rose told him, "and I don't like these insinuations. I dont seem to suit you people & I think I'll go in." At that moment Remington arrived on the scene and heard Dodge, stung by the word "insinuations," reply hotly, "Capt[ain] Rose I do not use insinuations. When I want to say anything I say it. If you want to leave this party, you can do so as soon & in any manner you wish." After a few more words Rose turned on his heel and left camp.

Still angry, Dodge wrote out an account of the confrontation, denouncing Rose as a "dogmatic, illiterate ill informed man, uncouth in manner dirty in person, & the most infamous 'blower' as to his own prowess & exploits I have ever met." However, he admitted his own part in precipitating the trouble:

> Remington & I don't think much of his shooting, & take him up on his "blowing" assertions not disagreeably, but enough to show him his own absurdity. . . . This kind of "taking up" has been of almost daily occurrence, & though all has apparently been pleasant they have evidently rankled in him. Added to this he has been about two thirds drunk ever since we left Sill. He has "blowed" about his skill as a shot, & success as a hunter, but has brought in very little game, & when hunting with Remington or I has not beat either of us. He "blows" about his woodcraft, & knowledge of country. Both of us know far more than he does. He brings in a lot of Spoon bills, & calls them Mallards & we laugh at him – & while not one single /really\ unpleasant thing has occurred, the accumulation of mortification at his want of success as a hunter, & his ignorance as a man, has driven him to the desperate resolve to seperate from us —

Dodge expressed regret, not at Rose's departure but at how it had taken place. By going off on his own, Rose was placing himself in some peril, for a short distance from camp he would have to cross the Canadian River, known to be dangerous when in flood.[41] Evidently Dodge had the case of Captain Lee in mind as he concluded his journal account, for he observed that Rose "has punished himself worse than any court would have punished him." He theorized that "my killing the goose yesterday instead of *him*" had set the stage for the falling out.[42]

On the next morning the ambulance and baggage wagon managed to negotiate the river crossing, but with some difficulty. The fate of Rose occupied Dodge's mind, and he asked the man aiding them across the ford whether he had heard anything of an individual who crossed on foot the night before. "A man with a gun," this local resident replied, "why, he came near being drowned." Rose had lost his footing while crossing and for a moment had gone completely out of sight, but he somehow righted himself and reached the other bank, where his waterlogged boots still stood. Moving into a stiff norther, around noon Dodge and Remington reached Fort Reno and were invited to stay the night at the quarters of Captain William H. Clapp, Sixteenth Infantry. As they entered Clapp's house, Rose opened a bedroom door and, half smiling, held out his hand to Dodge, who took it. "Well Rose," he said, "I am glad to see you have got safely out of your foolish scrape." Later he learned that Rose had arrived the night before in a half-demented state, having by his own account fallen and been semiconscious for some time after his ducking in the river. After being fed and comforted, he was placed in the care of Clapp, who asked him whether his quarrel with Dodge had been a serious one. "No, only a little one," he replied, "& I have no feeling in the matter. I got punished for it."[43] Perhaps fortunately for all, Rose was in no condition to attempt the next stage of the journey. He would remain at the post until sufficiently recovered to return by stage on a more direct route to Fort Riley.

The blustery winter wind continued, and the remainder of this day was spent indoors, in a manner pleasant to all concerned. The hospitality extended to the visiting officers at Fort Reno conformed to the description in the *Revised Army Regulations* of proper behavior on such occasions. Hosts and guests alike "maintained among themselves the courtesies and amenities of social life as it is observed among gentlemen."[44] Dodge and Remington called at the home of the post commander, Major Mizner, where they were introduced to his wife, took a drink together, and made conversation. Mizner and Dodge had been stationed within a few miles of each other in 1867, when the Union Pacific Railroad was beginning construction,[45] but their talk during this visit must also have touched upon the Northern Cheyennes, whose outbreak had brought troops from this post into the pursuit. After making himself more presentable, Dodge returned to Mizner's as a guest for a "most excellent dinner & good wines," then held an informal reception at Clapp's, where in approved fashion most of the officers stationed at the post called to pay their respects.[46]

The next morning Dodge observed another point of military etiquette, accompanying Mizner on an ambulatory tour of Fort Reno. He then said goodbye to Mrs. Mizner and the others who had come to see them off. Twelve miles into a cold ride up the river, he and Remington came within view of the sand hills where Dull Knife and his people had secretly built fortifications prior to taking flight. Near the end of the day's journey, Remington caught sight of a few turkeys but could not get a shot at them. Searching for more, in the morning he and Dodge went out ahead of the escort party, traveling on foot. Both found a small roost of perhaps twenty-five birds, both took shots at a distance, and both came away disappointed, and so after making camp they set out again. In an hour and a half Dodge returned, having found another small roost, but Remington claimed to have hit upon the very "paradise of deer & Turkeys." After supper they tried their luck a third time.

Dodge and his orderly entered the thicket where, he was sure, his birds passed the night. It was dark, the trees tall, the underbrush thick, and the prey widely scattered, but night shooting was said to be the best method of bagging them, so he went at it with a will. Later, in his journal entry for the day, he developed the comic possibilities of the situation:

> I shot & shot – sometimes a turkey would fall, sometimes the dead silence would proclaim that I had fired at a bunch of leaves or dead branch. Sometimes a fluttering commotion, & disappearance would indicate that I had only wounded my game. Twas pitch dark below in the thicket & I could only get along by feeling – one moment I'd run into a brush pile or lap of a dead tree – the next my eyes were assailed by numberless twigs of willow, & other small underbrush. A grape vine would tangle my legs, at one step – at the next a bamboo brier would catch me around the neck and try to throttle me. One limb would take my hat, another seize my gun another lay hold on my coat. I looked to Heaven so constantly & earnestly that like many other good people I became dizzy, lost my head & tumbled around indiscriminately. Oh, I had a glorious time, & came in by 7.30 wet to the skin with perspiration, to find the water in camp so frozen that I had to thaw it out to get a drink – but with 5 splendid Turkeys.[47]

At 9:00 P.M., just as Dodge was finishing his journal account, Remington returned to camp triumphantly, having bagged nine birds. Both men had worked—or played—hard, and both had won their rewards. If the cold weather held, at Camp Supply they would see the carcasses packed in ice and shipped to their respective posts.

As they moved up the river in the days that followed, Dodge and Remington devoted themselves enthusiastically to the pursuit of game—ducks, quail, and especially turkeys. On November 28, Thanksgiving Day, Dodge bagged nineteen turkeys and Remington eleven at a place known as Sheridan's Roost, named after a hunting excursion there by the general in 1869.[48] On December 2 seven inches of snow covered the ground, but the hunters' rage for sport continued almost unabated. Dodge was pleased with himself for successfully pursuing a flock of turkeys on horseback and killing three large birds by shots at long range. The total turkey count was sixty-six, Dodge having brought in forty.[49]

The Shadow of the Future

On the day he and Remington reached Camp Supply, Dodge's return journey through Indian Territory abruptly changed its character. The prime hunting country was behind him and ahead, he believed, lay only familiar territory in the vicinity of the post. Shortly after breaking camp, however, his party glimpsed a large group of people moving toward them. This proved to be Captain Sebastian Gunther, Fourth Cavalry, in command of two companies of troops who were escorting the "friendly Cheyenne prisoners" from Camp Supply to the Cheyenne and Arapaho Agency. These were the Northern Cheyennes who had departed from Fort Wallace on November 17 under the supervision of Captain Clarence Mauck. In conversation with Gunther, and later that day with Mauck at the post, Dodge heard a distressing account of a betrayal these native Americans had just suffered, and of the army officers whose duty had been to impose it on them.

Accompanied by Mauck, the Northern Cheyennes had arrived at Camp Supply on November 27 and remained there for two days, when Gunther assumed command of the escort and set out on the journey with them to the agency. They had gone only a short distance before a snowstorm forced them to encamp together and await better conditions. Meanwhile, General Pope's adjutant telegraphed to the commanding officer at Fort Dodge an order for Mauck, to be delivered at once by courier. The order, which reached Mauck at Camp Supply on the night of November 30, was "to seize and retain in your possession" all arms and war ponies then in possession of the Indians.[50] Mauck knew that Colonel Miles and subsequently General Sheridan had promised these people that they would be permitted to keep their guns and ponies while in Indian Territory. Moreover, traveling in their company during the past six weeks, he had come to respect them and deplore their plight. In this matter he shared the sentiments of Amos Chapman and Ben Clarke, the interpreters who had been his medium of communication with the Indians.[51] Compliance with General Pope's order would be deeply distasteful to him and dangerous as well, for the Northern Cheyennes would surely consider themselves betrayed and might react violently.

Pope later explained that he had no choice but to take the action he did. He was unaware of the promises made earlier to the Indians, and information he had received obliged him to issue the order to Mauck. On instructions from the Commissioner of Indian Affairs, the acting agent at the Cheyenne and Arapaho Agency, Charles E. Campbell, refused to receive the approaching Indians unless they were first disarmed and dismounted by the army. The Indian Bureau was determined to avoid a repetition of the violent outbreak of September, and that insistence underlay Pope's direction to Mauck "to take measures to be certain that you get possession of all arms."[52]

Like Pope, but without knowledge of the considerations that had dictated the general's action, Mauck had no choice, for he had received a lawful order. Accompanied by Chapman, on the morning of December 1 he rode out to Gunther's camp, then walked the few rods to the camp of the Indians and sat down with them in council. Another officer on the scene, Second Lieutenant Wilber E. Wilder, described the events that followed:

> The proposition was laid before them; was received with true Indian imperturbability, and rejected with dignity and decision. Chapman argued and protested with them a few minutes, until seeing the wrath of the bucks getting hotter, he said to Mauck that if they were going to get away alive they must be about it. So Mauck got up slowly and quietly moved toward the entrance, with Chapman after him. Not a moment too soon. He had scarcely risen from his place, when a knife slit down the canvass of the teepe from the outside, and a furious young buck sprang through the opening, crying: 'Let me kill —— —— thief! Let me kill him!' And he would have killed him if Mauck had not moved when he did. But that instant peril passed, the other chiefs restrained the hot head and Mauck and Chapman got back to camp and the protection of the troops.

From packages worn around their necks, the Indians pulled out their official military discharges attesting to their good character, but Mauck would not budge. At last the "friendly Cheyenne prisoners" tore up the documents in disgust, calling them "lying papers." They were surrounded by troops, but they would not give up their guns. They stalked back to their tents and donned war paint.

The Indians' head men—Little Chief, Crazy Mule, Iron Shirt, Ridge Bear, and Black Bear—had stated their position to Mauck, and he to them. For three hours he and his command stood in near silence, awaiting what might come. At 2:00 P.M. he called to the Indians that in one more hour he would commence to fight. All who chose to obey orders must come to his tents and lay down their arms; all who preferred violence should remain in their own camp. The choice was stark, but fortunately wise heads among the Northern Cheyennes, such as Little Chief, were able to see beyond it. Women, children, and then peaceably disposed men began moving toward the line of soldiers, and within the hour the entire band had subjected itself to the will of little Captain Mauck.[53]

For that brave officer, the bloodless victory he had won was painful. He told Dodge on the following day that imposing Pope's order on the Indians was "the most disagreeable duty of his life. The Indians were in the right, & an attack on them would simply have been a massacre." That night Dodge wrote out a summary of the incident as he had learned of it from Mauck, Gunther, and probably others. "From what I can gather," he concluded, "the whole affair was a strong commentary on the miserable inefficiency of a Govt, whose promises are not binding."[54]

Clarence Mauck. Courtesy U.S. Army Military History Institute.

Owing to a lack of transportation, Dodge and Remington remained at Camp Supply for three days before setting out on the military road north into Kansas. The post commander, Captain William J. Lyster, Nineteenth Infantry, proved no less gracious a host than Davidson and Mizner had been, though on the whole Dodge found his stay "extremely dull." His reputation as a billiards player had preceded him, and "for the delectation of the Off[icer]s & Ladies" he permitted himself to be matched against the post champion, whom he beat easily. On December 4 he intended to accompany Lyster and Remington on a quail hunt, but feeling "too tired & good for nothing," he remained behind, limiting himself to a few more games of billiards, the purchase of presents for Joe and Laura, and a nap in the afternoon. "Just a month since I left home," he wrote on the next day. "To look back on it, it seems like half a year."[55]

The final stage of Dodge's excursion through Indian Territory was to him the least interesting, consisting almost entirely of wagon travel over a well-known road. However, the scene at Bluff Creek Station, an overnight stopping point sixty-six miles out from Camp Supply, caught his attention as containing the material for a lively sketch of frontier life. "Ranche full of the wild element of the frontier," he wrote:

> Might draw a picture or make a story of it. At least 30 men, good bad and indifferent. Respectable men, sat cheek by jowl, in amiable conversation with horse thieves & train robbers.
>
> Until quite late, numbers were added to our party. One hard looking case came in, looking for prisoners escaped from the Dodge jail. Later two, half & half, might be anything from preachers to train robbers came in looking for a horse thief.

By silent acclamation of these citizens, Dodge and Remington were assigned the only decent room in the house, with two large double beds.[56]

On a cold and windy December 8 they reached Fort Dodge and went to Remington's house before making the obligatory courtesy call on the post commander, Major Henry A. Hambright, Nineteenth Infantry. Dodge was glad to see his old post but disappointed that Assistant Surgeon William S. Tremaine, his comrade during the hard winter of 1872–1873, was away on official business.[57] As he had ordered, an officer from Fort Hays was on hand with a small detachment of men as an escort along the old wagon road north. This was Second Lieutenant Calvin D. Cowles, Twenty-third Infantry, a native of North Carolina with whom Dodge had enjoyed some days of hunting during the summer.[58] Another hunt together had been planned for the return from Fort Dodge, but Cowles now recommended against it. He had seen no game, and in view of the bad weather he suggested that Dodge return to his post by train. That night, after humbling another officer at billiards, "one of the Crack young players of the present age," Dodge took Cowles's advice; he boarded a train for Topeka and a connection there back to Hays City.[59]

On the morning of December 10 Dodge administered to himself a walking tour of Fort Hays, wishing to observe the changes made during his five-weeks absence. All was in admirable shape, thanks to Trout and the good morale that prevailed. The improvements had been made every bit as well as if he had supervised them himself. "And now you see[,] dear Dad & Mam," he wrote in concluding his journal, "what constitutes a real good time on a hunt – for I have had a 'real good time' & enjoyed every moment of the outdoor life."[60] Weeks of strenuous activity had reduced his girth, leaving his pants and drawers much too wide at the waist, but he felt in excellent health. Part of his time away had resembled an officially sanctioned vacation tour, and clearly he regarded it in that light. Of course, army officers of his era were officially encouraged to make hunting excursions in order to keep themselves in good physical condition, maintain their skill as marksmen, and familiarize themselves with country where they might one day see action.[61] But as he diverted himself in search of game at Sheridan's Roost and elsewhere, he would not have credited that the rationale to promote field sport might apply especially to himself. He had no reason to believe he would ever be stationed in Indian Territory.

However, the shadow of the future rested on Dodge as he passed through that country. No doubt with interest, he viewed scenes that recalled the recent history of the Northern Cheyennes, met persons who had been involved in events that followed their outbreak, and even saw some of the tribespeople who had engaged him as soldier and author in recent years. His response to the predicament of Little Chief and his band was at the same time powerful and detached. He felt curiosity, pity, and anger at the double-dealing they had suffered, but he viewed them as a concerned observer, not as an officer who would play a direct role in their continuing history. Yet the "friendly Cheyenne prisoners" would soon become the object of his professional attention, causing him to pass this same spot on an urgent military mission. Without his suspecting it—and so far as can be determined, without General Pope's intending it—Dodge's tour through Indian Territory proved to be a preliminary reconnaissance. The convergence between his tour, the overland trek of the friendly Cheyennes, and the betrayal they suffered at the hands of U.S. authorities laid the basis for his challenging duties in the two years to come.

18

Cantonment North Fork Canadian River

The discord at Fort Sill and the apprehensions of violence in Indian Territory seemed distant as Dodge took up the threads of his activity at Fort Hays. The post trader had abruptly resigned, and a council of administration must now meet to select a successor. Company commanders reported that bread from the new bakehouse was inedible, and a board of survey should consider the matter. Space being at a premium in the officers' quarters, some of the younger men were jealous of the living arrangements others enjoyed. Mrs. O'Keefe, the authorized laundress and a "troublesome woman," was appealing her recent dismissal, but Dodge stood fast.[1] He convened a garrison court-martial to try men accused of minor infractions. He dealt with problems that arose from day to day, maintaining only general oversight on the improvements being directed by Trout. He was accustomed to performing the duties of a post commander and enjoyed the role. Fort Hays, though not without its bickerings and dissatisfactions, was on the whole a comfortable place to be.

The Potato Question

As a post commander, Dodge took seriously the injunction of the *Revised Army Regulations* that "the duty of every officer . . . [is] to exercise a rigid economy in the public expenses."[2] He was jealous of his prerogatives in the role and quite willing to engage in debate over matters of military procedure that he thought material.[3] As he once observed, "A good fight is a splendid sharpener of the intellect, & keeps a man from rusting out."[4] What was more, although capable of expressing himself with considerable subtlety, when aroused, he did not mince words. These traits of character were exhibited in a confrontation between him and a departmental staff officer in November and December 1878. Conducted according to official protocol and involving multiple bills of lading, receipts, affidavits, endorsements, and official and unofficial correspondence, as well as two reports from the proceedings of two boards of survey, each done in triplicate, this instance of friction between staff and line was a manifest waste of time and public funds. Its seriocomic character was heightened by the officious self-importance of the offended party, the departmental commissary of subsistence. Throughout the difficulty, Dodge kept his temper and showed a wise sense of proportion, even though some loose words of his own had fanned the initial flames. What he termed in private "the important potato question"[5] was hardly an earthshaking matter, but it did involve real issues of official responsibility and the proper conduct of government business.

The trouble began on October 25 with the shipment to Fort Hays of 123 sacks of peach blow potatoes by Captain C. A. Woodruff, the post commissary of subsistence at Fort Leavenworth. The potatoes had been purchased in the public market at Leavenworth, Kansas, at a price of sixty-three cents per bushel. Even before they reached Fort Hays, Dodge expressed alarm to Woodruff at their "exhorbitant" price. Enclosing slips cut from recent issues of Leavenworth newspapers that showed potatoes offered there on October 24 at twenty-five cents per bushel,[6] he noted that in requisitioning the shipment he had wished it furnished as reasonably as possible. Because potatoes were for sale at thirty cents a bushel in the vicinity of Fort Hays, Dodge wondered whether Woodruff's invoice price was an error. If not, "I must, in justice to the officers and men of my Command protest against it. They should not (and shall not if I can help it)" be required to pay extra for foodstuffs available at Hays City for half the price.[7]

To make matters worse, on the arrival of the potatoes, Trout reported that they weighed less than the gross amount shown on Woodruff's invoice, 16,668 pounds, and that they were very dirty. Accordingly, on November 1 Dodge appointed a board of survey to report on their condition and quality. The next day three officers, Captains Henton, Pollock, and Goodale, weighed all 123 sacks and, selecting three at random, emptied their contents onto the storeroom floor. The gross weight was only 16,283 pounds, and each of the three emptied bags was found to contain stones, coal clinkers, pieces of mortar, and dirt. Factoring the amount of foreign matter in the three bags, the board determined that a tare of 586 pounds, 13 ounces should be deducted from the shipment, leaving 15,696 pounds, 3 ounces of potatoes as the amount for which Trout should be responsible as post commissary of subsistence. The board also noted that potatoes for sale at Hays City and recently advertised at Leavenworth were much less costly than these, which were of "average" quality.[8]

Dodge's initial letter about the price of the potatoes reached Captain Woodruff on November 2. Forwarding it to his superior Captain Jeremiah H. Gilman, chief commissary of subsistence for the Department of the Missouri, Woodruff contented himself with observing that the market reports Dodge enclosed were "a most unreliable guide."[9] But Gilman took the matter more seriously, telegraphing Trout on the same day with a directive to return the potatoes at once. Even before the written proceedings of the board of survey at Fort Hays reached him on November 5, he had taken steps to vindicate himself against offensive statements made by Dodge. A few days earlier Dodge had written him an unofficial letter in which, assuming that Gilman had employed a purchasing agent, he asserted that the agent "was undoubtedly guilty of fraud, or most gross neglect of duty."[10] This incensed Gilman, for he had been his own purchasing agent. He resented the imputation of dishonesty or incompetence and at once wrote a reply that eventually reached Dodge at Fort Sill on November 18. Dodge responded that same day, withdrawing the charge of fraud but reiterating his objection to the high price.

A board of survey such as the one at Fort Hays had no power to dispose of property. Its function was simply to establish data through which questions of administrative responsibility could be answered and the adjustment of accounts made possible. Its work was complete upon approval of the commanding officer who had convened it, though a superior authority had the power to withhold his approval and order another board.[11] Thus, on November 6 Gilman recommended to General Pope that the Fort Hays proceedings be set aside and another board convened. His 1,000-word statement seethed with anger, not so much at the board members as at Dodge. He deemed it "my *duty, just* and *proper*" to report Dodge's objectionable actions: first, in requisitioning for potatoes from Leavenworth when he could get them cheaper at Hays City; second, in writing to Woodruff in a manner that reflected on Gilman and in basing his remarks on a mere newspaper quotation; and third, in ordering a board of survey about a matter—the price of potatoes at Leavenworth—he could not pretend to know from direct experience, and in denying Gilman "(whose efficiency or integrity . . . [was] apparently called in question)" or any other competent person an opportunity to appear before that board.[12]

The potatoes having been received at Fort Leavenworth on November 9, Pope agreed to appoint a new board of survey to examine them, especially with regard to the foreign matter alleged by the officers at Fort Hays to have been sacked with them. This body, consisting of Major D. G. Swaim, judge-advocate general of the department, Captain William McKee Dunn, Jr., Pope's senior aide-de-camp, and First Lieutenant Louis R. Stillé, Twenty-third Infantry, met at 11:00 A.M. on November 12 in the quartermaster's shed. The board weighed the potatoes and supervised the process as they were emptied sack by sack onto the storehouse floor. Members picked up some "clinkers and small stones" but found that the impurities totaled only 16 pounds for all 123 sacks. The 747 pounds net that had been lost by the shipment since being sent to Fort Hays two weeks before they attributed to shrinkage and the numerous times the potatoes had since been handled. In all, board members judged it "an exceptionally fine lot of 'Peach Blow' potatoes, of uniform size, apparently entirely free from disease, or decay, and unusually free from dirt."[13] Writing in the absence of Gilman, Woodruff recommended in his endorsement of the board's proceedings that the potatoes be sold at cost price to officers and employees at Fort Leavenworth, and on November 23 Pope approved that course.

Captain Gilman had now officially cleared himself and his office from blame, but not all the points at issue between him and Dodge had yet been resolved in his favor, for the proceedings of the Fort Hays board of survey remained to be disapproved by General Pope. That delay may have been owing in part to Gilman's absence while in Washington for consultations.[14] The more probable cause was Pope's unwillingness to perform any official act that might be countermanded by a junior officer of a staff department, such as Gilman. Acting on this principle, and despite a threat of court-martial leveled against him, Pope had recently declined to take action on two boards of survey that had been convened at Fort Leavenworth to condemn certain ordnance stores. General Sherman supported him in his stand, citing a comment made years before by General William H. Harrison, who had gone on to become president of the United States, that military commanders, not staff officers, must rule the army.[15] Of course, Pope recognized that except for its real organizational implications, the whole potato controversy was much ado over next to nothing. On December 16 he ended his involvement in the matter by disapproving the Fort Hays board of survey "and so much of the order convening it as directs it to report on the invoice price of the potatoes."[16]

Gilman was now in a position to declare triumph over Dodge, who appears to have taken no interest whatever in the potato shipment since being reminded of it at Fort Sill nearly a month before. On December 18 Gilman addressed him a lengthy letter, enclosing a copy of the board proceedings at Fort Leavenworth and emphasizing that the board "saw Every sack emptied, examined the *entire lot, sack by sack* and found the potatoes to be in excellent condition." He and his family had since dined on these potatoes at his own table, he wrote, and he judged them the best he had eaten that year. He ended by observing that the peach blows Dodge had objected to were the finest available variety, the quality of the original shipment excellent, and its price appropriate given market conditions.[17]

The peach blow incident ended with two letters by Dodge, one addressed to General Pope through his adjutant, the other directly to Gilman. To Pope he wrote that from his point of view the problem had been solved long before by the return of the potatoes from Fort Hays. Contrary to Gilman's early objections, "I believe that my action has been right and proper and but justice to my command." As to his having convened a board of survey whose proceedings Pope had disapproved, he offered no apology. In fact, he addressed the very topic that Pope himself had made an issue not long before—the power of staff officers—but vis-à-vis that of post commanders.

> I beg to remind the Department Commander that every post is to some extent at the mercy of the Department Staff, and that "Boards of Survey" are one of the means by which a Post Commander may protect his Command.
>
> If I have no power to order a Board to inquire into the invoice price of Articles sent for the purchase and use of my Command, I have no power to protect that command from any excessive (or even fraudulent) charge that the

> invoicing officer might make. The Staff Officer rises above investigation, & the troops suffer.[18]

Dodge's letter to Gilman was briefer and, though confined to the matter of potatoes, not unfriendly. Quoting a word and a phrase from Gilman's recent letter, he was "glad to be able to say that, 'while I yet regard the price of the potatoes as exhorbitant,' I am satisfied there was no intent to defraud or 'swindle.'"[19]

Consultations and a Midwinter Mission

On December 19, explaining to General Sheridan the circumstances that had dictated his ordering the "friendly" Northern Cheyennes under Little Chief to be disarmed and dismounted, General Pope pointed out that the army's reneging on promises was not the sole cause of the Indians' hostility and disposition to make trouble. So long as the Indian Bureau failed to supply sufficient food, violence was inevitable. Since the army was forbidden to issue rations to Indians unless they were prisoners of war, and then only until they could be turned over to the Indian Bureau, it was all but powerless to ease their desperate resentment. Pope warned that he considered affairs in the Indian Territory "critical" and the available military force, especially cavalry, "entirely inadequate" to protect the frontier should more Indians break away.[20]

In recent weeks post commanders at Forts Elliott, Reno, and Sill and at Camp Supply had all voiced their concerns on this matter. Midwinter was not ordinarily a season when military action was made necessary by Indian unrest, but 1878–1879 seemed a likely exception. Pope forwarded to Sheridan the reports of these men in the field, urging that something be done soon. Sheridan comprehended fully the misgivings of field officers who were expected to issue orders that could result in annihilation of their commands by a superior foe, and he shared Pope's belief that the troops in Indian Territory were too few to meet a crisis.[21] The question he faced was where to position his forces, given the constantly changing number and seriousness of trouble spots along a frontier that extended for more than 1,000 miles. Ultimately, of course, answering that question was the responsibility of the General of the Army and the secretary of war.

On December 23 General Sherman responded to the expressed concerns of his department and division commanders by directing Pope to send troops from Forts Leavenworth and Riley to the Indian Territory. The six companies then at Fort Leavenworth were all of an infantry regiment, the Twenty-third; the three at Fort Riley were also infantry, of the Sixteenth Regiment. Sherman was willing to commit almost a full regiment to the region as a deterrent force, but the problem yet remained of where to place them. On December 24 Sheridan telegraphed that the posts in the most dangerous sections had no quarters for more troops, but that the reinforcements could go into camp somewhere, occupying tents as they had done in far colder regions in the north.[22] On December 27 Sheridan modified his plan, reporting that ten companies from Fort Leavenworth and "other posts" would go to Camp Supply and Fort

Reno. He had directed Pope, he informed Sherman, to send the whole of the Twenty-third Infantry to those two places.[23]

The frequent communications of these days were passing between Sherman and Sheridan by telegraph, but on December 26 Pope sent Sheridan a written letter that addressed the present initiative in thoughtful fashion and strongly influenced the military policy then taking shape. Observing that deep snow and cold weather made travel away from main roads impossible for a time, he assured his immediate superior that the Twenty-third Infantry would move "as soon as it can be done, without unnecessary hardship and exposure." He proposed to send four companies to Camp Supply but to establish the other six in a temporary winter cantonment midway between Camp Supply and Fort Reno, along the North Fork of the Canadian River or else the Cimarron River a few miles north of it. He thought this course prudent both in a military view and because the troops could make themselves more comfortable during winter in the timber of that country than in an exposed camp near one of the posts. The cantonment would be a suitable site "for one of a cordon of posts which must soon be established around the Indian Territory if the present divided jurisdiction over the wild tribes be kept up." The proposed new installation would have a strategic advantage, being situated near the line of journey traditionally followed by the Cheyennes and Arapahos as they moved north and south through territory now part of Kansas. Without the deterrence promised by the cantonment, "this whole frontier is in constant danger."

Pope was convinced that the troops best suited to protect surrounding states from incursion by Indians were cavalry, but given their unavailability it was necessary "to do the best we can with the Infantry." Foot troops were of little value, he believed, for forced marches or rapid evolutions in the field, but they "would accomplish a most important task" if posted in "immediate contact" with the Indians and given power to control their conduct. Exactly how an infantry force was to exercise this control given the limitations imposed on the army by law, Pope did not address. "What we need here is Cavalry," he concluded. "Without it there is always danger of unavailing pursuit."[24]

Sheridan agreed wholeheartedly with Pope's assessment, and he inquired of General Ord whether six companies of cavalry could be spared from the Department of Texas. Ord suggested that they be posted within his own territory, in the Llano Estacado region of northern Texas, but on December 31 Sheridan telegraphed to Sherman that he preferred stationing the companies at Forts Sill and Elliott. He would do so, he added, if Sherman thought conditions in Texas warranted the reduction in force there.[25] But Sherman was satisfied with his own first determination. "The true policy," he responded, "is for Genl Pope to reenforce the Posts in the Indian Country, viz Sill, Elliott, Supply, Dodge &c, with his Reserve viz the 23rd Infantry, and not call for help till he has used every man subject to his orders. Meantime," he concluded, "the Indian Bureau will be asked to keep their Indians at home."[26]

Neither Sheridan nor Sherman commented in these exchanges on the proposal by Pope to establish a cantonment, except perhaps for the latter's "&c" at the end of his listing of posts. However, Sherman continued to reflect on Pope's letter of December 26, which he thought stated the case "fully and well." In an endorsement of January 8, 1879, he contrasted the notion of a line of facilities along the border of Indian Territory—Pope's "cordon of posts"—with the idea of placing troops well within the territory, near the agencies. The latter would be the more economical plan. "It will require ten or twenty times as many men on the Circumference, as it would at the Center, to control these or any other indians liable to become hostile, from provocation, hunger, desperation or any other cause."[27] A cantonment located as Pope had suggested would enable the army to stay in reasonably close touch with the Indians in their accustomed places of residence but would also permit troops to be sent to the frontiers of neighboring states with little delay.

Left free to pursue the plan he had outlined to his superiors, Pope followed that course. Suddenly the Twenty-third Infantry, Dodge's regiment, stood at the center of emerging events. On December 26 Dodge was informed by the departmental adjutant that the regiment would take posts in Indian Territory at "quite an early day" and that preparations for the move should begin.[28] Three days later he learned that Pope had entrusted to him the responsibility of selecting a site for the new cantonment. Except that the task was to be performed "without undue delay," the letter of instructions he received contained only general guidelines. Given the temporary post's remoteness from sources of supply, troops stationed there would need to provide shelter for themselves using whatever materials could be found in the vicinity. The cantonment might possibly be made a permanent facility, so questions of year-round healthfulness should be considered. He was to examine carefully a particular section of country, but a specific location remained for him to determine.

The receipt of these instructions began a flurry of activity by Dodge. Emphasizing that he was on urgent business, he contacted the post commanders at Fort Dodge and Camp Supply to bespeak transportation and an escort. He telegraphed the departmental engineer officer, First Lieutenant Ruffner, for a copy of the latest maps. He packed his winter clothing, and at 2:00 A.M. on December 31 he set out on the circuitous railroad journey to Dodge City.[29]

Although not without intervals of delay owing to poor train connections, snowdrifts, difficult terrain, and other causes, Dodge's schedule of activity in the month to come was punishing. The journey from Camp Supply to study the terrain around Barrel Springs on the North Fork of the Canadian River was through deep snow and often in wind and chilling cold. The country between that point and the Cimarron River, the vicinity of which he likened to a compartment of Dante's Hell,[30] was the most difficult he had ever passed over with wagons. Snow and bitter cold made the selection of a specific post site impossible, but he managed to identify an approximate location and was confident that in better conditions, making a final choice would be a simple matter. The return to Camp Supply, across terrain made treacherous by thawing ice and boggy soil, required exquisite caution and a measure of luck. More than once Dodge observed in his journal that he needed rest. Yet,

Amos Chapman. Courtesy Archives and Manuscripts Division, Oklahoma Historical Society.

despite the challenging physical difficulties he faced, he enjoyed the assignment. Reduced to reliance upon his own skill, he took pleasure in overcoming or circumventing the obstacles he met with. The mission also brought with it a genuine social satisfaction, for it placed him in close contact with Amos Chapman, the scout and interpreter at Camp Supply. Dodge would share many experiences with Chapman in the two years to come, but from the first he recognized in him "a remarkable man – a true frontiersman & Indian fighter."[31]

Chapman had been a fixture in the area for a decade, but he had won national attention for his courage on September 12, 1874, when he and five other men bearing dispatches to Camp Supply from Colonel Nelson A. Miles at McClellan Creek, Indian Territory, were attacked by Indians. Forced to take refuge in a buffalo wallow, they defended themselves under siege all that day. In a bold effort to rescue a disabled comrade, Chapman sprang from the depression, ran one hundred yards to the fallen man, and under intense fire shouldered him and returned with him to the place of safety. Only after reaching the buffalo wallow did he realize that during the excitement he had been badly injured. His foot was shot off just above the ankle joint, and he had made part of his return trip walking on the exposed bone. Chapman and four surviving comrades were rescued by troops late the next day. Shortly afterward, the post surgeon at Camp Supply amputated his wounded limb below the knee, and he was fitted with a wooden leg. Dodge described him in 1880 as "still in the government employ, as useful and as ready for a fight as any two-legged scout."[32]

Dodge returned to Fort Hays on January 21, in need of rest but well satisfied with what he had accomplished. Later that day he received a telegraph message summoning him to an interview with the department commander. "If ever a poor fellow was pushed about its me," he remarked in his journal, only half humorously.[33] The visit to Fort Leavenworth was itself filled with activity. It included a series of greetings from "the boys," his fellow officers, but its chief event was a three-hour conversation with Pope, on matters official and otherwise, that each seems to have found delightful. "He is an exceedingly interesting man," Dodge wrote, "well informed & a thinker. We differ on many points but agree in many more. He has broad views on Army questions & talks well – & has the faculty of inciting me to talk. Not that I cant do quite my full share at any time, but I seem to myself to talk better to Pope than to any one else."[34]

The meeting raised to a new level the mutual esteem between the two officers. Pope approved Dodge's report of his search for a post site,[35] and probably at this time he confirmed his intention to designate him the commander of the new post. Dodge was now to return to his station and prepare his men for departure. He would receive valuable assistance in that effort from Trout, who had agreed to delay ending his army career until the new cantonment was established and running smoothly. Dodge was grateful for his support at this critical time. A few days later he forwarded Trout's name to department headquarters, praising him as "an exceptionally valuable officer" but describing the incapacity that had resulted from his injury in the Black Hills, and therefore designating him a proper subject for future action by a Retiring Board.[36]

Establishing the Cantonment

For a short time after Dodge's departure from Fort Hays on December 31, preparations for the regimental change of station had continued apace. On January 2 a request reached the Adjutant General's Office for authority to purchase eighty mules for use on the march from Fort Dodge to Camp Supply and for later service there and at "Cantonment."[37] On January 3 Trout received orders to prepare estimates at Fort Leavenworth of the supplies that would be needed at the new post.[38] However, within a few more days the sense of urgency began to abate. On January 8 Sherman telegraphed to Sheridan that conditions in Indian Territory did not seem so pressing as to require Pope to send out the Twenty-third Infantry until the worst of the winter was over, perhaps in March. Sheridan returned that he had directed Pope not to put the troops into the field until February 1, when the weather ought to permit it. Sherman answered that Sheridan and Pope could decide together when the time was right. However, he added, "I have raided in Kansas, and have experienced in March weather of fearful severity. The fact that the troops are to go to that frontier will produce the necessary moral effect."[39]

This was a sensible view, and in regard to temporarily maintaining the peace in Indian Territory, it proved correct. Yet Sherman's reasoning failed to account for a disastrous sequence of events that commenced that same night at Fort Robinson, Nebraska. Undeterred by the bitter winter weather and unbowed by the "moral effect" of troops guarding them at the fort, a group of the Northern Cheyennes under Dull Knife broke away from their locked barracks and fled into the night once again. They had refused to return to Indian Territory, as the government now demanded

Little Chief, Northern Cheyenne. Courtesy Western History Collections, University of Oklahoma Libraries.

they do. To compel their acquiescence, their rations had been cut off, but they would not submit to starvation. They were determined to return to their ancestral hunting ranges or else to die in the attempt.[40]

The renewed escape of Dull Knife and many of his people underlined the potentially severe consequences should the Northern Cheyennes in Indian Territory also resort to flight. With concerns like these in the background, on December 30, 1878, the official name of Camp Supply was changed to Fort Supply, denoting its status as a permanent post.[41] The initial entry for 1879 in the register of letters received by the Adjutant General's Office at Washington related to "Cantonment," the new post at a site to be selected by Dodge.[42] These details of official action marked the heightened attention being directed to the western sections of Indian Territory bordering on Texas and Kansas.

Meanwhile, at the Cheyenne and Arapaho Agency, Little Chief, an astute politician, professed willingness to accept the decision of the U.S. government as to the place where his people were to live. However, he made known his unalterable desire to return north, as his people had been promised they might do if they wished.[43] On several occasions Little Chief assured authorities that he would never seek to take matters into his own hands in the foolhardy way Dull Knife had done. But he was not taken at his word—not so much because he was thought to be lying as because, according to report, his fellow tribesmen were responding badly to the constraints and privations of reservation life. Second Lieutenant Heber W. Creel, a young officer who was living with the newly arrived Northern Cheyennes, reported to General Sheridan in March that they were extremely discontented and made grave accusations against Agent Miles, from whom they received little charity or sympathy.[44] Ben Clarke, the post interpreter at Fort Reno, reported similarly to Pope, as did Mizner.[45] Even Charles E. Campbell, Miles's assistant, admitted the difficulties. On March 5 he warned the Commissioner of Indian Affairs that unless decided measures were taken at once, Little Chief and his people would attempt to escape. "Contemptible in numbers," he wrote, "they can yet repeat the effort of Dull Knife, Wild Hog & Co."[46] The *Army and Navy Journal* published a letter from a "well-informed correspondent" who had recently visited the Cheyenne and Arapaho Agency. This person assured the editor that "a more determined set of savages does not exist on the North American continent than the Northern Cheyennes." The likelihood of their sudden departure must be recognized at once, "so that in the next outbreak, which is considered inevitable, it will be known where to place the responsibility."[47]

The force of opinions like these led General Pope to move his reserve troops into Indian Territory with deliberate speed. Under command of Colonel Davis, the headquarters of the Twenty-third Infantry, with companies B, E, F, and H, began the march from Fort Dodge to Fort Supply on February 3, arriving there five days later. Davis assumed command of the post, and Fort Supply now housed a force of five companies, one of cavalry.[48] Dodge remained at Fort Hays until the wagon transportation for his battalion could return to Dodge City and be readied for further use. The work of preparing for the change of station left him no time for impatience. Before resigning command of Fort Hays he completed an estimate of value for the public property to be left there. He arranged with railroad authorities at Topeka for an empty baggage car to transport the goods and supplies that would accompany the troops with him, directing storage at the fort of the excess, which would be brought to the cantonment at a later date. He applied for delivery to the new post of ordnance stores from the depot at Jefferson Barracks, Missouri. He arranged with the departmental signal officer for issue of odometers and prismatic compasses. He requested an informational circular from the Medical Department, and from the Adjutant General's Office he requested a copy of the *Revised Statutes* and a variety of standard forms for office use. He ascertained that W. H. Keeling, his selection for post trader, had been confirmed in the position. Upon being informed that $3,000 earlier allocated for wood to build the cantonment was no longer available, he made the case for a steam-powered sawmill that would enable him to have boards cut from timber felled near the post site.[49]

On February 18, 1879, Dodge left Fort Hays with companies C and K, traveling by regular passenger car to Topeka, where they transferred to two chartered cars occupied by companies A, D, and G from Fort Leavenworth. Arriving at Dodge City the next day, the battalion went into camp nearby until February 21, when it began its march, moving twelve miles to Mulberry Creek. The next day it continued to Bluff Creek, fourteen miles; the next, to Bear Creek, eighteen miles; the next, to Cimarron Creek, fourteen miles; the next, crossing into Indian Territory, at Buffalo Springs, seventeen and one-half miles; and the next, at Wolf Creek near Fort Supply, twenty miles. The command remained in camp at the fort for one day before resuming its journey on February 28, keeping to the south side of the river. From this point Amos Chapman served as guide and scout.

On the first day out, the battalion marched eighteen miles and camped at Cedar Bluff, where it remained on March 1 owing to a snowstorm. The next day it moved eighteen and one-half miles farther along the military road, to Persimmon Creek. On March 3 a delay occurred when an inexperienced wagon master attempted to move two wagons at the head of the train across Sheep Creek, which flowed between steep banks. Using ropes held by troops, he ordered the loaded wagons to be eased down into the sandy creek bed, where they became stuck. Dodge appeared on the scene just as the men were about to unload the stranded supplies so that they and the wagons could be dragged up the incline on the opposite side. Recognizing that this action would occasion a long wait, he sent to the rear for Trout's right-hand man, Quartermaster Sergeant Christian F. Sommer, Company C. On the appearance of the quartermaster sergeant Dodge asked him whether he had any experience in situations like this one. Being answered in the negative, he informed Sommer that it was about time for him to acquire some. After considering the problem, Sommer directed twenty men with picks and shovels to begin cutting down the side of the opposite bank. Within an hour a wagon road had been hewn out—steep and narrow but capable of passing a government wagon. With some energetic encouragement of the pack teams, the creek was soon forded and the command back on the trail, camping at Muddy Creek that night after a march of thirteen miles.[50] The next day it moved eighteen more miles, to White Horse Creek, where it remained in camp one day.

On March 6, after four and one-half miles the command went into camp at the site Dodge had just selected for Cantonment North Fork Canadian River.[51] As he had anticipated, the final determination was not difficult once the terrain lay open to view. Two days later he reported his choice of location to departmental headquarters, characterizing it as "one of the best I have ever seen. It is high, well drained and should be perfectly healthy."[52] Already looking to the future, he added that as soon as he received a sawmill he could begin construction of a permanent post. The midwinter movement of 180 soldiers, with teamsters and wagons, over 167.5 miles of sometimes broken country had been a solid success.

In the days that followed, Dodge and his men played the role of Robinson Crusoe, gradually imposing human order on a wilderness.[53] Dodge assigned details to cut down trees, erect storehouses, construct a charcoal pit, burn lime, construct bridges, seek out building stone, begin a post garden, and plant peach trees around the perimeter of the future parade ground. As supplies continued to arrive from Wichita, he sketched plans for buildings and debated about their best locations. Writing and receiving letters by the dozen, he dispatched them first by courier to Fort Supply, but after experiencing irregular delivery, he instead dispatched to and from Fort Reno. "I am delighted with the way everything is going on," he wrote in his journal on March 30, "as smooth as possible – no hitch no jar – & everybody working."[54]

In the first weeks at the cantonment, the entire population—numbering more than 250 men, including civilians—lived in tents or in makeshift shelters under tarpaulins. Conditions were primitive, and when buffeted by dirt-laden wind or attempting to move over rain-sodden ground, officers and men alike must have recalled with nostalgia the comfortable times at Fort Hays and Fort Leavenworth. "One can't open eye or mouth without getting it filled with *Dust*," Dodge wrote early in April. "Every mouthful one eats is half dirt – & there is no remedy except houses."[55] Work went forward, however, alternating with a measure of daily amusement. The post trader had opened for business shortly after arrival, but the sale of liquor was illegal in Indian Territory, and Keeling had not yet been granted the special dispensation he sought.[56] For Dodge, hunting and fishing were natural accompaniments to his examinations of the near vicinity in search of resources that could be put to use. In his journal entries he gave such zestful accounts of these amusements that an uninformed reader would scarcely be aware of the potentially explosive state of affairs at the Indian agency. The name of Little Chief went unmentioned, as if Dodge were unaware of the Indian leader's existence. Emphases and omissions like these were his means of amusing his parents without alarming them.

One incident he recounted in detail occurred on March 25, in the course of a day's expedition in search of building stone. Upon reaching the flat top of a hill a few miles south of the post, he and his small party found the outcropping they hoped for and also, lying at the foot of a cairn, a young Indian man. Recognizing that the youth was "making medicine" and that their appearance was a bad omen for him, Dodge kept his men from approaching. They paid no further attention to the stranger but completed their examination, returned to the ambulance, and drove it to a sheltered spot where they took out a lunch basket and sat down to enjoy themselves. A short time afterward the young Indian stalked down the hill and also sat down, a short distance from them. Except for a blanket wrapped around him, he was naked. Using sign language, he told them that he was the son of Yellow Bear, an Arapaho chief whom Dodge had recently met. He had come to the hill without food or water three days before, and he would remain there three days longer. He had with him a musical instrument—Dodge called it an "Indian clarionet"—that produced a remarkably sweet tone.[57] However, he explained that he could not give them a fuller recital at that time since to play the instrument before sundown was against his medicine.

The young man had been fasting, but when Dodge placed a chunk of corned beef between two biscuits and offered it to him he accepted it without hesitation, along with a cup of cold coffee. If this encounter had compromised his act of devotion, it seemed to promise friendly relations between him and the soldiers. The son of

Yellow Bear assured Dodge that he would come to the post and see him—when, the latter observed in his journal, "I will have to feed him again."[58]

In the initial weeks at Cantonment North Fork Canadian River, Dodge was virtually powerless to provide material assistance to the army forces at Fort Reno should violence erupt at the agency or the Northern Cheyennes break away. Only one of the six companies under his command, Captain Randall's Company I, had been designated as mounted infantry and so could pursue a foe rapidly.[59] However, Randall's unit was not part of the battalion that had marched from Fort Dodge. Until he reached the post from another mission,[60] all Dodge could do in case of need was send some of his men to Fort Reno to swell the numbers there.

Meanwhile, other frustrations tested his mettle as commander of a post that had not yet established its sphere of influence within the region. The presence of Colonel Davis and regimental headquarters at Fort Supply implied precedence of that post over the cantonment, even though the latter housed a greater number of troops and was located closer to the source of military concern. Davis, a stickler for detail and an officer not above appropriating certain perquisites, created small inconveniences and interruptions that must either be ignored as beyond remedy or else somehow discouraged without disrupting the command structure. Dodge dealt with these irritations decisively and with success, thanks to support from General Pope.[61] One such incident concerned an almost new Dougherty spring wagon that Davis had ordered appropriated upon its arrival at Fort Supply from the cantonment, substituting an inferior article for the return journey. Dodge saw to it that the better wagon was returned.

At the cantonment he found himself an object of curiosity, naturally enough, to the Indians who resided in the vicinity. Many of these sought interviews, sometimes for no particular reason but on other occasions on matters evidently of real importance to them. Their visits could be frustrating on both sides, for communication was limited to sign language.[62] The need of a post interpreter was painfully evident, but as yet none had been authorized. A related embarrassment was that the Indians begged for food that, notwithstanding Dodge's courtesy to the young Arapaho, as post commander he had no authority to dispense.

Despite these difficulties, Dodge pursued his work at the new post with zest and confidence. The expeditions in search of building materials yielded pleasant surprises—lime, stone, and stands of white oak, all within practicable distance. The labor of creating a substantial fort moved ahead so rapidly that the stately leather-bound folio volumes that were to serve as repositories of the post records no longer seemed so presumptuous as symbols of an established military order. The sites of the temporary cantonment and the prospective permanent post were contiguous, so that work on the two could go forward simultaneously. Once the storehouses were erected, Dodge would begin directing the construction of barracks, officers' quarters, and his own commander's residence. Early in April he informed Joe and Laura, still at Fort Hays, that they could join him at the end of the month.[63]

By mid-April 1879, Cantonment North Fork Canadian River was becoming a credible new presence in Indian Territory. True, it had not yet been assigned a distinctive name, though a rumor circulated that it would soon be designated Fort Pelouze, after a recently deceased Civil War veteran.[64] In official communications the post was referred to in various ways, as "the new post," New Cantonment, Cantonment, Canadian River Cantonment, New Cantonement [*sic*] North Fork Canadian River, New Post on the North Fork of the Canadian, and "New Post" on North Fork Canadian River, among other permutations. The term "cantonment," ordinarily designating any temporary post, became by implicit acclamation the proper name of the one established by Dodge.[65] Although General Pope intended for it to be granted permanent status, it was marked by the name as permanently temporary.

Cantonment was isolated, with as yet no military road that connected it directly to a railroad depot. Fort Supply and Fort Reno both had such a connection, and for efficiency and economy, Cantonment must also be given one of its own. Other duties had kept Dodge from fulfilling his promise to Pope to lay out a road, but he was now ready to direct the survey of a route leading northeast to Skeleton Ranch, along the Wichita–Fort Reno trail not far south of the Kansas state line. Once that new route was passable, Cantonment would be on approximately equal footing with the older posts that flanked it along the river.

Divided Duties

For General Pope, the value of Cantonment lay in the strategic position it occupied should the Northern Cheyennes again bolt from their reservation, sixty miles distant. General Sherman also supported its establishment in terms of anticipated needs miles away. Some practical consequences of the generals' ideas manifested themselves in the spring of 1879: Although troops at the post were stationed almost seventy miles south of the Kansas state line, they were called into service there and also at Fort Reno. Increased military activity was proving necessary not only to secure the reservation tribes inside Indian Territory but also to keep intending settlers out. Thus, while still at work constructing the new post, Dodge and his men became caught up in the army's effort to cope with emergencies elsewhere. The six-company garrison of Cantonment gradually dwindled to three.

On his return in late April from the road surveying expedition, Dodge found projects at the post moving ahead satisfactorily. However, the physical strain of recent weeks had told on First Lieutenant Trout, sometimes bringing on fits of temper that brought him into conflict with other officers. According to Dodge, he "requires as much management as a balky horse. In his duty, he is like some people in their religion – not content to do the best he can for himself but continually & forever worrying over the short comings of others – He tries my patience terribly some times, but I put up with a good many peculiarities on account of his many extraordinarily good qualities."[66] Trout was at his best amidst plenty of activity and continued to work with a will. The sawmill was expected soon, and in the meantime fatigue details were erecting picket huts for temporary use by the troops—rows of raw logs stood on end in trenches forming rectangles, with roofs also of wood, covered by paulins and daubed with a layer of dirt.[67] If only sufficient wagons were at hand to transport the excellent stone that had been found, work could begin on a really handsome permanent post.

A stream of civilian laborers and artisans began flowing into Cantonment, looking for work. If hired, they were issued passes by the post provost marshal permitting them to remain on the military reservation, and their names, occupations, "peculiarities," and other data were recorded in a "Pass Book" kept at headquarters. Most of these employees were between twenty and forty years of age, and almost all were Americans without specialized skills.[68]

Families and furniture also began to make their way to the post as its inhabitants made themselves more comfortable. Early in June the spritely wife of First Lieutenant William L. Clarke professed herself to Dodge "agreeably disappointed" at what she saw.[69] Captain Gilman at Fort Leavenworth forwarded fifteen pounds of Old Judge smoking tobacco, his whole stock on hand. The post trader was doing a brisk business in miscellaneous articles, though he still lacked permission to sell alcoholic beverages. In March the officers and men had submitted a petition on his behalf, which after some delay was denied. They appealed, and this time Dodge provided them a vigorous statement of support. In a letter to the adjutant general, he warned that if liquor were to be officially prohibited, the word would spread and illegal sources would multiply: "Cut off the supply entirely and the old Adam is yet so strong in human nature, that even the habitually sober men will get beastly drunk from these contraband supplies, and my command will be debauched not only by the quantity but by the quality of the stuff sold to them by these Kansas pirates." On the other hand, he argued, moderate use of liquor could easily be ensured if its distribution could be regulated at the post.[70] Given additional persuasive force by favorable endorsements from Pope and Sheridan, these considerations prevailed. On May 24 notification reached Cantonment that henceforward Keeling could sell wines and liquors in accordance with policies to be established by Dodge.[71]

In fact, the most serious challenge to orderly administration of the post during the first months of its existence came not from drunken soldiers but from more serious delinquents— deserters. By the end of May approximately one-eighth of the enlisted men had absconded, and without sufficient manpower the post could not be built. Some men were captured, but more made good their attempts to flee, often carrying with them the clothes and supplies they had been issued. Given the poor living conditions and sometimes heavy labor imposed on them for low pay, their inclination to take up lives elsewhere is not surprising.[72] However, early in June Dodge decided to discourage further desertions by displaying publicly the ignominious result of a soldier's capture.

The man put on exhibit was Private George D. Myers of Captain Pollock's Company C. On the march from Dodge City to the new post, Myers had disobeyed positive orders from Pollock and the attending surgeon to remain with his company. Instead he stayed behind at Fort Supply, whence he was later transported to Cantonment, charged with desertion. A few days before his trial by court-martial, Myers wrote to Greenbury L. Fort, a congressman from Illinois, appealing for assistance in securing a discharge from the army. Since their arrival at Cantonment, he wrote, he and other men had been given hard work and treated like dogs, even as his own health had deteriorated. Congressman Fort forwarded Myers's letter to the secretary of war, who returned it through military channels for comment. Meanwhile, in court-martial proceedings that began on April 1, Myers was found guilty of desertion and placed in the guardhouse.

Captain Pollock, directed to make a statement about Myers's plea of ill health, responded that the soldier had reported at sick call almost constantly since December 1878. He had been examined by four different physicians, none of whom could find anything wrong with him. They judged, and Pollock agreed, that Myers was a chronic malingerer who was attempting to deceive them in order to obtain a discharge on grounds of incapacity.[73] On May 25, when Pollock wrote his endorsement, Myers was still confined in the guardhouse awaiting promulgation from department headquarters of his sentence—likely to be incarceration in the military prison at Fort Leavenworth for a period of years. However, on the night of June 5 he escaped, and upon learning of his absence Dodge acted at once. He alerted Amos Chapman, who quickly organized a posse of Indians to scour the vicinity, and as a result Myers's flight to freedom lasted only about twenty-four hours. At guard mounting on the morning of June 7, his capture and its immediate consequence were made public as he was placed in irons.[74] Whether as a result of this sobering sight or from other causes, the problem of desertion at Cantonment was much less serious thereafter.

In spite of aggravations from individual soldiers, in general Dodge was well pleased with his command, both officers and men. "My boys are good boys," he wrote of the former. "I treat them well, place confidence in them, & they repay me by an affection of which I am very proud. I can say from long & ample experience that comparatively few Comdg. Officers have the affection of their subordinates if they do their duty. I have a way of 'setting down' on my boys which is very telling, & never makes them mad or causes one to forfeit his self respect."[75] These rather boastful statements were of course addressed to an admiring inner circle of family members, yet from all other indications a mutual regard did prevail between Dodge and his subordinate officers.

In the escape of Private Myers and at other times, Dodge's task of maintaining order was made easier by assistance from small bands of Indians who were encamped along creeks near Cantonment. Beginning in May, five Southern Cheyenne scouts were regularly employed at the post; and within ten miles in either direction were twenty lodges of Southern Cheyennes under Stone Calf, ten under Coho, thirteen under Big Back, and five under Minimick. Of Arapahos within the same distance were fifteen lodges under Little Raven, four under Yellow Bear, and two under Lame Deer. These Indians were all peaceably disposed.[76] The appointment of Amos Chapman as post interpreter as of May 1 had deprived Fort Supply of a useful employee, but he was even more valuable in his new posting, for he related well to Indians, citizens, and soldiers. With the assistance of Chapman, Dodge was able to learn his neighbors' impressions of conditions at the Cheyenne and Arapaho Agency and gain insight into the mode of existence they chose to pursue along the river in preference to residing nearer the agency. Out of concern for their poverty and respect for their efforts to eke out a semi-independent existence, for a group under Minimick he devised a plan to promote their employment as woodchoppers outside the military reservation.[77]

Reports received by mail and by courier kept Dodge generally apprised of developments in the region, but in some respects his post remained in semi-isolation. Rumors that the Northern Cheyennes at the agency were quietly accumulating horses and hiding them in the blackjack timber for unspecified purposes reached the post in mid-May, but without Chapman, who was then absent, Dodge did not know what to make of them and so was "much in the dark about Indian affairs."[78] He "earnestly" urged Pope to consider assigning another company of mounted infantry to Cantonment, but none was forthcoming.[79] Matter for cynicism was here, had he chosen to view his assignment in that light. He was expected to pursue fleeing Indians without horsemen, and as he once noted, to build a $50,000 post without money.[80] Of course, he was inured to just such impossibilities as these. What concerned him most at present was that levies on his command for service elsewhere were interfering with the construction of Cantonment North Fork Canadian River.

On April 26, 1879, military authorities in Washington snapped to attention when President Hayes issued a proclamation warning prospective settlers in Indian Territory that their effort would be illegal and that trespassers would be expelled, by force if necessary.[81] A widely reprinted article in the *Chicago Times* of February 15 had alerted readers to the existence of some 14 million acres of unoccupied land in the heart of the territory. To persons like "Captain" Charles C. Carpenter, who in 1875 had organized a peaceable citizen invasion of the Black Hills, these federal lands offered another opportunity to promote settlement. Railroad companies that served towns along the borders of Kansas, Missouri, and Arkansas stood to profit handsomely should new communities grow up in Indian Territory, and they helped fan the enthusiasm. Advertisements in Kansas towns including Wichita, Caldwell, Coffeyville, Independence, Chetopa, and Baxter Springs encouraged homesteaders to enter the territory and set up claims. In April, Carpenter, who now called himself "Colonel," opened an agency in Independence, Kansas, to enroll settlers who would accompany him into the unoccupied lands and help establish a "colony" there.[82]

Though not ceded to particular tribes, the lands Carpenter and others had in view were part of Indian Territory as defined by Section 2147 of the *Revised Statutes* and were not open to general settlement. President Hayes considered that the good faith of the United States government was threatened by the attempt to occupy this region, which had been set aside for eventual use by Indians. On the basis of other provisions in the *Revised Statutes* he directed that the War Department, in consultation with the Indian Bureau, should repel any attempt to break the law.[83] Thus, acting on directions from the secretary of war, on May 2 General Sherman ordered General Sheridan to send detachments of troops to towns along the southern border of Kansas, with orders to warn emigrants that if they entered Indian Territory, they would be expelled. "Some judicious officer, say Col. C. H. Smith 19th Infty, or Lieut. Col. R. I. Dodge of the 23rd," with a few young officers, should patrol the border cautioning emigrants in the same manner.[84] In the Department of the Missouri, Sherman's orders were quickly complied with by the adjutant, General Pope then being absent in New York at a court-martial. Colonel Smith, who was currently posted at Fort Leavenworth, left for Coffeyville and other points on May 4, and companies from Forts Supply, Dodge, Reno, Lyon, and Gibson were soon in the field. On May 7 Sherman, with the president and the secretary of war standing in his office, telegraphed Sheridan to send out yet more troops, using whatever cavalry units could be spared from Forts Supply and Elliott. He added that army officers were free to act without consulting representatives of the Indian Bureau, and free also to use compelling force.[85]

Reports indicated that upon recognizing the government's determination to resist them, would-be settlers abandoned their plans at once. The prompt work of the military—even if against an unarmed and mainly invisible foe—thus won praise in Washington. The president and secretary of war were gratified at the result, especially since it had been achieved without violence to any emigrant. However, turning back new settlers had corrected only part of what General Pope believed could be a continuing problem—namely, settlers in Indian Territory who had been overlooked by the troops passing along its northern border. Pope ordered military units already away from their posts to search the areas where they were then located, removing any unauthorized citizens they came upon. For a similar purpose he also ordered Major Mizner to send a mounted detachment scouting east toward the Sac and Fox Reservation, since the prospective capital of the emigrant movement was said to be somewhere in that area. To round out the investigation, on May 12 Pope ordered Captain Randall's company of mounted infantry to move north from Cantonment to the state line in search of settlers, then east to the Wichita–Fort Reno road. Randall and his men, with Amos Chapman as guide, left the post four days later.[86]

Dodge had known little if anything of the citizens' invasion until May 9, when telegraphic instructions from General Sherman to post commanders in the region reached him by courier. He had instead been expecting a call for assistance from Fort Reno, where tensions had heightened for other reasons.[87] Most of the 5,000 Cheyennes and Arapahos attached to the agency were reconciled in varying degrees to their enforced new mode of life, but the unruly Northern Cheyennes under Little Chief continued to stir up sympathetic feelings in many of their neighbors. Little Chief's band had dwindled slightly, to about 175 persons, but its influence was disproportionate to its size. In recent weeks a new grievance had been added to the angry band's list of resentments. In accordance with the Indian Bureau's policy to educate its charges, Agent Miles was making a determined effort to enroll their children in the agency school. Little Chief objected strongly to this attempt, claiming General Sheridan had promised that no such requirement would ever be made of him. Some of his children had already died in Indian Territory, he said, and he would not give up his only remaining school-age child to do manual labor and be made a slave of at the school.[88] Miles could make no headway on this point. He considered withdrawing rations to force compliance, and he even thought of calling in the military. Prudently, however, he decided not to attempt compulsion.

What was to be done with these troublesome Indians, whose recalcitrance threatened to set back the Indian Bureau's civilizing mission at the agency? Agent Miles and his assistant, Charles E. Campbell, agreed that if the band was to be kept in Indian Territory, the use of force would eventually be necessary. On March 10 Miles inquired of the Commissioner of Indian Affairs what long-term policy the bureau intended to adopt with regard to Little Chief, and a few days later Campbell posed the same question in a different way. The chieftain wanted to know whether his wish to depart from Indian Territory would be granted by the authorities in Washington. Why not permit him to journey there and learn his fate "from the fountain head"?[89] Eventually this proposal was judged a good one, and the confrontation over school enrollment was set aside. Preparing for the journey as escort, Agent Miles reminded Commissioner Hayt that the policy to be made known to the visitors was still not known even to him. The Indians with him were aware, he added, that Dull Knife's comrade Little Wolf had recently been permitted to remain in the north, and they could see no reason why that rebellious segment of the tribe should possess any stronger claim to consideration than they.[90]

Agent Miles arrived in Washington, D.C., with Little Chief and five other head men on May 14 and remained there a fortnight. Several conferences with Secretary Schurz proved unsatisfactory, especially to the secretary. Schurz, whom the Indians named Big Eyes for his thick glasses, was unable to answer their chief question until he had conferred with the president, and when he had done so, he found it impossible to make them comprehend the federal statutes that applied to their case.[91] At last he turned them over to Commissioner Hayt, admitting that "I can do nothing more with them." By his own account, Hayt read to them the treaties and the law and told them "it was their duty to obey the law and go South." After a long conversation, Hayt later testified, they agreed to stay in the South and be "'good Indians.'" The question of school attendance was not resolved to everyone's satisfaction, but Little Chief was granted an exception for his one school-aged child. Hayt promised each visitor fifty dollars, a suit of clothes, and for Little Chief's band an extra supply of wagons and cattle that had been asked for. On the whole, the outcome of the Washington visit appears to have been acceptable to both sides even though the Northern Cheyennes had not been granted their wish. Before their return to Indian

Territory, Hayt and Miles took them to New York City, where from their hotel window they watched a Decoration Day parade, with several thousand former soldiers moving in uniform down a city street. The scene impressed the Indians greatly, Hayt reported, revealing to them "the power of the government."[92]

The policy of the Indian Bureau was now known to Miles and the Indian leaders, but the army had not yet been informed of it. Pope believed that if Little Chief was denied his wish he would resort to violence at the first opportunity, possibly with devastating results. It was essential to know what course Secretary Schurz had decided upon. Pope made this point in a telegram to Sheridan on May 14 and more urgently in another to the adjutant general two weeks later. At last, on June 2, Schurz informed the secretary of war that the Indians would remain on their reservation in Indian Territory.[93]

The next day, with the Indian delegation already en route to Wichita, Pope took action. Leaving infantry troops stationed along the Kansas border to repel any further efforts at invasion, he directed all cavalry units that had been brought to the state line to return to Fort Reno. In addition, he explained to the adjutant general that "our only course is to keep the Indian [Little Chief] and some of his principal men in some mild custody" for the present, at the same time disarming and dismounting the rest of the band. Adopting this course would set aside the army's mandate not to interfere with Indians unless requested by a representative of the Indian Bureau, and Pope therefore asked authorization from the General of the Army. "These measures may be necessary only for a short time," he urged, "but surely such precaution is better than the undoubted risk, especially after last year's experience."[94]

As part of the precautions, on June 3 Dodge received from Mizner a call for two companies from Cantonment to further reinforce the garrison at Fort Reno.[95] Little Chief's tribespeople had by now learned the government's decision in their case. They were quiet, but Mizner wished to be fully prepared in case of emergency. Dodge was chagrined to lose so many more of his troops, not because he underestimated the seriousness of the situation but because he judged that Mizner was unlikely to use them effectively. "He is a fuss & feathers kind of man," he wrote of his fellow officer, "always wanting more troops & swelling about his Command. There is no possible use for Infantry at Reno at present, & he knows it as well as I do."[96] Of course, the departure of two more companies from Cantonment would effectively put an end to construction work there. Begun so auspiciously, the effort had soon been impeded, first by the effort to repel the invaders and now by the need, in Mizner's phrase, to "overawe opposition" from Little Chief.[97] However, as Dodge remarked in a journal entry, "sich is life."[98] Within a few days he hoped to depart from Cantonment himself, on a long-awaited leave of absence.

He had done all he could at the post thus far, and indeed he had accomplished a great deal. If Cantonment was not yet what he had envisioned, the circumstances that had held back its construction were beyond his control. He would return, and perhaps at that time his plans for the permanent structures could be realized. Before his departure, he wrote out some instructions to Randall, his temporary successor as post commander, and paid a call on all the resident ladies, just as he would at a long-established post. He feared that Randall and Trout would not get along, both being quick-tempered, but after offering some advice to the former he washed his hands of the matter.

Dodge's most recent leave of absence had been in December 1877, eighteen months previous,[99] and he had not seen his wife, son, and other family members since. Absence from Cantonment would permit him to take up that other life in some measure. Traveling with his escort along the road past Skeleton Ranch, he saw for the first time Caldwell, Kansas, a frontier town on the verge of a boom in land speculation, railroad development, and other enterprises both legal and otherwise.[100] Continuing along the road to Wichita, he caught sight of Little Chief and his party riding in the opposite direction. The Indians "created a sensation" among lookers-on, he wrote some time afterward: "A brawny buck with white shirt, elaborate necktie and felt hat, had buckskin leggings, and moccasins, and held over his head a lady's parasol. Another buttoned to the chin in a thick coat, had his nether extremities covered in the same way, was without a hat, but fanned himself incessantly with a huge gaudily painted Chinese fan. Not one had a full suit of civilized clothing, and if each had studied his 'getup,' for a month, he could not have fitted himself out more ridiculously."[101] At that moment the Northern Cheyennes were objects more of mirth than concern to Dodge as they neared the end of their journey toward the "mild custody" Pope and Mizner had in store for them. Once he reached Wichita, he would travel at railroad speed eastward for a surprise reunion with his wife. Events in Indian Territory would follow a course of their own, but for Dodge the arduous first stage of his service there was over.

19

The Army and the Indian Bureau

Organizations at Odds

John De Bras Miles, the Indian Bureau's chief representative at the Cheyenne and Arapaho Agency, was in the opinion of most observers an able and industrious administrator who performed a difficult task about as well as anyone could. Assisted by his wife and brother, on a modest annual salary of $2,400 Miles directed the activity of fourteen agency employees and superintended the procedures to obtain and distribute food and supplies to more than 5,500 Indians, some of whom were acknowledged to be the most dangerous and least disposed to tolerate "civilizing" efforts of any on the continent. The greater number of his Indian wards were reasonably well satisfied with the programs he administered. They recognized that their traditional nomadic life was no longer viable, and they were growing accustomed to supporting themselves by farming, raising cattle, or earning money by employment made available through the agency. Miles, a Quaker, never grew close to the tribespeople under his charge, but he devoted himself energetically to the task of ensuring their survival and fostering their progress toward what he understood as a higher state of civilization. A tall, spare man forty-seven years of age in 1879, Miles drove himself, and his gaze shone with a quiet intensity.

During the spring of 1879 the threat of violence from the Northern Cheyennes under Little Chief was only one of several serious problems faced daily by Agent Miles. For the great majority of enrollees at the agency, his most intense effort was necessarily to provide for their physical wants. He had no authority to purchase food, clothing, farm implements, and medical supplies. He could only draw up estimates, submit requisitions, and store and distribute the provisions authorized by the Indian Bureau in Washington. In order to encourage Indians to take responsibility for their own livelihood through pursuits like farming, the bureau made provision for the issue of food rations that were not sufficient by themselves to sustain life. To complicate matters, its officials made little effort to ensure that supplies were delivered on time.

John D. Miles. Courtesy Archives and Manuscripts Division, Oklahoma Historical Society.

In short, the ration supplies were inadequate and their arrival was unpredictable, forcing Agent Miles to search for ways in which the Indians could feed themselves.

In the early years of his tenure, a fall buffalo hunt west and south of the agency was a recourse. It brought the hunters into perilous proximity to ranches and cattle herds along the Texas frontier, but it yielded an abundance of the food they preferred and enabled them to feel that some part of their former way of life was being preserved. However, with the depletion of the buffalo herds, the annual hunts began to prove unavailing. Miles made what compensations he could: he encouraged Indians to farm the fertile bottoms along the North Fork of the Canadian River; permitted them to sell cured hides and trinkets to the authorized Indian trader in return for credit at the agency store; arranged for their employment by contractors who served the agency; and obtained wagons and teams for their use as teamsters.

Technically, Agent Miles possessed authority to enforce federal law as it applied both to the inhabitants of the Cheyenne and Arapaho Agency and also to the lands themselves. However, with only a small contingent of Indian police he could not cope effectively with a range of abuses that beset the region. American citizens were not permitted to conduct business in Indian Territory without authorization, but taking advantage of long distances and feeble enforcement they did so anyway. Cattlemen from Texas drove herds over reservation lands without permission, sometimes causing damage. They grazed their herds in places they had no right to occupy, trespassing for weeks at a time while fattening their animals for market. Dealers in timber poached wood and carried it north across the Kansas border. Settlers built shelters and stables in remote locations, effectively establishing permanent residence. Outlaws from Kansas used the Indian Territory as a place for tactical retreat or else raided within it for horses and cattle. Miles understood the provisions of the *Revised Statutes* that governed all this behavior, but he had little power to combat it. Other than to waylay the occasional whisky peddler and destroy his wares,[1] he could accomplish little except to maintain at the agency an oasis of administrative order in a desert of lawlessness.

Miles versus the Army

Though formidable in themselves, the challenges faced by Agent Miles were in his view made more onerous by the efforts of other government representatives to interfere with his work. Like most Indian Bureau officials, he believed the army was inimical to his effort and sought to undermine it. Congressional hearings to consider the possibility of turning over to the army the conduct of Indian affairs were held almost annually, and the arguments in support of such a change were well known. In the military view, efforts to civilize Indians through moral example and gentle persuasion alone were a waste of time. Moreover, Indian agents supposedly qualified for office by their approved piety were administrative innocents, vulnerable to the chicanery and fraud of the unsavory interests with which the Indian Bureau was said to be afflicted.

Aware of contemptuous attitudes like these, Miles insisted, sometimes truculently, that he not be interfered with by army officers. More than once he emphasized that he, not they, possessed authority as the primary representative of the federal government in his section of Indian Territory.[2] In June 1879 Miles's latent antagonism toward the army rose up in response to events about to occur at Fort Reno, as Little Chief and his five companions approached the agency after their visit to Washington. In accordance with instructions from General Pope, on June 8 Mizner ordered Ben Clarke, who was accompanying the Indians as interpreter, to bring Little Chief and the other five men to him at once upon their return—by force if necessary. None of the Indians was to rejoin his people until he had first attended this meeting.[3] Mizner hoped to obviate any difficulty with Little Chief through the interview, which would not necessarily lead to "mild custody." Nevertheless, the effect of his order was to stir up trouble with Agent Miles. On June 12, having just returned to the agency from Washington, Miles informed Mizner that his instructions to Clarke could not be complied with, for the compulsion he contemplated would destroy whatever good effects the visit to Washington had worked upon the Indians, "and I must emphatically decline to allow, except under the strongest protest and only with the Consent of my superiors, the Execution of the line of action proposed by you." Reminding Mizner of his own authority in the matter, Miles directed him not to take part in actions that concerned the Indians until asked.[4]

Commissioner Hayt informed Secretary Schurz of this incident, emphasizing the importance of keeping faith with the Northern Cheyennes and recommending that Mizner be officially forbidden to meddle any further. Schurz obliged with a letter to the secretary of war deploring Mizner's "unnecessary interference" in areas not properly his concern.[5] Meanwhile, even as the assertions of Indian Bureau primacy re-echoed from official to official, Mizner arranged an interview with Little Chief in his post commander's office. Contrary to military expectation, the chieftain was clearly peaceable, even though he still hoped to return north at some time. Mizner informed Pope that danger seemed past for the present, but in view of the constant risk posed by the Northern Cheyennes he wished to reduce the enlarged garrison of Fort Reno only gradually during the summer.[6] For his part, Agent Miles was satisfied that the Indians' visit to the national capital had resulted in "great good."[7]

During the summer and fall of 1879, Agent Miles's chief army adversary, placed among the Indians within his jurisdiction by military authority and permitted to remain there against his wish, was Second Lieutenant Heber W. Creel, Seventh Cavalry. This officer was on duty as a linguistic-anthropological student of the Northern Cheyennes and also a confidential observer for General Sheridan of their behavior and disposition. He enjoyed the good will of the band, living in their camp, building himself a residence there, and even entering into negotiations for a Northern Cheyenne wife. His summary reports sometimes included criticism of Agent Miles. The initial assessment, in March, included claims that Miles showed no good feeling toward the recent arrivals and conducted agency business in a suspicious manner.[8] A month later he reported more favorably, granting that Miles seemed zealous in his labors but criticizing as unwise his insistence that children in the band of Little Chief should be sent to school.[9] In June, immediately after the return of Little Chief, Creel reported to an officer at Fort Reno that the angry Indians would surely make a break for the north soon. In view of his close association with the band, he suggested that he be permitted to run the agency school.[10]

Creel had little direct contact with Miles, but the agent was aware of his activities and heartily resented them. Beginning in September 1879, he wrote a series of letters complaining of Creel as "an acknowledged enemy" and protesting against his unsettling influence.[11] Miles accused Creel of attempting to prostitute the women he lived among and of conducting a campaign of insinuations and outright efforts to belittle and malign both himself and the Indian Bureau.[12] By whose authority, he demanded of Commissioner Hayt, had Creel ever been granted the right to live among these Indians? Miles wished him expelled from Indian Territory before any further damage was done. In November he wrote that he could "not submit to be harassed by the insidious attacks of this man. . . . I do not ask the assistance of Lt Creel or any other military officer, in the management of the Indians, but I must insist that he shall not be allowed to hinder me in carrying out the orders and policy of the Indian office."[13]

Frustrations like these led Miles to refer in his published annual report for 1879 to "enemies of the department" who had intensified the discontent of the Northern Cheyennes by counselling them that they had been denied their just dues.[14] Fortunately for his equanimity, an opportunity to set forth in a public forum the facts of his recent work occurred in August of that year, when a special Senate committee to examine the removal of the Northern Cheyennes from the Sioux Reservation to Indian Territory arrived at Fort Reno. The senators took testimony at the Cheyenne and Arapaho Agency between August 19 and 21, and those who appeared before them included Little Chief and five other Indians, Miles and three other agency employees, Mizner and two other army officers, and Ben Clarke. The committee's inquiries centered upon a few general subjects: the treatment in Indian Territory of the Northern Cheyennes—both the Dull Knife and the Little Chief bands; the Indian Bureau's conduct of the Cheyenne and Arapaho Agency; the unsuccessful effort by the military to intercept and capture Dull Knife and his people; and the policy of forcing a northern Indian tribe like the Cheyennes to take up permanent residence in Indian Territory. Agent Miles testified on these matters almost the entire day on August 20 and was recalled on August 21.

In its report, published months afterward following further testimony from Mizner, General Crook, Colonel Miles, and Colonel Mackenzie of the army, and Ezra Hayt and Carl Schurz of the Department of the Interior, the Select Committee found little fault with Agent Miles. It praised him for having "done his duty faithfully and bravely in almost every particular, [with] a most difficult task to perform." Mizner, too, was recognized for providing "the most enlightened and dutiful support" to measures intended to ensure the peace and promote the welfare of the Indians.[15] In the committee's view, the blame for the Dull Knife outbreak, the devastations that followed, and in part the continuing dissatisfaction of Little Chief and others rested on the federal government for not complying with its treaty obligations. More particularly, the committee concluded that the "neglect and indifference" of the Indian Bureau to requisitions and warnings from its own employees in the field had helped bring matters to a crisis.[16] It recommended that agents like Miles be made more independent of control by the Indian Bureau, whose derelictions they often felt obliged to conceal by shifting blame onto the Indians.

Cantonment: Intercessor or Interference?

As fall approached, conditions at the Cheyenne and Arapaho Agency were much as they had been before the brief interlude of official attention. Agent Miles had received expressions of support from the senators, but he must now contend with the same difficulties he had before their arrival. One of these, Cantonment and its large garrison, went unmentioned in published testimony before the Senate committee. Existing at a considerable remove and having been established in response to events whose causes the committee was considering, the new post was not central to its concerns. To Agent

Miles, however, Cantonment loomed as one more obstacle to his mission. For example, a letter written by Colonel Dodge concerning lands occupied by Indians along the North Fork near Cantonment had set in motion a process of official review that threatened to interfere seriously with arrangements Miles had already made.[17] On May 27, then in Washington with the Little Chief delegation, the agent explained to Commissioner Hayt his motives for encouraging the Indians to improve lands near the river, expressing hope that legislation could be enacted that would permit them to possess those properties in severalty. He tacitly granted the point Dodge had made, that the Indians possessed no valid title,[18] and subsequent investigation confirmed this fact. Through a complicated series of revisions, practical accommodations, and unratified adjustments since adoption of a treaty in 1867, the legally fixed reservation of these Indians remained in doubt and confusion.[19] As Commissioner Hayt informed Miles on July 31, the Cheyennes and Arapahos could claim no legal right to the lands they occupied and had improved.

Agent Miles's irritated response to that ruling was the first of several indirect attacks he made on Dodge, whom he came to regard as another official enemy. While not disputing the position Dodge had taken, he nevertheless asserted his own right to grant occupancy on the lands concerned by virtue of an executive order by President Grant dated August 10, 1869.[20] He noted that progressive Indians like Yellow Bear and Little Raven had occupied lands on Dodge's military reservation long before Cantonment ever existed. By the right of occupancy, he added, they had good reason "to object to the wholesale destruction of every stick of valuable timber adjacent to their farms." After all, Dodge had seen fit to "rob the best disposed of our Indians of the principal inducement that led them to locate and undertake farming." Miles wondered whether the Department of the Interior had ever sanctioned the establishment of Cantonment and expressed doubt as to the necessity of such a post. "I have the honor," he concluded, "to ask whether a military officer has any right to exercise any such interference over peaceable and industrious Indians."[21]

In raising the issue of land ownership, Dodge had sought to draw official attention to a potential cause of discontent among Indians who resided near Cantonment, not primarily to call into question the arrangements made by Agent Miles. Nevertheless, by his "interference" he had created a new set of problems for Miles, and like Creel and at times Mizner, he had roused the agent's ire. Miles was sensitive to criticism, aggressive in asserting his primacy as a representative of the U.S. government, and inclined to portray his detractors as morally deficient. Dodge was troubled by the sufferings of the Indians and regarded the Indian Bureau and its employees as incompetent if not dishonest. Both men were convinced of their own rectitude, expressed themselves with skill, and were not shy of official controversy. Ironically, both wished well to the Indians. Open conflict had not yet broken out between them, but given their ideas and the adversarial relationship of the organizations they represented, a clash was inevitable.

That confrontation did not occur during the summer of 1879, for Dodge's one-month leave of absence was extended twice, enabling him to remain in the eastern states through early September. After visiting his wife in upstate New York, he worked his way south toward the home of his parents in North Carolina, stopping for a few days in New York City.[22] His son, Fred, was busy at work there, making arrangements for a fall tour as the lead actor in a dramatic "traveling combination." The repertory company would perform in the opera houses, lyceums, and theaters of towns and cities connected by railroads across the east. While in England, Fred had studied the performances of both Henry Irving and the American tragedian Edwin Booth in Shakespearian roles that had won them fame, and he had developed his own fresh interpretation of the characters.[23] Under the stage name Frederick Paulding, he would be billed in the coming months as "The New Hamlet."

During the week of July 26 Dodge registered at the Ebbitt House and also at the War Department in Washington, D.C. Following the example of his friend Colonel James B. Fry, he examined the files of the Adjutant General's Office in search of documents that might serve him in drafting a future book about the army.[24] Earlier in the year, Fry had published a volume entitled *Army Sacrifices, or Briefs from Official Pigeon-Holes. Sketches Based on Official Reports—Grouped Together for the Purpose of Illustrating the Services and Experiences of the Regular Army of the United States on the Indian Frontier,* which included some of the same material Dodge hoped to deal with, all "Based upon official reports." That Fry's modest work had appeared in print before his own appears not to have distressed him in the least, for the subject was broad enough to accommodate other authors.[25] Then, after spending some quiet summer days near his childhood home, he reported at Fort Leavenworth and was assigned the task of superintending further construction and repair of the military road as he returned to Cantonment. Fortuitously, he reached his post on September 22, two days after the initiation of telegraph communication there.[26]

His arrival was timely, for dissatisfaction among Indians not only at the Cheyenne and Arapaho Agency but also around Cantonment was fast approaching a crisis. Earlier in the month Agent Miles had been directed by the Indian Bureau to reduce the rations he issued so as to make the budgeted supplies last through the current fiscal year. That meant cutting the weekly beef ration from three pounds to two, a reduction Miles believed would cause suffering, especially after the poor growing season just past. Before acting on the instructions, on September 15 he telegraphed Commissioner Hayt warning that the change of policy would create a serious disturbance and could lead to collisions with citizens away from the reservation. Four days later he addressed a letter to Hayt explaining his concerns in greater detail. He pointed out that news of the mandated reduction had already gone abroad and that the Indians were clamorous, asking many times daily whether the directive from Washington had been withdrawn. He appealed for some provision to make possible the delivery of additional food,[27] but he received no satisfactory reply. Because supplies of foodstuffs such as flour were already low, in the present week he had authorized the issue of additional beef to compensate. In the week that followed, he would be obliged to reduce the beef ration to a level below the normal amount.

Ben Clarke, who served as informal intermediary between the Indians, the agency, and Fort Reno, sensed the gravity of the situation and on October 1 reported to Mizner the views of several Indian leaders. Little Chief said he had not come south to beg and so would not make trouble even if he starved. Still, it was hard to see his children hungry. Whirlwind, another Northern Cheyenne, said it had been difficult enough to live on the rations before; he did not see how one could survive on them now. According to Clarke, all the Indians felt cheated. Some proposed to scratch along quietly in hope that the government would relent, while others urged breaking away for a hunt. Stone Calf said they should die on the prairie rather than remain at the agency and starve.[28]

These desperate sentiments quickly spread to the Indians around Cantonment. Interviews with some of their leaders, including Stone Calf, Minimick, White Horse, Raven, and others, convinced Dodge that prompt action was necessary. On October 4 he telegraphed an urgent message to departmental headquarters, the latter portion of which ran as follows:

> They say they cannot live on the rations furnished by the Agent. Chapman informs me that the general talk among them is becoming reckless, that they say they had better be killed than starved to death. He anticipates serious and widespread trouble unless something be done immediately. There are no buffalo. If the Indians are permitted to go west to hunt they will kill cattle and cause trouble in the Pan Handle. . . .
>
> Can I be authorized to issue a small quantity of subsistence stores to prominent Indians?
>
> This may prevent serious complications.

Dodge's message reached Washington on October 7,[29] accompanied by a recommendation from General Sheridan that emergency rations be distributed. However, the communication was referred to the Department of the Interior before being acted upon, and on the next day Secretary Schurz informed the adjutant general that steps had been taken to relieve the Indians' necessities.[30] Rations at the agency returned at once to their normal level, and the excitement dissipated. Dodge's intervention had helped correct a serious problem, yet however well intended, it had brought him to the brink of "interference" with Agent Miles and the Indian Bureau. To the Indians near Cantonment, he was winning reputation as a friend, but to Agent Miles he was becoming a competitor and by his association with agency Indians, potentially a disruptive influence on them.

The Case of Keeling and Company

Within one week after Dodge had telegraphed on behalf of Indians near his post, Agent Miles's chief subordinate, Charles E. Campbell, submitted an official complaint against alleged illegal trading with Indians at Cantonment by Henry C. Keeling, the post trader. Acting on information provided him by George E. Reynolds, the authorized Indian trader at the Cheyenne and Arapaho Agency, Campbell reported that the five Cheyenne scouts employed at the post regularly purchased from Keeling articles that were not for their own use.[31] This practice exposed the authorized Indian trader to competition from a concern that could claim no such warrant from the Indian Bureau. Campbell therefore asked the Commissioner of Indian Affairs whether the five scouts were in future to be regarded as in effect soldiers, rather than as Indians who were permitted to trade only at their agency. Two days later he wrote again, reporting information just received that Keeling had dispensed with the cover of selling only to the five scouts. He was conducting business "openly and above board" with any Indian who wished to purchase items from him. He kept in stock "stranding beads, paints &c" that were obviously intended for the Indian trade but were of no particular interest to the scouts.[32]

Petty accusations like these might seem frivolous at a time when a threat to the Indians' very survival had just been averted, but they involved two matters of serious concern to representatives of the Indian Bureau: protecting the privileges of its authorized traders, and ensuring that the army and persons associated with it, such as Keeling, did not interfere with its arrangements. The information from Campbell was taken seriously in Washington, with the eventual result that on November 19 Dodge received instructions from General Pope to investigate the charges and submit a report of his findings.[33] Accordingly, on the next day he informed Keeling of the accusations and requested a written response to them before he began further inquiries. Keeling answered at once that his store had sold goods to the scouts "for their own use," had indeed kept in stock a few beads at the request not only of the Indians but of officers of the garrison, and knew of no goods being sold except in a legitimate manner.[34]

On November 28 Dodge informed Assistant Agent Campbell of Keeling's denial and asked for documentary evidence and the names of witnesses "by whose evidence you expect to make good these charges."[35] On the same day he also responded to Miles, who had asked him to inform Indians in the vicinity of Cantonment that they must at once move closer to the agency. The agent's expressed rationale was that in future these Indians would be issued their rations weekly rather than monthly as heretofore. Whatever Miles's motives, Dodge replied to him with pointed politeness, expressing his willingness to pass on the message but making clear that he took no direct orders from officials of the Indian Bureau. He wrote, "I shall not however feel warranted in the use of force to carry out your wishes, until you shall have communicated with General Pope, and he with me. I shall be very greatly relieved if you succeed in getting these Indians away. They are a source of constant annoyance and trouble. Stone Calf says he cannot move, as the white thieves have stolen all of his ponies. I recommend that you send a few wagons from the agency for him; this will have a good effect I think on the other Indians."[36] Of course, Dodge was aware that sending "a few wagons" more than sixty miles over a primitive road was no small matter.

Resolution of the issues raised by Campbell and Miles concerning Keeling and Company was delayed by Dodge's departure from Cantonment on a short leave of absence. Late in November he took advantage of the opportunity for a reunion with his wife and son during Fred's dramatic tour of the western states.[37] The final preparations for performances by Frederick Paulding during the 1879–1880 season had been made in August, when his agent placed an advertisement in the *New York Dramatic Mirror* inviting theater managers having open dates to contact the agency office on Broadway.[38] Following its debut at Troy, New York, on September 27, the company moved north into Canada, with dates in Toronto, Hamilton, London, and Saint Catherines, Ontario. It returned to the United States for a booking at Erie, Pennsylvania, on October 18, followed by three weeks on "the Ohio circuit."[39] The routine of a nightly performance in a strange theater, often followed the next day by a railroad journey and performance that night in a new town, was taxing work. Nevertheless, Frederick Paulding won considerable praise for his efforts. Attendance was sometimes disappointing, but Julia Dodge, who accompanied the players, helped make up for losses by financial contributions of her own.[40] Being short of funds during the summer, she had prevailed upon her husband for a loan of $5,400.[41]

Dodge entertained some hope of witnessing his son's success on stage during the fall and had made tentative arrangements for a visit to Fort Leavenworth to coincide with Fred's appearances in the area. However, newspaper reports indicated that the dramatic troupe had failed financially and returned to New York.[42] He had set aside his anticipations when, on November 28, a telegram from Fort Leavenworth informed him that the reports were false and that Fred would appear in Leavenworth, Kansas, on December 1 and 2.[43] The result was a journey with all possible speed, leading to a moment of shocked recognition during the first night's entertainment.

The play was Tom Taylor's *The Fool's Revenge*, with Fred as Bertuccio, the malignant court fool of the title. Dodge reached the opera house before the curtain rose, but wishing to surprise his son he did not go backstage. When Fred came before the audience in the first act he was "so hideously made up" that his father hardly recognized him. Fascinated, he watched Fred perform as the plot unfolded until, in the intense final scene, Fred / Bertuccio overset a small table and fell with it to the stage floor. Dodge thought the fall intentional, for it merged seamlessly with the action, but when he hurried to the dressing room after the performance he learned the truth. Just as he turned to lean on the table, Fred had caught sight of him and was so surprised that he lost his balance.[44]

Dodge was a faithful, if uncritical observer of his son's performances in the days and nights that followed. On December 2 Fred played Hamlet, and Dodge judged him "simply grand" in the role, "better than any I have ever seen."[45] General Pope echoed this judgment, noting that he had witnessed interpretations of the tragic hero by some great actors including William C. Macready, Edwin Forrest, Edwin T. Booth, and Wilson Barrett. This was high praise indeed, but local newspapers were hardly less enthusiastic. Audiences at Kansas City, Saint Joseph, Atchison, and Omaha were appreciative, and proceeds were satisfactory.[46] Julia glowed with happiness and pride in her son, and to Dodge's delight she insisted on leaving Fred to be with him for a few days before he returned to his post. "I think my dear old wife has 'kinder' fallen in love with me again," he wrote in his journal. December 9 would be Dodge's last night with the show, and throwing economy to the winds he treated Fred's company to a champagne and oyster supper after the performance. The festivities continued until 3:00 A.M., when the elated host shook hands with all the men, "kissed all the (pretty) women," and returned to his hotel.[47]

On reaching Cantonment,[48] Dodge received the disappointing news that the post would not be designated as permanent. Rigid economy was necessary in the coming fiscal year, and the military situation in Indian Territory no longer seemed so explosive as it had a few months earlier. General Sheridan saw greater need for a post between Forts Concho and Elliott in Texas to help secure the western border of the territory from incursion by cattle herds being driven north to the railroads.[49] Though disappointing, the adverse decision was probably not surprising to Dodge, nor was it a source of deep personal regret. He had directed construction of the post with interest and even enthusiasm, but that was the approach he took to most initiatives. As he later wrote to Fred, "I get enthusiastic & ardent, work with all my might & main to attain my end, but if I fail there's an end to it. I never worry."[50]

An incitement to effort in the present was a letter from Agent Miles that also awaited him on his return to Cantonment. This was in reply to his request for documentary evidence and the names of persons who could supply testimony to support the charges against Keeling and Company. Miles sent no documentation, but he named several prospective witnesses. They included four Indians—Little Raven, Big Back, Mahminick [Minimick], and George Bent, a mixed-blood interpreter at the agency, and four "white men"—the agency trader, George E. Reynolds, Jake Zallwager, William Frass, and Amos Chapman, the latter three all married to Cheyenne women.[51] The list made possible a further investigation of Keeling's activity, and on December 20 Dodge assured the agent of his intention "to sift this matter to the bottom." Informing Miles that he had requested three of the "white men" to come to Cantonment and give evidence (Amos Chapman being already at hand), he asked his assistance in causing the Indians to make the journey as soon as possible. On December 30 Miles telegraphed that the Indians would report after New Year's Day.[52]

Thus far the army officer and the Indian agent had cooperated in businesslike fashion to set up the inquiry. However, the ten days that followed brought on a confrontation between them, caused in part by mere chance but intensified by their mutual suspicion and disrespect. On January 6 Dodge received from Amos Chapman a written deposition that he had on many occasions purchased goods of the post trader on behalf of his wife, her near relations, and other members of her band. According to Chapman, "squaw men" regularly assisted their wives' extended families in this way. He reported that in August, when he visited the agency in connection with the Senate committee's inquiry, Agent Miles had asked him to "do all he could to help the Indians along" back at Cantonment. In his opinion, the purchase of items like calico, flour, and bacon, either direct from Keeling or as surplus from company messes, was precisely the sort of help he had been called upon to give.[53] On January 7 three clerks at the trader's store submitted statements to Dodge that they had sold goods to the five Indian scouts but not to other Indians.

At this point Dodge believed he comprehended the nature of Keeling's business contacts with the reservation Indians. Having just received from George E. Reynolds, the original complainant, a note excusing himself from supplying testimony on account of illness in his family, on the morning of January 8 he telegraphed Agent Miles that the additional witnesses from the agency need not make the trip to Cantonment; he had examined several other persons and closed the case.[54] But later that same day the agency witnesses arrived at the post, accompanied by Miles. Arrangements were hastily made to accommodate the unexpected arrivals and secure their testimony. If at this point Miles suspected he had almost been circumvented by Dodge, who perhaps had not wished to consider evidence from persons at the agency, his suspicion was heightened by the hearings that ensued. Dodge examined the new witnesses—Zallwager, Frass, and in the presence of two interpreters, Minimick and Big Back—but in private. (George Bent, one of the interpreters, did not give testimony, for reasons later made clear.) Miles was miffed to be excluded from a formal inquiry into alleged practices that set at nought his authority to regulate trading by Indians in his care.

Dodge's report, dated January 9, 1880, was a model of due documentation, accompanied by twenty-two exhibits of his correspondence and the written and oral testimony he had received in the case. Drawing upon evidence that included testimony by Zallwager, Frass, and the two Indians, he related their statements to the deposition given him earlier by Chapman. He reported that Indians in the vicinity of Cantonment—scouts, farmers, wood contract workers, and the relatives of all these—had indeed purchased items from Keeling, not directly, for the post trader was "too shrewd" to do anything that would leave him liable to disciplinary action, but through intermediaries. Keeling's indirect patrons had been glad to trade with him, since they claimed to receive "four or five times as much for their money" as they did from Reynolds at the agency. "I have known of this all the time," Dodge wrote, "but have had no cause or right to interfere. There is no law prohibiting any white man from purchasing a hundred pounds of bacon, or one or more sacks of flour from the Post Trader—and if he then chooses to give it to the Indians I know of no law or power which can prevent him." Dodge concluded his report with a ringing statement of frustration with laws that in effect prohibited assisting the Indians: "It is simply impossible to prevent this trade. An Indian comes with a pitiful story of starvation and suffering of himself and family – somebody will be so charitably disposed as to help him. I and other officers of this post, have not infrequently bought small quantities of stores from the Post Trader for the benefit of Indians; and though the trader is thus really trading with, or for the benefit of Indians, the practice will continue just so long as the law of humanity is superior to the law of Congress."[55]

Forwarded through military channels to the Department of War, Dodge's report was not received by the Office of Indian Affairs until February 13.[56] Agent Miles was thus unaware of its precise contents, but he early suspected its drift.[57] Resentful of the treatment he had received at Cantonment, he was frustrated at his inability to stop a military trader like Keeling and Company from dealing with Indians. He had no recourse except to appeal for support from the Commissioner of Indian Affairs. On January 19 Miles therefore addressed a heated letter to Commissioner Hayt in which he branded Dodge's official inquiry a whitewash, designed to "Completely Exonerate Keeling." He trained his rhetorical firepower on Dodge, suggesting by innuendo and slanted statements that not all was what it should be at Cantonment. He mentioned that Amos Chapman, "a known representative of Keeling," had been permitted to attend the secret proceedings as interpreter while he—presumably more objective—had not been admitted. The accusations against the post trader were, he claimed, "evidently well founded and true in every particular." As proof of this statement Miles appended to his letter affidavits by four of the witnesses—Zallwager, Frass, Minimick, and Big Back—whose testimony before Dodge he had not heard. Ironically, these statements were virtually identical in content to the ones appended to Dodge's report. As the climax to his letter, Miles claimed that George Bent, an expected witness at the Cantonment proceedings, "was furnished with liquor" shortly after his arrival at the post and remained "intoxicated for five or six days."[58]

When Dodge's report reached the Office of Indian Affairs, it was filed without further action. However, Miles's statement of January 19 made its own way through official channels to the War Department and eventually back to Dodge for comment. On February 25, stung by Miles's claims but contemptuous as well, he did comment, and vigorously. Dispensing with official decorum, he responded in kind to the agent's accusations of favoritism and bias. He defended Amos Chapman as an honest man, "known for his gallantry and faithful service." He asserted that when at Cantonment, George Bent had first served as interpreter, then gotten himself drunk. Inquiry revealed that the alcohol he consumed came from a bottle of Jamaica Ginger and another of alcohol-laced red ink that he had induced a soldier to purchase for him. "As Bent is said to have drank the entire contents of both bottles within a few moments, his five or six days' 'intoxication' is easily accounted for." As to Miles and his affidavits—which Dodge had not seen and did not know essentially duplicated those he had obtained—he directed against the agent the same slur about "squaw men" that had been used to malign Chapman. "I have no doubt," he wrote, "that Mr. Miles can furnish an unlimited number of affidavits towards the proof of anything he may assert. . . . The Agency is surrounded by a number of squaw-men, offscourings of humanity that will make affidavit on demand." Miles had impugned Dodge's honesty; Dodge returned the favor, representing Miles as being thought by some "the most heartless and cruel of swindlers."[59] The war of words between these representatives of the army and the Indian Bureau had rapidly become unseemly. Meanwhile, Keeling and Company was permitted to continue operations at Cantonment on the same basis as before, but the controversy over the business it transacted was not over.

For the greater part of the year, a number of the Indians enrolled at the agency lived within a few miles of Cantonment. Concerned for their welfare at that considerable distance from their authorized source of purchased food and supplies and convinced also that they were being bilked by the trader at the agency, Dodge encouraged H. C. Keeling to apply for permission to sell goods directly to Indians at his Cantonment store. Accordingly, in February 1880, through an attorney in Washington, Keeling requested of Secretary Schurz that he be allowed to trade with Indians "subject to the regulations prescribed for traders with the Indians generally." Senator Preston B. Plumb, a valuable ally in such a petition, assured Schurz that Keeling was a sound businessman and a person of good character.[60] Nevertheless, this direct appeal by a military trader to the department that administered the Indian Bureau was quickly denied. Late in March, Keeling renewed his request, writing on his own behalf and intending for his letter to reach Schurz freighted with favorable endorsements from senior army officers. Dodge was the first to express support for the proposal, and in his endorsement he employed the strongest terms he could:

> It is very greatly to the interests of the Indian that this request be granted. At present there is practically but one firm of Traders on the Cheyenne & Arapahoe reservation. The Indian has to buy at highest and sell at lowest prices. Many come to this post who have no food, but have means to buy. I cannot permit them to buy of the Subsistence Department, and as Keeling and Co. cannot sell to them, they sometimes suffer greatly.
>
> In the interest of humanity, I approve and recommend a favorable consideration of this request.[61]

Unfortunately, Dodge's appeal flew in the face of political reality. General Pope had supported him on many occasions before, but in this instance he declined. Recently Pope had written to the secretary of war that, so long as the present system of managing Indian affairs existed, he could not approve of post traders selling to Indians. "It would only introduce a fresh element of dissension between the Post Commanders and Indian Agents and between the War and Interior Departments," he wrote. What was more, disputes would occur between the traders authorized by the army to sell to Indians and those authorized by the Indian Bureau. Through his adjutant, Pope informed Dodge that he had not changed his mind and could forward Keeling's request only with a negative endorsement.[62] On April 20 Dodge therefore returned Pope's comments to Keeling, ending the effort.[63] The appeal to principles that transcended political considerations had been a worthy one, but it seemed hopeless.

The Ute Woman

On January 20, 1880, the day after Miles had accused Dodge of dishonestly attempting to "Completely Exonerate Keeling" of trading with Indians, the agent took the offensive on a new front. Wishing, he wrote Commissioner Hayt, "to check, if not altogether to stop, the practice now so common, the prostitution of Indian women by U.S. soldiers," he enclosed an affidavit describing "the fatal result of excessive sexual intercourse" between men at Cantonment and a Ute woman.[64] The affidavit, made one month earlier by Minimick, concerned the death of this woman in November, a few days after she had visited Cantonment to earn money as a prostitute. Miles's reason for not informing his superiors of this distressing incident at the time he learned of it can only be guessed at, but his motives for sending it when he did were unmistakable. He wished to portray Cantonment as a sink of sexual license, probably both for the embarrassment his accusation would cause and so that Indians would be discouraged or prohibited from going there.

Miles's allegation received prompt attention in Washington. On January 30 Secretary Schurz forwarded it to the secretary of war with the request that in future all post commanders be instructed to keep Indians "without proper passes from their Agents, outside the lines" of military installations.[65] If the claims of Miles were true, as Schurz and Hayt appeared to assume, they constituted a mortifying reflection on army discipline. Presently the matter came before General Sherman, who reacted with cautious concern. It was easy for Indian agents to accuse soldiers of wrongdoing on the basis of "mere rumor," he wrote in his endorsement. He did not credit such claims, but they embarrassed the army as a whole, and "now that a direct charge is made in some detail I want the case investigated." On February 7 an order for a full investigation and report went out from army headquarters,[66] and after some delay the responsibility for the inquiry devolved upon Dodge.

The evidence he subsequently obtained through depositions from local Indians, Amos Chapman, and the post physician yielded a sordid but clear picture. As a girl, the Ute woman had been captured by the Arapahos and kept by them as a servant. Eventually they began selling her services as a prostitute, either directly or through Indians who took her to camps elsewhere for a few days at a time. Later she had been purchased from the Arapahos by Scabby, a Cheyenne, and on his death she became the property of his widow, Yellow Woman. Known as "Hobbled Woman" because of her slave status, the Ute woman was a fixture at the Cheyenne and Arapaho Agency, where she had done a steady trade for years. Witnesses agreed that she did not resent her place there. She was permitted to keep half of her earnings, and she seemed to like her work.

Stone Calf and Coho, Dodge's Indian witnesses, told a story of the few weeks preceding the woman's death that agreed in essentials with the testimony of Amos Chapman. Early in November, Yellow Woman came to Coho's camp and hired out Hobbled Woman to Indians who took her near the post at night and sold her to men there. Once in the daytime she had come to Chapman's house, begging. About three days before her death, Chapman visited Coho's camp and found her so ill that the occupants of the lodge had set her outside to die. Examining her, Chapman found that she was suffering "a most horrible case of Syphilis." He obtained medicine from Dr. Aaron I. Comfort at the post and sent it to her, but she died soon afterward.[67]

Dodge sought to ascertain from Dr. Louis La Garde, the chief physician at Cantonment, the part played by soldiers in the activities and final sufferings of this woman. According to hospital records, between November 6, 1879, and March 4, 1880, one soldier had received treatment for constitutional syphilis, one for gonorrheal orchitis, and one for gonorrheal cystitis. All three cases had been contracted long before. However, Dr. La Garde also mentioned in his report two civilians whose cases of gonorrhea he had treated in December. These, he emphasized, were "*doubtless contracted in the vicinity of this post.*" The physician was unable to specify the source of the infection,[68] but his clinical observations were strong if not conclusive evidence that while some men at Cantonment may have engaged in sexual intercourse with the deceased woman, soldiers had not.

Dodge's inquiry had not been difficult, but the charges were grave and taken seriously at army headquarters, so he drafted his report with care. Itemizing first the facts supported by direct evidence and second those by presumptive evidence, he next summarized the report of Dr. La Garde and the affidavits of Stone Calf, "a chief of standing, and one of the most reliable Indians of my acquaintance," Coho, "to whose band the owner of the Ute slave belonged," and finally Amos Chapman. Observing that further affidavits would be "simply cumulative," he proceeded to his conclusion: "The charges made by Mr. Miles are utterly unfounded."

In his report, Dodge did not give prominence to Agent Miles except as the source of statements whose validity he had investigated. However, at a few points he did refer ironically to Miles and his activities, suggesting that they might also warrant inquiry. For example, citing evidence that the agent had known for years of the Ute woman's prostitution at the agency and yet had done nothing to relieve her during her lifetime, he observed that his "new born zeal is scarcely to be accounted for." In regard to Secretary Schurz's request that Indians be kept outside the "lines" of military posts, he mentioned that in the spring just passed, Miles had actually encouraged the presence of reservation Indians near Cantonment. He had allowed Indians to continue cutting and racking wood after their contract to supply firewood to the post had been filled; he had in fact appealed to Dodge not to interfere with them. However, on that occasion his solicitude on behalf of the Indians lasted only until he learned that their labors would no longer benefit the contracting firm of Lee and Reynolds, at which point he directed them peremptorily to return to the agency. "To an unprejudiced observer," Dodge slyly suggested, "there would seem to be some connection between Lee and Reynolds and the authorities at the Agency."

He explained that as a cantonment, his post was without fortifications, and being situated along a public road, it could not possibly be made secure against intrusion. However, he enclosed documents that demonstrated a sustained effort to discourage Indians from entering the military reservation except during stated hours and on business. He granted that in spite of the efforts of provost officers and guards, every day Indian women came to the post begging for food or for work that would enable them to purchase it. They behaved themselves well, he wrote, and never entered the men's quarters. The danger of sexual contact, if any existed, was not on the post or near it—Secretary Schurz's "line"—but away from it, in bushes and ravines where detection of clandestine activities was impossible.

Dodge's report on the death of the Ute woman was detailed, tightly controlled, definitive. In concluding it, he permitted himself a rhetorical flourish:

> I do not believe that any Indian woman has been debauched by any soldier at this post. The Indian prostitutes brought to the vicinity at night by Indian pimps may have been used, and will probably continue to be used, as long as human nature is as it is. The social evil is an institution of savage as well as of civilized life, and if it cannot be stopped in the enlightened capital of this great country, it is hardly fair to expect post commanders to stop it among the savage tribes of the frontier.[69]

The report laid to rest the most recent set of accusations by Agent Miles.

"Undesirable Whites"

Undeterred, in February 1880 Miles launched a new campaign—an effort to rid the Cheyenne and Arapaho Agency of "undesirable whites . . . ostensibly engaged in work for the military."[70] He sought the expulsion, among other persons, of Robert L. Townsend, a civilian employee at Cantonment whom he described to Commissioner Hayt as a "worthless character," one who was "interfering with the effort to advance these Indians in civilization."[71] Townsend, a former soldier who had worked as a saddler while stationed at Fort Reno, had pursued his trade at the fort for some time after his discharge. Miles refused to legalize his marriage to an Indian woman whom he purchased, but the couple remained together and by 1879 had one small child. Recommended in September of that year for employment in the quartermaster's department at Cantonment, Townsend moved there with his small family and began work at sixty dollars per month.[72]

On March 8 Agent Miles informed Commissioner Hayt that Townsend had recently been brought to him by the Indian police, partially intoxicated. According to Miles, the police reported that he had entered an Indian lodge, "seized hold of an Arapahoe woman and evidently would have violated her person had he not been too drunk."[73] Townsend was taken to the guardhouse and two days later was brought before Miles for an interview. The agent's notes of this session included the information that Townsend's wife and child were enrolled at the agency and received rations there, but that the husband "[p]refers to have his wife live at the Military post where he is employed." Miles also recorded that Townsend habitually became intoxicated, buying his liquor at the "Military trading Establishment."[74] After five more days of detention, Townsend was released and permitted to return to Cantonment, but Miles wished to take further action. He asked Commissioner Hayt whether any means were available to rid Indian Territory of such persons as this.

During the period when Townsend resided near the Cheyenne and Arapaho Agency, he had not claimed the privileges due an Indian, as many other squaw men did. His only misdeeds noted by Miles were those that had led to his recent arrest, though certainly the alleged drunkenness and brutal behavior were serious matters, if true. Eventually the Townsend case was referred to Cantonment for investigation and report, this time not by Dodge but by the post provost marshal, First Lieutenant William L. Clarke. Upon Townsend's returning to work after more than a week's unexplained absence, Clarke had already made inquiries. At that time the only evidence he could obtain was a positive denial by Townsend that he had attempted to debauch the Arapaho woman. Through renewed investigation, Clarke succeeded in establishing what had prompted Townsend's journey to the agency. His wife had earlier gone there but wished to return to the military post, and he had requested permission at Cantonment to go and bring her back. Permission being granted, he left the post in a sober state and without liquor, arriving at the agency three days later, approximately when his alleged drunken misbehavior occurred. Clarke could obtain no further information about that incident, and in his report he therefore confined himself to describing Townsend's reputation and customary behavior. At Cantonment "he has performed his work faithfully, does not drink to any excess, is in no sense of the word a worthless character, works for his living, and so long as his wife remained here supported her decently."[75] These comments sufficed to end the matter. On June 7 the secretary of war informed the secretary of the interior that Townsend was "not regarded in any sense of the word as a worthless character" and so had not been removed from his position.[76]

In the spring of 1880 the contest of thrust and parry between Miles and Dodge was suspended when, for the second time in four months, the latter journeyed to Leavenworth, Kansas, for a rendezvous with his wife and son. Fred's company had enjoyed considerable success during its winter tour. Newspaper critics were now less inclined to comment archly on his youth and instead drew attention to his sensitive interpretation of the roles he played. As one put it, "Paulding is no doubt a rising young tragedian."[77] The traveling company had passed through the southern states, and by mid-March, when Dodge learned of its scheduled appearance in Leavenworth, it was moving northward from New Orleans.[78]

The death of his father on February 24 had deprived Dodge of the will to write in his journal,[79] but the prospect of witnessing the further development of Fred's ability as an actor and of seeing Julia again led him to resume his entries on March 25. He had been granted a twenty-day leave of absence beginning on that date, and he therefore made his way to Kansas City, where he arrived four days later. Julia was not yet in the city, having taken ill in New Orleans, but three days later she made her appearance, and with a series of adventures to relate including the loss of her valuable trunk. At Leavenworth she and Dodge shopped together for a replacement, attended social functions at the post, and took carriage rides together. They followed Fred's company to Topeka, then Atchison and north into Nebraska, first Lincoln and later

Omaha, where they were called upon by friends, including the wife of General Crook. Having obtained an additional five days' leave, Dodge accompanied Julia to performances in Des Moines, Iowa, and Rock Island, Illinois, before setting off on his return to Cantonment.[80]

Flying visits like these hardly qualified as domestic felicity in the traditional sense, but they gave satisfaction to all three Dodges. Fred, laboring as he was on a grueling theatrical circuit through the hinterlands, welcomed the contact with both his parents. Julia might be running through her inheritance, but she seemed to enjoy Dodge's attention and companionship. For Dodge, the interlude of travel with his wife and son was a hopeful augur for the future. He arrived back at his post on April 17, ending what he termed "a glorious trip without a flaw or accident."[81]

This spring the troops nominally at Cantonment were being called upon to help solve some of the same problems they had responded to one year before. The threat of the territory's invasion by land-hungry citizens was even more immediate than in 1879. The determination of Little Chief to win government approval of his desire to leave Indian Territory held firm. As an Atchison, Topeka and Santa Fe railhead neared Caldwell, the cattlemen of Texas blazed new trails across the Cheyenne and Arapaho Agency. However, these issues were receiving less attention from the army than they once had, for the focus of its crisis planning had shifted hundreds of miles westward. Political and military considerations dictated that troops be sent to occupy positions in the mountains of Colorado, where they would protect settlers from further attack by Ute Indians and guard against reprisals, depredations, and attempts at illegal settlement in Ute country by U.S. citizens. Within days of his return to Cantonment, Dodge received notification that "before long" he and three companies under his command would leave the post to join the Fort Garland Column in southern Colorado.[82]

As he awaited his orders, events in the vicinity followed a familiar pattern: it was spring and the Indians were agitated.[83] On April 20 Agent Miles received from the Indian Bureau a directive to enroll all school-age Indian children in the agency school, and on being informed of this plan, Little Chief was moved almost to violence. Captain Randall, in command at Fort Reno, telegraphed Pope that his company of mounted infantry had better be ordered back from Caldwell in case Miles asked him to make a roundup of the Indians, for he believed Little Chief would resist. Pope agreed that the order given Miles would surely cause serious trouble, "if not an open outbreak."[84] Dodge, who had gone to Fort Reno on an official errand, received there a request from Pope to use all his influence to dissuade Miles from attempting to put the order into effect.[85] Miles had grown impatient of Little Chief's "almost open defiance" and favored taking steps to "compel obedience" if the chief and his followers were to remain attached to the agency.[86] However, other views prevailed on this occasion, and the Indian Bureau directed him to defer the attempt to implement its educational policy until he received further instructions.[87]

Opinion was building that the interests of all parties would be best served if Little Chief and his followers were allowed to return north. Mizner had predicted in August

1879 that so long as the Indian leader remained at the agency, he would remain a source of "constant anxiety." In November of that year he concluded that, as a matter of prudence and "common justice," Little Chief and his people should be allowed to join their relations in their former home.[88] In February 1880 General Pope wondered what good could possibly accrue to the Indians or the government by keeping them in a place distasteful to them, and from which they continually spent time devising ways to escape. If they were allowed to return north, their absence would enable him to use elsewhere the forces now deployed to prevent their outbreak. Enumerating other military situations his troops were expected to deal with in Indian Territory and in New Mexico, Colorado, and along the border with Mexico, Pope made clear that the removal of the Northern Cheyennes from Indian Territory would be "an immense boon to them" and also to himself.[89]

Colonel Nelson A. Miles, a steady advocate of Little Chief and his followers, also urged compliance with their wishes, asserting that it would be "humane, just and wise to allow them to return north." He elaborated his views in testimony before the Senate committee on the Northern Cheyennes, and the committee's published report showed that he had been given respectful attention.[90] The Northern Cheyennes had not yet realized their hopes, but Little Chief's policy of firm but usually civil refusal to acquiesce was working its effect.[91]

Agent Miles would have said of most army officers in Indian Territory what General Pope had written of the unruly Northern Cheyennes—that it would be a relief to see them go elsewhere. At times of real crisis Miles cooperated with Mizner, Dodge, and other officers, but as a general rule he considered them adversaries. Determined to guard his official prerogatives and resentful of the army's interference with his work, he reacted to fresh irritations with hair-trigger hostility. His view of the army was distorted by the deep-seated suspicion of it within the Indian Bureau he served, and the converse was true of Dodge. Though mainly couched in polite official parlance, Dodge's endorsements, telegraphed messages, letters, and reports in regard to issues put forth by Miles formed one side of a verbal duel. That Dodge invariably got the better of Miles in these exchanges must have been galling to the agent, for his duties were challenging enough without the perception of powerlessness and lack of support that accompanied them.

Dodge's tour of duty at Cantonment deepened his conviction that the federal government's policy of dealing with the Indians through two different agencies was unwise. Incident after incident demonstrated to him that the Indian Bureau was not only inefficient but corrupt, swindling the Indians while enriching the licensed traders and contractors it employed and possibly also its agents. At the same time, contact with the Indians strengthened his personal regard for many of them and heightened his sympathy for them all. That Agent Miles openly opposed his efforts to improve their lot challenged his patience and also his pride as an army officer. It was intolerable that he should be called upon to help enforce a policy that obliged the Indians to "starve peaceably" or else resort to violence. Little wonder that while living with these stark perceptions as a daily reality, Dodge regarded his journeys to visit with Julia and Fred as delightful getaways. While in command at Cantonment North Fork Canadian River, he ably represented the army in its conflict with the Indian Bureau, but meanwhile the Indians suffered. Considering the situation, he might himself have uttered the lines he heard Fred declaim in the role of Hamlet: "The time is out of joint; O cursed spite / That ever I was born to set it right!"[92]

20

The Ute Expedition

During the 1870s the advent of prospectors, mining companies, railroads, and towns to the mountains of Colorado steadily increased the irritation felt by the loosely confederated bands of Ute Indians, to whom the mountain country was a birthright and an ancestral hunting range. Ouray, the respected chief of the Uncompahgre Utes, sought to moderate the resentment of his tribespeople and achieve through diplomacy some mutually satisfactory arrangement for coexistence between the tribe and the federal and state governments. However, not all bands were disposed to compromise. In September 1879 violence broke out at the White River Ute Agency in northern Colorado. The agent, Nathan Meeker, and other employees were murdered, buildings were pillaged and destroyed, and Meeker's wife and daughter were taken captive. Troops from the departments of the Platte and the Missouri were marching toward the scene at the time these events occurred, but one of the commands itself suffered heavy casualties at the hands of the Utes. On September 29 a force under Major Thomas T. Thornburgh, Fourth Infantry, was within a few miles of the agency when it was waylaid and attacked from impregnable positions by the Indians. Thornburgh was killed, and his men were besieged until October 5, when they were rescued by another body of troops under Colonel Wesley Merritt, Fifth Cavalry. Merritt pursued the retreating Indians south through the mountains, but his advance was halted on orders from Washington. To prevent further bloodshed, the Department of the Interior wished to open negotiations with the Ute bands at once.[1]

The Meeker massacre and the threatened annihilation of the force under Thornburgh excited intense alarm within the region and attracted nationwide attention. General Sheridan quickly concentrated a large contingent force at Fort Garland under Colonel Ranald S. Mackenzie, who had earlier been operating in Texas. Merritt's command remained stationed to the north as the White River Column, and by November 1879 two large bodies of troops occupied positions in the southern part of the state: the Fort Garland Column under Mackenzie, comprising six cavalry and seven infantry companies, and the Animas River Column, 120 miles west, under Colonel Edward Hatch, Ninth Cavalry, consisting of three cavalry and nine infantry companies.[2] Winter conditions where these commands were stationed made active operations all but impossible, but General Sherman intended to take no "halfway measures" against the Utes; he instructed Mackenzie to move toward Hatch at the first sign of an emergency.[3] If the Department of the Interior still wished the army to delay preparations for battle, so be it. But should the situation require it, he had determined to order General George Crook to command the three columns of troops, which would hem in the rebellious Utes in classic fashion, operating concentrically.[4] In this and other respects, the preparations being made suggested a reprise of the Sioux-Cheyenne conflict of four years before. Pressure from citizen leaders was already incessant to hurry troops into the fastnesses of the Colorado mountains. In January, Sherman informed General Pope that he would probably be called upon to supply 1,000 men to strengthen Mackenzie's command, even if he had to strip the Kansas border to do it.[5]

Meanwhile, attempts to achieve an accommodation between representatives of the Ute bands and the federal government moved ahead. On March 6 Ouray and other Ute leaders submitted to the Department of the Interior a proposal to sell to the United States the rights and title to the large Ute reservation in return for certain payments and a grant of other lands.[6] In order to be acted upon, this document would require ratification by Congress and by three-quarters of adult male Ute Indians. The work of securing the necessary approvals would take time, and the criminal acts at the White River agency remained to be dealt with. Still, a provisional basis for peaceful resolution of the crisis had been established.

To the army, however, peace remained only a possibility. On March 24 Sherman telegraphed to Sheridan that the continuing threat of violence between citizens and Utes necessitated the occupation, "with considerable force," of two as yet ungarrisoned locations in Colorado. These were the Los Pinos Ute agency on the Uncompahgre River and some other point north of it, near the junction of the Gunnison and Grand Rivers.[7] The general and lieutenant general spent the next weekend at Chicago discussing specific possibilities, and the result was a letter of April 3 to the secretary of war in which Sherman outlined his plans and specified his requirements for financial support of the operations in Colorado.

The three columns that had been deployed in November remained in their positions, but the southern column under Mackenzie was the strongest and most mobile since it could be supplied and reinforced by rail with relative ease. Sherman proposed to send Mackenzie to the Uncompahgre agency as soon as conditions in the mountains made wagon travel possible. From there, he would reconnoitre northward in search of the site for a new post, whose presence should go far toward ensuring peace in the region. Because troops could not live in that high country without adequate shelter, Sherman asked for an appropriation of $100,000 from Congress at the earliest date possible, so as to have buildings constructed and supplied for winter by September. Through that expenditure, he assured the secretary, "the whole of western Colorado, a country supposed to be rich in gold and silver, can be explored and utilized, paying back the cost of these forts a hundred fold."[8]

The United States was neither at peace nor at war with the Ute Indians, but in the foreseeable future a military presence in their homeland was imperative. As the senior officer of the Fort Garland Column, Mackenzie would act not under Crook but under Pope, in whose department the operations would take place. Pope had thus been involved for several months in the preparations for Mackenzie's march into remote country. As spring approached and the movement overland of supplies became more practicable, he took additional steps. Mackenzie had stressed the need for infantry in the mountain country, and so far as Pope could spare the men, he intended to oblige. During Dodge's visit to Fort Leavenworth in April, the general informed him of the possibility that he would be ordered to join the Fort Garland Column.[9] The addition of a brigade under Dodge would enable Mackenzie and his cavalry to patrol the Uncompahgre region, discouraging mischief from Indians and citizens alike. Dodge would supervise journeyman work at headquarters—transportation of supplies, erection of sheds and other buildings, and survey and construction of wagon roads. Of course, his service at Cantonment in the past year had prepared him well for tasks such as these. If the assignment lacked something in military glamor or brought to mind the secondary status accorded him in the Powder River Expedition, it would yet be an essential one.

Dodge cautioned himself against becoming too hopeful, but participation in the summer campaign interested him. He had never yet seen the country west and north of Fort Garland, which was said to be remarkable for its beauty, mineral wealth, and abundance of game. The San Luis Valley was the region William Blackmore had hoped to develop as grazing and agricultural country. Now being settled, it was becoming known as a garden spot.[10] Whether the expedition under Mackenzie would engage in combat with the unpredictable Utes who ranged that territory was of course uncertain. However, Dodge knew that if his former comrade under General Crook was called upon to subdue the Indians by force, he would be ready.

In late April, Dodge received confirmation that he would indeed take part in the summer campaign.[11] He was to march with two companies of his choice from Cantonment to the railhead at Wellington, Kansas, also bringing with him Company D, Twenty-third Infantry, then stationed along the state line near Caldwell. Following the 120-mile march to Wellington, a special train would carry his command, joined by other companies from posts along the way, six hundred miles west to Fort Garland. From that point, Mackenzie would move through rugged country toward the Los Pinos Agency for the Uncompahgre Utes near the southwestern corner of Colorado.

The Journey West

On May 7 Dodge and his men moved out onto the military road from Cantonment, accompanied by six six-mule wagons that carried their gear.[12] Anticipating that the summer's tour of duty would be filled with interest, he began writing entries in a fresh journal.[13] At Caldwell he camped adjacent to the site occupied by Company D, under Captain Thomas M. K. Smith. He liked Smith and thought him a potentially valuable officer, even though the illness and death of his wife at Cantonment a few months before had prostrated him and he had taken to drink. Dodge had tried to help him regain his equilibrium, but he was still not himself. On the march from Caldwell to Wellington, several of Smith's men were drunk, and once the train had left the station it was discovered that three of them had not boarded. "I am not sorry," Dodge wrote, "for they were miserable drunken wretches. S's Compy is in a horrible state of discipline – owing to his own bad habits. I had to set on him very heavily."[14]

Accompanying the command were a few citizens who had followed Dodge from post to post in recent years, securing what employment they could. Hugh Patton, who drove a six-mule wagon, had been the butcher at Fort Hays. Boon Tomlinson, another wagon driver, had been a teamster and scout at the same place. Henry C. Keeling, the post trader at Cantonment, had left the business there in other hands and planned to open up shop at Mackenzie's main camp. Joe and Laura, Dodge's domestic servants since the days at Omaha Barracks, were along and had with them their infant daughter, Ida. Dodge also brought with him his two hunting dogs, his hunting and fishing equipment, and other conveniences, all packed into small space. Captain Pollock, who commanded Company C, had once told him that he possessed the first requisite for a commanding officer—namely, that he knew how to take care of himself.[15] The same was true of the attention he gave his longtime civilian associates.

At Dodge City the train stopped for a few hours so that the mules aboard could be led from the cars, fed, and watered, and also to take on additional men and equipment. Here Dodge met some old acquaintances from his Fort Dodge days, including Bob Wright, once the post trader and now a leading citizen of the town, which had grown away from its lawless origins. The present post commander, Major Robert H. Offley, Nineteenth Infantry, boarded the train at this point. He was to be one of the three battalion commanders under Dodge, who would again "play Brigadier General" as in the Powder River Expedition. On May 15 the Atchison, Topeka and Santa Fe train reached Pueblo, Colorado, where everything on board was transferred onto the narrow-gauge cars of the Denver and Rio Grande Railway for the journey into the mountains. It was a tedious process, the government agent at Pueblo being, as Dodge remarked, "very obliging, but not extremely efficient."[16]

As a stockholder in the Denver and Rio Grande, Dodge took a proprietary interest in the performance of its trains. This was his first experience of narrow-gauge travel, and his reaction to it was mixed. On one hand, the nightlong clanking of the wheels robbed him of sleep. On the other, he was awestruck as the train clambered up Veta

Mountain the next morning. Impressed alike by the scenery and the feat of engineering that made possible the dizzying ascent from the village of La Veta, he declared the roadbed "the most remarkable work I ever saw."[17]

To this point, Dodge's impressions of mountain travel by rail were almost touristic in character. However, just past the summit the journey took on a more serious cast when the westbound train met another one traveling east and carrying General Pope and Colonel Mackenzie in conference together. The trains stopped, permitting a brief meeting between the three senior officers, after which Pope continued on to Fort Leavenworth and Mackenzie joined Dodge for the journey to Fort Garland. Impatient to put his long-delayed plans into operation, Mackenzie informed Dodge that the Fort Garland Column would march from the post the next day and that he was imposing strict limits on the facilities for transportation. Laura would not be permitted to accompany the troops, he said. "I know him well however," Dodge wrote to himself, "& am not scared." After the two had lunch together at the fort, Mackenzie relented, permitting Joe, Laura, and Ida to accompany the command and allotting Dodge an additional ambulance.[18]

Still, as commander of the column, Mackenzie was keeping tight control over its personnel and operations. His General Field Order 1, dated May 16, named Dodge as commander of the eleven-company infantry brigade[19] but denied him full authority over its battalions. Each of these would have its own headquarters staff and issue its own orders, receiving only nominal supervision from Dodge, so that the effective line of command passed directly from Mackenzie to the battalion leaders. Mackenzie had not taken exception to Pope's appointment of Dodge as commander of the infantry, but the limited authority he was entrusting to him, a well-tested officer who possessed twice his years of army experience, was hardly a vote of confidence.

On schedule, early in the afternoon of May 17 the Fort Garland Column moved north toward the Rio Grande, reaching in several days' march the little town of Saguache, at the upper end of a well-watered valley. The initial days of the journey, through sagebrush and sand, were uneventful. Dodge noted that May 19 was his fifty-third birthday and "by no means a hilarious one, but not unpleasant." However, on the following day a confrontation occurred that might have ended the good relations that had prevailed between him and his column commander thus far. That afternoon, Dodge was searching for a suitable campsite when Mackenzie overtook him, evidently in a foul mood, and berated him for permitting too many of his men to ride on the wagons. The privilege was customarily extended to a few designated soldiers, and others were not permitted to ride except in cases of special need. By his own account, Dodge made no attempt to defend himself from Mackenzie's tongue-lashing. "I told him," he wrote, "that I was perfectly loyal to my Comdg Offr, that I would do everything exactly as he wished, as long as I could conscienciously do so, & when he wanted me to do that which I believed to be wrong, I would apply to be relieved. That he is the responsible man, & I will do all I can to help him."[20] Mollified, and perhaps also flattered by this declaration of principled good will, Mackenzie went off in better humor. Later that day, Dodge issued an order prohibiting men other than the sergeant major, the headquarters clerk, and the company cooks from riding on the wagons unless by authority from him, one of the battalion commanders, or one of the two surgeons. To keep Mackenzie satisfied, he directed the officer of the day to "hold 'the boys' up a little stronger."[21]

Fenced ranches lined the road in the vicinity of La Garita Creek, approximately forty-five miles from Saguache. Depredations by Indians were not feared in this settled region; in fact, some residents viewed the passing soldiers as posing a greater threat. Later in the summer an aggrieved rancher submitted a claim against the government for certain fenceposts that, he alleged, Dodge's men had dug up for firewood.[22] Continuing along a wagon trail, Dodge camped outside Saguache on the night of May 23, and in two more days he arrived at Cochetopa Pass, 10,000 feet in elevation and an entryway into the interior of mountainous Colorado. Mackenzie had reached that point before him and intended to move forward on the following day, but he authorized Dodge to delay one day before following. Unshod mules needed attention if the wagon train was to proceed as it should, and after nine days on the march through high country, the infantry soldiers could use a rest.

After a conversation with Mackenzie, Dodge walked over to the cantonment that had been built at Cochetopa Pass under the direction of Captain Thomas E. Rose, his hunting companion in the fall of 1878. "He has done a good deal of work," Dodge allowed, "but not in as ship shape a manner as I would like." For the remainder of that day a succession of orders from Mackenzie kept him busy, but he did as he was told and was content. He took "a glorious hot bath" that night, and for the first time had a stove in his tent. "Tomorrow is our first days rest," he wrote in his journal, "& with it will close what I consider the first chapter of this expedition."[23]

The Summer Campaign

Dodge's journal record of the summer in Colorado ends with the entry for May 26, six days before he and his command reached the site on the Uncompahgre River near Los Pinos Agency that became the base of operations for the Fort Garland Column. Marching in advance of the infantry and supply train, Mackenzie had selected the position, and through his adjutant he urged Dodge to complete the journey as rapidly as possible without injury to the troops.[24] Despite the considerable distance between Mackenzie's battalion and the three under Dodge, he sent to the rear a series of directives that revealed his concern about details then under the immediate oversight of his subordinate officer. At Cochetopa Pass, Dodge was enjoined again not to permit his men to ride on the wagons. The next day he was instructed to ensure that his units stayed close together on the march so as not to be separated in the unlikely event of an attack.[25] Moving his troops and escorting a one hundred–man pack train with wagons that carried two Hotchkiss machine guns and tons of supplies over a primitive road was a demanding task in itself, not made easier

Ranald S. Mackenzie. Courtesy Western History Collections, University of Oklahoma Libraries.

by his commander's management at a distance. Mackenzie seemed to regard the entire operation as his own property.

Of course, as commander of the column, he did bear responsibility for its proper conduct. He took the mission seriously and, as Dodge had divined, personally. Dodge's assurance on May 20 that "he is the responsible man, & I will do all I can to help him" was just the message needed to ease him away from his nervous fault-finding and into better humor. Since his arrival at Fort Garland in October 1879, Mackenzie had found many other causes for complaint. He chafed at the delay in his being authorized to take the field, and wintering at an obscure, remote post like Fort Garland seemed to him a slight toward an officer of his rank.[26] He needed a pack train to be kept ready for service during the winter months, but Pope did not supply it; instead, he sent two companies of infantry that had not been asked for. Mackenzie objected, and at last he ruffled his departmental commander by appealing to General Sheridan for preemptive assistance.[27] Focusing on the task before him, he often discounted the needs of officers elsewhere. For example, he wished to make use of General Crook's chief civilian packer, Tom Moore, and his corps of men and animals. But Crook was a department commander fully occupied with the military demands of his own region. He responded tersely to an inquiry from Sheridan, observing that he had been training these men for twelve years and could not spare them now.[28] Mackenzie called for one hundred Indian scouts, preferably to be organized under Captain George Randall, but this was also not practicable. Randall had his hands full with the Indians at the Cheyenne and Arapaho Agency.[29]

Restive, and disposed to find fault with those who questioned his views or failed to comply with his demands, during the early months of 1880 Mackenzie gave offense to several of his superiors. In February the adjutant general commented archly on a complaint of his about recruits to be sent to Colorado, that "this is not the first time in which that officer has presumed to arraign the action of this office upon his assumption of facts that do not exist."[30] Mackenzie nettled even the General of the Army. In March, Sherman instructed his adjutant to inform the colonel that he himself gave attention to the assignment of all available recruits "and considers himself a better judge of the wants and necessities of each Regiment, and of each locality, than Col. Mackenzie can possibly be."[31] In short, Mackenzie could be a severe test of patience. His prospects for a generalship would have been dimmed by his pertinacious presumption, except that his views on most military questions were sound and his performance in the field consistently superior.

For reasons that remain in doubt, for a time Mackenzie was intensely critical of Dodge—"down on" him, in the words of the latter. To complicate the situation, he extended his disapproval to all persons whom he suspected of liking Dodge, including the teamsters who traveled with him. Dodge mentioned specifically Hugh Patton, toward whom, in Dodge's opinion, he "acted like a pig."[32] When Patton refused to take further abuse and quit, Mackenzie attempted to deny him his pay, refused to authorize his employment by the post trader, and even prohibited him from entering camp with a load of vegetables Dodge had given him permission to obtain. Exactly how Dodge managed to improve his own standing in Mackenzie's eyes and re-establish good relations with him remains a mystery. At any rate, after a consultation between the two officers, on June 23 Mackenzie revised his command structure in Dodge's favor, assigning him direct command over the three infantry battalions.[33] That delegation of authority left Mackenzie more free to range away from camp, as he had orders to do. Even so, he found himself hard pressed for ways to pass the time. Late in June he wrote to Pope that the campaign thus far had consisted only of "quiet uneventful weeks"—almost as quiet as the ones he had been forced to endure while waiting idle at Fort Garland.[34]

Although Mackenzie expected much from his troops and was not tolerant of failure to meet his standards, many officers and men were proud to accept the rigors of membership in what one soldier called the "McKinzie regiment."[35] On the other hand, the temptation to break away from the discipline he imposed could be strong, especially among soldiers who could desert with little risk of capture and find employment at a good wage in mining camps and towns not many miles distant. Indeed, the high desertion rate of the Fort Garland Column soon became a cause for alarm. Early in July, Dodge requested of the adjutant general that one hundred recruits be sent at an early date.[36]

Dodge knew from the Powder River Expedition that service under Mackenzie entailed the possibility of punishment for behavior that other commanders might consider cause for no more than a caution or rebuke. On June 23, Mackenzie gave an order by which battalion commanders were relieved of their command authority except in routine matters of drill and discipline. Reactions to this order produced demonstrations both of his capacity for diplomacy and also of his unwillingness to tolerate anything that approached insubordination. An instance of the former occurred on that same day. Dodge's adjutant returned unapproved to First Lieutenant George K. Spencer, Nineteenth Infantry, a request that a certain private be relieved from duty in the quartermaster's department. Spencer's battalion commander, Major Offley, had approved the request, but Dodge directed that "a more specific reason" for the desired transfer be stated. In his response, Spencer simply reiterated the request, noting that it had received his battalion commander's approval. In effect, he was defying Dodge by denying his authority over Offley. On learning of this, Mackenzie replied to Spencer with wry reserve: "Taking the fact of the return of this paper to Lt. Spencer by his superior, Lt. Col. Dodge, the Commanding Officer is somewhat surprised that Lt. Spencer should have deemed it judicious on no better ground to renew his request. The Commanding Officer of the Column regrets to feel obliged to express the opinion that such course was not very well advised."[37] Only weeks before, Spencer had been court-martialed at Fort Garland and judged guilty of conduct to the prejudice of good order and military discipline.[38] When provoked, however, Mackenzie enforced his rule with an iron hand. Presently Major Offley ran afoul of the column commander and found himself in arrest, threatened with a trial by court-martial.[39] Thereafter the records of the Fort Garland Column reveal no further questioning of the commanding officer's arrangements.

Dodge's duties during the summer were chiefly of the routine variety he had anticipated. Much of the construction he oversaw was road building, essential to permit communication between the three posts General Pope thought necessary to minimize the threat of violence in coming years.[40] Additionally, he took command of the column during Mackenzie's absences on patrol or on missions in search of a post site. After a thorough reconnaissance, Mackenzie decided that the best possible location for the cantonment and future post was the one now occupied by the supply camp. Thus, on July 21 the site was designated Cantonment Uncompahgre, and construction was begun shortly thereafter, under First Lieutenant Calvin D. Cowles.[41] Two additional camps were established during the summer, one for the cavalry on the Uncompahgre River seventeen miles north of Dodge's, the other for infantry and cavalry at Roubideaux's Crossing on the Gunnison River.

On June 15 Congress ratified a modification of the proposed agreement between representatives of the confederated Ute bands and the Department of the Interior,

Region of Dodge's service in Colorado, 1880

and a few days later five commissioners who had been appointed by President Hayes received their instructions from Secretary Schurz.[42] Their primary duty was to obtain in Colorado the signatures of three-fourths of all adult Ute men, signifying acceptance of the treaty's terms. This was a daunting task, both because the treaty provided for displacement of one band from its ancestral home and relocation of another on farming lands yet to be specified, and also because of the physical difficulties involved. In order to seek out the widely separated members of the tribe, the commissioners would have to pass over many miles of mountain terrain. A military escort would be imperative, and accordingly arrangements were made for troops and supplies from the Fort Garland Column to assist the Ute Commission. On June 29 Agent William H. Berry of the Los Pinos Agency received notice that the commissioners hoped to meet with the Uncompahgre Utes there on their first official stop. This was prudent, since the home of Ouray, the chief of the Uncompahgres, was only a mile from the agency and within three miles of the army's supply camp. It was thought that Ouray, who more than any other Ute wielded authority over his own and other bands, would be able to sway dubious tribesmen toward ratification and so help smooth the process from the beginning. On July 8 the commissioners reached the agency, and on July 21 they held their first council, which was attended by a large number of Uncompahgre and some White River Utes. The proceedings were orderly, but it was clear that some Indians were not ready to sign the instrument and others remained firmly opposed. Nevertheless, thanks largely to the influence of Ouray, by July 31 a total of 145 persons had given written consent to the treaty, an encouraging first step.

Mackenzie was impressed by the Uncompahgre Utes, for their civility and also their prosperity. Whatever his private views of "chronic commissioners" like George W. Manypenny and Alfred B. Meacham, who were on record as staunchly opposed to army involvement in Indian affairs, he did his part to facilitate the meetings between Indians and commissioners.[43] However, he played no part in the formal councils. Given to understand that the presence of his cavalry troops might frighten the Indians and disrupt the proceedings, on July 24 he rode north on a long patrol, crossing the Gunnison River and passing over Grand Mesa to Buzzard's Creek, within fifty miles of the White River Column of army troops. After making contact with the garrison there, he and his men returned across the range and scouted eastward for several days across the plateau above the Gunnison River. They arrived back at Cantonment Uncompahgre on August 8, having promoted the present effort to make peace with the Utes by their timely absence.[44]

The Ute Commissioners wished next to travel cross-country to the Southern Ute Agency on the Animas River. The agency was approximately sixty miles due south from Los Pinos but was accessible to them only by wagon roads over circuitous, sometimes precipitous former Indian trails that made the actual distance much greater. Dodge directed his quartermaster to issue the necessary provisions and supplies and named Captain Pollock's company as escort. In view of the still unstable relations between the federal government and the Indians, one hundred rounds of ammunition were issued each soldier in addition to those he carried on his person. For transportation, the infantrymen were assigned two wagons, each pulled by a six-mule team. The commissioners were more liberally provided, with a four-horse ambulance, a large Dougherty wagon, two six-mule teams, and two hospital tents for use as temporary residences.[45] The caravan left Los Pinos Agency on Tuesday, August 3.

On their journey the commissioners and their escort encountered no hostile Indians, but their passage through the mountains was a dangerous enterprise nonetheless. Twelve days of intense effort were required to cross 130 miles of terrain. Unable to pass over the San Juan Mountains using wagons, the party instead moved east to the Lake Fork of the Gunnison River, then south up that stream to its head and over Engineer Mountain, and finally southwest to its destination. Ten mules were required to pull each wagon to the highest point along the trail, which was well above timberline, and one morning the soldiers awoke to find seven inches of snow covering their blankets.[46] Three days after the commissioners reached the Southern Ute Agency, Ouray and a few of his subchiefs also arrived, intending to participate in the next round of meetings.

The effort to persuade the Indians to ratify an agreement that would deprive most of them of their reservation lands had now reached a delicate stage. At a preliminary meeting between the commissioners and 123 members of the Weenimuche, Muache, and Capote bands, a Weenimuche chief named Alahandra delivered a powerful speech against ratification. His opinions were neither affirmed nor opposed by the others, but it was decided to adjourn the meeting and reconvene three days later, after the several parties had taken time to confer. The next meeting, on August 23, was not promising. After a long discussion, the Weenimuche Utes declared that they were not disposed to accept the proposed terms, and representatives of the other bands kept silence. The success of the commission hung in the balance. Ouray had become gravely ill and was unable to sway the result. On the morning of August 24, the day agreed upon for resumption of talks, Ouray died, and the effect was electric. The Indian tipis ranged along the river were struck at once, and as the commissioners later reported, their occupants dispersed "as from a pestilence."[47]

Two days later only eight headmen met with the Ute Commissioners in the grove near their camp. In response to an invitation to sign the agreement, they were unwilling. Ignatio, head of the Weenimuche band, submitted that the tribe had already done all that could be asked of it. They had given up the mountains in which the valuable minerals were located, but they wished to retain what was left of their country. The meeting was then adjourned. On the following morning, August 27, the commissioners notified Pollock that they desired to move beyond the lines of the Ute reservation for a few days to await events, for evidently their efforts had reached an impasse. However, about noon that day about seventy-five Utes rode into camp in a body and requested a council session at once. Ignatio, cautioning that he hoped the commissioners would be careful to ensure that the government kept its word, announced that he and his companions had come to sign the agreement. They then stepped forward and made their marks on the documents, and by the next morning fifty-nine more men had done the same.

A breakthrough had occurred, and implementation of the pact was now likely. A census of the adult male population of the Utes remained to be completed, but by September 25 the commissioners were satisfied that the 581 names affixed to the document exceeded the necessary number. In a rare instance of cooperation between representatives of the Department of the Interior and the army, the Ute Commission had accomplished its difficult task. In their report to Secretary Schurz, the members gratefully acknowledged the "important and courteous aid given us by gentlemen of the Army."[48]

At the supply camp miles away from this quiet drama, Dodge had enjoyed time to spare from his official duties, diverting himself in hunting, fishing, and in other ways. He forwarded to Spencer Baird of the Smithsonian Institution a collection of unusual mountain herbs and flowers.[49] He often chatted with Agent Berry or with Ouray, at whose home he was a welcome guest. From Chipeta, Ouray's wife, he obtained a water jar made of grass, and from other Indians he purchased or was given additional specimens of Ute handcraft.[50] Exploring the vicinity of his camp, he came upon a Ute campsite where a death had recently occurred and examined closely the evidence it contained of the Indians' beliefs and funerary customs.[51] His residence near the Utes was a feast of opportunity to broaden his knowledge of Indian culture. Conversations with fellow officers yielded further insight, and he received from Pollock a written account of Ouray's death, funeral, and—so far as the Utes' strict secrecy would permit—his burial. Dodge himself observed the remarkable manner in which information about the Uncompahgre chief's deteriorating condition somehow made its way almost instantaneously to the Los Pinos Agency. He was on hand to witness the dramatic response at the agency to news of the chief's death.[52]

Jottings at the end of Dodge's journal on the march to Cochetopa Pass reveal that he was then considering a new literary undertaking, a book devoted to Indians of the western plains and mountains. During the summer, this project became an outlet for his spare energy. Further writing about events in the army's experiences in the West remained a possibility, but not one he would undertake at present. The Indians and their uneasy relationship with the U.S. government were topics he had come to know well and at first hand in the past two years. The federal laws governing Indian reservations were germane to the treatment he now had in mind, and accordingly for reference he requested from the Adjutant General's Office a copy of the *Revised Statutes*.[53] He planned to expand his earlier published account of Plains Indian culture, adding chapters on several topics not dealt with before. Coincidentally, at the time of Ouray's death he was drafting a discussion of burial customs.[54]

By early August, the site of Cantonment Uncompahgre had been selected and the Ute commissioners sent on their way under the care of Pollock and his men. On August 6 Dodge therefore addressed to his departmental headquarters a request to be relieved immediately from duty with the Fort Garland Column. He did not specify a reason for the request, but he made clear that it was "entirely personal to myself, and in no way connected with my duty in the field," adding that it was known to both Mackenzie and General Pope.[55] The unstated purpose was truly a personal one: he wished to return to Cantonment and finish his book there. He may have taken up the subject with Pope again when the general passed through the vicinity in mid-month,[56] but the arrival in camp of General Sheridan on August 23 accelerated the process of approval. Sheridan was on a tour of inspection, and though a stickler for tidiness and arrangements made according to rule, he was well satisfied with what he saw in "Col. Dodge's camp."[57] On that same day, Pope's adjutant directed the commanding officer at Fort Garland to notify Dodge that he was relieved from duty with the Fort Garland Column and ordered to take post at Cantonment.[58] Three days later, Sheridan and his party left the supply camp and proceeded downriver to that of the cavalry, where he reviewed the troops. Mackenzie once again had the satisfaction of witnessing his division commander's hearty approval.

Sheridan's visit effectively ended contributions by Mackenzie to the work of the Fort Garland Column. Construction of the cantonment was under way, and the five companies of Dodge's regiment that would garrison it through the winter should keep the region secure. Together with two companies of his own regiment as escort, Mackenzie accompanied Sheridan and other dignitaries on a hunting expedition that eventually took them to Gunnison City, where the general boarded a train for the east. After returning to Fort Garland and appearing later in September at a court of inquiry in Washington, D.C., Mackenzie spent the last months of the year in New York City, where he took steps to enlist support for his promotion to brigadier general, an event that took place on November 1, 1882.[59]

During the summer of 1880, Mackenzie had thus played a useful role in the government's effort to bring peace to the Colorado frontier. By maintaining a more than credible military presence and then absenting himself while the commissioners worked to secure an agreement with the Indians, he did all that could reasonably be expected of him. His success was of another sort than the exploits in battle that had won him fame in the Red River War and later on the Powder River Expedition, but it was success nonetheless, demonstrating versatility and prudent tact. His erratic behavior and sometimes harsh treatment of subordinates had won him few friends, but at least he had not further alienated his superiors. Though long delayed and devoid of action against an enemy, the Ute Campaign had been for Mackenzie and the army a costly but decided success.

For Mackenzie's second-in-command, the summer campaign had also been productive. As commander of the infantry battalion, Dodge had encountered no real difficulty, and under his superintendency wagon roads, post construction, and progress on a telegraph line were all well advanced. Five years earlier, while in command of the Black Hills Expedition, he had described his physically challenging and diplomatically delicate assignment without irony as a "delightful summer."[60] Probably he would have said much the same of the summer months now coming to a close. If his proximity to Mackenzie had necessitated circumspection and even on occasion swallowed retorts, the campaign in Colorado had offered many compensations, not the least of which was his progress on the new book. On September 1, accompanied by Joe, Laura, and Ida, he set out with his escort on the return to Cantonment.

Amusements in Transit

Dodge's second journal record of this summer, recording his return from Colorado to Indian Territory, reveals on every page his satisfaction at having completed the recent tour of duty. He began it with a witticism, that the two ambulances, five escort wagons, and three six-mule teams that accompanied his escort made him "feel bigger than" a Lieutenant General.[61] In fact, he was bound for Fort Garland with the identical transportation the diminutive Lieutenant General Sheridan had used on his journey to Cantonment Uncompahgre. He chose a return route that would ensure his not meeting Mackenzie on that officer's return from his hunting excursion with Sheridan. Stopping at Cimarron Crossing, he visited with a local resident, M. W. Cline, and heard testimonials from the rancher and his wife about the salubrious properties of Colorado's mountain air. Mrs. Cline, "a real nice oldfashioned work-woman of a wife," insisted on giving him a half dozen eggs as a parting gift. The weather that day was so "cool, crisp & bracing" that he gave his horse a gallop of a few miles in order to settle him down a little.[62] This was a wise precaution, since at many places along the road the animal's tendency to shy could result in a fall of from fifty to five hundred feet down a precipitous ledge. Upon reaching the Lake Fork of the Gunnison River, Dodge made camp and fished in what he pronounced "the finest trout stream I have ever seen."[63] In contrast to the intense westward march of three months before, the journey home had about it a holiday atmosphere.

At Lake City, Dodge was delighted to find Hugh Patton, who after being fired out of the Fort Garland Column had promptly found employment as a butcher. Hugh insisted on his visiting the billiard room at the American Hotel for a test of skill against the town's premier players, and the result was a few hours of suspenseful entertainment that tickled Dodge's vanity. For the benefit of family readers he recounted his triumph:

> Well, I went to the billiard room tackled the marker, who I was led to believe the best player. In spite of my lack of practice, composition balls, small table & bad light from lamps, I "walloped" him four straight games[.] He gave it up & handed the cue to another man, who I afterwards discovered could beat the marker & give him a third. As my games with the marker had been close, he thought he had an easy thing. We played one, very tight, but I beat him[.] He proposed another, & the drinks on it. Tight again but I beat him. Then he proposed a third, which I told him would be my last as I had to start early. I made two bad miscues in the start of the game, so we stood his 20 to my nothing. I felt sure he would beat me but I buckled myself to it, made two

> good runs, leaving me only one point to go. He had but 3 to go, & playing safe left me what he thought an almost impossible shot. I made it by cushion, & 'busted' my evening to the delight of Hugh, & many spectators.[64]

For some of the audience the sight of a senior army officer amusing himself among the rough and ready miners was probably an entertainment in itself.

Because Ida had become severely ill, the escort remained in camp near Lake City for one more night. "I am disgusted," Dodge wrote, "but must care for the dear baby. She is a great comfort to her 'Grandpap' & I would feel her loss, as severely as if she were my own child." Drawing upon a medicine kit he carried with him, he administered aconite to help break her fever and laudanum in solution to calm her system generally. That night she rested well, and on breaking camp the next morning he followed the advice of a physician to continue the aconite and dose her in addition with colocynth, a powerful cathartic.[65] Although she eventually recovered, Ida continued weak during the next few days, giving concern to the adults close to her.

After ascending a lengthy grade along a corduroy road over Slumgullion Mountain,[66] the party descended into the valley of the Rio Grande and moved east along a road that connected Fort Garland with far western Colorado. Dodge fished faithfully but with varying degrees of success; on one of the better days he helped Laura land her first trout, the largest of that afternoon's catch. At Hot Springs Creek his party met two officers who were returning from a tourist resort nestled in the mountains at the headwaters. They professed themselves "enchanted" with the place,[67] and Dodge was tempted to stop there. However, he decided against it since he thought Ida should be examined by another physician as soon as possible. His ambulance hurried ahead toward Fort Garland, leaving the rest of the party to come in behind him at the regular pace.

Second Lieutenant Lea Febiger, Twenty-third Infantry, commanded Dodge's escort and had orders to perform two additional duties upon his arrival at Fort Garland. He would first accompany four military convicts on the railroad journey to Fort Leavenworth, where they were to serve their sentences, and from there he would proceed to Cantonment. Since the three companies that had accompanied Dodge on his journey to Colorado were to remain at Cantonment Uncompahgre for the winter, Febiger was to supervise the transportation of their baggage and equipment from Cantonment North Fork Canadian River to the Colorado mountains.[68] The train from Fort Garland reached Pueblo at midnight September 12 and at noon the next day was at Dodge City, where Dodge parted with Febiger. Beginning the wagon journey to Fort Supply, that night he and his party reached Bluff Creek Station and went to bed early, all in the same room.

At Fort Supply, where he arrived on September 15, Dodge enjoyed a final few days of social diversion. Colonel Granville Haller, the post and regimental commander, was a gracious host and an agreeable companion.[69] In contrast to Fort Garland, which Dodge thought "a wonderfully stupid place" for lack of womenfolk, Fort Supply was well furnished in that regard. At a reception in his honor the evening of September 16, he counted seven men and seventeen women, a proportion that stirred him to feats of gallantry. "Danced flirted, talked sense & nonsense drank ale whisky et al until 12 pm," he wrote with satisfaction. That day and the next he was the guest at three meals, each served up by some obliging officer. He was, he wrote, "Stuffed like a Bologna. Have eaten more yesterday & today, than I have in any one week this summer." He was impatient at the delay caused by lack of an ambulance ready for his use, but he enjoyed himself nonetheless. He spent the evening of September 17 at Colonel Haller's residence, "listening to music, & gassing." Thinking over the work to be done on his book project, he approached Sebastian Berninger, principal musician of the regimental band, about the possibility of transcribing certain Indian songs into standard musical notation. Berninger assured him that neither he nor any other band member could do what he had in mind. However, he was not discouraged, being determined not to lose "a splendid chapter."[70]

On September 21 Dodge took a parting drink with Haller and sailed away in an ambulance that had just arrived, carrying the paymaster. Hunting and fishing along the North Fork were indifferent, but he was philosophical. On the evening of September 22 he, Joe, and Laura sat at a huge campfire, chatting pleasantly together until 11:00 P.M. on what would probably be the last night of the campaign. "The beauty of negro servants is that they do not presume on such familiarity," he observed.[71] Theirs was a delicate, perhaps unusual relationship: familiar, yet bounded by tacit interracial decorum; quasifamilial, yet involving payment for services rendered; marked by mutual regard and consideration, and apparently satisfactory to all.

The arrival of the party at Cantonment at midday on September 23 prompted general celebration. Sergeant Patrick Leonard, one of two noncommissioned officers who had been left behind at the post because of their ability to keep the severely reduced garrison in proper order, actually got tipsy in honor of the occasion.[72] A long-tried veteran and ordinarily a sober soul, Leonard was near the date of his discharge and no doubt regarded his commander's return as a harbinger of better times to come. "So Ended the Grand Campaign," Dodge wrote good-humoredly in the final entry of his summer's journal. He had reason for satisfaction, for in performing the duties assigned him by Mackenzie he had satisfied a demanding taskmaster whose emotional stability was fragile. Once again, he had acquitted himself ably as a top-level duty officer.

The quiet conditions at Cantonment in September 1880 were unique in the almost four years of Dodge's most recent tour of service in the Department of the Missouri. Thanks to the provision made on his behalf by General Pope, for the first time since 1876 he had before him an extended period of time to pursue a project of authorship. His observations of life in Indian Territory and in Colorado had afforded him new insight into Indian character and fired him with new passion as he witnessed the plight of the reservation tribes. He had a great deal to communicate, and the time was propitious for him to set about shaping it all into a book.

21

A Return to Authorship

In the fall of 1880, Cantonment conformed to De Benneville Randolph Keim's suggestive analogy between a frontier military post and an isolated ship at sea.[1] The post was in a sense autonomous, a rigorously organized little world by itself. Military forms and usages were observed, the days being subdivided by trumpet calls, drills, guard mountings, inspections, and other benchmarks of army routine. But this ship was becalmed, without a destination or mission except to continue in existence. The garrison was minimally staffed, mustering in November only forty-four men, and of these only sixteen available for general duty.[2] Events that required a military presence occurred fewer than one hundred miles north, east, and west of Cantonment and, in the case of the Cheyenne and Arapaho Agency, twice approached violence. Yet the post itself remained a place of relative calm, as if somehow hidden. Its location away from the swirl of affairs was exactly what Dodge required, for like many another intending author, he needed comfortable circumstances for an extended bout of deskwork. Fortunately for him, Amos Chapman remained at hand as post interpreter. Should Cheyennes like Stone Calf drop in for a chat, as was their habit, Chapman was there to translate, thus supplying possible new material for the book. Private Alexander Van Buren, formerly sergeant major of the regiment and a very able man, was present to serve as copyist.[3] After October 1 few special orders were issued from post headquarters to break the daily routine.

Following his return to the post in September, Dodge worked almost without interruption on his book project, grinding away at what he called "the description Mill."[4] Having ready access to his personal library, his notes and drafts, and a succession of Indian visitors to whom he could put queries, he pushed ahead. By December 12 he had completed a manuscript, and Private Van Buren had prepared a fair copy for submission to a publisher. In the preface he described his work as "a detailed account of the characteristics, habits, and—what I particularly desire to invite attention to,—a minute and careful study of the social or inner life of the wild Indian of the present day."[5]

The manuscript was almost 150,000 words in length, with fifty-one chapters and a "L'Envoi." At some points in it Dodge referred to the earlier writers whose works he had perused, as also to more popular figures like James Fenimore Cooper and George Belden,[6] but his comments on them were of a general nature and unsupported by documentation. He also acknowledged the assistance of other persons, chiefly on the basis of their unpublished observations. Among these were Major Robert S. Neighbors, a former agent to the Comanche Indians; William H. Berry, agent to the Uncompahgre Utes; Ben Clarke, the interpreter at Fort Reno; George Aschmann, leader of the regimental band; captains Pollock and Randall of his own regiment; and probably the most helpful of all, Amos Chapman, his employee and frequent companion.[7] When a conflict of opinion arose between himself and some printed authority, thanks to Chapman he could sometimes take the matter in dispute to the Indians themselves. "My position as commanding officer—'Big Chief'—enabled me always to get a hearing and an answer on any subject," he wrote; "and my well-known friendship for the race caused the Indians to give me more frank confidence than a white man usually obtains."[8] As his Indian collaborators, he named several men attached to the Cheyenne and Arapaho Agency, but those who gave him the most valued assistance were Buffalo (or Running Buffaloes), one of the post's scouts, and Stone Calf, the wise old Southern Cheyenne.[9] Other material incorporated in the manuscript included facts gleaned from private correspondence with army officers such as Major Mauck and Captain Pollock and from unpublished official reports.[10]

The preponderance of material in the work derived, however, from Dodge's own experiences. Examples abound, but a few will suffice to show that although he drew upon observations that went back over many years, recent experience yielded some of his most vivid descriptions. He sketched the scenes, recorded in his journals, of a young Indian man interrupted by soldiers while in his devotions atop a mountain, and of Indian women begging for food, picking through offal, or cutting meat from a horse that had drowned in quicksand.[11] Despite its many references to published and unpublished sources, Dodge's book manuscript was not primarily the fruit of scholarly research but a personal statement by a uniquely well-qualified amateur, based largely on firsthand observation.

He expressed his intention to portray the Indian "exactly as he is," judging him necessarily "from the civilized stand-point" but otherwise without bias. As steadily as his perceptions would permit, he wished to occupy a middle ground between two influential views of the Indian, both erroneous: on one side, "enthusiastic admiration for the 'noble Red Man,'" held by uninformed idealists; on the other, "prejudice against the ignoble savage," held by tacit exterminationists.[12] Writing here as a friend, he portrayed the Indian as a real creature, an "at least partially civilized" fellow human being.[13] Earlier writers, he submitted, had failed to represent the Indian accurately and fully. George Catlin, primarily a painter, produced vivid prose sketches of Indian life and costume but caught the surfaces only, failing to comprehend even a basic but essential Indian term like "medicine." The "ideal Indians" of Cooper were a conscious fiction, as were his fiendish Mingoes.[14] Those who credited the portrayals of Cooper and Catlin as representing real persons would turn with "loathing and disgust," he wrote, from a glimpse at Indian life in the present: "The peerless warrior with 'eye like the eagle,' whose name a few short years ago was a terror, and whose swoop destruction, may be found patiently plodding between the handles of a plough. The tender maiden,—wont in fiction to sacrifice herself to save her lover, or, reduced to despair, to fling herself from 'tallest cliff into the raging flood beneath,'—may now be seen following the plough of the father, nimbly plying the sportive hoe, intent only on getting through with a square day's work, and thinking fondly of the square meal that is to follow it."[15] Dodge proposed to strip away the veil of romance that obscured some readers' perception of the Indians, exposing to view their everyday existence.

As thus expressed, Dodge's aims in the book differed little from those of the chapters on Indians in *The Plains*. In fact, that work was the most fruitful published source for the new manuscript. Nineteen chapters were essentially identical to passages in the earlier publication, sometimes rephrased or reorganized but otherwise unchanged.[16] Lest he be accused of plagiarizing from himself or presenting as original a new book that contained sections already in print, in the preface he made clear his concerns on just those issues. Friends had overruled his scruples, he wrote, and he therefore contented himself with a general acknowledgment of self-indebtedness.[17] Eleven other chapters of the new manuscript also derived from *The Plains* but contained a large majority of fresh material. Several of these were 3,000-word treatments of topics that the earlier work had dealt with in a paragraph or two.[18] The remaining twenty-one chapters and the "L'Envoi" were without precedent in *The Plains*.[19]

The general manner in which Dodge went about incorporating passages from *The Plains* is evident from comparison of the two works. Of the first sixteen chapters in the new manuscript, roughly one-third the total length, nine included lengthy segments from *The Plains*.[20] However, of the thirty-five chapters that remained, all but ten were almost or entirely original.[21] That is, after writing two initial chapters expressly for the new work, through chapter 16 Dodge drew extensively upon the earlier one. After that point *The Plains* served him only to supplement discussions that he was drafting for the first time.

Early in the book manuscript he pointed out that the great diversity of customs and character among American Indian peoples made easy generalizations about "the Indians" always doubtful.[22] In his chapters he referred to a great many tribes—Algonquins, Apaches, Arapahos, Bannocks, Cherokees, Chickasaws, Chippewas, Choctaws, Comanches, Dakota Sioux, Delawares, Diggers, Gros Ventres, Hidatsas, Kickapoos, Kiowas, Minneconjou Sioux, Moquis, Navajos, Nez Perces, Oglala Sioux, Omahas, Osages, Pawnees, Poncas, Shoshones, Snakes, Tonkaways, Utes, Winnebagoes, and Zunis—but he did not pretend that his portrayal of Indian life was comprehensive. As in *The Plains*, the tribes he described the most fully were the native inhabitants of the western plains and mountains, and his most abundant source of examples was the Cheyennes.

Whether Dodge assigned a title to the book at this time is doubtful, but when published in 1882 it was named *Our Wild Indians*, followed by a lengthy subtitle that included the apt phrase "*A Popular Account*."[23] Dodge hoped *Our Wild Indians* would reach a much larger audience than *The Plains*, and the style of the later work reveals his effort to appeal to popular taste. When he wrote the earlier work, he was a novice author, but now, assured of his abilities and engaged in a process of composition he enjoyed, he wrote with easy confidence. Occasionally he reached after some happy effect or permitted himself a little elegancy of style. Wishing to evoke the predawn moments on November 25, 1876, when Colonel Mackenzie and his force were about to launch their attack, he began with an exclamation—"Imagine the scene!"[24] From time to time he alluded to passages from the Bible and the writings of Shakespeare and later authors, including Sterne, Hazlitt, Wordsworth, Dickens, and Bulwer-Lytton, often quoting a line or two. He delivered himself of neatly crafted, sometimes pungent aphorisms and phrases (Indian chiefs "suave as a crossroads politician"; "the Great American Buffalo Destroyer, fearless as Bayard, unsavory as a skunk").[25] The playful tone of observations like these conveys his awareness that the book was, after all, a performance.

The desire to produce a work that would appeal to the general reading public led Dodge to omit from the manuscript three of the five passages describing Indian sexual behavior that had offended some readers of *The Plains*. The two others appeared in condensed and sanitized versions and were given less emphasis than before.[26] Much of the new material was attractively set forth and inoffensive, including accounts of Indian games, handicrafts, cooking, dances, and clothing. The chapters on sign language and Indian chronology that William Blackmore had intended to write found a place in *Our Wild Indians* and added to its general interest.[27] George Aschmann and Ben Clarke assisted with the chapter on Indian music.[28] Dodge also included four chapters on frontiersmen and four more on the work of the army, thus rounding out in sketchy fashion the fourth and fifth segments of his original project of authorship.[29] If some of these discussions were at best tangential to his main topic, Indians, the discontinuity was hardly noticeable, for the book was splendidly miscellaneous throughout.

Naturally, Dodge portrayed himself in the manuscript, both implicitly through his narrative voice and explicitly through scenes and events he had witnessed. However, he rarely represented himself as a participant. For example, he introduced the outbreak and flight of the Northern Cheyennes in 1878 as "the most extraordinary feat of travel and pursuit within my knowledge," but in what followed he gave no hint of the part he had played in the effort to capture the Indians.[30] Similarly, he several times referred to events of recent years in the Black Hills but said nothing of the important role he had played there. On the other hand, in the chapters on the army and frontiersmen he paid generous tribute to men with whom he had shared experiences. He praised General Crook for his courage and independence of mind, especially in his use of Indian scouts in campaigns against other Indians. He introduced Amos Chapman as "One of the best and bravest, the most sober, quiet and genial of all scouts I have ever known."[31] He described the deeds of certain other officers without divulging their names but in a manner that would make their identities recognizable at once to informed readers.[32] He refrained from presenting detailed accounts of the army's performances in battle against Indians, except as instances of the tactics involved. Narratives of that stirring sort might easily be multiplied, he wrote, "but grateful as is the task of recording such noble deeds, I will leave it to other pens."[33]

Our Wild Indians touched upon a broad range of topics relating to Plains Indians—tribal government, warrior societies, medicine chiefs, rites and ceremonies, burial and mourning, training in childhood, the life of women, names and epithets, music, and cooks and cooking, to name only a few. In the diversity of its coverage, the work was a continuously interesting treatment. Some of its engaging character derived from the author's genial assurances that however outlandish the Indians might seem in their beliefs and practices, at bottom they were human beings like everyone else. Ordinarily he offered instances of this truth with double-edged irony. For example, in describing the great authority wielded by Indian soothsayers, he wrote: "Be he civilized or be he savage, man delights in being humbugged, and any pretender to mysteries, either medical or spiritual, is sure to find some one to believe him." Elsewhere, discussing items of personal decoration, he mentioned that the fortunate few Indian men who could ornament their war bonnets with eagle's quills "value them as a millionaire his estate, and they serve exactly the same purpose, often pushing forward a man who has no other claim to distinction." Women came in for a share of observations ("When the civilized woman would relieve her feelings by a 'good cry,' her savage sister enjoys a good howl").[34] But not all his comparisons between civilized persons and savages were intended to provoke a smile. Recounting a conversation between himself and Stone Calf wherein the old chief expressed his will to die fighting rather than submit to starvation, he recalled the admiration he felt for his friend's manly self-respect. "Were I an Indian," he wrote, "I fear that, with their provocations, I should be a bad Indian."[35]

At many points in *Our Wild Indians* Dodge wrote of the great changes that had occurred in Indian life in recent years. Exposure to new conditions brought on by the advance of modern civilization had inevitably affected some Indian customs and beliefs. The tomahawk, once a prime weapon, had become a mere ceremonial ornament, like a lady's fan. The medicine dance, once swathed in secrecy and mandatory for all young men as a rite of initiation into warrior status, had become optional, with the ceremony open even to casual observers from outside the tribe. The good old times of hunting for food were almost gone, for the buffalo and many other game animals had been all but exterminated.[36] He itemized developments like these with some regret, for they marked the far distance between the present and the times when the Cheyennes and other tribes had functioned well as independent societies.

Dodge adopted a different tone in enumerating changes that were directly attributable to the effects of reservation life on Indians. Here he wrote not as a detached anthropological observer nor as a genial fellow human being attuned to our mutual folly; rather, he expressed himself as an advocate of the Indian and a scandalized U.S. citizen. The most visible alteration in Indian life since their relocation onto reservations was, he wrote, the new importance they necessarily gave to food. As late as 1872 the question of access to food had been of small concern, but in the years since it had become "the paramount, and . . . I may say, the only question." He painted a grim picture of the poverty endured by Indians placed on reservations and forced to remain there. He pictured men and women examining the contents of slop barrels and dump piles at military posts, carrying off "stuff that a cur would disdain." At Fort Reno, where citizens in the eastern states might suppose hunger could never occur, "a dead horse or mule is no sooner dragged away from the vicinity of the post, than it is pounced upon, cut up and carried off by the starved Indians. They ask no questions, and meat is meat, even though it was killed for farcy or glanders. Nothing is too disgustingly filthy to come amiss to the starving Indian."[37]

Matter of this kind was painful to read, and deliberately so. By his insistent use of words like "starved," Dodge was portraying in dramatic fashion the abject state of Indians as the result of their treatment by the U.S. government. The varied tones of *Our Wild Indians* thus expressed multiple purposes. As an informal account of Indian beliefs, pastimes, and customs it was a comfortable work to peruse; as a critique of the nation's policy toward Indians it was not comfortable, for it resonated with angry frustration. Perhaps disconcertingly to casual readers, it often modulated from one tone and purpose to the other within a single chapter, invariably passing from inoffensiveness to corrosive criticism.[38] Viewed as a whole, the published work moved in the same direction. Passing from topics without political overtones, in its later chapters it became a tract for the times—an indictment of federal Indian policy and a call for reform.[39]

In Dodge's view, the historical root of the government's disastrous record of official contact with the Indians was its reliance on a treaty system that equated savage bands with sovereign states, as if they possessed the power to enter into legal relationships with great nations around the world. Often as the consequence of defeat in war, tribes had unwillingly entered into treaty agreements with the United States; in return for possession of the tribes' ancestral ranges, the government had undertaken to provide their members a new home and supply them rations, annuity goods, and perhaps other benefits. Professing a will to fair play, it then moved the defeated people to locations far from their homelands and confined them there. Gnawed by homesickness and unable to accustom themselves to the new style of life being forced on them, many of the Indian people grew ill and died. This was the consequence of treating the tribes as sovereign nations—a result "ludicrous, were it not so sad."[40]

To aggravate the wrong, the government had failed to abide by the terms of its solemn covenants with Indian tribes. As examples, Dodge cited provisions in the *Revised Statutes* designed to protect Indians by forbidding entry onto their reservations by commercial hunters and others who might victimize them. Poorly enforced, these laws were, in effect, misrepresentations of the national will, "the whole of that country having been constantly overrun by white men, who made their living by killing game and trapping the fur-bearing animals." The slaughter of 5 million buffalo in the early 1870s contravened Indian treaties, but Congress chose not to interfere, thus cutting off the tribes' traditional mode of subsistence.[41] By then appropriating too few funds to purchase food and other supplies for the Indians, also guaranteed by treaty, the government tacitly condemned tribes on reservations to helpless suffering. What wonder, Dodge asked, that the vision of their future drove some Indians to "aggressive desperation"? They resolved "to die fighting rather than by the slow torture of starvation to which the government condemns them."[42]

Dodge argued that the reservation system harmed Indians not only by failing to satisfy their physical needs but also by providing them an inadequate system of law enforcement. Having undermined tribal government by dispossessing the chiefs and intratribal organizations of their despotic powers, the United States had made all tribespeople equally subject to the tyranny of the Indian agent. That substitution had perhaps benefitted the Indians as a first step toward democratic rule, but it left almost no provision for the control of criminal behavior, earlier exerted by chiefs and tribal councils. Dodge offered several instances of the lawless conditions that prevailed within this legal vacuum, but the most telling was an incident recounted to him by Stone Calf. The chief's thirteen-year-old daughter, "his pet and jewel," was sent one day with another girl to deliver a message to a subchief seven miles away. The girls performed their errand, but on the return they were waylaid by a renegade member of Stone Calf's band who, pistol in hand, ordered the companion away. He then took the chief's daughter to his lodge and in the presence of his wives raped her repeatedly. Fearing reprisal, after two days he went in search of Stone Calf and took the girl to Cantonment, where she escaped to the tipi of one of the Indian scouts.

Later that day Stone Calf sought out Dodge and "begged for vengeance":

> "Have you among yourselves no remedy for such outrages?" I asked.
>
> "Yes," he replied, "I can kill him, and I ought to kill him, but the agent is not my friend, and if I do kill this scoundrel, the agent will put me in the guardhouse, and when I get out not only my daughter, but my wives and family will all be gone or outraged."
>
> "I am truly sorry for you, my friend," I said, "but I can do absolutely nothing. If this were a white villain I would put him in my guard-house, and turn him over to the civil authorities for trial, but he is an Indian, and there is no law to punish such acts when committed by Indians."
>
> Covering his face with his hands, the old man was bent and racked with emotion. Recovering himself he placed his hand on my arm, and in a quivering voice, said:
>
> "I am sick of the Indian road, it is not good;" then raising his eyes to Heaven, he added:

> "I hope the Good God will give us the white man's road before we are all destroyed."[43]

The predicament of Stone Calf was essentially that of any Indian man or woman on the reservation; when mistreated in any way, all were without recourse through a code of law.

An axiom of Dodge's conception of Indian character had long been that unlike civilized persons, Indians lacked a moral sense. By this he meant that whereas in civilized society a code of morality articulated the mutual obligations of individuals, the Indian had no conception of right and wrong as abstract realities. "All is right that he wishes to do, all is wrong that opposes him."[44] In the absence of social control, lawlessness must therefore prevail. As Dodge portrayed it, life on an Indian reservation was far from being a benign modification of traditional ways that gradually acclimated tribespeople to more progressive modes of living. Instead, quoting Wordsworth, he represented it as often brutal, where "he shall take who has the power, and he shall keep who can."[45]

In making his case against the reservation system, Dodge reserved the most bitter denunciation for its cruelest fixture, the authorized Indian trader. A trader's monopoly, he explained, was complete, enabling him to cheat at will the persons whom he was appointed to serve. As an instance of the mistreatment suffered by Indians at the hands of traders, he recounted an experience recently reported to him by the victim. This man had cut twenty cords of wood for a contractor at $1.25 per cord, and on delivering the wood he was given an order on the authorized trader for the agreed amount. But when he presented the warrant, he was issued not money, but supplies in kind amounting to one pint of brown sugar for each cord of wood. He had been grossly cheated, but he could do nothing since the trader was without competition and supervision. Dodge likened such merchants to harpies that "under the guise of friendship," devour their victims.[46]

In the incident of cordwood and brown sugar the unscrupulous trader was almost certainly George E. Reynolds, whose practices Dodge had interfered with at Cantonment to the extent he could. However, in *Our Wild Indians* he did not name Reynolds or any other abuser of delegated power, for the problem was widespread, and ultimate responsibility lay with the government that supported the system. Similarly, when discussing the necessity of stationing "a force of troops to watch and guard" the Indians on reservations, he clearly had in mind posts like Cantonment;[47] but he did not identify his post, for the situation was endemic to much of Indian Territory.

In concluding *Our Wild Indians*, Dodge expressed his desire as a citizen to preserve the honor of his nation. Americans, he maintained, were honorable, merciful, and readily aroused to sympathy for the plight of oppressed peoples elsewhere in the world. Yet, owing chiefly to the remoteness of Indian territory and their ignorance of conditions there, thus far they had permitted the Indians to suffer without sympathy. Dodge called upon his compatriots to consider the nation's treatment of the Indians in its full enormity and recognize their complicity in the wrong. Next to slavery, he held, "the foulest blot on the escutcheon of the Government of the United States is its treatment of the so-called 'Wards of the Nation.'"[48] By denying citizenship to the Indians and refusing them the right to possess land in severalty, the United States was failing to acknowledge their dignity as fellow human beings and condemning them to a cycle of degradation, impoverishment, and despair.

The "L'Envoi," far from an elegant coda to a neatly framed literary exercise, was a passionate call for reform. Here Dodge affirmed his awareness that in the body of the book, he had seriously offended certain classes of readers. Those good folk who, misled by Cooper, Catlin, and others, chose to embrace as reality a fanciful conception had been painfully disabused. They wished their supposed Indians to exist forever in some pristine state, but the laws of progress and the Indians' actual nature made that impossible. Another group, the professional humanitarians, served and were served by the status quo. They feathered their nests by victimizing the peoples whose condition they professed a wish to alleviate. To those persons Dodge declared his "unalterable hostility" and a determination "to use every faculty with which I am endowed to wrench the Indian from their sordid grasp."[49]

As a proponent of reform, Dodge addressed himself to a third group of readers, the great mass of Americans who, passing through life with their own preoccupations, had known little and cared less about the Indian. Here the double identity of *Our Wild Indians* as both a general account and a protest merged and became one. Only a few decades before, he pointed out, the term "Abolitionist" had been one of bitter reproach to some. Many honorable persons had doubted the wisdom of emancipating slaves and extending to them the rights and duties of citizenship. Yet the Negro race had already justified the nation's commitment to it, swelling the number of valuable citizens. The same future lay within reach of the Indians, if only the energies of "a few true men" could be brought to bear in their behalf. Like the Abolitionists, the friends of the Indian must prepare themselves for a long struggle, retaining faith in the wise decency of the American people. Dodge appealed to the press, the pulpit, and "every lover of humanity": "Arouse to this grand work. No slave now treads the soil of this noble land. Force your representatives to release the Indian from an official bondage more remorseless, more hideous than slavery itself. Deliver him from his pretended friends, and lift him into fellowship with the citizens of our loved and glorious country."[50]

Clearly the composition of *Our Wild Indians* had become for Dodge more than an ambitious project of authorship. It was also a private mission, an appeal for action on behalf of American Indians, many of whom he had come to know and respect. He included in his book a list of policy changes that he believed would benefit the tribes on reservations.[51] He knew that not all of these proposals would be acted upon in the near future, but at least he was using his status as a known author to advance a program for reform of the sorry arrangements that prevailed. Of course, some would dismiss his recommendations as merely a partisan appeal, as indeed it was. The first two of his ten policy suggestions were to turn over the care of Indians to the War Department and to abolish the Indian Bureau as then constituted, actions already often debated and with entrenched adherents on both sides. What gave his book unique power was the connection it established between his experience of actual conditions and the proposals he advanced to root out their underlying causes. *Our Wild Indians* was an authoritative report and recommendation from the field.

The completion of his book manuscript was a time of fulfillment for Dodge in several respects, for he could look back on his recent years in the Department of the Missouri as among the most eventful of his career. At Fort Riley, Fort Leavenworth, and Fort Hays he had been called upon to serve in several capacities and in every instance had acquitted himself well. As a field commander against the Northern Cheyennes he had faithfully followed orders that ran counter to his better judgment and when challenged, had vindicated himself from imputation otherwise. The move from Fort Hays and the establishment of Cantonment North Fork Canadian River had been accomplished efficiently. As post commander at Cantonment he had directed an ambitious construction program, effectively parried the attacks of Agent Miles, and promoted the welfare of the Indians living around him. If his stewardship on behalf of Keeling and Company had not been a complete success, the result was not for lack of high principle and due effort. In the summer just past, he had proved a faithful subaltern under the exacting eye of Colonel Mackenzie, and beginning in September he had drafted a substantial book on a topic that concerned him deeply. Certainly as a professional soldier and an author he had reason for satisfaction, and as a father and husband he had also prospered. Fred was well launched on a stage career, and Julia seemed more inclined toward a reconciliation.

The closing months of 1880 also brought Dodge hopeful anticipations for the future. Legislation then before Congress would make mandatory the retirement from active duty of army officers sixty-two years of age and over. Enactment of that law would help break the logjam for promotion that had demoralized the service for years,[52] and Dodge knew that it would make him a full colonel at once. What was more, early in November, General Pope had privately informed him of another, wholly unanticipated development. During the summer General Sherman had requested him to supply the name of an officer to replace the late Colonel Joseph C. Audenried, Sixth Cavalry, as a member of his personal staff. Pope had at that time named Dodge, and as he wrote in strict confidence, he had now done so again.[53] Service as aide-de-camp to the General of the Army carried with it the rank and salary of colonel, but to military men it was yet more highly prized as a mark of recognition by the army for the merits of one of its own. To have been nominated for the appointment was to Dodge a gratifying mark of his department commander's regard. Pope had recommended him to Sherman as "a fine writer & an active energetic man, of great personal fidelity."[54]

As with his two earlier books, once Dodge had a copy of the completed manuscript in hand for review, he planned a trip to New York City to secure a publisher. He therefore applied for a four-month leave of absence that would afford him time also to correct proofs, collect illustrations, and attend to details of production that he regretted not being able to oversee before *The Plains* was issued. An authorization for the requested period arrived early in December,[55] and he began preparations for a long absence. He was packed and ready to depart from Cantonment when, on December 15, the information arrived that General Pope had been directed to order him to report in person to the General of the Army.[56] Sherman had selected him to be a member of his staff, to replace Colonel Alexander McDowell McCook, who had just been promoted to command the Sixth Infantry. On the following day, Pope therefore ordered him by telegraph to report to Fort Leavenworth,[57] and Dodge set aside without regret his leave of absence and his book project, gathering his possessions for a permanent departure from the post. On December 17 he issued a final order as commander of Cantonment North Fork Canadian River, directing a sergeant and three privates to proceed to Caldwell, Kansas, the next day "as escort to public transportation."[58]

Dodge had left off writing his journal upon his return to the post three months earlier, devoting all his energies to quiet labor on the book manuscript. But on the evening of December 18, camped twenty-five miles from Cantonment, he opened his small pocket notebook and wrote an entry summarizing the period and recounting the recent events. "All has happened admirably," he concluded, "& I am a truly fortunate man."[59]

Part Six

On Duty with the General of the Army, 1881–1883

The appointment as an aide-de-camp to General Sherman conferred on Dodge the highest level of official status he had achieved in his career thus far. Perhaps more important to him, it marked recognition by a commanding officer he respected and whose good opinion he valued. In fact, Sherman had been aware of his versatile accomplishments for some time. Dodge's soldierly conduct at First Bull Run, the general's own initiation to Civil War combat, was an honorable exception to the lack of discipline that had turned the hard-fought battle into a rout. Since 1867, when the two officers had conferred at North Platte along the Union Pacific Railroad, Dodge's frontier duty had come to Sherman's attention with increasing regularity. By 1879 the general had formed a settled opinion of the younger man as a "judicious" and "active good officer" whose competence could be relied upon.[1] Dodge had a wide circle of friends in the army and was known for good fellowship and good sense. Hearty recommendations of him from General Pope and perhaps other of his superiors, including Brigadier General Randolph B. Marcy, made the selection as aide a natural one.

The privilege of membership on the army headquarters staff enabled Dodge to witness Sherman's efforts to round out his career by completing initiatives he had begun years before. As the general had envisioned, the Indian tribes that had contested the nation's development westward were now largely subjugated and confined on reservations. Trains passed freely along railroads that traversed the western portion of the continent, and more lines were under construction. The army that had helped bring about these transformations was itself in the midst of reforms that would help prepare it for service in a new era. Dodge had played a part in all these developments as an officer in the field, and as Sherman's subordinate, he would assist in the effort to establish a new equilibrium.

By advocating a more influential role for the army in fostering the welfare and cultural development of American Indians, Dodge's forthcoming book articulated a policy Sherman had long argued for. The general therefore chose to associate his name and the authority of his office with *Our Wild Indians*, lending it a semiofficial character while also strengthening its sales potential. As in this instance of cooperation, Sherman and Dodge shared beliefs, tastes, traits of personality, and identities as soldiers that led to a relationship of mutual effort, reciprocal admiration, and personal regard between them. Dodge exemplified a professional profile that Sherman wished to foster among army officers. In a revised edition of his *Memoirs* he expressed his respect for Dodge and other members of his staff "who were faithful, intelligent, and patriotic—not only an official respect, but a personal affection for their qualities as men, in the full belief that they were model soldiers and gentlemen, such as should ever characterize the headquarters of the army of the United States."[2]

The year 1883 was to be Sherman's last of active duty, and fittingly, one of his final major undertakings was at the same time valedictory and directed toward ensuring the nation's future security. Availing himself of the western railroads that paralleled the national boundaries on the north and south, he planned a summer-long inspection tour of the states and territories in that extensive region. The examination would afford him a view of the developments that had taken place during his tenure in office and would also provide a basis for recommendations on the location and strength of future military installations. Dodge was no longer on duty in Washington at the time this tour was scheduled to begin, having been relieved as an aide-de-camp some time before. However, a quirk of fate resulted in an unanticipated new assignment for him—namely, to accompany the general on the lengthy summer journey. He would thus join General Sherman in an experience the veteran leader regarded as in a sense the capstone of his career. As Dodge observed, it was a "very Bully" turn of events.[3]

22

Aide-de-Camp and Author

At the time he selected Dodge to be a member of his personal staff, General Sherman had served as the nation's highest-ranking army officer for eleven years. The worst of the conflicts and frustrations that had troubled his tenure as General of the Army—niggardly appropriations from Congress, subjection to the indifference or intrusive whims of civilian secretaries of war and the imperious wills of junior officers who commanded staff departments outside his control—were behind him now, accommodated as fully as he thought possible. His reputation as the fierce combatant whose march from Atlanta to the Atlantic coast in the winter of 1864–1865 had helped shatter the morale of the Confederacy was firmly established, but in the years since the conflict, the public's perception of him had mellowed. By many persons he was regarded with affection as the "old warrior," a grizzled, graying leader whose still-erect bearing, keen glance, and tart tongue evinced soldierly qualities that were somehow comfortable, a source of national pride. The postwar mandate of the army—to mediate between the advancing western tide of settlers and the Indian inhabitants whose ancestral lands they appropriated—was not yet fulfilled, especially on the nation's southwest and northwest frontiers. Yet events were verging toward a state of affairs wherein, as he declared in his annual report three years later, the Indians were "substantially eliminated from the problem of the Army."[1]

At sixty years of age, Sherman looked ahead to a few more years of active service in which, taking advantage of the generally peaceful times, he would set the army on a course to guarantee the nation's security in the foreseeable future. Even though he still deplored involvement in politics as potentially the ruin of soldiers like himself, he had developed skill in dealing with persons of influence and was active in the public sphere, serving on advisory boards, commissions, and planning committees. He attended receptions, dinners, and social gatherings of all kinds, often traveling hundreds of miles to preside at the annual reunions of military fraternities. Observers noted that

William T. Sherman. Reprinted from *Harper's Weekly*, November 3, 1883, p. 847.

the wiry general kept a schedule that would test most younger men. On occasion he admitted a wish to break free from the hurry and pomp of official life, but in some respects he had come to savor it. Amid all his activities, the chief focus of Sherman's attention as a public servant remained the army he led. He hoped, he often said, to be remembered first for his work as a soldier, and that work was not yet finished.

By law, the General of the Army was entitled to the full-time service of six aides-de-camp, and in recent years Sherman had availed himself of this privilege to the full. These officers were his executive assistants—senior subalterns who attended to routine office matters and performed such other duties as might be assigned them. All accompanied him to official functions in the national capital, and on his frequent trips outside Washington he was also joined by one or more, who made the arrangements for baggage, transportation, and lodging and kept track of expenses. The general and his staff were together regularly and developed a bond of official familiarity which, though modified by the differences in rank, verged in some instances toward personal friendship. Several of Sherman's aides had served him for years and now assisted him in capacities that suited their individual backgrounds and abilities. Captain John M. Bacon, Ninth Cavalry, an aide-de-camp since 1871, helped conduct the general's semiofficial correspondence and attended to some of his personal business affairs. Major Orlando M. Poe, of the Engineers, had been an aide since 1873 and took responsibility for keeping abreast of developments in that elite department. Captain

John E. Tourtelotte, Seventh Cavalry, had been a member of the headquarters staff since 1871. A widely traveled man of independent means, he often accompanied the general to social or diplomatic functions where his gentlemanly bearing would be an asset. From time to time, Tourtelotte was called upon to provide a legal opinion on some vexed question of policy not dealt with in army regulations.[2]

During 1880 the three other positions on Sherman's staff became vacant, and on December 15 he announced the new incumbents. He had selected one officer from each of the three arms of the field service. The infantry was represented by Lieutenant Colonel Dodge, who at once became the senior aide-de-camp in lineal rank. The successful candidate from the cavalry regiments was Major Albert P. Morrow, Ninth Cavalry, who had distinguished himself in recent operations against the Apache Indians. Major John C. Tidball, Second Artillery, represented that branch. He had just completed *A Manual for Heavy Artillery Service*, which was adopted as a textbook at his former duty station, the Artillery School at Fortress Monroe, Virginia, and also at West Point. Dodge and Tidball were West Point graduates—coincidentally, both in the Class of 1848—while Morrow had begun his military career during the Civil War as a volunteer enlisted man.[3] Sherman thus demonstrated that preferment in the officer corps lay within reach of individuals from all walks of life. All three officers satisfied the general's chief criterion for selection: long periods of duty in the field.[4]

Standing together in dress uniform, their dark blue dress jackets shining with brass buttons and epaulettes and hung with looped aiguillettes of gold braid, the general's staff formed a handsome group of men. Early in 1881 an observer remarked that Sherman "seems determined to keep up the reputation of his staff in all respects, good looks not excepted."[5] Dodge contributed to the favorable impression with his erect posture, broad chest, and neatly trimmed graying hair and beard. Though not inclined to personal display, he was familiar with the social requirements of military duty in major cities and was comfortable satisfying them. And as General Sherman once remarked to him, in times of peace the duties of an aide-de-camp were more social than military.[6]

The properly military work of the headquarters staff was transacted on weekdays at a not yet completed building on Pennsylvania Avenue that housed offices of the State Department, the army, and the navy. Dodge worked at a large, pigeon-holed desk in one of two rooms that flanked the general's office, at the end of the entry corridor on the main floor. The streams of visitors who presented themselves to an attendant outside Sherman's door were freely admitted. His large, shadowy office was furnished with spare simplicity and evidently dedicated to official business. Its furniture included a large roller desk, a revolving bookcase, a pine map case, and two converging rows of cane-bottomed chairs that together formed a V. A large window, equipped with a cloth shade on rollers but without curtains or draperies, offered a view of the president's mansion across an expanse of lawn. The only articles of decoration were engravings and paintings ranged along the walls, mainly the gifts of Sherman's war comrades but also including a few acquisitions of his own. Floor-to-ceiling panels in one corner concealed a clattering elevator, but the general read, wrote, and thought to himself as if oblivious to the racket. Smoking or chomping on an ever-present cigar, he sat at his desk against the wall, usually with his back to visitors. To those who announced themselves, he turned and offered a hearty welcome, but many citizens simply sat for a few moments on the cane-bottomed chairs, content to be witnessing the General of the Army at work.[7]

Each weekday morning, Sherman would arrive at headquarters at about nine o'clock, brimming with nervous energy and ready for the day's tasks. During the morning he would summon one member of his staff or another by a shouted surname—his invariable mode of address to them—or with short, quick steps would enter one of the side offices to declare his wants and perhaps pass a few moments in conversation. The atmosphere was businesslike but not formal, seemingly pleasant to all concerned. At one or two o'clock in the afternoon he took lunch, with sometimes a glass of neat whisky, at an eating place nearby. He returned to headquarters only on afternoons when some unusual matter required his attention. Ordinarily he devoted the later hours of the day to other commitments, and if possible to a few hours at home.[8]

In Dodge's initial weeks at army headquarters, a friendship began to develop between him and Sherman. Both were extroverts and masters of conversation who relished anecdotage, debate, and give-and-take on all topics, and who were aware of their talent in this area. Sherman considered himself "the best talker in seven states,"[9] but Dodge knew himself a strong competitor. The two men stimulated each other to feats of verbal performance, sometimes to the dismay of more taciturn types such as Tidball.[10] Both were wide readers, with more than casual knowledge on a range of subjects. Dodge was the more literary in his tastes; the texts of Shakespeare's plays were at his fingers' ends, while Sherman's enthusiasm for the drama ran more to performances than to reading. But here, fortuitously, another source of common interest presented itself. Dodge's son, Fred, was becoming known both as "the New Hamlet" and as "the Army Actor," his relationship to Dodge being noticed by newspapers like the *Army and Navy Journal*.[11] Sherman, an inveterate playgoer, may have attended performances by Fred during his repertory company's recent appearances in Washington. At any rate, as a lover of the theater he knew of Fred's accomplishments, if not at firsthand then certainly through newspaper notices and conversation with the proud father.

The themes richest with potential for elaboration by these two discussants were army stories and tales of life on the plains. Both men were drawn to the western wilderness, Dodge from long habitude, Sherman also from early associations but later as a respite from the constraints of life in eastern cities. Another officer, Colonel James F. Rusling, recalled the general's satisfaction when, on a visit to Fort Garland in 1866, he immersed himself in the mountain country just as he found it. "He threw off all reserve," Rusling wrote, and "entered fully into the life of the pioneer and Indian. He asked a thousand questions of everybody and was never at a loss for a story or a joke, and added to the effect of these by the twinkle of his eye, the toss of his head, and the serio-comic twitch of his many-wrinkled features, in a way indescribable."[12] Since assuming command of the army, Sherman had made several tours of inspection in the West. His desire to keep current about events and conditions in the region continued unabated, and in this respect Dodge, more than any other of his aides, was able to satisfy him.

The first major event in Washington, D.C., wherein the general and his new aides-de-camp appeared together in public was a peaceful one, the inauguration of James A. Garfield as president on March 4, 1881. A storm the night before dropped slushy snow on the city, soaking the drapes and bunting that had been hung along the parade route. At daylight, workers hurried to sweep the temporary bleachers and reviewing stands and then Pennsylvania Avenue, but the prospect was for a bedraggled procession at best until, in midmorning, wintry sunlight broke through the clouds and improved conditions somewhat. The national capital was crowded with visitors, many of whom soon lined the route of march and overflowed the galleries outside the capitol building. At approximately 10:30 A.M. the parade began, led by the president, the president-elect, and their military escort. General Sherman appeared next on a spirited gray horse, followed by his aides, also mounted, and then a division of regular troops. After these came the president-elect's party, in carriages, and then four more divisions of state troops and civic societies.

Arrived at the capitol, Sherman and his staff sat astride their mounts in front of the inaugural stand, their teeth chattering in the frigid wind. The inauguration ceremony took place, President Garfield addressed the crowd at some length, and at last the one-mile return march began. The sequence of marching units was the same as before, but additional participants now joined the rear of the procession and lent it a celebratory air. Amid the music of brass bands, the parade passed underneath thirty-three iron arches, draped with flags, that had been set in place to span the avenue. Several military brigades, among them the Pennsylvania state militia, the naval cadets, and a six-company contingent of marines, attracted attention for their bearing during this part of the day's observances.[13] Other groups won applause for their resplendent appearance. In front of the White House, General Sherman stood on a reviewing stand alongside the new president as the colorful procession made its way past, his aides-de-camp remaining behind the grandstand for another cold, tedious hour.[14]

Despite its inauspicious beginning and continuing discomforts, the day of the Garfield inauguration was a great success. The throng of spectators was unprecedented, and the procession of military and civic organizations was the largest ever to complement a presidential inauguration. It was agreed that Washington had not seen so fine a military display since the Grand Review of returning Union troops in May 1865.[15] True, these were palmy days of peace, but the army had at least shown that it could still add energy and snap to a parade. A few days afterward, Sherman and his staff took part in another ceremony, stiff with protocol, the president's annual reception for army and navy officers then in the city.

Once these events were over, it became possible to direct attention more specifically to army affairs. In addition to routine duties, each of the new aides was assigned responsibility for some project or area of activity within the service that related to his special competence. Morrow would assist Tourtelotte in reviewing court-martial proceedings so as to inform the general of cases or legal issues that required his attention. Tidball was to preside over a board of officers who would investigate possible changes in the light artillery equipment to be supplied the army.[16] Dodge would head up a similar board to study the practicability of adopting a single magazine gun design for use by troops in all branches of the army. The two latter assignments reflected Sherman's determination that despite the small likelihood of a major conflict in the near future, the army should keep pace with the times, moving beyond its dependence on outmoded arms that in some instances dated back to the Civil War era.

The idea of equipping soldiers with a reliable rifle that was capable of firing in rapid succession bullets stored in a reserve compartment, or magazine, had been of interest to Dodge for several years. He agreed with the recently retired Captain Charles King, Fifth Cavalry, that the magazine gun was "the weapon of the future," and he was acquainted with the work of two previous boards—one in 1876, another in 1878—that had inquired into the matter.[17] For himself, he knew firsthand the shortcomings of the differently styled breech loading rifles then in use by cavalry and infantry troops. In combat against Indians, neither the cavalry carbine, with its short range, nor the infantry rifle, with its size and heft, could perform satisfactorily in place of the other.[18] Meeting at various points in the eastern states including Troy, New York; Springfield, Massachusetts; and Governors Island, New York harbor, the Magazine Gun Board would conduct studies of weaponry submitted for its inspection by manufacturers in the United States and abroad. Should the board be able to recommend a design for general adoption, it would contribute measurably to the effectiveness of the nation's military force. The armies of France and Germany had already adopted magazine weapons, and to protect its credibility as an emerging international power, the United States should not be left behind.

Sherman and Dodge had discussed ideas like these by March 21, when an order was issued from army headquarters designating the membership of the Magazine Gun Board and directing it to assemble in New York City on July 5 to begin its work.[19] However, a few weeks later the general released Dodge from this important assignment and designated another senior officer, Colonel John R. Brooke, Third Infantry, to serve in his stead.[20] Sherman had known beforehand that Dodge was already pursuing a quite different project, one that also promised to advance the interests of the army. Releasing him from membership on the Magazine Gun Board would enable him to continue work on that undertaking—a book that would shed new light on the vexed Indian Question that had tasked the army since the Civil War.

Our Wild Indians

Commentaries on the Indians and their plight were being published frequently at just this time. George W. Manypenny's *Our Indian Wards*, a lengthy treatment by an apologist for the Indian Bureau, had appeared in 1880. Helen Hunt Jackson's indictment of the federal government, *A Century of Dishonor*, was issued in January 1881. The Military Service Institution, a semiofficial body, was offering a prize for the best essay on Indian affairs submitted to its review board that year.[21] The government's role in providing for the future of the American Indian was undergoing spirited discussion, and a contribution by Dodge, already an acknowledged authority, would be timely.

Sherman supported the publication of Dodge's book manuscript as both advancing the political interests of the army and also adding to the work of other army officers as a contribution to knowledge. General Sheridan was officially sponsoring cultural studies of Indian tribes by two talented young officers, First Lieutenant John G. Bourke, Third Cavalry, and Captain William Philo Clark, Second Cavalry.[22] Like Dodge, these younger men had already contributed to the anthropological record by collecting specimens of Indian material culture, many of which they donated to the Smithsonian Institution and other repositories. As for Dodge's political stance, Sherman knew from *The Plains* and from more recent conversations that his articulate aide-de-camp was a staunch supporter of the army's point of view.[23]

Dodge was eager to bring his work before the American reading public. Shortly after arriving in the capital, he lent the manuscript to a Professor Angel who recognized its value and communicated his judgment to Henry L. Dawes, chairman of the Senate Committee on Indian Affairs. Presently Dawes also borrowed a portion of the work, and upon returning it he assured Dodge that he had found in it a good many "nuggets" for use as a legislator. Gratifyingly, the senator predicted that when published, it would be a "valuable contribution to Indian literature."[24] Dodge intended to bring out this latest volume as a private venture, as he had *The Black Hills* and *The Plains*. However, since the new work meshed neatly with activities already under way under army auspices, Sherman authorized his aide-de-camp to move ahead on the book project as part of his regular duties. In the months that followed, he would also assist Dodge in other ways.

Although *The Plains* had been greeted enthusiastically by reviewers, its sales were disappointing. In 1881, four years after its publication, eighty-three copies of Putnam's modest second impression of the work remained in stock.[25] The firm had brought out the volume in creditable fashion, but in Dodge's view its conservative marketing practices had failed to realize its sales potential. He planned to find a another publisher that would ensure a wider audience for the new book.

To achieve this aim, he selected A. D. Worthington of Hartford, Connecticut, a former bank employee and traveling salesman whose firm marketed its publications through subscriptions and canvassing by agents. Unlike the Putnams, Worthington felt little concern to accumulate a list of titles whose solid merit would reflect lasting credit on his publishing house. So long as the books that appeared under his imprint gave no offense to reviewers or discouraged potential purchasers in any other way, he was relatively indifferent to their content. His publications were commodities, to be made attractive to the widest possible audience. He was not shy of proclaiming the merits of his products and extolling his methods of marketing them. In a pamphlet sent to persons who had expressed interest in enlisting as agents, he boasted that "In the hands of A. D. WORTHINGTON & Co., the subscription-book business has been raised to the order and dignity of a science." The principles of this science he expounded in a separate booklet, forwarded to agents, entitled *The Art of Canvassing, or What to Do and What Not to Do, to Achieve Success*. According to the advertising pamphlet, Worthington and his sales associates occupied a segment of the book trade that had grown "at a rate little dreamed of by the plodding publishers of fifteen years ago."[26] Dodge's would be the sixth book Worthington had offered for sale, and the first dealing with the American Indian.

The agreement between author and publisher specified that Dodge would supply an acceptable manuscript, cooperate in securing illustrations, and assist in marketing. In return, Worthington would bear all costs of production, advertising, and distribution and pay the author a royalty of ten cents per copy sold. Although the latter sum was far less than the twenty percent the Putnams had paid on copies of *The Plains* at the retail price of four dollars, if multiplied by a sufficient number of sales, it should yield the author a good long-term return.

Dodge therefore busied himself with final revisions of his text and with arranging for the illustrations. James E. Taylor of New York City, a well known illustrator for *Frank Leslie's Illustrated Weekly Magazine*, drew eleven sketches that, engraved by another artist, became part of the published work. The Matthew Brady studio in Washington produced a handsome three-quarter length portrait of Dodge in his dress uniform to serve as the frontispiece. At the Smithsonian Institution, Dodge secured an engraved facsimile of a curiosity in his possession, a chronological chart in hieroglyphics, which he believed the only calendar ever produced by Plains Indians. He had sent this object to William Blackmore five years earlier in hopes that the latter would make use of it in his projected contribution to *The Plains*.[27] He secured photographs of four military men, Brigadier General George Crook, Brigadier General Nelson A. Miles, Colonel Ranald S. Mackenzie, and the late Lieutenant Colonel George A. Custer, for engraving and publication together as a full-page illustration entitled "Famous Indian Fighters." General Sherman may have provided advice and assistance as Dodge assembled this diverse material. The general was himself in correspondence with James E. Taylor about watercolor depictions of Civil War scenes then being prepared by the artist for display at army headquarters.[28] Moreover, as a long-time regent of the Smithsonian Institution, he possessed considerable influence there, and a request for cooperation from a member of his staff would have received prompt attention.

Of course, Dodge was himself already well known at the Smithsonian, having corresponded with its employees and associates on several subjects. In the summer of 1881 he secured its cooperation in preparing illustrations of Indian artifacts for use in the forthcoming book. Spencer Baird, the director, made available to him a room wherein the designs for six full-page plates, each to be printed in fifteen colors, were meticulously etched onto stone tablets. Preparing the color plates was a laborious undertaking. A group of objects to be represented together was first photographed. A photographic print was then supplied to an artist who, with the original objects set before him as models, etched the stone chromolithographic tablets, with special attention to coloring and detail. To print each of the six plates that were prepared in this manner, fifteen separate impressions of the same sheets would be required.[29] The process increased the publisher's production cost, but if the results were as striking as hoped, the six varicolored illustrations should greatly enhance the book's appeal and strengthen its sales.

When Worthington or an employee of his firm read through Dodge's manuscript text, the publisher was troubled by the more polemic passages, which in his judgment posed a threat to sales. Dodge's undisguised contempt for the Indian Bureau and the "professional humanitarians" who supported it would surely offend many clergymen, for the bureau was a darling of the religious press.[30] These concerns led Worthington to insist that Dodge delete from the forthcoming book its first chapters, a discussion of the Indian Question, as "too argumentative, and not within the scope of a work designed to furnish to the vast reading public of the United States a popular account of the daily life of our Indians."[31] Dodge complied, but only in part, for he was unwilling to deprive his work of its political thrust. He pruned a few passages dealing chiefly with legislative history, but the greater part of the argument he simply moved to the back of the book. If Worthington ever noticed the maneuver, he made no objection. He had already developed plans to market *Our Wild Indians* without reference to the debate over federal Indian policy.

General Sherman was in regular contact with Dodge as these arrangements were being made, for he remained in Washington, D.C., during almost the entire summer of 1881. Ordinarily he passed a few weeks away from the capital, at some out-of-the-way resort with members of his family or else on an official errand that combined duty with pleasure, but this year the summer passed under a cloud of apprehension. On July 2, while standing in a Washington railroad station, President Garfield was shot and seriously wounded by a disappointed office-seeker, Charles J. Guiteau. In the weeks that followed, Garfield lingered and then rallied, inspiring hopes of his eventual recovery, but he was unable to perform official duties. In the Cabinet and elsewhere, the question was debated whether the vice president, Chester A. Arthur, should assume pro tem the executive functions of the presidency. Meanwhile fears were expressed that an angry mob might attempt to wrest Guiteau from custody. A crisis of some kind seemed imminent, and federal troops in the vicinity were made aware that duty in the city at short notice was a possibility.

Upon learning that General Sheridan proposed to undertake a tour to Yellowstone National Park with his family and a group of dignitaries, on July 15 Sherman approved at once, wishing him a good spell of "rest and recreation." He noted only that certain of Sheridan's immediate subordinates ought to remain within easy reach in case of need. For himself, he continued, he planned to remain "pretty close" to the capital all year "to give me a good excuse for a trip to Texas, Arizona, and California early next spring."[32] Fluctuations in Garfield's condition forced Sherman to cancel commitments he had made months before to attend various civic gatherings. Late in August he warned Governor Hobart B. Bigelow of Connecticut that, since Garfield was then "in extreme danger," as commanding general "I, of all officials" must be on hand in Washington and so might not be able to attend two upcoming events, the Groton Heights Centennial celebration at New London, on September 6, and the New England Fair at Worcester, Massachusetts, the next day.[33] However, the daily bulletins reporting the condition of the president soon took on a more optimistic tone, and on September 1 Sherman left the city, accompanied by Dodge. The two officers took rooms at the Fifth Avenue Hotel in New York City, the general's preferred place of residence there, and made short excursions before continuing on to Groton and Worcester. At the latter place, Sherman delivered an address at the grave of a Revolutionary hero, General Artemas Ward. On the return trip he conferred at Governors Island, New York harbor, with Major General Winfield S. Hancock, commander of the Military Division of the Atlantic, before arriving back in Washington on September 15.[34] Four days later President Garfield, lying in great pain at Elberon, New Jersey, sank into unconsciousness and died.

Contrary to the fears of some, the public mood at news of this dire event was sorrowful but not vindictive. On the afternoon of September 21, all officers of the army and navy on duty in the capital escorted the remains of the late president from the Baltimore and Potomac depot to the capitol building, where he was to lie in state. Sherman and Rear Admiral E. T. Nichols led the procession, followed by approximately two hundred officers, in ranks of two on either side of the hearse, army on the right, navy on the left. Bands sounded a funeral march as the streets of Washington again filled with militia corps, marine and artillery brigades, and civic societies. Two days later a yet longer procession including Cabinet members, the Supreme Court, members of Congress, and diplomatic representatives escorted the body back to the depot, whence it was transported to Cleveland, Ohio, for interment. Officers of the army were ordered to wear badges of mourning on their left sleeves and their sword hilts for six months.[35]

The resumption of routine that followed these anxious weeks coincided with a familiar ritual at army headquarters: preparation of the annual report, in which Sherman forwarded to the secretary of war, with his own remarks, the accounts he had received from commanders of the several military departments and divisions. In the introductory statement, Sherman always confined himself to topics that concerned the army at large, shifting his emphasis as circumstances changed from year to year. In the report for 1881, he observed that serious war conditions no longer existed between the army and tribes of Indians. True, another Apache outbreak in Arizona Territory had not yet been brought under control, but the troubles with more northerly tribes, such as the unruly Utes of Colorado and the recalcitrant Sioux under Sitting Bull, seemed largely past. Good progress had been made in locating formerly hostile Indians on their proper reservations. Sherman thus devoted his main attention to other matters of concern, chiefly the deployment, efficiency, and morale of the army as the period of Indian wars approached its close.

The enlisted force of the regular army was still limited to 25,000 enlisted men, a number that in his view was far too low. He asserted with pride that "in physique, in intelligence, in patriotic devotion to the honor and glory of the country," the fighting men of the army "will compare favorably with any similar establishment on earth." Still, the effectiveness of this body was inhibited by the dispersion of its fighting units, the inadequate numerical strength of the individual companies that comprised it, and the abject conditions under which some of those units were obliged to perform their duties. Sherman argued "most earnestly" that, in view of the army's contributions to the current national prosperity, increased attention should be paid to fostering its continued well-being. He called on Congress to pass a law authorizing each of the 430 companies in the regular forces to enroll at least fifty privates, a measure that would strengthen current artillery and infantry units by twenty-five percent. Second, he described difficulties encountered by the army in its attempt to reduce the number of its 190 posts. Communities threatened with closure of facilities in their vicinities objected so bitterly to their political representatives that the status quo often prevailed, even though the presence of troops there was no longer necessary to protect life and property. To enable the army to commit its limited manpower more effectively, Sherman proposed the formation of an impartial board, with authority to study "the whole problem of internal defense" and to dispose of forts and installations that did not warrant permanent occupancy. By "permanent" he of course referred to the indefinite future, in which he could foresee no utilization of army forces that was materially different from what was being required of them at present. With this long-term perspective in view, he also recommended that a statute still in force forbidding the construction of permanent army buildings except by special approval of Congress should be repealed. "The time for temporary structures has passed away," he declared. Construction of substantial stone or brick would be "true economy," for it would benefit the health and morale of soldiers and ultimately cost less than the frequent repair and replacement required by wooden structures.[36]

Not mentioned in Sherman's annual report were other problems that concerned him from year to year because of their negative impact on army morale. One was the slow rate of promotion through the officers' ranks, particularly at the lower levels. During peacetime, promotion came almost invariably from seniority in rank alone. This was the system Sherman thought most equitable. It might dampen some youthful ambitions, but it need not do so unduly, since forms of recognition other than promotion—special assignments, regimental staff details, desirable postings, commendations, mention in reports and general orders—were available to reward demonstrated merit. Simply earning the good opinion of one's fellow officers ought to remain a powerful incitement. Sherman wished to instill a code of thought and conduct that joined all commissioned officers in dedication to patriotic duty and personal honor.[37] But maintaining that esprit de corps was made difficult by a second demoralizing influence, the political machination and favoritism that often led to the award of plum assignments and made possible the avoidance of hard or disagreeable service. For himself, the general shunned even the appearance of seeking preferment for friends and family members. Brigadier General Miles, a relation by marriage, had tested this determination during a campaign to secure his recent promotion and had found it firm, despite Sherman's acknowledgment of his military ability.[38] However, other persons were less scrupulous. For example, Major David G. Swaim was serving at the rank of major in the judge advocate general's department at the time his boyhood friend James A. Garfield was elected president. Within a few weeks, he was nominated for promotion to brigadier general, with authority over the entire Bureau of Military Justice.[39] The action was in Sherman's view a blow to the professional spirit of the army. However, he had no real power in the matter, for even nominating a man to fill one of the rare vacancies in the list of general officers was still not a privilege he enjoyed.

Armed conflict between the army and the Indians might be almost a thing of the past, but within the service itself conflicts raged between senior officers, giving the commanding general a full measure of concern. Some antipathies expressed themselves through legal proceedings, such as the costly and time-consuming court-martial that pitted two infantry colonels, David S. Stanley and William B. Hazen, against each other in 1880. Others grew from events during the Civil War that had led to protracted campaigns for vindication or revenge. For example, the dismissal during the war of two officers, Fitz-John Porter and Granville O. Haller, resulted in long and ultimately successful efforts by both men to win reinstatement.[40] Sherman himself was embroiled in controversy, the publication of his *Memoirs* in 1875 having spawned a progeny of counterstatements and verbal assaults.[41] But the form of competition most distressing to him in 1881 was that among deserving senior colonels and brigadier generals for promotion to the ranks immediately below his.

Many men still on the active list had served temporarily during the Civil War as general officers, leading either regular army units or volunteers. Through that field service, they had developed military abilities that in too many cases had not been adequately utilized in the years since. Brigadier General Pope, who had served with distinction as commander of the Department of the Missouri, craved promotion to major general, with command over one of the three geographical divisions—of the Pacific, the Missouri, or the Atlantic. Major General Schofield had held his rank since 1869 and richly merited a new command commensurate with it—namely, one of the divisions. On Schofield's return from a visit to Europe, agreed to in order to buy time for Sherman, something suitable must be found for him.[42] The current commander of the Division of the Pacific, Major General Irvin McDowell, had assumed the position when Schofield vacated it, at the urgent request of Generals Sherman and Grant, to become commandant of cadets at West Point. But McDowell now showed no inclination to retire and so permit Schofield to reoccupy his old post.[43] Meanwhile, other generals, including brigadiers Crook, O. O. Howard, Miles, and Augur, all had their ambitions, their adherents, and their entitlements to consideration. Talented younger officers such as Colonel Mackenzie clamored for promotion and deserved it.

The army was top-heavy with military talent and experience, with too small a command organization to utilize it fully. As one means of correcting the problem, Sherman supported the measure that had come before Congress in its most recent session—to make mandatory the retirement of army officers at the age of sixty-two. As another solution, more limited in its effect, he was considering the possibility of vacating his own command.[44] Such an action would enable him to continue performing whatever special duties the president might assign him, and it would also permit his heir-apparent, Sheridan, to vacate his Chicago headquarters and each of the three major generals—Hancock, McDowell, and Schofield—to command a military division.

Sherman was an efficient administrator with a detailed knowledge of the units under his authority and a keen sense of priorities that enabled him to marshal his limited forces effectively. But the problems posed by cronyism, political influence, and the conflicting claims of other generals he found frustrating, for they admitted no easy solution. To officers who wrote him complaining of their slow promotion or soliciting his advice as to the best strategy for obtaining nomination to a higher rank, he could offer little encouragement or assistance. To Pope, whom he admired, he counseled finding some friend to make his case, preferably an influential senator. To Mackenzie he wrote frankly that when he had last recommended him for promotion, he was "overruled with almost an admonition" not to meddle. To Colonel Henry J. Hunt, a veteran artillery officer, he explained that only mandatory retirement for age would break the logjam of officers who ranked him on the lineal list. As to himself, he added, "I am in favor of compulsory retirement . . . at 62 or 65, don't care which."[45]

In view of his frustration at the lack of authority to correct problems that he saw so clearly, Sherman must have welcomed opportunities to assist deserving officers under his command. For example, in April 1881 he wrote Sheridan pointing out the personal difficulties then being faced by Colonel Alexander McDowell McCook, his former aide-de-camp. McCook's wife was seriously ill, and since his regiment had a just claim for transfer to a more desirable station, such a move might well assist him at a critical time. A few months later Sheridan acted on this suggestion, and an appropriate exchange of regimental stations was made.[46] Though in a sense less personal, Sherman's action to promote the forthcoming book by Dodge was no less effective.

By December 1881 Dodge had received proof sheets for review, and Sherman also read through them. Shortly afterward he addressed the author a 1,500-word letter, intended for publication, in which he praised the book and commended it heartily to the American reading public. Whether he volunteered this favor or acceded to a request is not known, but Dodge was deeply grateful for his commander's willingness to associate his name with *Our Wild Indians*. The published work was "dedicated (by permission) to William Tecumseh Sherman, General of the Army of the United States."[47]

In his commendatory letter, Sherman addressed both of the book's aims: to present factual data about its subject in a readable manner and also to advocate reform. Emphasizing the author's years of contact with Indians, he characterized the work as "the record of your personal observations, with dates, facts and figures, which constitute the very best testimony available on the subject-matter treated of." In the greater part of the letter, he discussed Dodge's criticism of U.S. Indian policy. He began, in statesmanlike fashion, by observing that he could not agree with Dodge "and the world generally in accusing our ancestors and the General Government with a deliberate purpose to be unjust to, and to defraud these people." Dodge's blanket condemnation of Indian agents as incompetent or dishonest was also an exaggeration, he wrote,[48] though he did register agreement with the book's criticism of the reservation system as it was then administered. The cause of the Indian Bureau's failure lay "elsewhere, in the nature of things, rather than in a systematic desire to do wrong."

Sherman went on to point out a connection between certain Indian beliefs and customs described by Dodge and the reforms to Indian policy he advocated. In the general's view, the absence in the Indian of "a moral sense as connected with religion"—a principle Dodge had developed at some length[49]—demonstrated the folly of efforts by the Indian Bureau to induce changes in behavior through religious instruction. He was convinced that "the military authorities of the United States are better qualified to guide the steps of the Indian towards that conclusion which we all desire, self-support and peaceful relations with his neighbors, than the civilian agents, most of whom are members of some one of our Christian churches." Congress, of course, exercised jurisdiction over Indian policy. Sherman expressed confidence that its members would welcome *Our Wild Indians* since it would afford them new comprehension of the issues surrounding the government's relationship with American Indians, a subject "which has always been involved in honest doubt."

Concluding his diplomatic statement, Sherman commended the book to all thinking Americans:

> The subject-matter of your volume has dramatic interest to a large class of the American people, is fair and just in its reasoning, and liberal in its tone; and I therefore take great pleasure in recommending it to the military student and to the general reading public, as by far the best description extant of the habits, manners, customs, usages, ceremonies, etc., of the American Indian as he now is.
>
> You are hereby authorized to use my name as authority for its publication and circulation; and I invite all persons interested in the subject of the North

> American Indian to read this book carefully, to the end that public opinion may aid the national authorities to deal justly and liberally with the remnants of that race which preceded us on this continent.[50]

Dating his letter at Washington, D.C., January 1, 1882, the general appended his signature in his flowing hand. Reproduced in facsimile, that signature concluded the letter as published in *Our Wild Indians*, where it served as the introduction.

When printed, bound, and ready for distribution, *Our Wild Indians* was a strikingly attractive book, richly decorated in the style of the era. Its binding was of deep red cloth, illuminated with designs in black ink and gold foil. On the front cover, between pressed patterns at top and bottom, appeared an engraving in gold of an Indian war shield, with a tomahawk and war club arranged crosswise behind it. To the right was the book's short title, and below it were the facsimile signatures of the author and the general. The spine was decorated in gilt from top to bottom, with the names of Dodge and Sherman printed in letters of equal size. At bottom, just above another engraving that showed a mounted Indian about to thrust his lance at a fleeing buffalo, appeared in conspicuous capital letters the word "illustrated," announcing a major feature of the work's sales appeal. The twenty-five pages of illustrations, listed following a brief preface by Dodge, included two engravings on steel, seventeen on wood, and the six chromolithographic plates. In a note preceding an enumeration of the plates' contents, the publisher emphasized the minute accuracy of the impressions, "no expense or pains having been spared."[51] The text, crisply printed and generally free of compositorial errors, filled 653 pages following the front matter. A. D. Worthington's boastful characterization of the volume as "the most artistic and sumptuous book ever issued from the American press" was of course transparent advertiser's hyperbole.[52] Still, *Our Wild Indians* was a creditable production and a good value at the prices offered. The extra cloth edition described here, printed on tinted paper with sprinkled edges, was for sale at $3.50. A leather-bound "library" edition was priced at $4.00, and a plain cloth edition, printed on white paper and without the steel engravings and fifteen-color plates, cost $2.75. The book was not available for sale in bookstores; it could be purchased only directly by mail from the publisher or else through one of his agents. The initial print run was an optimistic 20,000 copies.

To generate public awareness of *Our Wild Indians*, Worthington sent 150 copies of the library edition to newspapers from New England to Virginia and as far west as Illinois, soliciting reviews. This marketing effort proved effective, for in the early months of 1882 the book was widely and favorably noticed in the public press. The *New York Herald* praised Dodge's "bright, fresh, and frank" writing style and "painstaking labor" in compiling so thorough a treatment. The *Chicago Inter-Ocean* assured its readers that *Our Wild Indians* would be "considered the standard authority on its subject, as it deserves to be." The *New York Commercial Advertiser* thought the book "as entertaining as a well told history, as charming as a well written essay, and as attractive as an intensely interesting novel." Chaplain George G. Mullins, in charge of education in the army, suggested in the *Army and Navy Register* that copies of the book be placed in the reading rooms of military posts.[53]

Within the army, an awareness of the book's merits was assured by an extended review in the *Army and Navy Journal*, the lead article in its issue for February 18. According to the anonymous reviewer, *Our Wild Indians* was "one of the most valuable contributions ever made to the study of Indian life and character."[54] Two weeks later, the editors remarked that "Washington is an excellent missionary field for Gen. [*sic*] Dodge to work in. If the public business could be suspended for a day, and the time devoted by the members of Congress and other public officials to reading his book we might save time and money in the end by promoting a peaceful end of our Indian problem."[55] (As in this instance, throughout the 1880s Dodge was often referred to erroneously as "General," even on occasion by Sherman himself.)

The next stage of Worthington's sales program was to canvass in the national capital for subscriptions from well-known persons to purchase the book. His agent for this purpose, a Reverend Wilson, applied himself energetically to the task. Early in March the *Army and Navy Journal* remarked, perhaps archly, that the clergyman's subscription list "bids fair to be a most valuable autograph album." The Reverend Wilson obtained signatures of the president, members of his Cabinet, General Sherman and various other high-ranking army officers, former President Grant, and other individuals of special note. Worthington had now enlisted the support of major newspapers and public personages whose approval of the work would likely stimulate sales. By late June, 8,000 copies of *Our Wild Indians* had been spoken for, and new orders were pouring in.[56]

Little is known of the roles Dodge and Sherman played in this stage of the publisher's sales campaign. A widely attended reception at the general's home on January 17 afforded opportunity for conversation about the forthcoming book, whose issue within a few more weeks was common knowledge.[57] By writing his introductory letter, Sherman had lent *Our Wild Indians* a character, if not quite official, then at least ratified by official recognition and support. Beyond that point he could hardly pass if he were to preserve the dignity of his office. For his own part, as author of the work Dodge kept in mind possible outlets for distribution, especially to army officers and enlisted men. He called on Brigadier General Rufus Ingalls, the quartermaster general, to discuss the possibility of the government's purchasing copies for distribution to army posts.[58] Confident that he had written a work of real usefulness, he made no secret of his desire for its wide circulation.

Dodge was well pleased with the physical product of Worthington's bookmaking, but the publisher's emphasis in advertisements on the book's design, illustrations, and generally exciting contents satisfied him less fully. He had conceived *Our Wild Indians* as also a polemic work, a passionate call for change. Some reviewers had recognized this aim, but as the marketing campaign continued, he was troubled at representations of the book as, in effect, an attractive parlor table book. For this reason, he drafted a separate discussion of the Indian Question as he viewed it, issuing the result as a pamphlet, aptly entitled *A Living Issue*. In the preface to that work, dated May 20, 1882, he described Worthington's early objections to the political views expressed in the manuscript that became *Our Wild Indians*. However, he wrote, "The facts and arguments set forth in that MSS. are (in my opinion) of too much importance to the honor of the Country to be lost; and I am in too much earnest to remain silent under all the wrongs and outrages heaped upon the Indian."[59] Dodge thus sought to turn the popularity of *Our Wild Indians* to some positive legislative effect. He signed the pamphlet's prefatory statement not as an army officer but as a plain citizen, Richard I. Dodge. Issued early in June, *A Living Issue* bore on its title-page a quoted statement by Senator George F. Edmunds, chairman of the Judiciary Committee, affirming the value to civilized society of "the courage of sincere, individual opinion" expressed on matters of public affairs.[60] Worthington, keeping his eye on the main chance, purchased a full-page advertisement for *Our Wild Indians* that appeared on the final page of the pamphlet.

Inspection Tours, South and North

During these same months, General Sherman was bringing into sharper focus his views on the proper deployment of U.S. troops along the southern and northern national borders in the western states and territories. Three great railroad routes now spanned the region: the Southern Pacific, along the border with Mexico, and two branches of the Union Pacific, across the central plains. Two more railroads, the Atlantic and Pacific across central New Mexico and Arizona, and the Northern Pacific, passing west from Duluth, Minnesota, to Portland, Oregon, and Puget Sound in Washington Territory, were nearing completion. All these projects were powerful facilitators of national development. "No person," Sherman had written recently, "who has not been across the continent by the several routes, can possibly comprehend the changes there."[61] In response to these changes, Sherman intended to refine a plan for the housing and transportation of army units within convenient reach of railroads along the nation's southwestern and northwestern frontiers. As he had suggested in his annual report for 1881, only forts already existing at points of strategic importance—as, for example, at the junction of several rail routes—should be made permanent, all others being disposed of at once or else maintained for a few more years and then abandoned. Eventually, with a line of permanent posts within easy each of the Southern Pacific and Northern Pacific roads, the army could guarantee the nation's security along its continental borders.

Sherman had last traversed these approximate routes only a few years before. In 1879 he had passed along the southern road on a journey with President Hayes, but that fast-paced trip did not allow him to perform the onsite inspections necessary to make recommendations. The northern route he had not seen since 1877, when the Northern Pacific extended only as far west as Bismarck, Dakota Territory.[62] In the coming year he hoped to ride the length of both railroads in order to consider the military requirements there for the last time in his career. As a preliminary to the southern tour, early in 1881 he dispatched Colonel Poe, his specialist in engineering, to study several army posts in Texas and New Mexico that he intended to visit. Poe's report, with recommendations, appeared in the public press shortly after his return from the assignment, prompting outcries of alarm from communities he had identified as no longer in need of a nearby military presence.[63]

In February 1882 preparations for the general's initial inspection tour began in earnest. Post and departmental commanders along the itinerary received due notice, and railroad officials were asked what accommodations they could supply in regard to equipment and scheduling. Some of the latter correspondence Sherman conducted himself, asking for no special arrangements other than the use of a single car that could be left at railroad sidings at a convenient distance from posts he would need to reach by wagon. He volunteered to pay regular train fare for himself and his party, which would consist of Colonel Morrow, Colonel Poe, Poe's daughter Winifred, and his own daughter Lizzie. He noted, however, that the government reimbursed the travel expenses of army officers at the miserly rate of eight cents per mile. Most of his correspondents responded graciously to this tacit request, extending the privilege of their roads without charge. Sherman planned to devote the month of March to Texas, April to New Mexico and Arizona Territories, and a few days in May to California before returning to Washington.

Almost from its inception, the borderlands tour took on a public character. Demonstrations of good feeling greeted the celebrity general as he passed through these remote regions. In Texas he was feted at forts Clark, Ellis, and Bliss and welcomed exuberantly by the local citizenry. In speeches before the city fathers of San Antonio and El Paso, he expressed gratified wonder at the growth in those places since his last visit, in 1871. From El Paso he and his party made a 250-mile excursion on the Mexico Central Railroad, then under construction. Earlier, near Fort Clark, they had watched a Southern Pacific construction crew laying track toward New Orleans at the rate of two miles per day.[64] Truly, settlements along the border with Mexico were being linked together at railroad speed.

Residents of the towns west of El Paso greeted the Sherman train with sometimes alarming enthusiasm. On the party's arrival by wagon at Tombstone, Arizona Territory, a "cowboyish-looking individual" rode up and asked whether the general was present. Assured that he was, he raised his pistol and fired two shots in succession, the signal for a cacophonous welcome that included fireworks, ringing anvils, and discharge of guns of all types. That evening the celebration continued with a bonfire in the main street, an outdoors dinner, and a brief speech by Sherman.[65] The tour reached its end point in San Francisco, California, on April 23. At the Presidio, headquarters of the Division of the Pacific, Sherman conferred with General McDowell, attended a reception, reviewed the troops, and visited army colleagues before running a gamut of social engagements in the city proper. One of these, at the Poodle Dog restaurant, was organized in his honor by fifteen old friends, companions during his residence in San Francisco more than three decades earlier as a military officer and later a banker.[66]

Clearly the ten-week tour, which concluded in Washington on May 14, combined the official with the personal for Sherman. During its progress he addressed to Robert T. Lincoln, the secretary of war, a series of letters that exhibited this same hybrid quality, combining general description of travel and sightseeing with other matter, the results of his official inquiries. In the latter passages he set forth in plain terms and in considerable detail his analysis of military needs, together with recommendations for action by the secretary. Along the Texas frontier he identified six key posts: on the lower Rio Grande, forts Duncan, McIntosh, and Sam Houston; on the more northerly western section, Fort Davis, Camp Rice (later redesignated Fort Hancock), and Fort Bliss. He urged a $200,000 appropriation from Congress for further construction at these locations, recommending the abandonment of all intervening forts and other facilities. In New Mexico and Arizona he saw need for only four posts along the southern frontier, Forts Grant, Huachuca, Apache, and Thomas. To preserve and strengthen these, he recommended the expenditure of another $200,000, noting, however, that once General Crook had finished subduing the Apaches, the two latter forts could likely also be abandoned. Sherman thus accomplished his aim of identifying a line of posts within easy reach of the Southern Pacific Railroad that, without inordinate expense, would "put that whole frontier in a good and permanent condition of defense."[67]

Not long after his return to army headquarters, the general traveled to Detroit, Michigan, to attend a reunion of the Society of the Army of the Potomac, but then on his arrival back in the capital he expressed a resolve to stay put. "Got enough travelling," he brusquely informed a reporter; "got to stay at home and get to work."[68] Not mentioned in this interview was his eager anticipation of the second reconnaissance tour, which he expected to begin early in the fall. Although not yet made public, his plans for the northwestern excursion were already well advanced. Its official purpose was identical with that of the recently completed journey, to inspect military posts along the Northern Pacific Railroad so as to identify locations that would remain essential to the nation's permanent defense. The approaching completion of the Northern Pacific would make the examination far more convenient than it had been five years before. The road was now in service past Bozeman, Montana Territory, adjacent to Fort Ellis, and was under construction through difficult terrain toward Missoula, not far from another army post.

The late-summer tour would follow the railroad as far as Fort Ellis, but from that point it would involve travel by wagon, on horseback, and perhaps even afoot through the region where the construction crews had not yet penetrated. Sherman planned to retrace a part of the route he had followed in his 1877 reconnaissance expedition. From Fort Ellis he would proceed south, to renew acquaintance with Yellowstone National Park, then west across the continental divide to the Bitter Root valley. Passing along that valley north to Missoula, he would follow the old

Mullan wagon road that led west to Fort Coeur d'Alene, in Idaho Territory. The cross-country portion of the tour would be rugged, but Sherman relished the prospect of travel through the semiwilderness. Three official acquaintances, Morrison R. Waite, chief justice of the Supreme Court, and associate justices John Marshall Harlan and Horace Gray, had expressed interest in accompanying him. He promised himself satisfaction in introducing these distinguished easterners to the rigors of army-style travel.[69]

Sherman's plans for the second inspection tour were suddenly overset when, in conversation with Robert T. Lincoln on June 5, he learned that the secretary had accepted an invitation from Sheridan to join another expedition of his own to the Yellowstone National Park and points in its vicinity. That the nation's two highest ranking army officers should both be absent from their posts for weeks at a time was not to be thought of, and Sherman decided at once to postpone his northwestern journey until the following summer. After all, he had done his share of traveling in the months just past, and Sheridan's idea of introducing Lincoln to some of the undeveloped territory under his authority seemed wise in view of the close working relationship the two men would need to sustain in future years. Following an exchange of letters with Judge Waite to confirm the postponement of their journey until the summer of 1883, just after the adjournment of the Supreme Court's spring term, Sherman telegraphed Sheridan wishing him a good trip. He concluded this message with a statement that, while not unanticipated, was of considerable significance to both men and to the army generally. He had begun shaping his private affairs, he wrote, "so as to enable you to take my place" as General of the Army before Congress convened in December 1883.[70] From the date of this telegram, Sherman's inspection tour of the northwestern forts thus formed part of a planned sequence of events that would culminate in his retirement from the army on his sixty-fourth birthday, February 8, 1884.

By June it was clear that, when approved by Congress, the annual army appropriation bill would likely include a clause mandating the retirement from active service of commissioned officers upon their reaching the age of sixty-four. Sherman welcomed the development for several reasons, not least because the first general officer to be retired under the law would be Major General McDowell, the dog-in-the-manger commander of the Division of the Pacific. His departure would make possible Schofield's taking up his old command, placing an officer of appropriate rank in charge of all three military divisions. That arrangement should last out Sherman's tenure in office, when the vacancy created by Sheridan's departure from the Division of the Missouri would initiate another round of competition among the present brigadiers. As he wrote a departmental commander in late June, he hoped to "gracefully retire" with the military mosaic all in place, the divisions under major generals and the departments within them under brigadier generals or senior colonels.[71]

Assignment's End

It had been known for several months that Sherman would soon lose a popular member of his personal staff, Colonel Dodge, who was in line for promotion to a regular colonelcy and the command of a regiment. At the beginning of 1882, Dodge stood sixth in seniority among lieutenant colonels of infantry,[72] but by June several resignations had resulted in his imminent advancement, even without operation of the anticipated compulsory retirement law. The retirement on June 22 of Colonel Daniel Huston, Fifth Infantry, promoted Lieutenant Colonel John D. Wilkins to the command of that crack regiment, which had distinguished itself under its former colonel, now Brigadier General Nelson A. Miles. It was widely assumed that Wilkins would retire almost immediately, leaving Dodge to command the Fifth, as he hoped to do.[73] However, the resignation on June 26 of another officer, Colonel Thomas H. Wood, Eleventh Infantry, made Dodge eligible for promotion to that command, headquartered at Fort Sully, Dakota Territory.[74] At first he was inclined to apply for transfer back to the Fifth, but General Sherman dissuaded him, and presently he agreed.[75] President Arthur promptly forwarded his nomination for the position to Congress, but since the confirmation of appointments such as his was done in leisurely fashion, several more weeks would probably elapse before he could be ordered to join his new regiment.[76] Until then, he remained officially a member of the general's personal staff.

Sherman had received recommendations, and even some direct applications, to fill the anticipated vacancy among his aides-de-camp, when in mid-July he received a letter from General Pope, who named as a worthy candidate Dodge's friend Captain George M. Randall, Twenty-third Infantry. Responding to Pope, Sherman agreed that Randall's good standing was well deserved, he having "rendered a large share of that very kind of frontier service which ought to be rewarded, and which I have endeavored to do during my term of office." Still, he wrote, he had decided some time before that in times of peace like these the General of the Army required no more than three or perhaps four aides. He had let it be known that, barring unforeseen conditions, he would no longer fill vacancies on his staff. Colonels Tidball, Morrow, and Dodge would be his last appointments.[77]

Once Dodge joined his regiment in Dakota Territory, he was likely to remain on the north central plains for some time. Accordingly, in the interim before his confirmation, Sherman granted him permission to visit his family. He traveled first to North Carolina, where he saw his sisters and ailing mother, and then to the flat he maintained for Julia and Fred at 110 West 125th Street, New York City. On August 11 a telegram reached him there, containing the first order he received at his new rank. He had been designated a member of a blue-ribbon court-martial that would meet ten days hence at Newport Barracks, Kentucky, headquarters of the Department of the South.[78] The case was one of particular concern to Sherman, who remained determined to combat political influence and favoritism in the issuance of army appointments and assignments to duty.[79]

The accused officer, Major Joseph H. Taylor, was a respected West Point graduate with a solid record, but he would appear before the court to answer charges of conduct prejudicial to good order and military discipline. At the time of the alleged offense, Taylor occupied a responsible position, as assistant adjutant general for the Department of the South. On July 29 an order was issued by the Adjutant General's Office directing his transfer to the Department of the Platte to serve there in the same capacity. But having brought his family with him to Newport Barracks and made arrangements to remain in that location, he did not wish to move to Omaha.[80] On July 31 he addressed a letter to the adjutant general, Brigadier General Richard C. Drum, informing him that he could see no reason for the transfer other than to gratify the wishes of a junior officer who wished to remain in Washington. He informed Drum that he had asked the senators of his home state, Kentucky, to exert their influence to have the order revoked. Taylor assured General Drum that he had no wish to conceal his endeavor to enlist this political intervention.[81] Nevertheless, his appeal to the senators contravened a directive issued by Sherman forbidding evasive actions of this sort.[82] A military trial to consider the infraction was thus called for, and the judgment of the court, under the presidency of Brigadier General Augur, was awaited with interest since Taylor's behavior could be considered a test case. Private and semiofficial correspondence among army officers often dealt with dissatisfactions such as Taylor had expressed, and as all knew, the practice of rallying political support was pervasive. Inasmuch as Taylor's letter to General Drum was open and above board, exactly how reprehensible was his misconduct?

In sessions over three days, the court considered two sets of charges and specifications against the accused officer. To the first charge, that his correspondence with the senators was prejudicial to military discipline, Taylor held that his action was not subject to trial under the Articles of War, and the court sustained him. To the second, that the letter to General Drum manifested "contempt and disregard" for his orders and so was conduct prejudicial to good order and military discipline, he pled not guilty, but the court disagreed. Wisely, however, it recommended a light sentence, that Taylor was "[t]o be reprimanded in orders by the General of the Army." Sherman issued his public rebuke on August 31, Taylor reported to his new duty station,[83] and there the test case—but not abuses of influence more flagrant than the court had considered—ended.

Following the Taylor trial, Dodge returned to Washington for a few days before departing for Fort Snelling, Minnesota, headquarters of the Department of Dakota, where he was to report to his new commander, Brigadier General Alfred H. Terry. Sherman was himself about to depart with his family and the Tidballs for a few days' relaxation at Lake Winnipesaukee, New Hampshire. During his final days of service at army headquarters, Dodge no doubt expressed to the general his gratitude for various good offices, in the preparation of *Our Wild Indians* and in other ways. To his satisfaction, Sherman promised to make him a member of the following summer's official tour as far as Fort Missoula, at the western border of the Department of Dakota.[84] It had become the general's custom to address letters of thanks to departing members of his staff for whom he felt special regard. In full, the letter he wrote to Dodge appears below:

Headquarters Army of the United States,
Washington D. C., Sept. 2d, 1882.

Dear Dodge:

When McCook was promoted to the 6th Infantry, from my staff, I endeavored to frame a General Order congratulating him on his promotion, and thanking him for his services as A.D.C. on my staff, but the more I thought of it, it seemed tame and unprofitable;[85] for peace does not afford those opportunities for personal distinction which war does, and the duties of an A.D.C. in peace are, as you have discovered, more social than military. I do, however, congratulate you on your promotion to so good a regiment as the 11th, which is serving near the Indians, our only enemy, and where you can have many opportunities to apply your extensive knowledge of these aborigines, which you have already gained by a long experience with them. I shall endeavor during my remaining short period of command to strengthen existing companies by more "privates"; to encourage company officers to stay with their proper commands, and to collect our soldiers in larger garrisons at strategic points of the country where good comfortable permanent barracks should be built.

To reach this most desirable conclusion you can, at your new post of duty, aid me quite as much, if not more than if you remained here in Washington. Nevertheless I am none the less obliged for the assistance you have afforded me by your familiarity with the personnel of the Army, and the usages and customs which have grown up on our frontiers, as well as by the cheerfulness and good feelings you have inspired about you.

Wishing you eminent success in your new rank and sphere of action, I am

Sincerely your friend,
W. T. Sherman,
General[86]

The receipt of this congratulatory letter brought Dodge's tour of duty in Washington to a happy end. About to begin a new stage in an army career that now extended over thirty-four years, he boarded the first in a succession of trains that took him to Saint Paul, Minnesota, adjacent to Fort Snelling, and then to Pierre, Dakota Territory, not far from his new posting. On September 12 he arrived at Fort Sully, headquarters of the Eleventh Infantry, where on the next day he assumed command of the post and the regiment.[87]

23

At Headquarters and in the Field

Dodge's new duty station was situated on an elevated plain near the east bank of the Missouri River, approximately twenty-five miles north of Pierre, which had grown rapidly since the completion of the Chicago and Northwestern Railroad to that point two years before. Originally known as Fort Pierre, the town was the point of embarkation for stage and freight lines to the Black Hills, approximately 160 miles west. Fort Sully, established in 1863 by Brigadier General Alfred Sully during a campaign against the Sioux Indians, had remained a fixture in the army's effort to control the tribe.[1] The Sioux Reservation, encompassing more than one-third the territory of present-day South Dakota and much additional land to the north, extended west from the opposite shore of the Missouri River.[2] A subpost, Fort Bennett, adjoined the Cheyenne River Indian Agency nine miles north of Fort Sully. During the years of most serious Indian agitation, the threat of violence at the agency had necessitated maintaining a larger garrison at Fort Bennett than at the main post, but those conditions no longer prevailed. Fort Sully now housed four companies of troops, and Fort Bennett, one—all of the Eleventh Infantry.

Like other frontier posts, Fort Sully bore a double responsibility, to protect residents of its vicinity from Indians and other malefactors and, reciprocally, to help ensure that the treaty rights of the Indians were respected and that they were not victimized in other ways. Owing to the influx of settlers, the latter duties often devolved on troops at the fort. Stock ranches dotted the area, which was said to include "the finest agricultural land in the north-west, especially for the growth of wheat and other grains."[3] An effort to induce the Sioux to permit homesteading on their treaty lands had been rebuffed, but would-be farmers were disposed to take federal law into their own hands. As a result, during the summer of 1881 two companies of troops from Fort Sully were temporarily stationed at Pierre as a precaution against attempts

Fort Sully, Dakota Territory. Courtesy U.S. Army Military History Institute.

to defy the law.[4] The situation must have recalled to Dodge the army's operations to repel incursions of citizens into Indian Territory.

Dodge's duties as post commander were essentially the same as at Cantonment and the numerous other western forts where he had served in that capacity. Only two features of this assignment significantly distinguished it from those in his earlier career. First, he had never yet been stationed in the Department of Dakota, northernmost of the four departments that policed the Great Plains. Extremes of weather were endemic through the region, but they were worst in this country. Like many career officers of the line, Dodge had begun to suffer from rheumatic joints, the result of prolonged exposure to inclement conditions. How his constitution would react to a climate where winter temperatures dropped to minus forty degrees Fahrenheit for nights at a time was a matter for anxious doubt, since he was otherwise in good condition. In January 1883 he informed his wife that the weather had been "absolutely stunning" of late. Later in the year he assured her that the low temperatures "would kill off half New York."[5]

The second new feature of Dodge's posting was the concurrent command of a full regiment. The degree of responsibility was nothing new in itself, for during his nine years as a lieutenant colonel he had often commanded the Twenty-third Infantry in the absence of Colonel Davis, sometimes for months at a time. However, the continuing discipline and development of the Eleventh Infantry was now his to oversee. Just as a company of soldiers took its tone from the captain who led it, so a regiment bore the impress of its field officers, especially its colonel. Dodge looked forward to establishing a working relationship with the officers and men who would come under his leadership. Almost a decade of opportunity to make an impact lay before him, for according to the newly enacted law he was eligible to continue on active duty until his sixty-fourth birthday, May 19, 1891.

After almost a month at Fort Sully, Dodge summarized his impressions in a letter to General Sherman. No doubt mindful of Major Taylor's recent comeuppance in the court-martial proceedings, he began by assuring the general that "I would not presume to address you a personal letter, but for your request that I do so."[6] The prefatory disclaimer was more than mere punctilio, for he at once brought up a matter of administrative policy in which, as colonel of the Eleventh Infantry, he felt himself aggrieved. In a respectful but forthright manner he reminded Sherman of an earlier conversation in which the latter had mentioned the possibility of an exchange of stations between the Eleventh and the Twenty-first regiments of infantry. "Recent papers," he continued, stated that the Tenth, then stationed at Fort Wayne, Michigan, would exchange with the Twenty-first, then at Vancouver Barracks, Washington Territory, probably in the fall of 1883.[7] "I don't think that will be fair," he wrote. "According to received Army opinion, 'the Lakes' [for example, Fort Wayne] is the best station, Vancouver the next best. It does not seem just to the other Reg[imen]ts that the 10th & 21st should oscillate between the two best stations."

Advocating the claim of his new regiment, Dodge pointed out that the Eleventh had done hard service in the Department of Dakota for the past six years and in Texas and the Indian Territory for seven years before that. In his view, "no other regiment has a better claim for second choice"—meaning, apparently, second after the Twenty-first, which had served in Oregon, Washington, and Idaho for ten years and in Arizona for three years before that.[8] Dodge admitted that his informal appeal had a personal side. The recent death of his mother had severed the last of his close ties to the east, he wrote, and having always desired service in the Columbia River region he wished for it now more than ever. In what remained of his career, he hoped to accomplish "something besides mere guard duty," as at Fort Sully. However, lest he grow importunate, he dismissed the subject with a quotation applicable to soldiers on guard: "They also serve who only stand and wait."[9]

Dodge pronounced his regiment "a fine one" but in need of new blood and the salutary experience of service outside the confines of a post. The companies he had seen thus far betrayed the ill effects of a "long tour of mere guard duty, at posts so small that officers & men could not well be spared for those scouts, marches, & hunting expeditions which are absolutely necessary to teach officers & men *field duty*—to take care of themselves under all possible circumstances of danger, whether from the elements, or from human enemies." Moreover, many of his officers were permanently disabled and ought to be retired. Dodge went on to describe the rapid pace of change in the vicinity of Fort Sully, relating his comments to the debate over Indian policy that had engaged him and Sherman in the months surrounding publication of *Our Wild Indians*. Not only was the region being settled by outsiders, but Indians residing in the area also seemed anxious to establish farms and begin following "the white man's road." He confessed his amazement at the progress these people had made through adopting customs of the American culture that impinged on them. Optimistically, he looked forward to an end of federal mismanagement:

> This whole Indian business is now so easy of solution, that it seems strange that no statesman can be found, to place it in its proper light before the people. Every senator seems to regard the Indian from the standpoint he gained while a boy at school. The truth is that the Indian has progressed in his way as rapidly as the white, & all the old-fashioned notions & arrangements are now obsolete. A little common sense, fair dealing & courage enough to fight the Indian Ring, are all that can be wanted to settle the Indian problem forever. So rapid is the progress of these people that though constantly studying & writing about them for years, I as constantly find myself behind. And this progress is due not to schools churches or instruction but to their enforced contact with whites, & their inability from lack of game, to live their old usual style of life.[10]

Firsthand experience confirmed the thesis Dodge had advanced in print: that in a few years the formerly "savage" inhabitants of the plains would be ready for productive citizenship.

Sherman responded to this thoughtful letter, but what he wrote has not survived,[11] nor has additional correspondence between the two men during the next few months, if indeed there was any. Each was fully occupied in his own sphere of action, Dodge adjusting to his new command and Sherman leading the army while quietly making arrangements to end his active service.

During his assignment in Washington, Dodge had been without Joe and Laura, his domestic servants, who returned to Kansas and lived on a small farm they owned there. However, shortly after his arrival at Fort Sully they rejoined him. Laura was, in his estimate, "an excellent hand always ready for work, not a lazy bone in her body."[12] With her assistance, he established himself comfortably in the post commander's residence. Social calls and evenings at the home of the commanding officer were staples of the modest menu of entertainments at frontier posts, and on these occasions he became better acquainted with the officers' wives and families. A complimentary supper and dance arranged in his honor on December 5 marked his progress in winning the regard of his subordinates, who had served for twelve years under their former commander, Colonel Wood.[13] But in truth the gregarious Colonel Dodge was finding garrison life at Fort Sully a bit dull thus far.

He confided to Julia that neither the officers nor the ladies of the post entirely suited him. Though "good duty men," the officers were "very poor sticks socially," almost all being married and with their wives in residence. As to the women, with few exceptions they were "the most inveterate tattlers I ever knew . . . no *scandal*, but simply *tattle*. Some of the women seem to know what everybody has for dinner every day." Dodge had formed close friendships with several officers and ladies of the Twenty-third Infantry, but that closeness had not yet developed with those of the Eleventh. More satisfying were his occasional jaunts, accompanied by Joe, an orderly, and perhaps a fellow officer or two, in quest of grouse or rabbits. "These rabbits are delicious," he wrote Julia, adding that he and Ida "ate a whole one at dinner today & quarrelled over the remnants."[14] That Dodge sat at table with his servants' daughter no doubt provoked comment, but this was not the only instance of his unconventional behavior. On occasion he also shared a meal with an enlisted man—to traditionalists, a serious breach of decorum.

More actively than most field officers of his time, Dodge interested himself in the welfare and discipline of the private soldiers and noncommissioned officers of his command. Though far from lax in his exercise of authority, he took satisfaction in the low rates of occupancy in the guardhouses at posts where he was stationed, the result he believed of fair and impartial treatment. So far as practicable, he ensured that the men were assigned duties not always wanting in interest and variety.[15] He supported initiatives for amusement once the day's drill and other duty were completed. He permitted hunting parties, both to diversify company menus and to ensure the familiarity of his men with terrain in the vicinity. He promoted athletic events, including competition by a post baseball team, the Sully Blues, and he encouraged visits to the post library. On the evening of February 20, 1883, he surely attended the inaugural performance of the Fort Sully Minstrel and Variety Troupe, comprised entirely of enlisted men, which played to an overflow house. A published account of this entertainment predicted performances monthly, "if the fortunes of war permit."[16]

During the winter and spring of 1882–1883, Dodge's chief initiative as regimental and post commander was to encourage his men in target practice on the post's firing ranges, at 200, 300, and 600 yards. Stimulated by publication of Colonel Theodore T. S. Laidley's *Course of Instruction for Rifle Firing* (1879), a program for improvement in marksmanship was part of the army's effort to strengthen the professional competence of its troops.[17] Captain Stanhope E. Blunt, ordnance officer for the Department of Dakota, was an active participant in the movement. He administered a system of testing to certify levels of accomplishment, and he also organized an annual tournament at Fort Snelling wherein representatives from posts in the department vied for gold medals. Two of the four medals awarded in 1883 went to men from Fort Sully, and that year the overall performance of the Eleventh Infantry was the best in the entire army.[18] Of course, skill at rifle firing was an acquirement that had long interested Dodge. On May 17 he scored an average of eighty-three and one-third percent at the three standard distances, earning the right to wear the official Marksman's buttons.[19] Not long afterward he boasted to William C. Church that he was "the only Colonel in the U. S. A[rmy]" so honored.[20]

That spring Dodge came into arm's-length official contact with General Sherman as the result of a letter he wrote drawing attention to a problem that beset his regiment: namely, the low number of officers listed on its roster who were actually available for service with it. Forwarded through official channels, once the letter reached army headquarters it elicited a testy reaction. Dodge had pointed out that of thirty-four officers assigned to the Eleventh Infantry, only sixteen were on hand for company duty. Four others were physically present at their posts, but owing to one declared infirmity or another, they were performing "light duty" only, thereby creating an embarrassment and a source of dissatisfaction.[21] General Sheridan noted in his endorsement that of the remaining thirteen, only one officer not serving with his company could possibly be ordered back to it. This was Captain Warren C. Beach, the commander of Company D, who for more than a year had been assigned "temporarily" to a comfortable station, the headquarters of the Department of the East in New York harbor.

Dodge's letter with its endorsements touched on three areas of abuse by officers that especially provoked Sherman: not serving with their regiment; avoiding regular duty or obtaining sick leave on flimsy pleas of illness; and obtaining comfortable assignments through political influence.[22] Though fluent in the formal parlance of official interchanges, the general was not averse to delivering his opinions "with the bark on." He commented on the situation to Secretary Robert T. Lincoln, "inviting his attention to the fact that by his orders Capt. W. C. Beach, 11th Infantry, has been for a year on temporary duty at Genl. Hancock's Headquarters. There is no earthly reason for his being there except for his personal convenience – his father residing at Brooklyn. Being Capt. of a company of infantry[,] he should be with it."

As to the four officers who seemed to be accepting only those assignments they found congenial, Sherman exercised his authority as the official empowered to regulate the discipline and control of the army. He directed the adjutant general to inform all post commanders that "when officers are ordered to be at their posts for light duty, it is for the Com'dg officer, with the advice of his post Surgeon, to determine what that light duty shall be. The officer must obey orders, and he is not to be the judge of what constitutes 'light duty.'" Having delivered himself of these injunctions, Sherman ended on a sardonic note: "If we cannot have able-bodied officers for duty, we must get along the best we can with the halt and the lame."[23]

The effort to suppress political meddling with the assignments given well-connected army officers was a never-ending struggle. In the present case, a War Department order dated April 26 directed Captain Beach to rejoin his company at Fort Sully. However, a few days later the *Army and Navy Journal* announced that under recently issued new orders, Beach would continue as a member of General Hancock's staff. Quite possibly the influence of Beach's father, a prominent lawyer active in the Democratic Party that had nominated Hancock for the presidency in 1880, had caused the original directive to be revoked. Beach remained on duty at New York harbor until March 1885, when at last a new order to rejoin his company held firm, the intervening death of William Augustus Beach having deprived the captain of a powerful advocate. However, by that time the younger Beach had married a wealthy heiress, so one year later he resigned his commission.[24]

After his arrival at Fort Sully, Dodge remained in regular contact with his publisher in regard to sales of *Our Wild Indians*. A. D. Worthington had invested heavily in the volume, but he was confident that the attractiveness of the product and the sales momentum created by his marketing campaign would yield a rich reward. Following the initial effort to build public awareness of the book, he next sought to reach grassroots clients through saturation advertising. In a mass mailing to the editors of, he claimed, some 1,700 "country" newspapers, he offered to each a leather-bound copy of *Our Wild Indians* in return for placement in that newspaper's columns of an advertisement whose text he supplied. By his account, no fewer than 1,460 editors accepted this offer and so printed in their pages a notice that began "WANTED! AGENTS! AGENTS! AGENTS! for Gen. Dodge's bran' new book." With characteristic disregard for literal truth, Worthington informed prospective door-to-door solicitors that "*thousands of* EMINENT MEN" had subscribed for the work, the forty-third thousand copies of which were then in press. Persons interested in collecting additional orders were invited to contact the publisher in order to receive an informative circular that further described the book.[25] That four-page pamphlet, printed on an extra-large sheet, heralded *Our Wild Indians* as "A Standard, Superb Work of Great Value and Interest."[26]

In October 1882 Worthington assured Dodge that he was determined to give the work "such a lift as no book has ever received." He had sent out copies of the circular "by the cartload," he wrote, but his corps of agents, many of them young boys, had not yet produced quite the results he had anticipated. The reasons for the shortfall eluded him, especially since persons who did place orders were well satisfied. He thought perhaps "there have been so many cheap miserable blood & thunder Indian books sold" that the public had lost interest in the subject. In any case, he still hoped to sell at least 20,000 copies, which would enable him to recoup his investment. Meanwhile, he added, he was glad to learn from Dodge of some likely new outlets.[27]

Following up on his earlier interview with the quartermaster general, Dodge proposed to that official that 150 copies of *Our Wild Indians* be purchased by the federal government for distribution to army posts. His suggestion, forwarded with a favorable endorsement to the secretary of war, prompted an inquiry to Worthington as to what price he would require for that number of copies. The publisher submitted a bid he thought low, but in the end Secretary Lincoln decided against the expenditure. Dodge was informed in November that the secretary did not "feel justified in authorizing the purchase of *this* book."[28] No reason was given, and the emphasized "this" remains problematical. Secretary Lincoln may have considered *Our Wild Indians* too openly political in its approach to warrant patronage—and tacit approval—by an agency of the federal government. Though surprised, neither Dodge nor Worthington were much disappointed at the negative outcome. The publisher liked Dodge's suggestion that he seek to enlist the civilian traders at army posts across the country as agents. He would "go for them red hot," he wrote. Judging from Dodge's success in selling copies through the post trader at Fort Sully, Worthington thought thirty to fifty copies apiece might be worked off at other posts, a sales response out of all proportion to the modest purchase the secretary of war had declined to make.[29]

By the end of 1882, 18,072 copies of *Our Wild Indians* had been sold, yielding Dodge a goodly harvest of royalty payments that totaled approximately one-half his annual salary.[30] Worthington was within range of breaking even on his investment and now hoped for sales of perhaps 22,000 copies, but he was no longer very optimistic. Sales were "really about over," he informed the author on December 30. It was some satisfaction to receive praises of the book from many quarters, but now the publisher was short of funds. Protesting that he had done everything possible to market the work but had spent too much on it from the beginning, he asked Dodge to consider foregoing his royalty payments on future copies sold. When Dodge declined, sending along another order from the Fort Sully post trader and observing that Worthington seemed to him too pessimistic, the publisher assured him that any hopes of many more sales were doomed to disappointment.[31] Nevertheless, in April he declared his intention to mount one more campaign on a new front, one he had considered a lost cause. He would "salt" the religious press, he said, and take his chances, for at this late date the hostility of editors could do little harm.[32] Whether by that means or, more likely, through the activity of copublishers he enlisted in Chicago, Cleveland, Saint

Louis, and San Francisco, in the weeks that followed sales figures soared and swept away Worthington's mood of hopelessness. By August 1 a total of 30,149 copies had been sold, and the renewed surge in orders had not yet abated. *Our Wild Indians* was a resounding sales triumph.[33] Some time afterward, Worthington assured Dodge that it had "'taken the cake' from every other 'Indian book' published in the last 30 or 40 years."[34]

In September 1882 Dodge's celebrity as the author of *Our Wild Indians* led an editor for *Youth's Companion*, a popular weekly, to solicit contributions from him that drew upon his knowledge of Indian life. The editor, William H. Rideing, informed him that he had quoted a few paragraphs from *Our Wild Indians* in a forthcoming work of his own, *Boys in the Mountains and the Plains*, "giving, of course, full credit." Rideing suggested a series of perhaps three papers of 2,000 words each, to be entitled "The Boys of the Sioux" or some other tribe. Observing that *Youth's Companion* was a family magazine and not aimed specifically at children, he mentioned that the prose style "need not differ at all from that which you usually write" and offered a payment of thirty-five dollars per article.[35]

Dodge was intrigued by this proposal, which presented him an opportunity to prepare in shortened form the kind of work he and Blackmore had been considering as a sequel to *The Plains*. He wrote back that when his schedule permitted, he would certainly prepare some pieces that would give "a true picture of the condition of the Indians." Rideing responded at once, expressing eagerness to receive the material but also sounding a note of caution, that articles of a "controversial nature" would not be suitable for a magazine like *Youth's Companion*. Instead, "We hope that you will give us thrilling incidents & adventures and all that goes to make up *life* among the Indian boys and girls."[36]

Taking as his cue this formulation of the magazine's editorial preferences, Dodge prepared four installments and part of a fifth for a series he entitled "Indian Boys and Girls." He did his best to supply the kind of subject matter Rideing had asked for. Near the end of the first article, he explained that in future issues he would "give to the white boys and girls of our country an accurate account of Indian boys & girls in their natural savage condition." However, in attempting to realize that aim, he focused instead on describing the most effective means of enabling the Indian to develop from savagery toward civilization.[37] Struggling to achieve a compromise between his own inclinations and the requirements of *Youth's Companion*, he expressed hope that civilized children would someday use the knowledge he shared with them to help ameliorate the condition of the Indians.

Not surprisingly, Dodge's articles did not find favor with *Youth's Companion* and its publishers, Perry Mason and Company. They were "too ethnological, too philosophical, and too controversial for us," Rideing informed him. "What we want is incident—as thrilling and picturesque as possible."[38] Dodge was urged to get back in touch, for the management of the magazine wished to include his name in its prospectus for the coming year, but he never did so.[39] In future years he would continue to write for publication, for he enjoyed the process and the exposure it gave his ideas, but he would not write again about Indians, and not for popular magazines like *Youth's Companion*.

In the spring of 1883 Dodge addressed three letters to the editors of the *Army and Navy Journal* on subjects then under discussion among his army colleagues. The first, over the perhaps misprinted name "Dugge," related to recent initiatives in the Departments of Texas and the Missouri to adopt formulas limiting the number of soldiers assigned to "extra duty," as opposed to the "daily duty" tasks required for the normal functioning of a post. He took exception to the policy, arguing that the variety of conditions at posts within any military department made unworkable any single formula for allocating manpower. More importantly, department-imposed limits interfered with the prerogatives of post commanders. "'Hold me responsible, but don't fetter me with orders,' is the instinctive demand of every capable and valuable officer, and . . . it is neither fair nor just to hold a commander to a strict accountability, and yet allow him no latitude or discretion in his administration."[40] Over the pseudonym "Line," in the two other contributions he dealt with topics that also applied to enlisted men—namely, current recruitment policies and the causes of desertion. In both letters he set forth his views forcefully, arguing both from practical experience and principle and advocating changes in procedure. Communications like these were exactly the sort of material the editors of the *Army and Navy Journal* sought in order to keep up the magazine's reputation as a forum for debate about army policy. "Though we do not agree with all the suggestions of our correspondent," they wrote following the first of Dodge's "Line" letters, "we find sufficient in them to warrant us in commending them to the careful consideration of the superior military authorities."[41]

Meanwhile, the knowledge that Sherman would soon retire from the army redoubled the attentions lavished on the general in the national capital and elsewhere. At the president's annual reception on New Year's Day, the greetings he received from fellow officers brought tears to his eyes. On February 8, his sixty-third birthday, friends in Washington arranged a dinner in his honor. Responding in that month to an invitation to attend a meeting of the Society of the Army and Navy Officers in Cincinnati, he begged off. His "social obligations," he wrote, had become "simply overwhelming and imperative."[42] When in public, Sherman sought not to draw attention to himself, never appearing in uniform except when necessary and at some times even wearing a pair of large tortoise-shell glasses that partially concealed his features. Nevertheless, at theaters in the evenings he would often be recognized, applauded, even asked to say a few words. Though well intended, spontaneous marks of respect like these grew tiresome. Late in 1881 he had declined an invitation to a dinner at Delmonico's restaurant in New York City, making it no secret that he was weary of responding to toasts to the army.[43] Inevitably, his peaking popularity gave rise to renewed speculation that he might soon enter politics. For example, the *New York World* observed that when seated at his desk in the War Department, the general had an unobstructed view of the White House across the lawn. "Can he prevent his thoughts?" the reporter slyly wondered. But Sherman gave no encouragement to speculations of this kind. In one of his more measured responses on the subject, he assured an interviewer that he would never "soil my military record" by participation in politics.[44]

Early in 1883 Sherman began updating his arrangements for the more physically challenging portions of his postponed western tour. Developments in recent months had made clear that in order to perform a reconnaissance now regarded as necessary, he would need to cross the international boundary into Canada. Fort Colville, in northern Washington Territory, had recently been ordered abandoned, but amid some uncertainty its future had not yet been determined.[45] If in fact it was to be given no further military use, then a new post would need to be established to replace it. According to the imperfect maps of the region then available, the most eligible sites for such a facility were either near the point where the Columbia River crossed the international boundary or else to the west, in the Okinakane Valley. In either case, if Sherman were to examine that country, a mountain range yet further west would necessitate his passing into Canada in order to avoid delay by backtracking. He therefore directed General Schofield to determine whether an old road, shown on maps as leading from near the region he proposed to reconnoitre toward Fort Hope, on the Fraser River in British Columbia, was still in good enough condition for use by his party.[46]

Schofield's inquiries would require a few weeks, but by early March Sherman had otherwise "pretty well staked out" the rest of his itinerary.[47] As planned the year before, he would leave Washington in mid-June and be absent until about October 1. The members of his party would be few, including Justice Waite and possibly justices Gray and Harlan, with two aides-de-camp, colonels Bacon and Tidball. Other persons would join the tour and then drop away as it moved from region to region. Passing from Buffalo, New York, to Duluth via the Great Lakes, the party would board a Northern Pacific train for Saint Paul, where a reception was planned at Fort Snelling. From that point, augmented by General Terry and persons traveling with him, the group would continue by railroad to Fort Ellis, proceeding thence south by pack train through Yellowstone National Park. Following the course marked out the year before, it would next make its way back to Missoula, which the Northern Pacific had reached by this time.[48] The month of August would take the travelers through northern Idaho and Washington Territories and into Canada, then by sea aboard a U.S. revenue cutter toward Vancouver Barracks, Washington Territory, headquarters of the Department of the Columbia. After a series of events being planned there, the party would continue south, by a route yet to be determined, to San Francisco, where it would remain for a few days before proceeding by railroad to Los Angeles. It would then cross the southwestern territories to Santa Fe, New Mexico, and zigzag northwesterly to Salt Lake City, Utah, setting out from that point on the final leg of the journey back to Washington.[49] In all, the tour would cover approximately 11,000 miles. Sherman looked forward to passing through two stretches of country he had not yet seen, the region north of Fort Coeur d'Alene, Idaho Territory, and much of the mountain terrain between Santa Fe and Salt Lake City. Only months before, the Denver and Rio Grande Railroad had completed a 615-mile stretch of track that connected Pueblo, Colorado, and Salt Lake City, a bold feat of engineering and entrepreneurship. Writing to William J. Palmer, president of the Denver and Rio Grande, Sherman confessed himself "even yet incredulous" at the thought of rapid commercial travel in that "hitherto inaccessible" section of the country.[50]

Fortuitously, the Sherman tour in the summer of 1883 would coincide almost exactly with the completion of three major railroads, the Northern Pacific, the Denver and Rio Grande, and the Atlantic and Pacific, the latter connecting Needles, California, and Albuquerque, New Mexico. In view of Sherman's emphasis on railroad transportation as a key element of future army policy, this conjunction of events seemed fitting, the final links being connected just as he ended his career.[51] To register his sense of the railroads' crucial role in the development of the nation, he directed Colonel Poe to prepare a report describing the construction of the transcontinental lines and the implications of their presence for military operations. Poe's discussion would be published as part of the general's annual report to the secretary of war for 1883.[52]

Early in June, Sherman informed Major David S. Gordon, Second Cavalry, the post commander at Fort Ellis, Montana Territory, of the arrangements he wished made there prior to his arrival on July 1. "I fear too much preparation rather than too little," he wrote, but in issuing directions to Gordon and others he inclined to the former extreme. He specified the number and type of wagons, pack mules, and escort troops to be assembled, and declining an offer of overnight hospitality at Gordon's residence, he indicated the site on the post grounds where he wished to make camp. Once away from the railroad, he preferred to travel in relatively spartan fashion. "What I and all my party . . . want is to get away from dinners, parties and civilization; we are 'blasees,' and want to come down easily and gracefully to rations, to hard work, and in contact with nature." While at the fort, he would borrow a camp table and stools and perhaps a few other conveniences, but these were the only "luxuries" he would sanction.[53] Of course, he needed to bear in mind the judges who hoped to accompany him. Waite was sixty-seven years of age and unaccustomed to mountain travel, while Gray, though twelve years his junior and something of an outdoorsman, was a mountainous man, standing six feet five inches and weighing over three hundred pounds. He would need a sturdy horse. Meals on the pack-mule journey would consist of foodstuffs issued by post commissaries of subsistence, supplemented by whatever else might be bagged or purchased along the way.[54]

Official welcomes would necessarily occur at Fort Ellis and at other points, but Sherman felt these brought a certain satisfaction to all and need not be discouraged if kept within due limits. Receptions and testimonial dinners at towns and cities along the way were also part of the bargain, inseparable from his office and his fame. Having developed considerable skill in fashioning impromptu remarks before large audiences, he rarely failed to hit upon an observation or two that delighted those who came out to see him.[55] The only feature of his public appearances that he found genuinely painful was the beartrap handshakes he received from admirers. On more than one occasion the repeated pressure had forced him to break up a receiving line, briefly address all those present, and make his exit.[56]

That a superabundance of handshakes posed one of the worst threats to the general's well-being on a tour more than three months in duration argued the profound peace that prevailed along the proposed line of travel. Though escorted by only a small body of soldiers, whose main function was to conduct the pack train and attend to camp duties, Sherman was confident of traveling in security even in the northwestern wilderness. True, Indians on the Colville Reservation in Washington Territory had recently been aggravated almost to violence by incursions of illegal settlers, but the general was reasonably confident of a friendly reception from their representatives. Similarly, his reconnaissance of that region was in part to ensure its defensibility in the event of armed conflict, presumably with Canadian or British forces, but his reception by civil and military officials in British Columbia was expected to be cordial. In every regard, the inspection tour promised to be one long journey of good feeling.

A newspaper interviewer observed "a beam of satisfaction" in Sherman's eye as he outlined the plans for his approaching removal from the stresses and distractions of life in Washington.[57] He and his aides would leave the city on Wednesday, June 20. The core group of travelers had decreased by one, Justice Harlan having decided not to attempt the journey; but General Terry and his guests would still join it as far as Missoula. The Terry party would include Colonel Dodge, Sherman having informed the department commander of the promise to include him in the initial weeks of travel.[58] All was in readiness when, on June 19, a last-minute complication arose. The wife of Colonel Bacon, who was under orders to accompany the general on his entire trip, fell so ill as to preclude her husband's leaving Washington. Advised of the difficulty, Sherman remedied it promptly, telegraphing Terry that Dodge would replace Bacon and join him for "the whole round."[59] An order issued that day from army headquarters therefore incorporated mention of Dodge, who "will report in person to the General of the Army on the 28th instant, at Fort Snelling, Minnesota, and will accompany the General thence, as escort, until relieved."[60]

Sherman directed Terry to inform Dodge of the windfall duty that had been assigned him, but for some reason the department commander failed to do so. Hence, when Dodge left his post to board a train for Saint Paul, he looked forward eagerly to joining the Sherman-Terry expedition but was unaware of the revised orders. Having not yet seen the celebrated Yellowstone National Park or visited regions in its vicinity that were said to abound in fish and game, he anticipated an enviable outing, and for that reason he began writing a journal record of it.[61] But he would soon discover himself still more fortunate. A coincidence had destined him for daily association with the General of the Army during a summer that Sherman regarded as in a sense the high point of his career.

24

General Sherman's Inspection Tour

At Saint Paul, Dodge was met at the railroad depot by an officer who handed him a note from Tidball, informing him that he would accompany General Sherman as "caterer & general camp outfitter" for the whole trip. Delighted at the prospect, he declared the illness of Colonel Bacon's wife that had led to this result "a score in woman's favor."[1] While awaiting the arrival of the general, in the two days that followed he transacted some post and regimental business at Fort Snelling, obtained foodstuffs and camp supplies from the commissary, visited Minnehaha Falls and other local points of interest, and greeted old friends. Among these were Captain Frank S. Smith, Fourth Artillery, who had commanded a company of his brigade on the Powder River Expedition, and Brigadier General Richard W. "Sub" Johnson, now retired, a West Point classmate of his.[2] Like many other retired officers and other interested citizens, Johnson was on hand to greet the distinguished visitor. Following a series of renovations in the past two years and a thorough cleaning in recent weeks, Fort Snelling would look its best for the occasion.[3]

According to plan, Sherman and Tidball had left Washington on June 20 and were joined at Buffalo by Justice Gray, taking passage together on a Great Lakes steamer, the *Nyack*. Two days later Judge Waite boarded ship at Detroit, Michigan, making the core traveling party four-fifths complete. At this point the general began performing his official duties by inspecting Fort Wayne, a facility important for its strategic location between Lakes Erie and Huron. Here too, as in 1882, he began a series of letters to the secretary of war in which, with much other material, he reported his observations and reflections on the nation's military preparedness. After stops at Minnesota ports and visits to the Hecla and Calumet copper mines, the *Nyack* reached Duluth on June 27, almost exactly on schedule.[4] That night the party boarded a train for Saint Paul, where they were expected the next morning. At Fort Snelling, Dodge ended his journal entry for the day by observing that "there is going to be a —— of a time here tomorro."[5]

On the morning of June 28, four companies of infantry and one battery of light artillery, the entire garrison of Fort Snelling, greeted the Sherman party with a seventeen-gun salute and escorted them to General Terry's residence, where Terry and his headquarters staff, including Dodge, stood awaiting them. According to Dodge, there was "great cordiality and handshaking for a few moments, & then (as one of the Ladies down the line remarked) the circus was over." Later that day he returned to Saint Paul to take delivery of the provisions he had ordered, including "a few gallons of whisky."[6] Tidball and the two justices toured Minneapolis and visited the Washburn Flouring Mill, which in his published account of the tour Tidball described lamely as "one of the many that gives fame to this flour-producing city."[7]

Of the five travelers who comprised the Sherman party, three—Sherman, Tidball, and Dodge—would write day-to-day descriptions of the entire summer, each characteristic of its author and serving a purpose distinct from the others. Sherman's letters to the secretary of war emphasized military matters—officers he encountered, forts he visited and their place in future army policy, recommendations for appropriations from Congress. Tidball's narrative, prepared at the general's direction for publication with his annual report, was the lengthiest and least personal. Pleasant but not lively in tone, it expatiated in workmanlike fashion on the history and associations of the various places visited. Whatever his private thoughts may have been, Tidball sought to include some gracious or at least diplomatic remark about every participant on the tour and almost every person that came into significant contact with it. Individuals of foreign extraction and non-white race sometimes received less generous mention, however. Dodge's record was the most candid of the three about his impressions of scenes along the way and his personal likes and dislikes. As the journey proceeded, one or more periods of note-taking by the three men often formed part of a day's activities.

From Fort Snelling onward, the progress of the Sherman entourage received steady journalistic coverage, first in newspapers published at the towns and cities it visited and later in eastern newspapers through reprinted articles and the reports of correspondents. The *Army and Navy Journal* served up a steady sprinkling of reports from army posts and also quotations from articles in newspapers gleaned through exchange. Because no correspondent accompanied the touring party from place to place—an arrangement that would have been unthinkable to Sherman—successive newspaper reports often included similar material: description of the travelers' appearance and mood, especially those of the general; an account of a reception, inspection, or other event; a list of attendees; and sometimes a summary of remarks made on the occasion. The progress of the tour was thus national news, but the newspaper coverage emphasized its social or civic, rarely its military character, and conveyed no sense of its day-to-day flavor. However, taken together, the accounts by Dodge, Sherman, and Tidball supply that need.

After supper at Terry's residence, Sherman shook hands with a great many of the old soldiers who had come out to see him. At last, he announced that he was tired out and, in lieu of more handshaking, would address them all. Dodge, who admired the general's speechmaking ability, thought what followed a "characteristic" performance, with "[n]o eloquence but full of plain good sense." He was less impressed by Terry, who for a man trained as a lawyer seemed to him singularly wanting as an extemporaneous speaker. Justices Waite and Gray also made brief remarks, and when "the fuss was over," Dodge returned to his quarters to pack, finishing at midnight.[8]

On the morning of June 29, the party left Saint Paul aboard a Pullman Palace Car made available for their use by officials of the Northern Pacific Railroad. Despite suffocating heat and dusty wind, they passed time pleasantly as the train rolled west that day. Dodge and Terry lost decisively at whist to the two justices, while Sherman kept to himself, recovering from a spell of queasiness. Upon crossing the border into Montana Territory on June 30, Dodge pronounced the fervid descriptions of the territory's natural beauty by promotional writers as "bosh." The "bad lands" scenery in the vicinity of the Little Missouri River he considered "tame to monotony" in comparison to country he had passed through on the Black Hills Expedition. The high point of the day's travel was the whistle-stop visit to Fort Keogh, on the Yellowstone River just west of Miles City. Sherman had telegraphed the post commander, Colonel John D. Wilkins, Fifth Infantry, that his train would stop at the nearby railroad station, but for only one hour. Accordingly, on the arrival of the train at 10:30 P.M., Wilkins and his large garrison—eight companies of infantry and one of cavalry—were formed in line to welcome him. The general left the train and reviewed the troops by the light of lanterns. Dodge took particular interest in this stop, for the Fifth Infantry was the regiment he had been expected to command when he instead succeeded to the colonelcy of the Eleventh. "Met many old friends," he wrote of the brief visit.[9]

On the following afternoon, the train reached Fort Ellis, three miles west of Bozeman, and Sherman, Tidball, and Dodge went into camp on a site that had been prepared for them on high ground just south of the post. Judges Waite and Gray continued on for a visit to the territorial capital, Helena. Fort Ellis was the jumping-off place for the overland journey to Yellowstone National Park, so Dodge busied himself securing camp and mess equipment. In Bozeman he hired a Chinese man as mess cook, and another as waiter.[10] At the post, he had trestle beds made for the Sherman party, but the general refused the one intended for his use.[11] Dodge observed privately that he was "the only man I know who takes a positive delight in discomfort." As the two officers stood watching a troop of cavalry prepare to leave the post with a forty-mule pack train, Sherman noticed a wagon being loaded with rolls of bedding. "Why Dodge look at that," he exclaimed; "every private soldier has as much as a Major Genl ought to have."[12] This small force would make advance preparations along the road south and serve as escort during the party's trek through the national park.

On July 4 the judges returned from Helena, bringing with them two more travelers, Senator George F. Edmunds of Vermont and his nephew Lieutenant Elliott J. Arthur, U.S. Navy. This was a happy coincidence for Dodge; he had quoted a statement by Edmunds on the title page of his pamphlet, *A Living Issue*. Invited by Sherman to join the tour through the national park, the newcomers agreed at once. Edmunds purchased fishing tackle and other gear, rigging himself in what Tidball termed a "cow-boy suit" of leather-colored duck. According to Tidball, the senator "proved himself . . . such an enthusiastic sportsman that his singular outfit was entirely appropriate."[13] On the evening of July 4, Major David S. Gordon, Second Cavalry, hosted an Independence Day dinner at his post commander's residence, the concluding event of the party's stay at the post.

Yellowstone National Park

At four o'clock the next morning, Dodge awoke to the patter of rain on his tent and decided to take another snooze, uncertain how the general would react to the bad weather. One hour later he awoke again, this time to the sound of Sherman's voice, and learned that he wanted to break camp and push ahead, rain or no rain. Always an early riser, Sherman imposed this discipline on his companions during the portions of the summer journey made by wagons and on horseback; ordinarily reveille was at 4:00 A.M., breakfast at 5:00, and departure from camp at 6:00. Dodge described the first day of travel from Fort Ellis as "simply wretched," the wagons being delayed by slippery soil, but the second day was more satisfactory.[14] At noon on July 6, the travelers reached a local landmark, the ranch and lodging house of the Bottler brothers near the Yellowstone River. While the general renewed acquaintance with the Bottlers, whom he had met during his reconnaissance tour of 1877, Dodge and Gray went down to the river and fished. Dodge filled his twelve-pound basket with trout and whitefish or grayling, winning by acclamation the designation as principal fisherman of the party. Tidball noted that until its arrival at the Fraser River in British Columbia, Dodge "kept our mess well supplied with delicious trout."[15] As for Gray, Dodge wrote in his journal entry that "the fat old Baby" gave up after only a few casts, disliking the intense heat.[16] The originator of this nickname for the outsized judge is unknown, but "Baby" came into whispered use by the escort. Judge Gray was boastful, selfish, tended to find fault, and consumed volumes of food—all traits that alienated him from the others. Later in the wilderness segment of the journey, he seems to have made himself more agreeable.[17] However, during these early days the contrast was striking between him and Chief Justice Waite, who took things as they came and was grateful for any little comforts.

On July 7 the wagon road was almost continuously within sight of grading activity for a railroad that would soon run from Livingston, Montana Territory, to the entrance of Yellowstone National Park. On that day the Sherman party reached Park City, the intended terminus, which Dodge characterized as "a new town of one half a street," and literally so. Its buildings were strung out along one side of a line fifteen feet from the boundary of the park.[18] After a steep four-mile climb, the road reached Mammoth Hot Springs, where a three-story frame hotel was under construction. Neither Dodge nor Tidball was overly impressed by the scene. Dodge thought the expanse of hot springs "very wonderful" but "greatly over written," and Tidball commented that the hotel "has the disadvantage of occupying the most uninteresting site to be found within the limits of the park."[19] At this place the tour party split into two groups. Sherman, who had explored Yellowstone on his previous visit, would continue on with the ambulances and wagons to the Lower Geyser Basin, on the Madison River, and go into camp there. Everyone else would proceed on horseback, with a mounted escort, along mountain trails impassable by wagons.

The trail leading along the Yellowstone River toward the famous falls was, Dodge admitted, "very steep, sometimes dangerous."[20] The party had reached the falls and turned southwesterly onto another steep trail, toward Mount Washburn ten miles away, when despite all precautions an accident occurred. Chief Justice Waite's horse was moving uphill when the saddle slipped, causing the animal to buck. The judge was thrown to the ground and landed heavily, though fortunately not on the stones that lined the trail. He thought himself uninjured, but upon attempting to mount another horse, he felt a sharp pain in his side. A physician among a group of visitors not far away bandaged the old man's midsection, but with the caution that one or two of his ribs were probably fractured. Pluckily, Justice Waite remounted, and upon arriving at the fork in the trail that led to the ascent of Mount Washburn, he actually wished to join those who intended to reach the summit. His desire to complete the three-mile ascent was natural enough, for the effort led to a magnificent panoramic view. In the report of his 1877 visit, Sherman wrote that atop the peak one feels "as though the whole world were below him. The view is simply sublime; worth the labor of reaching it *once*, but not twice."[21] Dodge also wished to scale the summit but elected instead to remain with Waite while Terry, Tidball, and Terry's aide-de-camp, Captain Robert P. Hughes, Third Infantry, went ahead. Except for trouble breathing at that high altitude—the elevation where they left Dodge and Waite was 9,000 feet, and Mount Washburn rises to 10,317 feet—the three adventurers had no difficulty.[22]

Riding along a boggy trail through masses of snow, later in the day the party passed between mounts Washburn and Dunraven, the latter named after a former hunting companion of Dodge,[23] then down a steep grade to the river, where they made camp after a twenty-one-mile day's journey. "There is no doing justice to falls & Can[y]on in words," Dodge wrote that night. He had abandoned his skepticism about published reports of the park's scenic attractions. For the remainder of his stay, his comments on the beauty and natural wonders of the region were essentially those of other appreciative visitors then or since. In fact, adopting tourist vernacular, he reported that on the next morning he, Tidball, and the chief justice "remained to *do* again all the points of interest" before following the others toward the geyser basins.[24]

On the afternoon of July 11, Justice Waite's condition worsened, and it was decided to send for the army physician who accompanied the cavalry escort, then encamped ten miles away. Acting Assistant Surgeon J. C. McGuire arrived at nine o'clock that night and after examining the patient concluded that while the justice had suffered no broken bones, he was not in a condition to continue the tour. "We have all fallen in love with the old man," Dodge wrote, "& it has cast a gloom over the whole party."[25] On the next morning an ambulance arrived to transport Justice Waite to Sherman's camp, and by noon the entire group was congregated there—all except the general, who the day before had gone to the Upper Geyser Basin to camp within sight of Old Faithful and await his fellow travelers.

Dodge and Tidball were lying in their tent regretting the loss of the chief justice from their corps of travelers when, as if sent to replace him, a horseman rode into camp who proved to be Colonel Alexander McDowell McCook, Sixth Infantry, the aide-de-camp on Sherman's staff whose place Dodge had been appointed to fill. McCook now commanded his regiment at Fort Douglas, Utah Territory, adjacent to Salt Lake City, and was on a flying visit with a party of relatives and friends. They had taken the Utah Northern Railroad to Beaver Canyon, approximately one hundred miles west, and from that point had ridden in wagons along the same route the Sherman party would follow as it left the park. Jolly and affable, McCook would be a good companion. He went into camp near the general's, and that evening he, Tidball, and Dodge "made a night of it," in the words of the latter.[26]

On the morning of July 13 McCook and his party took the trail toward Yellowstone Falls, while all but one of the Sherman-Terry entourage made its way to the Upper Geyser Basin, where they found the general looking rugged and well, and glad to see them. He and Justice Waite were old acquaintances, both being officials of the Smithsonian Institution, and the general had been distressed to learn of the injury his friend had suffered. In hopes that Waite would be able to resume the journey after a few days' rest, he had reserved a room for him at the National Park House, a modest stopping place back at the Lower Geyser Basin.[27] However, a sufficient recovery was not to be. When the group bid farewell to the old gentleman two days later he almost shed tears, and all were touched. "He was so genial," Dodge wrote, "so kind, so winning, took everything so well, was so manly under all the novelty of camp life, & bore his hurt & pain with such plucky fortitude, that he had endeared himself to every one of us. He is the exact contrast to Judge Grey, who is a selfish grumbler, thinking only of his belly. If he had had the tumble & hurt, not a man of our whole party would have cared, & we would have regarded the parting as a good riddance."[28]

On July 13 and 14 Dodge and other party members admired the park's wonders, first those of Hell's Half Acre and then of the Upper Geyser Basin, whose most spectacular displays had already been given names—the Beehive, Giantess, Castle, Splendid, and others.[29] On July 15 he and Tidball left camp early to pay a parting visit to the geological curiosities, then returned to the National Park House. General Terry was experiencing difficulty breathing at the high altitudes and had decided not to cross the mountains toward Missoula. Instead he, his party, and the cavalry escort would accompany Justice Waite back to the railroad, while the Sherman and McCook groups traveled together to Beaver Canyon. From the Lower Geyser Basin to Missoula,

Giant Geyser, Yellowstone National Park. Reprinted from U.S. Geological and Geographical Survey of the Territories, *Twelfth Annual Report* (1883).

the military escort would include only a sergeant with ten infantry soldiers to do guard and police duty while in camp. To ensure a good supply of food during the coming days of travel, Dodge purchased some elk meat and bacon, and that night after dinner at the lodging house, he treated himself to a good bath.[30] His tourist experiences of recent days had been memorable, but the conditions of travel were primitive, and in the weeks to come they would be yet more so.

From Yellowstone to Missoula

The first day's travel out of Yellowstone was strenuous. The parties followed the Norris Road, named after an early superintendent of the national park, to the Tahgee or

Tarhee Pass at the western continental divide, then down a steep grade to Riverside Station on the Madison River. Tidball described the scenery just beyond the pass as "not particularly grand" but "exceedingly beautiful. The sky at this high altitude is of a peculiar depth of blue, and the clouds forming around the tops of the snow-peaked mountains are curiously billowy and fluffy."[31] The rigors of travel over bad roads on the next day were made worse for Dodge by riding in the general's ambulance, which he thought "very uncomfortable in every way." Compensation came when, crossing a fork of the Snake River, he and Justice Gray stopped to fish for trout and had what they agreed was the best sport of the kind they had ever seen. Gray landed three, Dodge seven, and he would have taken more had he not broken his fishing rod. Two of his fish weighed one and one-half pounds apiece. Recounting a witticism of his, Tidball wrote that "The most expert of our anglers complained that the trout of this Western country, although so beautiful and delicious, are clumsy at taking the bait; that although they strike with vigor, it is in an awkward country-like manner, entirely inferior to the more accomplished fish of the East."[32]

Crossing a low divide that separated the waters of the Snake River from those of Beaver Creek, on July 18 the McCook and Sherman parties reached Beaver City, where the former group would board a train for Salt Lake City at midnight. Sherman would see McCook again on his visit to Fort Douglas later that summer, but that evening McCook uncorked his last five bottles of champagne for a farewell celebration at the station house. Travel on the next day was "uninteresting" to Dodge, probably in part because the champagne had not agreed with him, but Tidball noticed suggestive evidence of the road's recent history. This was, he explained, "the old emigrant route to Oregon, and over its weary miles had toiled thousands of pioneers. . . . Now it is almost untraveled; railroads have superseded it. Some of the old stage stations remain, and their dilapidated block-houses and loop-holed walls tell of when the Indian held bloody sway over this land." The travelers passed fenced-in properties where Dodge purchased more mess supplies. Owing to mist and alkaline dust, the scenery was obscured, but he made a bright spot of the evening meal. "Spring chickens, fresh butter, milk, & cream for dinner," he wrote that night. "Judge Grey in good humor."[33]

As the Sherman party moved north through the valley of Beaver Creek, the chief point of interest, on July 21, was Bannock City, formerly the territorial capital but now in decay. Sherman, Tidball, and Dodge all regarded the scene as exemplifying the rapid rate of change in the western country. Sherman noted that Bannock City had once been famous as the place where gold was discovered in Montana, but that now it was no longer even a county seat. Tidball noticed "numerous signs of banks, assay offices, 'gold dust bought here,' still clinging to the decaying houses." Dodge described it as "a played out town of about 100 inhabitants. Once the proud capital of Montana, with 10,000 inhabitants."[34]

The next three days of travel brought the party past the Big Hole Basin, where Colonel John Gibbon, Seventh Infantry, had fought a pitched battle with the fleeing Nez Perce Indians in August 1877,[35] and then over the Bitter Root Mountains. The

The Tahgee Pass. Reprinted from U.S. Geological and Geographical Survey of the Territories, *Twelfth Annual Report* (1883).

pass across the mountain range was scenic, but wagon travel through it was difficult. Dodge described the descent into the Bitter Root valley as "a plunge into an abyss," estimating the rate of descent at 1,000 feet per mile. In camp that night, all agreed that the day's march had been the hardest yet, on both animals and men. The mountains were now behind them, their peaks outlined by sunset, and they had entered a setting that marked a climatic change. The valley was fenced and under cultivation with tomatoes, corn, berries, and other crops that could not survive in places like those just passed through, where frosty nights occurred throughout the year. Sherman wrote with pleased exaggeration that the party seemed "positively on the waters of the Pacific."[36]

They were now within an easy two days' march from Fort Missoula, which the general regarded as the endpoint of the first stage of his inspection tour.[37] The wagons, ambulances, some camp equipment, and the infantry escort would be shipped by rail back to Fort Ellis from Missoula, five miles from the post, and the core party would board a train there for Rathdrum, Idaho Territory, the station nearest the next army post on the itinerary, Fort Coeur d'Alene. Upon arriving at Fort Missoula, they were greeted by the customary salute, and Sherman inspected the post with more than ordinary interest, since he had directed major changes to it during his Yellowstone tour of 1877. In the absence of a railroad route across the continent at that latitude, he then regarded Missoula as "the door of the western frontier."[38] Accordingly, he had modified plans for the nearby post to permit its use as needed by a full regiment of infantry. However, the progress of the Northern Pacific Railroad had since lessened the importance of the fort, whose garrison now included four companies, all of the Third Infantry.

The post commander, Major William H. Jordan, expected to lodge the visitors at his own house and in other officers' quarters, but Sherman demurred. He explained to the secretary of war that "we were so used to tents that we preferred to stick to camp, and accordingly pitched our tents inside the Fort enclosure near the river bank."[39] Dodge was unimpressed by Fort Missoula, despite its scenic surroundings. "It is not nearly so pretty a post as Sully," he wrote, "& I think badly arranged. (Genl Sherman says he planned it, so I dont say this out loud). The only advantage over Sully is the hunting & fishing." He was glad to receive hearty greetings from some of his old Third Infantry comrades, including Jordan, who had greeted him at Camp Sheridan, Dakota Territory, near the end of the Black Hills Expedition. That evening Jordan held a reception at his residence, and afterward Dodge chatted and sipped whisky with another former comrade, First Lieutenant John P. Thompson. However, sensing Thompson's willingness to make it a long night, he ended the exchange on the plea of a need to sleep.[40]

At seven o'clock the next morning, the travelers checked their baggage in Missoula and strolled out for a look at the place. Dodge recorded no impressions, but the industrious Tidball took notes that yielded a colorful sketch of this northwestern frontier community. "It is a town of great business activity," he wrote, "combined, as we were informed, with an unusual amount of wickedness of every variety. . . . The streets, decorated with worn-out cards from the saloons, were picturesque with roughly clad miners, Indians with their squaws and papooses, flashily dressed gamblers, and the ubiquitous Chinaman."[41] Sherman, Tidball, and Dodge all described in glowing terms the 230-mile railroad journey that comprised that day's stint of travel. Dodge lavished adjectives upon his summary of the "[d]elightful trip in cars through a wonderfully beautiful & romantic country." Sherman characterized it as "thirteen hours of absolute comfort." Tidball touched upon the varied beauty of the region, but he also dwelt upon the feat of engineering represented by the mere existence of the railroad. He pointed out that the wooden truss bridge that spanned the Morentz Gulch, twenty miles from Missoula, was the highest in the United States and quite possibly the longest in the world.[42] Both the western wilderness and the enterprise that had created such structures were equally, he implied, sources of national pride.

In fact, the chief news event in the northwest during the approximate period of the Sherman party's presence there was a ceremony on September 9 at Last Spike, Montana Territory, marking completion of the Northern Pacific Railroad. The driving of a final spike, witnessed by President Arthur and other distinguished guests, including representatives of several foreign nations, was an occasion for celebration and a full measure of what Sherman termed "second wind oratory."[43] Asked to speak a few words, the usually taciturn former President Grant observed that railroads in the United States might have amounted to little even yet, had not Civil War veterans like Henry Villard, president of the Northern Pacific, sought out the western territories as their field of enterprise.[44] Although not present at the ceremony, Sherman also took satisfaction in the completion of the Northern Pacific, viewing it within a yet wider historical perspective. To him, the dreams of visionaries and surveyors in the 1840s and 1850s that had assumed solid reality in the great east-west railroads symbolized "a period of change." "The trapper, the Hunter, the miner, the buffalo, elk, deer, and antelope are gone," he wrote Secretary Lincoln on August 30. "Soon the Indian will disappear, or be absorbed as have been the Mexicans and Greasers of 1846." Some persons might view these almost magical evanescences in a more sober light, but Sherman expressed satisfaction at the "miraculous" developments, which brought with them the prospect of prosperity across the continent.[45]

Fort Coeur d'Alene

Reaching Rathdrum at 11:00 P.M., the train was greeted there by a bonfire local citizens had lit in the general's honor. The commander of Fort Coeur d'Alene, Colonel Frank Wheaton, Second Infantry, was on hand with an escort for the ten-mile journey to the post. Sherman had informed Wheaton of his desire to camp along the margin of Lake Coeur d'Alene, and the result was a set of hospital tents raised and ready for occupancy. Since its establishment in 1878, Fort Coeur d'Alene had become renowned for the beauty of its surroundings,[46] and the next morning brought an opportunity to view some of them. To Dodge the post quickly assumed the status of an ideal duty station. "This is certainly God's Country," he wrote, "& I would gladly compromise on it for my Heaven."[47] Happily, a few days' stop here would be necessary to complete preparations for the next stage of the journey, north into Canada. Wheaton was an "old compadre" of Dodge from the early days in Texas, and the two men passed one evening telling stories in the company of the bachelor officers. On one day Dodge fished in the lake for rainbow trout, reeling in forty-one in three hours. On another he joined a tour around the lake aboard a steamboat that had been constructed by men at the post, then attended a party at Wheaton's residence. He "flirted with all that would flirt, most desperately & I think carried away all the honors as flirt." But this judgment was perhaps vanity on his part, for he had returned to camp at the early hour of 2:00 A.M. Sherman, known to be an admirer of attractive young women, remained until the last dance, one hour later. According to a newspaper report, he passed the evening "with the zest of a young man," his eye "bright and keen" until the last moment.[48]

Earlier that day Brigadier General Miles, commander of the Department of the Columbia, had arrived at the post with a small party following a three-day journey from his headquarters at Vancouver Barracks. Miles had played an important role in making arrangements for the journey north from Fort Coeur d'Alene and would accompany Sherman into Canada. His chief engineer officer, First Lieutenant George W. Goethals, had just returned from a reconnaissance of the country to be passed through and had prepared a full set of maps.[49] The Miles party included Goethals; Major John Moore, medical director of the Department of the Columbia; Second Lieutenant John W. Mallory, an aide-de-camp; and a Mr. Saurin, first secretary of the British legation at Washington.[50] As the consequence of a recent ruling by Canadian authorities that any U.S. military organization wishing to visit Canada must first secure permission through diplomatic channels, Sherman had submitted the necessary application. A company of troops under Captain James Jackson, First Cavalry, would escort the combined Sherman and Miles groups as far as Fort Colville, near the international border, with a fifty-mule pack train transporting supplies. From Fort Coeur d'Alene to the first anticipated crossing of the Columbia River, a distance of 324 miles, the members of the official tour would ride on wagons. After that, they would continue by horseback or on foot.

On the morning of August 2, General Miles's disposition to take matters into his own hands made itself felt, to the irritation of Dodge. Checking over the wagons that had been loaded with the Sherman group's camping equipment, he discovered that Miles had appropriated about one-half the space on a wagon for his own use. The interview with Sherman that followed did not rectify matters to Dodge's satisfaction. "Well all right," said the General of the Army, who was wearily familiar with Miles and his ways, "let him have it." Dodge pressed the issue, warning that the main party would have to leave behind one-half its own things unless something was done, but Sherman was not to be drawn in. "Well it dont make any difference," he responded; "let it go." Dodge thought this typical of the general, "ready to be put to any inconvenience by any one who had cheek enough," but he quietly set things to rights by

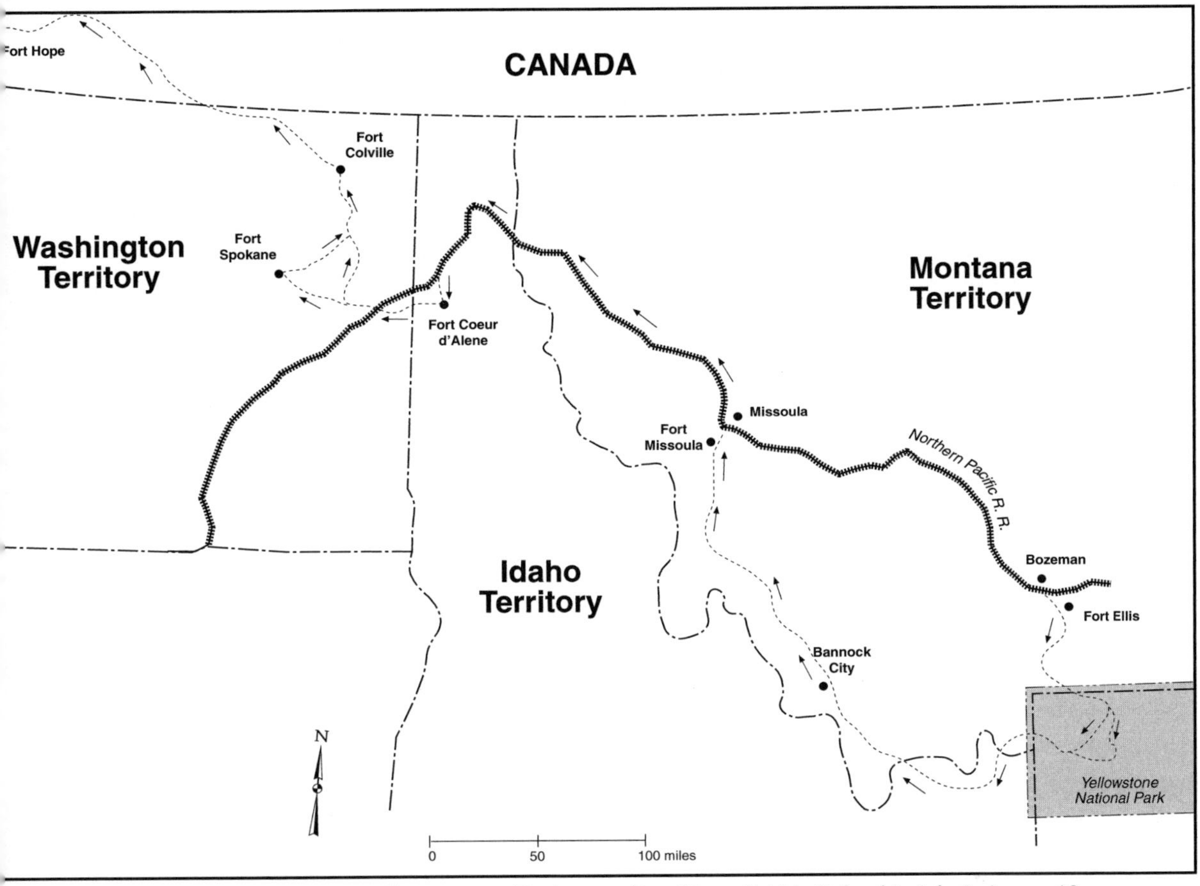

Inspection Tour Itinerary, Fort Ellis, Montana Territory, to Fort Hope, British Columbia, July 5–August 19, 1883

ordering another wagon.[51] After an hour's delay, at 7:00 A.M. Sherman, Miles, and those who were to accompany them left Fort Coeur d'Alene, Wheaton and others on hand to wish them a good journey. "I dont think I ever left a post with so much regret," Dodge wrote.[52]

Following the first day's march, to Spokane Falls, Washington Territory, the traveling party split into two. This was to enable Sherman, Miles, and Tidball to perform an inspection of Fort Spokane, sixty-five miles west. At issue was the possible role of that post in future army operations along the northern frontier.[53] The three officers planned to travel the entire distance by ambulance on this day and to rendezvous with Dodge's group on the next, taking advantage of a trail north that intersected with the road to Fort Colville. Dodge thus moved along the latter road, bringing with him a new member of the party, Bailey Willis, a geologist who was searching the region for coal deposits on behalf of the Northern Pacific Railroad. Willis would remain with the travelers as far as Osoyoos Lake, which straddled the international boundary.[54] Passing through the fertile Colville Valley, on August 5 Dodge reached the trail by which the two generals and Tidball were to arrive, then continued to a place known as Brown's Ranch, where the others joined him shortly afterward. For their own different reasons, Sherman and Justice Gray were both in ill humor, but an excellent dinner featuring trout that Dodge had just caught put everyone in a better mood.

Sherman was inclined to believe that if strengthened and provided with a better bridge across the Spokane River, Fort Spokane might well serve by itself the military needs in that section of Washington Territory.[55] However, another question also remained unanswered: whether to refurbish the recently abandoned Fort Colville, nearer the national frontier, or instead to establish another post in the region. Following a twenty-five-mile march, on August 6 the Sherman and Miles parties reached the old fort, and after encamping there, the commanding general looked it over. Miles had already secured an authorization to spend $50,000 on construction of a new post, but Sherman trumped that arrangement. What he saw was still potentially useful, especially since the abundant evidence of development in the region indicated a continuing need for assurance of civil order. If, as he had been informed, steam navigation proved feasible on the Columbia River as far north as to the rapidly progressing Canadian Pacific Railroad, "Fort Colville may again come into requisition, and some of the buildings are worth saving."[56]

As they approached the crossing of the Columbia River, the travelers passed the Indian mission of Saint Francis Regis, established many years before by the intrepid Jesuit missionary Pierre-Jean De Smet. Sherman resisted making unscheduled stops, but evidently elaborate preparations had been made here; and on the invitation of the priest and nun in attendance, he was persuaded to pay a short visit. Tidball recounted the entertainment that followed: "It was the season of summer vacation, and the boys, 50 in number, were absent, and so likewise the girls (also about 50) except 20, who, expecting us, had been arrayed in all their finery, neat, clean, and civilized. They were paraded in two semi-circular lines, the smallest in front, and received us with songs of greeting, accompanied by music on a parlor organ. After the songs[,] little speeches of welcome were pronounced in succession by several of the children, to which the General replied in appropriate words. The children ranged from four to fifteen years of age; some of them were half-breeds. After the singing one bright-eyed little girl, dressed as a beggar child, rehearsed a piece in the most effective and touching manner."[57] Dodge recorded some of the same details, adding that after the performance Sherman "showed his usual taste, & kissed the 2 prettiest girls. Color is no object to him."[58]

The Columbia River was 480 yards wide at the point the party crossed it by ferry, but despite its rapid current, all went smoothly. With First Lieutenant Goethals as guide, the final leg of the cross-country journey, 222 miles north and west to Fort Hope, British Columbia, would begin the next day.

Into Canada

Moving out ahead of the mule team, on August 8 Dodge and several others crossed Kettle River and, as he later wrote, "rode gaily forward" in search of game along a difficult trail. They expected to camp at a forage pile that had been left by a detachment of soldiers who were opening the road ahead of them. However, they were unable to locate the pile, and late in the afternoon they discussed the situation. Rather than backtrack to the main party, they elected to go into camp where they were, eat for dinner the game they had killed, and rely for breakfast on locating the road-openers, who ought to be not far ahead. "I made a bed of pine boughs," Dodge wrote in his journal, "& wrapped myself in my saddle blanket with saddle for pillow. Rowell constituted himself cook, & gave us an excellent supper of ducks & grouse, cooked on a tin plate, without salt, bread, or coffee. The only serious annoyance was the abundance & pertinacity of the flies & musquitoes."[59]

The campers *al fresco* were on the trail at dawn and soon came upon the road crew, all still asleep. After breakfast they loafed until early afternoon, when Sherman, Miles, and the rest came up and went into camp with them. Dodge was relieved to find that all the food and equipment, including a valued demijohn of whisky, was intact after passing over the terrible trail. As insurance against future mishaps, he decanted the liquor into a sturdier container. He and his fellow hunters were subjected to ridicule for "getting lost," but there had been no real danger. As Tidball remarked, "we all knew that such veteran woodsmen were not to be lost."[60]

The next morning Dodge and Miles, both determined to get some game and fish, rode ahead of the pack train along with another officer, First Lieutenant George B. Backus, First Cavalry. Dodge bagged nine grouse, but on this day he was outdone as a fisherman by the two others. His twenty small trout were a respectable catch, but Miles's eight or ten outweighed them, and the seventeen caught by Backus totaled about ten pounds. On that day Dodge had difficulty controlling his horse, which reared, plunged, and turned around at the slightest provocation, nor was he the only man whose mount gave him trouble. Bailey Willis recounted two accidents at this stage of the journey, suffered in succession by the two generals:

> General Sherman rode a lively bay mare Kentucky-bred, a beauty of the Bluegrass. She was . . . not exactly the mount I would have picked for a mountain trail. . . . In one tangle she got mad, reared, plunged wildly, stumbled, and threw the General. He saved himself adroitly & was not hurt, but General Miles was furious at the mare. He mounted her and we rode on, General Sherman having protestingly accepted the exchange.
>
> Toward noon we bivouacked for lunch in a grassy meadow. Miles rode out before the group of officers and squad of cavalry and, drawing attention, he proclaimed in a loud voice, "Now I'll take it out of her!"
>
> He jerked hard on the cruel curb. As the mare backed and reared he whipped and spurred. She, utterly frightened to be thus suddenly attacked by the demon astride her, plunged as before and threw the doughty general . . . upon the grass, where he lay a moment, the breath knocked out of him.
>
> "That's it! that's it!" cried Sherman, in ecstasy. "That's just the way she threw me!" But he turned away to hide his delight. The cavalrymen dashed after the mare in a body. They could not restrain their laughter.[61]

For all his admirable qualities as a soldier and a person, Miles's take-charge or, as Dodge expressed it, his "break neck – or more properly kill-horse" style[62] whetted his associates' appetite to witness a discomfiture such as this.

On August 12, the party reached Osoyoos Lake and visited the U.S. custom house there. This outpost of federal authority, the back shed of an unprepossessing log building, impressed no one. Sherman described the work of C. B. Bash, the customs officer, as consisting "chiefly if not wholly in stopping Chinese emigration, and in collecting the tax of one dollar a head on cattle sent from British Columbia into the United States. The whole place is sandy, dusty, and forbidding."[63] Four miles above the American custom house, the travelers reached its British counterpart and had more favorable impressions.[64] Judge J. C. Hayne came out to meet the party, which at that time numbered 81 men, 66 horses, and 79 mules, and invited the individuals of special note into his house. They were offered a variety of drinks, but Dodge confined himself to a personal favorite, "real Robertson Irish whisky." He took another glass at a toll facility two miles further on. "Consequently," he wrote, "when we took the trail again I was as drunk as I ever get – that is I could feel that I had been drinking."[65]

Traveling along the Similkameen River for the next two days, Dodge studied with interest the Indian inhabitants of the region. The scenes he witnessed contrasted sharply with those among reservation Indians in the United States. Here, he noted, they "live in houses, wear civilized clothing, & are Brittish subjects – with all the rights of citizens."[66] Despite difficult conditions for travel that included pestiferous insects, the campaigners into Canada were making good progress; in fact, they were ahead of schedule. Some travelers might welcome this state of affairs as leaving time for possible misadventures, but not Sherman. On the morning of August 16 all was packed and ready for travel at 5:30, but the general refused to begin the march until 6:00. "He is very curious in many respects," Dodge observed.[67]

The high point of this day was a stop at the Allison ranch at Princeton, formerly a gold mining community but now almost uninhabited and extremely isolated. Tidball was interested in the family of the ranch owner. "Allison himself was absent . . . but his courteous wife received us with hospitality. She is a rosy-cheeked English woman, apparently about twenty-five, but is old enough to boast of ten children, healthy, handsome urchins, another instance . . . that the more distant and difficult of access the place, the more prolific are the human inhabitants. . . . She appeared cheerful, happy, and contented, in her isolated home."[68] Sherman wished to revert to his schedule for progress toward Fort Hope, but he was overruled; as Dodge expressed it, Miles "got after him & fairly bullied him into going on."[69] It was rugged country, and for lack of anything better, they stopped that night at a place shown on the maps as Powder Camp. Fallen timber lay everywhere, but there was almost no grass for the animals.

The guide inside Canada was no longer First Lieutenant Goethals but a packer who, as he claimed, had passed over the trail to Fort Hope on one previous occasion. Unfortunately, this man's recollection of the experience proved imperfect. Several members of the party, including Sherman, had now become anxious to move forward as quickly as possible, as much for the welfare of the horses and mules as for their own comfort. On the afternoon of August 17 the guide dissuaded them from attempting to pass beyond another poor campsite that was, he said, the last possible stopping place before Lake House, sixteen miles away. They heeded his advice, but with unforgettable results. Dodge's journal account conveys the discomforts and frustrations of the next day's travel:

> Waked rather late to find the whole camp buried in snow – not less than 2 inches deep cold raw & disagreeable & still snowing.
>
> We got under weigh at 6.30, & such a journey! The trail was as bad as bad can be, barely passable in places, muddy boggy & very slippery, with rocks enough to make it dangerous – Sometimes on horseback, sometimes on foot, sometimes going up hill, sometimes down but always in rocks & bogs, we plodded our way not more than 2 miles an hour – making only about 9 miles by 1.30 pm. About six or seven miles from our camp we came to the true head of canon – & a very excellent camping ground[.] Our guide had made a mistake yesterday – & a very serious one for us. We could easily have made the distance, & the road was comparatively good & dry. Now everything is covered with snow & slush. . . .
>
> At 1.30 struck the old wagon road built years ago, by Her Majesty's Royal Engineers. It was a good road & cost a deal of money & labor, but is now barely passable for horses & pack mules.
>
> Ten miles of plodding brought us to the head of Suwallow River, at a shanty called the Lake House. Arrived 5 p.m. – Everybody used up except Miles & myself. Packs came in half an hour after – all right.[70]

"Taken all in all," Tidball wrote, "this was the most disagreeable day's march that we had encountered in our entire route."[71]

The fourteen-mile journey to Fort Hope on August 19 was almost as easy and uneventful as that on the day before had been challenging. Upon reaching the town at 2:00 P.M., the party was in good condition, and the animals addressed themselves to supplies of oats and hay that awaited them. In their official reports, both Sherman and Tidball expressed wonder at the strength of the steed that had carried Justice Gray all the way from the Columbia River crossing. According to Willis, the judge was "no doubt wise in the law but not exactly happy on a horse (it took a dray horse to carry him)." Gray, who was under the care of Goethals, had been nicknamed "Goethals' Baby."[72]

The Sherman party's arrival at this small center of population brought with it the usual invitations, some of which the general felt obliged to accept. But while he and the others visited the town of Yale, upstream on the Fraser River, Dodge pitched camp beside the river bank on the main street of the village. That evening Sherman and his fellow guests dined in style at a table that, he wrote, "would do credit to Washington"; no less pleased, Dodge took supper at the local hotel.[73]

From Fort Hope, Captain Jackson and the men of the army escort made their way back to Fort Coeur d'Alene while the principals of the Sherman and Miles parties continued their journey, now aboard the river steamer *Western Slope*. Their immediate destination was Victoria, the provincial capital of British Columbia, followed by a visit to the deep water bay of Esquimalt, home of the Northern Pacific fleet of the British.

Following a courtesy call on the lieutenant governor, at Victoria the party boarded a U.S. ship, the revenue cutter *Oliver Wolcott*, which been dispatched there with orders to carry General Sherman wherever he wished. Dodge was duly impressed with the display of naval might at Esquimalt. Anchored in the harbor were four warships: the *Swift-sure*, flagship of the admiral, and with it the *Sappho*, *Mutine*, and *Heroine*. Some residents of Washington Territory were apprehensive that these men of war could steam into American waters without significant resistance and quickly level the settlements on Puget Sound. However, neither Sherman nor his host, Admiral Sir Edmund Lyons, envisioned the slightest possibility of such an attack. The visiting Americans toured the *Swift-sure*, watched an exhibition drill, and attended a reception before returning to the *Oliver Wolcott*. A seventeen-gun salute, the tribute of respect to the commanding general of a friendly nation's army, sent the Sherman party on its way.[74]

Along the Pacific Coast

Smoke from forest fires combined with a blanket of fog to deny the *Oliver Wolcott* a tour of Puget Sound. The fog was so thick that the only means of reaching Fort Townsend, a two-company post on the western headland, was by sounding the ship's whistle and listening for an echo across the water. This post had been established in 1856 by Dodge's former regimental commander Colonel Haller, and it was now commanded by another former comrade of his, Lieutenant Colonel Alexander Chambers, Twenty-first Infantry.[75] After Sherman had inspected Fort Townsend, the steamer crossed the sound to Seattle, where representatives of the Grand Army of the Republic (GAR) chapter awaited him on the wharf, together with a crush of other citizens. Sherman was unenthusiastic about attending the reception there, but from what he could see of the place, he was optimistic about its future. He had visited Seattle twice before, in 1877 and 1880, and its rapid growth reminded him of San Francisco in the early days.[76] Late that afternoon, the *Oliver Wolcott* steamed with its passengers to Tacoma, at the southern end of Puget Sound. Hotel rooms were not to be had there, so the commander of the vessel, First Lieutenant James B. Moore, rigged beds for the guests on the floor of his cabin. According to Dodge, all were "very comfortable" on their last night aboard.[77]

On August 23, following a railroad journey south to Kalama and from that point a steam voyage up the Columbia River aboard the *Lurline*, the Sherman party arrived at Vancouver Barracks. General Miles had left Victoria in advance of the others, bringing with him the greater part of their baggage, and he stood at the head of those at the dock. Dodge was taken in hand by an old friend, Lieutenant Colonel Oliver D.

Greene, Second Artillery, the assistant adjutant general for the Department of the Columbia. Greene was a fellow West Pointer of the Class of 1848, and the two were eager to take up old ties, having recently been in correspondence.[78] Following a courtesy call at the home of Miles, that evening Dodge walked with Greene to the officer's club and, to his host's chagrin, beat him soundly at billiards. More satisfactory to both were the hours that followed at Greene's handsome residence, spent "gassing and drinking whiskey." On the next evening, General Sherman was Greene's guest at supper, the main item on the menu being native terrapin prepared by First Lieutenant E. S. Wood, Twenty-first Infantry. Dodge pronounced the dish "just as good as the Maryland article."[79]

The chief social event of Sherman's two-night stay at Vancouver Barracks was a reception at the home of Miles on the evening of August 24. Newspaper reports of the evening featured long lists of attendees, in the manner of a society column. Dodge was glad to encounter another old friend, the wife of First Lieutenant William L. Clarke, Twenty-third Infantry. However, he was not feeling well and thought it best not to dance with her, "as I would have had to dance with several." He and Greene returned to Greene's home at 1:30 A.M., abandoning the field to Sherman and other lively spirits. He was glad to renew contact with the Greenes, whom he thought "a model Army family," complete with a comely daughter who had wed a handsome lieutenant.[80]

On the afternoon of August 25, Sherman and his three tour companions crossed the Columbia River to Portland, Oregon, where they would stay that night and the next day. In the evening, Sherman and Gray dined as guests of Senator Joseph N. Dolph, while Dodge and Tidball found rooms at a hotel. To the satisfaction of both, they were not called upon to attend a G.A.R. reception at which Sherman addressed an audience of about 5,000 persons and shook hands with many of them. But following that event, Miles, Greene, and the post commander at Vancouver Barracks, Colonel Henry A. Morrow, Twenty-first Infantry, stopped at the hotel and brought Dodge and Tidball with them for a session at Eppinger's Saloon. Made riotous by what Dodge called "quantities of lush," this gathering lasted until just before midnight, when the Vancouver Barracks contingent hurried out to catch a boat across the river. Dodge and Tidball returned to their hotel, being in the words of the former "the worse for wear but not helpless."[81]

On Sunday, August 26, Dodge got up late, suffering from "a big head & disordered stomach." There was no hurry, for the fog and smoke made looking around the town almost impossible. A commercial vessel, the *State of Oregon*, was to sail with the party for San Francisco that night, but the bad weather rendered uncertain its exact hour of departure. After spending part of the day in preparations for travel, he and Tidball were among those invited to another dinner party at the home of Senator Dolph. Perhaps by this time Dodge was becoming jaded by the excellent fare set before him as a fellow guest with General Sherman. At any rate, he was unimpressed by Dolph's table. The company was pleasant enough, but the wines, being of local origin, were not to his taste. He was glad to board the ship just before midnight and retire to his stateroom. At 5:00 A.M. he awoke to find that the *State of Oregon* had gone aground a few miles below Portland, and went back to sleep. Five hours later, with the assistance of three tugboats, the ship's bow swung clear of the sand and mud that held it and pointed out again into the river. Its passage toward the Pacific Ocean resumed, and that night Dodge registered in his journal an uneasy prediction: "Good chance for sea sickness tomorrow."[82]

Alcoholic drinks had upset his system at Portland, but when the *State of Oregon* entered ocean waters and he began to feel white around the gills, they worked the opposite effect. He warded off illness by a regimen of moderate indulgence alternating with rest. He began the day with "a little drink," then had a "light breakfast" and a "little smoke," followed by a nap. Next, rising from bed, he "took a square drink" and found that the threat of seasickness had seemingly disappeared. He ate "a square lunch," slept two hours in the afternoon, then enjoyed "an excellent dinner" before going to bed early. He was well launched on the ocean traveler's circadian pattern of rest, leisure, and overconsumption. "Seafaring is most excellent for eating & sleeping," he wrote at 8:30 on the second night out from Portland, just before going to bed. He had eaten "three square meals since daylight" and had passed "at least 14 hours of sweet sleep since yesterday." Contrary to his fears, it had been "a most delightful voyage." He ended the first of his two journals describing experiences on the Sherman tour by noting that the ship's engineer hoped to catch sight of the Punta Arenas light in half an hour, "& if so we will sleep tonight in Frisco."[83]

At one o'clock that morning, Dodge was awakened by the sound of the anchor being dropped. Looking out his porthole, he saw the bright gaslights of the city. "It was a pretty sight," he recalled, "no houses, sea or shipping – only long rows of gaslights." The southerly segment of the inspection tour was beginning on schedule. This was fortunate, because a number of civic and military events had been arranged well in advance.[84] In respect of these, and also of San Francisco's importance as headquarters of the Division of the Pacific, General Sherman planned to remain in the vicinity more than a week. At the Palace Hotel his party was welcomed by Major General Schofield, who brought letters that had been sent in his care. Dodge was delighted to receive from A. D. Worthington a royalty check in the amount of $988.20; by June 30 a total of 30,149 copies of *Our Wild Indians* had been sold.[85] Then, in company with Major John Mendenhall, First Artillery, he made a brief tour of the city. On a walk by himself afterwards, he "fell into China – where I spent at least an hour examining a thousand curious things. Boy with baby strapped on his back – Vegetables – nice looking Chinese ladies – Queer shoes & costumes." The high point of Dodge's first day in San Francisco was his reunion that evening with Gus Bibby, an old friend whom he sought out at her home. He confessed himself "really touched by the demonstration of affection of herself & Mamie. They quite 'set me up' – I have not had so much kissing in many a day." He would pass time with Gus Bibby twice more during his stay in San Francisco.[86]

Among several other old acquaintances, he met Major Andrew S. Burt, Eighth Infantry, whose lively energy, multitude of interests, and prickly self-regard he had experienced on the Black Hills Expedition. Recently promoted, Burt was now attached to the regiment that had been Dodge's at the beginning of his career, commanding the small army post on Angel Island in San Francisco Bay.[87] Dodge spent the great part of September 5 on a visit across the bay, at Alameda, with Captain Otis W. Pollock and his family. Pollock was then on leave from his posting at Fort Bliss, Texas, a station Dodge recalled from his experiences there almost thirty years before. On the day after the perhaps bibulous visit with Pollock, he was miserable until midafternoon with "one of my old time Whiskey Belly aches," but by evening he was himself again. He attended a dinner party hosted by a retired army officer, Erasmus Darwin Keyes, where among other of the "biggest bugs," he encountered former major general of volunteers George Stoneman, now the governor of California.[88]

Because General Sherman's schedule was full and his hosts assiduous, Tidball and Dodge were sometimes left free to amuse themselves alone.[89] One morning they took breakfast together at what Dodge described as "a common restaurant where they don't charge a dozen prices." On the evening of the GAR reunion Tidball accompanied the general, but Dodge stayed away from their shared hotel room until the others had left, thus avoiding the event.[90] Nothing was said about his absence, but when on the next night he failed to attend a reception arranged by another veterans' organization, the Military Order of the Loyal Legion of the United States (MOLLUS), Sherman took him to task. "Glad to get out of it," Dodge commented in his journal.[91]

In company with the general, on two days in succession Dodge visited the estates of wealthy persons in Menlo Park, twenty-three miles south of the city. The first was Belmont, the palatial home of former senator William Sharon. Dodge thought it a "wonderful place," though the country around it interested him more. Although arid, it yielded superior crops thanks to irrigation and careful attention. "The desert blossoms as the rose," he wrote, borrowing a phrase from the Bible, then adding a less lyrical reflection: "Power of money."[92] Estates such as Belmont helped sustain the region's reputation as a haven for the wealthy, and the next day's visit was to a property that exemplified their extravagance. This was Flood's Palace, the home of James Clair Flood, a gold mining magnate who had once kept a saloon in San Francisco and now flaunted his wealth. Dodge and his companions were kindly entertained by the Flood family and shown around the grounds, with their gardens, statuary, stables, and "Regal state" generally. They returned to the city "gorged with splendor."[93]

More in tune with Dodge's accustomed tastes were the several military installations he saw in the course of the visit to San Francisco. At Black Point, the seat of Schofield's headquarters at the entrance to the bay, he and others guests were fêted in a style that, while not so lavish as at Flood's Palace, did credit to the tastes and means of high-ranking army officers. From that place they took carriages to the Presidio, a much larger post where they reviewed five companies of artillery. On another day, they boarded a boat to inspect the military prison on Alcatraz Island. Dodge thought "everything lovely" about the military post there, but in other respects he found it a "Horrible place – all up & down – a lonely rock prison." From there they steamed to Burt's post, which Dodge thought beautiful but Sherman dismissed as "of no particular use." The general was most impressed by the recently enlarged and refurnished Presidio, which he thought the proper place for consolidation of troops in future years.[94] On the whole, Dodge seems to have appreciated the scenic beauty of San Francisco but to have felt no strong desire to be posted there. For him, Fort Coeur d'Alene was the land of heart's desire, followed by Vancouver Barracks.

On September 9 the Sherman tourists boarded a car provided them by the Central Pacific Railroad and traveled south through the San Joaquin Valley to San Gabriel, a few miles past the rapidly growing town of Los Angeles. From there, they rode in carriages five miles to Sierra Madre Villa, a favorite stopping place of the general. He thought it "the most attractive spot for having a quiet, good time, of any place on the American continent."[95] No army posts being located in the vicinity, the two-night stay at this Spanish-style resort was purely for pleasure and for Sherman to renew contact with old friends. Dodge and Tidball were both captured by the setting—unlike the San Francisco suburbs, it was one of agricultural rather than architectural splendor.[96] Dodge characterized his first day at the villa as "Dolce far niente," a respite from the heat and confinement of the journey south.

The next morning featured a carriage ride around showplaces of the Los Angeles basin, all agricultural. The first stop was the ranch of E. J. "Lucky" Baldwin, so known for his successes as a trader. "A magnificent place[,] a small insignificant house" was Dodge's reaction. This was followed by visits to the vineyards and winemaking facility of L. J. Rose, then to properties owned by James de B. Shorb, B. D. Wilson, and their recent host in San Francisco, George Stoneman. Dodge was impressed by the variety of crops under cultivation: "wonderful vineyards – more wonderful orchards apples, peaches, pears, oranges lemons, limes, nectarines pomegranates, olives, figs Black & English walnuts almonds. Everything in the temperate & tropic zones." The travelers welcomed this interlude of relaxation in their tightly scheduled tour, now verging onto three months in duration. On his return to Sierra Madre Villa from this quiet day's amusement, Dodge was "tired out."[97]

On September 11, the special car returned the party to Los Angeles, where it was met by dignitaries including Horace Boughton, an acquaintance of the general from his early California days. After a carriage tour, they stopped at the Pico House, a three-story structure then considered by some the finest hostelry in the state. Sherman reacted characteristically to the improvements he saw, contrasting the "street cars, electric lights, and all . . . modern improvements" with the "small adobe town" he remembered from a visit there in 1847. Tidball, who had not seen Los Angeles before, perceived a different contrast. He noted that "the old Mexican town remains intact in its squalor, surrounded by a new, neat, and thrifty city." Dodge thought Los Angeles "very beautiful," marveling at the "endless variety" of fruit being grown there. He took special note of a banana plantation and an ornamental garden, the latter "the finest I have seen," owned by J. E. Hollanbeck, another old friend of Sherman.[98] A luncheon at the Pico House featured outsized evidence of the region's fertility—a watermelon that weighed 104 pounds.[99] Later that afternoon, a train carried the party to Mojave, a junction point at the edge of the Southern California desert, to await the Central Pacific's eastbound train the next morning.

The Army on the Fifth Frontier

The pace of the Sherman tour's travel now quickened. The eastbound train reached Needles, California, at 5:00 P.M. on September 12, and after transferring their baggage to a car provided them by the Atlantic and Pacific Railroad, the party crossed the Colorado River by a temporary bridge and entered Arizona. They followed a more northerly route than the one Sherman had taken on his inspection tour the year before, and the next afternoon they reached Wingate Station, New Mexico, three miles distant from Fort Wingate. On hand to greet them were the officers of the garrison, headed by Colonel Luther P. Bradley, Thirteenth Infantry, Dodge's gracious host at Fort Laramie during the Black Hills Expedition. That evening, Bradley hosted a reception where Dodge "met a lot of pleasant people."[100] These were military men and their wives, the society in which he, Tidball, and also Sherman were most at ease. However, the three officers' reactions following a tour of the post proper differed somewhat. Dodge, a severe judge in such matters, thought Fort Wingate only "fair to middling." Tidball admired the comfortable men's quarters of grayish blue clay, "very neat and pleasing to the eye." Sherman, for whom solidity of construction and strategic location were the paramount considerations, judged it "well built . . . well located . . . [and] all sufficient for that country."[101]

The next day's stop, Albuquerque, was not the seat of an army post but was nonetheless of professional interest to Sherman as the only place in that extensive territory where several railroads converged. A deputation of citizens took him and his party on a carriage tour of the old and new towns, then to the Armijo House for dinner, and finally to the Aztec Club for speeches and wine. Sherman agreed with local leaders that Albuquerque was destined to replace Santa Fe as the commercial hub of the region. "The old town on the river bank remains but little changed," he reported to Secretary Lincoln, "whilst the new town about a mile back shows all the activity, and go-aheaditiveness of Modern America, and its leading citizens expect it soon to rival Chicago."[102]

On September 15, the train reached Santa Fe, where a two-night stopover was planned. This was the headquarters of the District of New Mexico, then under the command of Brigadier General Mackenzie. Dodge was travel worn; he had been unable to sleep the night before, and to his frustration, the usually quiet Tidball "inflicted" him with conversation on the night of arrival. After a morning walk on the next day, he wrote some letters and took a nap. Roused at 1:30 by a message that the general wanted him at the midday meal, he complied and then went back to bed, and by late afternoon he was back to normal. In company with Tidball and Captain Charles J. Dickey, Twenty-Second Infantry, he called upon the ladies of Fort Marcy, at the edge of town, and spent the rest of the evening at a genteel gambling house. It being a Sunday, there was no play, only "drinks and conversation," but he chatted with "a pleasant lot of people."[103] The nature of Sherman's consultations with Mackenzie on this day was not recorded. Within a few weeks, the young general assumed command of the Department of Texas; but shortly after that, suffering under a delusion that he had been authorized to reorganize the U.S. Army, he was transferred to the government asylum in Washington for treatment.[104] Brilliant but brief, his career was almost at an end.

As the result of an agreement between the Atchison, Topeka and Santa Fe Railroad and the Denver and Rio Grande Railway that neither should pass within twenty miles of the other, a gap in the rail line north of Santa Fe forced the Sherman party to ride in ambulances to the southern terminus of the Denver and Rio Grande, at Espanola. Sherman was astonished at this arrangement, which greatly lessened the military usefulness of that railroad route. On his return to Washington, he urged speedy construction to close the gap, by public or by private means, a task that was accomplished not long afterward.[105]

Curiously, yet not illogically from his point of view, the general considered the United States of his time to possess five "frontiers": the Atlantic and Gulf, the northern, the Pacific, the southern or Mexican, and the interior.[106] At this stage of the tour, he was approaching the southern reaches of the fifth frontier, the mountain country formerly occupied by the unruly Utes. From Espanola, the Denver and Rio Grande Railway gave red-carpet treatment to the traveling party until its arrival in Denver ten days later. The route they traveled was along a zigzag course. First they rode west to Durango, Colorado, then east to Pueblo, then further west on a more northerly route to Salt Lake City, and finally back along the same route to Pueblo before making the run north to Denver. Tidball calculated the distance traveled on the Denver and Rio Grande at 2,088 miles.[107]

Owing to the superior adaptability of narrow-gauge track to broken country, the entire system of this railroad was narrow gauge. To all members of the Sherman party except Dodge, narrow-gauge travel was a novelty. According to Tidball, "greatly were we astonished at beholding [its] capabilities for climbing mountains, passing cañons and gorges, clinging to the edges of precipices and overcoming steep grades." At Antonito, just north of the New Mexico–Colorado border, the tracks passed through the rugged Toltec canyon. To a man, the travelers marveled at both the scenery and the route that had been carved through it. Later Dodge was struck by the contrast between the village of Durango he had visited three years before and the rapidly growing town of 2,500 inhabitants he now saw.[108]

Strangely, Fort Lewis, the military post a few miles outside Durango, had not been notified of General Sherman's intention to visit there. Established in July 1880 near the Southern Ute Agency to help preserve order in the region,[109] Fort Lewis

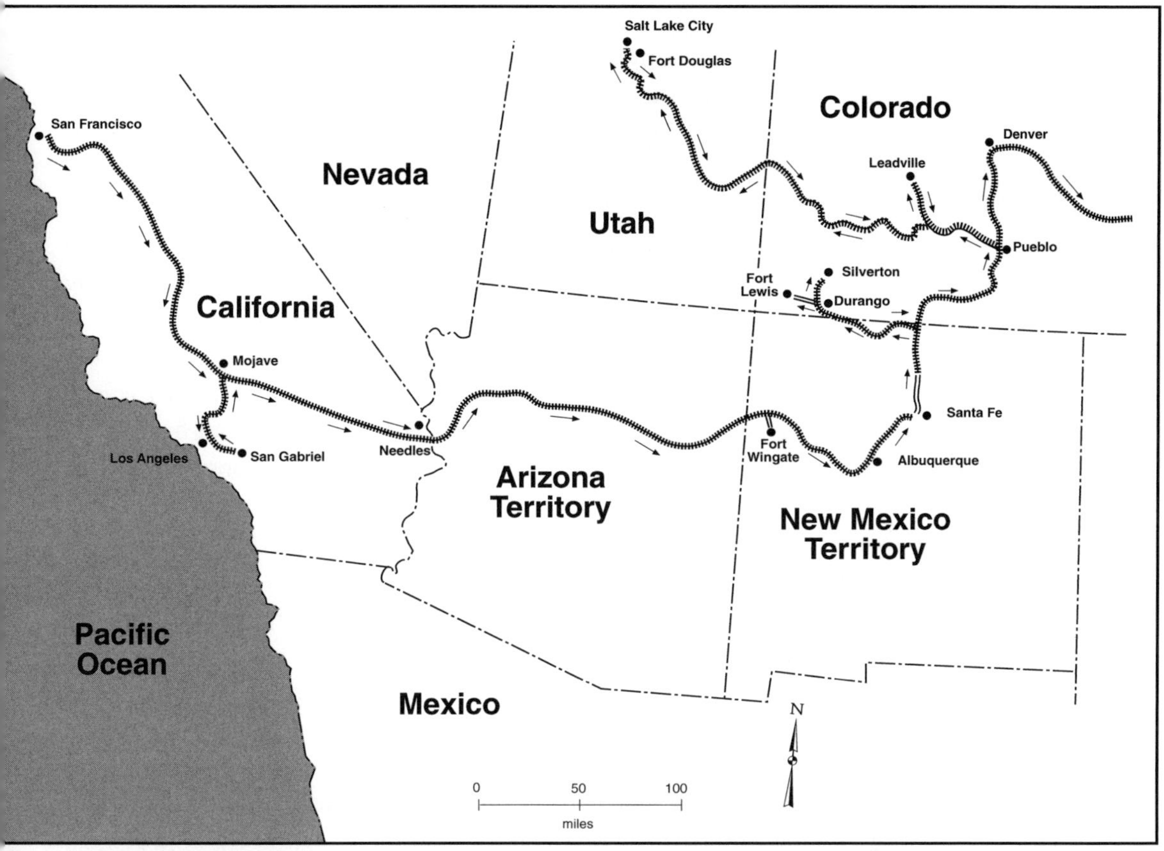

Inspection Tour Itinerary, San Francisco, California, to Denver, Colorado, September 8–26, 1883

was a busy place but, in the opinion of Sherman and his two military companions, not an attractive one. Tidball was mercifully vague, remarking on the excellent potatoes grown in the post garden. Dodge thought the post "badly located – badly built." Sherman found "nothing striking" in its location and, like Dodge, was not pleased with its design and construction. For all three visitors, the best feature of the post was its officers, including the commander, Major Robert H. Hall, Twenty-second Infantry. Dodge considered the Twenty-second "a dandy horse-riding Regt" but found the officers he met "a very pleasant set."[110] That evening, in bright moonlight, a drunken ambulance driver managed to return the party safely to Durango, where they spent the night on their railroad car.

The next day's activity was an improvement over the excursion to Fort Lewis, being strictly touristic and pleasantly eventful. The main feature was a white-knuckle railroad journey, forty-five miles north through the canyon of the Las Animas River to Silverton, a mining town at an elevation of 9,000 feet. That the train could pass safely along this precarious route excited Tidball's wonder, and Dodge declared the trip a "Splendid ride."[111] Sherman had thought of continuing north from Silverton to the town of Ouray, but upon learning that the route there was over a little-used mountain trail that would require a pack train and mules, he gave up the idea, and the party returned to Durango, continuing on to Pueblo.

While awaiting a westbound train across the mountains, they remained in that rapidly growing city almost a full day. Dodge recalled Pueblo from his Fort Lyon years, when it was a sleepy village; now he found it "improved out of my knowledge." Tidball noted that "the old Mexican pueblo, from which it takes its name, is gone—swept away by a superior civilization." The visitors watched the production of steel railroad tracks at the Bessemer steelworks of the Colorado Coal and Iron Company, then drove to the Pueblo Smelting and Refining Works, where they observed the process of reducing silver ore to base bullion. In the evening, while citizens called upon Sherman in the parlor section of the railroad car, Dodge strolled through the city streets and met several persons whom he had known years earlier. Still, he judged it "a pretty rough place."[112]

The following day's travel brought him into view of other locations he recalled, this time from his summer tour of duty in the Colorado mountains three years before. Passing through the canyon of the Arkansas River, the train ascended the Marshall Pass in dizzying fashion, then entered the precipitous Black Canyon of the Gunnison River. Dodge noticed that part of the railway along the Gunnison followed a military road whose construction he had supervised. He also recognized an old fishing spot of his, but he could not catch sight of the post on the Uncompahgre River, nor could he make out what he remembered as prominent landmarks.[113] During his absence, the vicinity had been settled and become farmland. That evening, at the crossing of the Grand River in western Colorado, a group of citizens clamored with drum and fife for a sight of General Sherman by light of their lanterns. Upon his appearance, they informed him that they needed a military post in the vicinity to protect them from Indians. But according to Tidball, the general "ridiculed the idea of such a lot of stalwart fellows wanting protection from a few miserable Indians. The ludicrousness of the idea struck them, and amid their shouts and laughter we steamed away."[114]

On the morning of September 22, the train came within sight of the Wasatch Mountains, covered with a dense growth of aspen, maple, and scrub oak. The fall colors were brilliant in the clear morning air. "With one voice we pronounced it the most beautiful picture we had ever seen," Tidball wrote, adding perhaps with irony that "Justice Gray, with aesthetic tastes, was enthusiastic over it, and readily admitted that there was nothing in or around Boston to excel it."[115] The sight helped compensate for the disappointment they had felt during the three weeks of travel from Fort Coeur d'Alene to Vancouver Barracks. During that entire period, views of the northwestern mountains were severely limited owing to dense smoke from forest fires.

At Salt Lake City, another two-night stop, Sherman and Gray were given rooms at Fort Douglas, on a height of land just to the east of the city, while Dodge and Tidball stayed at the Walker House, a well appointed hotel owned by G. S. Erb, an old acquaintance of the general.[116] Colonel McCook, who maintained a friendly relationship with Mormon leaders, was in his element as host. After "*doing* the city, the churches &c," Dodge attended a ball at the fort and "met all the people . . . talked

& drank and had a good time." On the next day, Sherman and the rest of his party lunched with Erb at the hotel, then attended a service at the Tabernacle. The general also enjoyed the good will of the Mormons, for although he did not share their religious faith, he respected their right to believe and worship as they chose. Privately at least, Dodge was less liberal. At the Tabernacle he "stood the nonsensical gabble" for an hour, then left to take an afternoon train ride by himself to the Great Salt Lake, where he admired the varied hues of the water at sunset.[117]

On the morning of September 24, the party set out on the return trip to Pueblo, the general having arranged to pass over by daylight the section of the railroad he had failed to see on the trip west owing to darkness. The journey included a side excursion north to the mining town of Leadville, Colorado, at an elevation of 10,300 feet, where Sherman was greeted by the GAR and others of what he called "the Boys," Civil War veterans. On the afternoon of September 26 the train reached Denver, where yet another crowd was on hand, and for the last time a cadre of importunate newspaper reporters. One of the latter presented himself at the door of the general's room at the Windsor Hotel, but in a few moments of byplay Sherman and Dodge sent him on his way. "Glad you called," Sherman greeted his uninvited guest. "Did you come by the elevator or climb the stairs?" Perhaps bemused, the young man answered that he had used the stairs. "Good!" exclaimed the general. "There can be only one witness, and one witness in Colorado don't count." Turning to Dodge, he called out, "Colonel, that last reporter I fired from the hotel window, he died; didn't he?" Dodge, seated at a table with a drink before him, looked up thoughtfully and took his cue. "You mean Hopkins, or that other chap?" he asked. "The other chap had his back broken, you know. Let's see, the distance, I believe, was just the same as this, four stories exactly, and . . ." But the newspaperman's hasty exit ended the performance of these jesters. That evening Tidball supplied the reporter with all the information he needed, while Sherman delivered a witty address that delighted his audience at a GAR reception.[118]

This would be the last of the two-night stops, and from the general's point of view, appropriately so. The tour of inspection had satisfied him that as he approached the end of his official career, the United States was on a steady course of development in its western states and territories. The system of railroads had brought with it the advance of civilization, opening up to peaceful development first the central region, then the south and the north, and finally the fifth or interior frontier. In his concluding letter to Secretary Lincoln, he held up Denver, Colorado, "the peer of any City of the Great West," as a worthy symbol of the nation's accomplishment. It offered "elegant hotels, thousands of fine brick stores and dwellings, lighted by electricity, with bountiful supply of purest water, and every thing that can make life agreeable."[119]

Dodge described Denver, and indeed the entire summer tour, from a less encompassing historical viewpoint than either Sherman or Tidball. His journal was almost entirely contemporaneous in its focus, a record of his personal experiences and reactions from day to day. Fortunately for himself, he had been given the opportunity to join these two officers and the two justices on a journey that most Americans of his time could undertake only through imagination. Reunions with army comrades like Lieutenant Colonel Greene and friends like Gus Bibby had been a great source of satisfaction for him, as had the wilderness travel, the hunting and fishing, and "doing" the tourist sites. Even more than these, his shared experiences of the summer with General Sherman brought to fruition a relationship in which he took pride. In all, the summer of 1883 was an experience without precedence or recurrence in his lifetime.

At the journey's end, as he remarked in journal entries for both his nights in Denver, Dodge was tired. The long succession of greetings, feasts, receptions, libations, packings, and repackings had taken their toll on a man who was unaccustomed to this peripatetic mode of public life. Like Sherman, Dodge was ready to open the next chapter of his life story—in his case, the duties as colonel of the Eleventh Infantry that would probably occupy him for the balance of his career. On September 28, aboard a train bound east to Saint Louis, he wrote the final entry in his journal record of the inspection tour, a dateline and the phrase "On cars."[120]

Part Seven

Regimental Commander, 1883–1891

Dodge passed the final years of his active service during a period that has become known, with considerable justification, as the twilight of the Old Army. The careers of veteran soldiers who had served in the War with Mexico, the Civil War, and the later Indian conflicts were coming to an end. The army now faced the challenges of maintaining its combat readiness, preserving its esprit de corps, and innovating—all in a time of profound peace.

Dodge welcomed these challenges, for he was not content to perform what he called "mere guard duty,"[1] and he refused to view his own career as crepuscular. Thus, as a post commander, he planned and directed ambitious construction programs. As a regimental commander, he fostered the professional development of his officers and men, adopting policies to advance that aim which later became standard throughout the army. He participated in several servicewide initiatives, including efforts to improve skill in marksmanship; programs to improve conditions for enlisted men; cooperation between the regular army and state militias; trials of new weapons; "practice marches" to ensure the familiarity of troops with the conditions of field duty; and experiments with post canteens, operated by the men themselves rather than by authorized traders. His published writings now focused almost entirely on military matters, and his varied involvements marked him as a veteran officer of reliable judgment, willingness to innovate, and devotion to the army.

In 1888 Major General John M. Schofield succeeded Lieutenant General Sheridan as commanding General of the Army. Schofield had not forgotten the good opinion of Dodge he had formed two decades before, and as a result Dodge performed a succession of special assignments in the following year, one of which marked a new high point in his career: Riding at the head of a brigade, he led the army contingent in a parade through New York City to celebrate the centennial of George Washington's inauguration there as president.

During his last two years of service, Dodge was sometimes tormented by rheumatism, an affliction he suffered along with many officers who had endured winter conditions on the plains. Whether his physical condition would permit him to remain on active duty until the legally mandated date of his retirement was one of two questions that largely defined the final months of his career. The other was made public in a series of articles in the *Army and Navy Journal*: In view of Colonel Dodge's distinguished services to the nation, would he be promoted to brigadier general?

25

In the Department of Dakota

Dodge left the inspection tour party at Saint Louis to return to his post via Chicago while the other members continued east to Washington, D.C. The resumption of regular duty brought with it a worrisome reinitiation to the exacting requirements of army office procedures. In Saint Louis he had written out for the general's signature two copies of an order directing him to proceed from there to his duty station, Fort Sully. One of these he carried with him, and the other the general was to place on file in the office of the adjutant general. Shortly after arriving at the post, however, he discovered that the order lacked one formula declaration—"This travel is necessary for the public service"—that was required by law in order to permit remuneration of his summer travel expenses. The omission was perhaps ironic in view of the light duty he had performed all summer, but he could ill afford the expense out of his own pocket. Accordingly, he wrote the adjutant general explaining the situation. He requested that the order left there by Sherman be amended to include the missing statement and that he be authorized to correct his own copy.[1]

This was a reasonable solution to the problem, but for administrative purposes it proved unacceptable. On November 6, five days after Sherman had relinquished command of the army, Brigadier General Drum informed Dodge that the order in question, issued by the former commanding general in Saint Louis, could not be amended by that office in Washington. Only the general himself could do so, and by that time he had left the city.[2] Dodge therefore addressed a note to Sherman at his new residence in Saint Louis, explaining the difficulty once more and enclosing for his signature two corrected copies of the original order.[3] All was now in due form. The revised orders were signed, the travel expenses authorized and, after two months' delay, repaid.[4] Clearly, the summer idyll of freedom from bureaucratic usages was over.

Perhaps emboldened by his friendly relations with Sherman and also bearing in mind that the general had set aside his role as commanding general, in the draft of his November 13 note Dodge included a familiar salutation, "Dear General," and a brief personal sentiment in closing. But before sending it, he thought better of both.[5] After all, he was addressing a senior in rank, and on official business; not to continue observing the formulae of accepted army usage might seem disrespectful. Now and afterward, the contacts between the two officers were friendly, familiar, and evinced mutual regard, but on Dodge's part they never lost the tone of respectful deference.

General Sheridan's change of station from Chicago to Washington created a vacancy in the Military Division of the Missouri that was filled, agreeably to Dodge, by his former commander Major General Schofield. With other officers, he was on hand at the Leland Hotel in Chicago to welcome the new division commander and his family on their arrival from San Francisco.[6] Despite the out-of-the-way location of Fort Sully, its access to the railhead at Pierre afforded a convenient avenue to points east that made possible brief journeys such as this. Moreover, the post was not without other real satisfactions. A reporter for the *Dakota Journal* of Pierre described it as "one of the handsomest and liveliest in the West." Commenting on its picturesque location overlooking the Missouri River, with the seemingly endless expanse of the Sioux Reservation to the west, this reporter wrote that "to live in such a romantic spot one need never weary or become lonesome."[7] Visitors from Pierre enlivened the scene at weekly performances by the regimental band, baseball games between the post team and the Pierre Reds, and other events. In 1883 the Thanksgiving celebration at the post featured a gargantuan meal, a game of football and other athletic contests, and in the evening a "grand ball" made possible by contributions of one dollar apiece by all who attended.[8] At Christmas the observances were equally varied. Assisted by Joe and Laura, Dodge hosted a gala supper party and dance. A correspondent of the *Army and Navy Journal* declared this entertainment "'simply immense,' the objects of particular mention being the many wreaths and mottoes of evergreens, made interesting by their beautiful design."[9]

Dodge was finding garrison life at Fort Sully more satisfying than during his first winter there. "My house is a little gem," he wrote Julia, "my servants all any man could wish in attention & in devotion to my interests."[10] The only continuing negative was the weather, which aggravated his rheumatism. However, the possibility of a change of station for the regiment offered hope of an improvement in that regard.

Events at Fort Sully stayed on a steady course until the night of February 11, 1884, when calamity struck. A fire broke out, destroying several buildings and much other government property. In the absence of sufficient barrack space, one company was ordered to Fort Bennett for temporary housing until something better could be provided.[11] This emergency in the dead of winter precipitated official tensions that cast a shadow over Dodge's service in the Department of Dakota for several years. A "Boom in economy," as he paradoxically termed it,[12] prevailed in the department. General Terry was attempting to stretch a small allotment of quartermaster's funds to continue the expansion of Fort Snelling while also giving due attention to other posts likely to be designated permanent in the army's program of consolidation.[13]

Fort Sully, which had strategic value only so long as the Sioux Reservation remained forbidden to settlement by non-Indians, did not rank high on Terry's priority list. In fact, in 1878 he had recommended its abandonment.[14]

In accordance with a telegraphed directive, on the day after the fire Dodge forwarded to departmental headquarters an estimate of the costs to replace quartermaster's sheds, barracks, and other essential buildings. The urgent need for action was not a matter for debate,[15] but it exacerbated an already strained fiscal situation. Assisted by his post and regimental quartermaster, First Lieutenant Ralph W. Hoyt, Dodge pressed the claims of Fort Sully forcefully[16]—so forcefully as to give offense to members of General Terry's staff. Dodge refused to accept as definitive the discouragements he received from two of the general's trusted subordinates, Major James M. Moore, the department's quartermaster general, and Captain Robert P. Hughes, Third Infantry, its acting inspector general. Hughes, a brother-in-law, aide-de-camp, and longtime friend of Terry's, appears to have taken umbrage at Dodge's persistence.[17] This miffed the bachelor general, who as Dodge later commented to Sherman was "as tender of his staff as he would be of his wife's honor—if he had one."[18] Undaunted, Dodge made his case directly to Terry and then, during that officer's absence at Washington, to General Schofield, who promptly granted him the authorization he required. Even though he had informed Terry of his intention to take this step, the department commander was offended by it,[19] especially as it resulted in an action he did not support.[20] In Terry's view, the determined advocacy of Dodge bordered on insubordination, but Dodge was not one to back away from a confrontation if he thought himself in the right. "The 'Powers' would be very glad to try me by Court Martial," he informed Fred in October, "& I am very willing to be tried."[21]

By that time, the repairs and new construction were already well advanced, and Dodge was proud of the results. He had "done wonderfully well," he wrote Sherman, with the funds that had been made available to him. True, he had alienated himself from General Terry's good will, and the likelihood of hearty support for any further initiatives from the departmental commander was slim. But efforts by Terry to make his continued service unpleasant had no effect on him, other than to confirm his readiness to be transferred elsewhere. "O! for Coeur d'Alene, or the Pacific," he exclaimed to Sherman in October.[22]

Publicity in the *Army and Navy Journal*

One feature of Dodge's service as a post and regimental commander that gave continuing satisfaction to General Terry was the superior performance of the Eleventh Infantry in target firing. Terry supported the army's efforts in this area, and the marksmanship program in the Department of Dakota was the strongest in the service. As in 1883, Dodge's regiment helped produce this enviable result in 1884 by recording the highest overall score in the army, and that despite marked improvement by other units. That year's Fort Sully contingent included 75 men classified as "sharpshooters," the highest level of attainment, 255 as "marksmen," and only 10 as "third-class" men.[23] By June 30, 1885, Fort Sully boasted 89 sharpshooters, 83 marksmen, and no third-class performers.[24]

Dodge took a keen interest in the marksmanship program, especially in the adoption of provisions to ensure that competitions were administered fairly.[25] Even so, he believed the value of target practice to the army was being overestimated. More useful for military purposes was practice in skirmish firing, which approximated the actual conditions of combat. In his view, the close attention being paid to marksmanship scores was another army fad, like the enthusiasm for instruction in signaling, or "wig-wag," of a few years before.

The success of Dodge's post and regiment in target firing received publicity and, inevitably, led to controversy. In August 1885 a letter from "Trigger" in the *Army and Navy Journal* cast doubt on the honesty of the officials who certified such high scores,[26] and his sly reference to "paper percentages" moved Dodge to write a detailed response. Attributing to "Trigger" the human tendency to denigrate an achievement one is unable to equal, he warned that rifle competitions were threatening to undermine army morale. "Regiments, posts, companies, individuals, officers and men are all becoming so leavened with doubt and suspicion, each of the other, that I am beginning to fear that by the time we have succeeded in making an army of sharpshooters, (which is only a question of time and work) we will have destroyed that brotherhood, that *camaradarie* which is at once the pride and happiness of every true man in the Service." While admitting that some persons would cheat at rifle firing if given the opportunity, he outlined elaborate measures he had taken to render cheating impossible. "There can be no false marking at Fort Sully," he submitted, "unless every officer and man at the post is sufficiently a scoundrel to enter into a grand conspiracy to that end."[27] A few weeks later, "Trigger," in an arch tone, professed his entire satisfaction with the explanation Dodge had given. He suggested that the standards for marksmen at Fort Sully were, however, a little less rigorous than those observed elsewhere, possibly a bit behind the times.[28]

As it happened, the first letter from "Trigger" appeared in the same issue of the *Army and Navy Journal* as the first installment of a feature series entitled "Chats around the Mess Table," later shortened to "The Mess." Although signed by a pseudonym, "The Caterer," these articles were clearly the productions of Major Andrew S. Burt, Dodge's energetic subordinate on the Black Hills Expedition.[29] Among several persons named in the portrayed gossip of the first article, Dodge received by far the fullest treatment. Two of his individual traits were featured—his style as a storyteller and his skill as a marksman. These came together in a dialogue between "Dickie Dodge" and "little Major B——":

> In the talk referred to Dickie took a long whiff of his pipe, threw back those big shoulders and orated:

> "Oh, balls, McCrackin! What's all this target business going to amount to? (This was in '75, round a camp fire in the Black Hills). What's it going to amount to? Just tell me. Now I can't hit a target at all—but I can make old Betsy Jane, there, speak pretty well at a deer jumping from one up to five hundred yards, and never alter the near sight." And he could, too.
>
> "Well, but you see, Colonel, you've got the buffalo by the horns, not by the tail, as you should, according to the highest *secundum artem* in that statement. Your ability to shoot that way is high art. That's way beyond target shooting. That's what a man "apes" to do after years of practice on a target. To start a man shooting your style is like the fool idea they've got in the cavalry of putting a raw recruit on horse bareback to give him the first lessons in riding. The recruit has as much idea of staying there as a "pfherd" has of a cyclone, and you want him to do that which Colonel May or General Bob Williams in their palmy days considered difficult. And they were men whom to see ride was seeing the dream of a Centaur."
>
> "Oh, pshaw, B——, what's the use of talking. You're stuck on this shooting boom; you're crazy as old Ord."
>
> "All pioneers are crazy to the crowd. But you'll see the day when anybody who talks the old Army out against target practice will go and hold a mass meeting at some prominent lunatic asylum, and pass resolutions that the service is going to—General Sheridan's paradise."
>
> "Where's that?"
>
> "Texas."

This dialogue was followed by a portrayed interchange between The Caterer and another officer in which the latter recalled Dodge's prowess as a hunter. "Why," he declares, "I knew Dodge to kill sixteen deer straight. Not all in one day, mark you, but shooting out on successive days. It was up in the Black Hills that year Jenny went up to make a survey. He hunts in a funny way too; goes mounted with an orderly; they seemingly pound along, and you'd think they'd scare every deer within a mile. He does jump 'em up. But it's all the same to Dodge. He lights off his horse and begins banging away with his old Army gun. The deer on the run jump and no matter how far off—any distance under five hundred yards. It's a big chance against the deer, every time."[30]

Evidently the description of Dodge's skill as a hunter piqued the interest of some readers. A few weeks after the first article in the series was published, "No-Shooter," a correspondent from Fort Bidwell, California, Burt's current posting, testified to that officer's skill in offhand shooting, the very style Dodge excelled in. In fact, Burt was a superior marksman. He had won a badge in a tournament sponsored by the Western Rifle Association, and in 1884 he attained sharpshooter status within the army.[31] On behalf of his fellow officers at Fort Bidwell, "No-Shooter" offered "to back Major Burt for ducats offhand or to rule" against any field officer in the army, "Colonel Dodge not barred."[32] But as Dodge had earlier remarked, contests such as the one proposed would strain the bond of comradeship that joined army men. The subjects of marksmanship and sometimes questionable target scores received treatment in later installments of "The Mess," but the issue of Burt's superiority to Dodge as a marksman, or otherwise, was never put to the test.

In the issue of the *Army and Navy Journal* for September 19, 1885, Burt took up another thread of memory from the Black Hills Expedition: Dodge's investigation of a incident wherein the manuscript of an article by Reuben B. Davenport of the *New York Herald* was supposedly lost in transit to Fort Laramie but later discovered there in good condition. The delay in delivery, the Caterer now alleged, resulted from collusion between Burt and Thomas C. MacMillan of the *Chicago Inter-Ocean* to "scoop" Davenport in a report of gold discoveries. "Col. Dodge says he was going to hang you and Mac for that scheme," the Caterer tells Burt in a conversation at the mess table.[33] Thus, through the playful portrayal of him in "The Mess," Dodge was gaining reputation among his army colleagues as a colorful character, an energetic commanding officer with ideas of his own and with deep roots in the army's past.

Dodge's interest in the development of a magazine gun for use by the army led to his post's participation in the testing of three models that had been recommended by the Magazine Gun Board in its 1882 report: the Lee, the Chaffee-Reese, and the Hotchkiss.[34] Although General Sheridan viewed the magazine rifle as "the arm of the future,"[35] the breech-loading Springfield rifle was still considered an excellent weapon, and many doubted whether any of the recommended designs warranted its replacement. In July 1885 the Adjutant General's Office issued directions for tests at selected posts, with the results to be forwarded to departmental headquarters for conflation.[36] In that month, R. T. Hare, an expert on the weapons, visited four posts in the Department of Dakota—Forts Sully, Randall, Keogh, and Missoula—to provide the necessary instruction in their use.[37] At Fort Sully as elsewhere, the tests yielded a clear conclusion: that the magazine gun as thus far perfected was not yet suitable for adoption.

Two years later, Sheridan, impatient at the slow progress of its development in the United States, reaffirmed his confidence in the magazine gun concept and suggested purchasing a supply from abroad.[38] As an officer in the field, Dodge was more practical in his outlook. He contended that whatever weapon was adopted, soldiers must have confidence in its use under all conditions, not merely on the firing range and in drill. As to the supply of test rifles he had been sent, since the test they were simply taking up storage space. He requested directions for their disposal, a matter that had not yet been attended to.[39]

In the U.S. Army of the 1880s, regimental commanders like Dodge possessed fewer powers than they had once enjoyed, and fewer than commanders in many foreign armies. Departmental commanders had usurped authority in several areas traditionally the prerogative of the colonels of regiments, such as the assignment of recruits to their respective duty stations. The inability to perform adequately the role of mentor to the officers and men of his regiment frustrated Dodge. After two years of service in the Department of Dakota, he had not even seen five of the ten companies that comprised the Eleventh Infantry, a situation that clearly required correction. The promotion of enlisted men to noncommissioned officer rank remained his responsibility, but except for the companies at Forts Sully and Bennett, he had no means of making firsthand judgments and had to rely on the recommendations of others. Some of his companies were stationed hundreds of miles apart,[40] making a cohesive sense of regimental identity almost impossible to preserve. For an officer like Dodge, who regarded his colonelcy as the culmination of an honorable life's work, these were serious disadvantages.

Nevertheless, he found means to promote the welfare of his regiment and sharpen its military preparedness. He recommended that officers who were no longer capable of performing active duty appear before a Retiring Board, thus performing a service both to them and to the army. Promotion remained agonizingly slow in the lower ranks, but the departure of the veterans, however regrettable, created vacancies that brought in new men and accelerated the advancement of their seniors. As a result of these and other actions, in October 1884 twenty-four of the Eleventh Infantry's officers were on duty with the regiment, a gain of eight in a single year.[41] When celebrations on behalf of his officers were in order, Dodge played his part. The promotion of Captain Charles A. Wikoff to major after twenty-two years as a company officer was such an occasion, prompting a complimentary hop.[42]

Dodge did what he could to advance the careers of deserving subordinates, even though their successes might result in transfer out of the regiment. Captain Theodore Schwan, a native of Germany, was one such officer. In 1886 Dodge recommended Schwan to fill a vacancy in the adjutant general's department, a much sought-after appointment that he eventually won.[43] In the same year, Dodge broke with army precedent by announcing that henceforward his regimental staff officers would be appointed for periods of no longer than three years. In a general order accepting the resignations of First Lieutenant George G. Lott as adjutant and First Lieutenant Ralph W. Hoyt as quartermaster, he made clear that he did so with personal reluctance, having been "long and intimately associated" with them both. However, despite his high estimate of their abilities, he believed that the current practice of retaining regimental staff officers in those positions until they were promoted to captaincies was ill advised. Rather, "the Colonel commanding believes that rotation in these positions is, in time of peace, directly in the interests of the Service, and of Army education; giving to each and every First Lieutenant an opportunity to make himself thoroughly proficient not only in line but in staff duties." Future appointments would go to those first lieutenants who, in his judgment, were "best fitted by habits, capacity, and attention to duty for these most responsible positions."[44]

Dodge's announcement of the new policy drew praise and stimulated further discussion of term limits for regimental appointments. In February 1887 a general order from army headquarters prescribed four years as the maximum term for service in regimental staff details.[45]

"The Enlisted Soldier"

Thoughts on the needs of the private soldiers and noncommissioned officers of his regiment led Dodge in 1885 to submit an essay entitled "The Enlisted Soldier" in a competition sponsored by the Military Service Institution for the best statement on that subject. The identities of the contestants were not made known to the three judges, all entrants adopting pseudonyms. Writing as "Waechter 91,"[46] Dodge won honorable mention in the contest, coming in second by a narrow margin to a medical officer, Surgeon Alfred A. Woodhull.[47] Subsequently his essay was published under his own name by the regimental press and somewhat later as an article in the *Journal of the Military Service Institution*.[48] Approximately 21,000 words in length, the work was a thoughtful, carefully organized overview of a topic that had long interested him.

"The Enlisted Soldier" was divided into eighteen sections followed by an enumeration of suggestions for change. Parts of the commentary elaborated ideas he had expressed in earlier years. One of these, under the heading "Rewards," recalled his support of Captain Pollock's 1875 proposal for an increase in the pay of noncommissioned officers. But here he presented the theme within his own philosophical framework, relating privates, on the one hand, and the corporals and sergeants who had authority over them, on the other, to the "two great classes" of humankind. The private's sole duty is obedience, whereas "The corporal commands, and his orders must be obeyed. He has crossed the great gulf. He was taken the first, greatest, most important step in mounting the ladder of ambition" (286–87). Dodge argued that the significance of this first step should be recognized by increasing the pay of a corporal to twice that of a private. When a corporal is properly paid, he predicted, "we shall see a struggle to obtain and keep these offices which will prove of inestimable value to discipline, and redound to the credit of the Army and the country" (288).

In another section, Dodge criticized the current focus on target firing as likely to produce an army of specialists, not soldiers. "The mass of our foot Army is well drilled, and composed of fair shots, but the men are not soldiers," he contended, "because, as a rule, they know nothing of field service" (300). He advocated not less than two months of instruction annually for every company, and not in drill and garrison duty but in campaign life. "This will give practical knowledge of that most important duty of the soldier, *how to take care of himself*. It will give real knowledge of advance and rear-guards, and flankers; of skirmish fighting as it actually occurs; of marching and camping; and make him a soldier instead of a specialist as now" (300–301).

Emphasizing that his intention was not to expose abuses but to identify practices that admitted of improvement and were liable to abuse, Dodge listed four ways to improve the condition of the enlisted soldier: permit men to purchase their discharges rather than requiring them to serve out full five-year terms of enlistment; punish desertion more severely, as the grave military offense it is; reduce the amount of manual labor required of soldiers; and provide regular changes of station and courses of instruction, so as to ward off monotony (316–18). Closely argued, crisply phrased, and demonstrating throughout his knowledge of enlisted men and the army's policies governing them, Dodge's essay was an impressive performance. He saved among his personal papers letters of praise from career army men who had read "The Enlisted Soldier" with appreciation.[49]

Except for this extended essay, Dodge wrote for publication only on occasion during his service in the Department of Dakota, in letters addressed to the editors of the *Army and Navy Journal* or else sent to them as copies for their information and possible use. For example, in December 1883, the newspaper reported that he had written the Humane Association at Washington, "calling attention to the wholesale destruction of buffalo still going on in the territories, and recommending that Congress pass a game law and direct the Army to enforce it."[50] In July 1886, the editors printed a letter he had written them, enclosing another to T. H. Hamersley, publisher of the *United Service* and *Century* magazines. He complained to Hamersley of his company's failure to supply copies of publications he had subscribed for. "If you conduct your business in this manner," he warned, "you cannot expect to receive the support of officers who, being on the frontier, are forced to rely on the promises of publishers for their reading matter."[51] Not surprisingly, during this period Dodge remained best known as an author for his major works, *The Plains* and *Our Wild Indians*. The "Indian Question" was no longer the burning issue it had been, but his recommendations for reform continued to receive mention. As late as October 15, 1887, the *Army and Navy Journal* observed that it would be "well to recall at this juncture the recommendations of General Dodge, to which so little attention has been given. He proposes to turn the Indians over to the War Department in peace as well as in war."[52]

In the fall of 1884, Dodge received from General Sherman a request for information and assistance concerning a group of topics that recalled their association in preparing *Our Wild Indians*. Sherman had agreed to preside at a convention of cattlemen that was to meet for the first time in November at Saint Louis, and he wished to acquaint himself beforehand with facts surrounding some of the issues that might come before that body. As part of his course of study he intended to reread *The Plains* and *Our Wild Indians*, but he had lent his copy of the latter to some friend and so had lost it. Stipulating that he wished to pay for a replacement, he asked Dodge to order one sent him.

In the remainder of his letter, Sherman set down some thoughts about the great historical forces that were determining the fates of the buffalo and the Indians, two populations on which Dodge was an authority. The general discerned the operation of these same forces in another development that now interested him—the increasing number of cattle and cowboys on lands that were once the preserve of the native inhabitants. The near-extinction of the buffalo seemed to him "almost a decree of the Almighty" in which, by Darwinian law, "the fittest survived." Moreover, he took the supposed inability of most breeding cattle to survive the birth of an offspring sired by a buffalo bull as evidence that the two species were distinct and could not intermingle. The sterility of buffalo-cattle hybrids confirmed this view. Sherman now extended his speculation to the Indian, formerly dependent for survival on the buffalo and other wild game, but with his future fate to be determined by the character of his interaction with the new possessors of his ancestral lands. Just as the doomed buffalo could not survive except through intermixture with cattle, so the Indian's doubtful future was "in the course of natural selection." American Indians must alter their customs and be absorbed into the successor population, or else they must die out. Sherman was convinced that it was "as idle to resist the Conclusion as it was for old Canute to command the tide to cease reaching his feet." What role the powerful cattle interests might play in the grand scheme of history Sherman did not address in his letter, but he was attempting to relate recent developments on the western plains to some larger pattern of development. "You and I have seen mighty things on this continent," he wrote Dodge; "and if there be useful lessons let us teach them to the rising generation."[53]

Sherman's statement initiated a thoughtful exchange of views in the months that followed. With his response to the initial letter, Dodge forwarded a handsomely bound copy of *Our Wild Indians*, from the twentieth thousand printed. He had just received a still more lavishly bound copy from the thirty-seventh thousand, he explained, and could readily spare the one he sent. Lest the general refuse to accept it, he noted also that the copy that had been lent and lost was one of two—one for Dodge, one for Sherman—sent by the publisher free of charge. He then set forth in considerable detail the results of his research into the history and total population of the Indians of North America, the practicality or otherwise of breeding buffalo with cattle, and other topics. Adopting a dispassionate point of view akin to Sherman's, he described the destruction of the great buffalo herds as a stage in the nation's development. "I was in the buffalo region during the great slaughter," he recalled, "and thought it . . . a National shame." However, he had since come to believe that, borrowing a phrase from R. W. Emerson, the nation's leaders "builded better than they knew."[54] By not interfering with the destruction of the buffalo, the U.S. government effectively conquered the rebellious Indian tribes by taking from them their traditional food supply. This radical solution to the Indian Problem made the nation "an absolute gainer of many millions of dollars, many valuable lives, & an extension of its settled area absolutely marvellous." Wild buffalo no longer roamed the plains, yet that setting now supported great herds of tame cattle that would provide food for millions of citizens. "Can any thinking man regret the change?" Dodge asked.

Still, in this and subsequent letters Dodge expressed hostility to the cattle interests, whose monopolistic practices he considered a threat to Indians and settlers alike. He knew from experience that unless secured by military force, the boundaries of Indian reservations were routinely ignored by cattle drivers moving their herds toward the railroads.[55] Nor were the cowboys' capitalist employers any more respectful of property occupied by homesteaders. Cattle interests that effectively denied farmers access to desirable lands were confronting a powerful force, he reminded Sherman—the tide of immigration. "When this happens, bloodshed is inevitable. A cattle-man with fifty or a hundred cow-boys at his back may easily over-awe and drive away a few would-be settlers, but that tide cannot be stopped & in a little while it will cut down those fences & kill those cattle men." In a country like the United States, no single interest, no matter how powerful, could ignore the rights of others. "But this is a question of Statesmanship, and in the absence of statesmen will probably finally eventuate as you said of the buffalo question, 'by the decree of the Almighty.'"[56] Thus these veteran officers discussed the continuing impact of historical developments that their military service and other official action had helped advance.[57]

Dodge also corresponded with other authors concerned with these issues. In his monograph *The Extermination of the American Bison*, William T. Hornaday of the Smithsonian Institution made use of both *The Plains* and *Our Wild Indians*.[58] In a letter to Dodge, he identified these works as comprising together "the most valuable popular account of the buffalo that has yet appeared in print."[59] The two men exchanged views on topics Dodge had dealt with in his books, including the probable total population of buffalo that had once ranged the plains and also the wild rushes of herds that for a time had endangered trains moving along the railroads. He assured Hornaday that any number of railroad men could corroborate his published descriptions. "I was then stationed at Fort Dodge," he wrote, "and I was personally cognizant of several of these 'accidents'" along the Atchison, Topeka and Santa Fe.[60] Hornaday requested his permission to reprint an engraving that had appeared in *The Plains*, showing a frantic buffalo herd being slaughtered for amusement by passengers who had alighted from a Kansas Pacific train.[61] When it eventually appeared in Hornaday's book, the image marked the evolution of Dodge's status as an historical witness. He had described a set of conditions that no longer prevailed as the transformation of the western frontier continued apace.

Probably other authors were less scrupulous than Hornaday in acknowledging their indebtedness to Dodge and his writings, but the degree to which *The Plains* and *Our Wild Indians* were drawn upon as source books can only be speculated upon.[62] The best-known instance of a fiction writer availing himself of material first presented by Dodge is Mark Twain, who made use of *The Plains* as part of his endeavor in 1884 to write a sequel to *Adventures of Huckleberry Finn*, set in "the Injun country."[63] Drawing almost exclusively upon Dodge for his representation of Indian character and behavior, he seized upon the passages that described the victimization suffered by women taken captive by Indians as a basis for horrified suspense. When Peggy, an innocent maiden whom Huck idolizes, becomes separated from her traveling party and is believed to be in the hands of fleeing Indian marauders, the inference about her immediate fate is clear. That suspicion is deepened by Huck's discovery of "a ragged piece of Peggy's dress as big as a big handkerchief, and it had blood on it" (328). Worse still, soon afterward Brace, a staunch frontiersman who is a fond admirer of Peggy, comes upon four stakes driven into the ground—a detail that clearly recalls Dodge's description of "staking out" as a preliminary to gang rape.[64] Always disposed to challenge accepted beliefs and ruffle the starched guardians of decorum, Twain had designed his narrative to explode the primitivist myth of Indian virtue. However, his reliance upon Dodge in pursuit of that aim was leading him into territory that even he preferred to traverse no further. Judging it best to retreat to the literary settlements, he broke off his tale before Huck Finn and his friends locate Peggy. He never finished the story, which remained unpublished until long after his death.[65]

In contrast with the "Injun country" of *The Plains* and of Twain's aborted experiment in melodrama, during the 1880s the territory around Fort Sully was no longer subject to marauding by Indians. In the five years of Dodge's service at the post, its troops were called upon to quell only a single disturbance, one caused not by Indians but by unruly American citizens. In April 1887 a group of persons who had settled on the Crow Creek–Winnebago Reservation, forty miles south of the post, refused to comply with the Indian agent's demand that they vacate their illegal homesteads. Accordingly, without resorting to violence but assisted by one company of troops, the agent and his Indian police arrested and expelled the intruders.[66]

When weather permitted, Dodge made many excursions from his post on horseback, some for as long as two weeks and as far east as the James River, one hundred miles distant. The region was being settled rapidly, but rabbits, field plover, and grouse of several varieties were abundant, red deer were to be found in the river bottoms, and in the rolling hill country one occasionally encountered lynx, wolf, prairie fox, and badger.[67] In December 1884 Dodge sent by express to General Sherman "a small token of my appreciation of your friendship & many kindnesses, more substantial than words"—namely, a box of grouse he had shot and had frozen. These, he explained, were "not the half-civilized 'pinnated' grouse (prairie chicken) but the wilder denizens of the northern wilds, the 'sharp-tailed' or willow grouse. You have been everywhere & eaten almost everything (with, I fear, *an almost equal relish*) but if you have not before hit upon these birds, I can assure you of a new sensation."[68] Probably the comment on Sherman's eating habits was a wry reference to the varied fare which, as chief caterer, Dodge had served up during the inspection tour.

Official Errands

In April 1886 Dodge went on a wagon trip west to Fort Meade, Dakota Territory, that afforded him a brief opportunity for hunting and fishing in the Black Hills. The journey's official purpose was to preside at a court-martial wherein an officer at the post, First Lieutenant Charles A. Varnum, was to be tried for alleged offenses seemingly without precedent.[69] The case attracted considerable attention even though, as the *Kansas City Times* observed, the charges were "such as to preclude them from publication in orders or the public prints."[70] Presently, upon publication of a general court-martial order, some inkling of the circumstances surrounding the case became known.

The charge, of conduct unbecoming an officer and gentleman, was based on a single specification: that on or about November 21, 1885, Varnum "did cause Mrs. Eugene Egan, wife of Sergeant Eugene Egan, Troop H, Seventh Cavalry, to be taken to the quarters at Fort Meade of Troop H . . . and did there direct Mrs. Egan to be placed on a table and whipped with a barrel stave by enlisted men." The accused officer pled guilty to this specification, but he declared himself innocent of the charge it allegedly supported. The published result of the court's deliberations did not specify the misbehavior of Mrs. Egan that had brought on the whipping, but First Lieutenant Varnum must have made a strong case on his own behalf. In accordance with his pleading, he was found guilty of the specification but not guilty of the charge. The court did adjudge him guilty of another punishable offense, conduct to the prejudice of good order and military discipline, but it imposed on him a light sentence: "To be reprimanded in orders by the reviewing authority"—in this case, Brigadier General Thomas H. Ruger, who had recently succeeded General Terry as departmental commander.[71]

Later in the summer, Dodge traveled from Fort Sully on another official errand, which was interesting for the insight it afforded him into the condition of the nation's volunteer forces. Since 1880 officers of the regular army had occasionally been assigned to visit the summer encampments of state militias, where they participated in inspections and provided instruction and counsel.[72] In 1884, as an indication that the program of cooperation between the regular army and the volunteer forces was being taken seriously at the highest level, Lieutenant General Sheridan himself visited the encampment of the Pennsylvania state militia at Mount Gretna.[73] Thus, in July 1886 Dodge was ordered to visit the two encampments of the Iowa National Guard.[74] This duty, the first of its kind he had performed in many years, surely recalled to him his experiences at the outset of the Civil War, when he had commanded a hastily organized camp of instruction for volunteer troops. Of course, in these later times the necessity of a volunteer army as a reserve force seemed remote. Nevertheless, several states and territories took pride in their home troops and welcomed the federal government's willingness to foster their training and discipline. Iowa, whose militia had been inspected in 1882 by Dodge's former commander, now Brigadier General John Gibbon,[75] supported one of the most enthusiastic state organizations. Dodge did not share the popular belief that a widely dispersed body of busy citizens could be maintained as an effective defense force with only a few days of training per year. Still, he supported the initiative in general and was glad to provide what assistance he could. He was to visit one brigade of troops from July 26 to 30, at Oskaloosa, and another from August 16 to 20, at Marshalltown, submitting a report of his observations at both.[76]

The adjutant general enjoined upon army officers the importance of maintaining cordial relations with officials of the state militias,[77] and Dodge was adept in this regard, both by temperament and from long experience. The Iowa brigade commanders, brigadier generals H. H. Wright and B. A. Beeson, were well instructed in their work and welcomed his presence. A newspaper reporter at the first encampment described the selection of Dodge as "fortunate," he being "one of the oldest officers in the active service" and "a gentleman whom it is a great pleasure to meet, as his conversation is of the most entertaining and instructive character."[78] The activities at the encampments, each numbering some 1,100 officers and men, consisted of drill, target firing, and guard duty, with a formal review by the governor and other high officials. Unfortunately, military operations at Oskaloosa were impeded at times by the choice of site, a fairgrounds adjacent to a race track where horses in training kicked up clouds of dust. The site at Marshalltown, in an abandoned beer garden, proved more suitable, allowing the regiments to arrange their tents in long streets according to rule. From 5,000 to 20,000 visitors crowded the grounds at both places daily, placing severe demands upon the hospitality and good nature of the headquarters staffs. Those officers had hoped to make the encampments, the sixth in as many years, more military than social in character.[79]

In his report on the proceedings, Dodge praised the headquarters personnel and noted that some of the forty-seven companies, each representing one of the state's counties, executed their drills with a crisp precision equal to that of crack units in the regular army. Inasmuch as the companies were in mutual contact only once annually, and that for a limited time, their performance together in regimental and brigade movements was in his estimation as good as could be expected. However, not all the companies participated in these drills; from lack of preparation, some were simply incapable of doing so. According to Dodge, the majority of company commanders were "more or less ignorant, some absolutely unfit for any position of command." The chief cause of this deficiency, he believed, was one that had beset volunteer companies during the Civil War: their commanding officers were elected by the men themselves, not on account of military ability but for their amiable social qualities. Because company commanders of the Iowa National Guard owed their positions to the good will of their subordinates, they failed to exert the necessary discipline, and their units suffered accordingly. Dodge observed, however, that the State of Iowa possessed full power to correct the problems he had identified. "Work, knowledge, ability"—and not personal popularity—"must be the pass words. These, backed by proper legislative action will ensure to the little army of Iowa a proud place in the Grand Army of the States."

Setting forth further observations in support of a second recommendation, Dodge mixed praise with criticism. He wrote that there existed "no better material for soldiers than is furnished by the State of Iowa," but he also insisted that soldiers are made, not born, and that sufficient time must be set aside for their instruction. To cause more than 2,000 private citizens to congregate annually, at minimal pay, for military training in times of peace was undoubtedly difficult in itself. Nevertheless, "the law making power of the State makes a grave mistake when it assumes that any very great real or permanent benefit can be effected by an encampment of five days."

He recommended that future encampments be not less than ten days in duration. Additionally, he urged that state authorities issue to volunteer troops uniforms identical with those in use by soldiers of the regular army; equip all companies of any regiment with arms of the same caliber; and pay all officers a sufficient amount to enable them to purchase uniforms.[80] Dodge's report was a discriminating statement that led General Beeson to address him a note of thanks, declaring it "just right."[81]

Except for two leaves of absence in 1884, both lasting only two weeks, Dodge had been on active duty without interruption since 1880.[82] He admitted that winter conditions on the northern plains were "very trying" to him,[83] but he resisted seeking out a warmer climate for the benefit of his health. He held to the belief that when disabled by rheumatism, he received better care from Laura and Joe than he would as a lodger at some anonymous hotel.[84] However, as the years passed, his physical condition deteriorated and enforced a change of attitude. Shortly after his return to Fort Sully from the assignment in Iowa, he was granted a six-month leave of absence, to commence in October.[85]

After a short visit to New York City, in November Dodge returned to Chicago and then Detroit to be with Julia and their son during Fred's professional visits to those cities. Following an appearance as a witness in court proceedings at Yankton, Dakota Territory, he returned to New York, spent a few days in Washington, and then traveled south to Greensboro, North Carolina, where he passed the rest of the winter.[86] To his surprise, while in New York City he came across a newspaper report that he was about to retire. In itself, this rumor was perhaps not surprising, for imminent army retirements were a rich theme for speculation, and he was one of only three members of his West Point graduating class still in active service.[87] Nevertheless, Dodge informed the *Army and Navy Journal* of the actual facts in regard to himself. He "says he is too sound and live a man to be retired just now," the editors reported, "and his 40 years limit of service will not expire until July, 1888, and he will not be retired for age until May 19, 1891."[88] The health reasons that had necessitated his lengthy leave of absence went unmentioned. Undoubtedly Dodge was still a "live" man, as he averred, but his physical condition did warrant some qualification of his public statement. Writing from Greensboro on December 19, he informed the adjutant general that he had left Washington "to escape winter." He had "improved somewhat on the climate," he added, "but not as I expected."[89]

Family Relations

As an admired senior member of his family, Dodge was assured of loving attention during the visit to his home country. With the assistance of his nephew Robert B. Glenn, an able young lawyer and a rising state politician, he had provided for his sisters as well as he could, in part by using funds left by his father for the purpose. Additionally, he had lent money to Jim, another of his sister Annie's sons, as well as to Annie herself.[90] In the spring of 1887, he reminded his wife Julia, through Fred, not to forget "to attend to Annie's check & china set. You know a little money is a big thing down South. Sis Annie has none to spare & is bothered & worried about her money—not that she fears to lose it, but because like the woman in scripture, 'she has it not.'"[91]

Even more than from his sisters and their families, Dodge derived personal satisfaction from the relationship that had grown up between him and his talented son, Fred. Since 1876 Fred had lived with his mother, but Dodge and he corresponded regularly, and they had passed time together during his western tours and on summer visits at Fort Sully. Twenty-nine years of age in 1886, Fred was well launched on his career as an actor. Ordinarily during the winter theatrical season he resided in New York City, and in the spring and early summer he went on tour as a leading member of a company under the direction of James M. Hill. Although no longer widely known as "the Army Actor," he was glad to hold onto that association. In 1883 he issued a public invitation to Brigadier General O. O. Howard, then commander of the Department of the Platte, to attend a performance at Omaha, mentioning as a motive his pleasant recollections of early experiences with the Officers' Dramatic Association there.[92] In 1884 he was a guest at the home of General Sherman during the company's stay in Saint Louis.[93] At that time he played the male lead opposite Margaret Mather, a young woman whose performances as Lady Macbeth and Juliet were attracting attention, thanks largely to the unstinting praise of her by Hill, who doubled as her publicist.[94] During the 1885–1886 season, Fred was the Romeo to Mather's Juliet more than seventy-five times at the Union Square Theater, New York. According to George C. D. O'Dell, annalist of the New York stage, "it became a sort of duty to see" the production.[95]

Of slight stature and uncertain health, Fred drove himself, to the concerned chagrin of his father. In affectionate letters Dodge often warned his son against overwork. In May 1887 he recommended that he try SSS, a patent medicine that he claimed was "doing wonders" for persons who were feeling run down. "Of course," he continued, "I take the most vital interest in all that concerns you, – your health first [*No 1*], your ambition [*No 2*] next. Now my private opinion is that Health is the first & greatest of Blessings – & I am very much afraid that you sacrifice No 1 to No 2." Dodge elaborated on this theme for two more pages, but Fred seems to have sensed the affection that prompted the flood of good advice. He preserved it among other keepsakes that, years afterward, he labeled "Father's letters to be kept."[96]

In her own way, Fred's mother was no less devoted to his welfare than Dodge. Besides sharing her home with him and keeping his costumes in good order, she attended rehearsals, accompanied him on some tours, and watched for developments in theatrical circles that might affect him. Both she and Fred were devout Roman Catholics, socially acquainted with clergymen and a circle of other devotees. Fred felt deep regard for his mother and understood that despite her prolonged separation from Dodge, he was himself the basis of a lasting bond between his parents. More than once in his letters to Dodge he expressed hope that a reconciliation would occur that would bring them all together permanently. Fred's intentions were good, but he did not comprehend the depth of frustration Dodge felt in just this matter. At last, in November 1884, Dodge confided to him his own sense of the situation.

"At present," he wrote of himself and Julia, "we do not quarrel, & there is nothing on my part to keep alive the animosity that she has exhibited toward me for some years." Nevertheless, he continued, neither he nor Fred was capable by himself of altering her settled attitude. He urged Fred not to appeal to her and so make matters worse: "If you now begin to *urge reconciliation* she will in true womanly perversity revive in her own mind those old animosities now dormant, or she will conclude that I am at the bottom of your appeal, will hate me worse than ever, & you may possibly come in for ill feeling, as a dupe & tool of mine. Be assured my dear boy, that I understand this matter better than you possibly can. The *only hope for future peace & reconciled life between us, is to let her entirely alone.*"

As he had done in his letter urging Fred not to work too hard, Dodge elaborated his point, passing more than once over the same paths of thought. He had traversed this lonely mental territory often in recent years; it was the reason why he had so rarely applied for leaves of absence. Julia and he were effectively estranged, and he felt powerless to change the situation, except possibly by allowing time to repair it. "I believe she has a strong womanly attachment for me," he wrote Fred, "now & of late years obscured by diseased imaginings. If not fixed in her by trying to turn her too suddenly, these ill feelings will probably wear away with the disease. The only hope of ever having her come back to her old time affection – *is to let her do it of her own accord.*"

Turning to a related topic of concern to his son, Dodge assured him that an improvement in Julia's feelings toward him would not necessarily result in their occupying a home together. His style of life as an army officer was itself a defining issue, and from his point of view one not subject to compromise. "I don't want her until she can come to me an affectionate wife happy in me & contented with her lot," he explained. Nor would his pride permit him to entertain the idea of her returning to him out of deference to the wishes of Fred. "If she is going to come around," he concluded, "time & good health may accomplish it. If not, not – & there's an end of it."[97]

What had aroused Julia's "ill feelings" toward her husband, and what were the "diseased imaginings" that he believed fueled them? Surviving statements by her provide no answers to these questions. Dodge's references to her "disease" and "imaginings" suggest a belief that she suffered psychological aberrations, perhaps associated in some way with her numerous maladies that had required care by physicians.[98] It seems evident that he considered himself innocent of whatever motives or misdeeds she imputed to him.[99] Even so, the known facts of their relationship do help account for her resentment of him. For one, she was unwilling to share Dodge's army life on the western frontier, and he was unwilling to abandon it for her sake. For another, should she elect to share the home he offered her, she must do so on his terms, not hers. Widely differing family backgrounds may also have contributed to the discord.

Julia, an only child and the darling of her grandparents, had grown up in privileged circumstances and was accustomed to indulgence. Dodge, one of four children, grew up in a much less prosperous family and was always conscious of the sacrifices necessary to make ends meet.

Beyond question, differences about money had placed a severe strain on the Dodges' marriage. The bequest Julia received upon the death of her mother gave her a lease on independence, and following her departure from Omaha Barracks in 1876 she had never again occupied his home. She traveled, entertained, contributed to charity causes, and otherwise spent freely, borrowing from Dodge to support her new lifestyle even as he warned her against extravagance. In January 1883 she informed him that she was sponsoring "musicales" in New York City at the rate of one per month but would be unable to pay him the interest on a debt she owed him. In response, he remonstrated with her. "I wish I could induce you to sit quietly down & think where you are drifting," he wrote. "You are spending six thousand a year on an income of nothing. . . . Your utter ruin, at the rate you are going on, is simply a matter of time, & possibly a very short time, for when the creditors who cant get their money find out how you are living & entertaining, they will naturally come down on you without mercy."

Dodge urged his wife to return to him and share his economy, but he seems to have understood that she would not do so as long as any other option remained to her. Frustrated, he accused her of setting aside her proper role as wife: "Your money has been only a curse to us both. It has seperated us, given me a solitary homeless life, & you a feverish desire for spending. You are your own mistress & can do as you please now. Run riot through all your means & then come to me. I believe you will be a happier & better woman when you have no money of your own, and I cant quarrel with your present extravagance, when I reflect that I may gain a wife & a home by it. With all my heart I wish you had never owned a cent of your own. Both our lives would have been more useful & more happy, had pecuniary necessity forced you to do your duty as a wife & at your proper home."[100] In light of reproachful words like these, it is understandable that Dodge should later caution Fred against urging Julia to make "what she will probably regard as concessions to me."

Coincidentally, only days before the exchange of views between Dodge and his son over the rift that divided their family, Julia had received notice of a possible windfall that if realized, would assure her of financial independence for life. A New York lawyer, Frederick A. Ward, informed her that she had an as yet unrecognized right to a portion of the estate of William Rhinelander, Jr., which after being held in trust for many years had been divided among twenty-four heirs in 1882.[101] The value of the property that might accrue to her was approximately $1.5 million, and Ward expressed confidence in the merits of Julia's claim. As the granddaughter of William Rhinelander, Jr.'s sister, Mary Rhinelander Paulding, Julia was the proper inheritor of certain waterfront property in New York City that had been owned by William Rhinelander, Jr., as trustee for Mary. The division of the estate had been made as if the property in question had been his, not hers, but Ward held that once the necessary documents were brought to light, the issue of succession and entitlement would surely be decided in Julia's favor.

This development brought to Julia's mind two incidents in earlier years that seemed to confirm the lawyer's statements. As early as 1859 William C. Rhinelander, a son of William Rhinelander, Jr., had mentioned to her that his father had been a trustee of Mary Rhinelander Paulding's estate. He remarked on the odd fact that no listing of the assets comprising the estate had come to light. Years later, in December 1877, this same man summoned Julia and Fred to his home and, obviously agitated, informed them that a portion of the Rhinelander trust that would be divided upon his death was properly hers. More strangely still, while looking through a chest that had belonged to her grandmother, in June 1884 Julia came across a document that seemed to prove the existence of a trust administered on behalf of Mary Rhinelander Paulding. She brought it home with her to show Fred, merely as a curiosity.[102]

Events across the years were linking themselves almost as in some fanciful work of fiction, and naturally Julia was eager to press the legal claim Ward had identified. Dodge, negotiating on Julia's behalf, entered an agreement that she would grant the attorney one-half the gross sum eventually realized in return for his performing all the labor and assuming all the expenses prior to recovery. At the same time, Dodge confided to Fred that he did not expect Julia would extract much money from the Rhinelander heirs. "They are a close money-loving set," he wrote, "& will squeeze hard."[103] Still, a demand upon the Rhinelanders was made, and in February 1886, now acting in concert with a cousin, Grace Paulding Brant, Julia filed suit in the Supreme Court of New York.[104]

In his letter to Fred advising him not to urge a reconciliation on Julia, Dodge did ask that he intervene with her on another financial matter. In the past five years she had kept up her independent lifestyle largely using her husband's funds, and Dodge hoped eventually to be repaid. Wisely or not, at her "earnest request" in July 1879 he had loaned her $5,400, which he raised by redeeming without interest certain U.S. bonds he had intended to hold for five more years. Subsequently he advanced her additional sums, always on her promise, as yet unfulfilled, of repaying him with interest. By November 1884 she owed him $9,650, and since Dodge assumed she had other creditors, he broached the matter to Fred. "I do not want to say anything to her about this at present," he wrote, "but I do want <u>you</u> to write as if of your own motion, speak to her of this debt & urge its payment out of the very first money she gets" from the action against the Rhinelanders. Dodge emphasized that he wanted the money not only for his own benefit but to enable him to support Julia and Fred should a future need arise. "Whatever her queerness," he wrote, "I know she is honest, & will see that I am paid if it is properly brought to her notice."[105] Ironically, the same funds Julia was seeking in order to maintain her independent lifestyle were valuable to him as a means of providing for his family in an emergency.

A Change of Station

Dodge's long winter's absence from Fort Sully yielded the physical benefits he had hoped for, and upon returning to the post in April 1887 he took up his duties with renewed vigor.[106] Life at the post had gone on well during his absence. As was customary in newspaper accounts, the correspondent writing as "Mars" at Fort Sully dwelt upon social and recreational rather than military endeavors in his reports to the *Army and Navy Journal*. Euchre parties, wedding anniversary celebrations, band concerts for the benefit of new musicians just arrived from Italy, and the triumphs of the post baseball team formed the staples of his accounts in the weeks following Dodge's return.[107]

Men stationed at the post were alert to a rumor that the Eleventh Infantry would at last be transferred to a new headquarters and a very desirable one, in the Division of the Atlantic. The regular exchange of regimental postings was a policy instituted by General Sheridan that was applauded by army men, even though the costs involved limited his ability to satisfy all parties. "I live in hope," Dodge informed Fred in late May, adding that he intended to write Sheridan a note reminding him of the regiment's strong claim to consideration.[108] Looking back, he had passed his period of service in the Department of Dakota agreeably enough, but he was ready for a change. If Fort Coeur d'Alene was not to be the station where he would round out his career, perhaps that was just as well, for he was no longer so fit to enjoy its wilderness surroundings as he had been a few years before.[109] And after all, "the Lakes" was still considered the most desirable posting the army had to offer. Interestingly, Fort Coeur d'Alene had just been renamed Fort Sherman in honor of the retired general who had ordered its establishment.[110] Now residing in New York City, Sherman informed a newspaper reporter in 1887 that he hoped eventually to locate his residence on Lake Coeur d'Alene, which he thought one of the most beautiful places in the world.[111] But like Dodge, he had lost some of his vigor. With its theaters, clubs, bustling army building, and schedule of social and ceremonial events, New York City was his home now.

Anticipating the new fiscal year that would make funds available, on June 28 General Sheridan announced four regimental changes of station that had been approved by the secretary of war. The Eleventh and Twelfth Infantry would exchange stations, with the new postings of their companies to be designated by the divisional or departmental commanders, and also the Fifth and Seventh Cavalry.[112] As Dodge had hoped, the almost 2,000-mile journey to his new headquarters, Madison Barracks, New York, would consist largely of summer travel by steamship—six days through the Great Lakes, much admired for their scenic attractions. After being transported by rail to Duluth, Minnesota, the regiment would cross Lake Superior, pass the Straits of Mackinac into Lake Huron, then sail past Detroit into Lake Erie, ending its summer voyage at Buffalo, from which designated companies would proceed by rail to their new stations. All these—Madison Barracks, Plattsburg Barracks, Fort Ontario, and

Fort Niagara—were located along the nation's northern frontier, on or near the south shore of Lake Ontario.[113]

News items in the *Army and Navy Journal* indicated that the troops of the Eleventh Infantry were as pleased with their approaching move as those of the Twelfth were regretful. Whereas "Mars" at Fort Sully reported that "[e]verybody is happy and the post is all astir," a writer who signed himself "Poca [*sic*] Tiempo" admitted that at Madison Barracks "the air is full of sighs—and hammering of packing boxes."[114] After five years of service at what they admitted were pleasant duty stations, the men of the Twelfth would soon be en route to Dakota, "the land of the festive blizzard." On the other hand, those of the Eleventh who accompanied Dodge to Madison Barracks would occupy one of the most comfortable posts in the eastern states. Its officers' quarters, rebuilt in 1876 after a fire, were handsome, as were its barracks and parade grounds. Located at Sackets Harbor and within ten miles of Watertown, a popular destination for summer travelers, it boasted a long history, its site having been occupied by U.S. troops since just after the War of 1812.[115] Dodge had a personal reason for satisfaction at his new posting, for during that early conflict, his grandfather, Richard Dodge, had served at Sackets Harbor as a brigadier general of volunteers.[116] If the convenience of rail connections between Watertown and New York City led to more frequent visits between him and his wife and son, so much the better.

During the 1880s the "Personal Items" columns of the *Army and Navy Journal* came to occupy more space than in earlier years. Reports of visits, leaves of absence, weddings, honors received, addresses delivered, reunions held, and similar miscellaneous matter helped compensate for the limited amount of more properly military news. As if he were about to begin a lengthy vacation, the issue for July 2, 1887, included the observation that "Colonel R. I. Dodge, 11th U.S. Infantry, whose stations have been mainly in the Far West for many years, will soon come with his headquarters to the pleasant post, especially in summer, of Madison Barracks."[117] Implicit in this bland announcement was the assumption that he had found his most recent twenty years of service in the West other than pleasant. But in fact, by taste, habit, and long experience he had thoroughly associated himself with the western country. The move east, although welcome, would end the period in which he had won his mature reputation as an army officer and author. He had no intention of putting himself out to pasture in the four years of active duty that remained to him, but he surely recognized, not without regret, that he had outlived his plainsman's prime and would be leaving behind him many pleasant associations. Other than Sheridan, of his senior commanders from earlier years, only Crook and Schofield remained on active duty.[118] Happily for him, the latter now commanded of the Division of the Atlantic.

On July 31, Dodge and all other troops at Fort Sully except a skeleton detachment set out for Buffalo, reaching there on August 8. From that point, with his headquarters staff, the regimental band, and companies A, D, G, H, and I, he traveled by rail to Madison Barracks, where on the morning of August 9 he arrived and assumed command.[119]

26

In the Division of the Atlantic

Dodge's service on the western frontier ended concurrently with a larger development, the final stage of the army's suppression of Indian resistance to settlement across the region. Incidents of violence continued to occur from time to time, but events such as the capture of the Apache leader Geronimo in 1888, the death of the Sioux chieftain Sitting Bull two years later, and the debacle at Wounded Knee, also in 1890, marked the end of an era. Posts where Dodge had served were being abandoned for military purposes as no longer of strategic value. Thus, Cantonment North Fork Canadian River was turned over to the Department of the Interior in 1882, Fort Dodge was decommissioned in 1885, Fort Fred Steele in 1886, and Forts Hays and Lyon in 1889. During the later 1880s, the frontier army took the field most often in small detachments, in response to troubles created by citizens attempting to appropriate Indian lands. Land hunger led in 1889 to the opening up to settlement of unceded tracts in Indian Territory and in 1890 to the Sioux tribe's agreement to give up the greater part of its reservation. The army's participation in the removal of potentially hostile Indians from the central plains had run its course.

General Sherman, an architect of this policy, remained convinced that inhabitants of the eastern states failed to estimate at its true value the army's postwar contribution to the growth and prosperity of the nation. Probably this perception accounts for the hyperbole of his assertion that the Indian wars "were of as much importance as our great civil war." He insisted that the officers and men of the army "should feel a just pride in the share they bore in this victory of civilization."[1] Dodge echoed that sentiment in "The Enlisted Soldier," characterizing the army as "the pioneer of the progress of civilization, standing like a guardian angel between the feeble settlements and the savages."[2]

Dodge and Sherman were in agreement on another principle, one that would motivate Dodge in the years of active service that remained to him. Sherman never tired of asserting the importance of maintaining the regular army in a state of preparedness, since crises requiring military intervention often arise unexpectedly. "I remember well the public apathy which immediately preceded the Mexican War and the Civil War," he wrote in 1881, urging that greater vigilance "may be of inestimable value in the *next* war." Sherman warned that Americans, in their pursuit of material gain, were "liable to forget the lessons" of those conflicts and fail once again to maintain a properly equipped standing army of sufficient size.[3] But on the whole, his statements were unavailing, for it was difficult to generate concern over wartime conditions that could not be foreseen. Throughout the 1880s, congressional appropriations for support of the army remained at low levels, and in 1890 the secretary of war, Redfield Proctor, actually proposed a further reduction in its authorized strength.[4] Under these circumstances, the efforts of career officers like Dodge continued to be inhibited by the inadequate resources made available to them. Nevertheless, they devoted themselves to improving the conditions of life in the ranks and to maintaining discipline, morale, and soldierly skills at the highest possible level.

The convenient access of Madison Barracks to the headquarters of the Division of the Atlantic at Governors Island, New York harbor, helped ensure Dodge's participation in innovative army programs and facilitated his making his voice heard. At the time of his transfer from Fort Sully, he was already well known within the army, but during his years in the east his contacts with the editors of the *Army and Navy Journal*, based in New York City, made him even more visible. The newspaper reported on his activities frequently and favorably, and as a result, his reputation within the service rose steadily. The reduced distance between Dodge's new duty station and the home of Julia and Fred in New York City also had an impact on their relations together. Shortly after his arrival at Madison Barracks they paid him a visit, laying a basis for future contact.[5] Madison Barracks—or Sackets Harbor as it was often called, after the nearby village—was indeed an attractive posting. Professionally and personally, Dodge's transfer to the Division of the Atlantic was propitious, if only his now chronic rheumatism did not betray him in the winters.

Because the Eleventh Infantry had served in the Department of Dakota for eleven years, its move to another military division could not be a clean break. For example, when the headquarters staff left Fort Sully, they took with them the back files of orders issued from division headquarters, and on leaving Madison Barracks, the staff of Colonel Orlando H. Willcox made the same mistake, necessitating an exchange.[6] Colonel Willcox had begun construction of a sewerage system at Madison Barracks,[7] but at the time of his departure the project and other improvements remained unfinished. The best known of these was beautification of the military cemetery on the post grounds. The dedication in 1886 of a monument to Brigadier General Zebulon Pike had attracted attention,[8] but for the cemetery to be made truly presentable, more work needed to be done.

The Eleventh Infantry brought with it to the Division of the Atlantic one unpleasant item of unfinished business, the trial by court-martial of one of its own officers, First

Lieutenant Benjamin F. Handforth. Probably to spare the regiment further embarrassment, all but two members of the court named for this purpose were officers of the Eleventh.[9] Handforth and the charges against him had received much attention from sensationalist newspaper commentators. Jealousy of his apparently unoffending wife had led him into bizarre behavior that included locking her in a room with him while he read aloud passages from scripture on the subject of marital infidelity.[10] The charges he now faced, of conduct unbecoming an officer and gentleman, were accompanied by specifications yet more strange. All related to behavior the previous spring, following his return to duty from four months of sick leave. While under arrest for breaking into the home of another officer and attacking him, Handforth was alleged to have sent letters to a young nun, a teacher at the Standing Rock Indian Agency, declaring his love for her and urging her to visit him privately at his residence. Further, ten days after this alleged indiscretion, Handforth was said to have sexually assaulted the wife of a soldier at his duty station, Fort Yates, Dakota Territory. When called upon at trial to declare his innocence or guilt of the charges against him, the accused officer stood mute, refusing to enter a plea, but he was subsequently found guilty on the charge and all specifications supporting it. Following a review by superior authorities, the court's sentence of dismissal from the service was approved by President Grover Cleveland,[11] and the unsavory Handforth case was closed.

No doubt to his relief, Dodge was not called upon to preside over the Handforth court, that duty being assigned to his immediate subordinate, Lieutenant Colonel Edward G. Bush. Since the proceedings were held at Madison Barracks, he did have the opportunity to take up old ties with the two court members who were not of his own regiment. These were his former subordinates at Cantonment North Fork Canadian River, Captain Thomas M. K. Smith and his namesake First Lieutenant Frederick L. Dodge, both of the Twenty-third Infantry.[12] That regiment was now also stationed in the Division of the Atlantic, at posts on the Great Lakes immediately west of those occupied by the Eleventh.[13] During his brief visits to Fort Leavenworth in 1879 and 1880, Dodge had been a welcome guest at the residence there of First Lieutenant Dodge and his wife. Another comrade from that time, Captain John J. Coppinger, Twenty-third Infantry, had since married a daughter of James G. Blaine, the former secretary of state. He was now a lieutenant colonel, and in 1888 he became superintendent of the General Recruiting Service on Governors Island, where Dodge would seek him out on his visits to New York City.[14] Another old friend from the Twenty-third was Captain Otis W. Pollock, who now commanded Fort Porter at Buffalo, New York, only a few miles away from one of the posts garrisoned by the Eleventh, Fort Niagara.[15] Officers and men of the Eleventh and Twenty-third Infantry would see much of each other in the coming years. If Dodge ever regretted his removal from the frontier West, the proximity of men who had served with him there must have helped allay the feeling.

Several junior officers and enlisted men of the Eleventh Infantry participated in the 1887 divisional rifle competitions at Fort Niagara. Two of its entrants scored among the ten best performers in the officers' revolver match, but the real distinction of the regiment was its onsite arrangements, which made the week-long event a success. Prominent among the event's attractions was the regimental band, under the direction of Chief Musician Achille La Guardia.[16]

The army's enthusiasm for target practice continued, as evidenced by the appointment of Captain Stanhope E. Blunt, formerly inspector of rifle practice for the Department of Dakota, to be an aide-de-camp to General Sheridan. Accordingly, during the greater part of his tenure at Madison Barracks, Dodge sought to purchase property contiguous to the post that would serve better as a firing range than the plot of land currently being leased for the purpose.[17] From year to year, companies stationed at Plattsburg Barracks and Fort Ontario were temporarily transferred to the post for use of the practice facilities there, and the regiment more than held its own in divisional competitions.[18] However, as Dodge had advocated, the army's focus on this limited area of expertise was gradually opening out to include a wider range of soldierly skills. Like his advocacy of increased attention to skirmish firing, his views on this subject accorded with those of General Sheridan.[19]

In the course of an inspection tour in 1884, Sheridan had expressed the idea that Madison Barracks could fulfill a unique function among army posts. Its scenic surroundings and the small likelihood of its garrison being ordered to field duty made it an ideal posting for the headquarters of regiments that had served for long periods in less desirable places. That conception of the post underlay the transfer there of Dodge and his staff.[20] However, in authorizing the move, Sheridan may not have reckoned with the Eleventh Infantry's reputation as industrious post-builders and Dodge's proclivities in the same area. Within weeks of his arrival at the post, Dodge, aided by his regimental and post quartermaster, First Lieutenant George LeRoy Brown, submitted for approval the plans for four new construction projects. Scarcity of funds necessitated a delay in beginning three of these—a quartermaster's storehouse, a commissary storehouse, and a new icehouse—but an appeal from no less influential a supporter than Major General Schofield yielded authorization to begin work on the fourth, a large new administration building.[21]

Thus, in October and November 1887 the post's expenditures for civilian labor suddenly rose to five times their usual level,[22] and within a few more months the two-story structure, located at the main gate, was complete. On its first floor, the building housed the post and regimental offices, the post library, and a schoolroom. On the second, running the building's 104-foot length, was a large meeting room, Dodge Hall. According to the *Watertown Times*, this space was "beautifully fitted up with stage scenery, [and] brilliantly lighted up with chandeliers, as occasion requires."[23] Dodge Hall become the scene of three weekly events, a dance on Monday evening for officers and ladies, a concert on Wednesday evening for all, and a dance on Saturday evening for enlisted men.[24] In matters military and otherwise, Dodge had set for himself the goal of making the post thoroughly up-to-date, and indeed, something of a showplace.

Family Relations: Toward a New Equilibrium

During Dodge's service at Madison Barracks, events occurred in the lives of his wife and son that altered his relationship with them. By 1887 Julia seems to have put behind her the animus she had felt toward him in earlier years. Utterly dependent on his assistance and the earnings of Fred, she continued to live with the latter in the New York City flat, assisted by one servant. Her lawsuit against the Rhinelander heirs had alienated her from some friends and relations, and when Fred was absent she was lonely. She told Dodge that most of the people they had once known were either dead or had moved away to avoid the expenses of the city. Her cousin Grace owned a twenty-room country house in White Plains, New York, but she could not afford to maintain it and so hoped to sell it. For the present, Grace and her son Paulding were boarding with her in the flat. Funds were scarce, leaving Julia "too poor to entertain" as in earlier years.[25] Her one hope for better times was the eventual success of her lawsuit.

In November 1887 a crisis occurred in Julia's legal challenge to one of the Rhinelander beneficiaries. After four months of research, including the taking of depositions in the presence of counsel for both sides, the referee appointed by the Supreme Court of New York to study the matter submitted his report, which did not support the claim of Julia and Grace. Still, their attorney remained convinced that the suit would prevail on appeal.[26] She and Grace were determined to press ahead, but when it became necessary to file with the court an administrative fee and also a guarantee for the payment of costs in case the appeal should fail, they lacked the necessary funds. Sensing their advantage, counsel for the Rhinelanders refused to support a request for even a few days' extension in the matter. At that point, on the Wednesday before Thanksgiving, it appeared that the case might be lost by default. Desperate, Julia telegraphed Dodge, who responded at once that he would guarantee her further expenses.

The case had not yet been decided by the court, but Julia now felt confident of its outcome in her favor. In her view, she had weathered this crisis through the intervention of her husband and the benign providence of God. "My dear Husband," she wrote Dodge on November 27, "I cannot express to you in words, the deep debt of gratitude I owe to you, for your prompt and generous assistance, in this sudden and unprepared crisis, of our case."

> But for your timely and most kind assistance, *just* at the *crisis*, we would have lost our *fortune, beyond a doubt*. – I have never *lost hope*, in our great case, *being finally decided*, in our lawful right to the property. –It has been *supernaturally* guided and *protected*, *all through* for *us*, and will be until the end, when the great *Arch* Angel Michael, and my own dear Angel Guardian, will win for us. – Every proof we have found, has been found in a most *marvelous* manner; the way in which every thing, *through* the *old letters*, and *papers* I *found*, have been *developed* to *prove* our *rights*, is most curious and interesting, and I *know* and

> *believe*, is in direct answer, to my prayers, devotion, and *faith* in, *Almighty God* and *my own* dear *Angel Guardian*.[27]

Several months would elapse before the court would publish its decision, but Julia believed that Dodge had done her a service that assured her future.

Julia had become as ardent in her devotion to Fred as she was now confident about the outcome of her lawsuit. After expressing her gratitude to Dodge, she recounted to him recent developments in Fred's troubled professional relationship with the actress Margaret Mather. Probably to do professional harm to her manager, Mather was covertly sabotaging performance after performance. Her behavior was well known by now and had excited public comment. According to the *New York Sun*, to detract from Fred's performance as Romeo opposite her she placed pins in her costume as Juliet, so that when he embraced her he would scratch his hands. She would lean her head against his chest in a manner that suggested languishing affection but actually impeded his efforts to breathe and speak his lines. Knowing, too, that he suffered from corns, she would press the heels of her slippers onto his toes as he shouted out his most passionate speeches.[28]

Behavior like this, repeated with variations, exacted a heavy emotional toll upon Fred, who wished to continue as James M. Hill's premier male actor and refused to imitate the behavior of his tormentor. Julia sought out Hill on behalf of her son and urged that something be done. He assured her that Fred would be well taken care of, and that he would not have the ill-natured actress to contend with in the coming season.[29] Hill proved as good as his word on the latter point, for in June 1888 Mather, having switched managers, filed a trumped-up suit against him for breach of contract.[30] Nevertheless, in the months that preceded that action, the actress continued to torment Fred on a tour that took the company as far west as San Francisco. For Julia, who accompanied her son, the early months of 1888 were thus doubly suspenseful. Both Fred's continued ability to cope with Mather and the outcome of her own lawsuit against the Rhinelanders remained in doubt.

During the summer, Julia was gratified by the publication in the *New York World* of a long article that set forth some of the facts and legal issues that inhered in her case. The exposure given her lawsuit was clearly motivated by an editorial intention to embarrass the wealthy Rhinelander family, but Julia regarded the *World's* attention to her as another act of God on her behalf. "I am very thankful to God, and the great Arch Angel Michael," she wrote Dodge, "for obtaining for me, such a powerful influence as the World newspaper, to protect my interests in this case." She added that she had saved a copy of the issue that contained the article, intending to send it to him, but that by mistake it had been used for some other purpose. "God grant dear Rich," she continued, "that I may be able to pay you every thousand dollars, that Jordan bargained of you, to use for Fred." Evidently Fred had successfully impressed upon his mother the need to place Dodge first in line among her creditors. Whether the money he had made available to her had been for her benefit or Fred's was probably no longer worth debating. "God bless you dear Rich," she wrote, "for your *kindness* and *forbearance* to me, in never haveing reproached me, for this disasterous transaction."[31]

Clearly the fond regard Julia was now expressing in her letters to Dodge marked a major change in her attitude toward him. Two decisive events in the fall of 1888 brought on a further change. The first of these, early in November, was the unanimous judgment of the Supreme Court of New York against the appellants in the case of *Dodge et al v. Gallatin et al.* As summarized in the court's decision, the case turned upon statutes and precedents that antedated the documents that Julia, Grace, and their lawyers had adduced in proof of their claim. At the time William Rhinelander, Jr., made the will that established the Rhinelander trust, he had legitimately owned the water lots in his own right. Because these lots did not form part of the property he administered for his sister Mary, Julia and Grace had inherited no claim to them.[32]

This was indeed a "severe reverse of fortune," as Julia expressed it in December. Thanking Dodge for a cash gift he had sent her and Fred as a Christmas present, she assured him that they would do with it "*just* what you advise and wish us to *do*; *spend* it upon *ourselves*, in getting *necessary* clothing, which we both need." The golden vision of lifelong wealth had come to nothing, leaving Julia to grasp, perhaps not altogether consciously, at another fond hope. "I would so much like to see you, dear Richie, and wish that you *could* and *would arrange it*, so that you, and I, might meet, my dear husband, and have a visit together. — It would give me much pleasure to see your dear, kind, face again. — Instead of looking at your large picture, I have handsomely framed, in our library."[33] With her husband now stationed at a post generally considered desirable and in a region known for its social advantages, Julia was revolving the possibility that she and Dodge might resume life together under the same roof.

A second event brought this issue to a head. Following the successful debut of a production at the Fifth Avenue Theater of Mary Fiske's play *Philip Herne*, Fred continued performing in this "modern melodrama" through early November 1888, when Hill took the play on the road. It had been sufficiently well received in New York City that he believed it would succeed in a tour of one- and two-night stands before audiences in the provinces. Little as Fred enjoyed travel of this kind, he was also optimistic. He was now free of Margaret Mather's interference, and he thought *Philip Herne* was quite possibly the vehicle that would propel him to stardom. After leaving New York City, the company played in New England and then turned south for appearances along an itinerary Fred knew well, bringing it back to Chicago for a run at the end of the season.[34]

Julia planned to leave New York City on December 20 in order to meet her son at Atlanta and, as she said, "rush through the South with him" as in earlier years. However, on December 19 she received a telegram from Fred, then in Charlotte, North Carolina, telling her not to make the trip. Audiences outside New York City had not liked the play, and Hill had decided to cut his losses and end the tour, leaving members of the company out of work. Fred informed his mother than he would be home within two weeks, and on the same day he also informed Dodge of the development. Deeply disappointed, Fred feared that he and Julia would not be able to make ends meet through the winter. He asked Dodge whether it would be possible for them to live with him until he could find new employment.[35]

On December 20, before Dodge had received Fred's letter, Julia sent him one of her own in which she made the same appeal, framing it in terms of the great good an extended visit would do Fred: "I wish so much, dear Rich, you would let Fred and I, come to visit you for the next two months; we would both like so much, to see you, and I know, the entire rest and change of life, and scene, would be of great benefit, to our dear Son, for you know, from what I have written you, how much the dear boy requires, mental and physical refreshment." Julia was aware that her earlier visits had not been entirely satisfactory to Dodge, for she also assured him that she would not "disarrange" his household by her bad habits or inconvenience his cook. "I am on time for my meals when I travel with Fred, and I shall do the same while I am visiting you, as I do not wish or mean, to give trouble, in your most comfortable and well appointed home." As to her parrot, whose "screaming and whistling" had irritated both Dodge and Fred, it had died a year before, and she had not gotten another.[36] Having no other recourse, Julia hoped to confide herself to the care of her husband, whom she knew was devoted to her, and she was willing to do so on his terms.

When Dodge responded to Fred's letter, on December 23, he had not yet received Julia's; he assumed she was not in New York but with Fred on the dramatic tour. His response to Julia has not survived, if indeed he wrote one, but in the present instance what he wrote to Fred applied to her as well. Characteristically, as when addressing other matters that concerned him deeply, in his letter Dodge repeated himself here and there. In fact, he had previously conveyed the entire substance of his message more than once. "As regards your future this winter," he wrote, "we must do the best we can, but you may as well once for all abandon the idea of bringing your mother to live with me. I have already explained my position with reference to her. I fully recognize all her good qualities, & her bad habits. I have already explained to you that these habits are such as to render me constantly uncomfortable & unhappy when with her, & I do not think you treat me right when in almost every letter you revert in some way to your desire to get her here."

In asserting the right to view the situation from his own perspective, Dodge admitted to feeling taken for granted. "You don't seem to care at all for *my* happiness," he wrote, "but altogether for *hers*. You constantly refer to the great sacrifices she has made for you – & you are right to be grateful. You dont recollect that nearly every cent of money that I have been able to save for years has gone to her & to you – amounting all told to more than twenty thousand dollars. I do not begrudge this in the slightest, but while I shall do all in my power to help her & you, I insist on my right to be comfortable & happy in my own house. And you know I would be neither were she in it."

Dodge declared his willingness to send Fred and Julia all the money he could save from month to month, including the usual sixty dollars rent on the flat and as much as one hundred dollars additional. He understood their wish not to give up the flat, but should that prove necessary, they could surely find some agreeable place to board in the country. "I will do every thing in my power for the comfort & happiness of you both," he continued, "except borrow money or sacrifice my own happiness, without far better reason than is now presented." Noting Fred's tendency "to be '*way up*' or '*way down*,'" he assured him that the present predicament was far from hopeless. A spell of rest would do him no harm, and an actor of his standing would probably find a new engagement within a month. "You understand," he concluded, "that my only objection to your mother is her habits."[37]

Dodge's prediction of better times to come for Fred proved accurate, for on March 1, 1889, he opened in a new production in New York City. Three weeks later he opened in another, this time as a leading actor in a top-level organization, the Jefferson-Florence Company, which specialized in staging revivals of dramatic classics.[38] Although he never became a star, "Frederick Paulding" now occupied a respectable place in the second rank of the city's actors that assured him of continued employment for years to come, and with it a home for himself and his mother. In future years he would continue to visit Dodge during the summers, and Dodge would stay with him and Julia while visiting New York. Her hope to take up residence with him in the winter of 1888–1889 had been prompted more by necessity than by desire to adopt a new mode of life as an army wife. Still, the new relationship between her and Dodge was mutually supportive, and although it continued to be focused primarily on Fred, it was affectionate as well.

During Dodge's remaining years at Madison Barracks, their mutual regard expressed itself in exchanges of anecdotes about their physical infirmities and earnest injunctions, especially from Julia, that each should try patent medicines and other forms of treatment that the other had found beneficial. Julia suffered from gout, among other ailments, and Dodge from rheumatism. Similarities in the treatment of these conditions prompted her to urge that he put himself on a regular regimen of two products, Ayers's Sarsaparilla and Salicilica.[39] In return, Dodge recommended to his wife a "rheumatic ring" made of "a *secret* combination of metals" that he wore on the little finger of his left hand. "It would seem to be a matter of faith," he admitted, "but faith or not, so long as good effect is produced – I wear mine & I certainly have been less troubled with rheumatism this year [1890] than the last." Offering to send a ring to her, he suggested that she have a jeweler take her exact size.[40] In their letters to each other they now signed themselves "Your affectionate wife" and "Yr affec hub."

Improvements—and Amusements—at Madison Barracks

In November 1888 Dodge wrote Julia that he had been exceedingly busy of late, supervising construction at the post. Owing to the delay by Congress in approving the annual army appropriation bill, funds for the purpose had not become available until September. Meanwhile, he had sent in the plans and estimates for "innumerable

Richard Irving Dodge, 1888. Courtesy The Newberry Library, Chicago.

alterations and repairs"—so many, indeed, that "one after another several of the Big Bugs (principally the Quarter Master General himself) dropped in on me for a casual visit." His plans were approved, and in the next six weeks several projects went forward at a rapid pace. By the time he wrote Julia, one of two new storehouses was in use and the other would be finished in a few days. A new wharf, porches for the men's barracks, a complete system of sewerage, paling fences that enclosed the lawns and gardens in front of the officers' residences, and a new set of quarters for the band leader were all in place.[41] Like most of the older buildings at Madison Barracks, those just built were of stone. They conveyed an air of permanence, as if the post would remain in use indefinitely. In the following year, a correspondent for the *New York Times* described it as "one of those delightful lake posts to which Army men are always anxious to be appointed."[42]

The most publicized of Dodge's enhancements of his post's appeal was a monument to the approximately 1,400 unknown soldiers who had died of wounds or disease in the vicinity during the War of 1812. An attack of rheumatism kept him from presiding at the dedicatory observances, on Decoration Day, 1888,[43] but in the following year he was able to supervise the installation of a valued embellishment to the cemetery. While on a visit to Washington, he obtained for installation at the post an ornamental iron fence that had once enclosed Lafayette Park in that city. It was then badly rusted and in 130 pieces, but it arrived safely; and when scoured, painted, and set in place, it lent a new civic dignity to the grounds.[44] Not long before, Dodge had informed the adjutant general that a collection of captured British guns from the War of 1812, currently lying in a post storehouse, might be of interest to the persons who were then assembling exhibits for a national military museum.[45] In more than one respect, Madison Barracks was itself becoming a living monument of American history.

Dodge was on duty at Madison Barracks almost the entire summer of 1888, during which period the post was a center for social and official contact among military men, and also between them and visitors to the area. Two general courts-martial held sessions there during those months, and the garrison was enlarged from time to time by companies of troops who came to practice on the firing range. A number of army families took rooms at the Earl House in Sackets Harbor, including those of some officers formerly stationed at the post. On July 18 the men currently on duty at Madison Barracks sponsored a "magnificent" hop at Dodge Hall, complete with printed programs cut to resemble drums and soldier caps. Later in July, the resident officers and their families made the annual boat excursion to the scenic Thousand Islands on Lake Ontario, and on August 23 Mrs. Colonel Mason of Sackets Harbor gave a reception at her historic home. Dancing was the order of that evening, the music being supplied by the regimental band. According to an observer, "The uniforms of the officers, together with the handsome dresses of the ladies, made a picturesque sight as they strolled about the spacious grounds enjoying the moonlight."[46]

The death of Lieutenant General Sheridan on August 6 had been anticipated for several weeks and did not seriously interrupt the ongoing affairs of the army. For a time his successor, Major General Schofield, attempted to perform the duties of General of the Army while also retaining command of the Division of the Atlantic. However, the double responsibility exceeded even his considerable ability and stamina, and he assigned the latter position to another experienced leader, Major General O. O. Howard.[47] A thoughtful pragmatist, Schofield continued to foster programs that Sheridan had set in motion, in some cases varying the degree of emphasis being placed upon them. Thus, while improvement in rifle firing remained a priority, other initiatives took on added importance. Among these were scheduling one month per year of practical instruction in field duty, organizing practice marches across country, and causing regular army units and the states' volunteer militias to encamp together during the summer. Dodge supported these new emphases, having advocated them all in "The Enlisted Soldier." Further, although the increased salary and perquisites he had advocated for noncommissioned officers had not yet become army policy, he had taken a step in that direction at Madison Barracks. The post now housed a noncommissioned officers' club that, according to a correspondent of the *Army and Navy Journal*, "affords a pleasant and convenient lounging place for non-coms and obviates the necessity of visiting the village to enjoy a good cigar or a game of checkers or chess."[48]

John M. Schofield. Courtesy U.S. Army Military History Institute.

As that newspaper observed, the work that went forward at Madison Barracks through the spring of 1889 owed its extent and variety to the presence of its activist commander.[49] By March the construction of a pier on the post grounds was well advanced, obviating the necessity of hauling supplies from an old pier in the village. Installation of steam heating in all the permanent structures later in the year brought the campaign of modernization almost to an end. "Should Col. R. I. Dodge . . . remain a few years longer," the *Watertown Times* observed, "Madison Barracks will rank number one in the United States, as never since their erection at any one time has any other commander made so many improvements. Col. Dodge has the matter very much at heart, and whatever improvements are made are made with intelligence and taste and at the same time are just what were needed."[50]

Assignments Afield

Whereas in 1888 Dodge spent almost the entire year in the vicinity of his post, in 1889 he traveled widely and repeatedly on special assignments while also maintaining a busy schedule when at home. This was the year of his greatest prominence and visibility in the army, but the physical demands of his duties taxed his energies severely, bringing him to the limit of his strength.

Notice of Dodge's first errand away from Madison Barracks arrived on March 2, when he was detailed as a member of a blue-ribbon general court-martial that would convene in Washington later that month. The accused officer was Major Garrett J. Lydecker of the Engineers, who was alleged to have been derelict in his duty as supervisor of civilian labor on an underground aqueduct to conduct fresh water to the national capital. Lydecker, the son of a former deputy collector of customs in New York City and himself a commissioner of the District of Columbia, had been a fixture in Washington's social circle for years. His competence and diligence had never been impugned,[51] and the case therefore attracted considerable attention, both within the army and outside it.

Under the presidency of Major General George Crook, who now commanded the Military Division of the Missouri, the court began its sessions in the War Department building on March 25 and, under intense newspaper scrutiny, continued in session through April 3. For Dodge, the tedium of the proceedings was alleviated somewhat by the opportunity they presented him to mix with fellow court members, several of whom were old comrades. Besides Crook, these included Colonel Edwin F. Townsend, Twelfth Infantry, formerly lieutenant colonel of the Eleventh; Colonel John Mendenhall, Fifth Artillery, his host at San Francisco in 1883; and Colonel Orlando M. Poe of the Engineers, a former fellow aide-de-camp under General Sherman. The testimony heard by the twelve-man court was primarily technical in nature, best interpreted by the engineer officers who predominated on it. Nevertheless, all recognized that none of the evidence seriously discredited Lydecker. Inspections had been made on sections of the aqueduct tunnel that had later proved defective in construction; but the lighting was so poor, and the contractors so deft in concealing their derelictions, that responsibility for the failure of the project could not be placed upon the accused officer alone. Even so, since Lydecker had assumed full charge over construction but had not himself regularly conducted examinations of its progress, the court found him guilty of neglect of duty. It recommended a light sentence—one that, when confirmed by the president, pleased almost no one.[52] Lydecker resented his transfer soon afterward to Vancouver Barracks, for in his opinion an exile on the Pacific coast amounted to punishment for performance of duty in a case that had warranted no punishment at all.[53]

Probably Dodge's convenient presence in Washington played a part in his appointment as president of a second court that began its meetings only a few days after the Lydecker court was dissolved. Unlike Lydecker, who enjoyed general respect within the army both before and after his trial, the defendant in this case, Captain George A. Armes, had become a byword for emotional instability and self-destructive impertinence. Armes had won attention for bravery and pluck as a combat officer during the Civil War and on the western plains for a few years afterward. In fact, Dodge had probably not forgotten a courageous exploit of his at Fort Sedgwick, Colorado, just prior to his own tour of duty there in 1867. But by the time of his forced retirement for incapacity in 1883, Armes had been court-martialed six times, with a separate inquiry conducted as to his mental state.[54] General Sherman had twice approved sentences of dismissal from the service against him, both mitigated by the president. Armes was fortunate not to have been dismissed earlier, but he considered himself an aggrieved party when a Retiring Board recommended his removal from active service just when he was about to be promoted to major after seventeen years at the rank of captain.[55] In the years following his forced retirement he resided in Washington, where he conducted a real estate business, but he held fast to his self-image as a soldier who had been treated unfairly.[56]

In the court proceedings presided over by Dodge, Armes pled not guilty to charges of conduct unbecoming an officer and gentleman. These charges related to his behavior during the inaugural parade on March 4 for the newly elected president, Benjamin Harrison, and also in related incidents in the weeks that followed. Wearing the dress uniform of a captain of cavalry and mounted on a fine bay horse, during the parade Armes rode as an aide to the grand marshal, Governor James Adams Beaver of Pennsylvania, taking a position only a short distance from the presidential carriage. However, once Beaver discovered his presence in the line, he ordered him removed by two officers, Colonel Horatio G. Gibson, Third Artillery, and Captain John G. Bourke, Third Cavalry, which was done forcibly. Outraged, Armes had Gibson and Bourke arrested for assault and addressed a heated letter to the adjutant general, subsequently published in the *Washington Critic*, in which he accused them of drunkenness and unsoldierly conduct. Then on March 27, at the Riggs House in Washington, Armes confronted Beaver and demanded an apology for the part he had played in the incident at the parade. The governor refused, and as he turned away, Armes was alleged to have pulled his nose, an act that delighted Beaver's political enemies but was characterized in the charges against Armes as "a cowardly and disgraceful violent public assault upon his excellency."[57] Earlier in the month, Bourke had responded to Armes's initial complaint with a countersuit, but this had seemed unlikely to be acted upon until the confrontation with the governor occurred.[58] An order detailing a court to hear charges against Armes was issued from army headquarters on April 3.[59]

Understandably, the ten days of testimony before the Armes court, which met between April 11 and 24, included moments of angry confrontation and also tense levity. Notwithstanding the accused officer's brash behavior, testimony elicited from him and other witnesses brought to light mitigating circumstances. Weeks before the inauguration, Armes had applied to Governor Beaver to serve as a mounted aide; and in due course, though under a misapprehension of his identity, a member of the governor's staff had sent him an appointment. Moreover, Armes had declined a second appointment before being informed, without explanation, that the one from Beaver was being withdrawn. Furthermore, testimony in closed session established that he had participated in the inaugural parade under separate, secret orders, as one of ten picked men who comprised a special body guard to the president. In view of facts like these, Major George B. Davis, the judge advocate, declined in his summation of the case even to argue its legal merits. Instead, he urged court members to give the accused officer the benefit of every doubt and every piece of extenuating testimony.[60] But it remained clear to Dodge and his fellow court members that in three of the four specifications of the charge against him, Armes was guilty of conduct unbecoming an officer, and that by his extravagant behavior he had sullied the service. The court sentenced him to dismissal.[61]

Dodge had now been absent from Madison Barracks for more than a month, but as a mark of regard General Schofield selected him to perform one more task before returning to his regular duty station. Dodge would represent the U.S. Army more prominently than he had ever done before, this time in a great civic parade. A celebration was forthcoming in New York City on April 30, the centennial of George Washington's inauguration there as the nation's first president. The day's observances would include thanksgiving services, concerts, fireworks, a display of warships, and a banquet, but the chief event would be a five-mile procession up Broadway and Fifth Avenue, from the Battery to 57th Street. Comprised of army and navy units, militia brigades representing twenty-four states, veteran's organizations, and various high officials, including state governors, Supreme Court justices, and members of Congress, the parade would include 50,000 persons. It would be the largest quasi-military demonstration in the United States since the Grand Review in Washington at the close of the Civil War. As its grand marshal, Schofield would take the lead position, accompanied by his aides and a cavalry escort. Next after him would come a body of regular army troops, with Dodge at their head, and then the rest of the participants. At Twenty-third Street, near Madison Square, President Harrison would occupy a reviewing stand with other dignitaries and would receive the tributes of the passing units.

Preparations in the city were extensive, and on the morning of April 30 the relief was palpable when a rainbow appeared, an auspicious promise of good weather. Along the parade route, portraits of George Washington were hung out by the thousand, in festoons of U.S. flags. The housetops were packed with spectators, while wreaths, banners, mottoes, shields, and more flags, all red, white, and blue, enlivened the scene below. As those who would march in the parade searched out their designated assembly points, the streets filled with more than 1 million spectators. Shortly before noon the presidential party reached the reviewing stand. The crowd nearby, packed to suffocation on the sidewalks and in rows of bleachers, greeted individual members of the group as they came into view and were recognized. President Harrison and former President Cleveland received a thunderous welcome, but General Sherman was also among the invited guests, and the shout that went up for him was one of the heartiest.

Now was heard the roar of voices drowning out the martial music as the body of the parade came into distant view. According to the *New York Times*, the sight down Fifth Avenue from the reviewing stand was memorable. "The effect produced by the compact mass of waving plumes of the helmetted troops was that of a moving bed of flowers. First there was a strip of bright yellow, next a strip of white, then one [of] red, and away beyond could faintly be discerned successive repetitions of those streaks of color."[62] The approaching pattern of colors gradually took on human form, and in a few more minutes General Schofield, an expert horseman, moved past the reviewing stand with graceful dignity. He saluted the president, who in response removed his hat and bowed, to great applause. Schofield and his aides rode forward, leaving behind them a free space, and then came Dodge, leading 265 West Point cadets and three battalions of regulars—cavalry, artillery, and infantry, the latter group including virtually the entire five-company garrison of Madison Barracks together with other units of the Eleventh Regiment.[63] As he had done on occasion in earlier years, Dodge was again "playing brigadier general." Presidents Harrison and Cleveland exchanged comments on the fine marching and soldierly bearing of the West Pointers, and the *Times* reporter noted that Dodge "looked as if he was proud of them."[64]

After all these, up the avenue came units of the Marine Corps, with its famous band, followed by the various bodies of state troops extending for more than a mile. Detailed instructions circulated by Schofield several days before the parade had specified that the leaders of various military contingents should acknowledge the president all in the same fashion, by a salute with drawn sabre.[65] Dodge was thus the second officer to recognize the chief executive in this manner. As his mount reached the reviewing stand, he drew his sword, turned his head to the right, lifted his gaze, and raised, then dipped the sword in salute to his commander in chief.

Possibly in that long moment Dodge also caught sight of General Sherman among the official party; but whether he did so or not, thoughts of his former commander must have entered his mind as he led the army troops through the streets of New York City. The position Dodge occupied near the head of the parade was a great honor, but it invited comparison to other, perhaps even more valued distinctions he had enjoyed during his association with the general not many years earlier. What Sherman had written of Dodge in his *Memoirs* was true in reverse: his regard had become not only professional but personal. However, whether the two veteran officers met and conversed during that event-filled day of patriotic celebration cannot be stated with certainty. So far as is known, the centennial parade was the last occasion in which they appeared together in public.

Shortly after his return to Madison Barracks, Dodge received from division headquarters an order to inspect the companies of his regiment at Fort Niagara, Fort Ontario, and Plattsburg Barracks. Two days later another order arrived: that upon completing this errand, he was to return to Fort Wood, on Bedloe's Island in New York harbor, to inspect the one company of his regiment now stationed there.[66] These duties keep him fully occupied for the greater part of June, but at the end of the month he was back at Madison Barracks to greet General Howard on his arrival for a three-day visit. Howard returned in July for another short stay that included a fishing excursion on Lake Ontario,[67] but Dodge was unable to join him then. He was performing yet another inspection, this time of state troops.

The governor of North Carolina, Daniel G. Fowle, had secured the approval of the secretary of war for the appointment of Dodge as inspector at the state militia's summer encampment.[68] Probably Dodge's nephew James Dodge Glenn, now adjutant general of the North Carolina volunteer force, had played a part in securing this nomination.[69] At any rate, between July 2 and July 26, Dodge was on detached service, combining official duties with visits among his family and old friends. He arrived at Camp Latimer, near Wilmington, North Carolina, well in advance of the encampment's first day of organized activity, July 9. The commander, Brigadier General W. H. Anthony; Dodge's nephew Jim; and other prominent citizens were already on hand and gave him a hearty welcome.[70]

The military exercises that had been planned for the ten-day encampment were seriously impeded by heat and wind, as well as fleas and ticks, but none of these dampened the high spirits of the citizen soldiers and the thousands of persons who visited their sprawling tent camp. To Dodge, the contrast between the holiday atmosphere of this gathering and the sober earnestness of the Iowa encampment three years before must have been striking. Bathing in the ocean, horseplay, flirting, and sleep agreeably filled the hours when the various companies were not engaged in their military maneuvers. On one afternoon, three companies of Confederate veterans, numbering 240 men, paraded in light marching order, carrying with them the national colors and two Confederate battle-flags. One of these old soldiers was asked by a reporter for the *Wilmington Star* whether the youths he saw around him measured up to the fighting Southrons of a generation before. He may have had his doubts, but he cloaked any reservations within a flattering classical comparison. If, he replied, "the boys now at Wrightsville [*i.e.*, Camp Latimer] are worthy descendants of noble sires, they stand to the rest of the world as the soldiers of Leonidas and Pausanias, the Spartans[,] did to those of other Grecian States."[71]

Within days of his return to Madison Barracks, Dodge advised his divisional headquarters of plans he had developed over the past several months for a fifteen-day practice march by the troops stationed at Madison Barracks.[72] The route he had chosen was approximately 125–150 miles in length and triangular, involving four days of travel northeast, five days due south, and finally a northwesterly return to the post. "In selecting this route," he explained, "I attain several desirable ends. I get my command by the shortest route away from grain fields and wire fences and onto grounds w[h]ere skirmish lines can be extended without subsequent demand for damages. Many, if not most, of my camps will be in the woods without the usual demand for payment for fuel and for rent of ground. The roads, little used, will be free from dust and the country healthy."[73] As these considerations make clear, Dodge understood that a practice march was but a pale imitation of the conditions experienced by an army in the field in wartime. However, he believed that valuable lessons could be learned by troops unaccustomed to movements of this kind. Summarizing the marching order he issued on August 17, the *Army and Navy Journal* declared it "a model of sound military common sense."[74]

On the morning of August 20, the Madison Barracks headquarters staff, the regimental band, and companies A, D, G, H, and I, totaling thirteen officers and 156 men, set out on the first day's march, eleven miles to the village of Brownsville, New York. On subsequent days the marches ranged in distance from eight to fourteen miles and presented no unforeseen difficulties. At Castorland, New York, on August 27, Dodge ordered Captain Erasmus C. Gilbreath to return to the post; the strain of the march had aggravated old wounds and made him unable to continue.[75]

The passage of armed soldiery through the quiet country of upstate New York proved of much interest to the local residents. According to the *Watertown Times*, "The available fences in the vicinity of the camps were lined with vehicles of all sorts which had brought people from miles around to see the soldiers in their picturesque camp, their outdoor life, the morning roll call and inspection, the evening guard mount, and to hear the beautifully rendered music by the regimental band. The courtesy of Col. R. I. Dodge and his gallant officers and men in giving all information to every query was most gratifying to visitors."[76] On the afternoon of September 1, following a thirteen-mile journey that day from Adams, New York, the command returned to Madison Barracks, ending what was described as "a highly instructive and successful practice march."[77]

In the few weeks' interval before some junior officers departed for the rifle competitions at Fort Niagara, Dodge enjoyed a respite from the rigors of the summer. Fred was on hand, having been the guest of the evening at an entertainment just prior to the march and remaining at the post through September. Late that month, two senior officers, Inspector General Robert P. Hughes and Assistant Quartermaster General Charles H. Tompkins, spent several days at the post in connection with the vexed problem of securing land for a new rifle range.[78] "P.," a correspondent of the *Army and Navy Journal*, remarked that Madison Barracks was "unusually dull" at this time, the summer residents having departed.[79] To Dodge the relative peace and quiet was welcome, providing him a space of time—scarce since his transfer from Fort Sully—to read, think, and write.

One subject that engaged his attention was the experimental post canteen that had been established in March.[80] The idea of a designated place of resort on the post grounds for enlisted men, where they could purchase food, incidental items, and perhaps beer and wine, was hardly new. The term itself derived from *cantina*, designating an institution within the army of Spain, and a canteen system had long been in operation among British forces. The first trial of its practicability in the U.S. Army had been made in 1880 by Colonel Henry A. Morrow, Twenty-first Infantry, at Vancouver Barracks. The postwar army had earlier relied entirely upon authorized post traders, under supervision, to provide facilities similar to those supplied by canteens. However, various problems with that arrangement eventually opened up the possibility of dispensing with licensed traders and administering a system from within the army itself.[81] Dodge, who had been on friendly terms with many traders at posts he had commanded, knew that not all of them were the opportunistic rogues some persons alleged.[82] Still, his interest in the welfare of enlisted men led him to authorize organization of the canteen at Madison Barracks and observe its effect on discipline and morale.

He was frankly surprised at the extent of the improvements he witnessed, and in common with post commanders across the nation, he registered hearty support for general adoption of the canteen system.[83] "In my opinion," he wrote the House Committee on Military Affairs,

> no step has been taken for the improvement of the moral, social, and intellectual condition of the enlisted men more efficacious than the establishment of the canteen. With pride, I am able to say that in discipline and general good conduct, I have a command superior to any I have ever seen in the Army. As my general rules and mode of command have not changed, [and] as this post differs from others only in being surrounded with even more grog-shops and other temptations, I can attribute the very marked improvement only to the very wonderful influence of the canteen. I hope that this powerful influence may be extended to the whole Army, and that posts now controlled by the political, social, or moneyed power of post-traders may soon enjoy the benefits accorded to my command.[84]

In conversation with a reporter for the *New York Times*, Dodge cited the presence of the canteen as a cause of the unusually low number of garrison courts-martial and desertions at the post. "There is a freedom and conviviality about the post canteen," this observer wrote after a visit, "that makes it homelike for the soldier who is not the fortunate possessor of mother, wife, or sweetheart. There is now no asking for a short furlough to sneak away to the neighboring town to squander the month's pay in reckless debauchery." Dodge informed the *Times* reporter that in the canteen's six months of operation, three saloons in Sackets Harbor had closed.[85]

During this lull in activity, Dodge also addressed another concern long-standing in army circles. Over the signature "Ancient," in the *Army and Navy Journal* for September 28 Dodge rejoined the discussion of desertion from the army and the best ways to address that chronic problem. Responding to an article he had read in the *Journal of the Military Service Institution*, he approached the subject of desertion from a different point of view than he had in "The Enlisted Soldier." Here he submitted that the root cause was "social ostracism, and a generally unfavorable sentiment" among the American people toward the regular army.[86] Later in the year he made another published comment on desertion, this time in response to an unnamed officer who had identified "military caste" as the root cause. Here Dodge distinguished between "caste" as a social institution of India and the use of the term to denote rank, grade, or place in society generally. Difference in military rank, he insisted, was not to be confused with difference in social standing. "An officer of the Army," he wrote, "once covered himself with the contempt of myself and other officers present, by refusing, at a public hotel, to dine at the same table with two enlisted men, all of us being in uniform and the enlisted men behaving with perfect propriety." Association between officers and men was not necessarily prejudicial to good order and military discipline, he urged, even though in many cases it might well be. "I have had a private soldier a guest at my dinner table, and I contend that I have violated no military law or principle."[87]

"A Duty to Myself"

Probably Dodge had not intended to provoke controversy by referring to his occasional social contacts with enlisted men. However, his published remarks prompted further comment in the *Army and Navy Journal*, including reproaches of his admitted behavior. At last, the editors expressed their own views in an essay entitled "Officer and Man" in the issue of June 21, 1890.[88] Deeply as the issues involved may have interested him, Dodge had neither time nor energy to debate them further in print. His exertions since spring had worn him down to such a degree that, reluctantly, he obtained from the post surgeon a certificate stating that he suffered from chronic subacute articular rheumatism of both ankles and that to prevent permanent disability, he required a four-month change of climate.[89] In hopes that the symptoms would abate, he waited a full month before submitting an application for a medical leave of absence supported by the surgeon's certificate, but at last he gave in. "For several years" he wrote the adjutant general on November 7, "I have suffered greatly in winter from attacks of rheumatism. Since being stationed in this most trying of winter climates, these attacks do not yield to treatment. It is therefore as a duty to myself that I ask permission to seek a climate, where if not permanently cured I can at least be free from suffering for the winter."[90] An order granting him a four-month leave of absence was issued ten days later.[91]

In one sense, this action represented a personal defeat, for Dodge had not been obliged to apply for a medical leave since his bout with tuberculosis more than thirty years earlier.[92] On the other hand, the time away from Madison Barracks offered hope of relief from suffering. He left the post on December 3, spent a few days in New York, then made his way further south. The post surgeon had mentioned Hot Springs, New Mexico, as a place that might benefit him, but as his health resort he chose the Hot Springs in western North Carolina, near his childhood home.[93] Worn down by a level of activity he was no longer able to maintain, he spent the winter months recuperating.

Events during Dodge's absence from his post brought sobering reminders of time's passage. In February, General Sherman celebrated his seventieth birthday, and in March, General Crook died, still in harness, creating a vacancy for the promotion of Nelson A. Miles to major general.[94] Following the retirement in 1895 of General Schofield, Miles would become the last veteran of Civil War action to command the army. Dodge was by now the only graduate of his West Point class still in active service. Having completed forty years of duty, he was eligible for placement on the Retired List, but he hoped to continue in his present position until his sixty-fourth birthday. In part this was a matter of pride, but a financial motivation also existed. Over the years he had helped support family members using funds from his salary that he might otherwise have saved, and now he needed to conserve what he could for himself.

On March 31, 1890, Dodge resumed command at his post, much improved in health. Fortunately for him, that year proved as quiet and routine as the one before had been strenuous. During the summer months one company and then another left the post for a session of target practice at Fort Niagara. In August two companies were added to the garrison, lending new impressiveness to battalion drills and the weekly dress parade, and in September Dodge led another practice march. "Adonis," writing from Madison Barracks to the *Army and Navy Journal*, lamented that "[o]ur pleasant summer has come to an end . . . and all look forward to the practice march . . . with dismal forebodings, anticipating a cold, wet time. We snatch all enjoyment possible from our pleasant agreeable surroundings, and shout 'On with the dance!'"[96]

Two of Dodge's close relations made extended visits to Madison Barracks this summer. After convalescing in New York City from a physical breakdown brought on by overwork during the spring season, Fred completed his recuperation as his father's guest. He was a valued accession to the community of officers' families and visitors that passed back and forth between the post and the village. After a hop at Dodge Hall on July 12, Fred was among the guests for refreshments at the home of Captain and Mrs. Erasmus Gilbreath, helping round out the evening "most agreeably" by a series of recitations.

The cottages and hotels of Sackets Harbor were filled in the summer, chiefly with families who returned from year to year.[97] With its broad streets lined by stately trees, its quiet harbor dotted by boats and yachts, its picnic grounds, and its convenient access to Lake Ontario, Sackets Harbor was an attractive summer resort. When Dodge's sister, Annie Glenn, visited the post later in the summer, she enjoyed herself immensely. She had seldom traveled outside North Carolina, and when she returned home, her sons reported her equipped with anecdotes and impressions to fill out the balance of her lifetime. "Well," Dodge wrote Julia, "she made herself a general favorite at the post, & did have a good time."[98]

Dodge reported to his wife in October that he had been feeling "unusually well" of late and hoped to "stick it out here this winter." The weather was interfering with outdoor amusements by now, but his house was "quadruply" fortified against the rigors of winter. It boasted steam heat, a furnace, fire places in most of the rooms, "& a garret full of stoves."[99] He carefully monitored himself in the months that followed, conserving his energy. In January and February 1890, the retirement for disability of four officers in his regiment served as incitements to persevere.[100] Yet no matter how firm his resolution, he knew that the close of his army career was not far off.

The death of General Sherman on February 14 came as a shock, for observers had anticipated his ability to keep up a brisk pace of activity for several more years. The distinguished soldier's passing occasioned demonstrations of regret at army posts across the nation. By direction from headquarters in Washington, D.C., on the day of Sherman's funeral seventeen-gun salutes sounded every half hour from 8:00 A.M. until sunset.[101] For Dodge, the official tributes to his former commander rang out with deep personal resonance. Fittingly, the end of his own active service would come close upon the end of his general's lifetime.

"He Deserves Well of His Country"

In its issue for the week that followed coverage of memorial tributes to Sherman, the *Army and Navy Journal* published under the heading "He Deserves Well of His Country" a letter to the editor devoted, not to the late leader, but to Colonel Richard I. Dodge, Eleventh Infantry. The anonymous author, who signed himself "A Loving Nephew of Uncle Sam," expressed satisfaction that Dodge, "one of the most deserving patriots, one of the best and truest soldiers, one of the most honest, upright, faithful officers of our little Army," had been mentioned as a candidate to fill the next vacancy at the rank of brigadier general. The author related an event in Dodge's personal history that had never before been mentioned in print but that entitled him to the respect and gratitude of the nation:

> Very few know how unflinchingly loyal and true this talented officer proved himself to be under the most trying circumstances. At the breaking out of the War of the Rebellion, Col. Dodge, then a lieutenant of infantry, and considered one of the brightest and most promising young officers of the Army, declined the offer of a brigadier-generalship in the Southern Army and served as a captain under the old flag. Though from the South, Col. Dodge came from old line Whig stock. Loyalty to the Union was bred in the bone and he remained faithful to the flag because he loved it and believed implicitly in the principles underlying the Government, whose Army bore it to glorious victory.

In light of Dodge's commitment to democratic principles and long service to his country, the writer concluded that it "would be eminently fitting and appropriate to crown the last days of active service of this gallant soldier and single minded and noble hearted patriot with the promotion so well earned and richly deserved."[102]

Whoever the author of this statement may have been, the editors of the *Army and Navy Journal* shared his respect for Dodge.[103] In a subsequent issue they noted that the colonel's "many friends" still hoped that upon the retirement for age of Brigadier General Gibbon on April 20, the promotion to a generalship would be Dodge's, enabling him "to round off his career in a manner befitting his distinguished services."[104] A short-term commission such as the newspaper proposed was not without precedent in recent years; in fact, some colonels had been awarded the rank of brigadier general on the very day of their retirement.[105] The promotions acknowledged work well done and expressed the nation's esteem for these veteran soldiers. According to the *Army and Navy Journal*, a rumor was circulating in April that all colonels scheduled to retire in 1891 would be promoted to brigadier general on their final day of active duty.[106]

Inasmuch as Dodge had devoted his entire adult life to the army, he would unquestionably have been gratified to receive the tribute being urged by his adherents.

However, at the time the measure was being advocated, his physical condition rendered it uncertain whether he would be able to serve out the few weeks that remained to him. Racked with pain, on April 6 he again secured from his post surgeon a completed certificate that would be required should he apply for a medical leave of absence. Apparently the physician counted the days that must elapse until Dodge's retirement, for he recommended a forty-five-day leave—that is, until just beyond his birthday.[107] Dodge had hoped not to make use of the document, but after five more days of suffering he gave up the fight and left the post for Hot Springs, North Carolina.[108]

During his absence, Colonel August V. Kautz, Eighth Infantry, was announced as the successor to Brigadier General Gibbon. At the beginning of 1891, Kautz had stood third in lineal rank among colonels of infantry, Dodge eighth; and whereas Dodge had only one month of service before him in April, Kautz had nine.[109] He was a solid selection. Regarding the possible promotion of Dodge, it remained only to await a decision that might still be made at the War Department. William C. Church of the *Army and Navy Journal* saw to it that his friend's claim to recognition received due publicity at this perhaps critical time. "Two distinguished officers of the Army," he wrote in the issue of May 16, "will be retired for age next week, both still vigorous and able for service—Colonel Richard I. Dodge, 11th U. S. Infantry, on May 19, and Colonel Horatio G. Gibson, 3d U. S. Artillery, May 22. Both are so well known throughout the Army, that it seems hardly necessary to refer to their military careers, which have done so much honor to themselves and to their country." In the sketch of Dodge's career that followed, Church praised him as "a duty officer second to none," a "fearless, experienced, practical and hardy soldier," and an author whose "reminiscences of a soldier's life in the far West" had been read by "many thousands."[110] Beyond question, he implied, such a man richly merited whatever special tribute the U.S. government might choose to bestow on him.

In mid-May, Dodge passed through New York City on his way back to Madison Barracks, but on his arrival there he did not resume command. He had decided to spend the summer in the village before selecting a permanent home, and his career as an active duty officer was now behind him. On May 19 Special Order 119 from the Headquarters of the Army announced in a single formula sentence that "[b]y direction of the Secretary of War," Dodge was no longer in active service.[111] Colonel Dodge he had been for a quarter of a century, and Colonel Dodge he would remain. In its issue for May 23, the *Army and Navy Journal* announced the end of his "distinguished military career," placing his name first in a list of those to whom it extended birthday greetings and a wish for "[m]any happy returns of the day."[112] Having reached sixty-four years of age, Colonel Dodge was permanently at ease.

Part Eight

In Retirement, 1891–1895

27

Career's End

Living in a comfortable house attended to by Laura and a cook, Dodge remained a local celebrity in Sackets Harbor following his retirement from active service. In the fall, when it was announced that the Eleventh Infantry would exchange stations with the Ninth, then serving in the Department of Arizona,[1] a citizens' meeting adopted resolutions of thanks to several persons who had served the community during the regiment's four-year stay in its midst. Among those so honored were the secretary of war, Dodge's successor, Colonel Isaac De Russy, Eleventh Infantry, and especially Dodge himself. Introducing its resolution, the committee of trustees characterized the Eleventh as "a superior body of men," the equal of any in the army:

> As every command reflects its "commander," so we would, at this meeting, express to Col. R. I. Dodge, now honorably retired after a long and eventful career, our high appreciation of his soldierly qualities and of his efforts to maintain and vastly improve the military reservation at this place. We thank him for his appreciation of this locality, for its historic associations, and his interest in the commemorative services that secured to history the honored names that found a sepulchre here in the memorable War of 1812–15, and with whom his grandsire was a distinguished compatriot.
>
> *Resolved*, That, in his retirement, we beg to assure him of our sincere desire, that length of days, with good health and cheer, may be a part of the reward for his faithful service to his country during his active command. Also for his literary achievements in presenting to the world his incomparable works illustrating the habits of the "Indians of the Plains."[2]

Like many other military men, Dodge had chosen to live out his lifetime amid scenes that had witnessed years of his activity as a soldier. Insofar as local sentiment reflected due regard for the work of the army, he could not have selected a more congenial home.

In the fall of 1891, Dodge performed another act characteristic of persons recently retired after long years in harness—he traveled. More than one motive moved him to set out on this long journey. For him, the besetting threat to year-round comfort in Sackets Harbor was its winter weather, and caution enjoined him to avoid it. At the same time, a passage to warmer locations in the West would take him through scenes of his earlier career and enable him to greet old friends and comrades. Since improvement in his physical mobility was a cherished long-term goal, he had decided to adopt the advice of his post surgeon two years before and make the hot springs at Las Vegas, New Mexico, the place of his first extended stay.[3] Las Vegas was not many miles distant from Fort Union, which he had visited on more than one occasion, and the railroad journey there would carry him past old haunts like Saint Louis, Kansas City, and Dodge City, possibly with stops along the way. It was a happy prospect, even though he would be traveling alone. Following a short visit to New York, where Fred was starring in a successful new play, *The Struggle for Life*,[4] at the end of October he traveled west.

Following a few weeks in New Mexico, early in December Dodge continued on to San Antonio, Texas, where he remained almost three months. For a time he took a room at the Menger Hotel, but later he was the guest of fellow officers, either retired or on duty in the city, which remained a center for army activity. The headquarters of the Department of Texas were located here, now under command of Brigadier General David S. Stanley. Additionally, the newly enlarged Fort Sam Houston was the headquarters of the Twenty-third Infantry, Dodge's former regiment, now commanded by his friend Colonel John J. Coppinger.[5] Dodge had much in common with both these senior officers. Like him, Stanley had passed the greater part of his career on the western plains, having in fact commanded at Fort Sully for several years during the 1870s. And Coppinger, besides being in Dodge's opinion a talented officer, was a colorful figure, a true soldier of fortune.[6] Now a widower, he may have opened his home to Dodge, as he had in earlier years, and at any rate he was a genial host and a valued companion. The same was true of other officers who had served under Dodge, including captains William H. Clapp, Joseph T. Haskell, and Otis W. Pollock, and first lieutenants J. Rozier Clagett and Edwin P. Pendleton, all still attached to the Twenty-third Infantry. These fellow soldiers had a wealth of memories to share, and conversation was a pastime they had learned to value. A lecture series featuring presentations by resident officers enlivened the social scene at Fort Sam Houston this winter. In February, Haskell discussed "The Coddling System in the Army" in a talk that must have produced an animated response, for it was declared the most interesting of the season.[7]

Because Dodge's health had not yet benefitted as markedly as he hoped, before leaving San Antonio he availed himself of services provided by the medical dispensary at the fort.[8] Seeking further treatment, he then traveled to Hot Springs, Arkansas, a popular center for civilians in search of a water cure and also the site of a government hospital. On February 19 he applied for authorization to be admitted to the Army and Navy Hospital as a patient, and one week later the necessary order was issued at Washington. Upon his admission, his malady was identified as "chronic muscular rheumatism."[9] The exact regimen he underwent during the six weeks that followed is not known, except that it involved prolonged exposure to hot mineral water. All patients were expected to drink from three to five glasses daily and were required to bathe in the heated pools every day of the week except Sunday. While bathing, they were free to adjust the water temperature to as high a level as they wished, though the attending physician recommended ninety-eight degrees Fahrenheit as the upper limit. After sitting in a tub for about fifteen minutes, a patient was administered a rubdown to stimulate blood circulation and then ushered into a sweating room, where he remained for an hour or more. Finally, in another room, he cooled off and was given dry clothing.[10] Dodge remained at the hospital almost two months, until April 20, when at his own request he was discharged. The government physician recorded his condition on that date as "not materially changed."[11]

Continuing a long geographical loop, in April Dodge journeyed eastward, visiting friends and relations in North Carolina before reaching Washington in the following month and continuing north.[12] At about this time his wife and son left their flat in New York City to occupy a small house in New Rochelle, on Long Island Sound, conveniently located only a few miles from the city.[13] Dodge must have helped make possible the move, for in the years that followed his place of residence alternated between Sackets Harbor and New Rochelle, with an occasional journey to North Carolina. Julia and Fred visited him from time to time during the summer months, and in the winter he came south and made his home with them, leaving Laura to keep his residence in order until his return.[14] Only a few years earlier, there had seemed no likelihood that he and his wife would reside together again under the same roof, but ultimately they did so, at least for a part of each year. Nevertheless, Dodge valued the time he had to himself at Sackets Harbor during the warmer months.

He had ceased to write for publication, but he remained an active correspondent, taking care to ensure that interested readers of the *Army and Navy Journal* were informed of his whereabouts. In January 1894 he requested of the Adjutant General's Office a copy of the most recent listing of army officers' addresses and also a copy of the official list showing the anticipated retirement date of field officers.[15] Meanwhile, the ranks of his former associates grew thinner. His fellow aide-de-camp John E. Tourtelotte had died in 1891, General Pope in 1892, and James B. Fry would pass away later in 1894.[16] Even so, at events like MOLLUS reunions and in impromptu meetings and visits, old comrades were still to be met with, and for Dodge there was always plenty to talk about.[17]

Beginning in 1890, a topic of interest to many army officers who had served in the West after the Civil War was the possibility that deserving men would be awarded brevet commissions for their distinguished performance of duty during the Indian wars. The late General Crook had long advocated this form of recognition, but so far without success. At the close of the Big Horn and Yellowstone Expedition in 1876, he had eloquently described the claims of the men who had served under him. "Indian warfare," he then wrote, "is of all warfare the most dangerous, the most trying and the most thankless. Not recognized by the high authority of the United States Senate as war, it still possesses for you the disadvantages of civilized warfare, with all the horrible accompaniments that barbarians can invent and savages can execute. In it you are required to serve without the incentive to promotion or reward. You have been on the side of the weak, the sparsely settled frontier, against the strong and numerous enemy, and those few on the frontier will remember your efforts with gratitude. If in the future it should transpire that the avenues for recognition of distinguished service and gallant conduct are opened, those rendered in this campaign will be recommended for suitable reward." Despite such appeals by Crook and others, Congress failed to act on a brevet bill for service against Indians until shortly before his death in 1890.[18]

After a further delay, necessitated in part by the difficulty of assembling testimony that related to events years earlier, in February 1894 General Schofield forwarded to the secretary of war a list of 151 recommended appointments to brevet commissions, ranging in rank from first lieutenant to brigadier general. Among the men so nominated, some for more than one commission, were many whom Dodge had known or served with, including Captain Frederick W. Benteen, Seventh Cavalry, recommended for brigadier general; Captain George M. Randall, Twenty-third Infantry, for lieutenant colonel and colonel; and First Lieutenant John G. Bourke, Third Cavalry, for captain and major. Only one officer, William B. Royall, Third Cavalry, had ranked as high as lieutenant colonel at the time of the action for which he was now being recognized; Royall was subsequently confirmed a brevet brigadier general.[19] In June. the *Army and Navy Journal* reported that General Schofield was drawing up a second list of nominees but was impeded in his work by a statutory requirement, that the file for each candidate must include a recommendation from his department commander. "In many cases it is almost absolutely certain that the officers are entitled to the rank," the article continued, "but the failure of the departmental commander to certify to this fact makes it impossible under the law for General Schofield to recommend that the honor be conferred."[20] The supplementary list, including fifteen nominations, was submitted shortly afterward, but by the end of the year forty other cases still awaited action by Schofield.[21] The difficulty was that current department commanders often could not vouch for alleged conspicuous services they had no record of.

In the meantime, the fairness of the entire process of awarding brevets came under debate, as it had after the Civil War. Some officers refused the honorary commissions being offered them, either because the brevets were at ranks no higher than the ones they now held or because they were not being awarded brevets for services they considered more important. Some departmental commanders had sent in long lists of recommendations, while others submitted none. One officer suggested that the law requiring involvement by department commanders be rewritten, permitting the

General of the Army to base his decisions solely on records available at army headquarters.[22] However, by that time Congress had adjourned until the coming year, and nothing further could be done. Although well intentioned, the process was a muddle, and it was never brought to a satisfactory conclusion. In March 1895 more than thirty cases still awaited action by the War Department but could not receive consideration by Congress until after the retirement of General Schofield in September. Optimistically but inaccurately, the *Army and Navy Journal* predicted that these possible nominations would surely be acted upon by his successor.[23]

On many occasions during his career, Dodge had met the sole criterion for consideration as a potential brevet recipient by taking the field against hostile Indians. However, he was not one of the hundred-odd officers awarded brevets by Congress, nor does surviving evidence indicate that he was considered for such an award. Some formal recognition of his services would no doubt have been gratifying to him, and yet in all likelihood he was neither surprised nor disappointed at the omission of his name from the lists of nominees. After all, none of generals Augur, Pope, Crook, and Terry were alive to write on his behalf, and in any case he had already received a generous share of official rewards and recognitions. Like General Sherman, Dodge wished to be known for his work as a soldier, and he would be remembered with fond regard among those best able to judge of him in that capacity.

Following a springtime visit to North Carolina, in May 1895 Dodge celebrated his sixty-eighth birthday in New Rochelle.[24] A few days later he boarded a train to Albany and thence to Watertown, where he expected to see Laura on hand with his carriage for the ride to Sackets Harbor. Not finding her, he telegraphed his safe arrival to Julia and sat down to await the morning train to the village. In a letter written to Julia on the next day, he sketched the scene and the events that followed it in a style that exhibited all his good humor and easy verbal ability:

> There were many people, & I was a little tired when my attention was attracted by a large fine looking female, gorgeous in appearance, & wearing a pair of Angel's Wings big enough for a sail boat.[25] There was something familiar in the face & appearance, & I was saying to myself, "I ought to know that woman" when I noticed that she was followed by a small dog, that I recognized. So I called out, "Laura." She turned & came back to me – & there was my old Laura – but so swelled out with fat & fashionable clothing that I did not know her. She is about twice as big, as when you last saw her. In fact I was about to relegate her to my list of *fatnesses* when getting home, I was introduced to the new cook, who is such a monster that though Laura is apparently about as big as my own better Half, she is a perfect sylph by comparison.

Dodge confessed himself "still weak as to walking," but he had heartily enjoyed himself on the ride to his house and was glad to be home. "Everything is lovely," he reported; "house in perfect order, flowers flourishing, garden all planted, & the vegetation is not so advanced as at New Rochelle. The world here is very beautiful – & the weather yesterday & today is all that could be desired." After finishing his letter, he wrote, he planned to go out fishing for dace.[26]

Three weeks later, at 3:30 A.M. on June 16, Dodge died suddenly at his home; the cause of death was reported as apoplexy.[27] A former subordinate, First Lieutenant Pierce Butler Travis, Eleventh Infantry, was visiting him at the time, and in the days that followed Travis remained with the body of his former commander and with Julia and Fred. The post commander at Madison Barracks, Lieutenant Colonel Jacob Kline, Ninth Infantry, made preparations for a military funeral at the post on June 18, to be followed by interment at Arlington National Cemetery, Virginia. The national flag at the post was flown at half mast, and officers wore the customary black crepe on their sword hilts and left sleeves. At the funeral, largely attended by the local citizenry, a full regiment of troops marched to the sound of muffled drums, alternating with military airs played by the regimental band. At the close of the ceremony, three rifle volleys sounded a parting salute to the fallen soldier.[28]

Upon being informed that Travis wished to accompany Dodge's remains to Arlington, the Adjutant General's Office at first balked, informing Kline that under decisions in similar cases the lieutenant could not be so ordered. However, Lieutenant General Schofield pre-empted his administrative staff, and as a result Travis accompanied Julia and Fred on the train to Washington. In accordance with a directive from Schofield, the commanding officer at Fort Myer, Virginia, detailed six noncommissioned officers to serve as pallbearers at the burial, which took place on the afternoon of June 19.[29] At the grave site a trumpeter from the post sounded taps, and a firing party again sounded a triple salute to Dodge, who had indeed "deserved well of his country," both North and South. At Arlington, bordering on both regions, he rested where he would have wished.

The *Army and Navy Journal* published two notices of Colonel Dodge's passing. The first, in the June 22 issue, described him as "a gallant and very popular officer" and recounted the highlights of his career. The second set forth details of his family history, sketching a long tradition of honorable military service from within both the northern and southern branches. His loss, this notice began, had occasioned "much grief."[30]

The final contemporary tribute to Dodge was a generous statement by his fellow aide-de-camp Colonel John C. Tidball, for publication in the 1896 *Annual Report* of the Association of Graduates of the United States Military Academy. After reciting the facts of his classmate's parentage, birth, and death, Tidball summarized Dodge's army career through the outbreak of the Civil War:

> Graduating in 1848, he was assigned to the infantry arm and served on frontier duty in Texas until 1856. This was at a period when frontier service in Texas meant constant activity against the Comanche Indians, and it proved to him, then a Lieutenant, a training which made him a most skillful frontiersman. A brief tour of recruiting service and of duty as a tactical instructor at the Military Academy brought him to the outbreak of the Rebellion in 1861.

> Although of Southern birth and surrounded by that strange hallucination which carried so many of his brother officers into hostility to their government, he remained loyal to the Union and gave his best energies to a successful prosecution of the war. Promoted now to a captaincy, he commanded his company at the first Bull Run battle, July 21, 1861. This, however, closed his active field service, for now the government had other important duty for him to perform.

Tidball next described Dodge's unheralded service during the greater part of the Civil War:

> When, at last, it became necessary for the Federal Government to call into existence vast armies to preserve the nation, officers of experience, executive ability, and, above all, of integrity, were sought for to organize and give martial shape to the raw material from which the armies were to be created. To such responsible duty Dodge was assigned: First, as commandant of Camp of Instruction at Elmira, N. Y.; and soon as Chief Mustering and Disbursing Officer for the State of Pennsylvania, and subsequently for the State of New York. The glamour of warlike campaigns and of battles is but too apt to belittle such service, but fortunate was the nation in having a class of officers capable of its efficient performance. Dodge was one of these, and his faithful services were rewarded by the brevets of Lieutenant-Colonel and Colonel.

In his comments on the quarter-century of Dodge's postwar service, which had formed the chief basis for his reputation within the army, Tidball surely did not intend to convey faint praise. Still, he failed to capture the energy, versatility, resourcefulness, courage, and humanity the deceased officer had demonstrated during the period of his frontier duty and afterward. He emphasized instead the writings that had grown out of it:

> After the return of peace he resumed his duties upon the frontier and commanded many posts upon the plains and in the mountains, extending from Arizona to the Dakotas. This period of his life embraced explorations, expeditions to suppress Indian hostilities, and a variety of other duty which familiarized him with the vast West and the habits and character of the Indians who then roamed over it. He was a close and thoughtful observer of such things, and, being free and forcible in description, was able to contribute much valuable information upon these interesting subjects. Among his works may be mentioned the "Plains of the Great West," the "Black Hills," and "Our Indian Wards" [*sic*]. Having reached the age limit, he was retired in 1891.

The concluding sentence of the obituary notice touched the core of Colonel Dodge's appeal to his fellow officers and friends, his hearty sociability: "His many points of good fellowship made him a marked figure upon the frontier," Tidball wrote, "and a new generation who did not know him will have to spring up before memory of him passes away."[31]

Tidball's prediction proved accurate in the twentieth century, for the recollection of Dodge as a living man gradually faded away. He remained known, if at all, as the author of writings about American Indians and about conditions on the Plains of a bygone time. But as set forth in the foregoing pages, Dodge's life history enables us to envision him anew, both in himself and as he appeared to his contemporaries.

In some respects, Dodge's more than four decades of service to his nation exacted of him a high personal price. He was a dedicated outdoorsman, but his duties on the western frontier had as their visible result the taming of an environment whose very wildness he valued. He was troubled by the wholesale slaughter of the buffalo and other species, but he was all too powerless to allay it. A friend to the Indians, he seethed with indignation as he witnessed their sufferings, and so far as the performance of his duty as a military officer enabled him, he did all he could on their behalf. But they remained effectively imprisoned on the reservations allotted to them, dispossessed of their ancestral lands and unable to pursue their traditional mode of life.

Probably in his later years Dodge, a thoughtful man, reflected over the lost opportunities and unrealized hopes of his lifetime, the consequences either of choices he had made or of circumstances he could not control. For example, had he continued bearing arms against the Confederacy following the first Bull Run battle, he might well have distinguished himself in the field and been known thereafter as General Dodge. This was a sobering thought to a man who valued the esteem of his fellow officers as highly as Dodge did. Still, he had reason to be content with his lot. Having served with credit in the remainder of the war, in the years that followed he won a reputation as a stalwart soldier's soldier, and meanwhile, the ties of affection that had bound him to his family and friends in the southern states held firm.

The chief disappointment of Dodge's lifetime was his flawed marriage and the solitary domestic existence he endured because of it. To some degree, of course, his unhappiness in this regard was of his own making. Even though he knew Julia was unwilling to reside at most of the army posts where he was stationed, he never considered seriously the possibility of resigning his army commission to pursue a lifestyle more congenial to her. As a result, despite his continued devotion to her and the fatherly interest he took in Fred, he passed years of lonely separation from his wife and son. To a gregarious man like Dodge, this lack of a family life was a source of deep regret. To compensate, he made virtual family members of his domestic servants, and his army colleagues and other friends became to him a kind of extended family. Even so, the comfortable home life he eventually managed to fashion for himself was a makeshift, and not what he had once hoped for.

Whatever misgivings and regrets Colonel Dodge may have felt, his career was on the whole a happy and successful one. Thanks to his solid good sense, sunny disposition, enjoyment of activity and stir, and patriotic zeal, Dodge's army service record was filled with productive undertakings. Moreover, not only did he win the regard of military leaders like Generals Sherman and Pope, but he participated in events that he knew would be of lasting historical significance. Like Sherman, he believed that the army's support of westward development was a source of legitimate pride, being service in furtherance of the nation's high destiny. In this and other respects, Dodge was thoroughly a man of his own era. But in matters that aroused his passion, he also saw beyond his time. The fervor of a visionary patriot rings through his repeated calls for the fair treatment of American Indians. He was committed to promoting in the United States a just society open to all persons—what President Lincoln had termed "the last, best hope of earth."[32]

"The conditions of frontier life are constantly changing," Dodge wrote in 1878, when he hoped to compile a history of the U.S. Army in recent years. "Advancing civilization and railroads have modified all the surroundings of the frontier Army, and no record will be complete which does not show the labors and privations of the 'old' Army [i.e., before the Civil War], but the thousand complications arising from the restraining position which the 'New' Army occupies between the great opposing forces, civilization and barbarism." Beyond question, Dodge's own record of service eventually earned him an honorable place in the history he once envisioned, for his career was almost in itself "an epitome of frontier and Army life, of Army services and experiences in that most arduous and thankless of all duties, frontier work."[33] The years of varied duty on the western plains were thus the chief legacy of this humane warrior, this talented soldier-author, this engaging personality who became so well known to his army comrades, Richard Irving "Dickie" Dodge.

Notes

The following abbreviations are employed in citations:

AAAG	Acting Assistant Adjutant General
AAG	Assistant Adjutant General
ACP	Appointment, Commission, and Personal
AG	Adjutant General
AGO	Adjutant General's Office
ANJ	*Army and Navy Journal*
BHE	Black Hills Expedition
BHJ	Dodge, *The Black Hills Journals*
C&A	Cheyenne and Arapaho Agency
CNFCR	Cantonment North Fork Canadian River
C.O.	Commanding Officer
DMO	Department of the Missouri
DP	Department of the Platte
FPD	Frederick Paulding Dodge
GCMO	General Court-Martial Order
G.O.	General Order
Graff	Dodge Papers, Everett D. Graff Collection of Western Americana, Newberry Library, Chicago, Illinois
HQA	Headquarters of the Army
I.T.	Indian Territory
ITJ	Dodge, *The Indian Territory Journals*
JMSI	*Journal of the Military Service Institution of the United States*
JRPD	Julia Rhinelander Paulding Dodge
LC	Library of Congress, Washington, D.C.
LR	Letters Received
LS	Letters Sent
MDM	Military Division of the Missouri
MNM	William Blackmore Papers, History Library, Museum of New Mexico, Santa Fe
NARA	National Archives and Records Administration
NYPL	New York Public Library, New York
OIA	Office of Indian Affairs ("Indian Bureau")
O.R.	*The War of the Rebellion. A Compilation of Official Records*

OWI	Dodge, *Our Wild Indians*
PNA	Dodge, *The Plains of North America and Their Inhabitants*
PMG	Provost Marshal General
PRE	Powder River Expedition
PREJ	Dodge, *The Powder River Expedition Journals*
Reg	Register
RG	Record Group
RID	Richard Irving Dodge
SI	Secretary of the Interior
S.O.	Special Order
STJ	Dodge, *The Sherman Tour Journals*
SW	Secretary of War
USAMHI	United States Army Military History Institute, Carlisle Barracks, Pa.
USMA	United States Military Academy, West Point, New York
WTS	William Tecumseh Sherman
Yale	Dodge Papers, Yale Collection of Western Americana, Beinecke Library, Yale University, New Haven, Connecticut

Preface

1. "Frontier Army Life," *Army and Navy Journal*, February 23, 1878, p. 459. For further discussion of this project of authorship, see below, chapters 15 and 21.

Chapter 1

1. Aderman, *A Genealogy of the Irvings of New York*, pp. 2, 7; *ITJ*, p. 303.
2. Wheeler, *Reminiscences and Memoirs of North Carolina*, pp. 394–95; for a genealogical sketch of the Williams family, see pp. 418–20. See also Moore, *History of North Carolina*, II, 135.
3. Reid to SW, February 22 and March 27, 1844; Mitchell to Col. J. G. Totten, February 26, 1843, and January 8, 1844; RID to W. Wilkins, SW [April 1844] (RID Application File, USMA).
4. *The Papers of Thomas Ruffin*, II, 253–56, 269–70.
5. Ebenezer Irving to Katrina Irving, November 6, 1857 (Irving Family Papers W 229, Historic Hudson Valley).
6. According to a descendant, Richard Irving Dodge's parents often visited New York during his cadet years (John P. Frothingham to Grace Sheldon Potter, August 26, 1935—Frothingham Family Papers, Manuscript Division, NYPL).
7. Tidball, "Getting through West Point," pp. 24, 65–66, 90, 96, 129; "On General Sherman's Staff as Aide-de-Camp," p. 73 (Tidball Papers, USMA).
8. Tidball, "Getting through West Point," p. 122 (Tidball Papers, USMA); Cullum, *Biographical Register* (1891), p. 217.
9. Tidball, "Getting through West Point," pp. 156–57 (Tidball Papers, USMA).
10. Eighth Infantry Regimental Return, August 1848. Dodge accepted his commission as a brevet second lieutenant in an August 28, 1848, letter to the adjutant general (AGO LR).
11. Wilhelm, *Eighth U.S. Infantry*, pp. 29–40.
12. See Waugh, *The Class of 1846*, pp. 73–75 passim.
13. Eighth Infantry Regimental Return, November 1848.
14. The right wing consisted of Companies A, E, G, I, and K; the left, the other five companies.
15. Eighth Infantry Annual Return, 1848 Eighth Infantry Regimental Returns, November 1848–January 1849; Wilhelm, *Eighth U.S. Infantry*, pp. 40–42; R. H. Wilson, "Eighth Regiment of Infantry" in Rodenbough, *The Army of the United States*, p. 519.
16. RID to AG, January 6, 1849 (AGO LR).
17. RID to AG, January 21, 1849 (AGO LR).
18. Alvord to AG, April 10, 1849 (AGO LR); Heitman, *Historical Register*, I, 891.

19. Eighth Infantry Regimental Return, April–July 1849. Dodge acknowledged the receipt of his commission as second lieutenant, Eighth Infantry, on July 16, 1849 (AGO LR).

20. Crimmins, "The First Line of Army Posts," p. 122; *Frontier Forts of Texas*, pp. x–xi; Ball, *Army Regulars*, p. xxvii.

21. Ball, *Army Regulars*, pp. xx, xxi, xxx.

22. See House, *Report of the Secretary of War,* 1852, pp. 58–59; see also Doubleday, *My Life in the Old Army*, p. 179. Major General Winfield Scott emphasized in 1850 that "The great extent of our frontiers, and the peculiar character of the service devolving on the troops, render it indispensable that the *cavalry* element should enter largely into the composition of the army" (Scott to SW, November 30, 1850—quoted in Ball, *Army Regulars*, p. xx).

23. *PNA*, p. 160.

24. *PNA*, p. 112; see also Ball, *Army Regulars*, p. xxxi.

25. *PNA*, p. 112.

26. *PNA*, p. 115; see also pp. 81, 90–91, 121, 160, 162, 189. Elsewhere in this work Dodge observed that his knowledge of plains life had been drilled into him "by the sharp point of a bitter experience" (p. 112).

27. *PNA*, p. 342. See also *OWI*, pp. 566–67.

28. On April 20, 1850, Dodge transmitted from Fort Lincoln to the Adjutant General's Office a muster roll for a company of Texas Rangers under Captain J. B. McConn (AGO LR).

29. *PNA*, pp. 345–46; *OWI*, pp. 240, 416, 566–69.

30. *PNA*, pp. 351–52.

31. *PNA*, p. 312.

32. Eighth Infantry Regimental Return, April 1851; Crimmins, "The First Line of Army Posts," p. 123. Dodge was stationed at Fort Martin Scott through February 1852.

33. *OWI*, pp. 33–35.

34. *PNA*, pp. 342, 380; *OWI*, p. 554.

35. *PNA*, pp. 273–74, 352.

36. *OWI*, p. 99. According to Rupert Richardson, a "better man could not have been found" than Neighbors to perform his dangerous and almost unprecedented duties (*The Comanche Barrier to South Plains Settlement*, p. 149).

37. *OWI*, pp. 160–61.

38. *PNA*, pp. 281, 283.

39. Dodge spelled the word "greazer" and defined it as "A term of contempt applied by Americans to the lower class of Mexicans" (*PNA*, p. 331).

40. Eighth Infantry Regimental Returns, July and August 1851.

41. House, *Report of the SW,* 1852, p. 58.

42. House, *Report of the SW,* 1852, p. 4.

43. *PNA*, pp. 296–97. For an account of Pa-ha-yu-ca see Richardson, *The Comanche Barrier to South Plains Settlement*, pp. 118–20, 128–29.

44. Eighth Infantry Regimental Returns, January–April 1852.

45. On March 4, 1847, Dodge had been admitted to the post hospital at West Point, suffering from "pleuritis"; he was released two days later. On other occasions he was treated for cephalgia, catarrhus, and subluxatio—the latter denoting a dislocation in a joint (RID ACP File, AGO).

46. Eighth Infantry Regimental Returns, April–August 1852.

47. Q. Simpson to AG, October 11, 1852 (AGO LR).

48. RID to AG, October 26, 1852 (AGO LR).

49. RID to AG, November 1, 1852 (AGO LR).

50. Eighth Infantry Regimental Returns, June–August 1853.

51. A veteran of service in Texas during this period wrote that "the hard work necessary to accomplish, apparently, so little" made it difficult to bear. "It was the long marches, the fatigue, the exposure, the hunger and thirst, the desolation and loneliness of the stations, and, finally, the loss of health, that made it so very trying and so thankless" (Lane, "Frontier Service in the Fifties," p. 522). Further details about the conditions of a young officer's service in Texas can be found in Doubleday, *My Life in the Old Army*, pp. 4–7, 175–81, 215–21, 236–37, 275–77.

52. *PNA*, pp. 90–91.

53. RID Journal, September 22, 1878 (*ITJ*, p. 19).

54. *PNA*, p. 92.

55. *PNA*, pp. 161–63. Haynes died in Mexico City in September 1850, aged twenty-five (Cullum, *Biographical Register* (1891), p. 211).

56. *PNA*, pp. 275, 336.

57. *PNA*, pp. 279–80.

58. *PNA*, pp. 287–88.

59. *OWI*, pp. 546–47.

60. A description of Fort Davis and a sketch of its history can be found in *Frontier Forts of Texas*, pp. 111–34.

61. Eighth Infantry Regimental Return, October 1854; Wilhelm, *Eighth U.S. Infantry*, pp. 49–51.

62. *OWI*, pp. 521–22. Additional details relating to Sam Cherry can be found in Johnson, *A Soldier's Reminiscences*, pp. 116–17.

63. *PNA*, p. 333.

64. Lee, *Fort Davis and the Texas Frontier*, p. 4.

65. William Butler Yeats, "Easter 1916."

66. See Morrison, *"The Best School,"* p. 22.

67. Washington Seawell to AG, October 15, 1854 (AGO LR); Eighth Infantry Regimental Returns, November 1849, January 1850.

68. Old Soldier, "The Trials of an Army Officer," *ANJ*, May 11, 1867, p. 606.

69. See *PREJ*, pp. 173, 179; "The Quartermaster," *ANJ*, December 30, 1865, p. 293.

70. Eighth Infantry Regimental Return, September 1854.

71. The official head of the Eighth Infantry, Colonel John Garland, then commanded the Ninth Military District from headquarters at Santa Fe, New Mexico.

72. See "The New Army Regulations," *ANJ*, April 11, 1874, p. 551.

73. RID to AG, May 26, 1855 (AGO LR); Cullum, *Biographical Register* (1891), p. 217; Eighth Infantry Regimental Returns, September 1854–October 1855.

74. For example, see *STJ*, p. 112.

75. See Wilhelm, *Eighth U.S. Infantry*, pp. 270–73.

76. Upon the expiration of his term of enlistment, Private Reeves was discharged at Fort Bliss on June 18, 1856 (Eighth Infantry Regimental Return, June 1856).

77. RID to Col. S. Cooper, AG, May 9, 1857 (AGO LR).

78. Reeves to Col. S. Cooper, AG, September 27, 1856; RID to Cooper, May 9, 1857 (AGO LR).

79. RID to James B. Fry, February 6, 1865 (*O.R.*, ser. III, vol. 4, p. 1151).

80. Eighth Infantry Regimental Return, July 1856; William McE. Dye to AG, September 25, 1856 (AGO LR); Order 37, General Recruiting Service, received by AGO August 27, 1856 (AGO Reg LR).

Chapter 2

1. House, *Report of the SW,* 1856, p. 3.

2. Utley, *Frontiersmen in Blue*, pp. 29, 36, 39–41.

3. Reeves to Col. S. Cooper, AG, September 27, 1856 (AGO LR).

4. House, *Report of the SW,* 1856, p. 3.

5. The files of the Adjutant General's Office contain various items relating to this assignment and a similar one at Fort Davis. See RID to AG, December 20, 1854; March 3, April 3, June [15], September 1, September [25], and October 1, 1855; April 30, 1856 (AGO LR).

6. House, *Report of the SW,* 1858, pp. 786–87.

7. See RID to AG, November 6, 1856 (AGO LR).

8. See RID to AG, February 14, 1857, relating to the disposition of government property, and April 29, 1858, relating to an advertisement for recruits that he had placed in the *New York Daily News* (AGO LR). See also RID to AG, September [15] and November 1, 1856; January 5, March 31, July 1, and September 30, 1857; April 2 and April 29, 1858 (AGO Reg LR).

9. Ebenezer Irving to Katrina Irving, November 6, 1857 (Irving Family Papers, Historic Hudson Valley).

10. RID to AG, November 1, 1856, with endorsements (AGO LR).

11. RID to AG, January 13, 1858, with endorsements and attachments (AGO LR).

12. Dodge was also occasionally confused with yet another army officer, Colonel Henry Dodge (1762–1867).

13. Kime, *Pierre M. Irving and Washington Irving*, p. 129; Ebenezer Irving to Katrina Irving, November 6, 1857 (Irving Family Papers, Historic Hudson Valley).

14. Aderman, *A Genealogy of the Irvings of New York*, p. 1.

15. Frederick William Paulding (1809–1859) married his first cousin Maria Paulding (1812–1876) on July 10, 1834. Their only child, Julia, was born on October 17, 1837. (Details on the Paulding family are supplied to the author by Alice R. Aderman.)

16. Ebenezer Irving to Katrina Irving, November 6, 1857 (Irving Family Papers, Historic Hudson Valley).

17. Ebenezer Irving to Katrina Irving, March 4–5, 1858 (Irving Family Papers, Historic Hudson Valley).

18. RID to AG, February 15, 1858, with endorsements (AGO Reg LR).

19. Eighth Infantry Regimental Return, August 1858.

20. Delafield to Col. J. G. Totten, August 20, 1857; Totten to AG, August 22, 1857 (AGO Reg LR); Delafield to AG, April 2, 1858 (AGO LR); "Report of the Board of Visitors to the Military Academy," in House, *Report of the SW*, 1858, pp. 842–43.

21. For a semester-by-semester summary of the West Point curriculum between 1833 and 1854, see Morrison, *"The Best School,"* pp. 160–63; for a synopsis of the course of studies in 1854, see House, *Report of the SW*, 1855, pp. 248–49. After 1855, William J. Hardee's *Rifle and Light Infantry Tactics*, issued in that year, superseded the teachings of the French theorist Antoine H. Jomini as adapted by the influential West Point professor Dennis Hart Mahan.

22. Tidball, "Getting through West Point," pp. 113–14 (Tidball Papers, USMA).

23. Wilson to George W. McCrary, SW, September 23, 1877 (RID ACP File, AGO).

24. H. G. Wright to Col. Richard Delafield, January 13, 1860 (AGO, Records Relating to the USMA).

25. Aderman, *A Genealogy of the Irvings of New York*, p. 19; Pierre M. Irving, Diary, September 28, 1859, in Kime, *Pierre M. Irving and Washington Irving*, p. 229.

26. Morrison, *"The Best School,"* pp. 126–31; Sargent, *They Lie Forgotten*, pp. 89–90.

27. S.O. 181, AGO, August 29, 1860, relieving Dodge and other officers from duty at West Point, is cited in RID to AG, October 7, 1860, and its endorsements (AGO LR).

28. Selden, a Virginian, had recently obtained a leave of absence through January 13, 1861 (Eighth Infantry Regimental Return, October 1860). On April 27, 1861, he resigned his commission, and subsequently he joined the Confederate army (Wilhelm, *Eighth U.S. Infantry*, p. 169).

29. Eighth Infantry Regimental Returns, July and October, 1860. According to Wilhelm, the precipitating cause of the disbandment was the murder of a soldier by a civilian (*Eighth U.S. Infantry*, p. 62). But in a memorandum of March 26, 1861, the adjutant general identified "riotous conduct" as the cause (RID to AG, March 23, 1861—AGO LR).

30. RID to AG, October 7, 1860 (AGO LR). On October 13 Dodge applied for a thirty-day leave of absence (AGO Reg LR).

31. Morrison, *"The Best School,"* pp. 126–29.

32. RID to AG, January 1, 1861 (AGO LR).

33. *North Carolina Troops*, p. 365; Aderman, *A Genealogy of the Irvings of New York*, p. 19.

34. Wheeler, *Reminiscences and Memoirs of North Carolina*, p. 393.

35. Summary of Dodge's army career, dated August 22, 1895 (RID ACP File, AGO).

36. "He Deserves Well of His Country," *ANJ*, March 7, 1891, p. 480. See below, chapter 26.

37. RID to AG, March 23, 1861 (AGO LR).

38. Wilhelm, *Eighth U.S. Infantry*, pp. 63–65.

39. Circular, Commissioners on Behalf of the Committee on Public Safety, San Antonio, February 18, 1861 (Reprinted in Wilhelm, *Eighth U.S. Infantry*, pp. 63–65; the quotation is from p. 64).

40. RID to AG, November 10, 1860 (AGO LR).

41. Grinnell to Seward, March 9, 1861 (AGO LR).

42. RID to AG, March 23, 1861, with endorsements (AGO LR). For more on the serious shortage of manpower available to the War Department in the spring of 1861, see Meneely, *The War Department, 1861*, pp. 29–31.

43. RID to AG, March 30, 1861 (AGO Reg LR).

Part 2

1. RID to AG, July 27, 1861 (AGO LR).

2. James G. Blaine to E. B. Washburne, September 20, 1864 (*O.R.*, ser. III, vol. 4, p. 607).

Chapter 3

1. Heitman, *Historical Register*, II, p. 285.

2. Wilhelm, *Eighth U.S. Infantry*, pp. 66–93; Rodenbough, *The Army of the United States*, pp. 519–20.

3. *PNA*, p. 343.

4. Regimental returns of the Eighth Infantry from January to August 1861 have not survived. Following their capture by Confederate forces, the majority of the regiment's officers and men were detained as prisoners of war, the rest being released on parole. Company F was reorganized in July at Newport Barracks, Kentucky, and later joined Dodge's Company G (Wilhelm, *Eighth U.S. Infantry*, p. 91).

5. Wilhelm, *Eighth U.S. Infantry*, pp. 174–75.

6. RID to AG, May 13, 1861 (AGO Reg LR).

7. *O.R.*, ser. III, vol. 1, p. 8; Crook, *General George Crook: His Autobiography*, pp. 83–84; Eisenhower, *Agent of Destiny*, pp. 382–83.

8. In his proclamation of May 3, 1861, President Lincoln also authorized the addition to the regular Army of ten regiments—eight infantry, one cavalry, and one artillery (*O.R.*, ser. III, vol. 1, pp. 145–46, 154–57).

9. Eisenhower, *Agent of Destiny*, p. 382.

10. See G.O. 15, AGO, May 4, 1861, which publishes a "Plan of organization of the volunteer forces called into the service of the United States by the President" (*O.R.*, ser. III, vol. 1, pp. 151–54).

11. Davis, *Battle at Bull Run*, pp. 20–22.

12. *O.R.*, ser. I, vol. 2, pp. 670–71; Parker, "The Regular Infantry," p. 522; Eisenhower, *Agent of Destiny*, p. 430 n. 10.

13. Wilhelm, *Eighth U.S. Infantry*, pp. 90–91.

14. The indispensable source of documentary evidence relating to this sequence of events is *O.R.*, ser. I, p. 2; a reliable one-volume narrative is Davis, *Battle at Bull Run*.

15. Sykes's battalion consisted of seven companies: C and G, Second Infantry; B, D, G, and H, Third Infantry; and Dodge's Company G, Eighth Infantry (Parker, "The Regular Infantry," p. 521).

16. Parker, "The Regular Infantry," p. 524, where the exclamation is attributed to "Captain D——." In later years Dodge was inclined to use the expression "damned fool" when roused to anger; see chapter 4; *ITJ* pp. 82, 84.

17. Parker, "The Regular Infantry," p. 524.

18. For a detailed map of the battle site and surrounding areas, see U.S. Army, *Atlas*, I, plate 3.

19. Davis, *Battle at Bull Run*, p. 192.

20. Parker, "The Regular Infantry," p. 520.

21. *O.R.*, ser. I, vol. 2, pp. 390–91.

22. Beauregard, "The Battle of Bull Run," p. 80; see also pp. 93, 99.

23. A Union soldier recalled: "There was no confusion or panic then, but discouragement. . . . They fell back steadily, cursing their generals because no reënforcement were sent to them. Our men began to feel it was no use to fight without reënforcements" (Goss, "Recollections of a Private," p. 112).

24. *O.R.*, ser. I, vol. 2, p. 368.

25. "A Square Formed at Bull Run," *ANJ*, December 30, 1882, p. 498.

26. Parker, "The Regular Infantry," p. 529.

27. *O.R.,* ser. I, vol. 2, p. 391.

28. Davis, *Battle at Bull Run*, pp. 251, 252.

29. Fry, "The First Battle of Bull Run," in *Military Miscellanies*, pp. 393–94.

30. Davis, *Battle at Bull Run*, p. 253.

31. These statistics are from Sykes's official report (*O.R.,* ser. I, vol. 2, p. 390). Parker, writing in 1885, gave the total of wounded, missing, and killed as eighty-three ("The Regular Infantry," p. 539).

32. Parker, "The Regular Infantry," p. 531.

33. The Sixth North Carolina Regiment was reported in a Raleigh, North Carolina, newspaper as sustaining losses of sixteen men killed, fifty-three wounded, and one missing (*New York Times*, August 18, 1861, p. 3).

34. RID to AG, July 27, 1861 (AGO LR).

35. RID to AG, August 7, 1861 (AGO LR).

36. RID to AG (private), August 17, 1861 (AGO LR).

37. Notation by Lt. Col. E. D. Townsend, AAG, on disposition sheet for RID to AG, August 7, 1861 (AGO LR).

38. RID to AG, August 16, 1861 (AGO Reg LR).

39. RID to Townsend, August 17, 1861 (AGO LR).

40. G.O. 58, AGO, August 15, 1861, reprinted in *O.R.,* ser. III, vol. 1, p. 412.

41. Endorsements and notations by Townsend, AAG, and Absalom Baird, AAG, on RID to AG, July 27, 1861 (AGO LR).

42. RID to AG, September 7, 1861 (AGO LR).

Chapter 4

1. J. Tidball to AG, August 26, 1861 (AGO LR); *O.R.*, ser. II, vol. 4, pp. 66–75; III, 1, pp. 69, 369, 412.

2. Eighth Infantry Regimental Returns, September–October 1861; Cullum, *Biographical Register*, II, p. 219; Summary of Dodge's Army career, August 27, 1895 (RID ACP File, AGO).

3. In *Civil War City*, William Miller describes Harrisburg during the Civil War years and provides much information relating to Camp Curtin, the volunteer camp on its outskirts.

4. *O.R.*, ser. III, vol. 4, p. 1269. According to this source, the population of Pennsylvania in 1860 was 2,906,215. New York, with a population of 3,880,735, furnished 448,850 men to the Union armies.

5. Cullum, *Biographical Register*, II, p. 737; Summary of Dodge's Army career, August 27, 1895 (RID ACP File, AGO). What was termed the "western division" of Pennsylvania was actually the entire state, excepting Philadelphia and its immediate vicinity.

6. Curtin to Cameron, December 11, 1861; Cameron to Curtin, December 11, 1861 (*O.R.,* ser. III, vol. 1, p. 738).

7. Stanton to Governor David Tod, October 21, 1862 (*O.R.*, ser. III, vol. 3, p. 677).

8. Curtin to Stanton, May 20 and May 26, 1862 (*O.R.*, ser. III, vol. 2, pp. 69, 80).

9. Lincoln to state governors, July 1 and July 3, 1862 (*O.R.,* ser. III, vol. 2, pp. 187–88, 200–201).

10. Curtin to Edwin M. Stanton, August 9, 1862; C. P. Buckingham, AAG, to RID, August 16, 1862 (*O.R.*, ser. III, vol. 2, pp. 343, 400).

11. L. Thomas, AG, to RID, September 17, 1862 (*O.R.*, ser. III, vol. 2, p. 563).

12. RID to AG, September 19, 1862 (*O.R.*, ser. III, vol. 2, p. 574).

13. T. M. Vincent, AAG, to RID, September 26, 1862 (*O.R.,* ser. III, vol. 2, p. 589).

14. G.O. 105, AGO, December 15, 1861, directed that no more volunteer regiments should be raised by state governors until further notice. G.O. 49, AGO, May 1, 1862, provided that "upon requisition by commanders" in the field, governors were authorized to recruit for regiments then in service. G.O. 60, AGO, June 6, 1862, restored the Volunteer Recruiting Service to activity (*O.R.*, ser. III, vol. 1, pp. 722–23; 2, pp. 28, 108–9).

15. Thomas M. Vincent, AAG, "Statement showing the number of troops that have been mustered into the service from the loyal states," August 6, 1862 (*O.R.*, ser. III, vol. 2, p. 314).

16. Halleck to Wool and Ketchum, August 13, 1862 (*O.R.*, ser. III, vol. 2, pp. 379–80).

17. G.O. 94, AGO, August 4, 1862 (*O.R.*, ser. III, vol. 2, pp. 291–92); Murdock, *Patriotism Limited*, p. 6.

18. Curtin to General C. P. Buckingham, October 6, 1862 (*O.R.*, ser. III, vol. 2, p. 651).

19. See *O.R.*, ser. III, vol. 5, p. 693; A. Lincoln to Horatio Seymour, August 7, 1863 (*O.R.*, ser. III, vol. 3, p. 635).

20. G.O. 104, AGO, August 13, 1862 (*O.R.*, ser. III, vol. 2, p. 370).

21. Thomas to Stanton, November 3, 1862 (*O.R.*, ser. III, vol. 2, p. 735; see also pp. 739–41).

22. Stanton to Curtin, September 10, 1862 (*O.R.*, ser. III, vol. 2, p. 509).

23. On January 14, 1863, Dodge, then on duty as mustering and disbursing officer for the state of Maryland, acknowledged an order assigning him as assistant inspector general of the Fourth Army Corps. On February 2 he telegraphed the Adjutant General's Office from New York City that, "if not too late," he would accept the offer of "the position at Harrisburg" that, he had just learned, had been offered him several days before. On March 3 he reported that in accordance with S.O. 89, AGO, February 24, 1863, he had entered on his duties as mustering and disbursing officer for the state of Pennsylvania (AGO LR).

24. The text of this legislation is reprinted in U.S. Army, Office of the PMG, *Revised Regulations*, pp. 67–74, and in *O.R.*, ser. III, vol. 3, pp. 88–93.

25. Murdock, *Patriotism Limited*, pp. 8–9.

26. G.O. 17, AGO, March 17, 1863 (*O.R.*, ser. III, vol. 3, p. 74). An Office of the Provost Marshal General under the authority of the adjutant general had earlier been created by G.O. 140, AGO, September 24, 1862 (*O.R.*, ser. III, vol. 2, p. 586).

27. Murdock, *Patriotism Limited*, p. 8; Fry, *The Conkling and Blaine-Fry Controversy*, pp. 6–7, 156.

28. Grant to [J. W. Nesmith], December 14, 1865, quoted in Fry, *The Conkling and Blaine-Fry Controversy*, p. 64; see also p. 158.

29. G.O. 105, AGO, April 28, 1863, authorizing the Invalid Corps, is reprinted in *O.R.*, ser. III, vol. 3, pp. 170–72.

30. House, *Report of the PMG*, p. 92.

31. Fry to Stanton, April 2, 1863 (*O.R.*, ser. III, vol. 3, pp. 113–14); House, *Report of the PMG*, pp. 14–15.

32. House, *Report of the PMG*, p. 132.

33. *O.R.*, ser. III, vol. 3, pp. 321, 360–61, 681; Couch to AG, November 13, 1863, and December 11, 1863 (AGO Reg LR).

34. Fry to T. G. Pitcher, J. V. Bomford, et al., July 3, 1863; Fry to Bomford, July 14, 1863 (*O.R.*, ser. III, vol. 3, pp. 467, 491, 543, 556).

35. For Fry's summary account of these events and his bureau's response to them, see House, *Report of the PMG*, pp. 26–28. In *The Armies of the Streets*, Adrian Cook offers a one-volume account of the violence in New York City.

36. "The Conscription," *ANJ*, August 20, 1863, p. 11.

37. WTS to Edwin M. Stanton, September 13, 1864; Grant to Stanton, September 13, 1864 (*O.R.*, ser. III, vol. 4, p. 713).

38. Thomas M. Vincent, AAG, to RID, June 19, 1863 (*O.R.*, ser. III, vol. 3, p. 388).

39. "Charges and Specifications against Captain Richard I. Dodge," enclosed with Isaac J. Neall to Col. Charles M. Prevost, August 14, 1863 (AGO LR). Correspondence and other material relating to this incident is in a consolidated file, 573 P 1863, available in NARA microform publication M619, Roll 204.

40. Couch to Brigadier General L. Thomas, AG, September 22, 1863 (AGO LR).

41. Endorsements by Fry, October 15, and Halleck, October 17, of Couch to Col. E. D. Townsend, AAG, October 14, 1863 (AGO LR).

42. "The General-in-Chief does not deem it expedient at this time that you should be brought to trial," Assistant Adjutant General Townsend wrote Dodge. "But he directs me to say that he cannot omit the expression of his strong disapprobation of your conduct. He regrets that an officer who has been so long in the service, and who should have set an example of courtesy and discipline, should have forgotten himself so far as to be guilty of the language used. A moment's reflection should have caused you to commend an inexperienced guard for over zeal, rather than encourage it to neglect of duty by an untimely reproof" (AGO LS).

43. Churchill to RID, March 4, 1864, with endorsements by RID, March 4, and Thomas, n.d. (AGO LR).

44. In September 1864 Dodge joined other officers stationed at Harrisburg in requesting that their allowances for quarters and fuel be doubled. Owing to "the enhanced price of all the necessaries of life, we are no longer able from our pay and allowances to support ourselves as becomes Officers and Gentlemen" (RID et al. to AG, September 9, 1864—AGO LR). Secretary Stanton elected to defer consideration of the request.

45. RID to Fry, February 6, 1865 (*O.R.*, ser. III, vol. 4, p. 1151).

46. The photograph is dated August 5, 1865 (Graff).

47. Curtin to Fry, January 12, 1864 (*O.R.*, ser. III, vol. 4, p. 27).

48. Cameron to Lincoln, July 15, 1864, quoted in George D. Ruggles, AAG, to Fry, July 19, 1864 (*O.R.*, ser. III, vol. 4, p. 519).

49. Ruggles, AAG, to Fry, July 19, 1864 (*O.R.*, ser. III, vol. 4, pp. 520–23, with enclosed documents, pp. 523–27).

50. Cullum, *Biographical Register*, I, p. 217; *ANJ*, February 25, 1865, p. 427; RID to AG, November 1, 1864 (RID ACP File, AGO).

51. House, *Report of the PMG*, p. 132; J. V. Bomford to AG, July 25, 1864 (AGO LR).

Chapter 5

1. Waugh, *Reelecting Lincoln*, pp. 272, 276.

2. William Silver to RID, August 1, 1864, with endorsement by RID, August 3 (AGO LR).

3. RID to Fry, August 10, 1864; Fry to RID, August 16, 1864 (*O.R.*, ser. III, vol. 4, pp. 607, 620–21).

4. RID to Fry, August 10, 1864 (*O.R.*, ser. III, vol. 4, p. 607).

5. Blaine to E. B. Washburne, September 20, 1864 (*O.R.*, ser. III, vol. 4, p. 742).

6. Cuthbertson to James B. Fry, August 15, 1865 (Office of the PMG, Historical Reports). This letter, with other summary reports by district provost marshals in the western division of Pennsylvania, is available in NARA microform publication M1163, Roll 5.

7. Fry to Edwin M. Stanton, November 15, 1864 (*O.R.*, ser. III, vol. 4, p. 928). Excepting certain tables, Fry's report is reprinted on pp. 925–34 of that volume.

8. RID to AG, August 13, 1864, concerning his requested detail of Captain Snyder; RID to AG, September 20, 1864 (AGO LR).

9. Dodge noted that the "ideas" of the refractory officials "are being improved" (RID to Fry, December 12, 1864—*O.R.*, ser. III, vol. 4, p. 992).

10. RID to Fry, December 12, 1864 (*O.R.*, ser. III, vol. 4, p. 991).

11. RID to Fry, December 12, 1864 (*O.R.*, ser. III, vol. 4, p. 992).

12. George B. Eyster to James B. Fry, July 26, 1865 (Office of the PMG, Historical Reports).

13. G.O. 301, AGO, December 19, 1864 (*O.R.*, ser. III, vol. 4, p. 999).

14. RID to Fry, December 12, 1864 (*O.R.*, ser. III, vol. 4, 990–91).

15. RID to Fry, February 6, 1865, with enclosures: Eli Slifer to Speaker of the House of Representatives, February 1, 1865; transcript of proceedings, Pennsylvania state legislature, February 2, 1865 (*O.R.*, ser. III, vol. 4, pp. 1151–54).

16. Curtin to Stanton, February 8, 1865; Hardie to Curtin, February 8, 1865 (*O.R.*, ser. III, vol. 4, p. 1157).

17. Benedict to Stanton, February 9, 1965 (AGO LR). The resolution forwarded by Benedict was the same one Dodge had sent to Fry on February 6.

18. RID to Fry, February 15, 1865 (AGO LR).

19. RID to Fry, February 6, 1865 (*O.R.*, ser. III, vol. 4, p. 1151).

20. RID to Fry, February 15, 1865, with notations and endorsements by Fry and James Hardie (AGO LR).

21. Fry to Stanton, February 27, 1865 (AGO LR); House, *Report of the PMG*, p. 132.

22. A map showing the thirty-one provost marshal districts in the state of New York, 1863–1865, can be found in Murdock, *Patriotism Limited*, p. 214.

23. *O.R.*, ser. III, vol. 4, pp. 118, 600–605, 611, 1099–1100, 1121–28; House, *Report of the PMG*, p. 18; Murdock, *Patriotism Limited*, p. 65.

24. *O.R.*, ser. III, vol. 4, pp. 1129–44. The quotation (p. 1142) is from an addendum by Lincoln to a note he had written to Fry on February 6.

25. Hinks to Blunt, March 3, 1865 (*O.R.*, ser. III, vol. 4, pp. 1220–21).

26. House, *Report of the PMG*, pp. 85–87; Murdock, *Patriotism Limited*, pp. 20–23, 81, 134–35.

27. Baker to Fry, March 11, 1865; Fry to Baker, March 11, 1865 (two messages) (*O.R.*, ser. III, vol. 4, pp. 1231–32); House, *Report of the PMG*, p. 87; Murdock, *Patriotism Limited*, pp. 134–35.

28. Office of the PMG, *Revised Regulations*, p. 74.

29. "It must be recollected," Dodge wrote to Fry on April 18, "that every step I have taken has been combated covertly, but most earnestly, by Mr. Blunt and the people at large. Every obstacle has been thrown in my way. Money has been refused by merchants and bankers, and even when they have placed it in the hands of Mr. B's committee the district provost-marshals have in many cases been unable to procure it" (*O.R.*, ser. III, vol. 4, p. 1273).

30. See, for example, *New York Times*, March 18, 1865, p. 10; March 22, pp. 4–5; March 28, p. 8.

31. To his consternation, in most of the districts under his charge the draft went ahead during his absence. "This greatly injured the chances of success of my plans by rendering indifferent all whose names had not been drawn from the wheel" (RID to Fry, April 18, 1865—*O.R.*, ser. III, vol. 4, p. 1272).

32. See Fry to RID (confidential), March 16, 1865 (*O.R.*, ser. III, vol. 4, p. 1242). Dodge employed the phrase "fully occupied" in a letter of March 17 to C. Godfrey Gunther, mayor of New York City (*New York Times*, March 19, 1865, p. 8).

33. RID to Col. R. D. Goodwin, April 8, 1865 (*New York Times*, April 11, 1865, p. 8).

34. See *New York Times*, April 8, 1865, p. 6. This nuance of policy appears to have originated with Fry; see *O.R.*, ser. III, vol. 4, p. 1170.

35. "The Era of Peace" and "The Surrender," *New York Times*, April 14, 1865, p. 1.

36. *New York Times*, April 15, 1865, pp. 1, 8.

37. Edwin M. Stanton to Andrew Johnson, November 14, 1866 (*O.R.*, ser. III, vol. 5, p. 1031).

38. RID to Fry, August [20], 1865, pp. 23, 56–57 (Office of the PMG, Historical Reports).

39. James B. Fry to Edwin M. Stanton, September 11, 1865 (*O.R.*, ser. III, vol. 5, pp. 108–12).

40. RID to James B. Fry, August [20] 1865, p. 17 (Office of the PMG, Historical Reports).

41. RID to AG, August 25, 1865 (AGO LR).

42. RID to Fry, August [20], 1865, pp. 19–21 (Office of the PMG, Historical Reports).

43. RID to Fry, August [20], 1865, p. 43 (Office of the PMG, Historical Reports).

44. RID to Fry, August [20], 1865, pp. 23–24 (Office of the PMG, Historical Reports).

45. RID to Fry, August [20], 1865, pp. 23, 44, 57 (Office of the PMG, Historical Reports). Dodge was implicitly distinguishing between lineal rank, an officer's status as recorded in the official register on file on the Adjutant General's Office, and local rank, the degree of command authority accorded to the incumbent of a particular position.

46. House, *Report of the PMG*, p. 5.

47. Several years afterward, Senator George F. Edmunds ofVermont referred ironically during debate to Conkling's "sweetness of disposition" (*Congressional Globe*, January 19, 1870, p. 574).

48. "The Provost Marshal's Bureau," *ANJ*, April 28, 1866, p. 570. The debate in the House of Representatives on April 24, 1866, is reprinted in Fry, *The Conkling and Blaine-Fry Controversy*, pp. 179–286.

49. See Fry to Blaine, April 27, 1866, in Fry, *The Conkling and Blaine-Fry Controversy*, pp. 188–94.

50. Fry presented the documentary evidence surrounding the incident in *The Conkling and Blaine-Fry Controversy* (1893); see especially pp. 6–7, 156.

51. Fry, *The Conkling and Blaine-Fry Controversy*, p. 157.

52. *ANJ*, December 22, 1866, p. 286. On August 28, 1866, the functions of the Office of the Provost Marshal General, and also many of its employees, were transferred to the Adjutant General's Office.

53. Utley, *Frontier Regulars*, pp. 21, 37.

54. A review of Fry's career and services to the army is found in an obituary notice, *ANJ*, July 14, 1894, p. 908. For the brevet commissions, see Heitman, *Historical Register*, I, p. 439.

55. RID Journal, April 8, 1879 (*ITJ*, p. 196).

56. Dodge acknowledged receipt of his appointment as brevet lieutenant colonel on April 3, 1865, and as colonel on August 22, 1867 (ACP File, AGO). See also Heitman, *Historical Register*, I, p. 377; *ANJ*, September 1, 1866, p. 31; and March 14, 1868, p. 499.

57. *ANJ*, December 22, 1866, p. 286; Thirtieth Infantry Regimental Returns, December 1865–December 1866.

58. RID to AG, January 31 and April 1, 1866 (AGO LR); *ANJ*, February 17, 1866, p. 411.

59. *Official Register of the United States* (1867), p. 107.

60. Grant to Stanton, October 20, 1865 (*O.R.*, ser. III, vol. 5, pp. 126–27).

61. Stanton to Andrew Johnson, October 22, 1865 (*O.R.*, ser. III, vol. 5, p. 512).

62. "Size of the Army," *ANJ*, August 5, 1865, p. 792.

63. Heitman, *Historical Register*, III, pp. 601–5.

64. G.O. 92, AGO, November 23, 1866, summarized in "The Reorganization of the Army," *ANJ*, December 8, 1866, p. 253.

65. "Memoranda of Special Orders" with copy of a telegram, AGO to RID, January 2, 1867; on January 3 Dodge acknowledged receipt of the message (AGO LR).

66. RID to George P. Fountain, January 16, 1867 (Yale).

67. Thirtieth Infantry Regimental Returns, January–February 1867.

Chapter 6

1. H.V.N.B[oynton]., "Letter from Omaha," *Cincinnati Gazette*, June 7, 1867, p. 1.

2. Ambrose, *Nothing Like It in the World*, pp. 141, 190, 191, 254.

3. WTS to G. M. Dodge, January 16, 1867, in Dodge, *How We Built the Union Pacific Railway*, p. 14.

4. Ambrose, *Nothing Like It in the World*, pp. 184, 214.

5. *ANJ*, February 16, 1867, p. 411; Athearn, *Sherman and the Settlement of the West*, pp. 39, 55, 70–71, 99–100.

6. "Directions for Trains Crossing the Plains," *ANJ*, March 16, 1867, p. 471. This article reprinted G.O. 29, DMO, February 25, 1867, designating rendezvous points for wagon trains.

7. See Utley, *Frontier Regulars*, pp. 93–110.

8. WTS to John Sherman, n.d., quoted in Ambrose, *Nothing Like It in the World*, p. 226.

9. WTS to John A. Rawlins, August 31, 1866, quoted in Athearn, *Sherman and the Settlement of the West*, p. 67.

10. House, *Report of the SW,* 1866, pp. 21–22; *ANJ*, January 5, 1867, p. 317; Athearn, *Sherman and the Settlement of the West*, pp. 96–97.

11. House, *Report of the SW,* 1866, p. 22. Sherman was referring to the Union Pacific Railroad, passing west from Omaha, and the Eastern Division of the Union Pacific, later the Kansas Pacific, passing west from Kansas City, Missouri. On January 15, 1867, General Grant informed Sherman that he was then drafting a letter to the secretary of war, to be submitted to the secretary of the interior, "endorsing your recommendations as to colonizing hostile and friendly Indians."

> In the mean time you may go on with your preparations to carry out your views in the matter and if you receive no further instructions you may regard your plans sustained.
>
> In conversation with the Secretary of War on the subject of treatment of Indian affairs, more than six months since he said that in general the whole matter would be left to you being satisfied that with your facilities for information you would know better what should be done than he could by any possibility (SW LS).

12. A considerable body of literature exists relating to Sherman's career and character. Especially valuable for their account of his military service after the Civil War are a biography (Marszalek, *Sherman*) and a specialized study (Athearn, *Sherman and the Settlement of the West*). Other recent biographies include Hirshson, *The White Tecumseh*, Fellman, *Citizen Sherman*, and Kennett, *Sherman: A Soldier's Life.*

13. The quotation is taken from a review of Swinton's *The Twelve Decisive Battles* (1867) in *ANJ*, May 4, 1867, p. 582.

14. WTS to D. R. Garrison, August 10, 1865 (Sherman Papers, LC).

15. Ambrose, *Nothing Like It in the World*, p. 188.

16. In 1867 the Department of the Platte, with headquarters in Omaha, encompassed the state of Nebraska, that portion of Dakota Territory soon to be designated Wyoming Territory, and Utah Territory. Wyoming Territory, with boundaries identical with those of the later state of Wyoming, was established by Congress on July 25, 1868 (House, *The Public Domain*, p. 457).

17. The distribution of troops in the Department of the Platte on March 1, 1867, is summarized in *ANJ*, March 30, 1867, p. 505.

18. "It is almost a miracle to grasp your purpose to finish to Fort Sanders (288 miles) this year," Sherman wrote Grenville Mellen Dodge on January 16, 1867, "but you have done so much that I mistrust my own judgment and accept yours. I regard this road of yours as the solution of the Indian affairs and the Mormon question" (Dodge, *How We Built the Union Pacific Railway*, p. 14).

19. Fort Sedgwick Post Return, March 1867. A total of 248 officers and men were attached to the post at that time.

20. Fort Sedgwick Post Return, May 1867.

21. Ambrose, *Nothing Like It in the World*, pp. 207, 210.

22. Fort Sedgwick Post Returns, February and March 1867; *PNA*, pp. 84–85; *OWI*, pp. 504–7.

23. Fort Sedgwick Post Return, January 1867.

24. WTS to George K. Leet, AAG, April 3, 1867; WTS to G. M. Dodge, May 7, 1867, quoted in Athearn, *Sherman and the Settlement of the West*, pp. 112, 149.

25. Athearn, *Sherman and the Settlement of the West*, p. 167.

26. The *Oxford English Dictionary* defines "officer of the day" as "an officer whose immediate duty is to attend to the interior economy of the corps to which he belongs, or of those with which he may be doing duty." More specifically, the commissioned officer so designated bore responsibility for ensuring that stints of guard duty, scheduled drills, and all other features of a day's activities were properly performed. Assignment as officer of the day was on a rotating basis, usually daily.

27. "The Army," *ANJ*, May 11, 1867, p. 598.

28. Heitman, *Historical Register*, I, p. 742.

29. Fort Sedgwick Post Returns, February–April 1867.

30. These subposts (Sidney Barracks was later made a permanent installation) were adjacent to the third and fifth of twelve supply bases established by the Union Pacific for its construction crews. The first two, no longer in intensive use after 1866, were Fremont and Fort Kearny, Nebraska. Those active during the 1867 season were North Platte, Julesburg, Sidney, and Cheyenne (G. M. Dodge, *How We Built the Union Pacific Railway*, p. 31).

31. RID to J. H. Potter, June 9, 1867 (North Platte Station LS); G.O. 1, Headquarters, Detachment Thirtieth Infantry, September 9, 1867 (North Platte Station Orders).

32. G. M. Dodge, *How We Built the Union Pacific Railway*, p. 32.

33. Stanley, *My Early Travels*, quoted in Ambrose, *Nothing Like It in the World*, p. 218.

34. RID to Major William Myers, Chief Quartermaster DP, September 9, 1867 (North Platte Station LS); S.O. 17, October 2, 1867 (North Platte Station Orders); Office of the Surgeon General, *A Report on Barracks and Hospitals*, p. 337.

35. Edwin M. Stanton to Secretary of the Treasury, n.d. [after November 26, 1867] (SW LS to President and Executive Departments).

36. G. M. Dodge, *How We Built the Union Pacific Railway*, pp. 118–19.

37. RID, "Railroad Towns" (Graff). Balaklava was renowned as the site of an allied victory (1854) in the Crimean War and for the suicidal charge of an English light cavalry brigade there, the subject of Tennyson's poem.

38. WTS to Grant, June 11, 1867, quoted in Athearn, *Sherman and the Settlement of the West*, pp. 161–62. See also "The Indian War," *Cincinnati Gazette*, June 29, 1867, p. 3.

39. C.H., "Gen. Augur's Expedition," *New York Times*, June 24, 1867, p. 1. Augur held the brevet rank of major general.

40. Flogging was abolished by G.O. 56, AGO, August 12, 1861 (*O.R.*, ser. III, vol. 1, p. 401).

41. "Flogging at Fort Sedgwick," *ANJ*, July 6, 1867, p. 725.

42. For example, on June 17 Lantz requested that Sergeant Thomas Gaynor of his company be reduced to the ranks for insubordination, a move ordered that day by Dodge (Lantz to AAAG, June 17, 1867—North Platte Station Endorsements; S.O. 8, June 17, 1867—North Platte Station Orders).

43. RID endorsement, July 15, 1867, of Lantz to AAAG, Thirtieth Infantry, June 26, 1867 (North Platte Station Endorsements).

44. In the summer of 1867 the military operations in the Department of the Missouri were more extensive than along the Union Pacific line, the former being denominated "Hancock's War" after the commander of that department, Major General Winfield S. Hancock. See Utley, *Frontier Regulars*, pp. 111-29.

45. RID to Joseph H. Potter, June 24, 1867 (North Platte Station LS).

46. Thirtieth Infantry Regimental Returns, June and July 1867.

47. Dodge later wrote a brief account of the fate that befell Kidder and his men; see *PNA*, pp. 278–79 and *OWI*, pp. 219–23.

48. See "The War on the Platte," *ANJ*, June 6, 1867, p. 668; "The Indian War," *ANJ*, June 15, 1867, pp. 684–85.

49. The activities of the Pawnees and their citizen leaders, Frank and Luther North, are described by Grinnell in *Two Great Scouts*; see also Danker, ed., *Man of the Plains*.

50. See *PNA*, pp. 326–27; *OWI*, pp. 456–58.

51. *PNA*, p. 296; *OWI*, pp. 276–77.

52. C. C. Augur to WTS, August 8, 1867, enclosed with WTS to AG, August 8, 1867 (AGO LR); *ANJ*, August 24, 1867; p. 12; Grinnell, *Two Great Scouts*, pp. 145–46; Ambrose, *Nothing Like It in the World*, pp. 222–23.

53. *OWI*, pp. 443–44.

54. The efforts of this Indian leader on behalf of his people are described by Hyde in *Spotted Tail's Folk*.

55. *PNA*, p. 146.

56. WTS to Edwin M. Stanton, June 17, 1867, quoted in *ANJ*, July 20, 1867, p. 770 and in Athearn, *Sherman and the Settlement of the West*, p. 162.

57. "Personnel of the Indian Peace Commission," *ANJ*, December 7, 1867, p. 251.

58. The members of the Indian Peace Commission authorized by Congress on July 20, 1868, were N. G. Taylor, president; J. B. Henderson, John B. Sanborn, and S. F. Tappan; and from the army, Lieutenant General William T. Sherman, Brevet Major General William S. Harney, and Brigadier General Alfred H. Terry. In October 1867 Colonel C. C. Augur took the place of Sherman, who was called to Washington.

59. Sherman's attitude toward his duties as a peace commissioner was unsentimental. "I don't care about interesting myself too far in the fate of the poor devils of Indians, who are doomed from the causes inherent in their nature, or from the natural and persistent hostility of the White Race. All I desire to accomplish is to so clearly define the duties of the civil and military agents of Govt so that we won't be quarrelling all the time as to whose business it is to look after them" (WTS to Ellen Ewing Sherman, September 14, 1867—Sherman Family Papers).

60. *OWI*, p. 299.

61. *PNA*, p. 300.

62. C. H., "The Indian Commission," *New York Times*, September 27, 1867, p. 2.

63. See House, *Report of Indian Peace Commission*, pp. 3–4; Sherman, *Memoirs*, II, pp. 434–35.

64. The end of track reached Cheyenne on November 14, 1867 (Ambrose, *Nothing Like It in the World*, p. 227).

65. RID to Captain H. G. Litchfield, AAG DP, September 9, 1867 (North Platte Station LS).

66. RID to Major William Myers, Chief Quartermaster DP, June 26 and September 15, 1867 (North Platte Station LS).

67. S.O. 21, North Platte Station, October 21, 1867.

68. *PNA*, pp. 172–74.

69. *OWI*, pp. 274–75.

70. S.O. 484, AGO, November 1, 1867, and S.O. 252, DP, December 25, 1867, cited in Fort Sedgwick Post Returns, November and December 1867.

71. *PNA*, p. 187.

72. "North Platte Station" in U.S. Army, *Outline Descriptions*, p. 104.

73. *PNA*, p. 270.

74. D. [RID], "Religion among Indians," *ANJ*, July 6, 1878, p. 778.

75. Athearn, *Sherman and the Settlement of the West*, pp. 197–98.

76. Augur to G. M. Dodge, April 16, 1868, quoted in Murray, "Fort Fred Steele," p. 145; see also Augur to WTS, April 7, 1868 (Sherman Papers, LC). A listing of regiments and companies "employed in connection with Indian hostilities in protecting the Missouri traffic and the Union Pacific railroad" is found in U.S. Senate Executive Document No. 7, 40th Cong., 2nd sess., 1868.

77. Ambrose, *Nothing Like It in the World*, pp. 254, 259, 263.

78. Ambrose, *Nothing Like It in the World*, p. 254.

79. A history of this important post, which remained in use until 1930, is provided by Adams in *The Post Near Cheyenne*.

80. S.O. 48, DP, March 4, 1868, cited in Thirtieth Infantry Regimental Return, March 1868.

81. Thirtieth Infantry Regimental Return, April 1868.

82. Murray, "Fort Fred Steele," p. 146.

83. Field Return, battalion commanded by RID, April 1868, with Thirtieth Infantry Regimental Returns, 1868.

84. G.O. 16, DP, May 12, 1868, cited in Murray, "Fort Fred Steele," p. 147.

85. For a description of the post once construction was completed, see U.S. Army, *Outline Descriptions*, p. 94.

86. The first passenger train arrived on July 21, 1868 (Ambrose, *Nothing Like It in the World*, p. 263). A pencil sketch of Fort Fred Steele in 1871, by Philippe Régis De Trobriand, can be found in his *Military Life in Dakota*, p. 229.

87. Murray, "Fort Fred Steele," pp. 149–51. The town of Benton was for a short time one of the twelve supply depots along the Union Pacific route. Those active in 1868 were all in Wyoming Territory and included Cheyenne, Laramie, Benton, Green River, and Evanston (G. M. Dodge, *How We Built the Union Pacific Railway*, pp. 31–32).

88. Thirtieth Infantry Regimental Return, July 1868.

89. The Rocky Mountain District was established on May 23, 1868, by G.O. 16, DP; Gibbon assumed command of it on June 1, and Dodge was appointed its acting assistant inspector general on July 26 (G.O. 1 and 5, Rocky Mountain District, cited in Fort Sanders Post Returns, June and July 1868).

90. Shortly after Gibbon's birth in Pennsylvania, his parents moved to Charlotte, North Carolina, where he spent his childhood and youth. Like Dodge, at the outbreak of the Civil War he elected to serve with the Union army, at the cost of alienation from many of those close to him in the South. See the biographical sketch in Gaff and Gaff, eds., *Adventures on the Western Frontier*, pp. ix–xvi.

91. Fort Sanders Post Return, July 1868. For descriptions of Fort Sanders at this period see *ANJ*, January 5, 1867, p. 313; and May 18, 1867, p. 618.

92. *PNA*, pp. 165, 168, 199, 209, 215, 230.

93. Ambrose, *Nothing Like It in the World*, pp. 272–73.

94. Marcou, *Louis Agassiz*, I, p. 170–71; *PNA*, pp. 62–66, 378.

95. For the benefit of potential investors, Blackmore wrote a pamphlet, *Suggestions for a United States Government Loan; made in January, 1864, to Salmon P. Chase, Esq., Secretary of the Treasury of the United States* (London: Witherby & Co., [1864]).

96. Brayer, *William Blackmore*, pp. 35–39.

97. Brayer, *William Blackmore*, p. 40. See also Stevens, *Flint Chips*, pp. xix–xx; *Some Account of the Blackmore Museum*. The contents of the Blackmore Museum have since been transferred to the British Museum.

98. Blackmore, Diary 1 (1868), n.d. [September 25] (No. 074, MNM).

99. Blackmore noted that "Jake – (Col's servant) – good tempered – handled the cart" on the hunting trip. Beneath this entry he wrote "orderly," probably indicating that the man was an enlisted soldier (No. 074, MNM).

100. Brayer, *William Blackmore*, pp. 50–54; Ambrose, *Nothing Like It in the World*, p. 276.

101. Blackmore, Diary, October 14, 1868 (No. 071, MNM).

102. Blackmore, Diary, n.d. [September 1868], p. 32 (No. 070, MNM). An account of the Forsyth engagement can be found in Dixon, *Hero of Beecher Island*, pp. 76–87; see also Keim, *Sheridan's Troopers on the Borders*, pp. 50–57.

103. Blackmore, Diary, October 14, 1868 (No. 071, MNM).

104. Brayer, *William Blackmore*, pp. 73–74.

105. Blackmore, Diary, October 18, 1868 (No. 071, MNM).

106. G.O. 11, Rocky Mountain District, November 27, 1868, cited in Fort Sanders Post Return, November 1868; *ANJ*, December 26, 1868, p. 290.

107. See *ANJ*, March 13, 1869, pp. 466–67, and above, chapter 1.

108. Memorandum by R. Williams, AAG, October 31, 1867 (AGO LR).

Chapter 7

1. Meigs to SW, October 9, 1868 (Orders and Endorsements, Office of SW). The report by Parkinson was forwarded to the Adjutant General's Office on October 13.

2. Moyers and Dedrick to SW, October 20, 1869 (Office of SW Reg LR).

3. See the editorial comments in *ANJ*, May 7, 1864, pp. 614, 616.

4. See "Rules and Regulations for the Payment of Bounties under the Act to Equalize Bounties, Approved July 28, 1866," *ANJ*, September 29, 1866, p. 100.

5. The Freedmen's Bureau was withdrawn from the formerly rebellious states on January 1, 1869. In his official report for that year, the commissioner of the organization, Brigadier General O. O. Howard, described some of the means by which freedmen were deprived of money from the bounty and pension claims legally due them: "Some attorneys, after getting possession of a large number of claims, held the papers, and then, by representing that it would require years to untie the red tape in Washington, and get them settled, they bought them at a small percentage of their value. Others charged exorbitant fees, which often ate up nearly the whole amount paid. Others with apparent generosity, offered to collect the claims for a share of the proceeds, or to advance a part of the sum due, taking a note for the amount, with interest, at the rate of fifty, one hundred, and in some cases as high as one hundred and fifty per cent. By numerous crafty devices, dishonest villainy imposed upon confiding ignorance, and the colored soldiers became the victims" (House, *Report of the SW*, 1869, p. 507).

6. In June 1868 Arkansas, Alabama, Florida, Georgia, Louisiana, North Carolina, and South Carolina were readmitted to representation in Congress. The other seceding states had been granted the privilege earlier except Texas, which was not readmitted until March 30, 1870.

7. Ferraro, foreword to *Forty-Six Years in the Army*, by John M. Schofield, pp. xv–xix.

8. AG to SW, January 4, 1869 (AGO LR); AG to WTS, January 5, 1869 (AGO LS).

9. Dodge was ordered to Memphis by S.O. 3, AGO, January 5, 1869 (AGO LR). He left his regiment on January 10 (Thirtieth Infantry Regimental Return, January 1869).

10. Memorandum, February 23, 1869, by Thomas M. Vincent, AAG; Memorandum, June 1, 1869, by Edwin D. Townsend, AG (AGO LR).

11. The quoted phrase is from RID to AG, August 6, 1869 (AGO Reg LR).

12. AGO to RID, June 1, 1869 (AGO Reg LR); AG to SW, March 6 and June 15, 1869 (Office of SW Reg LR from the President, Executive Bureaus, and War Department Bureaus). On April 12 the paymaster general forwarded to the Adjutant General's Office papers implicating the firm of Moyers and Dedrick in "gross frauds on the government in collection of claims of colored solders" (AGO Reg LR).

13. *ANJ*, March 13, 1869, p. 466.

14. *ANJ*, March 20, 1869, pp. 482, 483.

15. In 1867 General Grant had prevailed upon Grenville Mellen Dodge to allow Rawlins to accompany him on a summer tour along the Union Pacific line, hoping the dry plains atmosphere would improve his friend's health (G. M. Dodge, *How We Built the Union Pacific Railway*, pp. 19, 89).

16. Coincidentally, the same issue of the *Army and Navy Journal* that announced the appointment of Rawlins as secretary of war also reprinted G.O. 16 and 17, HQA, March 10, 1869, detailing the consolidation of infantry regiments in the re-reorganized army (March 20, 1869, p. 483).

17. RID to AG, August 6, 1869 (AGO Reg LR). The quoted phrase was written by a clerk summarizing Dodge's letter with its enclosures.

18. AG to SW, June 15, 1869 (Office of SW Reg LR from the President, Executive Bureaus, and War Department Bureaus).

19. AGO to RID, June 1, 1869 (AGO Reg LR); *ANJ*, June 12, 1869, p. 674.

20. Moyers and Dedrick to SW, May 11, May 14, and June 30, 1869 (Office of SW Reg LR).

21. Moyers and Dedrick to AG, July 27, 1869 (AGO Reg LR); Moyers and Dedrick to SW, July 31, 1869 (Office of SW Reg LR).

22. Parkinson to AG, July 23, 1869 (AGO Reg LR). See also Parkinson to AG, October 7, 1869 (AGO Reg LR).

23. Howard to SW, August 6, 1869 (Office of SW Reg LR).

24. RID to AG, August 6, 1869 (AGO Reg LR); RID to AG, August 9, 1869 (AGO LR).

25. Memorandum by Vincent, August 11, 1869, on RID to AG, August 8, 1869 (AGO LR). Dodge gave as his address until further notice Clarendon Hotel, Branch Shore Post Office, New Jersey.

26. Endorsement No. 1608, September 11, 1869 (Orders and Endorsements by SW).

27. AG to SW, September 5, 1869 (Office of SW Reg LR from the President, Executive Departments, and War Department Bureaus).

28. Marszalek, *Sherman*, p. 385. G.O. 11, HQA, signed by Secretary Schofield, was reprinted in *ANJ*, March 13, 1869, p. 466.

29. "The Army," *ANJ*, March 13, 1869, p. 466.

30. Marszalek, *Sherman*, pp. 383–85; Athearn, *Sherman and the Settlement of the West*, pp. 240–41; Hirshson, *The White Tecumseh*, p. 340.

31. Endorsement No. 1608, September 11, 1869 (Orders and Endorsements by SW).

32. WTS to Attorney General, September 16, 1869 (LS by SW to the President and Executive Departments).

33. Memorandum by Thomas M. Vincent, September 13, 1869 (AGO LR); S.O. 222, AGO, September 15, 1869, cited in Third Infantry Regimental Returns, September and October 1869.

34. Dodge's association with Schofield while in Washington soon became known at his new posting, Fort Lyon, Colorado. In October 1869 the general's brother visited that post and inquired about Dodge's "character & disposition," not having met him previously. According to Dodge, this person was curious "*because Schofield liked me so much, while the others of the family hated me so much*" (RID to JRPD, October 14, 1869—Yale).

35. WTS to Attorney General, September 16, 1869 (Office of SW LS).

36. Dunn and Swayne to E. B. French, Second Auditor, U.S. Treasury, et al., October 13, 1869 (LR by SW from the President, Executive Departments, and War Department Bureaus).

37. Dunn and Swayne to SW, October 26, 1869 (Orders and Endorsements by SW). Approved by WTS on October 26, this recommendation was forwarded to the Freedman's Bureau.

38. For example, see Marszalek, *Sherman*, pp. 422–25; Hirshson, *The White Tecumseh*, p. 380.

39. For example, see *ANJ*, November 18, 1882, p. 348.

40. *Congressional Globe*, December 22, 1869, Part 1, p. 320.

41. *Congressional Globe*, January 10, 1870, Part 1, p. 348.

42. *Congressional Globe*, Part 7, Appendix, pp. 679–80.

Chapter 8

1. Coffman, *The Old Army*, pp. 220–22.

2. Heitman, *Historical Register*, II, pp. 604–607.

3. See Utley, "Operations on the Southern Plains, 1868–69" in *Frontier Regulars*, pp. 142–62. The Medicine Lodge Treaties were signed in October 1867 following council sessions at a site approximately seventy miles south of Fort Larned, Kansas. See Jones, *The Treaty of Medicine Lodge*; Nye, *Plains Indian Raiders*, pp. 105–12.

4. Sheridan to E. D. Townsend, AG, November 1, 1869 (AGO LR). In his annual report for the same year, General Sherman described the conditions on the western plains that persons in the eastern states seemed to ignore or regard with indifference: "While the nation at large is at peace, a state of *quasi*

war has existed, and continues to exist, over one-half its extent, and the troops therein are exposed to labors, marches, fights, and dangers that amount to war" (House, *Report of the SW*, 1869, p. 24).

5. RID to JRPD, December 5, 1869 (Yale). In accordance with S.O. 184, DMO, October 5, 1869, Dodge assumed command of Fort Lyon on October 12 (Third Infantry Regimental Return, Fort Lyon Post Return, October 1869).

6. Frazer, *Forts of the West*, pp. 39–40; Roberts, *Encyclopedia of Historic Forts*, pp. 109–10.

7. This event, which poisoned relations with the Cheyenne tribe for decades, is described by Hoig in *The Sand Creek Massacre*.

8. For more on the army's activities in this region, see Oliva, *Soldiers on the Santa Fe Trail,* and Connor and Skaggs, *Broadcloth and Britches*.

9. RID to JRPD, May 5, 1870 (Yale). Dodge and Woods were fellow graduates from West Point in the class of 1848.

10. Penrose had established Fort Lyon at its new location. The original post, known severally as Fort Fauntleroy, Fort Wise, and finally Fort Lyon, was built in 1860 near Bent's New Fort, twenty miles upriver from the site of its successor. It was abandoned due to flooding.

11. RID to JRPD, November 21, 1869 (Yale).

12. Office of the Surgeon General, *Report on Barracks and Hospitals*, p. 314; RID to JRPD, December 5, 1869 (Yale).

13. RID to JRPD, December 5, 1869 (Yale).

14. RID to JRPD, October 14, 1869 (Yale).

15. RID to JRPD, December 5, 1869 (Yale). Dodge later observed that "one does not realize the pleasure of army life until he gets to a be a field officer – I know by experience, having been a Subaltern for sixteen years" (RID to JRPD, January 16, 1870—Yale).

16. RID to JRPD, October 14, 1869 (Yale).

17. RID to JRPD, April 17, 1870 (Yale).

18. RID to JRPD, October 14, 1869 (Yale).

19. For example, see McCrae, *Dear Belle*, pp. 236–37; Stallard, *Glittering Misery*, pp. 11–13.

20. RID to JRPD, October 14, 1869 (Yale).

21. RID to JRPD, November 21, 1869 (Yale).

22. RID to JRPD, November 21, 1869 (Yale).

23. RID to JRPD, December 5, 1869 (Yale).

24. RID to JRPD, January 16, 1870 (Yale).

25. See RID to JRPD, December 5, 1869 (Yale).

26. RID to JRPD, January 16, 1870 (Yale).

27. RID to JRPD, April 17, 1870 (Yale).

28. RID to JRPD, May 29, 1870 (Yale).

29. RID to JRPD, June 12, 1870 (Yale).

30. RID to JRPD, July 17, 1870 (Yale).

31. RID, "The Enlisted Soldier," p. 263.

32. RID to JRPD, July 17, 1870 (Yale).

33. A summary of Kent's army career is in *ANJ*, October 18, 1890, p. 119; see also *ANJ*, March 20, 1869, p. 483; Hamersley, *Records of Living Officers*, pp. 244–45.

34. RID to JRPD, August 14, 1870 (Yale).

35. James Dodge did not lose his position. He remained employed in the New York custom house until 1873 (*Official Register of the United States,* 1873, p. 160).

36. RID to JRPD, July 24, 1870 (Yale).

37. RID to JRPD, August 24, 1870 (Yale).

38. RID to JRPD, August 7, 1870 (Yale).

39. RID to JRPD, September 2 and September 17, 1870 (Yale).

40. RID to JRPD, May 27, 1870 (Yale); *ANJ*, May 28, 1870, p. 638; House, *Report of the SW,* 1870, p. 6; U.S. Army, *Record of Engagements with Hostile Indians*, pp. 26–27.

41. RID to JRPD, May 1 and September 2, 1870 (Yale). For a biography of Palmer, later president of the Denver and Rio Grande Railway, see Fisher, *A Builder of the West*; see also Athearn, *Rebel of the Rockies*.

42. RID to JRPD, May 1, May 5, and May 27, 1870 (Yale).

43. RID Journal, September 2, 1875 (*BHJ*, p. 197).

44. RID to JRPD, September 11, 1870 (Yale).

45. In April 1870 Penrose's was judged the best of the sets of equipment submitted to an army board for examination, but none was recommended by the board for general adoption (Memorandum, Penrose's Infantry Equipment, April 26, 1871—AGO LR).

46. The letter, he added, was "quite equal to some of the old lucubrations which Hardie appropriated" (RID to JRPD, January 16, 1870—Yale). He was alluding to Colonel James A. Hardie, formerly inspector general of the army. The Tactics Board completed its work in November 1870 (*ANJ*, November 12, 1870, p. 199). For further discussion of this board and its report, see chapter 9.

47. "Two of my Companies have been ordered out, the Cavalry to hunt up & whip Mr Indian, & one Infantry Co. to guard the supply trains" (RID to JRPD, May 27, 1870—Yale).

48. Tilton, "Fort Lyon, Colorado Territory" in Office of the Surgeon General, *Report on Barracks and Hospitals*, pp. 314–15.

49. RID Journal, January 20, 1880 (*ITJ*, p. 315).

50. *ANJ*, May 14, 1870, p. 607.

51. See Connor and Skaggs, *Broadcloth and Britches*, pp. 134–35; Oliva, *Fort Larned*, p. 3. A detailed description of both the Raton and the Cimarron routes can be found in J. C. McFerran to Montgomery C. Meigs, July 27, 1865 (*O.R.*, ser. III, vol. 5, pp. 442–44).

52. In his annual report for 1872, General Pope discussed the potential savings in transportation costs resulting from completion of the Atchison, Topeka and Santa Fe and Denver and Rio Grande railroads; see House, *Report of the SW*, 1872, pp. 47–48.

53. RID to JRPD, May 17, 1870 (Yale).

54. *PNA*, pp. 60–61.

55. RID to JRPD, May 5 and May 27, 1870 (Yale).

56. On June 7, 1865, Lieutenant Colonel William H. Grier, First Cavalry, relieved Brigadier General Edward W. Hinks as acting assistant provost marshal general, Western Division of Pennsylvania—the post Dodge had held prior to exchanging assignments with Hinks in February of that year (House, *Report of the PMG*, p. 133).

57. *ANJ*, November 26, 1870, pp. 232–33.

58. RID to JRPD, May 17, 1870 (Yale).

59. RID to JRPD, May 27, 1870 (Yale).

60. "I have felt very uneasy – I can say now – about the safety of my Post. It is a terrible responsibility to place a man in, to expect him to hold a position, with so few troops. . . . I am happy to say the danger is past now" (RID to JRPD, July 24, 1870—Yale). See also Fort Lyon Post Return, July 1870; *ANJ*, July 30, 1870, p. 782.

61. Fort Lyon Post Return, July, October 1870; *ANJ*, October 15, 1870, p. 136.

62. RID to JRPD, October 14, 1869 (Yale); Schofield to WTS, December 15, 1869 (Sherman Papers, LC). The other officer stationed at the post and tried by court-martial was First Lieutenant D. W. Wallingford, Seventh Cavalry, who was dismissed from the army on May 10, 1870 (Fort Lyon Post Return, June 1870).

63. Members of the Bothwell court arrived at Fort Lyon on October 25 and remained there until the court's adjournment on December 5 (Fort Lyon Post Returns, October–December 1870). Bothwell was cashiered on December 29, 1870 (Heitman, *Historical Register*, I, p. 232).

64. RID to JRPD, May 1, 1870 (Yale).

65. RID to JRPD, June 12, 1870 (Yale).

66. Office of the Surgeon General, *Report on Barracks and Hospitals*, p. 313.

67. RID to JRPD, May 27, 1870 (Yale).

68. *PNA*, pp. 102–103, 119.

69. *PNA*, pp. 64, 66.

70. *PNA*, p. 68.

71. Fort Lyon Post Return, December 1870; *ANJ*, November 26, 1870, p. 231.

72. A few years afterward, Dodge compared the development of the West to "a huge cuttle fish, [that] has passed its arms of settlements up almost every stream, grasping the land, killing the game, driving out the Indian, crushing the romance, the poetry, the very life and soul of the 'plains,' leaving only the bare and monotonous carcass" (*PNA*, p. 126).

73. See Oliva, *Fort Larned*, pp. 34–42.

74. Bryant, *History of the Atchison, Topeka and Santa Fe Railway*, pp. 24–25; Miner, *West of Wichita*, pp. 30–32.

75. Bryant, *History of the Atchison, Topeka and Santa Fe Railway*, pp. 25, 30.

76. A table supplied by the paymaster general and showing the salaries of army officers can be found in *ANJ*, April 15, 1882, p. 829. These rates of pay, fixed in 1870, remained unchanged until 1898 (Coffman, *The Old Army*, p. 265).

77. *PNA*, pp. 323–25.

78. *PNA*, pp. 328–29.

79. *PNA*, pp. 120–21.

80. *PNA*, pp. 141–42.

81. *PNA*, p. 120.

82. Dodge commanded at Fort Larned from March 13 to July 9, 1871 (Cullum, *Supplement to the Biographical Register*, p. 194).

83. *PNA*, pp. 140–41.

84. RID to Hornaday, September 21, 1887, quoted in Hornaday, *The Extinction of the American Bison*, II, pp. 389–91.

Chapter 9

1. Fellman, *Citizen Sherman*, pp. 322–23; Marszalek, *Sherman*, pp. 430, 441; Hirshson, *The White Tecumseh*, p. 345.

2. WTS to Sheridan, April 10, 1869, quoted in Athearn, *Sherman and the Settlement of the West*, p. 242.

3. Sherman's order directing the Schofield board to convene at Fort Leavenworth to harmonize the systems of tactics in use by the army was issued on August 6, 1869 (AGO LR). The papers accumulated by all three boards are gathered into a single consolidated file, 312 A 1869, in the records of the Adjutant General's Office, available in NARA microform publication M619, Rolls 680–85.

4. WTS to William W. Belknap, January 18, 1871 (AGO LR); WTS endorsement, December 5, 1872, of Wesley Merritt to AG, December [1?], 1872 (AGO LR).

5. G.O. 2, AGO, January 14, 1871 (AGO LR).

6. House, *Report of the SW,* 1869, p. 25. The papers relating to the Sherman board of 1867–1868 form part of a consolidated file, 723 A 1866, in the records of the Adjutant General's Office, available in NARA microform publication M619, Rolls 448–50.

7. Fry, "Notes on Theoretical and Practical Matters," in *Military Miscellanies*, p. 58.

8. S.O. 260, AGO, July 3, 1871, reprinted in "Abstract of Special Orders," *ANJ*, July 15, 1871, p. 764.

9. Kroeker, *Great Plains Command,* pp. 104–106.

10. Belknap to W. D. Whipple, AAG, July 8, 1871; WTS endorsement of that communication, n.d. (AGO LR). Correspondence and other material relating to the Army Regulations Board is in a consolidated file, 2308 AGO 1871, available in NARA microform pulication M666, Roll 19.

11. *ANJ*, July 15, 1871, p. 769.

12. See Marcy's official report in House, *Route from Fort Smith to Santa Fe*, pp. 31, 33, 44, 71–72, 75. A more general account of Marcy is by Hollon, *Beyond the Cross Timbers*.

13. Scharf, *History of St. Louis*, II, p. 1486.

14. Marcy's book was reviewed in *ANJ*, December 23, 1871, p. 310.

15. RID Journal, July 8, 1875 (*BHJ*, pp. 120–21).

16. The communications signed by "Infantry" appeared in *ANJ*, July 22, 1871, p. 783; July 29, p. 799; August 5, pp. 814–15; August 12, p. 831; and September 2, p. 39. The quotation is from the first letter.

17. Infantry, "Army Regulations. No. III," *ANJ*, August 5, 1871, p. 814.

18. "Acting Assistant Surgeons, U.S. Army," *ANJ*, September 9, 1871, p. 59.

19. "Improved Barracks," *ANJ*, October 28, 1871, p. 171.

20. "Our Non-Commissioned Officers," *ANJ*, December 2, 1871, p. 251.

21. "The Rights of Company Officers," *ANJ*, December 2, 1871, p. 251.

22. Correspondence and other material relating to the Marcy board's deliberations on the uniform and dress of the army is in a consolidated file, 3028 AGO 1872, available in NARA microform publication M666, Roll 75. The changes recommended by the board were officially adopted in G.O. 76, AGO, July 27, 1872.

23. Memorandum by an unknown hand accompanying WTS endorsement of James Van Voast to AG, September 14, 1872 (AGO LR).

24. R. B. Marcy to AG, December 6, 1871; memorandum by H. Crosby, chief clerk, December 7, 1871 (AGO LR).

25. Brayer, *William Blackmore*, p. 95. Blackmore's involvement with the Denver and Rio Grande Railway is the subject of another volume by Brayer, *William Blackmore: The Early Financing of the Denver and Rio Grande Railway and Ancillary Land Companies* (Denver: Bradford-Robinson, 1949).

26. Newspaper clippings, *Washington Daily Morning Chronicle*, May 28, [29], 1872 (Nos. 517a, 520, MNM); Brayer, *William Blackmore*, p. 116.

27. Blackmore to Belknap, April 16, 1872 (AGO LR); Joseph Henry to SW, April 17, 1872 (AGO LR).

28. Blackmore Diary, August 23–September 1, 1871, p. [1] (No. 323, MNM).

29. In 1871 Blackmore was a fellow passenger with Sheridan aboard the SS *Russia*, bound for New York. On August 7 of that year he called upon the general and "arranged for buffalo hunt about 20th of September Fort McPherson to Fort Hays" (Diary, August 7, 1871—No. 263, MNM).

30. Hutton, *Phil Sheridan and His Army*, pp. 212–16.

31. AG to Sheridan, April 19, 1872 (AGO LR).

32. Sheridan to E. D. Townsend, AG, April 22, 1872 (AGO LR); Blackmore Diary, April 25, 1872 (No. 496, MNM).

33. Blackmore to Sheridan, May 1, 1872 (copy) (AGO LR).

34. Notation by an unidentified official in the Adjutant General's Office, with Joseph Henry to AG, April 17, 1872 (AGO LR). In April 1872 Fort Garland was garrisoned by Company F, Eighth Cavalry, and Company D, Fifteenth Infantry.

35. Sheridan to Blackmore, May 10, 1872 (AGO LR).

36. Sheridan to Belknap, May 11, 1872 (AGO LR). For an anonymous 1873 statement accusing Blackmore of concealing mercenary motives in his professions of interest in scientific exploration, see Brayer, *William Blackmore*, pp. 201–202.

37. Blackmore Diary, May 10, 1872 (No. 496, MNM).

38. Early in 1871 Blackmore proposed to Ferdinand V. Hayden that they make a "grand tour" together along the valley of the Rio Grande through Colorado and New Mexico, accompanied by William J. Palmer and "our mutual friends Col. Dodge and Col. Bridges" (Brayer, *William Blackmore*, p. 147). A "Map Showing Private Land Claims" in Colorado, New Mexico, and Arizona and identifying the Sangre de Christo and Costilla tracts owned in 1872 by Blackmore is available in House, *The Public Domain*, facing p. 1155.

39. These included Article XVII, Retirement of Officers; Article XX, Naturalization of Alien Soldiers; Article XXVII, Hospital Stewards; Article XXVIII, Superintendents of National Cemeteries; Articles XXIX and XXX, On Veterinary Surgeons of Cavalry and the Purchase and Care of Horses; Article XXXII, Civilian Employees; Article XLIV, Course of Instruction to Troops; Article XLV, Soldiers' Home; Article XLVI, Government Hospital for the Insane; Article LIV, Miscellaneous; Article LVII, Inspector General's Department; and Article LXV, Signal Service.

40. For example, compare Articles LIII, Military Obligation and Etiquette; XXXIII, Interior Economy of Regiments; XXXIV, Interior Economy of Companies; and LXIV, Bureau of Military Justice, in the revised regulations to Articles I, XII, XIII, and XXXVIII in *Revised United States Army Regulations of 1861* (1863).

41. S.O. 116, AGO, May 17, 1872, cited in Third Infantry Regimental Return, May 1872; the order was summarized in *ANJ*, May 25, 1872, p. 648.

42. For a summary discussion of the changes in style, production, and distribution of army clothing in these years see the foreword by Jerome A. Greene to Office of the Quartermaster General, *U.S. Army Uniforms and Equipment*, pp. v–ix. More detailed information can be found in Emerson, *Encyclopedia of United States Army Insignia and Uniforms*.

43. Athearn, *Sherman and the Settlement of the West*, pp. 257–60; Hutton, *Phil Sheridan and His Army*, pp. 296–97; Marszalek, *Sherman*, pp. 386–87.

44. Athearn, *Sherman and the Settlement of the West*, pp. 257–58. Under the heading "Powers of the Commanding General," Sherman's letter to Belknap was published in *ANJ*, July 4, 1874, p. 742.

45. WTS to Belknap, January 18, 1871 (AGO LR).

46. WTS endorsement, August 12, 1871, of Emory Upton to AG, August 9, 1871 (AGO LR).

47. WTS endorsement, September 20, 1872, of James Van Voast to AG, September 14, 1872, with undated memorandum by H. Crosby, chief clerk; Crosby to Van Voast, September 24, 1872 (AGO LR).

48. WTS endorsement, December 5, 1872, of W. Merritt to AG, December 1, 1872 (AGO LR).

49. WTS to Emory Upton, January 3, 1873 (Sherman Papers, LC).

50. Belknap to House of Representatives, February 17, 1873, in House, *Revised Army Regulations*, p. 1.

51. The testimony by Sherman was published in full in *ANJ*, February 7, 1874, pp. 406–8. The text of the bill for the reduction of the army was also published in *ANJ*, March 28, 1874, p. 516.

52. *OWI*, pp. 469–70. On February 22, 1874, Dodge's former commander at Bull Run, Colonel George Sykes, Twentieth Infantry, thanked General Sherman for his advocacy of the Line of the Army in his recent testimony before a congressional committee: "You said very truly that our branch of the Service looks to you as its defender, and I am sure every officer of it will appreciate all that you have done to prevent unwise legislation towards us" (Sherman Papers, LC).

Chapter 10

1. House, *Revised Army Regulations*, pp. 5–8.

2. *ANJ*, September 22, 1888, p. 68.

3. Frazer, *Forts of the West*, pp. 52–53; Roberts, *Encyclopedia of Historic Forts*, p. 294; Office of the Surgeon General, *Report on Barracks and Hospitals*, pp. 301–303; U.S. Army, *Outline Descriptions*, p. 143.

4. J. C. McFerran to Montgomery C. Meigs, July 27, 1865 (*O.R.*, ser. III, vol. 5, p. 443).

5. Bristol to C.O. Fort Dodge, April 11 and 14, 1873 (Fort Dodge Unregistered LR); S.O. 46, Fort Dodge, April 21, 1873.

6. RID to AAG DMO, September 10, 1872 (Fort Dodge LS). Orders, reports, correspondence, and other records of Fort Dodge during this period are available in NARA microform publication M 989, Rolls 1–25.

7. AAG DMO to RID, April 4, 1873 (Fort Dodge Unregistered LR); see also AAG DMO to RID, April 15, 1873 (Fort Dodge LR).

8. For example, see S.O. 90, Fort Dodge, June 25, 1873.

9. The Atchison, Topeka and Santa Fe Railroad reached the Kansas-Colorado line on December 28, 1872. The company's first annual report, dated March 31, 1873, showed 497 miles of completed track, as far west as Granada, a few miles into Colorado (Bryant, *History of the Atchison, Topeka and Santa Fe Railway*, p. 30).

10. See Miner, *Wichita: The Early Years*, pp. 51–61.

11. See Utley, *Frontier Regulars*, pp. 188–91.

12. In recent years spokesmen for the army had objected strenuously to the transfer of its former controlling authority over Indians to representatives of the Indian Bureau; for example, see House, *Report of the SW*, 1868, pp. 6–7, 20–21; *ANJ*, June 2, 1866, p. 653; July 31, 1869, p. 792; May 28, 1870, p. 657; and April 26, 1873, pp. 582–83. Their dissatisfaction intensified with the introduction in 1869 of President Grant's so-called "Peace Policy," which provided for the appointment as Indian agents of persons representing various religious denominations. A history of army attitudes toward federal Indian policy in the latter decades of the nineteenth century is provided by Wooster in *The Military and United States Indian Policy*.

13. S.O. 45, Fort Dodge, April 19, 1873.

14. RID to AAG DMO, April 28, 1873 (Fort Dodge LS).

15. John R. Brooke to AAG DMO, April 5, 1873 (Fort Dodge LR); S.O. 45, Fort Dodge, April 19, 1873.

16. RID to AAG DMO, June 13 and July 1, 1872 (Fort Dodge LS).

17. S.O. 119, Fort Dodge, August 8, 1872; G.O. 24, Fort Dodge, September 2, 1872; RID to AAG DMO, September 3, 1872 (Fort Dodge LS).

18. RID to AAG DMO, July 1, 1872 (Fort Dodge LS).

19. RID to U.S. Marshal, Topeka, Kansas, June 19, 1872 (Fort Dodge LS).

20. RID to AAG DMO, July 28, 1872 (Fort Dodge LS).

21. RID endorsement, July 30, 1872 (Fort Dodge Endorsement Book).

22. RID to AAG DMO, July 28, 1872 (Fort Dodge LS); First Lieutenant William Krause endorsement, July 28, 1872 (Fort Dodge Endorsement Book).

23. AAG DMO to RID, August 30, 1872 (Fort Dodge LR).

24. *PNA*, p. 84.

25. RID endorsement, February 13, 1873 (Fort Dodge Endorsement Book).

26. RID endorsement, May 21, 1873 (Fort Dodge Endorsement Book).

27. RID endorsement, September 26, 1873 (Fort Dodge endorsement Book).

28. *PNA*, pp. 131–32.

29. RID notation, June 3, 1873, on Eugene B. Allen to Post Adjutant (Fort Dodge Unregistered LR).

30. "This is absolutely necessary for the preservation of discipline and good order at this post," he urged (RID to AAG DMO, June 18, 1872—Fort Dodge LS). For a map showing the boundaries in question, see House, *Fort Dodge Military Reservation*, following p. 4.

31. First Lieutenant William Krause, post adjutant, to Robert M. Wright, June 19, 1872 (Fort Dodge LS).

32. Heitman, *Historical Register*, I, p. 974.

33. RID to AAG DMO, July 29, 1872 (Fort Dodge LS).

34. S.O. 114, Fort Dodge, July 29, 1872.

35. RID to AAG DMO, August 3, 1872, transmitting charges and specifications against Turner (Fort Dodge LS); AAG DMO to C.O. Fort Dodge, August 23, 1872 (Fort Dodge LR); S.O. 139, Fort Dodge, September 10, 1872. Second Lieutenant Turner owed his commission to the influence of General Sherman, who requested it of President Grant out of friendship for the young man's father, Henry S. Turner of Saint Louis, Missouri, and his uncle, Admiral Turner of the U.S. Navy. By 1878 the lieutenant had been tried repeatedly by court-martial and had acquired a reputation as a "quarrelsome and insubordinate" individual (WTS, Endorsement No. 254, February 9, 1878—Sherman Papers, LC). He resigned his commission in that year.

36. RID endorsement, June 26, 1873, of Alexander Johnstone to General John Pope, June 5, 1873 (copy) (Fort Dodge Unregistered LR).

37. RID to AAG DMO, May 24, 1873 (Fort Dodge LS). With endorsements by several superior officers, Dodge's suggestion reached the secretary of war, who elected to preserve the status quo "as there are strong arguments on both sides" (AG to RID, June 25, 1873—Fort Dodge Unregistered LR).

38. E. H. Ruffner to RID, April 16, June 17, and June 28, 1873 (Fort Dodge Unregistered LR); RID to Ruffner, April 13, 25, and 26, 1873 (Fort Dodge LS).

39. For example, see S.O. 62, Fort Dodge, May 10, 1873.

40. Fort Dodge Post Return, November 1873. The circular was reprinted in *ANJ*, November 15, 1873, p. 212.

41. Additionally, to ensure the security of prisoners being transported for arraignment in federal courts, they were caused to board trains on sections of track that lay within the military reservation. John R. Brooke to RID, February 18, 1873 (Fort Dodge Unregistered LR); R. Williams, AAG DMO, to C.O. Fort Dodge, October 16, 1873 (Fort Dodge LR); *PNA*, pp. 282–83.

42. "Author's Preface," *OWI*, p. v. These articles have not been identified.

43. *PNA*, p. 303.

44. The names of these and other Indian leaders are recorded in the reports of scouts from Fort Dodge during the period of Dodge's posting there; see NARA microform publication M989, Roll 25.

45. *OWI*, p. 40.

46. According to Dodge, these were the earliest of his published writings about Plains Indians (*OWI*, p. 40). They have not been identified.

47. Brayer, *William Blackmore*, pp. 191–92.

48. S.O. 145, Fort Dodge, October 5, 1872.

49. *PNA*, pp. 138–39.

50. *PNA*, pp. 100–1. See also Blackmore, introduction to *The Plains of the Great West*, by RID, pp. xiv–xv.

51. RID, "Railroad Towns" (Graff).

52. For more on the role of Dodge City and environs in the settlement of the region, see Haywood, *Trails South,* and Skaggs, *The Cattle-Trailing Industry*.

53. RID, "Railroad Towns" (Graff). See also *PNA*, p. 148; *OWI*, p. 650.

54. Hazen's letter to Henry Bergh, president of the society, was published in *ANJ*, February 3, 1872, p. 397.

55. Floyd-Jones to Sheridan, June 3, 1872; Sheridan to SW, June 11, 1872 (Fort Dodge Unregistered LR).

56. RID to AAG DMO, June 10, 1872 (Fort Dodge LS).

57. E. D. Townsend, AG, to Commanding General MDM, July 3, 1872, with endorsements (Fort Dodge Unregistered LR); Pope to AG, June 20, 1872 (AGO Reg LR).

58. Section 2137 of the *Revised Statutes* of the United States provided that persons other than Indians who hunted in Indian Territory except for subsistence there were liable to confiscation of their supplies and peltries and a penalty of five hundred dollars. Section 2118 provided that settlers on lands belonging, secured, or granted by treaty to an Indian tribe were liable to a penalty of $1,000 and to be removed from those lands by military force. Section 2147 provided that representatives of the Office of Indian Affairs had authority to remove from the Indian country all persons found there contrary to law and to call upon military forces to effect the removal (*Revised Statutes*, pp. 373, 370, and 374, respectively).

59. *OWI*, p. 296.

60. Blackmore, introduction to *The Plains of the Great West*, by RID, p. xv.

61. Blackmore, Diary, October 14 and 15, 1873 (No. 717a, MNM).

62. Blackmore, Diary, October 20, 1873 (No. 717a, MNM).

63. Blackmore, Diary, October 3, 1873 (No. 717a, MNM); *ANJ*, October 25, 1873, p. 164.

64. Blackmore estimated the number of buffalo slaughtered for their hides in Kansas and Nebraska in the past year at 1 million (Diary, October 20, 1873—No. 717a, MNM).

65. R. Williams, AAG DMO, to RID, October 3, 1873 (Fort Dodge LR)

66. RID to AAG DMO, October 27, 1873 (Fort Dodge LS).

67. Pope endorsement, October 30, 1873, of RID to AAG DMO, October 27, 1873 (AGO LR).

68. See "A Buffalo Campaign," *ANJ*, June 26, 1869, p. 704.

69. WTS endorsement, November 6, 1873, of RID to AAG DMO, October 27, 1873 (AGO LR); Belknap to SI, November 14, 1873 (AGO LR; Fort Dodge Unregistered LR).

70. *OWI*, p. 296.

71. U.S. Army, *Official Army Register* (1873), p. 185; Heitman, *Historical Register*, I, p. 1036.

72. RID to AAG DMO, October 30, 1873 (Fort Dodge LS); RID ACP File (AGO).

73. RID to AG through headquarters MDM, November 5, 1873 (Fort Dodge LS).

74. Robinson, *General Crook and the Western Frontier*, p. 137.

75. See *STJ*, pp. 30–31.

76. Crook commanded the department in respect of his brevet rank of major general.

77. "General Crook as an Indian Fighter," *ANJ*, August 26, 1871, p. 27. The description is attributed to a correspondent of the *Chicago Tribune*.

78. S.O. 216, AGO, November 1, 1873, cited in Fort Dodge Post Return, November 1873; *ANJ*, November 8, 1873, p. 196.

79. S.O. 171, DMO, November 3, 1873 (RID ACP File, AGO); *ANJ*, November 15, 1873, p. 212.

80. Thomas M. Vincent, AAG, to RID, November 11, 1873 (RID ACP File, AGO).

81. RID to AG, November 9, 1873 (RID ACP File, AGO).

82. On November 15 Woods, who had been a division commander under General Sherman during the Civil War, informed him in an unofficial note that he would not consent to the removal from the Fifth Infantry which General Pope was said to have in mind. He asked Sherman to prevent the action "should it be in your power" (Sherman Papers, LC). Woods's immediate superior, Colonel Nelson A. Miles, took umbrage at Pope's evident intention to adjust the roster of officers in the Fifth Infantry to suit his own tastes. "Colonel Dodge informed me that J[ohn] P[ope] had promised him this [reassignment] some time ago," he complained to Sherman. "There seems to be a strong feeling for Dodge and no friendship for [Brevet] Genl Woods. I would much prefer to be associated with Genl Woods" (Miles to WTS, November 8, 1873—Sherman Papers, LC).

83. G.O. 29, Fort Dodge, November 13, 1873.

Part 4

1. Twain to Howells, February 22, 1877, in Clemens, *Mark Twain–Howells Letters*, I, p. 172.

Chapter 11

1. Two regiments, the Twenty-third Infantry and the Fifth Cavalry, occupied posts in the Department of Arizona at the time of Dodge's transfer ("Stations of the Regiments . . By Companies," *ANJ*, December 27, 1873, p. 319). John G. Bourke described Arizona at the time of his arrival there in 1871 as a place "separated from 'God's country' by a space of more than fifteen hundred miles, without a railroad, and the officer who once got out there rarely returned for years." He characterized the Department of Arizona as "the most woe-begone of all in the Army" (*On the Border with Crook*, p. 2).

2. Bourke, *On the Border with Crook*, pp. 232–33.

3. Simon Cameron to W. W. Belknap, December 26, 1873; Belknap to Cameron, January 2, 1874; memorandum by E. D. Townsend, AG, January 2, 1874 (RID ACP File, AGO).

4. RID to Thomas A. Vincent, AAG, March 30, 1874 (RID ACP File, AGO). Dodge was at Fort Wingate on April 21 (*ANJ*, May 23, 1874, p. 645).

5. Fanny Dunbar Corbusier accompanied her husband, Assistant Surgeon William H. Corbusier, on a journey from Las Animas, Colorado, to Fort Whipple, Arizona, in August and September 1874. Her evocative account of the experience is found in *Fanny Dunbar Corbusier: Recollections*, pp. 46–57. According to Mrs. Corbusier, Dodge's itinerary of the route from Fort Wingate to Fort Whipple proved "very reliable. It told us where he had found wood for his fires, food for his animals, and water" (p. 54).

6. As a further coincidence, at the time of his promotion to lieutenant colonel in 1866, Crook was major, Third Infantry—the identical post occupied by Dodge at the time of his recent promotion.

7. Twenty-third Infantry Regimental Return, May 1874; *ANJ*, June 20, 1874, p. 710.

8. In November 1873 Companies A and B were stationed at Camp Verde; Company C, at Camp McDowell; Companies D and E, at Camp Lowell; Company F, at Camp Bowie; Company G, at Fort Yuma, California; Company H, at Camp Grant; Company I, at Camp Apache; and Company K, at Fort Whipple (Twenty-third Infantry Regimental Return).

9. See *ANJ*, January 11, 1868, p. 328; December 24, 1870, p. 294; April 19, 1873, p. 569; and May 31, 1873, pp. 663, 665. General Canby, then in command of the Department of the Columbia, was killed on April 11, 1873, during negotiations with the Modoc Indians, who refused to return to their Klamath Reservation in Oregon and had taken sanctuary in the lava beds of northern California.

10. The fullest biographical treatment of Crook is Robinson, *General Crook and the Western Frontier*. See also the general's uncompleted autobiography, brought to a close by its editor, Martin Schmitt, *General George Crook: His Autobiography*, and Bourke's informative but adulatory *On the Border with Crook*.

11. "Regiments are the primary schools of all armies. The companies are the classes. In them the military education is taught, order and military discipline instituted, subordination enforced, and the soldier created. The colonels are the teachers. By them the Army is molded and military character impressed. They make the dies that stamp on all armies character and invincibility" ("The New Army Regulations," *ANJ*, April 11, 1874, p. 551).

12. See *PREJ*, pp. 65–66; Hutton, *Phil Sheridan and His Army*, pp. 126–29, 325–26. Within the army a wide divergence of opinion existed over the reliability and usefulness of Indian scouts and auxiliaries. For a survey, see Dunlay, *Wolves for the Blue Soldiers*, pp. 59–69.

13. Crook's report, dated August 31, 1874, was reprinted in *ANJ*, December 5, 1874, pp. 266–67.

14. Representatives of the Indian Bureau who served in Arizona during this period are listed in Bourke, *Diaries*, I, p. 458; but see also Bourke, *On the Border with Crook*, pp. 213–17, 221.

15. See *ANJ*, June 20, 1874, p. 710; December 5, 1874, p. 257; Bourke, *On the Border with Crook*, pp. 201, 208–9, 217; Robinson, *General Crook and the Western Frontier*, pp. 135–36. Another officer well attuned to the Indians and their needs was Second Lieutenant Walter S. Schuyler, Fifth Cavalry, who according to Bourke showed "wonderful aptitude" in helping them adapt to civilized ways (*On the Border with Crook*, p. 215).

16. *ANJ*, August 1, 1874, p. 810.

17. *ANJ*, February 7, 1874, pp. 406–407.

18. *ANJ*, March 28, 1874, p. 516.

19. *General George Crook: His Autobiography*, p. 83.

20. G.O. 1, HQA, June 10, 1874, reprinted in *ANJ*, June 20, 1874, p. 708. The Twenty-third was to exchange stations with Dodge's old regiment, the Eighth Infantry.

21. Like his promotion to brigadier general, Crook's transfer to the Department of the Platte would be at the behest of President Grant. In the winter of 1874–1875 Crook made an inspection tour of posts in the Department of Arizona, observing the operation of programs he had established there on behalf of the Indians (Bourke, *On the Border with Crook*, p. 230). Crook relinquished command of the department on March 27, 1875 (Bourke, *Diaries*, I, p. 136).

22. Twenty-third Infantry Regimental Returns, July–September 1874; *ANJ*, September 5, 1874, p. 53.

23. Omaha Barracks Post Return, September 1874.

24. A general account of the 1874 Black Hills expedition is provided by Jackson, *Custer's Gold*; the published reports of correspondents who accompanied Custer have been gathered and reprinted by Krause and Olson in *Prelude to Glory*; see also Parker, *Gold in the Black Hills*, and *ANJ*, June 27, 1874, p. 723; July 4, 1874, p. 744–45.

25. Custer's dispatches of August 2 and 15, 1874, are included in his report to the U.S. Senate, *Report of the Expedition to the Black Hills*, pp. 1–9; the quotation is from p. 8. See also *ANJ*, August 15, 1874, p. 3; August 22, p. 26; and August 29, p. 38.

26. Brayer, *William Blackmore*, p. 216.

27. Receipt, Iler & Co., Liquor and Cigar Merchants, Omaha, October 3, 1874; List of grocery articles purchased, October 5, 1874 (Nos. 0842, 0843, MNM).

28. Cardboard card, dated "Oct 5/ 74" (No. 844c, MNM).

29. Blackmore, Diary, October 7–9, 1874 (No. 0837, MNM); *PNA*, pp. 303–304.

30. *PNA*, pp. 304, 321.

31. Among the Blackmore Papers (No. 0845, MNM) is an envelope labeled by the Englishman "*Oct. 8. 1874* Scrapings from buffalo hide made by Squaw of 'Two Lance' Chief of Whistler's band of Ogallala Sioux—in camp on South Platte Colorado near Riverside Station."

32. Blackmore, Diary, October 12, 14, 1874 (No. 0837, MNM).

33. One of these Blackmore recorded in cipher as "Dodge's experience of an Indian maiden" (Diary, p. 28—No. 0848, MNM).

34. Among these was *Colorado: Its Resources, Parks, and Prospects as a New Field for Emigration* (1869), promoting land grant properties he had recently purchased. Another, published anonymously, was *The Denver and Rio Grande Railway of Colorado and New Mexico* (1871).

35. Blackmore's pertinacity, Dodge later recalled good-naturedly, amounted almost to "bullying" (RID to Blackmore, February 3, 1877—No. 918, MNM).

36. Twenty-third Infantry Regimental Return, November 1874; Omaha Barracks Post Return, November 1874; *ANJ*, November 11, 1874, p. 228.

37. Cooke's best-known work was *Scenes and Adventures in the Army.*

38. Moore, *History of North Carolina*, II, p. 135.

39. RID to Blackmore, March 21, 1875 (No. 0899, MNM).

40. See *PNA*, pp. 303–4, 321–22.

41. Author's manuscript, "The Plains," p. 243 (MNM), cited hereafter as MSA. See also *PNA*, p. 235.

42. MSA, p. 255a; see also *PNA*, p. 239n.

43. For example, the Indian's "views on chastity might well have been derived from a close study of the ancient Hebrew records" (MSA, p. 344); see also *PNA*, p. 267.

44. MSA, pp. 123–24; see also *PNA*, pp. 302–303.

45. MSA, pp. 425; see also *PNA*, p. 303.

46. RID to Blackmore, January 31, 1875 (No. 0898, MNM).

47. MSA, pp. 498, 490; see also *PNA*, pp. 320, 318.

48. MSA, p. 566; see also *PNA*, p. 341.

49. MSA, pp. 542, 546–49, 554; see also *PNA*, pp. 333, 334–35.

50. MSA, p. 623; see also *PNA*, p. 354.

51. MSA, p. 605; see also *PNA*, p. 350.

52. MSA, p. 639; see also *PNA*, p. 359.

53. MSA, pp. 641–42; see also *PNA*, p. 360.

54. MSA, p. 662; see also *PNA*, p. 366.

55. RID to Blackmore, March 21, 1875 (No. 0899, MNM).

56. MSA, pp. 210–14; see also *PNA*, pp. 117–18.

57. MSA, p. 2; see also *PNA*, p. 59.

58. MSA, p. 242; see also *PNA*, p. 126.

59. S.O. 52, DP, May 1, 1875, forms part of a consolidated file relating to the Black Hills Expedition, 1356 AGO 1875, available in NARA microform publication M666, Roll 192.

60. MSA, p. 241; see also *PNA*, p. 126.

Chapter 12

1. The activities of this controversial figure (1839–1890) have been detailed by Anderson, "Samuel D. Hinman," and by Parker, "Report of the Reverend Samuel D. Hinman."

2. Custer's letter, dated December 13, 1874, was reprinted in *ANJ*, January 9, 1875, pp. 341–42.

3. For Henry's report of this almost disastrous errand, see *ANJ*, January 30, 1875, p. 387.

4. Mix to Post Adjutant, Fort Laramie, in MDM Papers, pp. 244–51 (USAMHI). Mix's report was published in *ANJ*, May 8, 1875, p. 613; see also Parker, "The Report of Captain John Mix."

5. Turchen and McLaird, *The Black Hills Expedition of 1875* (hereafter *Black Hills Expedition*), p. 2.

6. Sherman's March 17 letter to Sheridan forms part of G.O. 2, MDM, March 17, 1875 (AGO LR).

7. Quoted in *ANJ*, May 1, 1875, p. 596.

8. "Report of the Commission Appointed to Treat with the Sioux Indians for the Relinquishment of the Black Hills," in House, *Report of the SI,* 1875, p. 691. The speaker was Fast (or Quick) Bear, of Red Cloud Agency.

9. "The Indians," *ANJ*, June 12, 1875, p. 698.

10. C. Delano to SW, March 22, 1875 (AGO LR).

11. A protégé of the geologist J. S. Newberry, who nominated him for the position, Jenney (1849–1921) had only limited field experience. He had spent fourteen months in western Texas and New Mexico, participating in explorations and surveys for the projected Texas and Southwest Railroad.

12. WTS to W. W. Belknap, April 9, 1875 (AGO LR).

13. Sheridan to WTS, March 25, 1875, in *ANJ*, April 3, 1875, p. 533.

14. *ANJ*, May 15, 1875, p. 632.

15. E. D. Townsend, AG, to Sheridan, May 13, 1875 (AGO LR).

16. E. D. Townsend, AG, to A. H. Terry, May 17, 1875; Terry to AG, May 17, 1875; Sheridan to W. W. Belknap, May 17, 1875 (AGO LR). The source of confusion was a reference to a forthcoming "Black Hill's [*sic*] Expedition" under Custer in S.O. 83, Department of Dakota, May 11, 1875 (AGO LR).

17. In a general order relinquishing command of the Department of the Platte on April 6, 1875, General Ord noted that "until the arrival of Brigadier-General Crook, the command of the Department of the Platte will be exercised by the Lieutenant-General"—that is, Sheridan (*ANJ*, April 24, 1875, p. 580).

18. Crook's junior aide-de-camp Second Lieutenant Bourke recorded the journey to Omaha; see *Diaries*, I, pp. 133–57. Additionally, he sketched a vivid scene just following the general's arrival at Omaha: "Scarcely had we been shown to our rooms in the Grand Central Hotel when the notes of the 'General Crook March', played by the band of his old regiment, the 23d. Infantry, broke upon the air and a long line of officers, most of whom had served under General Crook from British America to Mexico, filed up the main stairway headed by the soldierly figure of Colonel R.I. Dodge" (I, p. 157). See also *ANJ*, May 8, 1875, p. 613.

19. S.O. 52, DP, May 1, 1875 (AGO LR).

20. These journals, with entries from May 6 to October 19, 1875, have been published together as *The Black Hills Journals of Colonel Richard Irving Dodge* (BHJ).

21. See Article LII, "Journal," in House, *Revised Army Regulations*, p. 102.

22. RID to Blackmore, May 1 and May 19, 1875 (Nos. 900, 901, MNM). Dodge's reference to "the Big Horn country," many miles west of the Black Hills, is problematical. Possibly he considered the northern reaches of the hills as a portion of the Big Horn country.

23. RID Journal, May 8, 1875 (*BHJ*, pp. 38–39).

24. See "The Dispatches of Walter P. Jenney" in Turchen and McLaird, *Black Hills Expedition*, pp. 9–13.

25. RID Journal, May 9, 1875 (BHJ, p. 39).

26. RID Journal, May 12, 1875 (BHJ, p. 41).

27. Bourke, Diary, May 16, 1875 (Bourke Papers, USMA). The career of Bourke has been described by Porter in *Paper Medicine Man*. Much information concerning this officer should also be made available in subsequent volumes of his *Diaries*, the first of which, covering the period November 20, 1872, to July 28, 1876, appeared in 2003.

28. Bourke, Diary, May 16, 1875 (Bourke Papers, USMA).

29. See Custer, *My Life on the Plains*, pp. 134–35 passim.

30. RID Journal, June 8, 1875 (*BHJ*, p. 70); Milner, *California Joe*, pp. 222–29.

31. The General and Special Orders issued during the BHE can be found in NARA RG 393, Part 1, Entry 3749.

32. Bourke, Diary, May 24, 1875 (Bourke Papers, USMA). The corresponding passage in *Diaries*, I, p. 169, differs in some details from the text as given here. Further citations of Bourke's diaries refer to my own transcription but for convenience also include references to the published texts.

33. Guerin reached the command on June 23. His photographs were later offered for sale by Robert Benecke of St. Louis. An almost complete set is included in Turchen and McLaird, *Black Hills Expedition*, pp. 96–121.

34. RID Journal, May 25, 1875 (*BHJ*, p. 46).

35. G.O. 2, BHE, May 24, 1875.

36. G.O. 2, BHE, May 24, 1875; Bourke, Diary, May 31, 1875 (Bourke Papers, USMA); *New York Tribune*, June 7, 1875, p. 3.

37. Bourke, Diary, May 31, 1875 (Bourke Papers, USMA); see also Bourke, *Diaries*, I, pp. 173–74.

38. See RID Journal, May 29, 1875 (*BHJ*, p. 51).

39. RID Journal, May 26–27, 1875 (*BHJ*, pp. 47–48).

40. According to Henry Newton, assistant geologist of the Black Hills Expedition, Warren's route north from Fort Laramie in 1856 was much the same as that followed by Dodge and his command, and Warren's camp of September 12, 1856, was "almost the same as our first [permanent] camp in the Hills, known as Camp Jenney" (Newton and Jenney, *Report*, p. 11). In 1859 Captain William F. Raynolds of the U.S. Army Topographical Engineers had led an expedition from Fort Pierre, on the Missouri River, to explore the Yellowstone region. But as Dodge soon discovered, Raynolds did not pass anywhere near Rawhide Butte. See RID Journal, May 28, 1875 (*BHJ*, pp. 49–50).

41. RID Journal, May 30, 1875 (*BHJ*, p. 53). For an account of the wagon road established by Colonel James A. Sawyer, see Hafen and Hafen, *Powder River Campaigns.*

42. RID Journal, May 31, 1875 (*BHJ*, p. 55).

43. RID Journal, June 2, 1875 (*BHJ*, p. 59). In a report of July 31 to the Commissioner of Indian Affairs, Jenney explained that he had lacked both the time and the instruments necessary to establish the

Wyoming-Dakota boundary in the field. He noted that the boundary "as placed on the various maps issued from time to time is from eight to twenty miles too far west" (Turchen and McLaird, *Black Hills Expedition*, pp. 21–22).

44. Bourke, Diary, June 3, 1875 (Bourke Papers, USMA). See also Bourke, *Diaries*, I, p. 177.

45. RID, *The Black Hills*, p. 29.

46. RID Journal, May 31, 1875 (*BHJ*, pp. 55–56). McGillycuddy's striking relief map of the Black Hills country was included in the *Atlas* that accompanied Newton and Jenney's *Report*.

47. See Jenney to E. P. Smith, May 2 and May 9, 1875 (Turchen and McLaird, *Black Hills Expedition*, pp. 11–12).

48. *New York Herald*, July 8, 1875, p. 4.

49. RID Journal, June 8, 1875 (*BHJ*, p. 69).

50. RID Journal, May 31, 1875 (*BHJ*, p. 56).

51. RID Journal, May 31, 1875 (*BHJ*, p. 57). MacMillan's activities during the Sioux campaigns of 1876 have been described by Knight in *Following the Indian Wars*, pp. 164–93.

52. McGillycuddy, *McGillycuddy, Agent*, p. 34.

53. *Chicago Inter-Ocean*, July 2, 1875, p. 9. See also the *Chicago Tribune*, June 19, 1875, p. 8; and Young, *Hard Knocks*, pp. 169–72.

54. RID Journal, July 12, 1875 (*BHJ*, p. 125).

55. RID Journal, June 24, 1875 (*BHJ*, p. 98). MacMillan described Brown as "heavy-set . . . possessed of sterling physiognomy, has heavy hair, plentifully sprinkled with gray, and is altogether a Brown" (*Chicago Inter-Ocean*, May 29, 1875, p. 7).

56. The fullest account of this legendary figure is Milner, *California Joe*; see also Collins, *My Experiences in the West*, pp. 131–37.

57. *New York Herald*, June 20, 1875, p. 6.

58. *Chicago Inter-Ocean*, May 29, 1875, p. 7.

59. *Chicago Tribune*, August 21, 1875, p. 2.

60. McGillycuddy, *McGillycuddy, Agent*, p. 34.

61. RID Journal, June 3, 1875 (*BHJ*, p. 60).

62. Bourke, Diary, June 3, 1875 (Bourke Papers, USMA). See also Bourke, *Diaries*, I, p. 179.

63. *New York Tribune*, June 21, 1875, p. 5. An account of Burt's career that draws largely upon the edited memoirs of his wife, Elizabeth, can be found in Mattes, *Indians, Infants, and Infantry*.

64. Bourke, Diary, June 3, 1875 (Bourke Papers, USMA). See also Bourke, *Diaries*, p. 178.

65. RID Journal, June 5, 1875 (*BHJ*, p. 63).

66. RID Journal, June 3, 1875 (*BHJ*, p. 61). See Proverbs 26:12.

67. RID Journal, June 9, 1875 (*BHJ*, pp. 72, 73).

68. RID Journal, May 31, 1875 (*BHJ*, p. 55).

69. Bourke, Diary, June 1, 1875 (Bourke Papers, USMA). See also Bourke, *Diaries*, I, p. 176–77.

70. RID Journal, June 7, 1875 (*BHJ*, p. 66).

71. See *PNA*, pp. 93–97.

72. RID Journal, June 9, 1875 (*BHJ*, p. 72).

73. RID Journal, June 10, 1875 (*BHJ*, pp. 74–76).

74. RID to AAG DP, December 22, 1875 (AGO LR). Dodge's official report has been published in Turchen and McLaird, *Black Hills Expedition*, pp. 30–93; the quoted passage is on p. 40.

75. Forsyth's official report and diary were published in the *Chicago Tribune*, August 27, 1874; the diary has been reprinted in Krause and Olson, *Prelude to Glory*, pp. 253–59.

76. *New York Tribune*, July 1, 1875, p. 1.

77. RID Journal, June 13, 1875 (*BHJ*, p. 84).

78. RID Journal, June 14, 1875 (*BHJ*, p. 88).

79. RID Journal, June 14, 1875 (*BHJ*, pp. 86–89). On the same day Bourke wrote in his diary that "these streams are now full of miners, whose fires send up volumes of smoke from the glens to the South, S.E., and S.W. of us" (Bourke Papers, USMA). See also Bourke, *Diaries*, I, p. 190).

80. Dodge's message was relayed to army headquarters in a letter from William D. Whipple to AG, June 23, 1875 (AGO LR). On June 24 the *New York Herald* reprinted (p. 7) a telegram from the correspondent of

the *Chicago Inter-Ocean*, dated June 16 and announcing the gold discovery; a telegram from Jenney, dated June 17 and announcing his discovery of gold on Castle Creek; and a report of Dodge's telegram of June 17. A dispatch from the *Herald* correspondent, also dated June 17,was not published until July 1 (p. 4). For the cause of this delay, see below, chapter 25.

81. S.O. 7, BHE, June 16, 1875.

82. RID Journal, June 23, 1875 (*BHJ*, p. 97).

83. RID Journal, June 14, 1875 (*BHJ*, p. 88).

84. RID Journal, June 16, 1875 (*BHJ*, pp. 90–91).

85. RID Journal, July 8, 1875 (*BHJ*, p. 120).

86. RID Journal, June 24, 1875 (*BHJ*, p. 97).

87. S.O. 8, BHE, June 23, 1875.

88. "The Sioux Chieftains," *New York Herald*, June 4, 1875, p. 10.

89. Probably Dodge read an article, "The Visiting Sioux," that described a conversation between Professor Marsh and President Grant concerning Marsh's allegations (*New York Herald*, June 1, 1875, p. 7).

90. RID Journal, June 22, 1875 (*BHJ*, p. 108). Dodge placed within quotation marks a phrase from *Julius Caesar* III.ii.88.

91. *BHJ*, pp. 108–109.

92. RID Journal, n.d. (*BHJ*, p. 109).

93. G.O. 4, BHE, June 25, 1875.

94. RID Journal, June 22, 1875 (*BHJ*, p. 95). Taken from "Lo, the poor Indian!" in Pope's *Essay on Man*, Epistle I, line 99, the epithet "Mr. Lo" was often used in reference to American Indians.

95. RID Journal, July 10, 1875 (*BHJ*, p. 122).

96. RID Journal, July 18, 1875 (*BHJ*, p. 132).

97. Dodge had written similar comments on June 18 and 21.

98. RID Journal, June 25, 1875 (*BHJ*, p. 99).

99. RID Journal, June 26 and July 3, 1875 (*BHJ*, pp. 100, 115). In the latter entry Dodge indicated that one section of the chapter on buffalo remained to be written, "statistics of the hide and meat business" (see *PNA*, pp. 148–57).

100. RID Journal, July 4, 1875 (*BHJ*, p. 117). The extract was published under the title "The Doomed Buffalo" in the *Chicago Inter-Ocean*, August 5, 1875, p. 2.

101. RID Journal, July 22, 1875 (*BHJ*, p. 147).

102. RID Journal, June 19, 1875 (*BHJ*, p. 92. A sketch of Colonel Bullock appeared in the *New York Herald*, August 19, 1875, p. 6.

103. RID Journal, June 20 and July 12, 1875 (*BHJ*, pp. 93, 123–24).

104. RID Journal, July 19, 1875 (*BHJ*, p. 133). Compare *PNA*, p. 126.

105. RID Journal, June 26, 1875 (*BHJ*, p. 100).

106. *Chicago Tribune*, July 8, 1875, p. 4.

107. RID Journal, June 24, 1875 (*BHJ*, p. 97).

108. RID Journal, July 3, 1875 (*BHJ*, p. 116).

109. RID Journal, June 27 and July 8, 1875 (*BHJ*, pp. 100–101, 120).

110. RID Journal, July 15, 1875 (*BHJ*, p. 127).

111. Jenney to E. P. Smith, July 31, 1875, quoted in "The Black Hills," *New York Tribune*, August 20, 1875, p. 1.

112. RID Journal, July 19, 1875 (*BHJ*, p. 134).

113. RID Journal, July 6, 7, and 15, 1875 (*BHJ*, pp. 118–19, 128).

114. Dodge copied the letter to Crook into the third of his Black Hills journals following its last dated entry, for July 20. See *BHJ*, pp. 136–38; the quotation is from p. 138.

115. RID Journal, July 17, 1875 (*BHJ*, pp. 129–30).

116. RID Journal, July 20, 1875 (*BHJ*, p. 135); Turchen and McLaird, *Black Hills Expedition*, p. 57.

117. RID Journal, July 20, 1875 (*BHJ*, p. 134).

118. An account of this official errand can be found in Parker, "Report of the Reverend Samuel Hinman." According to the *Chicago Tribune* (August 10, p. 2), the deputation of Indians included Red Dog,

No Flesh, Little Eagle, The-Man-Who-Kills-The-Hawk, and "eight other red devils with fantastic sounding names."

119. RID, July 22, 1875 (*BHJ*, pp. 145–47).

120. Dodge wrote in his official report: "The Commissioners wanted my Guide, Joe Merivale, as interpreter, and as he was of no use to me, I discharged him to go with them" (Turchen and McLaird, *Black Hills Expedition*, p. 50).

121. RID Journal, July 23, 25, and 27, 1875 (*BHJ*, pp. 148, 150, 151).

122. When established, the new post, Camp Collins, was garrisoned by Pollock's company of infantry; Company E, Second Cavalry, under Captain Elijah R. Wells; and Company D, Third Cavalry, under Captain Guy V. Henry. Captain Pollock did not endear himself to the Black Hills miners, one of whom described him as the "most famous wretch I know of . . . the devil in disguise" (Brown and Willard, *The Black Hills Trails*, pp. 87–88).

123. RID Journal, July 29, 1875 (*BHJ*, pp. 152–53).

124. The text of Crook's proclamation, dated July 29, 1875, was published in the *Chicago Tribune*, August 4, 1875, p. 4, and the *New York Tribune*, August 4, 1875, p. 4.

125. RID Journal, July 30, 1875 (*BHJ*, p. 155).

126. J. R. L., "Departure of Troops," *Chicago Tribune*, August 21, 1875, p. 2.

127. "The root or leaves of Aconitum Napellus. . . . As an internal remedy aconite is very valuable in sthenic fever from any cause" (Wood and Bache, *Dispensatory*, p. 128).

128. S.O. 22, BHE, August 6, 1875.

129. RID Journal, August 7–8, 1875 (*BHJ*, pp. 161–64).

130. J. R. L., "The Military and the Miners," *Chicago Tribune*, August 21, 1875, p. 2; "Spotted Tail and the Miners," *New York Tribune*, August 19, 1875, p. 4; "The Gold Seekers," *New York Herald*, August 26, 1875, p. 1.

131. "He was undoubtedly right in his shrewd penetration," Davenport wrote (*New York Herald*, August 26, 1875, p. 1).

132. *New York Tribune*, August 19, 1875, p. 4.

133. *Chicago Tribune*, August 21, 1875, p. 2.

134. Turchen and McLaird, *Black Hills Expedition*, p. 53. As published, this passage reproduces misspellings in Dodge's manuscript report, which was prepared by a copyist (AGO LR).

135. First Lieutenant Christopher T. Hall, Second Cavalry, commanded a company of the Black Hills Expedition but would remain at the stockade. Later in the summer Dodge relieved the unit from duty with the command (S.O. 28, BHE, August 26, 1875).

136. RID Journal, August 13, 1875 (*BHJ*, p. 172).

137. Dodge's journal entry for August 18 conveys vividly the difficulties confronted by his command. Recounting his strenuous but unsuccessful efforts, he registered the opinion that "to go through these hills is a matter of accident as well as knowledge" (*BHJ*, p. 182).

138. RID Journal, August 22, 1875 (*BHJ*, p. 186). Harry (Sam) Young, who drove the headquarters wagon and was privy to some of the commander's private conversations, claimed to have overheard an interchange between Dodge and California Joe. "Joe," the commander declared at the beginning of a day's march into new country, "I would follow you through the wilds of Africa." With a shrug the scout allowed in reply, "Well, I could take you and the outfit through there" (*Hard Knocks*, pp. 167–68).

139. RID Journal, August 21, 1875 (*BHJ*, p. 185); Turchen and McLaird, *Black Hills Expedition*, p. 58.

140. RID to Crook, September 4, 1875, in *BHJ*, pp. 207–208.

141. S.O. 187, AGO, September 9, 1876, cited in Twenty-third Infantry Regimental Return, September 1876; RID Journal, November 26, 1876 (*PREJ*, p. 88).

142. See below, chapter 20.

143. RID Journal, August 27 and 29, 1875 (*BHJ*, pp. 191, 192).

144. RID Journal, (*BHJ*, p. 200).

145. RID Journal, September 1, 1875 (*BHJ*, p. 196).

146. RID Journal, September 2, 1875 (*BHJ*, p. 197).

147. RID Journal, September 5, 1875 (*BHJ*, p. 199).

148. S.O. 32, BHE, September 4, 1875.

149. RID Journal, September 5, 1875 (*BHJ*, p. 199).

150. RID Journal, September 18, 1875 (*BHJ*, p. 248). "Sam" may have been Harry Young, the headquarters wagon driver, who was known familiarly by that name.

151. RID, September 28, 1875 (*BHJ*, p. 227).

152. See Parker, *Gold in the Black Hills*, p. 64; and for an earlier account, see King, *Campaigning with Crook*, pp. 154–55.

153. S.O. 34, BHE, September 27, 1875.

154. RID Journal, October 2, 1875 (*BHJ*, pp. 229–31).

155. RID Journal, October 6, 1875 (*BHJ*, p. 236).

156. RID Journal, October 8 and 9, 1875 (*BHJ*, pp. 238, 239).

157. S.O. 35, BHE, October 9, 1875.

158. RID Journal, October 13, 1875 (*BHJ*, p. 241).

159. RID Journal, October 13, 1875 (*BHJ*, p. 244). In G.O. 6, BHE, October 15, 1875, Dodge congratulated his command "on their generally very faithful and efficient performance of duty" and thanked his staff for their "cordial cooperation and assistance."

160. Turchen and McLaird, *Black Hills Expedition*, p. 92.

161. See Jenney, "Report of Geological Survey of the Black Hills," in House, *Report of the SI,* 1875, pp. 683–85. On April 25, 1876, the U.S. Senate ordered a portion of Jenney's interim assessment to be printed. The result was *Report on the Mineral Wealth, Climate, and Rainfall, and Natural Resources of the Black Hills of Dakota*. The final document remained unpublished until 1880 (Newton and Jenney, *Report on the Black Hills).*

162. See "Report of the Commission Appointed to Treat with the Sioux Indians for the Relinquishment of the Black Hills," in House, *Report of the SI,* 1875, pp. 686–702.

163. Turchen and McLaird, *Black Hills Expedition*, p. 92.

Chapter 13

1. RID Journal, October 19, 1875 (*BHJ*, p. 247).

2. Omaha Barracks Post Return, October 1875; Twenty-third Infantry Regimental Return, October 1875.

3. RID to AAG DP, December 22, 1875 (AGO LR).

4. RID to Crook, September 4, 1875 (*BHJ*, p. 208).

5. These officers, all of the Third Cavalry, were Second Lieutenants John G. Bourke, Charles Morton, and James E. H. Foster.

6. The map Dodge transmitted to the Adjutant General's Office bears at the lower right the inscription "drawn and traced by Wm Schwerdtfeger, Pvte. Co 'K,' 3d Cavalry" (AGO LR).

7. Brigadier General A. A. Humphreys, Chief of Engineers, wrote on May 1, 1876: "Inasmuch as the interesting work [Dodge's *The Black Hills*] recently published . . . contains the map accompanying this report and much of the information furnished in the latter, it is not recommended that the expense be incurred of their publication by this office" (Endorsement of RID to AG, February 16, 1876—AGO LR). However, the itinerary of the Black Hills Expedition and topographical features from Dodge's Black Hills map such as Dodge's Peak and Devils Tower were shown on Sheet No. 3, Western Territories Map, issued in 1876 by the Corps of Engineers.

8. Omaha Barracks Post Return, January 1876; *ANJ*, January 15, 1876, p. 365.

9. RID, "Preface," *The Black Hills*, p. [iii].

10. The passage continues: "The approaches from every direction are through long stretches of inhospitable plains, treeless and broken, in which the supply of water is so saturated with bitter and nauseous alkalies as to be unfit for the continuous use of the white man" (*The Black Hills*, p. 149). This statement may be compared to the original in *BHJ*, p. 109.

11. RID, *The Black Hills*, p. 151.

12. RID Journal, October 11, 1875 (*BHJ*, p. 240). "Structure of the Black Hills," pp. 29–43 in Dodge's *The Black Hills*, was the work of Newton.

13. RID to William Blackmore, February 7, 1876 (No. 0906, MNM).

14. Duplicated by the American Photo-Lithographic Company, the map was also offered for sale separately.

15. See House, *Revised Army Regulations*, p. 65.

16. The copy Dodge kept for reference has been lost; the second, MSA, survives among the Blackmore Papers, MNM.

17. See Putnam, *Authors and Publishers: A Manual*, pp. 36–37; Gohdes, *American Literature in Nineteenth Century England*, pp. 16–18; Nowell-Smith, *International Copyright Laws and the Publisher in the Reign of Queen Victoria*, pp. 15, 32.

18. RID to Blackmore, January 20, 1876 (No. 904, MNM).

19. Blackmore to RID, February 5, 1876, copy (No. 905, MNM).

20. Twenty-third Infantry Regimental Returns, January–April 1876; *ANJ*, February 19, 1876, p. 449.

21. RID to Blackmore, February 7 and 18, 1876 (Nos. 906, 908, MNM). Dodge's brother-in-law, Captain Chalmers Glenn of the Thirteenth North Carolina Regiment, died in 1862 at the Battle of South Mountain. In 1876 his widow, Ann Dodge Glenn, lived in Leakesville, Rockingham County, North Carolina.

22. RID to Blackmore, February 7, 1876 (No. 906, MNM).

23. Blackmore to RID, April 1, 1876, copy (No. 911a, MNM).

24. Gohdes, *American Literature in Nineteenth Century England*, pp. 24, 25, 95–96.

25. This summary of the agreement is given on the basis of information in several sources in the Blackmore Papers, MNM: Blackmore to RID, April 1, 1876, copy, No. 911a; RID to Blackmore, April 16 and June 11, 1876, Nos. 913, 915; Chatto & Windus to Blackmore, May 6, 1876, No. 999; George H. Putnam to Blackmore, April 22, 1876, No. 1037; Putnam to Blackmore, June 22, 1876, No. 1039; Statement of account between Chatto & Windus and Blackmore, October 16, 1877, No. 1262.

26. RID to Blackmore, June 11, 1876 (No. 915, MNM).

27. Among the material Dodge forwarded to Blackmore were the texts of his dedication and preface, a table of contents, photographs of plains scenes for possible use as illustrations, a diagram to assist Blackmore in preparing his chapter on Indian chronology, a correction of an omission in the main text, and a photograph of himself (Nos. 906, 908, 909, 910, 912, 913, MNM).

28. RID to Blackmore, March 10, 1876 (No. 909, MNM). Lithographed in London, the map was published in the English and U.S. editions of *The Plains*, following p. xiv.

29. George H. Putnam to Blackmore, February 15, 1876 (No. 1033, MNM); Blackmore to G. P. Putnam's Sons, March 4, 1876 (No. 1034, MNM); Chatto & Windus to Blackmore, May 6, 1876 (Nos. 999 and 1000, MNM); RID to Blackmore, January 20 and February 7, 1876 (Nos. 904, 906, MNM); RID to Blackmore, April 20, 1876 (No. 914, MNM).

30. RID to Blackmore, February 15 and 18, 1876 (Nos. 907, 908, MNM).

31. RID to Blackmore, March 23, 1876 (No. 910, MNM).

32. George H. Putnam to Blackmore, April 13, 1876 (Nos. 1036, 1036a, MNM); RID to Blackmore, April 16, 1876 (No. 913, MNM).

33. RID to Blackmore, February 15, 1876 (No. 907, MNM).

34. RID to Blackmore, March 23, 1876 (No. 910, MNM).

35. RID to Blackmore, March 23, 1876 (No. 910, MNM). The passages in question occur at the following points in *PNA* (citations are to page and line numbers): 267.38–271.29 (The Indian . . . discontinued.); 275.24–276.29 (The natural . . . back.); 334.33–336.20 (No words . . . subject.); 350.24–30 (I have . . . inflicted.); 353.21–44 (The ringleader . . . improbability.) (Appendix, MSA).

36. Blackmore created this passage by adapting one he had published in 1869. For the original and the revised versions, see *PNA*, p. 399, note 21 and p. 453, "List of Rejected Variants," 336.20.

37. RID to Blackmore, April 20 and June 11, 1876 (Nos. 914, 915, MNM).

38. RID to Blackmore, August 2, 1876 (No. 916, MNM).

39. Blackmore to RID, April 1, 1876, copy (No. 911a, MNM).

40. A receipt showing the payment of five pounds for copying the manuscript was signed by Blackmore's secretary, Andrew Chinn, on April 7, 1876 (No. 1049, MNM). The recopied manuscript survives as a part of the Blackmore Papers.

41. In his initial review of the manuscript, Blackmore altered it at 134 points. For a detailed account of changes to the manuscript text as it moved toward publication, see "Textual Commentary," *PNA*, pp. 382–401.

42. See *PNA*, p. 145.25–39 and the "List of Rejected Variants" corresponding to this passage, p. 431.

43. See *PNA*, p. 137.22 and the "List of Rejected Variants," p. 422.

44. Chinn was responsible for 976 word changes to the manuscript; see *PNA*, pp. 387–88.

45. See *PNA*, "List of Rejected Variants," 296.36, 329.17 (pp. 449, 453).

46. As eventually issued by G. P. Putnam's Sons, the book incorporated 1,921 changes to the words in the manuscript Dodge had sent Blackmore, not counting mechanical matters such as revisions of chapter titles and the table of contents. In a book approximately 137,000 words long, that total represents an emendation of one word in every seventy-one ("Textual Commentary," *PNA*, p. 391).

47. Putnam to Blackmore, June 22 and 30, 1878 (Nos. 1039, 1040, MNM).

48. Brayer, *William Blackmore*, pp. 241–42, 299–303, 311.

49. Spottiswoode & Co. to Chatto & Windus, August 23, 1876 (No. 1002, MNM); Chatto & Windus to Blackmore, August 25, 1876 (No. 1005, MNM); George H. Putnam to Blackmore, September 23 and October 26, 1876 (Nos. 1041, 1042, MNM); *Times* (London), November 23, 1876, p. 4.

50. Among the Dodge Papers in the Everett D. Graff Collection is the photograph of a trim, elderly woman taken by Sarony & Co., New York. On the reverse side is written "Dear Grandma Paulding. Died at Omaha Barracks Saturday eve, August 5th 1876."

51. RID to AG, September 20, 1876; AG to RID, September 22, 1876; RID to Major Thomas M. Vincent, AAG, January 31, 1877 (RID ACP File, AGO); *ANJ*, September 9, 1876, p. 69.

52. RID to Blackmore, January 31, 1877 (No. 917, MNM). The subtitle of the American edition was *Being a Description of the Plains, Games, Indians, &c., of the Great North American Desert.*

53. RID Journal, November 1, 1876 (*PREJ*, p. 52).

54. RID Journal, December 11, 1876 (*PREJ*, p. 122).

55. "Forthcoming Publications of G. P. Putnam's Sons," *Publisher's Weekly* 10 (September 16, 1876), 439.

56. *Publisher's Weekly* 10 (November 18, 1876), 848–49. The entire first page of the advertisement was devoted to *The Plains of the Great West and Their Inhabitants.*

57. *New York Times*, January 10, 1877, p. 6; George H. Putnam to Blackmore, January 31, 1877 (No. 1042, MNM).

58. "Col Dodges Book—Hunting Grounds of the Great West" heads a listing by addressee of sixty-five complimentary copies the editor distributed between November 17, 1876, and June 18, 1877 (No. 1196, MNM).

59. G. H. Kingsley to Blackmore, December 6 and 7, 1876 (Nos. 1138, 1141, MNM). Kingsley was the author of various works, including a posthumous *Notes on Sport and Travel* (1890).

60. Lawley to Blackmore, November 27, 1876 (No. 1122, MNM). Probably Lawley was referring to George F. Ruxton's much admired *Adventures in Mexico and the Rocky Mountains* (1847), though he may have meant the later *Life in the Far West* (1849).

61. This discussion of the critical reception of *Hunting Grounds* is based on the following notices: *Edinburgh Daily Review*, November 24, 1876; *London Daily News*, November 24, 1876; *Nonconformist*, November 29, 1876, pp. 7–8; *London Daily Telegraph*, December 12, 1876; *Field*, December 23, 1876, pp. 771–72; *London Globe*, December 29, 1876; *Pall Mall Gazette*, January 2, 1877; *Saturday Review* 43 (January 13, 1877), 54–55; *Westminster Review* 107 (January 1877), 113; *Spectator*, February 24, 1877; *Times* (London), April 9, 1877, p. 4; *Land and Water Illustrated*, n.d., pp. 7–8. Citations lacking either dates or page numbers are to newspaper clippings thus identified in No. 1156, MNM.

62. George H. Putnam to Blackmore, January 31, 1877 (No.1042, MNM).

63. This discussion of the critical reception of *The Plains of the Great West and Their Inhabitants* is based upon the following notices: *ANJ*, January 20, 1877, p. 378; *Publisher's Weekly* 11 (January 20, 1877), 91–92; *New York Tribune*, January 30, 1877, p. 1; *Nation* 24 (February 8, 1877), 91–92; *Chicago Inter-Ocean*, February 10, 1877, p. 9; *New York Times*, February 12, 1877, p. 3; *Galaxy* 23 (March 1877), 425–27; *Eclectic Magazine* 25 (April 1877), 504–5; *Harper's New Monthly Magazine* 54 (April 1877), 768–69; *Popular Science*

Monthly 10 (April 1877), 754; *Scribner's Monthly Magazine*, 13 (April 1877), 875; *Atlantic Monthly* 39 (June 1877), 756–57.

64. RID to Blackmore, January 31, 1877 (No. 917, MNM).

65. RID to Blackmore, February 3, 1877 (No. 918, MNM).

66. RID to Blackmore, January 31, 1877 (No. 917, MNM).

67. "Recent Publications," *Atlantic Monthly* 29 (June 1877), 757.

68. "Literary Notices," *Eclectic Magazine* 25 (April 1877), 504.

69. "Literary Notices," *Popular Science Monthly* 10 (April 1877), 754.

70. Thoreau, *The Illustrated Walden*, p. 3.

Chapter 14

1. Dodge was on court-martial duty between October 19 and 27; the conversation summarized here occurred on October 29 (Omaha Barracks Post Return, October 1876; RID Journal, October 31, 1876—*PREJ*, p. 49).

The fullest account of Crook's campaign, the Powder River Expedition, is Greene, *Morning Star Dawn*. Other important sources of information include Bourke, "Mackenzie's Last Fight"; Smith, *Sagebrush Soldier*, and *PREJ*.

2. Dodge copied the telegraphed messages into his journal entry for October 31, 1876, beginning the first of his four journals describing the campaign; see *PREJ*, p. 50.

3. A narrative history of the Sioux War of 1876–1877 is Robinson, *A Good Year to Die*. Contemporary accounts include Bourke, *On the Border with Crook*, pp. 241–423; and Finerty, *War-Path and Bivouac*. Other standard discussions of events during the period include Vaughn, *With Crook at the Rosebud*; Utley, *Frontier Regulars*, pp. 236–79; and Greene, *Slim Buttes* and *Yellowstone Command*. For a summary account of U.S. military operations during the war, see Greene, ed., "The Great Sioux War: A Military Perspective," in *Battles and Skirmishes of the Great Sioux War*, pp. xv–xxvi.

4. One of the accused officers, Captain Henry E. Noyes, Second Cavalry, was tried shortly afterward and given a light sentence. The trial of Colonel Reynolds and Captain Alexander Moore, Third Cavalry, was delayed until January 1877. See Robinson, *General Crook and the Western Frontier*, pp. 169–72.

5. RID Journal, undated entry (*PREJ*, p. 173).

6. The other two commands, operating from within the Department of Dakota, were under Brigadier General Alfred H. Terry and Colonel John Gibbon, Seventh Infantry.

7. A useful volume detailing the locations of engagements in this year-long conflict is Hedren, *Traveler's Guide to the Great Sioux War*. For the Rosebud and Custer battles, see pp. 48, 52, 63.

8. RID Journal Four (*PREJ*, p. 174).

9. Robinson, *A Good Year to Die*, p. 243.

10. See Greene, *Slim Buttes*, pp. 40–46.

11. Mills, "The Indian Campaign," *New York Times*, October 11, 1876, p. 5. See also Finerty, *War-Path and Bivouac*, p. 49; King, *Campaigning with Crook*, pp. 57, 130; Bourke, *On the Border with Crook*, p. 370; Robinson, *Bad Hand*, p. 102.

12. Increasing the proportion, this same writer went on to declare that one hundred infantry "will 'stand off' one thousand savages when mounted" ("From the Indian Country," *Philadelphia Press*, November 7, 1876, p. 2—Scrapbook of Mrs. George Crook, Crook-Kennan Papers, USAMHI). The same article is pasted into Bourke's diary, vol. 16, December 28, 1876–January 3, 1877 (Bourke Papers, USMA).

13. RID Journal, November 10, 1876 (*PREJ*, p. 57).

14. Bourke, *On the Border with Crook*, pp. 130, 158, 284; Greene, "George Crook" in *Soldiers West*, ed. Hutton, pp. 121–22; Robinson, *General Crook and the Western Frontier*, pp. 86, 92, 98, 127. See also Crook, *Autobiography*, pp. 177–78; Greene, *Slim Buttes*, pp. 57–58.

15. Biographical accounts of Mackenzie include Nohl, "Bad Hand"; Pierce, *The Most Promising Young Officer*; and Robinson, *Bad Hand*.

16. Hedren, *Fort Laramie in 1876*, pp. 170–71.

17. "The Indian Campaign," *New York Times*, October 11, 1876, p. 5. See also "Gen. Crook's Campaign," *New York Tribune*, October 2, 1876, p. 1; Hutton, "Philip H. Sheridan," in *Soldiers West*, p. 92.

18. For description of the winter clothing distributed for use on the Powder River Expedition, see McChristian, *The United States Army in the West,* pp. 157, 173–77.

19. Bourke, Diary, December 16, 1876 (Bourke Papers, USMA); Crook estimated the amount required at 26,000 pounds per day (Greene, *Morning Star Dawn*, p. 75).

20. A map showing the anticipated operations by Crook and Miles is located in Greene, *Morning Star Dawn*, p. [2].

21. "I prefer to have direct comd but cant help myself," he wrote, perhaps with a bit of humor (RID Journal, November 10, 1876—*PREJ*, p. 57).

22. Bourke, Diary, November 9, 1876 (Bourke Papers, USMA).

23. RID Journal, November 17, 1876 (*PREJ*, p. 68).

24. RID Journal, November 14, 17, 1876 (*PREJ*, pp. 62, 67–68).

25. RID Journal, November 19, 1876 (*PREJ*, p. 75).

26. Bourke, who recorded Frank White's translated speech, was impressed with his appearance: "Like most of the others, he wore the military uniform, but his face and head were grotesquely daubed with paint. Eyelids and Ears painted vermillion, which also daubed the median line of head and chin, forehead and cheek-bones, dark brown, and whole lower part of face, yellow. Hair, in two pig-tails, one on each side, wrapped in yellow tape. . . . [He had] a good face, prominent cheek bones, aquiline nose, large mouth, and frank, open eyes, not so piercing as one usually notices among the aborigines. His general expression is that of a far-seeing, judicious – lawgiver, one who takes note of all he has seen and whose advice may be relied on. Still, he is no lamb, as the stern lines of his countenance plainly show. If aroused, he would be a bad enemy" Bourke, Diary (Bourke Papers, USMA). The sentences preceding the ellipsis are from the entry for November 18, 1876; those that follow, November 21.

27. RID Journal Four (*PREJ*, p. 172).

28. RID Journal, November 16, 1876 (*PREJ*, p. 66).

29. *New York Herald*, October 2, 1876, p. 2.

30. RID Journal, November 16, 1876 (*PREJ*, pp. 65, 66).

31. Writing in the summer of 1876, a correspondent of the *Cheyenne Leader* commented on Crook's inexpressiveness: "While apparently frank to all who approach him, he is never communicative, except occasionally to his aids. To all others he is a Sphinx" (undated clipping in the scrapbook of Mrs. George Crook, Crook-Kennan Papers, USAMHI).

32. Circular 3, November 22, 1876, Headquarters, Infantry and Artillery Battalions (PRE Field Records, DP).

33. RID Journal, November 23, 1876 (*PREJ*, p. 82); Greene, *Morning Star Dawn*, pp. 81–84; Bourke, "Mackenzie's Last Fight," p. 13. The latter work, which originally appeared in *Journal of the Military Service Institution* (1890), was reprinted as a pamphlet, with new pagination, in the same year. The latter text, itself reprinted in 1970, is cited here.

34. RID Journal, November 23, 1876 (*PREJ*, p. 82).

35. Among his own people this Indian leader was known as Morning Star, but the Sioux and nineteenth-century Americans knew him as Dull Knife. Both names have their validity, but I have elected to use the one by which Dodge knew him, Dull Knife.

36. In his diary entry for November 30, Bourke wrote a summary account of the battle, recalling conditions during its most intense stage: "It would be tedious to enumerate all the narrow escapes. It would be easier to say that everybody had one or more. General Mackenzie was constantly and, to my mind, often needlessly, exposed. Those officers who served on his staff that morning will long remember the whistling of the bullets flying about their heads as they carried the General's orders from point to point" (Bourke Papers, USMA).

37. The most authoritative account of the Dull Knife battle is Greene, *Morning Star Dawn*, pp. 106–40, which incorporates information from many sources representing both sides of the engagement.

38. RID Journal, November 26, 1876 (*PREJ*, pp. 87–88).

39. RID Journal, November 28, 1876 (*PREJ*, p. 91).

40. RID Journal, November 28, 1876 (*PREJ*, pp. 91–92). Bourke later characterized the rapid movement by Dodge and his troops, "twenty-six miles over the frozen, slippery ground in twelve hours, much of the distance by night," as a "wonderful march" (*On the Border with Crook*, p. 393).

41. Roche, "The Indian War," *New York Herald*, November 29, 1876, p. 7; "M'Kenzie's Victory," December 1, 1876, p. 3; and "General Mackenzie' Fight," December 11, 1876, p. 6.

42. RID Journal, November 30, 1876 (*PREJ*, p. 98).

43. RID Journal, November 29, 1876 (*PREJ*, p. 97). For Dodge's published account of the Dull Knife battle, see *OWI*, pp. 494–99.

44. RID Journal, November 30, 1876 (*PREJ*, p. 100).

45. RID Journal, December 1, 1876 (*PREJ*, p. 101).

46. Bourke copied these messages, both dated December 3, into the PRE Order Book, p. 67, and also into his diary for December 4, 1876 (Bourke Papers, USMA).

47. RID Journal, December 5, 1876 (*PREJ*, pp. 107–108).

48. Clipping in Bourke Diary No. 17, marked as from the *Cheyenne Sun*, December 28, 1876 (Bourke Papers, USMA). The same text appeared in *ANJ*, December 30, 1876, p. 325, where it was attributed to "the *Tribune* reporter."

49. Bourke, "Mackenzie's Last Fight," p. 36.

50. RID Journal, December 7, 1876 (*PREJ*, p. 113).

51. Bourke, Diary, December 22, 1876 (Bourke Papers, USMA); Bourke, "Mackenzie's Last Fight," pp. 14, 40–41; Bourke, *On the Border with Crook*, pp. 138, 150, 154, 166, 244; Robinson, *General Crook and the Western Frontier*, p. 117; Hooker, *The Bullwhacker*, p. 51.

52. RID Journal, December 8, 1876 (*PREJ*, p. 115).

53. See RID Journal, December 11, 1876 (*PREJ*, pp. 118–22).

54. See *New York Herald*, December 23, 1876, p. 6; *ANJ*, December 30, 1876, p. 325. Captain Randall and the Crows might well have perished in a severe storm, had they not happened upon a small herd of buffalo. They shot some of the animals and thrust their legs into the carcasses for warmth, subsisting for a time on raw meat.

55. RID Journal, December 15, 1876 (*PREJ*, p. 127).

56. RID Journal, November 30, 1876 (*PREJ*, p. 99).

57. RID Journal, December 20, 1876 (*PREJ*, p. 133); RID to William Blackmore, January 31, 1877 (No. 917, MNM).

58. Bourke, Diary, December 20, 1876 (Bourke Papers, USMA); Greene, *Morning Star Dawn*, pp. 163–64; RID Journal, December 20, 1876 (*PREJ*, p. 130). In a reprise of an incident between him and Frank White almost a decade before, on this day Dodge was offered the granulated liver of a just-killed elk by a Pawnee named Ralph Weeks. Upon his declining the gift, according to Bourke "Ralph looked at him with an air of compassion and then swallowed the mess himself, leaving nothing but the dirty handkerchief" (Diary, December 11, 1876—Bourke Papers, USMA). See also Danker, *Man of the Plains*, p. 235.

59. RID Journal, December 21, 1876 (*PREJ*, p. 134).

60. RID Journal, December 21, 1876 (*PREJ*, pp. 134–36).

61. RID Journal, December 22, 1876 (*PREJ*, p. 138).

62. RID Journal, December 7, 1876 (*PREJ*, pp. 113–14).

63. "No one frozen today," he added, "which is a wonder" (RID Journal, December 23, 1876—*PREJ*, p. 142).

64. RID Journal, December 28, 1876 (*PREJ*, p. 155).

65. RID Journal, December 24, 1876 (*PREJ*, pp. 142–45).

66. Bourke, "Mackenzie's Last Fight," p. 42.

67. Dodge recounted this confrontation twice, in his journal entry for December 25, 1876, (*PREJ*, pp. 147–48) and in the undated Journal Four (*PREJ*, pp. 177–78). The present account incorporates material from these complementary sources.

68. RID, "The Enlisted Soldier," p. 261.

69. RID Journal Four (*PREJ*, p. 178).

70. RID Journal, December 25, 1876 (*PREJ*, pp. 147–48).

71. RID Journal, December 26, 1876 (*PREJ*, pp. 151–52).

72. *ANJ*, January 20, 1877, pp. 372–73. Bourke, "Mackenzie's Last Fight," pp. 41–42.

73. RID Journal, December 26, 1876 (*PREJ*, pp. 150–51). Colonel Joseph J. Reynolds, Third Cavalry, would have agreed with Dodge's assessment. Shortly after the close of Crook's operations in the

previous March, Reynolds declared to General Sherman that "winter campaigns in this latitude should be prohibited. Cruelty is no name for them. The month of March has told on me more than any five years of my life" (Reynolds to WTS, April 11, 1876—Sherman Papers, LC).

74. RID Journal, December 26, 1876 (*PREJ*, p. 152).

75. In proceedings that continued through January 19, 1877, Reynolds was found guilty of the charges against him and sentenced to be suspended from his rank and command for one year. His subordinate, Captain Alexander Moore, Third Cavalry, was also found guilty and was sentenced to be suspended from command and confined to his post for six months. But in view of the officers' honorable records of service, President Grant remitted their sentences (AGO, GCMO 30 and 39, March 3, 1877). A discussion of the Reynolds-Moore court-martial proceedings is provided by Vaughn in *The Reynolds Campaign on Powder River*, pp. 166–90.

76. RID Journal, December 28, 1876 (*PREJ*, p. 157).

77. Bourke, Diary, December 28, 1876 (Bourke Papers, USMA).

78. Nohl, "Bad Hand," pp. 228–30; Pierce, *The Most Promising Young Officer*, p. 194; Robinson, *Bad Hand*, p. 232.

79. Order Book, Headquarters Infantry and Artillery Battalions (PRE Field Records, DP).

80. RID Journal, January 3, 1877 (*PREJ*, p. 167).

81. S.O. 164, DP, December 5, 1876, and S.O. 140, MDM, both reprinted in *ANJ*, December 23, 1876, p. 309.

82. RID Journal, January 6, 1877 (*PREJ*, p. 168).

83. RID Journal, January 6 and 7, 1877 (*PREJ*, p. 169).

84. RID Journal, January 8, 1877 (*PREJ*, p. 170).

85. See *OWI*, pp. 85, 492, 493–97.

86. RID Journal Four (*PREJ*, pp. 171–79).

Part 5

1. *Army and Navy Journal,* May 16, 1891, p. 649.

Chapter 15

1. The article had appeared in *ANJ*, December 2, 1876, p. 269; Dodge read it on December 27 (*PREJ*, p. 154).

2. "It was impossible that there should not be errors," Dodge wrote to his friend, "unless I could have proof-read myself, for no one but myself could possibly have known just what I wanted to say" (RID to Blackmore, February 3, 1877—No. 918, MNM).

3. Fort Riley Post Returns, February–April 1877; RID ACP File, AGO; *ANJ*, March 10, 1877, p. 493.

4. See *PNA*, pp. 31–32, 391–92, 400 n. 33.

5. For example, in the section on hunting, Dodge four times changed the published "bay" to his own "bag," which Blackmore's copyist had mistranscribed. Only the author could have noticed that particular error, or indeed could have known that "ravines" at one point should be "streams," or "partially" elsewhere should be "specially," or "supported by lead-work" should be "supporting by bead-work." See "Textual Commentary," *PNA*, p. 397.

6. "Col Dodges Book—Hunting Grounds of the Great West" (No. 1196, MNM).

7. Statement of account between Chatto & Windus and Blackmore, October 16, 1877 (No. 1259, MNM).

8. Brayer, *William Blackmore*, pp. 317–18. The last known communication between Dodge and Blackmore was a letter written by the former on September 14, 1877 (No. 920, MNM).

9. "New Books," *ANJ*, January 20, 1877, p. 378.

10. *ANJ*, January 27, 1877, p. 390; February 3, p. 411; February 10, pp. 423–24. The quotation is from p. 429.

11. Compare Farrow, *Mountain Scouting*, pp. 101–2 to *PNA*, pp. 93–95; *Mounting Scouting*, pp. 213–27 to *PNA*, pp. 247–50 passim; *Mountain Scouting*, pp. 228–38 to *PNA*, pp. 343–47; *Mountain Scouting*,

pp. 339–48 to *PNA*, pp. 318–32. At one point in *Mountain Scouting*, pp. 103–4, Farrow acknowledges Dodge in introducing a quotation from *The Plains*.

12. Mallery to RID, December 1, 1879, and April 10, July 6, and November 18, 1880 (Graff). Mallery's *Sign Language among North American Indians* was issued as part of the Bureau of American Ethnology's *First Annual Report* (1881), pp. 263–552. For Mallery's use of Dodge's private letters in this work, see pp. 316–17, 335, 339–40.

13. Allen to RID, October 30, 1877 (Graff). Dodge informed General Sherman that he and Allen had conducted "a long & very interesting correspondence" about the buffalo (RID to WTS, November 8, 1884—Sherman Papers, LC). For Allen's use of *The Plains*, see *History of the American Bison*, pp. 464, 467, 469, 543–44, 555–57.

14. Baird to RID, March 22 and October 25, 1880; August 31, 1881; and May 4, 1882 (Graff). Dodge's contributions to the Smithsonian Institution collections are recorded in its *Annual Report . . . for the Year 1881*, p. 138; *Annual Report . . . for the Year 1882*, p. 239. In return for Dodge's cooperation, Baird forwarded to him complimentary copies of studies published by the Smithsonian Institution.

15. RID to Blackmore, January 31, February 3, and September 14, 1877 (Nos. 917, 918, 920, MNM).

16. Bourke, Diary, May 16, 1875 (Bourke Papers, USMA); *ANJ*, December 1, 1883, p. 347.

17. *New York Times*, February 26, 1879, p. 5.

18. Dodge informed Blackmore of Julia's wish for him to accompany her to England but added that "I am too poor just yet – & I am waiting until you are ready to make the 'grand tour' with me" (RID to Blackmore, January 31, 1877—No. 917, MNM).

19. *PREJ*, pp. 130, 168.

20. Fort Riley Post Return, January 1877; House, *Report of the SW*, 1877, p. 16; Frazer, *Forts of the West*, p. 57; Dobak, *Fort Riley*, pp. 112–13. A map showing the rail connections at Junction City to other towns and military posts in Kansas during the late 1870s is found in Dobak, *Fort Riley*, p. [2].

21. RID to AAG DMO, May 17, 1877, quoted in House, *Report of the SW*, 1877, p. 218; Inspector General to AG, March 21, 1877 (AGO LR).

22. RID to AAG DMO, June 3, 1877, quoted in *Report of the SW*, 1877, pp. 218–19; AAG MDM to AG, June 11, 1877 (AGO Reg LR).

23. Fort Riley Post Return, May 1877; House, *Report of the SW*, 1877, p. 219. The affair of the deteriorating bridge is further described in Dobak, *Fort Riley*, pp. 142–48; a photograph of the bridge is on p. 146.

24. Fort Riley Post Return, June 1877; Fort Leavenworth Post Return, June 1877. Dodge took post at Fort Leavenworth on June 13 in accordance with S.O. 107, DMO, June 7, 1877.

25. House, *Report of the SW*, 1877, pp. 219–20.

26. Fort Leavenworth Post Return, July 1877; Frazer, *Forts of the West*, p. 56.

27. See House, *Report of the SW*, 1877, pp. 58, 63–64.

28. An account of this emergency and the army's response to it in the eastern states appeared in *ANJ*, July 28, 1877, pp. 817–20.

29. Twenty-third Infantry Regimental Returns, June–July 1877; *Report of the SW*, 1877, pp. 62–63; *ANJ*, August 4, 1877, p. 829.

30. Twenty-third Infantry Regimental Return, June 1877; House, *Report of the SW*, 1877, p. 62.

31. G.O. 9, DMO, reprinted in *ANJ*, July 21, 1877, p. 797.

32. RID to Blackmore, September 14, 1877 (No. 920, MNM).

33. Marszalek, *Sherman*, pp. 388–90; *ANJ*, February 3, 1877, p. 409.

34. *ANJ*, February 5, 1876, p. 417; February 3, 1877, p. 411.

35. The questions were included in House, *Report of a Subcommittee . . . Reorganization of the Army* (1878), pp. 22–27, cited hereafter as *Reorganization of the Army*.

36. See *Reorganization of the Army*, pp. 22–27 (Schofield), 27–35 (Pope).

37. *Reorganization of the Army*, pp. 147–48. In 1876 Dodge was required by the Ordnance Department to pay the money value of eighty cartridges he had ordered expended to kill wild beef cattle during the Black Hills Expedition. He did so, but in protest he called the attention of the War Department to the injustice being done officers of the line like him by the staff bureaus' "merely technical" interpretations of policy such as this (AGO Reg LR). General Sherman supported him unreservedly. "It is simply absurd

[to say] that General [*sic*] Dodge had not the absolute right to expend his ammunition as he did in killing his beef cattle," he wrote. "Every officer of the Army does this very thing, and always has done, and the order of the Comdg Officer *must* be final, unless there be waste under the 15th and 16th Articles of War" (Endorsement No. 31, June 2, 1876—Sherman Papers, LC).

38. Pollock to AG, November 28, 1875, with endorsements; William W. Belknap to House of Representatives, December 30, 1875 (AGO LR).

39. "Our Non-Commissioned Officers," *ANJ*, February 5, 1876, pp. 416–17.

40. *ANJ*, December 1, 1877, p. 252. Pollock's letter was reprinted in *Reorganization of the Army*, pp. 141–42. See also *ANJ*, February 3, 1877, pp. 408–409.

41. *Reorganization of the Army*, pp. 139–40. The reprinted text of Pollock's original proposal followed Davis's letter, pp. 140–41.

42. Coffman, *The Old Army*, p. 348.

43. Marszalek, *Sherman*, pp. 432–34. The text of the Banning bill was reprinted in *ANJ*, February 9, 1878, pp. 421–22.

44. Schutz and Trennery, *Abandoned by Lincoln*, pp. 109, 175; Ellis, *General Pope and U.S. Indian Policy*, pp. 206–8; *ITJ*, p. 151; *ANJ*, April 12, 1879, p. 656.

45. In 1862 a journalist wrote of Pope that he "talks rapidly and is rather fond of it, as an exercise or diversion" (quoted in Schutz and Trenerry, *Abandoned by Lincoln*, p. 169). For Pope as an orator, see *ANJ*, November 22, 1879, p. 303. Colonel Edwin P. Pendleton, who met Dodge in 1879 following his graduation from West Point in that year, later described him as "a famous raconteur and brilliant conversationalist" (Shirk, "Military Duty on the Western Frontier," p. 121).

46. A "Bird's Eye View of Fort Leavenworth, 1881" is reproduced in Hunt and Lorence, *History of Fort Leavenworth*, opposite p. 132. See also Schindler, *A Guide. Description of Fort Leavenworth.*

47. RID Journal, January 25, 1879 (*ITJ*, pp. 151–52).

48. See Sheridan to WTS, December 24, 1878 (AGO LR). In March 1880 Sherman was attempting to obtain answers from the secretary of war to queries he had received from Pope, when to his alarm he received another set. He telegraphed to Pope, "please don't ask any more questions till the old ones are answered" (WTS to Pope, March 6, 1880—AGO LS).

49. RID, "To Officers and Ex-Officers of the Army," February 8, 1878, in "Frontier Army Life," *ANJ*, February 23, 1878, p. 459.

50. Dodge continued: "The people of the country are not hostile to the Army, but deceived by the arts & lies of demagogues, they regard us as a lazy set of loafers, whom it would be wise to get rid of. Such a book as I propose will have a tendency to set us right before the Country & may do us all good" (RID to Church, March 12, 1878—Church Papers, LC).

51. "Author's Preface," *OWI*, p. vi; *PREJ*, pp. 133–34.

52. Osborne, "The Exile of the Nez Percé," p. 452; *OWI*, p. 124; Fort Leavenworth Post Return, December 1877.

53. The pursuit of the Nez Perce Indians and the events leading up to their journey east from their homeland are described in Beal, *"I Will Fight No More Forever,"* and Greene, *Nez Perce Summer*.

54. Dodge later described Randall as one "who, in knowledge of Indians and success in their management, is second to no man on the frontier" (*OWI*, p. 111).

55. "Religion among Indians," *ANJ*, July 6, 1878, p. 778; see above, chapter 6. Dodge later incorporated the anecdote in *OWI*, pp. 111–12.

56. Joseph, "An Indian's Views of Indian Affairs," *North American Review* 128 (1880), 412–33, quoted in Osborne, "The Exile of the Nez Percé," p. 457.

57. The official correspondence relating to this subject forms a consolidated file, 1620 AGO 1878, available in NARA microform publication M666, Roll 401.

58. Dorsey to G. W. McCrary, SW, March 1, 1878 (AGO LR); Dorsey to WTS, March 1, 1878 (AGO LR).

59. WTS endorsement, March 5, 1878, of Schurz to SW, March 2, 1878 (AGO LR).

60. WTS endorsement, March 27, 1878, of Schurz to SW, March 25, 1878 (AGO LR).

61. Schurz to SW, April 8, 1878 (AGO LR).

62. Hatch endorsement, April 4, 1878, of B. M. Thomas to Hatch, April 1, 1878 (AGO LR).

63. Hatch to Pope, April 18, 1878 (AGO LR).

64. Hatch to Pope, April 19, 1878 (AGO LR).

65. Pope to Sheridan, April 18, 1878; Sheridan to E. D. Townsend, April 18, 1878 (AGO LR).

66. William M. Leeds, Acting Commissioner of Indian Affairs, to SI, April 19, 1878 (AGO LR).

67. Sheridan to E. D. Townsend, April 20, 1878; Townsend to Sheridan, April 20, 1878 (AGO LR). The officer named to served in Dodge's place on the St. Louis board was Captain John J. Coppinger, Twenty-third Infantry.

68. E. R. Platt, AAG DMO, to C.O. Fort Leavenworth [RID], April 23, 1878 (AGO LR).

69. G.O. 2, Fort Hays, July 24, 1878.

70. E. A. Hayt to SI, April 30 and May 28, 1878 (AGO LR); S.O. 82, DMO, May 8, 1878 (AGO LR), reprinted in part in *ANJ*, May 18, 1878, p. 657.

71. E. D. Townsend to Sheridan, May 9, 1878; S.O. 84, DMO, May 10, 1878 (AGO LR).

72. Weaver to E. A. Hayt, May 6, 1878 (AGO LR).

73. Endorsement No. 338, June 5, 1878 (Sherman Papers, LC).

74. C. Schurz to SW, July 10, 1878 (AGO LR).

75. Hatch to AAG DMO, July 19, 1878, in Pope to AAG MDM, July 19, 1878 (AGO LR).

76. RID to Church, August 5, 1878—Church Papers, LC.

77. Fort Leavenworth Post Return, July 1878; Fort Hays Post Return, July 1878; RID to AAG DMO, July 22, 1878 (Fort Hays LS); *ANJ*, July 27, 1878, p. 81.

78. Oliva, *Fort Hays*, pp. 41–45; Frazer, *Forts of the West*, p. 54; Keim, *Sheridan's Troopers on the Borders*, pp. 22–24.

79. See *ANJ*, May 11, 1878, p. 650.

80. RID to Chief Commissary of Subsistence, DMO, August 11, 1878; RID to J. T. Odell, Assistant Superintendent, Kansas Pacific Rail Road, August 27, 1878 (Fort Hays LS).

81. First Lieutenant Charles Hay, Post Adjutant, to Wilson, August 25, 1878 (Fort Hays LS).

82. RID to Adjutant, Twenty-third Infantry, July 22, 1878 (Fort Hays LS). During the spring Dodge had supervised rifle target practice at Fort Leavenworth, with superior results. He forwarded a tabular summary of the several companies' shooting records to the *Army and Navy Journal* for publication in its April 13 issue, p. 569.

83. RID to Church, August 5, 1878 (Church Papers, LC).

84. Senate, *Testimony . . . Concerning the Removal of the Northern Cheyenne Indians,* hereafter cited as *Removal of the Northern Cheyenne Indians*, p. 113.

Chapter 16

1. See chapter 14.

2. In *The Cheyenne and Arapaho Ordeal*, Donald Berthrong recounts the experiences of the Northern Cheyennes in the three decades that followed their forced move to Indian Territory.

3. General Crook denied that the Northern Cheyennes had received such a promise; see *Removal of the Northern Cheyenne Indians*, pp. 224–25. Nevertheless, the Indians clearly believed they had been assured of the freedom to return to their homeland if they chose.

4. Lawton to Post Adjutant, Fort Sill, October 11, 1877, with endorsements (OIA LR, C&A).

5. Schurz to SW, October 20, 1877 (AGO LR). Schurz was quoting from a letter by William Nicholson of the Central Superintendency at Lawrence, Kansas, to the Commissioner of Indian Affairs.

6. Carriker, *Fort Supply*, pp. 117–18.

7. Pope to AAG MDM, July 11, 1877, with endorsements (AGO LR).

8. Mackenzie to Mizner, September 15, 1877 (AGO LR).

9. John D. Miles to Mizner, September 20, 1878 (OIA LR, C&A).

10. Miles to E. A. Hayt, September 10, 1878 (OIA LR, C&A).

11. Carriker, *Fort Supply*, pp. 122–23; Wright, "The Pursuit of Dull Knife," pp. 147–48. Volumes devoted to the events described in this chapter include Sandoz, *Cheyenne Autumn*; Hoig, *Perilous Pursuit*; Monnett, *Tell Them We Are Going Home*. Much testimony by persons involved in events leading up to the

outbreak and by participants on both sides in the escape and pursuit was published in *Removal of the Northern Cheyenne Indians*, pp. 45–47, 53–152.

12. *Removal of the Northern Cheyenne Indians*, p. 113; Hoig, "The Northern Cheyenne Exodus," pp. 86–94.

13. Carriker, *Fort Supply*, pp. 123–24; *Removal of the Northern Cheyenne Indians*, pp. 127–18.

14. Mizner to Pope, September 10, 1878 (AGO LR).

15. Sheridan to AG, September 12, 1878, transmitting Pope's report on his disposition of troops (AGO LR).

16. Wright, "The Pursuit of Dull Knife," pp. 148–49.

17. Pope to Sheridan, September 18, 1878 (AGO LR).

18. Sheridan to WTS, September 19, 1878 (OIA LR, C&A).

19. AAG DMO to RID, September 18, 1878 (Fort Hays LR).

20. This journal, with entries dated from September 18 to October 13, 1878, is the first of eight by RID included in *ITJ*.

21. For partial texts of Van Voast's telegraph messages to Dodge, see *ITJ*, p. 18, notes 15 and 16.

22. RID Journal, September 25, 1878 (*ITJ*, p. 22). Later in the entry Dodge wrote: "I am not 'spilin' for a fight, but I want the Comd. of this exp[editio]n."

23. RID Journal, September 27, 1878 (*ITJ*, p. 24). On September 25 Pope had directed Davis to assume general charge of operations within the Department of the Missouri to intercept and capture the fleeing Indians (DMO LS).

24. RID Journal, September 28, 1878 (*ITJ*, p. 25). In naval usage, a chase from astern is proverbially a long one.

25. Davis to AAG DMO, September 29, 1878 (MDM Cheyenne Outbreak Special File).

26. RID Journal, September 29, 1878 (*ITJ*, pp. 26–28); Davis to RID, September 29, 1878 (DMO LR). In the fairy story of Hop o' My Thumb, a magical pair of boots enables the wearer to cover seven leagues at each step.

27. RID Journal, October 2, 1878 (*ITJ*, p. 32).

28. RID Journal, October 3, 1878 (*ITJ*, p. 33).

29. RID Journal, October 3, 1878 (*ITJ*, p. 8). As William Chalfant has shown, the Northern Cheyennes had reason to take vengeance on the inhabitants of the Sappa country; see *Cheyennes at Dark Water Creek*, especially pp. 174–75.

30. RID Journal, October 4, 1878 (*ITJ*, pp. 35–36).

31. Davis had written: "The indications are that the Indians are pushing for the Whiteman's or Frenchman's fork of the Republican, with one day's march ahead of Mauck. Yet it is possible they may retreat in the direction of Fort Macpherson [northeastward]—in either case on receipt of this you will assume command of Major Dallas' Column, as soon as possible, and push forward in pursuit without regard to Capt. Mauck's movement as far as the U.P. R. R. at least, and report to both Genls. Pope and Crook" (Enclosure, RID to AAG DMO, October 12—DMO LR).

32. RID to P. T. Brodrick, Post Adjutant, Fort Hays, October 5, 1878, enclosed with Davis to AAG DMO, October 17, 1878 (DMO LR).

33. Pope to Sheridan, October 8, 1878 (MDM Cheyenne Outbreak Special File).

34. WTS to Sheridan, October 7, 1878 (AGO LS); Pope to AAG MDM, October 8, 1878 (Cheyenne Outbreak Special File); House, *Report of the SW*, 1878, p. 43.

35. Dodge's private assessment of the failed campaign in its immediate aftermath forms part of his lengthy journal entry for October 11, 1878 (*ITJ*, pp. 41–43).

36. AAG DMO to RID, October 10, 1878 (DMO LS).

37. RID to AAG DMO, October 12, 1878 (DMO LR).

38. Pope to AAG MDM, October 10, 1878 (DMO LS).

39. In proceedings at Fort Supply on March 10 and 14, 1879, Captains William Hemphill and Sebastian Gunther were acquitted of charges brought against them for their activities in the early stages of the chase. See *ANJ*, April 12, 1879, p. 633; April 19, 1879, p. 652; and April 26, 1879, pp. 671–72. However, on March 24 a court at the same post found Captain Joseph Rendlebrock guilty on special specifications

connected with his field duty between September 14 and October 13, 1878. He was sentenced to dismissal, but on recommendation of the court and subsequently General Sherman, the punishment was remitted in view of his long and creditable service and poor physical condition. On June 30, 1879, Rendlebrock was ordered to appear before a Retiring Board, and shortly thereafter he was removed from active duty. See *ANJ*, July 1, 1879, p. 884; AGO, GCMO 36 (1879).

40. RID Journal, October 13, 1878 (*ITJ*, pp. 45–47).

41. Fry, "Killed by a Brother Officer (Nelson and Davis)," in *Military Miscellanies*, pp. 486–505; the quotation is from p. 489.

42. See AAG to Jeff. C. Davis, February 5, 1873, with endorsement by WTS (HQA LS).

43. RID to AAG DMO, October 12, 1878 (DMO Reg LR).

44. Davis to AAG DMO, October 17, 1878 (DMO LR). The dispositions of the statements by Davis and Dodge are shown in DMO Reg LR.

45. The text of Dodge's previously unpublished account of the Northern Cheyennes comprises Appendix A in *ITJ*, pp. 436–44.

Chapter 17

1. An account of the peaceful surrender of Little Wolf and his people, by Second Lieutenant William P. Clark, Second Cavalry, is found in House, *Report of the SW*, 1879, pp. 55–58. See also Powell, *People of the Sacred Mountain*, II, pp. 1245–61.

2. A lucid account of the army's foray into Nebraska sand hills, written before the Northern Cheyennes had yet been discovered, is First Lieutenant John G. Bourke to AAG DP, October 15, 1878 (MDM Cheyenne Outbreak Special File). For a report of the capture, see George Crook to Philip H. Sheridan, October 26, 1878, with enclosures (MDM Cheyenne Outbreak Special File); see also *ANJ*, November 2, 1878, p. 201; and November 9, 1878, pp. 217–18.

3. Sheridan endorsement, Crook to Sheridan, October 26, 1878 (OIA LR, C&A); Senate, *Letter . . . in Relation to the Escape of the Northern Cheyenne Indians from Fort Robinson,* hereafter, *Escape of the Northern Cheyenne Indians*, pp. 2–6.

4. Sheridan to WTS, November 13, 1878; S.O. 93, DP, October 14, 1878; John P. Hatch to Mauck, November 28, 1878 (OIA LR, C&A); *ANJ*, November 30, 1878, p. 267; *ITJ*, p. 96.

5. Mizner to AAG DMO, September 19, 1878 (DMO LR).

6. Miles to Hayt, September 24, 1878 (OIA LR, C&A). This message was included in *Escape of the Northern Cheyenne Indians*, pp. 35–36.

7. Lewis to AAG DMO, September 15, 1878 (MDM Cheyenne Outbreak Special File).

8. Miles to Hayt, October 2, 1878 (OIA LR, C&A). The term *squaw man* denoted a white man married to an Indian woman, but it carried connotations of lawlessness, opportunism, and moral degeneracy.

9. "The Refractory Cheyennes," *New York Times*, October 15, 1878, p. 4.

10. Miles to Hayt, November 1, 1878 (OIA LR, C&A). In this communication Miles listed the names of all the Indians who had left the reservation. Except for the list, his letter was published in *Escape of the North Cheyenne Indians*, pp. 36–38.

11. Hayt to SI, November 16, 1878 (*Removal of the Northern Cheyenne Indians*, pp. 290–91).

12. Miles to Hayt, December 9, 1878 (OIA LR, C&A).

13. The bitterness revealed itself at the highest official levels. In his annual report, Secretary Schurz publicly attacked General Sheridan, who had pointed out instances of the Indian Bureau's mismanagement. See "The Army and the Indian Office," *ANJ*, November 30, 1878, pp. 372–73.

14. AAG MDM to AG, December 17, 1878 (AGO Reg LR).

15. AAG MDM to AG, December 30, 1878, with enclosure (AGO Reg LR).

16. Manypenny to Hayt, December 19, 1878 (OIA LR, C&A).

17. WTS to AG, January 2, 1879 (AGO LR).

18. Anthony to Sheridan, November 11, 1878 (AGO LR).

19. WTS endorsement, Sheridan to AG, November 18, 1878 (AGO LR).

20. RID to J. T. Odell, Assistant Superintendent, Kansas Pacific Railroad, November 13, 1878 (Fort Hays LS); RID Journal, December 10, 1878 (*ITJ*, p. 104).

21. RID Journal, November 3, 1878 (*ITJ*, p. 62).

22. RID's record of the trip, with daily entries from November 5 to December 10, 1878, is Journal Two in *ITJ*, pp. 70–105.

23. S.O. 197, DMO, October 30, 1878; Fort Hays Post Return, November 1878; *ANJ*, November 9, 1878, p. 217.

24. RID Journal, November 5, 1878 (*ITJ*, p. 71); RID, *A Living Issue*, pp. 25–26.

25. RID Journal, November 10, 1878 (*ITJ*, p. 74).

26. See *ITJ*, pp. 63–67. A summary of Davidson's military career can be found in *ANJ*, July 2, 1881, p. 999.

27. "I do hate a Ct Martial of all things" (RID Journal, December 14, 1876—*PREJ*, p. 125).

28. See RID, "The Enlisted Soldier," pp. 260–61, 279–80, 286, 288.

29. War Department, Office of the Judge-Advocate General, Registers of Army General Courts-Martial (NARA, RG 153); *ANJ*, July 20, 1878, p. 805.

30. *ANJ*, August 31, 1878, p. 52; Division of Military Justice to Lee, July 31, 1878 (AGO LR).

31. Baldwin to AG, August 8 and September 22, 1878 (AGO LR).

32. Fort Sill Post Returns, September and October 1878; GCMO 22, AGO, April 10, 1879.

33. RID Journal, November 19 and 20, 1878 (*ITJ*, pp. 77–78).

34. President Hayes commuted Lee's sentence generously, to a single forfeiture of fifty dollars (GCMO 22, AGO, April 10, 1879). For further developments in Lee's campaign against his commanding officer, see *ITJ*, pp. 65–67.

35. "Everybody is quarrelling at the Post," Dodge wrote after the event. "It is in a most wretched condition socially. Faults on every side" (Journal, November 19, 1878—*ITJ*, p. 78).

36. RID Journal, November 20, 1878 (*ITJ*, p. 78).

37. Enclosures, SW to SI, December 2, 1878—OIA LR, C&A.

38. RID Journal, November 22, 1878 (*ITJ*, p. 88).

39. *ANJ*, October 20, 1883, p. 224; September 3, 1887, p. 99; and January 5, 1889, p. 367.

40. Hamersley, *Records of Living Officers*, pp. 308–309.

41. This was the Canadian River, not the North Fork of the Canadian, which lay twelve miles further north. A contemporary characterized the former as "a most treacherous stream, liable to rise at any moment, and whose channel changes from hour to hour" (*ANJ*, December 3, 1881, p. 381). See also Seger, *Early Days among the Cheyenne and Arapahoe Indians*, p. 109.

42. RID Journal, November 23, 1878 (*ITJ*, pp. 81–84). "Verily," Dodge wrote in another of his Bible-inspired aphorisms, "the folly well punishes the fool" (p. 84); see Proverbs 13:16, 22:15.

43. RID Journal, November 24, 1878 (*ITJ*, pp. 86–87).

44. House, *Revised Army Regulations*, p. 103.

45. Mizner was then stationed at Fort McPherson, Nebraska. See G. M. Dodge, *How We Built the Union Pacific Railway*, p. 19; Hamersley, *Records of Living Officers*, p. 121.

46. RID Journal, November 24, 1878 (*ITJ*, pp. 86–87); see House, *Revised Army Regulations*, p. 103.

47. RID Journal, November 26, 1878 (*ITJ*, pp. 88–90).

48. De Benneville Randolph Keim, who witnessed the hunt, recounted it in his *Sheridan's Troopers on the Borders*, a classic account of that winter's military campaign against the Cheyennes and allied tribes. According to Keim, in one night's shooting the general's party bagged sixty-three birds, Sheridan himself claiming eleven (pp. 303–4). See also Strong, *Canadian River Hunt*, p. 23; Aldridge, *Life on a Ranch*, pp. 162–66.

49. RID Journal, November 27–December 1, 1878 (*ITJ*, pp. 90–95).

50. AAG DMO to C.O. Fort Dodge, November 29, 1878 (OIA LR, C&A).

51. *Removal of the Northern Cheyenne Indians*, p. vi.

52. Pope to AAG MDM, December 19, 1878 (OIA LR, C&A). See also Pope to AAG MDM, November 29, 1878 (OIA LR, C&A), which confirms Pope's later account of the position taken by officials at the Cheyenne and Arapaho Agency. The quoted phrases are from Pope's order of November 29 to Mauck (OIA LR, C&A).

53. Wilder, "The Experience of Major Mauck in Disarming a Band of Cheyennes on the North Fork of the Canadian River in 1878," in *The Papers of the Order of Indian Wars*, pp. 91–92.

54. RID Journal, December 2, 1878 (*ITJ*, pp. 97–98).

55. RID Journal, December 3–5, 1878 (*ITJ*, pp. 99–100).

56. RID Journal, December 7, 1878 (*ITJ*, pp. 101–102).

57. Tremaine was a witness before a Retiring Board then meeting at Fort Leavenworth (*ANJ*, December 7, 1878, p. 283).

58. S.O. 40, Fort Hays, December 2, 1878. For the hunting excursions Dodge and Second Lieutenant Cowles took together, see Jordan, "A Soldier's Life on the Indian Frontier," p. 153. The wagon road between Forts Hays and Dodge had been in existence since 1867, but completion of the Atchison, Topeka and Santa Fe Railroad to Dodge City had greatly reduced its military value. See Clapsaddle, "The Fort Hays–Fort Dodge Road," pp. 101–12.

59. RID Journal, December 8, 1878 (*ITJ*, p. 103).

60. RID Journal, following the entry for December 10, 1878 (*ITJ*, p. 104).

61. In August 1879 General Sherman directed that permission given officers to hunt should not be charged to them as leaves of absence. Hunting was to be encouraged, being "in many ways so advantageous to the Service." See G.O. 9, MDM, August 27, 1879; *ANJ*, September 4, 1880, p. 79.

Chapter 18

1. Hill P. Wilson to C.O. Fort Hays, October 30, 1878 (Fort Hays LR); S.O. 42, Fort Hays, December 18, 1878; Calvin W. Cowles to Post Adjutant, Fort Hays, November 27, 1878 (AGO Reg LR); RID to AAG DMO, December 12, 1878 (Fort Hays LS); RID endorsement, November 2, 1878 (Fort Hays LS). Mrs. O'Keefe, who had been discharged for bad conduct, was the wife of a private who had been transferred from Fort Leavenworth without consultation with his new company commander. Dodge suspected the transfer was a means of "getting rid of a troublesome woman."

2. House, *Revised Army Regulations*, p. 98.

3. For example, on June 23 he drew attention to a conflict between paragraphs of the *Revised Army Regulations* of 1873 and Upton's *A New System of Infantry Tactics*, then in use as a textbook (AGO LR). See also AG to RID, July 11, 1878 (AGO LS).

4. RID Journal, April 13, 1879 (*ITJ*, p. 202).

5. RID Journal, November 18, 1878 (*ITJ*, p. 77).

6. In its "Home Markets" section, the *Leavenworth Times* quoted the current local price of potatoes at twenty-five cents per bushel between October 20 and 26. Peach blow potatoes were not listed as for sale until November 1, when they were quoted at fifty cents per bushel.

7. RID to Woodruff, October 31, 1878 (Fort Hays LS).

8. "Proceedings of a Board of Survey, Convened at Fort Hays, Kansas" [November 2, 1878] (Fort Hays LR).

9. Woodruff endorsement, November 2, enclosed with Gilman to RID, December 18, 1878 (Fort Hays LR).

10. The quotation is from RID to AAG DMO, December 19, 1878 (Fort Hays LS). Dodge explained here that he had lost the first letter he wrote Gilman.

11. House, *Revised Army Regulations*, pp. 101–2.

12. Gilman endorsement, November 6, 1878, with "Proceedings of a Board of Survey Convened at Fort Hays, Kansas" [November 2, 1878] (Fort Hays LR).

13. "Proceedings of a Board of Survey Convened at Fort Leavenworth, Kansas" [November 12, 1878] (Fort Hays LR).

14. See *ANJ*, November 23, 1878, p. 247; November 30, 1878, p. 267.

15. WTS to George W. McCrary, SW, December 7, 1878 (AGO LS). The power of staff departments even over departmental commanders had long been a sore point for General Pope. "I have never during my service known the Army to be reduced to such abject & humiliating subordination to the Staff Depts." he wrote General Sherman on October 12, 1872. "It seems to me that I have no more control over the administration of this Dept than I have over the administration of the Pacific RR & it will not be long before I cease to feel any interest in it" (Sherman Papers, LC). See also *Reorganization of the Army*, p. 28; *ANJ*, January 18, 1879, p. 409; Utley, *Frontier Regulars*, pp. 28–33.

16. Pope endorsement, December 16, "Proceedings of a Board of Survey, Convened at Fort Hays, Kansas" [November 2, 1878] (Fort Hays LR).

17. Gilman to RID, December 18, 1878 (Fort Hays LR).

18. RID to AAG DMO, December 19, 1878 (Fort Hays LS).

19. RID to Gilman, December 21, 1878 (Fort Hays LS).

20. Pope to AAG MDM, December 19, 1878 (OIA LR, C&A).

21. Sheridan to AG, November 19, 1878 (AGO LR).

22. Sheridan to WTS, December 24, 1878 (AGO LR).

23. Sheridan to WTS, December 27, 1878 (AGO LR).

24. Pope to Sheridan, December 26, 1878 (AGO LR).

25. Sheridan to AG, December 31, 1878 (AGO LR).

26. WTS to Sheridan, January 1, 1879 (AGO LR).

27. WTS endorsement of Pope to Sheridan, December 26, 1878 (AGO LR).

28. AAG DMO to C.O. Fort Hays, December 26, 1878 (Fort Hays LR).

29. Aboard the train that day, Dodge began a journal record of his experiences on this official errand, writing "Site for New Post" on the front cover of the notebook. The text, with entries dated December 31, 1878, to January 31, 1879, is Journal Three in *ITJ*, pp. 123–57.

30. "In all the world there is not a man I hate sufficiently to wish to condemn him to live on the Cimarron," he wrote. "So I dont recommend it very highly to Pope" (RID Journal, January 12, 1879—*ITJ*, p. 139).

31. RID Journal, January 6, 1879 (*ITJ*, p. 129).

32. *OWI*, p. 632. For other accounts of Chapman see *The Papers of the Order of Indian Wars*, pp. 90–91; Carriker, *Fort Supply*, pp. 97–100; *OWI*, pp. 628–32.

33. RID Journal, January 21, 1879 (*ITJ*, p. 148).

34. RID Journal, January 23, 1879 (*ITJ*, p. 149).

35. A copy of this report, dated at Fort Hays on January 22, 1879, is among the Dodge Papers (Graff).

36. RID to AAG DMO, February 9, 1879 (Fort Hays LS); RID endorsement of John F. Trout to AAG DMO, June 5, 1879 (CNFCR LS).

37. AAG MDM to AG, January 2, 1879 (AGO Reg LR).

38. AAG DMO to C.O. Fort Hays, January 3, 1879 (Fort Hays LR).

39. WTS to Sheridan, January 8, 1879; Sheridan to WTS, January 9, 1879; WTS to Sheridan, January 9, 1879 (AGO LR).

40. Official documents relating to the incident, in which thirty-five Northern Cheyennes had been recaptured and thirty killed by January 13, can be found in *Escape of the Northern Cheyenne Indians*, passim. Modern accounts include Grinnell, *The Fighting Cheyennes*, pp. 414–27; Sandoz, *Cheyenne Autumn*, pp. 194–230; Powell, *Sweet Medicine*, I, pp. 241–77, and *People of the Sacred Mountain*, II, pp. 1202–1208.

41. G.O. 9, MDM, December 30, 1878 (AGO Reg LR).

42. AAG MDM to AG, January 2, 1879 (AGO Reg LR).

43. The *Caldwell (Kansas) Commercial* described Little Chief in 1881 as possessing "more brain power than some of the white milksops the newspapers advertise as great statesmen. If we could only place a few Little Chiefs into Congress, it is possible the Indian question would be solved" (quoted in Hoig, *The Peace Chiefs*, p. 176).

44. Creel to AAG MDM, March 7, 1879 (AGO LR).

45. SW to SI, enclosing an affidavit by Clarke, January 4, 1879 (SW LS); Mizner to AAG DMO, April 12, 1879 (OIA LR, C&A). See also SW to SI, January 4, 1879, transmitting the text of a daunting speech to Mizner by Little Chief (SW LS).

46. Campbell to Ezra A. Hayt, March 5, 1879 (OIA LR, C&A).

47. *ANJ*, March 22, 1879, p. 587.

48. Twenty-third Infantry Regimental Return, February 1879; Fort Supply Post Return, February 1879; *ANJ*, February 1, 1879, pp. 452–53.

49. Documentation of Dodge's duties, in the order listed in the text, is as follows: RID to AAG DMO, February 10, 1879 (AGO Reg LR); RID to W. B. Strong, February 17, 1879 (Fort Hays LS); Circular 1, January 27, 1879 (Fort Hays Orders and Circulars); Ordnance Office, War Department, to RID, February

17, 1879 (Fort Hays LR); AAG DMO to C.O. Fort Hays, February 10, 1879 (Fort Hays LR) and RID to AAG DMO, February 15, 1879 (Fort Hays LS); RID to Surgeon General, February 5, 1879 (Fort Hays LS); RID to AG, February 7, 1879 (Fort Hays LS); RID to AAG DMO, February 15, 1879 (Fort Hays LS); RID to Chief Quartermaster DMO, February 4, 1879 (Fort Hays LS).

50. Sommer, "Cantonment North Fork of the Canadian River" (Thoburn Papers, Oklahoma Historical Society).

51. Twenty-third Infantry Regimental Returns, February and March 1879; Fort Supply Post Return, February 1879; CNFCR Post Return, March 1879.

52. RID to AAG DMO, March 8–10, 1879 (CNFCR LS).

53. In journal entries dated from March 16 to April 14, 1879, Dodge recorded the early stages of this effort. See Journal Four, *ITJ*, pp. 169–205.

54. RID Journal, March 30, 1879 (*ITJ*, p. 186).

55. RID Journal, April 6, 1879 (*ITJ*, p. 193).

56. Dodge had requested the exception on behalf of his men while still at Fort Hays (RID to AAG DMO, February 15, 1879—Fort Hays LS).

57. Elsewhere Dodge described an Indian "pipe or flute, ingeniously constructed" that conforms to the "Clarionet" referred to in this journal entry. "The only music on them is the repetition again and again of a few chords, low, slow, and sometimes very sweet and weird" (*OWI*, pp. 349–50).

58. RID Journal, March 25, 1879 (*ITJ*, pp. 181–83).

59. Randall's was one of three companies in the Department of the Missouri designated as mounted infantry, "services of mounted troops being absolutely necessary . . . and there not being any cavalry at the disposal of the Department Commander" (S.O. 66, DMO, April 6, 1879, reprinted in *ANJ*, April 19, 1879, p. 653).

60. On March 6, then at Fort Leavenworth, Randall had received orders to take post with his company at the new cantonment. On his way there he was to escort fourteen additional Northern Cheyenne prisoners to a point on the Wichita–Fort Reno trail, where he would be relieved of responsibility for them by a detachment from Fort Reno (S.O. 43, DMO, March 6, 1879).

61. See *ITJ*, pp. 191, 200–201.

62. See *ITJ*, pp. 198, 203.

63. RID Journal, April 9, 1879 (*ITJ*, p. 196).

64. RID Journal, March 19, 1879 (*ITJ*, p. 174). A summary of the military career of Brevet Brigadier General Louis H. Pelouze (1831–1878) is in *ANJ*, June 15, 1878, p. 721.

65. For the army's customary use of "cantonment," see Frazer, *Forts of the West*, p. xxi. Nevertheless, on official maps issued during Dodge's era, the post he established was identified simply as "Cantonment," and in later years it has continued to be known by that name. See Morris, Goins, and McReynolds, *Historical Atlas of Oklahoma*, Nos. 33, 51.

66. RID Journal, April 14, 1879 (*ITJ*, p. 203).

67. Sommer, "Cantonment North Fork of the Canadian River" (Thoburn Papers, Oklahoma Historical Society); *ITJ*, p. 207.

68. For further discussion of the civilian laborers, see *ITJ*, pp. 207–8.

69. RID Journal, June 7, 1879 (*ITJ*, p. 234). (Entries dated May 28–June 18, 1879, are found in Journal Five in *ITJ*, pp. 222–44.)

70. AAG MDM to AG, March 27, 1879, forwarding the petition (AGO Reg LR); RID to AG, April 30, 1879 (CNFCR LS).

71. AG to C.O. CNFCR, May 14, 1879, cited in CNFCR Post Return, May 1879.

72. A summary discussion of this topic is by McDermott, "Were They Really Rogues?" pp. 165–74; see also Coffman, *The Old Army*, pp. 192–97.

73. Entry No. 103, March 25, 1879 (CNFCR Reg LR); Pollock endorsement, May 25, 1879 (CNFCR Reg LR).

74. RID Journal, June 7, 1879 (*ITJ*, p. 233). General courts-martial were convened twice more to consider charges against Private Myers. On August 27, 1879, he was sentenced to two years in confinement and dishonorably discharged from the army (Office of the Judge Advocate General, Registers of General Courts-Martial; CNFCR Post Return, August 1879; *ANJ*, November 1, 1879, p. 237).

75. RID Journal, June 9, 1879 (*ITJ*, p. 235). Nine years earlier, when less accustomed to the role of post commander, Dodge had discussed the same topic in a letter to his wife from Fort Lyon. It was a pleasure, he wrote then, "to know that while I am doing what I think is right, I should also secure the approbation and good will of my subordinates. . . . I do deserve commendation for my conduct in com[man]d of this post, more than I ever have before. I have controlled with more dignity, impartiality, & success than ever before, & the result is that I *command*. I have no trouble, & my will is law to everyone about me, not as that of a Tyrant, but as that of a Brother Officer, who has the interests of all at heart, but who will permit no question or cavil" (RID to JRPD, January 16, 1870—Yale).

76. This enumeration describes the Indian population around Cantonment in November 1879, after crops had been harvested. Most of the Indians ordinarily in the vicinity had already returned to the agency for the winter. R. B. Marcy to WTS, November 25, 1879, enclosing part of an inspection report by Major John J. Coppinger (AGO LR).

77. See *ITJ*, pp. 211, 227–28, 326; RID to AAG DMO, January 9, 1880 (CNFCR LS).

78. RID to C.O. Fort Reno, May 16, 1879 (CNFCR LS).

79. RID to AAG DMO, May 16, 1879 (CNFCR LS).

80. RID Journal, June 3, 1879 (*ITJ*, p. 230).

81. *The Statutes at Large*, XXI, p. 797.

82. Rister, *Land Hunger*, pp. 36–49.

83. Section 2149 of the *Revised Statues* authorized the Commissioner of Indian Affairs, with approval of the secretary of the interior, to remove by force from a tribal reservation any person there without legal authority or judged detrimental to the peace and welfare of the Indians. Section 2150 authorized military forces to be employed in Indian Territory as directed by the president, to apprehend intruders, seize property, repel persons attempting entry, and destroy distilleries (p. 374). For a map showing the "Unassigned Lands," see No. 33, "Indian Territory, 1866–1889," in Morris, Goins, and McReynolds, *Historical Atlas of Oklahoma*.

84. WTS to Sheridan, May 2, 1879 (MDM Settlers in I.T. Special File).

85. WTS to Sheridan, May 7, 1879 (MDM Settlers in I.T. Special File).

86. Pope to Sheridan, May 14, 1879 (MDM Settlers in I.T. Special File); CNFCR Post Return, May 1879. Documents relating to the citizen invasion of Indian Territory in 1879 are gathered in Senate, *Occupation of Indian Territory by White Settlers*.

87. On April 2 Dodge had pledged to Mizner his assistance "to the extent of the whole available force at my command" in the event of Indian trouble near Fort Reno (CNFCR LS).

88. Charles E. Campbell to E. A. Hayt, March 14, 1879; Miles to Hayt, April 24, 1879 (OIA LR, C&A); *Removal of the Northern Cheyenne Indians*, pp. 52, 87, 188.

89. Campbell to Hayt, March 4, 1879; Miles to Hayt, March 10, 1879; Campbell to Hayt, March 14, 1879 (OIA LR, C&A).

90. Miles to Hayt, April 24, 1879 (OIA LR, C&A).

91. *New York Times*, May 16, 1879, p. 5; May 20, 1879, p. 1; *Removal of the Northern Cheyenne Indians*, pp. 86, 146–47, 188. According to the *Army and Navy Journal*, Little Chief told Schurz that he would rather die than conform to the white man's ways (May 24, 1879, p. 745).

92. *Removal of the Northern Cheyenne Indians*, pp. 87, 186, 188–89.

93. Pope to Sheridan, May 14, 1879 (MDM Settlers in I.T. Special File); Pope to AG, May 27, 1879 (AGO LR); Schurz to SW, June 2, 1879 (AGO LR).

94. Pope to AG, June 3, 1879 (AGO LR). Endorsing Pope's letter, General Sherman withheld approval of the course he advised unless it was requested by the secretary of war and the secretary of the interior. "Meantime all precautionary measures to guard against a flight are very proper" (Endorsement No. 553, June 7, 1879—Sherman Papers, LC).

95. CNFCR Post Return, June 1879; S.O. 47, CNFCR, June 6, 1879.

96. RID Journal, June 3, 1879 (*ITJ*, p. 229).

97. Mizner to AAG DMO, June 4, 1879 (AGO LR).

98. RID Journal, June 6, 1879 (*ITJ*, p. 233).

99. Twenty-third Infantry Regimental Returns, November–December 1877; RID ACP File (AGO).

100. For a contemporary account of Caldwell during this yeasty period of its history, see Freeman, *Midnight and Noonday*.

101. *OWI*, p. 300.

Chapter 19

1. Seger, *Early Days Among the Cheyenne and Arapahoe Indians*, p. 27.

2. Miles expected adherence to G.O. 28, issued by General Pope on September 26, 1870, as the framework for working relations between army officers and Indian agents like himself. This order specified that Indian agents held sole jurisdiction over all matters of conduct and the protection of rights on reservations, and that military forces were placed there solely to assist the agents in preserving order. Pope's order is reprinted in *ITJ*, Appendix B, pp. 445–46.

3. Mizner to Clarke, June 12, 1879 (OIA LR, C&A).

4. Miles to Mizner, June 12, 1879 (OIA LR, C&A).

5. Hayt to SI, June 19, 1879; Schurz to SW, June 19, 1879 (AGO LR).

6. Mizner to AAG DMO, June 15, 1879, and June 18, 1879 (AGO LR).

7. Miles to Hayt, June 25, 1879 (AGO LR).

8. Creel to AAG MDM, March 7, 1879 (AGO Reg LR).

9. Creel to AAG MDM, April 22, 1879 (OIA LR, C&A).

10. Creel to Major Barbar [Captain Merritt Barber, Sixteenth Infantry], June 15, 1879 (OIA LR, C&A).

11. Miles to Mizner, September 10, 1879 (OIA LR, C&A).

12. Miles to E. A. Hayt, September 16, 1879. On September 19 Miles wrote again to Hayt, protesting Creel's baneful influence (OIA LR, C&A).

13. Miles to Hayt, November 1, 1879 (OIA LR, C&A).

14. House, *Report of the Commissioner of Indian Affairs,* 1879, p. 164.

15. *Removal of the Northern Cheyenne Indians*, p. xxv. The members of the Select Committee were Senators Samuel J. Kirkwood, John T. Morgan, H. L. Dawes, and Preston B. Plumb.

16. The committee also recorded its judgment that the annual reports and testimony of Agent Miles refuted statements by Commissioner Hayt that the Northern Cheyennes had no real cause for dissatisfaction (*Removal of the Northern Cheyennes*, p. xv).

17. RID to AAG DMO, April 4, 1879 (CNFCR LS). See *ITJ,* p. 298 n. 65.

18. Miles to Hayt, May 27, 1879 (OIA LR, C&A).

19. An undated "Brief history of Cheyenne & Arapahoe Reserve" documents the Indian Bureau's effort to ascertain which lands these Indian tribes were legally entitled to (OIA LR, C&A). The Senate committee observed in its report that "no part of [the land then occupied by the Cheyennes and Arapahos] is included in either of the treaties with these tribes, and it has never been conferred on them by act of Congress" (*Removal of the Northern Cheyenne Indians*, p. ii). The results of the original survey were published in House, *Survey of Lands for Cheyenne and Arapahoe Indians*.

20. This order was reprinted as an appendix to *Removal of the Northern Cheyenne Indians*, pp. 229–32; see also pp. 307–12.

21. Miles to Hayt, August 14, 1879 (OIA LR, C&A).

22. CNFCR Post Returns, June and July 1879; *ANJ*, July 12, 1879, p. 885; July 19, p. 909; and July 26, p. 930.

23. "Lyceum Theatre," *New York Times*, February 26, 1879, p. 5.

24. *ANJ*, July 31, 1879, p. 93. Surviving evidence of Dodge's activity includes the copied proceedings of a military commission, convened at Denver, Colorado, on February 9, 1865, to investigate the conduct of Colonel John M. Chivington in his campaign of the previous year against the Cheyenne Indians. It refers to "fiendish atrocities" and "atrocious barbarities" by the force under Chivington (Graff).

25. Fry's book was reviewed in *ANJ*, February 22, 1879, p. 519. On April 9 Dodge received a "splendid letter" from Fry (*ITJ*, p. 196). The letter has not survived, but in view of Dodge's recently published desire to recount army exploits in the frontier West, it seems likely that Fry referred in his letter to their shared interest.

26. S.O. 177, DMO, September 11, 1879; CNFCR Post Return, September 1879.

27. Miles to Hayt, September 15, 1879, and September 19, 1879 (OIA LR, C&A).

28. Clarke to Mizner, October 1, 1879 (OIA LR, C&A).

29. RID to AAG DMO, October 4, 1879, with endorsements (CNFCR LS). General Sherman learned of the situation from a second source, Colonel James B. Fry, who was then assistant adjutant general for the Division of the Atlantic. Writing on October 21 to Major General Winfield S. Hancock, commander of that division, Sherman enclosed an extract from a private letter Dodge had sent Fry. "I am not certain," he wrote, "that he, Dodge, has reported the identical facts to his Department Commander, but I know that General Pope has reported similar cases, again and again, but the Indian Bureau will turn around and prove to *their* satisfaction that the Indians are *over* fed" (Sherman Papers, LC).

30. SW to SI, October 7, 1879; Schurz to AG, October 8, 1879 (AGO Reg LR).

31. Campbell to E. A. Hayt, October 9, 1879 (OIA LR, C&A).

32. Campbell to Hayt, October 11, 1879 (OIA LR, C&A).

33. RID to AAG DMO, January 9, 1880 (OIA LR, C&A).

34. Keeling and Co. to RID, November 20, 1879 (CNFCR LR).

35. RID to Campbell, November 28, 1879 (CNFCR LS).

36. RID to Miles, November 28, 1879 (CNFCR LS).

37. Dodge's daily record of his experiences from November 6 to December 10, 1879, comprises Journal Six in *ITJ*, pp. 274–303.

38. *New York Dramatic Mirror*, August 23, 1879, p. 7.

39. *New York Dramatic Mirror*, October 11, 1879, p. 4; October 25, p. 4.

40. *Atchison (Kansas) Globe*, April 6, 1880. See also RID Journal, December 10, 1879 (*ITJ*, p. 303 n. 61).

41. RID to FPD, July 17, 1884 (Graff).

42. "Earlier dates cancelled" appeared beside the entry for the Frederick Paulding Company in the "Dates Ahead" column of the *New York Dramatic Mirror* for November 8 and 15, 1879.

43. RID Journal, November 28, 1879 (*ITJ*, p. 294).

44. RID Journal, December 1, 1879 (*ITJ*, pp. 297–98).

45. RID Journal, December 2, 1879 (*ITJ*, p. 298). The *Leavenworth Times* was hardly less positive, entitling its notice of the performance "He Is a Wonder" (December 3, 1879, p. 3).

46. RID Journal, December 2–9, 1879 (*ITJ*, pp. 299–301).

47. RID Journal, December 10, 1879 (*ITJ*, p. 303).

48. Dodge's journal record of the period from December 11, 1879, to May 26, 1880, comprising Journal Six in *ITJ*, pp. 304–65, includes four month-long hiatuses, between the entries dated December 19, 1879, and January 20, 1880; January 27 and February 18; February 24 and March 25; and April 5 and May 7, 1880.

49. For the official communications that preceded the decision not to designate Cantonment a permanent post, see *ITJ*, p. 309.

50. RID to FPD, July 17, 1884 (Graff).

51. Miles to RID, December 2, 1879 (OIA LR, C&A). Although his assistant had precipitated the inquiry by his complaints against Keeling, from this point Miles himself acted on behalf of the agency.

52. RID to Miles, December 20, 1879 (OIA LR, C&A); Miles to RID, December 30, 1879 (OIA LR, C&A).

53. Chapman to C.O. CNFCR, January 6, 1880 (OIA LR, C&A).

54. Reynolds to RID, January 6, 1880 (OIA LR, C&A); RID to Miles, January 8, 1880 (CNFCR LS).

55. RID to AAG DMO, January 9, 1880 (OIA LR, C&A).

56. SW to SI, February 10, 1880, with inked stamp showing date of receipt (OIA LR, C&A).

57. See *ITJ*, p. 313 n. 25.

58. Miles to Hayt, January 19, 1880 (OIA LR, C&A).

59. RID to AAG DMO, February 25, 1880 (CNFCR LS).

60. J. H. Gillpatrick to Carl Schurz, February 4, 1880, with endorsement by Plumb (OIA LR, C&A).

61. Keeling and Co. to Commissioner of Indian Affairs, March 25, 1880, with RID endorsement (Yale). Dodge's endorsement is also recorded in CNFCR Reg LR.

62. E. R. Platt endorsement [after April 6, 1880] of Keeling and Co. to Commissioner of Indian Affairs, March 25, 1880 (Yale).

63. RID endorsement, April 20, 1880, of Keeling and Co. to Commissioner of Indian Affairs, March 25, 1880 (Yale).

64. Miles to Hayt, January 20, 1880 (OIA LR, C&A).

65. Schurz to SW, January 30, 1880 (AGO LR).

66. Disposition sheet with endorsements by WTS and others, RID to AAG DMO, March 4, 1880 (AGO LR).

67. Depositions by Stone Calf, Coho, and Chapman, all dated March 3, 1880, enclosed with RID to AAG DMO, March 4, 1880 (AGO LR). Stone Calf and Coho both deposed that Agent Miles had long known that the Ute woman was a prostitute. According to Coho, Miles's informant, Minimick, had twice pimped for the woman during her stay near Cantonment.

68. La Garde to C.O. CNFCR, March 4, 1880, enclosed with RID's report (AGO LR).

69. RID to AAG DMO, March 4, 1880 (AGO LR). The correspondence in this case is a consolidated file, 768 AGO 1880, available in NARA microform publication M666, Roll 550. Copies of Dodge's report with its enclosures are found in OIA LR, C&A, and CNFCR LS.

70. Miles to Commissioner of Indian Affairs, February 24, 1880 (OIA LR, C&A).

71. Miles to Commissioner of Indian Affairs, March 8, 1880 (OIA LR, C&A).

72. William L. Clarke endorsement, n.d. [March 1880] (CNFCR Reg LR).

73. Miles to Commissioner of Indian Affairs, March 8, 1880 (OIA LR, C&A).

74. Miles, Notes on an interview with Robert L. Townsend, March 1, 1880 (OIA LR, C&A).

75. Clarke endorsement, n.d. [March 1880] (CNFCR Reg LR).

76. SW to SI, June 7, 1880 (SW LS).

77. Unidentified newspaper article reprinted in *New York Dramatic Mirror*, April 10, 1880, p. 5. Fred's relationship to Dodge occasionally received comment. For example, the *Army and Navy Journal* noted in is January 10, 1880, issue that the young man's success had "attracted considerable notice in Army circles at Washington" (p. 452).

78. *New York Dramatic Mirror*, January 31, 1880, p. 4; February 7, 1880, p. 4; and March 13, 1880, p. 4.

79. In 1870, when James R. Dodge and his wife were settled in New York City, Dodge feared for his father's welfare if he were to lose his position at the custom house. "The transition from life & bustle & business, & the intercourse of pleasant friends & relations, to the monotony of backwoods life in Yadkin [County], the companionship of secessionists – without occupation, without hope – I'm sure he could not live through it six months" (RID to JRPD, July 24, 1870—Yale). However, the younger Dodge underestimated his father's adaptability and genial good nature, for the latter did return to North Carolina, and happily. His reputation as a man of solid trust and a lively wit had not been forgotten, and his last years were serene. He died peacefully at the home of his eldest daughter, Annie S. Glenn (Wheeler, *Reminiscences and Memoirs of North Carolina*), p. 393).

80. RID Journal, March 25–April 13, 1880 (*ITJ*, pp. 339–46).

81. RID Journal, April 15 [17], 1880 (*ITJ*, p. 346).

82. AAG DMO to C.O. CNFCR, April 13, 1880 (CNFCR Unregistered LR).

83. This observation was Sheridan's; see *ANJ*, April 24, 1880, p. 773.

84. Miles to R. W. Trowbridge, Commissioner of Indian Affairs, April 20, 1880 (OIA LR, C&A); Randall to Pope, April 20, 1880, with endorsement (OIA LR, C&A). Randall's letter was published in *ANJ*, April 24, 1880, p. 773.

85. C.O. to RID, April 21, 1880 (CNFCR LS). Dodge was away from the post on his own authority between April 21 and 25 (CNFCR Post Return, April 1880).

86. Miles to R. E. Trowbridge, April 20, 1880 (OIA LR, C&A).

87. *ANJ*, May 1, 1880, p. 794; House, *Report of the Commissioner of Indian Affairs*, 1880, p. 68.

88. *Removal of the Northern Cheyenne Indians*, p. 122; Mizner to Pope, November 17, 1879 (OIA LR, C&A).

89. Pope to WTS, February 12, 1880 (AGO LR).

90. Miles endorsement, January 26, 1880, of Ben Clarke to Nelson A. Miles, January 14, 1880 (OIA LR, C&A); *Removal of the Northern Cheyenne Indians*, pp. 202–16; *ANJ*, May 1, 1880, p. 794. The testimony of Miles figures prominently in the Senate committee's summary of its findings; see *Removal of the Northern Cheyenne Indians*, pp. xxi–xxiv.

91. In October 1881 Little Chief and his people were permitted to move from Indian Territory to the Pine Ridge reservation in Dakota Territory, where the chieftain continued his agitation for a return to his homeland further north. At last, in 1891, he was successful. His group of Northern Cheyennes moved to the Tongue River Reservation in eastern Montana in that year. See Hoig, *The Peace Chiefs*, pp. 140–41.

92. *Hamlet* I.v.188–89.

Chapter 20

1. House, *Report of the SW,* 1880, pp. 79–81, 83–85; Sprague, *Massacre*, pp. 179–288 passim.

2. DMO, *Roster*, November 1879, pp. 14–15.

3. WTS to AAG MDM, December 29, 1879 (AGO LS).

4. A force under Colonel Merritt would push the White River Utes southward, and the two units under Mackenzie and Hatch's successor, Colonel George Buell, Fifteenth Infantry, would press the southern bands by moving northwest and northeast respectively.

5. Sherman expected no useful results from the negotiations then under way, but he planned to defer any "systematic campaign" against the Utes until the Department of the Interior had confessed its inability to deal with them. WTS to Pope, January 6, 1880 (AGO LS).

6. Sprague, *Massacre*, p. 307. For the act approved by Congress on the basis of this proposal, see *The Statutes at Large*, XXI, pp. 199–205.

7. WTS to Sheridan, March 24, 1880 (AGO LS).

8. WTS to A. Ramsay, April 3, 1880 (AGO LR). This letter was published in *ANJ* as "The Plan for the Ute Campaign," May 15, 1880, p. 844.

9. RID Journal, May 7, 1880 (*ITJ*, p. 353).

10. For contemporary descriptions see Crofutt, *Crofutt's Grip-Sack Guide*, pp. 92, 138; Bancroft, *History of Nevada, Colorado, and Wyoming*, pp. 495, 636. A more complete account is provided by John Dietz and Albert Larson, "Colorado's San Luis Valley," in Wyckoff and Dilsaver, eds., *The Mountainous West*, pp. 349–67.

11. S.O. 93, DMO, April 27, 1880; CNFCR Post Return, April 1880; *ANJ*, May 8, 1880, p. 810.

12. S.O. 67, CNFCR, May 5, 1880.

13. Dodge's daily record of the journey to Colorado, with entries dated May 7 to May 26, 1880, is Journal Seven in *ITJ*, pp. 353–65.

14. RID Journal, May 13, 1880 (*ITJ*, p. 357).

15. RID Journal, March 30, 1879 (*ITJ*, p. 188).

16. RID Journal, May 15, 1880 (*ITJ*, p. 350).

17. RID Journal, May 16, 1880 (*ITJ*, p. 358). A description of the train's ascent from La Veta that helps account for Dodge's superlative is found in Crofutt, *Crofutt's Grip-Sack Guide*, p. 63.

18. RID Journal, May 16, 1880 (*ITJ*, p. 359).

19. By Order 1, Headquarters Infantry Column, on May 16, 1880, Dodge assumed direct command over the infantry units in compliance with General Field Order 1 issued by Mackenzie. He divided the troops under him into three battalions, under Major Charles A. Webb, Sixteenth Infantry; Captain George K. Brady, Twenty-third Infantry; and Major Robert H. Offley. Dodge's adjutant was First Lieutenant Charles Hay, Twenty-third Infantry (Fort Garland Column, DMO).

20. RID Journal, May 19 and 20, 1880 (*ITJ*, p. 361).

21. Order 5, Headquarters Infantry Column, May 20, 1880 (Fort Garland Column, DMO); RID Journal, May 20, 1880 (*ITJ*, p. 362).

22. P. H. Wilcox to C. O. Fort Garland Column, July 11, 1880, with endorsements (Fort Garland Column LR).

23. RID Journal, May 25, 1880 (*ITJ*, pp. 364–65).

24. AAAG to RID, May 27, 1880 (Fort Garland Column LR); *ANJ*, June 12, 1880, p. 917. A day-by-day record of Dodge's marches from Cochetopa Pass to the supply camp is in Twenty-third Infantry Regimental Returns, May and June, 1880.

25. AAAG to RID, May 27 and 28, 1880 (Fort Garland Column LR); Order 9, Headquarters Infantry Battalions, May 28, 1880 (Fort Garland Column).

26. Pierce, *The Most Promising Young Officer*, p. 206; Robinson, *Bad Hand*, p. 267.

27. Pope to Sheridan, October 30 and 31, 1879; Mackenzie to AAG DMO, October 30, 1879; Pope to AAG MDM, November 5, 1879; Pope to Sheridan, November 7, 1879 (MDM Ute Campaign Special File); WTS to Pope, January 13, 1880 (AGO LS).

28. Crook to Sheridan, November 30, 1879 (MDM Ute Campaign Special File).

29. Mackenzie to AAG DMO, October 30, 1879 (MDM Ute Campaign Special File). For Randall's activities at Fort Reno in the summer of 1880, including a confrontation with a large body of angry Indians, see *ITJ*, pp. 407–10.

30. AG to Pope, February 19, 1880 (AGO LS).

31. AG to Pope, March 17, 1880 (AGO LS).

32. RID Journal, September 3, 1880 (*ITJ*, p. 388).

33. Order 19, June 23, 1880, Headquarters Infantry Column (Fort Garland Column).

34. Mackenzie to Pope, June 29, 1880 (Nohl, "Bad Hand," p. 272).

35. Wallace E. Bingham, "Early Days on the Frontier" (Don Rickey Papers, USAMHI).

36. RID to AG, June 27, 1880 (Fort Garland Column LS).

37. Endorsements, Spencer to AAAG, June 23, 1880 (Fort Garland Column LR).

38. *ANJ*, May 29, 1880, p. 876.

39. For the circumstances surrounding this incident, which concluded with Major Offley's release from arrest after he had submitted an abject apology, see *ITJ*, pp. 371–72.

40. Pope to AG, May 15, 1880 (AGO LR); House, *Report of the SW*, 1880, pp. 91–92.

41. Order 49, Fort Garland Column, August 9, 1880. For descriptions of the buildings constructed under the supervision of Cowles and in later years see Nankivell, "Fort Crawford," pp. 57–61.

42. The commissioners were John B. Bowman, George W. Manypenny, Alfred B. Meacham, Otto Mears, and John J. Russell.

43. Mackenzie to AAG MDM, May 21, 1880 (Nohl, "Bad Hand" p. 271).

44. *ANJ*, July 24, 1880, p. 1048; and August 28, 1880, p. 61; Parker, *The Old Army*, pp. 124–31, 134–35. A day-by-day record of Mackenzie's journey through the mountains can be found in the July 1880 Field Return of the Fort Garland Column.

45. Order 44, Fort Garland Column, July 31, 1880.

46. Bingham, "Early Days on the Frontier" (Don Rickey Papers, USAMHI).

47. "Report of the Ute Commission" in House, *Report of the Commissioner of Indian Affairs*, 1880, p. 261.

48. "Report of the Ute Commission," p. 264.

49. Baird to RID, October 25, 1880 (Graff).

50. *OWI*, pp. ix–xi, 264; *Annual Report of the Board of Regents of the Smithsonian Institution*, 1881, p. 138; *Annual Report of the Board of Regents of the Smithsonian Institution*, 1882, pp. 46, 239.

51. *OWI*, p. 163.

52. *OWI*, pp. 175–76.

53. RID to AG, August 10, 1880 (AGO Reg LR).

54. *OWI*, p. 167.

55. RID to AAG DMO, August 6, 1880 (Fort Garland Column LS).

56. *ANJ*, July 31, 1880, p. 1061; and August 14, 1880, pp. 2–3. In the course of an inspection tour, Pope arrived at Fort Garland on July 29 and left there on August 1 (Fort Garland Post Returns, July, August 1880).

57. *ANJ*, September 11, 1880, p. 83.

58. AAG DMO to C.O. Fort Garland, August 23, 1880 (Fort Garland Column LR). Dodge's relief from duty with the Fort Garland Column was made official by S.O. 185, DMO, August 24, which was reprinted in part in *ANJ*, September 4, 1880, p. 81.

59. Nohl, "Bad Hand," pp. 275–77; Robinson, *Bad Hand*, pp. 270–73.

60. Turchen and McLaird, *The Black Hills Expedition,* p. 92.

61. Dodge's daily record of his return to Cantonment, with entries dated September 1–23 and December 18, 1880, is Journal Eight in *ITJ*, pp. 382–404, 435–36. The quotation is from p. 382.

62. RID Journal, September 1–2, 1880 (*ITJ*, pp. 382–84).

63. RID Journal, September 2, 1880 (*ITJ*, p. 386).

64. RID Journal, September 3, 1880 (*ITJ*, p. 389). Dodge's journal entry for this day was about 1,200 words in length, a measure of his leisure now that the summer's work had ended.

65. RID Journal, September 4, 1880 (*ITJ*, pp. 390–91). For descriptions of the medicines Dodge used, see Wood and Bache, *Dispensatory*, pp. 128, 793, 977–78.

66. This landmark was so named for bright yellow dirt on its northern face, which according to Crofutt "seems to have no bottom" when wet and stuck to the footsoles like glue. The toll road over the mountain, completed in 1877, was celebrated locally as a feat of engineering (*Crofutt's Grip-Sack Guide*, p. 143).

67. An engraving that depicts the resort nestled among its scenic surroundings is found in Crofutt, *Crofutt's Grip-Sack Guide*, p. 154.

68. S.O. 205, DMO, September 16, 1880; RID Journal, September 11, 1880 (*ITJ*, p. 398).

69. Upon the death of Colonel Jefferson C. Davis on November 30, 1879, Dodge had commanded the Twenty-third Infantry on an interim basis until Colonel Haller took command in February 1880 (Twenty-third Infantry Regimental Returns, January–February 1880; RID to Haller, February 7, 1880—CNFCR LS; S.O. 20, CNFCR, February 11, 1880). See *ITJ*, pp. 321–22; Hamersley, *Records of Living Officers*, pp. 389–90.

70. RID Journal, September 12, 16, and 17, 1880 (*ITJ*, pp. 399–401).

71. RID Journal, September 22, 1880 (*ITJ*, p. 403).

72. RID Journal, September 23, 1880 (*ITJ*, pp. 403–404). The other stalwart noncommissioned officer left behind was the quartermaster sergeant, Christian F. Sommer.

Chapter 21

1. Keim, *Sheridan's Troopers on the Borders*, p. 59.

2. CNFCR Post Return, November 1880.

3. S.O. 113, CNFCR, November 3, 1880; S.O. 115, CNFCR, November 29, 1880; *ANJ*, March 13, 1880, p. 643.

4. RID Journal, December 18, 1880 (*ITJ*, p. 435).

5. "Author's Preface," *OWI*, p. vi. Except for a few pages of material omitted from the published work or else included in fragmentary form, Dodge's manuscript has not survived. However, by December 1880 he considered his work complete, ready for review, and essentially ready for publication. Only one sentence in the printed text of *Our Wild Indians*, a detail added to a longer discussion (p. 86), was certainly written after that time. It is therefore assumed here that, except for initial chapters that his publisher thought too argumentative—see below, chapter 22—the contents and organization of the manuscript were the same as appear in the published book.

6. Though little remembered now, George P. Belden's *Belden, The White Chief, or, Twelve Years Among the Wild Indians of the Plains*, edited by Major James S. Brisbin, Second Cavalry, was a popular work at the time of its issue in 1870, selling over 20,000 copies.

7. *OWI*, pp. 99, 128, 163, 353, 608.

8. "Author's Preface," *OWI*, p. v.

9. *OWI*, pp. 74, 95, 202, 214, 279, 310, 345, 398, 540, 581.

10. *OWI*, pp. 122, 164, 446, 484, 582, 628.

11. *OWI*, pp. 79–80. See Dodge's journal entries for March 25 and May 31, 1879 (*ITJ*, pp. 182–83, 227).

12. *OWI*, p. 41.

13. *OWI*, p. 67.

14. *OWI*, pp. 43, 54.

15. *OWI*, p. 258.
16. These are chapters 3–6, 9, 10, 13, 15, 16, 22, 25, 26, 33, 34, 38, 40, 41, 43, and 44.
17. "Author's Preface," *OWI*, p. v.
18. These are chapters 1, 17, 23, 24, 28, 32, 39, 42, and 45–47.
19. These are chapters 2, 7, 8, 11, 12, 14, 18–21, 27, 29–31, 35–37, and 48–51.
20. These are chapters 1, 3, 4, 6, 9, 10, 13, 15, and 16.
21. These are chapters 17–21, 23, 24, 27–32, 35–37, 39, 42, and 45–51.
22. *OWI*, p. 53. In a preliminary jab at federal Indian policy, Dodge wrote that the various Indian tribes were alike only in that "all are savage, all are swindled, starved and imposed upon."
23. The full title of the book was almost certainly the work of Dodge's publisher, A. D. Worthington, who employed verbal grandiloquence as a marketing tool. The title was *Our Wild Indians: Thirty-three Years' Personal Experience among the Red Men of the Great West. A Popular Account of Their Social Life, Religion, Habits, Traits, Customs, Exploits, etc. with Thrilling Adventures and Experiences on the Great Plains and in the Mountains of Our Wide Frontier.* See below, chapter 22.
24. *OWI*, p. 492. At some points Dodge presented narrative material in monologue or dialogue form, as when he portrayed Amos Chapman describing his adventures in the Buffalo Wallow fight, pp. 631–32.
25. *OWI*, pp. 76, 608. Among Dodge's wry apothegms are these: "Religious faith (or what we call superstition when applied to any religion but the one we happen to believe in) is strongest among the uneducated" (p. 149); "In all ages and climes the blessed sex have arrogated to themselves the right of exaggeration in all matters of sentiment or affection" (p. 171).
26. Compare *OWI*, pp. 210–13 ("I have . . . pleasure.") to *PNA*, pp. 267–71 ("The Indians . . . discontinued."); *OWI*, pp. 530–32 ("Indians . . . deserved.") to *PNA*, pp. 334–36 ("No words . . . subject."). For the three passages omitted from *Our Wild Indians*, see above, chapters 13 and 15. These changes and other efforts by Dodge to bring the book into conformity with popular taste are discussed in Kime, "'Not Coarse . . . but Not Delicate,'" pp. 79–81).
27. *OWI*, Chapters 29 and 30, pp. 379–405.
28. *OWI*, Chapter 27, pp. 348–55.
29. *OWI*, Chapters 47–50, pp. 596–638 (frontiersmen); Chapters 35–38, pp. 468–511 (army).
30. *OWI*, pp. 572–73.
31. *OWI*, pp. 492–93, 628. See also the tribute to Captain George M. Randall on p. 111.
32. For example, see *OWI*, p. 164 (Captain Pollock), 310 (Captain Randall).
33. *OWI*, p. 472. In the first of his chapters describing army life on the plains, Dodge did write a brief statement of the U.S. Army's contributions to the nation's century of unexampled progress. See *OWI*, pp. 469–70. No evidence exists that after completing this manuscript he resumed work on his ambitious project to narrate incidents in the history of the army on the western frontier.
34. *OWI*, pp. 125, 305, and 172, respectively.
35. *OWI*, p. 424. Of course, Dodge was here referring to an imaginary situation. Elsewhere, without making the identification explicit, he described a prominent feature of Indian character that matched his own approach to life: "The Indian is proud, sensitive, quick-tempered, easily wounded, easily excited," he wrote, "but though utterly unforgiving, he never broods. This, in my opinion, is the whole secret of his happiness" (p. 248). Compare the latter portion of this statement to Dodge's assertion of his own refusal to worry, in chapter 19 above.
36. *OWI*, pp. 143, 153, 420, and 578.
37. *OWI*, pp. 279–81.
38. For example, see chapter 15, entitled "Love-Making in an Indian Camp—Courtship and Marriage," pp. 194–203; chapter 22, "The Buffalo and Its Destruction," pp. 282–96.
39. It should be noted, however, that according to Dodge the concluding chapters were originally placed at the beginning of the book. See RID, "Explanatory," in *A Living Issue*, p. [2], and below, chapter 22.
40. *OWI*, pp. 89–91, 267.
41. *OWI*, pp. 265, 296.
42. *OWI*, pp. 259, 313.
43. *OWI*, pp. 95–97.
44. *OWI*, pp. 57–58.

45. *OWI*, p. 601. See William Wordsworth, "Rob Roy's Grave."

46. *OWI*, pp. 269, 296. Elsewhere Dodge described the Indian trader as "the monster devised by the government to keep the Indian in abject penury" (p. 281).

47. Dodge was here describing the Nez Perces, a tribe "which for generations has lived in the most amicable relations with white men, [but] is, for a single outbreak, forced on it by injustice, greed and aggression, exiled to a strange land. Despairing and desperate, men who have been our life-long friends are converted into unforgiving enemies. Hoping, almost praying, for an excuse for outbreak, willing to risk death for even the slightest chance of regaining their loved homes, these fragments of bands are a constant source of anxiety to States containing over two millions of inhabitants, and require a force of troops to watch and control them, at an expense ten times greater than would feed, clothe, house, make them valuable citizens in the countries for which they yearn" (*OWI*, p. 314).

48. *OWI*, pp. 639–40.

49. *OWI*, p. 652.

50. *OWI*, p. 653.

51. See *OWI*, pp. 646–47.

52. Evidence of junior officers' desire for brighter prospects for advancement in rank appeared often in the *Army and Navy Journal*, especially during this period. For example, see the issues for August 21, 1880, p. 49; November 6, pp. 268–69; and December 11, p. 377; see also Coffman, *The Old Army*, pp. 230–34.

53. Pope to RID, November 2, 1880 (Graff). Audenried had died on June 3, 1880; for a summary of his career see *ANJ*, June 5, 1880, p. 897.

54. Pope to WTS, November 2, 1880 (Sherman Papers, LC).

55. S.O. 257, DMO, November 24, 1880, granted Dodge one month's leave of absence, with permission to apply for an extension of three months.

56. William G. Whipple, AAG MDM, to RID, December 15, 1880 (Graff).

57. Pope to RID, December 16, 1880 (Graff).

58. S.O. 119, CNFCR, December 17, 1880.

59. RID Journal, December 18, 1880 (*ITJ*, p. 436).

Part 6

1. Sherman to Philip H. Sheridan, May 2, 1879 (MDM, I.T. Operations Special File).

2. Sherman, *Memoirs*, II, p. 460.

3. Dodge Journal, June 25, 1883 (*Sherman Tour Journals*, p. 87).

Chapter 22

1. House, *Report of the SW*, 1883, p. 45.

2. Tidball, "On General Sherman's Staff as Aide-de-Camp," pp. 65–67 (Tidball Papers, USMA); *ANJ*, January 4, 1873, p. 323; and May 31, 1873, p. 663; Heitman, *Historical Register*, I, pp. 179, 195, 966; *ITJ*, p. 202.

3. Cullum, *Biographical Register*, II, pp. 212–14, 217–18; Hamersley, *Records of Living Officers*, p. 159.

4. See *ANJ*, November 19, 1881, p. 345; WTS to John Pope, July 15, 1882 (HQA LS).

5. *ANJ*, January 15, 1881, p. 477.

6. See WTS to RID, September 2, 1882 (HQA LS).

7. Tidball, "On General Sherman's Staff as Aide-de-Camp," pp. 12–19 (Tidball Papers, USMA).

8. *ANJ*, May 20, 1882, p. 956; and March 31, 1993, p. 799; Tidball, "On General Sherman's Staff as Aide-de-Camp," pp. 12–19, 21–22, 34–36, 50, 79–81 (Tidball Papers, USMA).

9. *ANJ*, June 30, 1883, p. 1082, quoting an article attributed to the *Washington Republican*.

10. In his memoirs, Tidball mentioned the verbal fluency of both Sherman and Dodge, but whereas he praised the general's habits of speech and noted his enjoyment of "sprightly conversation and amusing anecdotes," the similar qualities of his fellow aide evidently irritated him. He wrote a generally unflattering sketch of Dodge that focused on him as a tiresome talker:

> His proclivity for talking and laughing, possessed by him as a cadet, seems to have increased as time advanced, making him one of the greatest talkers in the army, and he indulged this propensity on all occasions and at all times. It was simply talk not conversation; a sort of monologue, a constant clatter in which those around could take but little part. He was not given to long stories, but rattled along relating trifling incidents, generally of his own experience, and of but little importance or interest to his listeners, keeping up all the while a constant laughing by way of accompanym[en]ts. Having a rapid utterance he covered much ground in a short space of time, in fact so much that at the end of any given period no one was able to make head or tail of what he had been saying, except only now and then he let drop some remark that could be jotted down as a kind of oasis in the great desert of his remarks. His long service upon the plains and among the mountains of the West had educated him in the ways of that kind of life. To this was added an enthusiastic fondness for hunting and fishing in both of which he had uncommon skill. Upon these subjects, as upon some others of a kindred nature his talk, when restrained within bounds, was interesting and instructive. I never knew why the general was persuaded to make him an aid, but he evidently did fancy him, although I thought he did weary a little of his clattering talk. ("On General Sherman's Staff as Aide-de-Camp," pp. 51, 73–77—Tidball Papers, USMA).

Eugene C. Tidball speculated that his namesake, "who had a reputation for taciturnity, was amused, frustrated, or bored" when in continued contact with Dodge and Sherman ("General Sherman's Last March," p. 8).

11. See *ANJ*, January 10, 1880, p. 452; April 9, 1881, p. 745; and April 16, 1881, p. 766.

12. Rusling, *Men and Things I Saw in Civil War Days*, pp. 139–40. The visit of Sherman to Fort Garland occurred in September 1866, in the course of an inspection tour.

13. As the marines marched crisply past Willard's Hotel, a country visitor was heard to allow, "Well, now, them fellers are doin' purty good walkin'" (*ANJ*, March 19, 1881, p. 668).

14. *ANJ*, March 5, 1881, p. 638; *New York Times*, March 4, 1881, p. 1; and March 5, pp. 1–2; *Washington Herald* (Army and Navy Edition), March 6, 1881, p. 1; Tidball, "On General Sherman's Staff as Aide-de-Camp," pp. 121–38 (Tidball Papers, USMA).

15. *New York Times*, March 4, 1881, p. 4; and March 5, p. 2; *ANJ*, March 19, 1881, p. 688.

16. The Light Artillery Board submitted a report of its findings in September 1881. Sherman and Brigadier General Stephen V. Benét, the chief of ordnance, approved the board's proceedings and suggested that the guns it recommended be given a series of tests. *ANJ*, August 6, 1881, p. 12; WTS to SW, September 19, 1881 (AGO Reg LR).

17. See the reprinted statement by King, "Arms or Tactics?" in *ANJ*, March 27, 1880, p. 685. For the work of earlier magazine gun boards, see *ANJ*, November 13, 1876, p. 229; December 22, 1877, p. 307; and May 4, 1878, p. 634.

18. For example, see *ITJ*, p. 27.

19. G.O. 31, HQA, March 21, 1881, reprinted in *ANJ*, March 26, 1881, p. 697.

20. S.O. 98, HQA, April 29, 1881 (Graff). The two orders pertaining to Dodge were included in the Magazine Gun Board's report; see House, *Report of the SW*, 1882, pp. 331–32.

21. The winning entrant was Colonel John Gibbon, Seventh Infantry, whose prize essay, "Our Indian Question," appeared in *JMSI* 2 (1881), 101–20; it has been reprinted in Gaff and Gaff, eds., *Adventures on the Western Frontier*, pp. 236–50.

22. Hutton, *Phil Sheridan and His Army*, pp. 341–42. See also *ANJ*, September 27, 1881, p. 147; and December 31, 1881, p. 472.

23. WTS to RID, September 16, 1884 (Sherman Papers, LC).

24. H. L. Dawes to RID, March 27 and April 4, 1881 (Graff).

25. Statement of account, G. P. Putnam's Sons with RID, October 22, 1885 (Graff).

26. A.D. Worthington & Co., *Illustrated Descriptive Catalogue of Popular and Standard Books*, pp. [1–2] (Trade Catalogs, Special Collections, University of Delaware Library). For a listing of Worthington's earlier publications, see *STJ*, p. 22, note 53.

27. See RID to Blackmore, March 23, 1876 (No. 910, MNM); *PNA*, pp. 20, 46, 388. For the provenance of this item, see *ANJ*, April 21, 1877, p. 593. Dodge's account of the copy in his possession is in *OWI*, pp. 399–401; a facsimile illustration appears on p. 403.

28. For example, see *ANJ*, August 28, 1880, p. 62, and WTS to Taylor, June 23, 1881, both concerning the artist's watercolor representation of the Grand Review in Washington, D.C.; WTS to Taylor, July 28, 1881, concerning another painting in progress, of Union troops crossing the Big Black River in May 1863 (HQA LS).

29. Baird to RID, August 31, 1881 (Graff); [A. D. Worthington & Co.], "Thirty-Three Years' Personal Experience among Our Wild Indians," p. [1] (Graff).

30. *OWI*, p. 653; see also *PNA*, pp. 364–66.

31. RID, "Explanatory," in *A Living Issue*, p. [1]. The words quoted here are Dodge's, not the publisher's.

32. WTS to Sheridan, July 15, 1881 (HQA LS).

33. WTS to Bigelow, August 26, 1881. See also the letter from WTS to George F. Hoar, of Worcester, Massachusetts, dated the same day (HQA LS).

34. *ANJ*, September 3, 1881, p. 95; and September 17, 1881, p. 147; WTS to John E. Tourtelotte, September 11, 1881 (HQA LS).

35. *ANJ*, September 24, 1881, p. 160.

36. House, *Report of the SW*, 1881, pp. 32–36.

37. For example, see the general's reprimand of Captain Philip L. Lee, Tenth Cavalry, on his being found guilty of conduct unbecoming an officer and gentleman; *ITJ*, p. 67.

38. See Johnson, *The Unregimented General*, pp. 214–15; Fellman, *Citizen Sherman*, p. 281; De Montravel, *A Hero to His Fighting Men*, pp. 137–54. Miles was promoted to brigadier general in December 1880.

39. Ironically, shortly after Garfield's election to the presidency Swaim, who was then assisting with his friend's correspondence, complained of the need to fight off office-seekers (*ANJ*, November 20, 1880, p. 311).

40. For a description of the Hazen-Stanley controversy, see Kroeker, *Great Plains Command*, pp. 154–63. For Haller, see Hamersley, *Records of Living Officers*, pp. 389–90; *ANJ*, March 30, 1878, p. 537; March 8, 1879, p. 548; July 5, 1879, p. 867; and February 11, 1882, p. 612. For Porter, see Eisenschiml, *The Celebrated Case of Fitz-John Porter*, and Schofield, *Forty-Six Years in the Army*, pp. 460–66.

41. Marszalek, *Sherman*, pp. 461–67; Fellman, *Citizen Sherman*, pp. 316–40.

42. Schofield, *Forty-Six Years in the Army*, pp. 446–51; WTS to W. S. Hancock, June 13, 1881 (HQA LS); *ANJ*, December 25, 1880, p. 418; November 19, 1881, p. 343; and May 13, 1882, p. 932.

43. "McDowell has held on with a selfishness and tenacity that seemed to me at times almost indecent," Sherman wrote to Schofield on September 29, 1882 (HQA LS).

44. WTS to W. S. Hancock, June 13, 1881 (HQA LS).

45. WTS to Pope, October 24, 1881; WTS to Mackenzie, September 28, 1882; WTS to Hunt, April 20, 1881 (HQA LS).

46. WTS to Sheridan, May 10, 1881 (HQA LS); *ANJ*, March 16, 1881, p. 698; August 6, 1881, p. 12; and September 10, 1881, p. 114.

47. *OWI*, p. [iii].

48. Actually Dodge did not make this claim in *Our Wild Indians*, as an anonymous correspondent of the *Army and Navy Journal* pointed out (April 22, 1882, p. 870).

49. See *OWI*, pp. 101–15; see also *PNA*, pp. 247–48.

50. *OWI*, pp. xxxv–xxxix.

51. "List of Chromo-Lithographic Plates, with Descriptions and Explanations," *OWI*, p. ix.

52. [A. D. Worthington & Co.], "Thirty-Three Years' Personal Experience among Our Wild Indians," p. [1] (Graff).

53. RID, *A Living Issue*, p. [1]; [A.D. Worthington & Co.], "Thirty-Three Years' Experience among Our Wild Indians," p. [2] (Graff); *ANJ*, April 22, 1881, p. 880; May 6, 1882, p. 916; and June 17, 1882, p. 1055. See also *New York Times*, May 21, 1882, p. 11; *JMSI* 3 (1882), 287.

54. "Our Wild Indians," *ANJ*, February 18, 1882, pp. 640–41. An equally favorable review, signed by H.O. P. [Horace O. Porter], appeared in *JMSI* 3 (1882), 287.

55. *ANJ*, March 4, 1882, p. 681. In its issue for May 6, the newspaper quoted a similar observation in the *New York World* (p. 916).

56. [A.D. Worthington & Co.], "Thirty-Three Years' Personal Experience among Our Wild Indians," p. [1] (Graff); Statement of account, A. D. Worthington & Co. with RID, January 1, 1883 (Graff).

57. *ANJ*, January 21, 1882, p. 536.

58. Alexander J. Perry, Deputy Quartermaster General, to RID, November 18, 1882 (Graff). General Ingalls had subscribed for a personal copy of *Our Wild Indians*.

59. "Explanatory," in *A Living Issue*, p. [2]. Dodge noted that the wording in some portions of the pamphlet "is identical with that in 'Our Wild Indians.' That book, designed to be a minute and careful study of the interior life of the Wild Indians, gives only general conclusions as to their management and ultimate destination. This pamphlet gives the facts and arguments on which those conclusions are based."

60. In full, the quoted statement by Edmunds was as follows: "There is, perhaps, no one thing so valuable to the right progress of civilized society as the courage of sincere, individual opinion; and, as regards public affairs, the man who tries honestly to form an accurate conclusion, and bravely to maintain and advance it, without counting the number of his adversaries, will fulfill the best mission of a citizen."

61. House, *Report of the SW*, 1882, p. 5. Sherman had made virtually the same statement in a report from the Pacific Northwest in 1877; see his *Travel Accounts*, p. 69.

62. The general's report of this journey, in a series of letters to the secretary of war, was published the following year in *Reports of Inspection Made in the Summer of 1877 by Generals P. H. Sheridan and W. T. Sherman of Country North of the Union Pacific Railroad*. It has been reprinted in *Travel Accounts*, pp. 41–83, to which further citations of *Reports of Inspection* refer.

63. *ANJ*, February 26, 1881, p. 619; April 2, 1881, p. 728; and April 9, 1881, p. 749. As a consequence of the Poe report, General Augur, commander of the Department of Texas, directed expeditions in the southwestern section of Texas in search of suitable post sites (*ANJ*, June 18, 1881, p. 963).

64. WTS to Robert T. Lincoln, March 18, 1882; and March 26, 1882 (HQA LS). A consolidated file that includes the general's inspection reports and recommendations for posts along the Rio Grande frontier is 1513 AGO 1882, available in NARA microform publication M989, Roll 91. See also *ANJ*, April 8, 1882, pp. 803, 809, 815.

65. *ANJ*, April 22, 1882, p. 860; and April 29, 1882, p. 880. The quotation is from the latter.

66. *ANJ*, May 13, 1882, p. 932.

67. WTS to Lincoln, March 18, 1882; March 26, 1882; March 30, 1882; and April 14, 1882 (HQA LS). The quotation is from WTS to Lincoln, October 16, 1882 (HQA LS), which was published in House, *Report of the SW*, 1882, pp. 10–17.

68. *ANJ*, June 24, 1882, p. 1080. The interview was acknowledged as from the *New York World*.

69. WTS to Irvin McDowell, February 21, 1882; WTS to Alfred H. Terry, March 7 and May 20, 1883; WTS to Philip H. Sheridan, May 20, 1883 (HQA LS). Brigadier General Alfred H. Terry, who commanded the Department of Dakota, cautioned Sherman that the justices, being unaccustomed to camp life, "will need much more to make them comfortable . . . than you would think at all necessary for yourself." Terry suggested that Colonel Tidball or Colonel Dodge be sent in advance, with appropriate instructions, to supervise preparations (Terry to WTS, June 8, 1882—Sherman Papers, LC).

70. WTS to Waite, June 6 and June 15, 1882; WTS to Sheridan, June 15 and June 19, 1882 (HQA LS).

71. WTS to Orlando B. Willcox, June 27, 1882 (HQA LS).

72. *Official Army Register*, 1882, p. 343.

73. *ANJ*, June 24, 1882, p. 1081. Wilkins, a graduate of West Point in the class of 1842, had completed forty years of active service.

74. *ANJ*, July 1, 1882, pp. 1104, 1109.

75. "I advise him to take his chances," Sherman wrote his wife, Ellen, on June 29, 1882, "and go where accident and the chances of War carry him" (Sherman Family Papers).

76. *ANJ*, July 1, 1882, p. 1110; and July 8, 1882, p. 1133.

77. WTS to Pope, July 15, 1882 (HQA LS). See also *ANJ*, July 22, 1882, p. 1180.

78. RID to AG, August 11, 1882 (AGO LR); *ANJ*, August 19, 1882, p. 52. Dodge was relieved as aide-de-camp by S.O. 163, HQA, July 15, 1882, which was reprinted in *ANJ*, July 22, 1882, p. 1183.

79. See *ANJ*, July 15, 1882, p. 1155.

80. *ANJ*, August 12, 1882, p. 17; and August 26, 1882, p. 72.

81. Taylor to Drum, July 31, 1882 (*ANJ*, September 9, 1882, p. 128). Taylor had appealed for assistance not only to Senators James B. Beck and John S. Williams of Kentucky, but also to a congressman from that state, John G. Carlisle. Moreover, as son-in-law of Brigadier General Montgomery C. Meigs, the recently retired quartermaster general, Taylor may have had access to yet more intervention.

82. *ANJ*, August 26, 1882, p. 72; see also July 15, 1882, p. 1155.

83. GCMO 54, HQA, August 31, 1882, was reprinted in full in *ANJ*, September 9, 1882, p. 128. In his reprimand, Sherman defined the issue at stake in the Taylor trial: "To seek outside influence, or to accept outside influence when a sure mode of redress for all real grievances is given by the statutes and usages governing the army, is destructive to all good discipline, and the higher the officer, the more exalted the reputation and fame, the worse the example."

84. WTS to Alfred H. Terry, May 20, 1883 (HQA LS).

85. Sherman paid tribute to Alexander McD. McCook in G.O. 82, HQA, December 15, 1882, the same order in which he announced his three new staff members. In the present letter his phrase "tame and unprofitable" was an allusion Dodge would have recognized, to *Hamlet* I.ii.130.

86. WTS to RID, September 2, 1882 (HQA LS).

87. Fort Sully Post Return, September 1882; Eleventh Infantry Regimental Return, September 1882.

Chapter 23

1. Frazer, *Forts of the West*, pp. 137–38. General histories of this important frontier post include Schuler, *Fort Sully*, and Hoeckman, "The History of Fort Sully." See also *ANJ*, January 3, 1880, p. 424; October 9, 1880, p. 180; and November 27, 1880, p. 331.

2. In 1880 the Sioux Reservation covered an area of 31,408,511 acres in Dakota Territory, by far the largest reservation of public land allotted to any single tribe (House, *The Public Domain*, p. 245). A map showing Indian reservations west of the Mississippi River in 1883 follows p. 726 in that work.

3. *ANJ*, July 30, 1881, p. 1093.

4. Schuler, *Fort Sully*, pp. 17–18.

5. RID to JRPD, January 20, 1883; and December 20, 1883 (Yale).

6. RID to WTS, October 7, 1882 (Sherman Papers, LC).

7. See *ANJ*, September 30, 1882, p. 196. The anonymous source quoted in this article summarized remarks recently made by Sherman during a visit to Fort Porter, New York. The exchange of stations eventually did occur as anticipated. See *ANJ*, August 4, 1883, p. 53; and September 1, 1883, p. 92.

8. In its issue for February 23, 1889, the *Army and Navy Journal* published a useful table showing the stations of infantry, cavalry, and artillery regiments since 1865 (p. 511).

9. This is the concluding line of John Milton's sonnet, "When I Consider How My Light Is Spent." A few months afterward, a rumor did circulate that the Eleventh Infantry was about to be transferred; see *ANJ*, April 21, 1883, p. 859. However, no action was taken at that time.

10. RID to WTS, October 7, 1882 (Sherman Papers, LC).

11. Beneath Dodge's signature at the end of the letter, Sherman did write "Ansd—" for "Answered," a formula notation he employed regularly.

12. RID Journal, September 11, 1880 (*ITJ*, p. 398).

13. *ANJ*, December 16, 1882, p. 440.

14. RID to JRPD, January 20, 1883 (Yale).

15. RID, "The Enlisted Soldier," pp. 282–83, 316.

16. Schuler, *Fort Sully*, pp. 160, 162–63; RID, "The Enlisted Soldier," p. 317; *ANJ*, September 24, 1881, p. 163; and March 10, 1883, p. 724. The quotation is from the latter article.

17. The implementation of this initiative is described by Douglas C. McChristian in *An Army of Marksmen*, pp. 41–79. For G.O. 44, HQA, May 10, 1881, establishing annual marksmanship competitions within the army, see *ANJ*, May 14, 1881, p. 847.

18. *ANJ*, December 13, 1884, p. 385; Schuler, *Fort Sully*, p. 105.

19. Certificate No. 35, Office Chief Ordnance Officer, Headquarters Department of Dakota, May 17, 1883 (Graff).

20. RID to Church, June 8, 1883 (Church Papers, LC).

21. The original of Dodge's letter, dated March 26, 1883, has not been located. Its date and contents are noted in a summary that precedes the text of the Sherman endorsement of it as copied into the general's collected papers. See Endorsement No. 87, April 14, 1883 (Sherman Papers, LC). See also Eleventh Infantry Regimental Return, March 1883.

22. G.O. 114, HQA, December 12, 1877, regulating the award of sick leaves, was reprinted in *ANJ*, December 22, 1877, p. 307. See also *ANJ*, November 19, 1881, p. 345; January 7, 1882, p. 493; March 4, 1882, p. 680; and July 15, 1882, p. 1155.

23. Endorsement No. 87, April 14, 1883 (Sherman Papers, LC).

24. *ANJ*, April 28, 1883, p. 889; May 5, 1883, p. 901; August 4, 1883, p. 53; December 8, 1883, p. 379; and March 14, 1885, p. 645; Heitman, *Historical Register*, I, p. 201; *STJ*, p. 61 nn. 147, 148.

25. A. D. Worthington to RID, October 24, 1882 (Graff). A printed copy of the newspaper advertisement is attached to the letter.

26. A. D. Worthington & Co., "Thirty-Three Years' Personal Experience among Our Wild Indians" (Dodge Papers, Graff).

27. A. D. Worthington to RID, October 24, 1882 (Graff).

28. Alexander J. Perry, Deputy Quartermaster General, to RID, November 18, 1882 (Graff).

29. A. D. Worthington to RID, October 24, 1882, and December 30, 1882 (Graff).

30. Statement of account, A. D. Worthington & Co. with RID, January 1, 1883 (Graff). As a colonel with less than five years' experience at that rank, Dodge earned $3,500 per year (*ANJ*, July 22, 1882, p. 1185).

31. A. D. Worthington to RID, December 30, 1882, and January 19, 1883 (Graff). Not mentioned in either of these letters was the publisher's acute need of funds to finance an upcoming publication, *Our Famous Women*, which appeared in the spring.

32. A. D. Worthington to RID, April 20, 1883 (Graff).

33. Statement of account, A. D. Worthington & Co. with RID, August 1, 1883 (Graff). The statement of July 1, 1884, showed 38,185 copies sold (Graff).

34. A. D. Worthington to RID, March 10, 1884 (Graff).

35. Rideing to RID, September 22, 1882 (Graff). Rideing's book was entitled *Boys in the Mountains and on the Plains: Or, The Western Adventures of Tom Smart, Bob Edge and Peter Small* (1882).

36. Rideing to RID, October 10, 1882 (Graff). Dodge's initial response to Rideing has been lost. The phrases attributed to him in the text are Rideing's, evidently reproducing the content of a statement in that letter.

37. The following paragraph preceded Dodge's expression of intent to supply an "accurate account":

> The Indians are now rounded up on Reservations, herded fed and cared for as if so many cattle. One good results from the cordon of troops. Indian wars such as horrified the country even less than fifteen years ago can never occur again. Animosities and prejudices will gradually die out, & we may well hope that when those white Boys, of whom I have spoken, shall have taken their places as Rulers of this country they will if properly educated see that both policy and humanity point to the treatment of the Indian as a man and not a mere brutish animal. Break up the Tribal relations, Erect the Indian into an American Citizen, give him the ballot, and a home in severalty, and make him individually amenable to the Laws of the county and state in which he dwells. There is in my mind no doubt of this final solution to the Indian problem. The wild Indian, as he lived when free and untrammelled on his western home exists no longer ("Indian Boys and Girls"—Graff).

38. Perry Mason & Co. per William H. Rideing to RID, November 28, 1882 (Graff). Coincidentally, the phrase "thrilling adventures" formed part of the sesquipedalian subtitle of *Our Wild Indians*, devised in all probability by A. D. Worthington. It did not accurately describe the book's contents, nor did it suit Dodge's taste.

39. In response to a letter from Dodge that has been lost, on March 3, 1883, Rideing assured him that "I fully understand and appreciate your views." He urged him to send along for review any future writings he thought might be suitable for *Youth's Companion* (Graff).

40. "Details of Extra Duty Men," *ANJ*, April 21, 1883, p. 836. Dodge's authorship of this letter is confirmed by an unpublished letter he wrote on April 1, 1883, to William C. Church of the *Army and Navy Journal*. In the March 24 issue of the newspaper, two letters had appeared under the heading "Extra and Daily Duty Men," both calling into question recent directives by department commanders concerning the numbers of men assigned at posts to these types of duty (p. 779). Additionally, an editorial statement urged the War Department to consider the issues these correspondents had raised (p. 777). "Let us have more discussion on these subjects," Dodge wrote Church in regard to the recent issue. "If you will open up a discussion on this subject, I will say my say" (Church Papers, LC). The letter in the April 21 issue, signed by "Dugge," was his promised contribution to the interchange of opinion.

41. Line [RID], "Enlistments," *ANJ*, April 21, 1883, p. 868; Line [RID], "Causes for Desertion," *ANJ*, May 19, 1883, p. 957. I have attributed these items to Dodge on account of the virtual identity between the ideas expressed in them and those in his other writings, notably "The Enlisted Soldier"; their vigorous style; the applicability to him of the pseudonym, he being an officer of the line; and his other known contributions to the *Army and Navy Journal*.

42. *ANJ*, January 13, 1883, p. 525; January 27, 1883, p. 576; and February 10, 1883, p. 625.

43. *ANJ*, December 24, 1881, p. 481.

44. *ANJ*, November 18, 1882, p. 348.

45. *ANJ*, December 9, 1882, p. 393.

46. WTS to Schofield, February 17, 1883 (HQA LS).

47. WTS to Alfred H. Terry, March 7, 1883 (HQA LS).

48. WTS to Alfred H. Terry, March 7 and May 20, 1883; WTS to Philip H. Sheridan, May 20, 1883; WTS to Thomas H. Ruger, May 29, 1883 (HQA LS).

49. WTS to Alfred H. Terry, March 7 and May 20, 1883; WTS to Philip H. Sheridan, May 20 and June 2, 1883; WTS to John M. Schofield, May 20, 1883; WTS to Thomas H. Ruger, May 29, 1883 (HQA LS). Plans for the summer tour were made public in *ANJ*, March 31, 1883, p. 798, and June 23, 1883, p. 1069.

50. WTS to Palmer, May 21, 1883 (HQA LS); Poor, *Manual of the Railroads*, 1883, pp. 886–89.

51. Sherman appreciated the historical symmetry suggested here, as he indicated in his annual report for 1883: "The recent completion of the last of the four great transcontinental lines of railway [the Atlantic and Pacific] has settled forever the Indian question, the Army question, and many others which have hitherto troubled the country" (House, *Report of the SW*, p. 46). See also Athearn, *Sherman and the Settlement of the West*, pp. 343–48.

52. Poe, "Report on Transcontinental Railways, 1883," in House, *Report of the SW*, 1883, pp. 253–330.

53. WTS to Gordon, June 3, 1883 (HQA LS).

54. Sherman wrote to Terry on May 20: "I want to put these Judges on army diet, for they are over fed now, and I want them to experience the usual privations of camp life. . . . The nearer we get to 'first principles' the better will I be pleased" (HQA LS).

55. In 1875 the *New York Herald* named Sherman "the best random speech-maker in the country" (*ANJ*, October 9, 1875, p. 138; see also *ANJ*, October 27, 1883, p. 250). Dodge later commented on the general's "numerous speeches (wonderful for their 'infinite variety')" ("The Enlisted Soldier," p. 286). The quoted phrase within Dodge's parentheses is from *Antony and Cleopatra* II.ii.244.

56. *ANJ*, February 23, 1886, p. 617.

57. *ANJ*, June 30, 1883, p. 1082. The article was acknowledged as from the *Washington Republican*.

58. WTS to Terry, May 20, 1883. See also WTS to Philip H. Sheridan, May 20, 1883 (HQA LS).

59. WTS to Terry, June 19, 1883 (HQA LS); *ANJ*, June 23, 1883, p. 1059.

60. S.O. 140, HQA, June 19, 1883 (Graff).

61. "If I get time from the sight seeing, fishing & hunting," Dodge wrote William C. Church of the *Army and Navy Journal*, "I may give you a letter or two" (RID to Church, June 8, 1883—Church Papers, LC).

Chapter 24

1. RID Journal, June 25, 1883 (*STJ*, p. 88). The first of Dodge's two journals describing the inspection tour, with entries dated from June 23 to August 29, 1883, is found in *STJ*, pp. 86–136.

2. Johnson, who had retired in 1875, later published a volume of memoirs, *A Soldier's Reminiscences in Peace and War* (1886).

3. *ANJ*, June 30, 1883, p. 1076. See also *ANJ*, July 20, 1878, p. 805.

4. Sherman judged the first week of the journey "most successful and agreeable" (WTS to Robert T. Lincoln, July 2, 1883—HQA LS). The letters addressed by Sherman to Secretary Lincoln during the summer of 1883 are available in NARA microform publication M857, Roll 9.

5. RID Journal, June 27, 1883 (*STJ*, p. 89).

6. RID Journal, June 28, 1883 (*STJ*, pp. 89–90).

7. Tidball, "Report of Journey Made by General W. T. Sherman in the Northwest and Middle Parts of the United States in 1883" (hereafter cited as "Report"), *Report of the SW,* 1883, p. 206. This narrative has been reprinted, but with inaccuracies, in Sherman, *Travel Accounts*, pp. 152–213.

8. RID Journal, June 28, 1883 (*STJ*, pp. 90–91).

9. RID Journal, June 30, 1883 (*STJ*, pp. 91–92).

10. Employing contemporary vernacular, Dodge referred to the cook as "a heathen Chinee." See Bret Harte's poem, "Plain Language from Truthful James."

11. Sherman informed Secretary Lincoln that in respect of "the two distinguished judges, we will carry tents and a few more of the ordinary comforts of life than I usually approve on such trips" (WTS to Lincoln, July 2, 1883—HQA LS).

12. RID Journal, July 4, 1883 (*STJ*, p. 94).

13. Tidball, "Report," p. 208.

14. RID Journal, July 5 and 6, 1883 (*STJ*, pp. 94–95).

15. Tidball, "Report," p. 209.

16. RID Journal, July 6, 1883 (*STJ*, p. 95).

17. See Dodge's journal entry for August 4, 1883 (*STJ*, p. 117).

18. The south side of the single thoroughfare lay within the government reservation and so was unoccupied. Tidball remarked that businesses were housed in "every conceivable manner of shanty, the majority of which are drinking saloons" ("Report," p. 209).

19. RID Journal, July 7, 1883 (*STJ*, p. 96); Tidball, "Report," p. 209.

20. RID Journal, July 9, 1883 (*STJ*, p. 97).

21. *Sherman, Travel Accounts*, pp. 50–51.

22. RID Journal, July 9, 1883 (*STJ*, pp. 97–98); Tidball, "Report," p. 212.

23. In July 1876 Dodge received from the Earl of Dunraven a letter proposing a hunt from Fort Fred Steele that October. In response, he assured the nobleman that he would find out the most likely vicinities in the area and that he expected William Blackmore to join them. Shortly afterward he wrote Blackmore: "Now[,] old fellow entre nous, I would'nt give a snap to go with him, unless you are of the party – He is too quiet too abstemious & too hard working a hunter for my taste – I like hunting, but I don't propose to make my pleasure a labor – I shall do my best to make him have a good time & a successful hunt but I want *you*. *You* suit my style of hunting – & *you* are the fellow I am after" (RID to Blackmore, August 2, 1876—No. 916, MNM).

24. RID Journal, July 10, 1883 (*STJ*, p. 98).

25. RID Journal, July 11, 1883 (*STJ*, p. 99).

26. Poor, *Manual of the Railroads,* 1883, pp. 900–901; RID Journal, July 12, 1883 (*STJ*, p. 100); Tidball, "Report," p. 216.

27. WTS to Robert T. Lincoln, July 29, 1883 (HQA LS). In 1881 Chief Justice Waite was chancellor of the Smithsonian Institution, and Sherman a member of its board of regents (U.S. Department of the Interior, *Proceedings of the United States National Museum* [1881], Appendix 5, p. 1).

28. RID Journal, July 13, 1883 (*STJ*, p. 101). For a time Waite hoped to rejoin the tour in San Francisco, but he abandoned the idea in deference to the wishes of his wife. "Remember me most kindly to all the party," he wrote to General Sherman on August 1. "I hope Dodge found use for his gun after he

got out of the [Yellowstone] park, and tell Gray there are many things in this world worse than a frying pan" (Sherman Papers, LC).

29. The named geysers of the Lower and Upper Basins are mapped in U.S. Geological and Geographical Survey, *Twelfth Annual Report* (1883), Part II, "Yellowstone National Park," pp. 178, 240.

30. RID Journal, July 14 and 15 (*STJ*, pp. 103–104); Tidball, "Report," pp. 217–19.

31. Tidball, "Report," p. 220.

32. RID Journal, July 17, 1883 (*STJ*, p. 105); Tidball, "Report," p. 221.

33. RID Journal, July 19 and 20, 1883 (*STJ*, pp. 106–107); Tidball, "Report," p. 222.

34. WTS to Robert T. Lincoln, July 29, 1883 (HQA LS); Tidball, "Report," pp. 222–23; RID Journal, July 21, 1883 (*STJ*, p. 107). The name of the settlement was spelled either Bannock or Bannack City.

35. On August 9–10, 1877, Gibbon fought a pitched battle in the Big Hole Basin against the Nez Perce Indians under Chief Joseph. Both sides suffered heavy casualties, and Gibbon himself was wounded. His official report of the engagement is found in the *Report of the SW,* 1877, pp. 501–505; see also *ANJ*, August 18, 1877, p. 21; and Beal, *"I Will Fight No More Forever,"* pp. 112–27. A monument commemorating the battle and the men who died there was subsequently constructed. However, in 1883 it had not yet been placed on the battlefield, owing to difficulty transporting it from the Northern Pacific Railroad; see *ANJ*, October 14, 1882, p. 237.

36. RID Journal, July 24, 1883 (*STJ*, pp. 108–109); WTS to Robert T. Lincoln, July 29, 1883 (HQA LS); Tidball, "Report," pp. 224–25.

37. WTS to Robert T. Lincoln, July 29, 1883 (HQA LS).

38. Sherman, *Travel Accounts*, p. 47.

39. WTS to Robert T. Lincoln, July 29, 1883 (HQA LS).

40. RID Journal, July 26, 1883 (*STJ*, p. 110). For a description of improvements to Fort Missoula since the first visit there by Sherman, see *ANJ*, October 30, 1880, p. 241.

41. Tidball, "Report," pp. 225–26.

42. RID Journal, July 27, 1883 (*STJ*, p. 111); WTS to Robert T. Lincoln, July 29, 1883 (HQA LS); Tidball, "Report," p. 226. According to Tidball, the bridge over the Morentz Gulch was 226 feet high and 868 feet long.

43. *ANJ*, May 27, 1882, p. 982.

44. *New York Times*, September 10, 1883, p. 1.

45. WTS to Robert T. Lincoln, August 30, 1883 (Sherman Papers, LC).

46. See *ANJ*, October 30, 1880, p. 241; and April 22, 1882, p. 260. The fort was established in accordance with a directive by Sherman; see House, *Report of the SW,* 1878, p. 259.

47. RID Journal, July 28, 1883 (*STJ*, p. 112). Sherman wrote that "General Dodge" pronounced Fort Coeur d'Alene "perfect, as near Heaven as he ever expects to get" (WTS to Robert T. Lincoln, July 29, 1883—HQA LS).

48. RID Journal, July 31, 1883 (*STJ*, p. 113); *ANJ*, August 25, 1883, p. 65, summarized from the *Portland (Oregon) News*. Sherman later acknowledged his liking for young women, pronouncing them "God's most perfect handiwork" (*ANJ*, October 1, 1887, p. 190).

49. George W. Goethals (1858–1928) later won fame as supervisor of construction for the Panama Canal, which was opened for use in 1914 after seven years under construction. In recognition, Goethals was promoted to major general; in the following year he was appointed the first governor of the Canal Zone.

50. *ANJ*, August 18, 1883, p. 47; *STJ*, p. 113 n. 94.

51. RID Journal, August 2, 1883 (*STJ*, p. 114). Sherman was inured to the aggressive officiousness of Miles and considered him "too apt to mistake the dictates of his personal ambition for wisdom. . . . He will absorb all power to himself and ignore his immediate commanders if not supervised and checked" (WTS to P. H. Sheridan, July 19, 1879—Sherman Papers, LC). He once told Miles that evidently the only way to satisfy his ambition was "to surrender to him absolute power over the whole Army with President and Congress thrown in" (Robert M. Utley, "Nelson A. Miles," in *Soldiers West*, ed. Hutton, p. 222).

52. RID Journal, August 2, 1883 (*STJ*, p. 114).

53. A Senate document, *Report of Brig. Gen. Nelson A. Miles, September 1881*, summarizes General Miles's inspection of Camp Spokane at that time.

54. Willis (1857–1949), son of the New York literary journalist Nathaniel Parker Willis, recounted his participation in the Sherman tour in *A Yanqui in Patagonia*, pp. 20–23.

55. For the comments of Sherman on Camp Spokane, see *STJ*, p. 116 n. 103.

56. WTS to Robert T. Lincoln, August 30, 1883 (HQA LS). The feasibility of steamboat transportation on the upper Columbia River had recently been evaluated by First Lieutenant Thomas W. Symons, the engineer officer of the Department of the Columbia. His report was issued as a Senate document, *Report of an Examination of the Upper Columbia River* (1882).

57. Tidball, "Report," p. 231.

58. RID Journal, August 7, 1883 (*STJ*, p. 119).

59. RID Journal, August 8, 1883 (*STJ*, pp. 120–21). Dodge refers here to First Lieutenant Charles W. Rowell, Second Infantry.

60. RID Journal, August 9, 1883 (*STJ*, p. 121); Tidball, "Report," p. 233.

61. Willis, *A Yanqui in Patagonia*, p. 21.

62. RID Journal, August 6, 1883 (*STJ*, p. 118).

63. WTS to Robert T. Lincoln, August 30, 1883 (HQA LS); see also Tidball, "Report," p. 234.

64. According to Tidball, the British custom house was "a neat, comfortable frame building, with brick chimneys and broad piazzas. It occupies a beautiful site on the shore of the lake, which is here a clean sandy beach" ("Report," p. 236).

65. RID Journal, August 13, 1883 (*STJ*, p. 124).

66. RID Journal, August 15, 1883 (*STJ*, p. 124).

67. RID Journal, August 16, 1883 (*STJ*, p. 125).

68. Tidball, "Report," p. 238.

69. RID Journal, August 16, 1883 (*STJ*, p. 125).

70. RID Journal, August 18, 1883 (*STJ*, pp. 126–27).

71. Tidball, "Report," p. 240.

72. WTS to Robert T. Lincoln, August 30, 1883 (HQA LS); Tidball, "Report," p. 240; Willis, *A Yanqui in Patagonia*, p. 20.

73. WTS to Robert T. Lincoln, August 30, 1883 (HQA LS); RID Journal, August 19, 1883 (*STJ*, pp. 128–30).

74. RID Journal, August 20 and 21, 1883 (*STJ*, pp. 130–31); Tidball, "Report," pp. 240–41.

75. Chambers had been Dodge's host at Camp Sheridan late in the Black Hills Expedition; see *BHJ*, pp. 236–45 passim.

76. WTS to Robert T. Lincoln, August 30, 1883 (HQA LS).

77. RID Journal, August 22, 1883 (*STJ*, p. 133).

78. *ANJ*, August 18, 1883, p. 44.

79. RID Journal, August 23 and 24, 1883 (*STJ*, pp. 132–33).

80. RID Journal, August 24, 1883 (*STJ*, pp. 133–34). The marriage of Mamie Greene, the eldest daughter of Lt. Col. and Mrs. Greene, to First Lieutenant Charles H. Bonesteel, Twenty-first Infantry, had been a brilliant social event; see *ANJ*, May 13, 1882, p. 931; and July 8, 1882, p. 1135.

81. RID Journal, August 25, 1883 (*STJ*, p. 134); *ANJ*, September 15, 1883, pp. 128, 133.

82. RID Journal, August 26 and 27, 1883 (*STJ*, pp. 134–35).

83. RID Journal, August 28 and 29, 1883 (*STJ*, p. 136).

84. RID Journal, August 29, 1883 (*STJ*, p.136); *San Francisco Chronicle*, September 4, 1883, p. 8. The second of Dodge's journals describing the inspection tour, with entries dated from August 30 to September 28, 1883, is found in *STJ*, pp. 137–60.

85. Statement of account, A. D. Worthington & Co. with RID, August 1, 1883 (Graff).

86. RID Journal, August 30, 1883 (*STJ*, pp. 138–39). Dodge referred to Gus Bibby in a journal entry of April 13, 1879, as "a dear old girl, and has a hard life of it. They have failed to realize the bright future they hoped was in store for them" (*ITJ*, p. 304). Probably she was the widow of Alfred Bibby, who lived at 418 Post Street and ran a store dealing in kid gloves for ladies and gentlemen (Langley, *Langley's San Francisco Directory for 1881*, pp. 107, 151).

87. *ANJ*, February 17, 1883, p. 651; and April 4, 1883, p. 837; Heitman, *Historical Register*, I, p. 267.

88. RID Journal, September 3–6, 1883 (*STJ*, pp. 140–42).

89. Together with Judge Gray, the two officers considered the possibility of visiting Monterey, on the Pacific coast south of San Francisco, and also Yosemite, in the Sierra Nevada to the east, but decided against both. As General Sherman explained in a letter of September 5 to his wife, Ellen, "the atmosphere continues so smoky that they have not felt inclined to risk the mountains with the probability as in Oregon of seeing nothing. They however have been fully occupied with the specialities of this city" (Sherman Family Papers).

90. RID Journal, September 4, 1883 (*STJ*, p. 141). An account of the G.A.R. meeting appeared in the *San Francisco Chronicle*, September 11, 1883, p. 3.

91. RID Journal, September 5, 1883 (*STJ*, p. 141). For an account of the Military Order of the Loyal Legion of the United States, a veteran's organization founded in 1865, see Davies, *Patriotism on Parade*. Dodge was not at this time a member of MOLLUS, but eventually he did become one (Aubin, *Register*, p. 73).

92. RID Journal, September 1, 1883 (*STJ*, p. 140). RID was quoting Isaiah 35:1.

93. RID Journal, September 1 and 2, 1883 (*STJ*, pp. 139–40). According to a contemporary observer, "The dwellings, furniture, tables, and dress of the people, indicate very liberal expenditure. San Francisco has the reputation of buying the most costly wines, cigars and silks. A saying, not deserving to be dignified as a proverb, declares that 'New York dresses better than Paris, and San Francisco better than New York.' The magnificent hotels and the palaces of a dozen millionaires are unsurpassed, if equaled, by anything short of royalty in the luxury of their appointments" (Hittell, *A History of the City of San Francisco*, p. 457).

94. RID Journal, September 3 and 4, 1883 (*STJ*, pp. 140–41); WTS to Robert T. Lincoln, October 1, 1883 (HQA LS).

95. *Los Angeles Herald*, September 12, 1883, p. 3.

96. Tidball tasked his descriptive powers to convey his impression of the view from Sierra Madre Villa: "This place is elevated some 500 feet above the valley of the San Gabriel, which stretches out below some 20 miles to the Pacific. In clear weather Santa Catalina and other islands can be seen breaking the horizon to the westward. Over this entire region nature smiling has bestowed her richest gifts—a tropical climate, tempered by ocean breezes, to perennial spring, and a soil securing the broadest and highest agricultural and horticultural possibilities. As far as the eye can see, the plain below is a vast field of vineyards and orange groves, interspersed with lemons, pomegranates, limes, and other trees of semi-tropical growth" ("Report," p. 242).

97. RID Journal, September 10, 1883 (*STJ*, p. 144).

98. WTS to Robert T. Lincoln, October 1, 1883 (HQA LS); Tidball, "Report," pp. 242–43; RID Journal, September 10 and 11, 1883 (*STJ*, pp. 144–45).

99. *Los Angeles Herald*, September 12, 1883, p. 3.

100. RID Journal, September 13, 1883 (*STJ*, p. 146).

101. RID Journal, September 13, 1883 (*STJ*, p. 146); Tidball, "Report," p. 245; WTS to Robert T. Lincoln, October 1, 1883 (HQA LS).

102. WTS to Lincoln, October 1, 1883 (HQA LS); RID Journal, September 14, 1883 (*STJ*, pp. 146–47).

103. RID Journal, September 16, 1883 (*STJ*, pp. 147–48).

104. *ANJ*, December 29, 1883, p. 440; January 5, 1884, pp. 459–60, 461; February 23, 1884, p. 601; March 15, 1884, pp. 664, 672; and March 29, 1884, p. 715. See also Nohl, "Bad Hand," pp. 323–30; Pierce, *The Most Promising Young Officer*, pp. 224–25.

105. WTS to Robert T. Lincoln, October 1, 1883 (HQA LS); Poor, *Manual of the Railroads*, 1883, p. 892; Bryant, *History of the Atchison, Topeka and Santa Fe Railway*, pp. 60–62.

106. See WTS to Robert T. Lincoln, October 16, 1882 (HQA LS). This letter, which contained the general's recommendations to that date of the army posts to be made permanent along the five "frontiers," was published in House, *Report of the SW*, 1882, pp. 10–17.

107. Tidball, "Report," p. 252.

108. Tidball, "Report," p. 246; RID Journal, September 17 and 18, 1883 (*STJ*, pp. 148–49).

109. The post was named after Lieutenant Colonel William H. Lewis, Nineteenth Infantry, who had been mortally wounded in action against the Northern Cheyennes in September 1878. Upon learning of

Lewis's death, Dodge wrote in his journal: "Poor Lewis, he was a noble fellow, & died a noble death, the death of all others that a soldier should desire" (*ITJ*, p. 28).

110. RID Journal, September 18, 1883 (*STJ*, p. 149); Tidball, "Report," p. 247; WTS to Robert T. Lincoln, October 1, 1883 (HQA LS).

111. Tidball, "Report," p. 248; RID Journal, September 19, 1883 (*STJ*, p. 149).

112. Tidball, "Report," p. 248; RID Journal, September 20, 1883 (*STJ*, pp. 150–51).

113. RID Journal, September 21, 1883 (*STJ*, p. 151); see also *ITJ*, pp. 372–79.

114. Tidball, "Report," p. 249.

115. Tidball, "Report," p. 250.

116. The Walker House boasted a "Passenger Elevator and all other modern improvements," with the "Largest Billiard Hall in the City" (*Salt Lake City Directory for 1879–80*, p. 11).

117. RID Journal, September 23, 1883 (*STJ*, p. 152–53); *Salt Lake City Deseret News*, September 22, 1883, p. 5; and September 24, 1883, p. 3.

118. *Denver Tribune*, September 27, 1883, p. 1.

119. WTS to Lincoln, October 1, 1883 (HQA LS). A survey of Denver's development as a regional center is provided by Rodman Paul in *The Far West and the Great Plains in Transition*, pp. 94–104.

120. RID Journal, September 28, 1883 (*STJ*, p. 156).

Part 7

1. RID to WTS, October 7, 1882 (Sherman Papers, LC).

Chapter 25

1. RID to AG, October 21, 1883 (RID ACP File, AGO). The original order, dated October 2, also forms part of the file.

2. R. C. Drum to RID, November 6, 1883 (RID ACP File, AGO).

3. RID to WTS, November 13, 1883 (Graff).

4. The amended order bearing Sherman's signature was received at the Adjutant General's Office on November 22 (RID ACP File, AGO).

5. He deleted "Dear" and the following statement: "With best wishes for your health & happiness in your new sphere of life." Other revisions exhibit a similar intention to maintain a tone not personal but official. For example, Dodge began the letter's penultimate statement with the phrases, "Will you please do me the favor to sign these . . ." but revised them to "You will please sign these . . ." (RID to WTS [draft], November 13, 1883—Graff).

6. *ANJ*, November 10, 1883, p. 286.

7. *Dakota Journal*, September 21, 1883, quoted in Schuler, *Fort Sully*, p. 63.

8. Schuler, *Fort Sully*, p. 165.

9. *ANJ*, January 3, 1884, p. 455.

10. RID to JRPD, January 20, 1883 (Yale).

11. John M. Schofield to AG, February 15, 1884, forwarding a report by Dodge dated February 13 (AGO LR). A consolidated file relating to the fire at Fort Sully, 688 AGO 1884, is available in NARA microform publication M689, Roll 260. An account of the fire appeared in *ANJ*, February 28, 1884, p. 603.

12. RID Journal, June 26, 1883 (*STJ*, p. 88).

13. *ANJ*, April 12, 1884, p. 760.

14. See *ANJ*, May 11, 1878, p. 650. Terry's priorities had long favored the larger posts in his department and some of those along the Northern Pacific Railroad. See *Report of the SW*, 1884; Bailey, *Pacifying the Plains*, pp. 196–98. However, General Sherman had listed Fort Sully among the posts in the interior of the United States that should be considered permanent; see *ANJ*, November 25, 1882, p. 373.

15. Forts Sully and Bennett had been inspected only one month before (Inspector General to AG, January 26, 1884—AGO Reg LR).

16. In addition to documents in the consolidated file concerning the fire at Fort Sully, see letters from Dodge forwarded by Schofield to the Adjutant General's Office on March 25 and 27, May 6, June 23 and 26, and August 30, 1884 (AGO Reg LR).

17. For a description of Terry's close relationship with Hughes, see Bailey, *Pacifying the Plains*, p. 135.

18. RID to WTS, December 10, 1884 (Sherman Papers, LC).

19. RID to FPD, October 12, 1884 (Yale); RID to WTS, December 10, 1884 (Sherman Papers, LC).

20. On August 30, 1884, Schofield forwarded to the adjutant general, with his approval, a communication from Terry reporting that he had reconsidered his earlier recommendation against the rebuilding of Fort Sully. Terry now believed that the garrison at the fort should be maintained at its present strength. In addition, he asked authority and funds to construct a barracks at the fort in addition to the structures already authorized (AGO Reg LR). The summary of these documents in the register of letters received by the Adjutant General's Office indicates a capitulation by Terry.

21. RID to FPD, October 12, 1884 (Yale).

22. RID to WTS, October 21, 1884 (Sherman Papers, LC). See also RID to WTS, November 8 and December 10, 1884 (Sherman Papers, LC).

23. *ANJ*, November 29, 1884, p. 341; and December 13, 1884, p. 385.

24. *ANJ*, July 18, 1885, p. 1034.

25. Rifle competitions that relied upon the unverified reports of company commanders for determining the relative levels of attainment among units throughout the army were "simply premiums on lying & fraud," Dodge declared in 1883. He advocated a more closely monitored system that, being "perfectly fair," would ensure that "the best man wins" (RID to William C. Church, June 8, 1883—Church Papers, LC).

26. "Sharpshooters," *ANJ*, August 8, 1885, p. 34.

27. RID, "Rifle Firing at Fort Sully," *ANJ*, August 29, 1885, p. 90. In the issue for August 22, the editors noted that "a very interesting and conclusive answer" to "Trigger" had been received from "General Richard I. Dodge," but that it had arrived too late for that week's issue (p. 69).

28. "Fort Sully Sharpshooters Again," *ANJ*, September 19, 1885, p. 149.

29. A variety of evidence identifies Burt as the author of "Chats around the Mess Table." Burt, whom Dodge once referred to as "a literary & Artistic cuss" (*ITJ*, p. 302), was an experienced newspaper journalist with a lively wit. He was known personally by the editors of *the Army and Navy Journal*, who gave generous coverage to his activities and characterized him as an "all-round good fellow" (July 14, 1894, p. 806). In its issue for August 21, 1875, the newspaper had reprinted a letter by Burt for the *New York Tribune* describing Dodge's skill as a marksman and hunter (p. 21). Burt figures as a character in several of installments of "Chats," some of which recount information only he could have known.

"Chats around the Mess Table" soon moved away from its satirical comments on named individuals. In addition to the articles cited in the notes that follow, "Chats" appeared in *ANJ*, August 22, 1885, p. 69; September 26, 1885, p. 172; October 10, 1885, p. 210; October 17, 1885, p. 229; February 27, 1886, p. 617; and August 21, 1886, p. 80.

30. "Chats around the Mess Table," *ANJ*, August 8, 1885, p. 34.

31. See *ANJ*, April 15, 1882, p. 828; November 22, 1884, p. 320; and September 12, 1885, 127.

32. "Offhand Shooting," *ANJ*, September 12, 1885, p. 124.

33. The column continues: "How did Caterer know that? Well, in part, so: Morris Foote told Miss Maud Harrison, the divine soubrette. Did you know that he met her at the riots in Chicago in _77? No? The strikers raised the riot. Miss Maud was there playing with the Madison Square Company, and Foote was working with an infantry one. That does account for it, as Miss Harrison told Clara Belle, and, and, so the oft-told tale went glacing [glancing?]" (*ANJ*, September 19, 1885, p. 144). See also *BHJ*, pp. 111–17. First Lieutenant Morris C. Foote, Ninth Infantry, was Dodge's adjutant during the Black Hills Expedition but was officially attached to Burt's company.

34. *ANJ*, November 15, 1884, p. 309.

35. *ANJ*, November 19, 1887, p. 320. The phrase is from Sheridan's annual report, reprinted in that issue.

36. A consolidated file relating to the tests of magazine guns, 7565 AGO 1885, is available in NARA microform publication M689, Roll 302.

37. *ANJ*, July 11, 1885, p. 1013; and July 25, 1885, p. 1052; Fort Sully Post Return, October 1883.

38. *ANJ*, November 19, 1887, p. 320.

39. RID to AG, December 10, 1885 (AGO LR).

40. In May 1884 the companies of the Eleventh Infantry were posted as follows: A, D, E, and K at Fort Sully; B and F at Camp Poplar River, Montana Territory; C and H at Fort Buford, Dakota Territory; G at Fort Leavenworth, Kansas; and I at Fort Bennett (Eleventh Infantry Regimental Return). Dodge had seen only the companies at Forts Sully and Bennett.

41. Eleventh Infantry Regimental Return, October 1884; *ANJ*, November 22, 1884, p. 320. For the number of the regiment's officers serving in 1883, see above, chapter 23.

42. *ANJ*, December 11, 1886. Wikoff had been attached to the Eleventh Infantry since 1867. On the deaths of regimental officers, Dodge fashioned fitting official tributes of respect. See, for example, his statement concerning the late Second Lieutenant Frederick F. Kislingbury, who had died in the Arctic regions as a member of the Greely Expedition in search of Sir John Franklin; *ANJ*, August 9, 1884, p. 22.

43. *ANJ*, June 5, 1886, p. 924; and July 10, 1886, pp. 1017, 1020. See also the issues of December 13, 1884, p. 385; and December 26, 1885, p. 430.

44. *ANJ*, May 13, 1886, p. 852.

45. *ANJ*, February 26, 1887, p. 607; see also February 12, 1887, p. 575; and May 7, 1887, p. 815; *New York Times*, February 7, 1887, p. 4.

46. In German, *Wächter* means "guard," as in guard duty; "91" indicated the year of Dodge's retirement.

47. Woodhull's prize essay was summarized in *ANJ*, April 2, 1887, p. 718, and published in full in *JMSI* 8 (March 1887), 18–70.

48. RID, *The Enlisted Soldier* (Fort Sully, 1886); "The Enlisted Soldier," *JMSI* 8 (September 1887), 259–318. Parenthetical page-references in the text that follows are to the journal article.

49. A. A. Woodhull to RID, September 27, 1887; R. L. Kilpatrick to RID, September 29, 1887 (Graff).

50. *ANJ*, December 15, 1883, p. 388.

51. *ANJ*, July 31, 1886, p. 13.

52. "The Army and the Indians," *ANJ*, October 15, 1887, p. 226.

53. WTS to RID, September 16, 1884 (Sherman Papers, LC).

54. See Emerson, "The Problem."

55. See *ITJ*, pp. 414–15. In May 1884, Running Buffalo, a Cheyenne Indian with whom Dodge became friends while stationed in Indian Territory, was slain by a cattle herder near Fort Supply. Running Buffalo was attempting to resist a herd's being driven across land he considered his own.

56. RID to WTS, September 30, 1884 (Sherman Papers, LC). See Emerson, "The Problem." Dodge returned to his criticism of the cattle industry in letters to Sherman dated October 14, October 21, and November 8, 1884 (Sherman Papers, LC). For a survey of the industry's impact on the Great Plains in the 1870s and 1880s, see Paul, *The Far West and the Great Plains in Transition*, pp. 193–206.

57. In his remarks before the cattleman's convention, Sherman recalled his regret at seeing the buffalo, elk, and antelope disappear from the plains. However, he continued, he had since discerned "a decree of nature" in the replacement of these animals by "twenty millions of fine breeding cattle which supply the world with meat" (*ANJ*, November 22, 1884, p. 317). See also "The Round-Up," *St. Louis Post-Dispatch*, November 17, 1884, p. 2; *STJ*, pp. 169–70.

58. See Hornaday, *The Extermination of the American Bison*, II, pp. 389–90, 392, 400, 407, 409–11, 424, 433–34, 471–72. 495–96, 498–500.

59. W. T. Hornaday to RID, September 14, 1887 (Graff).

60. RID to Hornaday, September 21, 1887, reprinted in Hornaday, *The Extermination of the American Bison*, II, p. 392.

61. Hornaday to RID, September 14, 1887 (Graff). The illustration borrowed by Hornaday appeared in *The Extermination of the American Bison*, II, following p. 392; for a modern reprint, see *PNA*, following p. 149.

62. Certainly the partial translation of *The Plains* into German, by Karl Müller, contributed to the enthusiasm for western tales that prevailed in Europe at that time. See *Die Heutigen Indianer des Fernen Westens: Aus Dreisjähriger Anschauung Geschildert von Richard Irving Dodge . . . Mit Einer Einleitung von W. Blackmore* (Vienna: A. Hartleben, 1884). Without acknowledgment though probably with Dodge's assent, Nelson A. Miles included four of the full-page color plates from *Our Wild Indians* in his *Personal Recollections and Observations* (1896); see pp. 99, 185, 410, and 531.

63. On July 15, 1884, Twain informed William Dean Howells that on his "off days" he was at work on "a new story (Huck Finn & Tom Sawyer among the Indians 40 or 50 years ago.)" (Clemens, *Mark Twain-Howells Letters*, II, p. 496). "Huck Finn and Tom Sawyer among the Indians" was first published in *Life* magazine (65 [December 20, 1968], 32–50). Parenthetical page references in the text that follows are to Blair, ed., *Mark Twain's Hannibal, Huck and Tom*, pp. 92–140.

64. See above, chapter 13.

65. Walter Blair thought *Our Wild Indians* to be Twain's chief authority for the Indian material in "Huck Finn and Tom Sawyer among the Indians" (*Mark Twain's Hannibal, Huck and Tom*, p. 85). In fact, *The Plains* was his main source. See Kime, "Huck among the Indians," pp. 324–32.

66. A consolidated file relating to this removal, 5765 AGO 1885, is available in NARA microform publication M689, Roll 384. See also Fort Sully Post Returns, April and May 1887.

67. "Hunting at Army Posts," *ANJ*, March 6, 1886, p. 649. The article, including the summary of a report by Dodge on hunting in the vicinity of Fort Sully, was "condensed from an interesting series of letters published in *Forest and Stream*." On August 3, 1884, Dodge reported to his son, Fred, that he had shot 122 grouse thus far that season and that "I have never seen such good grouse shooting anywhere" (Graff).

68. RID to WTS, December 10, 1884 (Sherman Papers, LC). For the events that led to Dodge's sending this gift of appreciation, see *STJ*, pp. 171–73.

69. The detail for the court, which convened on April 20, was published in *ANJ*, April 3, 1886, p. 728. The Varnum trial was described elsewhere in the issue as an "important General Court-Martial" (p. 725), but from an official point of view, it was probably more embarrassingly visible than intrinsically important.

70. *Kansas City Times*, quoted in *ANJ*, April 17, 1886, p. 767.

71. Ruger could find no flaws in the court proceedings and therefore directed that Varnum be restored to duty. Nevertheless, in the official reprimand he took exception to the court's interpretation of what constituted proper conduct by an army officer. "In his opinion," Ruger wrote, "the acts of Lieutenant Varnum, as admitted in his defence, were so disgraceful to the Service, and injurious to discipline in nature and degree, as to sustain the charge set aside by the court; and he cannot, by his approval, aid in establishing so low a standard for estimating propriety of conduct on the part of officers of the Army" (GCMO 24, Department of Dakota, June 16, 1886; reprinted in *ANJ*, June 23, 1886, p. 986). The proceedings of the Varnum court—file number V 1960 (1886)—are among the records of the Judge-Advocate General, NARA, RG 153.

72. See *ANJ*, September 11, 1880, p. 108; February 4, 1882, p. 593; September 9, 1882, p. 116; March 29, 1884, p. 711; and November 14, 1885, p. 313. An overview of the subject is provided in Cooper, *The Rise of the National Guard*, pp. 75–86.

73. *ANJ*, November 15, 1884, p. 309.

74. A letter of instructions went out to Dodge from the Adjutant General's Office on July 12, 1886 (AGO Reg LR).

75. *ANJ*, September 9, 1882, p. 116.

76. *ANJ*, July 31, 1886, p. 2; and August 21, 1886, pp. 79–80; William L. Alexander to AG, July 16, 1886 (AGO Reg LR).

77. Cooper, *The Rise of the National Guard*, p. 89.

78. *Iowa State Register (Des Moines)*, August 7, 1886, p. 2.

79. Accounts of the encampments appeared in the *Iowa State Register (Des Moines)*, July 31, 1886, p. 6; August 4, p. 2; August 7, p. 2; August 17, p. 6; and August 19, p. 2.

80. Dodge's official report, dated September 4, 1886, was duly received at the Adjutant General's Office but has been lost (AGO Reg LR). However, a copy dated at Fort Sully August [*sic*] 5, 1886, is among the Dodge Papers (Graff). This copy was written by an amanuensis and signed by Dodge, who probably

by oversight added "5" in a space left blank between "August" and "1886" but neglected to change "August" to "September."

81. B. A. Beeson to RID, September 3, 1886 (Graff). Beeson wrote that he had "just received" the report.

82. RID ACP File (AGO); *ANJ*, May 17, 1884, p. 857; and November 20, 1884, p. 320; Fort Sully Post Returns, May 1884, December 1884, and January 1885.

83. RID to WTS, September 30, 1884 (Sherman Papers, LC).

84. RID to FPD, October 12, 1884 (Yale).

85. Fort Sully Post Return, October 1886; *ANJ*, September 25, 1886, pp. 166, 170.

86. *ANJ*, October 30, 1886, p. 267; O. D. Greene, AAG, to D. W. Maretta, U.S. Marshal, November 12, 1886; RID to AG, December 14, 1886; RID to R. C. Drum, December 19, 1886 (RID ACP File, AGO).

87. The others were Brigadier General James C. Duane, the Chief of Engineers, who retired on June 30, 1888, and Colonel John C. Tidball, First Artillery, who retired on January 25, 1889.

88. *ANJ*, December 4, 1886, p. 344. In 1882 Congress had provided for retirement on application by army officers upon their completing forty years of service (Coffman, *The Old Army*, p. 320).

89. RID to R. C. Drum, December 19, 1886 (RID ACP File, AGO).

90. Robert B. Glenn to RID, March 31, 1883; James D. Glenn to RID, January 4, 1884; RID to James D. Glenn (draft), June 13, 1884 (Graff); *ITJ*, p. 320.

91. RID to FPD, May 27, 1887 (Yale).

92. *ANJ*, December 1, 1883, p. 347; *Omaha Republican*, November 18, 1883, p. 4; November 21, p. 4; November 24, p. 4; and November 25, p. 5.

93. General Sherman briefly described Fred's visit of November 27, 1884, in a letter to his wife, Ellen, who had not been at home at the time. "Now that he does not play the part of Star," he wrote of Fred, "but simply one of the troupe he has gained reputation and is considered a promising actor. Neither his mother or Father is with him and he goes on his own hook" (Sherman Family Papers).

94. *STJ*, pp. 171–72.

95. Odell, *Annals of the New York Stage*, XIII, p. 25.

96. RID to FPD, May 27, 1887 (Yale). Fred's notation is dated September 8, 1894, on the back of an envelope received at the Kansas City, Missouri, post office on November 20, 1884, addressed to "Frederick Paulding [/] Margaret Mather Com [/] Opera House [/] Kansas City, Mo" (Graff).

In a letter addressed to Fred at Milwaukee, Wisconsin, on November 2, 1884, Dodge offered advice on getting ahead as a professional actor: "I want you to cultivate as you go, the very best society attainable. It is a *bore* I know, but it will pay you. When Managers find that boxes are nightly filled with *your* friends, the nicest people of each place, it will not be long until some one will find it to his interest to *star* you. You are young & can afford to 'bide your time,' but bread cast upon Societie's waters now while you are a young & fascinating object of adoration of fair damsels, will be returned with interest at the Box Office" (Collection of Paul R. Hedren).

97. RID to FPD [November 1884] (Dodge Papers, Graff). As filed in the Graff Collection, this letter is written on both sides of four sheets of paper, the first of which bears the date July 17, 1884. However, the three subsequent sheets are of a different style of paper, and their contents make clear that they form part of another letter, written in November of the same year.

98. Some insight into what Dodge considered Julia's "diseased imaginings" may be afforded by his comments in a letter to Fred of November 2, 1884. There he characterized as "a monomania" her determination to deny him any knowledge of her financial affairs and any influence over them. Her fierce independence, he observed, had "relieved me of all responsibility & her of all her fortune" (Collection of Paul R. Hedren).

99. Dodge's frequent references in his journals to flirting at parties may point to a cause of jealousy on Julia's part, but that seems unlikely. No evidence exists that he had a romantic attachment to any other woman, and the comments about flirting, often intended to be read by family members, simply indicated his enjoyment of the social occasions.

100. RID to JRPD, January 20, 1883 (Yale). In a letter of December 20, 1883, to a New York attorney, A. B. Cruikshank, Dodge sought to obtain for his wife's use the funds remaining in the estate of her late mother. He informed Cruikshank that Julia had "an immediate & most pressing need of $1000" (Graff).

101. *New York Times*, June 21, 1878, p. 5; June 23, 1878, p. 2; and June 24, 1878, p. 8; Q. A. Gillmore to RID, October 17, 1884 (Graff); "Suing the Rhinelanders," *New York World*, June 3, 1888, p. 23.

102. "Suing the Rhinelanders," *New York World*, June 3, 1888, p. 23.

103. RID to FPD [November 1884], pp. 3, 4 (Graff). On October 17, 1884, an army colleague of Dodge's, Colonel Quincy A. Gillmore, wrote Ward a letter of introduction to him (Graff).

104. The demand on the Rhinelanders had passed into the hands of two New York lawyers, William G. Bussey and Edward Stephens, who negotiated with representatives of the Rhinelander family in hopes of a compromise, but without success. See Stephens to RID, July 23, 1886, and Bussey to RID, July 28, 1886 (Graff). A test case was therefore brought against one of the heirs, Mrs. Mary L. Gallatin, for property that had been awarded her under the provisions of the Rhinelander trust ("Suing the Rhinelanders," *New York World*, June 3, 1888, p. 23).

105. RID to FPD [November 1884], pp. 3–4 (Graff).

106. Fort Sully Post Return, April 1887; RID to FPD, May 27, 1887 (Yale).

107. *ANJ*, April 9, 1887, p. 735; May 7, p. 815; and May 21, p. 855.

108. RID to FPD, May 27, 1887 (Yale).

109. However, Dodge's affection for the region continued; on April 18, 1888, he joined other officers of the Eleventh Infantry in petitioning for passage of a Senate bill to ensure the protection of Yellowstone National Park (AGO Reg LR).

110. G.O. 30, HQA, reprinted in *ANJ*, April 16, 1887, p. 754; Frazer, *Forts of the West*, p. 46.

111. *ANJ*, July 23, 1887, p. 1030. The interview was acknowledged as from the *Washington (D.C.) Critic.*

112. G.O. 46, HQA, June 28, 1887, reprinted in *ANJ*, July 2, 1887, p. 973.

113. *ANJ*, July 2, 1887, p. 974.

114. *ANJ*, July 9, 1887, p. 995; and July 16, p. 1012.

115. *ANJ*, September 30, 1882, p. 187; October 14, 1882, pp. 236–37; and September 22, 1888, p. 68. The post was named after James Madison, president of the United States at the time of its establishment.

116. Hough, *History of Jefferson County, New York*, pp. 466–68.

117. *ANJ*, July 2, 1887, p. 970.

118. Brigadier General Christopher C. Augur retired on July 10, 1885; Major General John Pope retired on March 16, 1886; Major General Alfred H. Terry did not retire until April 5, 1888, but was in declining health and unable to perform his duties as commander of the Military Division of the Missouri (Bailey, *Pacifying the Plains*, pp. 202–3).

119. Fort Sully Post Returns, July and August, 1887; Eleventh Infantry Regimental Returns, July and August 1887; Madison Barracks Post Return, August 1887; *ANJ*, August 6, 1887, p. 18. The distance from Fort Sully to Madison Barracks along the route taken was 1,992 miles.

Chapter 26

1. "Indian Warfare," *ANJ*, April 26, 1890, p. 654.

2. RID, "The Enlisted Soldier," p. 318. For an early commentary on the postwar army's contribution to development in the West, see *ANJ*, August 20, 1881, p. 54. A comprehensive modern treatment is provided in Tate, *The Frontier Army in the Settlement of the West.*

3. *ANJ*, June 11, 1881, p. 945. For earlier statements by Sherman on the need to maintain military preparedness, see *ANJ*, October 24, 1874, p. 167; and August 4, 1877, p. 832.

4. *ANJ*, September 13, 1890, p. 40; and September 20, pp. 56–57.

5. JRPD to RID, October 23, 1887 (Graff).

6. Headquarters Division of the Atlantic to AG, November 16, 1887; Headquarters Department of Dakota to AG, October 25, 1887 (AGO Reg LR).

7. Heiner, *Madison Barracks*, p. 61.

8. Heiner, *Madison Barracks*, pp. 61–63. The Pike monument was dedicated on Independence Day, 1886.

9. The detail for the court, in S.O. 170, Division of the Atlantic, August 15, 1887, was reported in *ANJ*, August 20, 1887, p. 63.

10. *ANJ*, December 17, 1887, p. 399, reprinting an article on Handforth's personal history from the *Kansas City Times*.

11. GCMO 88, HQA, November 30, 1887, pp. 1–4. The text of this order was reprinted in full in *ANJ*, December 10, 1887, p. 388.

12. Madison Barracks Post Return, August 1887; *ANJ*, August 20, 1887, p. 63; and September 3, 1887, pp. 99, 108.

13. *ANJ*, September 3, 1887, p. 108; and February 23, 1889, p. 511.

14. See *ITJ*, pp. 306, 342 (Lt. Dodge); pp. 149, 152, 241, 298 (Coppinger). The activities of Coppinger after 1880 were reported in *ANJ*, December 30, 1882, p. 484; February 10, 1883, p. 625; December 15, 1883, p. 388; March 6, 1886, p. 649; and July 14, 1888, p. 1010. The 1883 Coppinger-Blaine wedding in Washington, D.C., was attended by General Sherman and other persons of note.

15. At the time of Dodge's arrival at Madison Barracks, Pollock was on temporary duty with his company at Fort Niagara, engaged in preparations for the annual rifle competition there; see *ANJ*, July 23, 1887, p. 1030; July 30, p. 2; and September 17, p. 138.

16. Madison Barracks Post Return, September 1887; *ANJ*, September 3, 1887, p. 108. Under the direction of La Guardia, the Eleventh Infantry's band maintained a busy schedule of performances at Fort Sully and later at Madison Barracks. See *ANJ*, January 23, 1886, p. 516 (reporting a performance of "The Eleventh Regiment March," composed by La Guardia and dedicated to Dodge); May 14, 1887, p. 834; and August 25, 1888, p. 1134; *STJ*, p. 178. La Guardia's son Fiorello, later the mayor of New York City, resided at the band's postings as a boy.

17. Communications from Dodge concerning the firing range were forwarded from the Division of the Atlantic to the Adjutant General's Office on December 2, 1887; April 27, May 1, and December 13, 1888; January 4 and July 3, 1889 (AGO Reg LR).

18. For example, in 1888 the Eleventh Infantry helped the Department of the East, an organization within the Division of the Atlantic, achieve the highest overall score among departments of the army. See G.O. 73, HQA, October 3, 1888, reprinted in *ANJ*, October 20, 1888, p. 145.

19. Sheridan emphasized practice marches, field camps, and skirmish firing in his annual report for 1887, reprinted in *ANJ*, November 19, 1887, p. 320.

20. Heiner, *Madison Barracks*, p. 61; RID to FPD, May 27, 1887 (Yale).

21. Communications from Dodge and Brown relating to proposed construction at Madison Barracks were forwarded by the Division of the Atlantic to the Adjutant General's Office on September 2, 1887 (administration building); September 17 (quartermaster's storehouse and office); September 17 (workshops); September 17 (commissary storehouse). On September 20 a telegram from headquarters of the Division of the Atlantic requested speedy approval for the administration building, and on September 24 those headquarters acknowledged receipt of the approval (AGO Reg LR).

22. Madison Barracks Post Returns, September–November 1887.

23. *Watertown (New York) Times*, September 13, 1888, as summarized and quoted in *ANJ*, September 22, 1888, p. 68.

24. RID to JRPD, November 22, 1888 (Yale).

25. JRPD to RID, October 23, 1887 (Graff).

26. JRPD to RID, November 27, 1887 (Graff); "Suing the Rhinelanders," *New York World*, June 3, 1888, p. 23).

27. JRPD to RID, November 27, 1887 (Graff).

28. *New York Sun*, quoted in *ANJ*, June 9, 1888, p. 910.

29. JRPD to RID, November 27, 1887 (Graff).

30. In March 1888 Margaret Mather signed a contract with Messrs. Gilmore and Tompkins of the Academy of Music, New York City, even though she remained under engagement to J. M. Hill through 1893. The court proceedings in her suit against Hill were described in the *New York World*, June 23, 1888, p. 1; June 27, 1888, p. 3; and June 28, 1888, p. 5. The latest of these articles included a summary of testimony by "Mrs. Julia W. Dodge, wife of the late Gen. [*sic*] Dodge, and mother of Frederick Paulding, the actor."

31. JRPD to RID, July 23, 1888 (Graff). Robert C. Jordan was a Nebraska businessman whom Dodge had entrusted for a time to serve as administrator of the late Maria Paulding's estate; see *ITJ*, pp.

282–97 passim. Dodge believed Jordan had profited at his expense and in 1883 was concerned over the possibility that he would lay claim to yet more funds as a service fee. See RID to A. B. Cruikshank, December 20, 1883 (Graff).

32. "Dodge *et al.* v. Gallatin *et al.* (Supreme Court, General Term, First Department, March 29, 1889)," in the *New York Supplement*, V, pp. 126–27. Julia and Grace intended to bring their suit before the New York State Court of Appeals, and on October 1890 Dodge inquired of Julia for any news about "your great case" (Graff). However, the published decisions of the court through 1895 include no reference to *Dodge et al. v. Gallatin et al.*

33. JRPD to RID, n.p., n.d. (Graff). Taken together with other evidence, the contents of this letter indicate that it was written shortly before December 20, 1888.

34. *New York World*, August 26, 1888, p. 13; Odell, *Annals of the New York Stage*, XIV, pp. 29, 166; JRPD to RID, October 12, 1888 (Yale); RID to JRPD, November 22, 1888 (Yale).

35. JRPD to RID [December 1888] (Graff); RID to FPD, December 23, 1888 (Yale).

36. JRPD to RID, December 20, 1888 (Graff).

37. RID to FPD, December 23, 1888 (Yale).

38. Odell, *Annals of the New York Stage*, XIV, pp. 153, 259; *Chicago Times*, April 12, 1891, p. 14. On March 19, 1890, General Sherman attended a performance of Sheridan's *The Rivals* by the Jefferson-Florence Company, with Frederick Paulding Dodge in the role of Captain Absolute (Sherman Diary, Sherman Family Papers).

39. JRPD to RID, May 18, 1888 (Yale).

40. RID to JRPD, October 19, 1890 (Graff).

41. RID to JRPD, November 22, 1888 (Yale). The Madison Barracks Post Return for November 1888 records a visit there by Colonel Robert P. Hughes, inspector general of the Division of the Atlantic, but not by the quartermaster general, Brigadier General S. B. Holabird.

42. "The Post Canteen System," *New York Times*, October 6, 1889, p. 20. This article was reprinted in *ANJ*, October 12, 1889, p. 123.

43. *ANJ*, May 19, 1888, p. 855; JRPD to RID, May 30, 1888 (Graff); Heiner, *Madison Barracks*, p. 62.

44. *ANJ*, October 26, 1889, p. 163; Heiner, *Madison Barracks*, p. 63. A photograph showing the iron fence is in Haddock, *History of Jefferson County, New York*, p. 598.

45. RID to AG, August 23, 1888 (AGO Reg LR).

46. *ANJ*, July 21, 1888, p. 1031; July 28, p. 1052; August 11, p. 1116; and August 25, p. 1134.

47. General Schofield assumed command of the army on July 14, 1888, and General Howard assumed command of the Division of the Atlantic on November 12 (Madison Barracks Post Returns).

48. *ANJ*, August 18, 1888, p. 1115–16. The writer, "Paddler," observed that facilities like it "tend to elevate and increase the efficiency of the non-com. officers" (p. 1116).

49. *ANJ*, September 22, 1888, p. 68.

50. *Watertown Times*, quoted in *ANJ*, March 16, 1889, p. 577; see also *ANJ*, October 26, 1889, p. 163.

51. *ANJ*, May 13, 1882, p. 942; May 20, 1882, p. 956; November 3, 1883, p. 273; and March 9, 1889, p. 557.

52. *ANJ*, March 9, 1889, p. 552; March 30, p. 615; April 6, pp. 643–44; and May 11, p. 765. The findings of the court were published in GCMO 21, HQA, May 2, 1889. Lydecker was sentenced to forfeit one hundred dollars of his pay for nine months and to be reprimanded in orders (p. 9). The findings were reprinted in *ANJ*, May 11, 1889, p. 760.

53. *ANJ*, July 13, 1889, p. 939. For a more balanced analysis of the proceedings, see the issue for June 8, 1889, p. 848.

54. *ANJ*, June 12, 1880, p. 916; January 15, 1881, p. 475; and July 9, 1881, pp. 1022, 1025; *New York Times*, June 9, 1889, p. 3.

55. *ANJ*, August 18, 1883, p. 43; September 8, p. 105; September 22, pp. 144, 147; November 10, p. 291; and November 24, p. 331. General Sherman came to view Armes as a "pestiferous fellow . . . utterly worthless for good, but seemingly powerful for mischief" (WTS to John Sherman, March 10, 1884—Sherman Papers, LC). Armes recounted his career in a volume aptly entitled *Ups and Downs of an Army Officer.*

56. The *Army and Navy Journal* reported from time to time on Armes's activities, including efforts to secure reinstatement. See the issues of September 29, 1883, p. 165; November 10, 1883, p. 291; November 24, 1883, p. 331; January 8, 1887, p. 466.

57. GCMO 31, HQA, June 7, 1889, pp. 1–3; the quotation is from p. 3. See also *ANJ*, March 16, 1889, p. 574; and June 15, 1889, p. 863; *New York Times*, April 9, 1889, p. 2; April 13, 1889, p. 3; and April 24, 1889, p. 3. Armes included in *Ups and Downs of an Army Officer* an illustration of "a beautiful gold medal" that was sent him by one hundred subscribers in Pittsburgh, Pennsylvania, "in approval of his pulling Gov. Beaver's nose" (p. 593).

58. *ANJ*, March 16, 1889, p. 574.

59. S.O., HQA, April 8, 1889, reprinted in *ANJ*, April 13, 1889, p. 659. The court included thirteen members in addition to Dodge and the judge advocate or prosecutor, an unusually large number that reflected the gravity of the matter under review.

60. *ANJ*, April 20, 1889, pp. 684, 694; and April 27, 1889, p. 706; *New York Times*, April 9, 1889, p. 2; and April 24, 1889, p. 3; Armes, *Ups and Downs of an Army Officer*, pp. 590–93.

61. Armes was convinced that the court's members had been "specially picked out" to return a sentence of dismissal (*Ups and Downs of an Army Officer*, p. 591). However, President Harrison commuted the sentence to confinement within such limits as the secretary of war might designate and deprivation of the right to wear the army uniform and insignia of rank for a period of five years. Armes, the father of a large family, would thus lose none of his retirement pay. The secretary of war later designated the place of confinement as to be within a radius of fifty miles of the District of Columbia (GCMO 31, HQA, June 7, 1889, pp. 3–4). A portion of the court-martial order was reprinted in *ANJ*, June 15, 1889, p. 863.

62. *New York Times*, April 29, 1889, p. 1; April 30, 1889, p. 1; and May 1, 1889, pp. 1–2. The quotation is from "The Great Procession. The Military Parade as Seen by the President and Those with Him," May 1, p. 11.

63. Eleventh Infantry Regimental Returns, April and May 1889; Madison Barracks Post Returns, April and May 1889.

64. *New York Times*, May 1, 1889, p. 11.

65. The full text of Schofield's circular containing an elaborate set of directions for parade participants was reprinted in the *New York Times*, April 25, 1889, p. 9.

66. *ANJ*, May 18, 1889, p. 783; May 25, 1889, p. 808; and June 1, 1889, p. 818.

67. Madison Barracks Post Returns, June and July 1889; *ANJ*, July 20, 1889, p. 960.

68. Fowle to AG, March 21 and March 23, 1889 (RID ACP File, AGO); S.O., HQA, May 15, 1889, reprinted in *ANJ*, May 18, 1889, p. 783.

69. In company with the governor of his state, Brigadier General James Dodge Glenn had led the North Carolina troops in the George Washington Centennial parade in New York City on April 30 (*New York Times*, May 1, 1889, p. 10).

70. Madison Barracks Post Return, July 1889; *Wilmington (North Carolina) Morning Star*, July 8, 1889, p. 1; and July 9, 1889, p. 1; *ANJ*, July 13, 1889, pp. 938, 951; and July 20, 1889, p. 958.

71. *Wilmington (North Carolina) Morning Star*, July 12, 1889, p. 1; July 13, p. 1; July 14, p. 1; July 16, p. 1; July 17, p. 1; and July 18, p. 1. The quotation is from the July 13 article.

72. In response to S.O. 33, Division of the Atlantic, February 9, 1889, plans were formed for practice marches through settled country surrounding army posts throughout the division.

73. RID to AAG, Division of the Atlantic, July 29, 1889 (AGO LR).

74. *ANJ*, August 24, 1889, p. 1064.

75. Field Order 2, Headquarters Eleventh Infantry, August 27, 1889, summarized in *ANJ*, August 31, 1889, p. 4.

76. *Watertown (New York) Times*, quoted in *ANJ*, September 7, 1889, p. 23.

77. Madison Barracks Post Returns, August and September 1889; *ANJ*, September 7, 1889, p. 18.

78. Madison Barracks Post Return, September 1889; *ANJ*, October 5, 1889, p. 103.

79. *ANJ*, October 5, 1889, p. 103.

80. G.O. 10, HQA, February 1, 1889, published "rules and regulations for the establishment and government of post canteens"; the order was reprinted in *ANJ*, February 9, 1889, pp. 468–69.

81. The history of supplying the incidental needs of soldiers at army posts through authorized traders and canteens was summarized in a report to the adjutant general by Major Theodore Schwan, dated December 31, 1888 (AGO LR).

82. Statements for and against retaining post traders were part of a spirited discussion of the canteen system featured in the *Army and Navy Journal* during 1889. See the issues of March 9, pp. 552, 557; March 23, p. 597; April 13, p. 664; April 27, p. 704; May 11, p. 764; May 27, p. 800; August 31, p. 10; and November 16, p. 229. A list of canteens then in operation was published in *ANJ*, January 4, 1890, p. 309. An editorial in the issue of March 15, 1890, declared the new system "now fairly established" (p. 549).

83. AAG, Division of the Atlantic, to AG, August 15, 1889, forwarding Dodge's comments on the canteens at Madison Barracks (AGO Reg LR).

84. House, *Report . . . Relating to Army Appropriations* (1890), Appendix C, p. 31. A copy of the published report forms part of a consolidated file, 364 AGO 1889, on the subject of post canteens, available in NARA microform publication M989, Roll 666.

85. "The Post Canteen System," *New York Times*, October 6, 1889, p. 20.

86. "Ancient" [RID], "Excuses for Desertion," *ANJ*, September 28, 1889, p. 80. Dodge identified himself as the author of this anonymous statement in a later article, "The Desertion Question," p. 163. See the following note and *ANJ*, January 11, 1890, p. 389.

87. RID, "The Desertion Question," *JMSI* 11 (December 1889), 163–65. This article was one of several published responses to an essay by First Lieutenant William D. McAnaney, "Desertion in the United States Army," *JMSI* 10 (1889), 450–65.

88. See "Military Caste," *ANJ*, February 15, 1890, p. 471; "Officer and Man," *ANJ*, June 21, 1890, p. 812.

89. "Form of Medical Certificate to Accompany Application for Leave of Absence," dated October 5, 1889, and signed by Major Clarence Ewen (RID ACP File, AGO).

90. RID to AG, November 7, 1889 (RID ACP File, AGO).

91. Dodge's leave of absence was "to take effect about December 1, 1889" (S.O. 270, HQA, November 19, 1889, in RID ACP File, AGO).

92. In 1852 and 1853; see above, chapter 1,.

93. Madison Barracks Post Return, December 1889; *ANJ*, November 30, 1889, p. 266; February 1, 1890, p. 434; and February 22, 1890, p. 486.

94. Sherman celebrated his seventieth birthday by hosting a dinner party at his new house on West 71st Street, New York City; see *ANJ*, February 15, 1890, p. 478, and Marszalek, *Sherman*, p. 487. The secretary of war's obituary tribute to General Crook was issued in G.O. 33, HQA, March 22, 1890, reprinted in *ANJ*, March 29, 1890, p. 577. On April 5 President Harrison sent to the Senate a nomination of Brigadier General Miles for promotion to major general (*ANJ*, April 12, 1890, p. 623).

95. Madison Barracks Post Return, March and April 1890; *ANJ*, April 5, 1890, p. 594.

96. Madison Barracks Post Returns, July–September 1890; *ANJ*, July 19, 1890, p. 875; September 6, p. 18; September 13, p. 38; and September 20, p. 54. The quotation is from the latest of these articles.

97. *ANJ*, July 19, 1890, p. 875.

98. RID to JRPD, October 19, 1890 (Graff).

99. RID to JRPD, October 19, 1890 (Graff). Apropos his hope to "stick it out," six years earlier Dodge had used the phrase "stave it off" in reference to the pain brought on him in the winter by rheumatism; see RID to FPD, October 12, 1884 (Yale).

100. These were Captain George G. Lott, Captain Charles F. Roe, Captain William H. Wheeler, and First Lieutenant John J. Dougherty (Eleventh Infantry Regimental Returns, December 1889–February 1890).

101. G.O. 16, HQA, February 14, 1891, published President Harrison's tribute to Sherman. This was reprinted, with other orders and official statements, in *ANJ*, February 21, 1891, p. 445. See also *STJ*, pp. 189–90.

102. *ANJ*, March 7, 1891, p. 480.

103. Who was the anonymous author of this generous tribute to Dodge? The heading's somewhat unusual phrase "deserves well of his country" was characteristic of William C. Church, the coeditor and editorial copywriter of the *Army and Navy Journal*. It had been used in the newspaper's obituary tribute to

Colonel Jefferson C. Davis (*ANJ*, December 6, 1879, p. 341). A much later tribute, to Major Thomas E. Rose, also noted that he "deserved well of his country" (March 10, 1894, p. 478). Editorial commentary on the death of General Pope described him as a "faithful servant of his country . . . deserving of the fullest commendation" (October 1, 1892, p. 90). Thus, Church may have written the letter about Dodge, for the two men had been personally acquainted since Civil War times. However, the dateline ("United States Army, Feb. 28, 1891") suggests that, unlike Church, the author was someone officially connected with the army at that time.

104. *ANJ*, April 4, 1891, p. 543.

105. See "Who Should Be Brigadiers?" *ANJ*, December 13, 1884, p. 392.

106. *ANJ*, April 18, 1891, p. 581.

107. "Form of Medical Certificate to Accompany Application for Leave of Absence," dated April 6, 1891, and signed by Captain and Assistant Surgeon Henry S. Turrill (RID ACP File, AGO).

108. Madison Barracks Post Return, April 1891; *ANJ*, April 18, 1891, p. 574.

109. *ANJ*, April 25, 1891, pp. 598–99; *Official Army Register,* 1891, p. 255.

110. *ANJ*, May 16, 1891, p. 649.

111. S.O. 114, HQA, May 19, 1891 (RID ACP File, AGO); *ANJ*, May 23, 1891, pp. 660, 661.

112. *ANJ*, May 23, 1891, p. 659.

Chapter 27

1. *ANJ*, June 20, 1891, p. 734; August 15, 1891, p. 871; and March 19, 1892, p. 520.

2. "Madison Barracks," *ANJ*, October 10, 1891, p. 117.

3. *ANJ*, November 21, 1891, p. 210.

4. Odell, *Annals of the New York Stage*, XV, pp. 33–34, 69, 74, 75, 82, 215, 244, 345; Bordman, *American Theatre*, p. 317. Fred was a nephew of the play's author, William Irving Paulding, and revised the work for production.

5. *ANJ*, December 12, 1891, pp. 268, 269, 271; February 6, 1892, p. 409; March 12, 1892, p. 503.

6. For a summary of Coppinger's early career following his youth in Ireland, see *ANJ*, February 6, 1892, p. 409. He had been promoted to colonel in January 1891.

7. *ANJ*, February 27, 1892, p. 469.

8. Three prescription slips, all dated February 16, 1892, at the U.S. Dispensary, Post of San Antonio, Texas, are among the Dodge Papers (Graff).

9. RID to AG, February 19, 1892; RID to AG, February 26, 1892; AG to RID, February 26, 1892; Medical record card, Government Hospital, Hot Springs, Arkansas (RID ACP File, AGO); *ANJ*, March 12, 1892, p. 503.

10. "Hot Springs, Ark.," *ANJ*, December 17, 1887, p. 404; see also February 16, 1889, p. 486.

11. Medical record card, Government Hospital, Hot Springs, Arkansas (RID ACP File, AGO).

12. *ANJ*, May 14, 1892, p. 666.

13. *ANJ*, May 24, 1890, p. 734; and January 27, 1894, p. 376; *Trow's New York City Directory,* 1891, pp. 324, 963; and 1892, pp. 339, 1063; RID to AG, January 23, 1894 (RID ACP File, AGO). The Dodges' new home was at 25 Elm Street, New Rochelle.

14. *ANJ*, August 13, 1892, p. 881; November 19, 1892, p. 205; June 10, 1893, p. 698; October 14, 1893, p. 120; January 27, 1894, p. 376, 377; March 3, 1894, p. 461; May 12, 1894, p. 613; and November 10, 1894, p. 168.

15. RID to AG, January 23, 1894; AAG to RID, January 25, 1894 (RID ACP File, AGO).

16. For obituary tributes to these officers see, respectively, *ANJ*, July 25, 1891, p. 821; October 1, 1892, p. 90; and July 14, 1894, p. 808.

17. Dodge was a member of the New York Commandery of MOLLUS (Aubin, *Register*, p. 73). Writing in 1894, First Lieutenant J. H. McRae acknowledged his assistance in preparing an historical sketch of the Third Infantry, which appeared in Rodenbough, *The Army of the United States*, pp. 432–51; McRae's acknowledgment appears on p. 451.

18. *ANJ*, October 28, 1876, p. 198; "Indian Warfare," *ANJ*, April 26, 1890, p. 654.

19. "Brevets for Indian Service," *ANJ*, April 28, 1894, pp. 607–608. The article includes the full text of General Schofield's recommendations for brevet commissions, dated February 28, 1894.

20. *ANJ*, June 2, 1894, p. 694.

21. *ANJ*, July 7, 1894, p. 782; and December 29, 1894, p. 290.

22. *ANJ*, June 16, 1894, p. 743; and January 26, 1895, p. 395.

23. *ANJ*, March 2, 1895, p. 434.

24. *ANJ*, April 20, 1895, p. 552; RID to JRPD, May 25, 1895 (Yale).

25. Angel's wings were puffy sleeves on a dress or blouse.

26. RID to JRPD, May 25, 1895 (Yale).

27. Lt. Col. Jacob Kline to AG, June 16, 1895 (RID ACP File, AGO).

28. *ANJ*, June 22, 1895, p. 711; "Funeral Honors," in Farrow, *Farrow's Military Encyclopedia*, I, pp. 718–19.

29. Kline to AG, June 17, 1895; AAG to Kline, June 18, 1895; AAG to C.O., Fort Myer, Virginia, June 18, 1895 (RID ACP File, AGO).

30. *ANJ*, June 22, 1895, p. 711; and June 29, 1895, p. 729. In later years Dodge's widow continued to reside with Fred, who never married. She died in 1926 at his home, then in Rutherford, New Jersey. For many years, Frederick Paulding Dodge continued to work as an actor, writer, and lecturer. Some of his engagements in New York are detailed by Odell in *Annals of the New York Stage*, volumes 10–14. After 1910 he devoted his energies to dramatic recitation, giving one-man performances in New York hotels, including the Waldorf Astoria, and in schools, colleges, and clubs across the country. For his contributions to the drama he was awarded an honorary doctorate of letters degree by Holy Cross College. He died in 1937 (*New York Times*, January 7, 1926, p. 25; and September 8, 1937, p. 23).

31. Tidball, "Richard I. Dodge," in *Twenty-seventh Annual Reunion*, pp. 13–14. A one-paragraph summary of Dodge's career appeared in *Appleton's Annual Cyclopaedia,* p. 569.

32. Lincoln's message to Congress, December 1, 1862, quoted in Foote, *The Civil War*, I, p. 810.

33. RID, "Frontier Army Life, *ANJ*, February 23, 1878, p. 459.

Bibliography

Manuscript Materials

Blackmore, William. Papers. Manuscript Division, Museum of New Mexico, Santa Fe.

Bourke, John G. Diary. Powder River Expedition Order Book. U.S. Military Academy Library, West Point, N.Y.

Bradley, Luther P. Papers. USAMHI, Carlisle Barracks, Pa.

Church, William Conant. Papers. Manuscript Division, Library of Congress, Washington, D.C.

Crook, George. Papers. USAMHI, Carlisle Barracks, Pa.

Crook-Kennan Papers. USAMHI, Carlisle Barracks, Pa.

Dodge, Richard Irving. Papers, 1865–1949. Everett D. Graff Collection of Western Americana, Newberry Library, Chicago.

———. Papers, 1867–1895. Yale Collection of Western Americana. Beinecke Library, Yale University, New Haven, Conn.

Frothingham Family Papers. Manuscript Division, New York Public Library, New York.

Indian Wars Miscellaneous Collection. USAMHI, Carlisle Barracks, Pa.

Irving Family Papers. Historic Hudson Valley, Tarrytown, N.Y.

Mackenzie, Ranald S. Papers. USAMHI, Carlisle Barracks, Pa.

Miles, Nelson A. Papers. USAMHI, Carlisle Barracks, Pa.

Military Division of the Missouri Papers. USAMHI, Carlisle Barracks, Pa.

Order of the Indian Wars Collection. USAMHI, Carlisle Barracks, Pa.

Ovenshine, Samuel J. Papers. USAMHI, Carlisle Barracks, Pa.

Palmer, William J. Papers. USAMHI, Carlisle Barracks, Pa.

Rickey, Don. Papers. USAMHI, Carlisle Barracks, Pa.

Sherman, William T. Microfilm Edition of the William Tecumseh Sherman Family Papers, 1808–1891. University of Notre Dame Archives, 1967, Notre Dame, Ind.

———. Papers. Manuscript Division, Library of Congress, Washington, D.C.

Thoburn, Joseph C. Papers. Oklahoma Historical Society, Oklahoma City.

Tidball, John C. Papers. Special Collections, U.S. Military Academy Library, West Point, N.Y.

Trade Catalogs. Special Collections, University of Delaware Library, Newark.

United States Army. Cantonment North Fork Canadian River. Endorsements. General Orders and Circulars. Letters Received. Letters Sent. Monthly Report of Schools in Operation. Monthly Statement of Persons in Arrest or Confinement. Pass Book: Descriptive List of Civilian Employees. Register of Letters Received. Special Orders. Unregistered Letters Received. NARA. RG 393.

———. Cantonment North Fork Canadian River Post Returns, 1879–1882. NARA. RG 94. Microcopy 617, Roll 870.

———. Department of the Missouri. Fort Garland Column Field Records. Endorsements. Letters Received. Letters Sent. Special Orders. NARA. RG 393.

———. Department of the Platte. Black Hills Expedition Field Records. General and Special Orders. NARA. RG 393.

———. Department of the Platte. General and Special Orders, 1875. NARA. RG 393.

———. Department of the Platte. Powder River Expedition Field Records. Letters Sent. Endorsements Sent. Letters Received. General and Special Orders Issued. Charges and Specifications. Field Returns. NARA. RG 393.

———. Department of the Platte. Powder River Expedition. Field Records: Headquarters, Infantry and Artillery Battalions. Order Book. Endorsement and Letter Book. NARA. RG 393.

———. Eighth Infantry Regimental Returns, 1848–1865. NARA. RG 94. Microcopy M 665, Rolls 91, 92.

———. Eleventh Infantry Regimental Returns, 1873–1892. NARA. RG 94. Microcopy M665, Rolls 126, 127.

———. Fort Crawford Post Returns, 1880–1890. NARA. RG 94. Microcopy M617, Roll 263.

———. Fort Dodge, 1871–1873. Endorsements. General Orders and Circulars. Letters Sent. Registered Letters Received. Registers of Letters Received. Reports Relating to Indians and to Scouts and Marches. Special Orders. Unregistered Letters Received. NARA. RG 393. Microcopy M989, Rolls 1, 3, 5, 7, 15, 16, 22, 23, 25.

———. Fort Dodge Post Returns, 1866–1882. NARA. RG 94. Microcopy M617, Roll 319.

———. Fort Fetterman Post Returns, 1867–1882. NARA. RG 94. Microcopy 617, Roll 365.

———. Fort Garland Post Returns, 1873–1883. NARA. RG 94. Microcopy M617, Roll 395.

———. Fort Hays. Letters Received, 1876–1880. Letters Sent, 1874–1883. Orders, 1871–1889. NARA. RG 393. Microcopy T713, Rolls 2, 11–12, 21.

———. Fort Hays Post Returns, 1876–1889. NARA. RG 94. Microcopy M617, Roll 470.

———. Fort Laramie Post Returns, 1861–1876. NARA. RG 94. Microcopy M617, Roll 596.

———. Fort Leavenworth Post Returns, 1870–1890. NARA. RG 94. Microcopy M617, Roll 612.

———. Fort Lyon Post Returns, 1860–69, 1870–1880. NARA. RG 94. Microcopy 617, Rolls 659, 660.

———. Fort McPherson Post Returns, 1866–1872. NARA. RG 94. Microcopy M617, Roll 708.

———. Fort Reno Post Returns, 1874–1884. NARA. RG 94. Microcopy M617, Roll 998.

———. Fort Riley Post Returns, 1872–1884. NARA. RG 94. Microcopy M617, Roll 1013.

———. Fort Sanders Post Returns, 1866–1882. NARA. Microcopy M617, Roll 1094.

———. Fort Sedgwick Post Returns, 1864–1871. NARA. RG 94. Microcopy M617, Roll 1144.

———. Fort Sill Post Returns, 1876–1887. NARA. RG 94. Microcopy M617, Roll 1174.

———. Fort Sully Post Returns, 1877–1884, 1885–1894. NARA. Microcopy M617, Rolls 1239, 1240.

———. Fort Supply Post Returns, 1868–1879, 1880–1894. NARA. RG 94. Microcopy M617, Rolls 1243, 1244.

———. Fourteenth Infantry Regimental Returns, 1873–1882. NARA. RG 94. Microcopy M744, Roll 43.

———. Fourth Cavalry Regimental Returns, 1877–1883. NARA. RG 94. Microcopy M744, Roll 43.

———. Headquarters. Letters Received, 1883–1884. NARA. RG 108. Microcopy M1635, Roll 121.

———. Headquarters. Letters Sent, 1871–1883. NARA. RG 108. Microcopy M857, Rolls 8, 9.

———. Madison Barracks Post Returns, 1887–1891. NARA. RG 94. Microcopy M617, Roll 724.

———. Military Division of the Missouri. Cheyenne Outbreak Special File, 1878–1879. NARA. RG 393. Microcopy 1495, Roll 6.

———. Military Division of the Missouri. Indian Territory Operations Special File, May–December 1879. NARA. RG 393. Microcopy M1495, Roll 10.

———. Military Division of the Missouri. Sioux War Special File, 1876–1877. NARA. RG 393. Microcopy 1495, Roll 4.

———. Military Division of the Missouri. Ute Campaign Special File, 1879–1880. NARA. RG 393. Microcopy 1495, Roll 7.

———. Nineteenth Infantry Regimental Returns, 1871–1888. NARA. RG 94. Microcopy 665, Rolls 204, 205.

———. Ninth Infantry Regimental Returns, 1870–1879. NARA. RG 94. Microcopy M665, Roll 104.

———. North Platte Station. Endorsements. General and Special Orders, 1867–1868. Letters Sent. NARA. RG 393.

———. Office of the Adjutant General. Dodge, Richard Irving. Appointment, Commission, and Personal File. NARA. RG 94.

———. Office of the Adjutant General. Indexes to Letters Received (Main Series), 1861–1889. NARA. RG 94. Microcopy M725, Rolls 1–9.

———. Office of the Adjutant General. Letters Received (Main Series), 1848–1860. NARA. RG 94. Microcopy M567, Rolls 415, 461, 557, 577, 578, 622.

———. Office of the Adjutant General. Letters Received (Main Series), 1861–1870. NARA. RG 94. Microcopy M619, Rolls 15, 16, 28, 92, 93, 169, 204, 240, 251–53, 346–48, 379, 395, 448–450, 467, 468, 534, 546, 547, 565, 672, 680–85, 698, 699, 802, 812.

———. Office of the Adjutant General. Letters Received (Main Series), 1871–1880. NARA. RG 94. Microcopy M666, Rolls 4, 19, 58, 75, 126, 130, 148, 192, 239, 335, 401, 428–30, 459, 463, 539, 541, 550, 552, 558.

———. Office of the Adjutant General. Letters Received (Main Series), 1881–1889. NARA. RG 94. Microcopy M689, Rolls 18, 30, 43, 54, 77, 121, 214, 260, 287, 302, 319, 384, 425, 472, 647, 653, 666, 675, 732.

———. Office of the Adjutant General. Letters Sent (Main Series), 1863, 1868–69, 1878–1881. NARA. RG 94. Microcopy M565, Rolls 22, 36, 37, 349–52.

———. Office of the Adjutant General. Records Relating to the U.S. Military Academy, 1858–1861. NARA. RG 94. Microcopy M91, Rolls 22, 23.

———. Office of the Adjutant General. Registers of Letters Received, 1848–89. NARA. RG 94. Microcopy 711, Rolls 21–56, 62–85.

———. Omaha Barracks Post Returns, 1874–1885. NARA. RG 94. Microcopy M617, Roll 880.

———. Second Cavalry Regimental Returns, 1872–1879. NARA. RG 94. Microcopy M744, Roll 19.

———. Sixteenth Infantry Regimental Returns, 1870–1889. NARA. RG 94. Microcopy M665, Rolls 175, 176.

———. Third Cavalry Regimental Returns, 1868–1884. NARA. RG 94. Microcopy M744, Rolls 30–31.

———. Thirtieth Infantry Regimental Returns, 1866–1869. NARA. RG 94. Microcopy M 665, Roll 281.

———. Twelfth Infantry Regimental Returns, 1864–1867. NARA. RG 94. M665, Roll 135.

———. Twenty-third Infantry Regimental Returns, 1866–1882. NARA. RG 94. Microcopy M665, Rolls 236, 237.

United States Military Academy. Archives. Richard Irving Dodge Application File. West Point, N.Y.

United States Office of Indian Affairs. Inspection Reports, Cheyenne and Arapaho Agency, 1873–1882, 1883–1890. NARA. RG 48. Microcopy M 1070, Rolls 4, 5.

———. Letters Received, Central Superintendency, 1878–1880. NARA. RG 75. Microcopy M234, Rolls 69–70.

———. Letters Received, Cheyenne and Arapahoe Agency, 1878–1880. NARA. RG 75. Microcopy M234, Rolls 123–26.

United States War Department. Office of the Judge-Advocate General. Registers of Army General Courts-Martial, 1869–1889. NARA. RG 153. Microcopy M1105, Rolls 7, 8.

———. Office of the Provost Marshal General. Historical Reports of the State Acting Assistant Provost Marshal Generals and District Provost Marshals, 1865. NARA. RG 110. Microcopy M1163, Rolls 3, 5.

———. Office of the Secretary of War. Letters Received by the Secretary of War from the President, Executive Departments, and War Department Bureaus, 1869–1870. NARA. RG 107. Microcopy M 494, Rolls 110–14.

———. Office of the Secretary of War. Letters Sent (Main Series), 1867–1869, 1875–1876, 1878–1880, 1881–1883. NARA. RG 107. Microcopy M6, Rolls 59, 60, 70–73, 76–81, 82–87.

———. Office of the Secretary of War. Letters Sent by the Secretary of War to the President and Executive Departments, 1869. NARA. RG 107. Microcopy M 421, Roll 5.

———. Office of the Secretary of War. Orders and Endorsements by the Secretary of War, 1868–1869. NARA. RG 107. Microcopy M 444, Roll 12.

———. Office of the Secretary of War. Registers of Letters Received by the Secretary of War, Main Series, 1869. NARA. RG 107. Microcopy M 22, Rolls 131, 132.

———. Office of the Secretary of War. Registers of Letters Received by the Secretary of War from the President, Executive Bureaus, and War Department Bureaus, 1868–1869. NARA. RG 107. Microcopy M 493, Rolls 11, 12.

Government Publications

Annual Report of the Board of Regents of the Smithsonian Institution . . . for the Year 1881. Washington, D.C.: GPO, 1883.

Annual Report of the Board of Regents of the Smithsonian Institution . . . for the Year 1882. Washington, D.C.: GPO, 1884.

Annual Report of the Board of Regents of the Smithsonian Institution . . . for the Year Ending June 30, 1887. 2 vols. Washington, D.C.: GPO, 1889.

Bureau of American Ethnology. *First Annual Report . . . to the Secretary of the Smithsonian Institution 1879–'80.* Washington, D.C.: GPO, 1881.

———. *Seventeenth Annual Report . . . to the Secretary of the Smithsonian Institution 1895–'96.* Washington, D.C.: GPO, 1898.

Department of the Interior. *Proceedings of the United States National Museum.* Volume IV. *1881.* Washington, D.C.: GPO, 1882.

Official Register of the United States, Containing a List of Officers and Employés in the Civil, Military, and Naval Service. Washington, D.C.: GPO, 1867–1875, 1879–1881.

Report of an Exploration of Parts of Wyoming, Idaho, and Montana, in August and September, 1882, Made by Lieut. Gen. P. H. Sheridan. Washington, D.C.: GPO, 1882.

Report of Lieut. General P. H. Sheridan, Dated September 20, 1881, of His Expedition Through the Big Horn Mountains, Yellowstone National Park, etc. Washington, D.C.: GPO, 1882.

Reports of Inspection Made in the Summer of 1877 by Generals P. H. Sheridan and W.T. Sherman of Country North of the Union Pacific Railroad. Washington, D.C.: GPO, 1878.

Revised Statutes of the United States. Second edition. Washington, D.C.: GPO, 1878.

The Statutes at Large of the United States of America, from October, 1877, to March, 1881, and Recent Treaties, Postal Conventions, and Executive Proclamations. Volumes XX, XXI. Washington, D.C.: GPO, 1879, 1881.

United States Army. Department of Dakota. *Roster of Troops Serving in the Department of Dakota, July 20, 1882.* Fort Snelling, Minn.: The Department, 1882.

———. Department of the Missouri. *Roster of Troops Serving in the Department of the Missouri.* Fort Leavenworth: The Department, 1878, 1879.

———. Department of the Platte. *Tables of Distances and Itineraries of Routes between the Military Posts in, and to Certain Points Contiguous to, the Department of the Platte.* By W. S. Stanton. Omaha, Nebr.: The Department, 1877.

———. Military Division of the Missouri. *Outline Descriptions of the Posts in the Military Division of the Missouri.* Chicago: The Division, 1876.

———. *Official Army Register.* Washington, D.C.: GPO, 1848–1891.

———. Office of the Adjutant General. *General Orders, Circulars, and General Court-Martial Orders.* Washington, D.C.: Office of the Adjutant General, 1864–1891.

———. Office of the Provost Marshal General. *Revised Regulations for the Government of the Bureau of the Provost Marshal General of the United States.* Washington, D.C.: GPO, 1864.

———. Office of the Quartermaster General. *U.S. Army Uniforms and Equipment, 1889.* Reprint. Foreword by Jerome A. Greene. Lincoln, Nebr.: University of Nebraska Press, 1989.

———. Office of the Surgeon General. *A Report on Barracks and Hospitals, with Descriptions of Military Posts.* Washington, D.C.: GPO, 1870.

———. *Outline Descriptions of the Posts and Stations of Troops in the Geographical Divisions and Departments of the United States.* Compiled by R. B. Marcy. Washington, D.C.: GPO, 1872.

———. *Record of Engagements with Hostile Indians within the Military Division of the Missouri, from 1868 to 1882, Lieutenant-General P. H. Sheridan, Commanding.* Washington, D.C.: GPO, 1882.

———. *Regulations of the Army of the United States and General Orders in Force on the 17th of February 1881.* Washington, D.C.: GPO, 1881.

———. *Revised United States Army Regulations of 1861. With an Appendix Containing the Changes and Laws Affecting Army Regulations and Articles of War to June 25, 1863.* Washington, D.C.: GPO, 1863.

———. War Department. *Atlas to Accompany the Official Records of the Union and Confederate Armies.* 3 vols. Washington, D.C.: GPO, 1891–1895.

———. War Department. *Reports of Explorations and Surveys, to Ascertain the Most Practicable and Economical Route for a Railroad from the Mississippi River to the Pacific Ocean.* Washington, D.C.: Beverly Tucker, 1855–1860.

———. War Department. *The War of the Rebellion. A Compilation of the Official Records of the Union and Confederate Armies.* 70 vols. Washington, D.C.: GPO, 1881–1901.

United States Congress. House. *Fort Dodge and Fort Wallace Military Reservations.* Ex. Doc. 225, 47th Cong., 1st sess., 1882.

———. House. *Fort Dodge Military Reservation.* Ex. Doc. 195, 47th Cong., 1st sess, 1882.

———. House. *The Public Domain. Its History, with Statistics . . .* By Thomas Donaldson. Third ed. Misc. Doc. 45, Part 4, 47th Cong., 1st sess., 1882.

———. House. *Report of a Subcommittee of the Committee on Military Affairs Relating to the Reorganization of the Army.* Misc. Doc. 56, 45th Cong., 2nd sess., 1878.

———. House. *Report of Indian Peace Commission.* Ex. Doc. 97, 40th Cong., 2nd sess., 1868.

———. House. *Report of the Commissioner of Indian Affairs* (1875). Ex. Doc. 1, Part 5, 44th Cong., 1st sess.

———. House. *Report of the Commissioner of Indian Affairs* (1876). Ex. Doc. 1, Part 5, 44th Cong., 2nd sess.

———. House. *Report of the Commissioner of Indian Affairs* (1877). Ex. Doc. 1, Part 5, 45th Cong., 2nd sess.

———. House. *Report of the Commissioner of Indian Affairs* (1878). Ex. Doc. 1, Part 5, 45th Cong., 3rd sess.

———. House. *Report of the Commissioner of Indian Affairs* (1879). Ex. Doc. 1, Part 5, 46th Cong., 2nd sess.

———. House. *Report of the Commissioner of Indian Affairs* (1880). Ex. Doc. 1, Part 5, 47th Cong., 1st sess.

———. House. *Report of the Committee on Military Affairs Relating to Army Appropriations.* Report 529, 51st Cong., 1st sess., 1890.

———. House. *Report of the Provost Marshal General.* Appendix to Ex. Doc. 1, Parts 1 and 2, 39th Cong., 1st sess., 1866.

———. House. *Report of the Secretary of the Interior* (1875). Ex. Doc. 1, Part 5, 44th Cong., 1st Sess.

———. House. *Report of the Secretary of the Interior* (1879). Ex. Doc. 1, Part 5, 46th Cong., 2nd Sess.

———. House. *Report of the Secretary of War* (1852). Ex. Doc. 1, 32nd Cong., 2nd sess.

———. House. *Report of the Secretary of War* (1853). Ex. Doc. 1, 33rd Cong., 2nd sess.

———. House. *Report of the Secretary of War* (1854). Ex. Doc. 1, 33rd Cong., 3rd sess.

———. House. *Report of the Secretary of War* (1855). Ex. Doc. 1, 34th Cong., 1st sess.

———. House. *Report of the Secretary of War* (1856). Ex. Doc. 1, 34th Cong., 3rd sess.

———. House. *Report of the Secretary of War* (1857). Ex. Doc. 2, 35th Cong., 1st sess.

———. House. *Report of the Secretary of War* (1858). Ex. Doc. 2, 35th Cong., 2nd sess.

———. House. *Report of the Secretary of War* (1868). Ex. Doc. 1, Part 2, 40th Cong., 3rd sess.

———. House. *Report of the Secretary of War* (1869). Ex. Doc. 1, Part 2, 41st Cong., 2nd sess.

———. House. *Report of the Secretary of War* (1870). Ex. Doc. 1, Part 2, 41st Cong., 3rd sess.

———. House. *Report of the Secretary of War* (1872). Ex. Doc. 1, Part 2, 42nd Cong., 3rd sess.

———. House. *Report of the Secretary of War* (1873). Ex. Doc. 1, Part 2, 43rd Cong., 1st sess.

———. House. *Report of the Secretary of War* (1875). Ex. Doc. 1, Part 2, 44th Cong., 1st sess.

———. House. *Report of the Secretary of War* (1876). Ex. Doc. 1, Part 2, 44th Cong., 2nd sess.

———. House. *Report of the Secretary of War* (1877). Ex. Doc. 1, Part 2, 45th Cong., 1st sess.

———. House. *Report of the Secretary of War* (1878). Ex. Doc. 1, Part 2, 45th Cong., 3rd sess.

———. House. *Report of the Secretary of War* (1879). Ex. Doc. 1, Part 2, 46th Cong., 2nd sess.

———. House. *Report of the Secretary of War* (1880). Ex. Doc. 1, Part 2, 46th Cong., 3rd sess.

———. House. *Report of the Secretary of War* (1881). Ex. Doc. 1, Part 2, 47th Cong., 1st sess.

———. House. *Report of the Secretary of War* (1882). Ex. Doc. No. 1, Part 2, 47th Cong., 2nd sess.

———. House. *Report of the Secretary of War* (1883). Ex. Doc., No. 1, Part 2, 48th Cong., 1st sess.

———. House. *Report of the Secretary of War* (1884). Ex. Doc. 1, Part 2, 48th Cong., 2nd sess.

———. House. *Revised Army Regulations.* Report 85, 42nd Cong., 3rd sess., 1873.

———. House. *Route from Fort Smith to Santa Fe.* Doc. 45, 31st Cong., 1st sess., 1849–1850.

———. House. *Survey of Lands for Cheyenne and Arapahoe Indians.* Ex. Doc. 104, 40th Cong., 2nd sess., 1867.

———. House. *Survey of the Black Hills.* Ex. Doc. 125, 44th Cong., 1st sess., 1876.

———. House. *Testimony in Relation to the Ute Indian Outbreak, Taken by the Committee on Indian Affairs.* Misc. Doc. 38, 46th Cong., 2nd sess., 1880.

———. House. *Transfer of Indian Bureau.* Report 240, 44th Cong., 1st sess., 1876.

———. Senate. *The Civil Service of the United States*. Report No. 576, 47th Congress, 1st sess., 1882.

———. Senate. *Letter from the Secretary of the Interior, Transmitting in Compliance with a Resolution of the Senate of December 8, 1879, Correspondence Concerning the Ute Indians in Colorado*. Ex. Doc. No. 31, 46th Cong., 2nd sess., 1880.

———. Senate. *Letter from the Secretary of War to the Chairman of the Committee on Indian Affairs Communicating Information in Relation to the Escape of the Northern Cheyenne Indians from Fort Robinson*. Misc. Doc. 64, 45th Cong., 3rd sess., 1879.

———. Senate. *Memorial of Fitz-John Porter*. Misc. Doc. 91, 47th Cong., 1st sess., 1881.

———. Senate. *Occupation of a Portion of Indian Territory by White Settlers*. Ex. Doc. 20. 46th Cong., 1st sess., 1879.

———. Senate. *Report of an Examination of the Upper Columbia River and the Territory in Its Vicinity in September and October, 1881, to Determine Its Navigability, and Adaptability to Steamboat Transportation . . . by Lieut. Thomas W. Symons, Chief Engineer of the Dept. of the Columbia*. Ex. Doc. 186. 47th Cong., 1st sess., 1882.

———. Senate. *Report of Brig. Gen. Nelson A. Miles, September 1881, of an Inspection of Forts Coeur d'Alene and Colville and Camp Spokane, Washington Territory*. Ex. Doc. 1, 47th Cong., 1st sess., 1882.

———. Senate. *Report of the Expedition to the Black Hills of Dakota, Under Command of Bvt. Maj.-Gen. G. A. Custer*. Ex. Doc. 32, 43rd Cong., 2nd sess., 1875.

———. Senate. *Report of the Joint Committee Appointed to Consider the Expediency of Transferring the Indian Bureau to the War Department*. Report 693, January 31, 1879, 45th Cong., 3rd sess., 1879.

———. Senate. *Report of the Joint Committee on the Conduct of the War*. Report 142, 38th Cong., 2nd sess., 1866. "Massacre of Cheyenne Indians," pp. 3–108.

———. Senate. *Report on the Mineral Wealth, Climate, and Rainfall, and Natural Resources of the Black Hills of Dakota*. By Walter P. Jenney, E. M., Geologist in Charge. Ex. Doc. 51, 44th Cong., 1st sess., 1876.

———. Senate. *Testimony Taken by a Select Committee Concerning the Removal of the Northern Cheyenne Indians*. Report 708. 46th Cong., 2nd sess., 1880.

———. Senate. *Troops Employed in Connection with Indian Hostilities in Protecting the Missouri Traffic and the Union Pacific Railroad* Ex. Doc. 7, 40th Cong., 2nd sess., 1868.

United States Geological and Geographical Survey of the Territories. *Ethnography and Philology of the Hidatsa Indians*. By Washington Matthews. Misc. Pub. No. 7. Washington, D.C.: GPO, 1877.

———. *Fourth Annual Report . . . Preliminary Report of the . . . Survey of Wyoming*. By Ferdinand V. Hayden. Washington: GPO, 1872.

———. *Sixth Annual Report*. By Ferdinand V. Hayden. Washington: GPO, 1873.

———. *Twelfth Annual Report . . . Progress of the Exploration in Wyoming and Idaho for the Year 1878*. By Ferdinand V. Hayden. Washington: GPO, 1883.

Newspapers and Periodicals

Army and Navy Journal, 1863–1895

Atchison (Kansas) Globe, 1879–1880

Atlantic Monthly, 1877

Caldwell (Kansas) Post, 1879–1880

Chicago Inter-Ocean, 1875–1880, 1883

Chicago Tribune, 1876

Cincinnati Gazette, 1867

Congressional Globe, 41st Cong, 2nd sess., 1869–1870

Eclectic Magazine, 1877
Field, 1876
Galaxy, 1877
Harper's New Monthly Magazine, 1877
Harper's Weekly, 1872, 1875–1881, 1883, 1889
Iowa State Register (Des Moines), 1880, 1886
Journal of the Ethnological Society of London, 1868–1869
Journal of the Military Service Institution of the United States, 1881, 1882, 1886, 1887, 1889, 1890
Land and Water, 1876
Leavenworth (Kansas) Times, 1878–1880
Life, 1968
Los Angeles Herald, 1883
Nation, 1877
Nature, 1876
New York Dramatic Mirror, 1879–1889
New York Herald, 1875–1876, 1878–1880
New York Times, 1865, 1867, 1875–1889, 1898
New York Tribune, 1875–1877, 1879–1880
New York World, 1883, 1887–1889
Nonconformist, 1876
North American Review, 1878
Omaha Herald, 1867, 1875,1880, 1883
Omaha Republican, 1883
Pall Mall Gazette, 1876
Popular Science Monthly, 1877
Publisher's Weekly, 1876–1877, 1881–1883
St. Louis Post-Dispatch, 1884
Salt Lake City Deseret News, 1883
San Francisco Chronicle, 1883
Saturday Review, 1876
Scribner's Monthly Magazine, 1877, 1887
Seattle Post Intelligencer, 1883
Times (London), 1876–1877
Topeka (Kansas) Weekly Commonwealth, 1880
Washington (D.C.) Daily Morning Chronicle, 1872
Washington (D.C.) Herald (Army and Navy Edition), 1881
Wilmington (N.C.) Morning Star, 1889
Youth's Companion, 1882–1883

Articles

Anderson, Grant K. "Samuel D. Hinman and the Opening of the Black Hills." *Nebraska History* 60 (1979): 520–42.

Ayres, Mary C. "History of Fort Lewis, Colorado." *Colorado Magazine* 8, no. 3 (May 1931): 81–90.

Beauregard, P. G. T. "The Battle of Bull Run." *Century* 29 (November 1884): 80–106.

Blackmore, William. "The North American Indians: A Sketch of Some of the Hostile Tribes." *Journal of the Ethnological Society of London* 1 (1869): 287–320.

Bourke, John G. "Mackenzie's Last Fight with the Cheyennes: A Winter Campaign in Wyoming and Montana." *Journal of the Military Service Institution of the United States* 11 (January 1890): 29–49; (March 1890): 198–221; reprint, Fort Collins, Colo.: Old Army Press, 1970.

Brayer, Herbert O. "Exploring the Yellowstone with Hayden, 1872. Diary of Sidford Hamp." *Annals of Wyoming* 14, no. 4 (1942): 1–47.

Buecker, Thomas R. "The Journals of James S. McClellan, 1st Sgt., Company H, 3rd Cavalry." *Annals of Wyoming* 57 (spring 1985): 21–34.

Clapsaddle, David K. "The Fort Hays-Fort Dodge Road." *Kansas History* 14, no. 2 (summer 1991): 100–12.

Covington, James Warren. "Causes of the Dull Knife Raid." *Chronicles of Oklahoma* 26, no. 1 (March 1948): 13–22.

Crimmins, Martin L. "The First Line of Army Posts Established in West Texas in 1849." *West Texas Historical Association Year Book* 19 (1943): 121–27.

Dodge, Richard Irving. "Causes for Desertion." *Army and Navy Journal*, May 19, 1883: 957.

———. "The Desertion Question." *Journal of the Military Service Institution of the United States* 11 (December 1889): 163–65.

———. "Details of Extra Duty Men." *Army and Navy Journal*, April 14, 1883: 836.

———. "The Enlisted Soldier." *Journal of the Military Service Institution of the United States* 8 (May 1886): 259–318.

———. "Enlistments." *Army and Navy Journal*, April 21, 1883: 868.

———. "Excuses for Desertion." *Army and Navy Journal*, September 28, 1889: 80.

———. "Frontier Army Life." *Army and Navy Journal*, February 23, 1878: 459.

———. "Religion among Indians." *Army and Navy Journal*, July 6, 1878: 778.

———. "Rifle Firing at Fort Sully." *Army and Navy Journal*, August 29, 1885: 90.

Goss, Warren Lee. "Recollections of a Private (Including the Battle of Bull Run)." *Century* 29 (November 1884): 107–13.

Grange, Roger T., Jr. "Fort Robinson: Outpost on the Plains." *Nebraska History* 39, no. 3 (September 1958): 191–240.

Henry, Guy V. "A Winter March to the Black Hills." *Harper's Weekly* 39 (July 27, 1895): 700.

Hoeckman, Steven. "The History of Fort Sully." *South Dakota Historical Collections* 26 (1952): 222–77.

Hoig, Stan. "The Northern Cheyenne Exodus and the 1878 Battle of Turkey Springs." *Chronicles of Oklahoma* 80 (spring 2002): 86–101.

Irvine, R. J. "11th Infantry Regiment." *Journal of the Military Service Institution of the United States* 12 (1891): 379–81.

Johnson, Walter A. "Brief History of the Missouri-Kansas-Texas Railroad Line." *Chronicles of Oklahoma* 24, no. 3 (autumn 1946): 340–58.

Jordan, Weymouth T., Jr. "A Soldier's Life on the Indian Frontier, 1876–1878: Letters of 2Lt. C. D. Cowles." *Kansas Historical Quarterly* 38 (summer 1972): 144–55.

Keeling, Henry C. "My Experiences with the Cheyenne Indians." *Chronicles of Oklahoma* 3 (March 1925): 59–68.

Kime, Wayne R. "Huck among the Indians: Mark Twain and Richard Irving Dodge's *The Plains of the Great West and Their Inhabitants*." *Western American Literature* 24 (February 1990): 321–34.

———. "'Not Coarse . . . But Not Delicate': Richard Irving Dodge's Portrayal of Plains Indians in *The Plains of the Great West and Their Inhabitants*." *Platte Valley Review* 17, no. 1 (winter 1989): 69–83.

King, James T. "Needed: A Re-Evaluation of General George Crook." *Nebraska History* 45, no. 3 (September 1964): 223–35.

Lane, W. B. "Frontier Service in the Fifties." *The United Service Magazine* 10 (December 1893): 522–45.

McDermott, John D. "Were They Really Rogues: Desertion in the Nineteenth Century U.S. Army." *Nebraska History* 78 (winter 1997): 165–74.

McLaird, James D., and Lesta V. Turchen. "Exploring the Black Hills, 1855–1875: Reports of the Government Expeditions." *South Dakota History* 4 (1974): 161–97, 281–319, 403–38.

Mattes, Merrill J. "The Sutler's Store at Fort Laramie." *Annals of Wyoming* 18 (July 1946): 93–132.

Murray, Robert A. "Fort Fred Steele: Desert Outpost on the Union Pacific." *Annals of Wyoming* 44 (fall 1972): 139–206.

Nankivell, John H. "Fort Crawford, Colorado, 1880–1890." *Colorado Magazine* 11 (March 1934): 54–64.

Osborne, Alan. "The Exile of the Nez Percé in Indian Territory, 1878–1885." *Chronicles of Oklahoma* 56, no. 4 (winter 1978–79): 450–71.

Parker, Daingerfield. "The Regular Infantry in the First Bull Run Campaign." *United Service* 12 (1885): 521–31.

Parker, Watson. "The Report of Captain John Mix of a Scout to the Black Hills, March–April 1875." *South Dakota History* 7 (fall 1977): 385–401.

———. "Report of the Reverend Samuel D. Hinman of an Expedition to the Black Hills during August, 1874." *Bits and Pieces* 5 (November 1969): 5–9.

Pennington, William D. "Government Policy and Indian Farming on the Cheyenne and Arapaho Reservation, 1869–1880." *Chronicles of Oklahoma* 57, no. 2 (summer 1979): 171–89.

Reade, Philip. "Chronicles of the Twenty-third Regiment of Infantry." *Journal of the Military Service Institution of the United States* 35 (1904): 422–27.

Shirk, George H. "Military Duty on the Western Frontier." *Chronicles of Oklahoma* 57 (summer 1979): 171–89.

Thoburn, Joseph B. "The Story of Cantonment." *Chronicles of Oklahoma* 3 (1925): 68–73.

Tidball, Eugene C. "General Sherman's Last March." *Colorado History* 46 (1997): 1–29.

Woodhull, Alfred A. "The Enlisted Soldier." *Journal of the Military Service Institution of the United States* 8 (March 1887): 18–70.

Wright, Peter M. "The Pursuit of Dull Knife from Fort Reno in 1878–1879." *Chronicles of Oklahoma* 46, no. 2 (June 1968): 141–54.

Books

Adams, George Rollie. *General William S. Harney, Prince of Dragoons*. Lincoln: University of Nebraska Press, 2001.

Adams, Gerald F. *The Post Near Cheyenne: A History of Fort D. A. Russell, 1867–1930*. Boulder, Colo.: Pruett, 1989.

Aderman, Alice R. *A Genealogy of the Irvings of New York: Washington Irving, His Brothers and Sisters, and Their Dependents*. N.p.: privately printed, 1981.

A. D. Worthington and Company. *Illustrated Descriptive Catalog of Popular and Standard Books*. Hartford, Conn.: Worthington, 1877.

Agassiz, Elizabeth, ed. *Louis Agassiz, His Life and Correspondence*. 3rd ed. Boston: Houghton Mifflin, 1886.

Aldridge, Reginald. *Life on a Ranch: Ranch Notes in Kansas, Colorado, the Indian Territory, and Northern Texas*. New York: D. Appleton, 1884.

Allen, Joel Asaph. *History of the American Bison, Bison Americanus.* Washington: GPO, 1877.

Ambrose, Stephen B. *Nothing Like It in the World: The Men Who Built the Transcontinental Railroad, 1863–1869.* New York: Simon & Schuster, 2000.

Appleton's Annual Cyclopedia and Register of Important Events of the Year 1895. New York: D. Appleton, 1896.

Armes, George A. *Ups and Downs of an Army Officer.* Washington, D.C.: n.p., 1900.

Athearn, Robert G. *Rebel of the Rockies: A History of the Denver and Rio Grande Western Railroad.* New Haven, Conn.: Yale University Press, 1962.

———. *William Tecumseh Sherman and the Settlement of the West.* Foreword by William M. Ferraro and J. Thomas Murphy. Norman: University of Oklahoma Press, 1995.

Aubin, J. Harris. *Register of the Military Order of the Loyal Legion of the United States.* Boston: Commandery of the State of Massachusetts, 1906.

Bailey, John W. *Pacifying the Plains: General Alfred Terry and the Decline of the Sioux, 1866–1890.* Westport, Conn.: Greenwood Press, 1979.

Baird, Spencer F. *Catalogue of North American Birds, Chiefly in the Museum of the Smithsonian Institution.* Washington, D.C.: Smithsonian Institution, 1859.

Ball, Durwood. *Army Regulars on the Western Frontier, 1848–1861.* Norman: University of Oklahoma Press, 2001.

Bancroft, Hubert Howe. *History of Nevada, Colorado, and Wyoming, 1540–1888.* Vol. 25 of *Works* (39 vols., 1882–1890). San Francisco: History Company, 1890.

Battles and Leaders of the Civil War. Edited by Robert Underwood Johnson and Clarence Clough Buel. 4 vols. New York: Century Company, 1887–1888.

Beal, Merrill D. *"I Will Fight No More Forever": Chief Joseph and the Nez Perce War.* Seattle: University of Washington Press, 1963.

Belden, George P. *Belden, The White Chief: or, Twelve Years among the Wild Indians of the Plains.* Edited by James S. Brisbin. Cincinnati: C. F. Vent, 1870.

Berkeley, George Charles Grantley. *The English Sportsman in the Western Prairies.* London: Hurst and Blackett, 1861.

Berthrong, Donald J. *The Cheyenne and Arapaho Ordeal: Reservation and Agency Life in the Indian Territory, 1875–1907.* Norman: University of Oklahoma Press, 1976.

———. *The Southern Cheyennes.* Norman: University of Oklahoma Press, 1963.

Bigelow, Donald N. *William Conant Church and the Army and Navy Journal.* New York: Columbia University Press, 1952.

Blackmore, William. *Colorado: Its Resources, Parks, and Prospects as a New Field for Emigration; with an Account of the Trenchara and Costilla Estates, in the San Luis Park.* London: Sampson Low, Son, and Marston, 1869.

———. *Investments in Land in Colorado and New Mexico; with Especial Reference to Their Prospective Increase in Value in Consequence of the Extension of Railroads through These Regions; Combined With Their Salubrious Climate, and Mineral, Pastoral, and Agricultural Resources.* London: privately printed. 1876.

———. (Published anonymously.) *The Denver and Rio Grande Railway of Colorado and New Mexico.* London: G. Norman and Sons, 1871.

Blair, Walter, ed. *Mark Twain's Hannibal, Huck and Tom.* Berkeley and Los Angeles: University of California Press, 1969.

Bordman, Gerald. *American Theatre: A Chronicle of Comedy and Drama, 1869–1914.* New York: Oxford University Press, 1994.

Bourke, John G. *The Diaries of John Gregory Bourke.* Vol. 1, *November 20, 1872, to July 28, 1876.* Edited by Charles M. Robinson III. Denton: University of North Texas Press, 2003.

———. *Mackenzie's Last Fight with the Cheyennes: A Winter Campaign in Wyoming and Montana.* Governors Island, New York Harbor: Military Service Institution, 1890.

———. *On the Border with Crook.* New York: Charles Scribner's Sons, 1891.

———. *The Snake-Dance of the Moquis of Arizona; Being a Narrative of a Journey from Santa Fé, New Mexico to the Villages of the Moqui Indians of Arizona, with a Description of the Manners and Customs of This Peculiar People, and Especially of the Revolting Religious Rite, the Snake-Dance, to Which Is Added a Brief Dissertation upon Serpent-Worship in General, with an Account of the Tablet Dance of the Pueblo of Santo Domingo, etc.* New York: Charles Scribner's Sons, 1884.

Boyd, William H., comp. *Boyd's Directory of the District of Columbia.* Washington, D.C.: Boyd, 1882.

Brandes, T. Donald. *Military Posts of Colorado.* Fort Collins, Colo.: Old Army Press, 1973.

Brayer, Herbert Oliver. *William Blackmore: A Case Study in the Economic Development of the West.* 2 vols. Denver: Bradford-Robinson, 1949.

Brown, Jesse, and A. M. Willard. *The Black Hills Trails.* Rapid City, S.D.: Rapid City Journal Co., 1924.

Bryant, Keith L., Jr. *History of the Atchison, Topeka and Santa Fe Railway.* Lincoln: University of Nebraska Press, 1974.

Buecker, Thomas R. *Fort Robinson and the American West, 1874–1899.* Lincoln: Nebraska State Historical Society, 1999.

Burton, Jeffrey. *Indian Territory and the United States, 1866–1906.* Norman: University of Oklahoma Press, 1995.

Butler, David F. *United States Firearms: The First Century, 1776–1875.* New York: Winchester Press, 1971.

Butterfield, Consul W. *History of the City of Omaha, Nebraska.* New York: Munsell and Co., 1894.

Carriker, Robert C. *Fort Supply, Indian Territory: Frontier Outpost on the Plains.* Norman: University of Oklahoma Press, 1970.

Cassin, John. *Illustrations of the Birds of California, Texas, Oregon, British, and Russian America.* Philadelphia: J. B. Lippincott, 1856.

Catlin, George. *Last Rambles Amongst the Indians of the Rocky Mountains.* London: Sampson, Low, Son, and Marston, 1868.

———. *Letters and Notes on the Manners, Customs, and Conditions of the North American Indians; Written during Eight Years' Travel (1832–1839) Amongst the Wildest Tribes of Indians in North America.* 2 vols. Reprint, New York: Dover, 1973.

The Centennial of the United States Military Academy at West Point, New York, 1802–1902. 2 vols. Washington, D.C.: GPO, 1904.

Chalfant, William Y. *Cheyennes at Dark Water Creek: The Last Fight of the Red River War.* Foreword by Father Peter John Powell. Norman: University of Oklahoma Press, 1997.

Check List of Publications of the Smithsonian Institution. Smithsonian Misc. Collections, No. 745. Washington, D.C.: GPO, 1890.

Chittenden, Hiram M. *The Yellowstone National Park.* Edited by Richard A. Bartlett. Norman: University of Oklahoma Press, 1964.

City Directories of the United States, 1860–1901: Guide to the Microfilm Collection. Woodbridge, Conn.: Research Publications, 1983.

Clark, William P. *The Indian Sign Language: With Brief Explanatory Notes of the Gestures Taught Deaf-Mutes in Our Institutions for Their Instruction, and a Description of Some of the Peculiar Laws, Customs, Myths, Superstitions, Ways of Living, Code of Peace and War and Signals of Our Aborigines.* Philadelphia: L. R. Hamersley and Co., 1885.

Clemens, Samuel L. *Mark Twain–Howells Letters. The Correspondence of Samuel L. Clemens and William D. Howells, 1872–1910.* Edited by Henry Nash Smith and William M. Gibson. 2 vols. Cambridge, Mass.: Harvard University Press, 1960.

Coffman, Edward M. *The Old Army: A Portrait of the American Army in Peacetime, 1784–1898.* New York: Oxford University Press, 1986.

Collins, John S. *My Experiences in the West.* Edited by Colton Storm. Chicago: Lakeside Press, 1970.

Connelly, William E. *A Standard History of Kansas and Kansans.* 5 vols. Chicago and New York: Lewis Publishing Co., 1918.

Connor, Seymour V., and Jimmy M. Skaggs. *Broadcloth and Britches: The Santa Fe Trade.* College Station: Texas A & M University Press, 1977.

Cook, Adrian. *The Armies of the Streets: The New York Draft Riots of 1863.* Lexington: University of Kentucky Press, 1974.

Cooke, Philip St. George. *Scenes and Adventures in the Army; or, Romance of Military Life.* Philadelphia: Lewis & Blackiston, 1857.

Cooper, Jerry. *The Army and Civil Disorder: Federal Military Intervention in Labor Disputes, 1877–1900.* Westport, Conn.: Greenwood Press, 1980.

———. *The Rise of the National Guard: The Evolution of the American Militia, 1865–1920.* Lincoln: University of Nebraska Press, 1997.

Corbett and Ballenger's Denver City Directory for 1881. Denver: Rocky Mountain News Printing Co., 1881.

Corbusier, Fanny Dunbar. *Fanny Dunbar Corbusier: Recollections of Her Army Life, 1869–1908.* Edited by Patricia Y. Stallard. Norman: University of Oklahoma Press, 2003.

Crabtree, Beth G. *North Carolina Governors, 1585–1974.* Raleigh, N.C.: Division of Archives and History, 1974.

Crofutt, George A. *Crofutt's Grip-Sack Guide of Colorado. . . . A Complete Encyclopedia of the State.* Denver: Alvord & Co., 1881.

Crook, George W. *General George Crook: His Autobiography.* Edited by Martin E. Schmitt. Norman: University of Oklahoma Press, 1960.

Cullum, George W. *Biographical Register of Officers and Graduates of the U.S. Military Academy at West Point, from Its Establishment to the Army Re-organization of 1866–67.* 2 vols. New York: D. Van Nostrand, 1868.

———. *Biographical Register of the Officers and Graduates of the U.S. Military Academy from 1802 to 1890.* Boston: Houghton Mifflin, 1891.

———. *Supplement to the Biographical Register.* New York: D. Van Nostrand, 1868.

Custer, George A. *My Life on the Plains; or, Personal Experiences with Indians.* New York: Shelton, 1874.

———. *My Life on the Plains; or, Personal Experiences with Indians.* Edited with an introduction by Edgar I. Stewart. Norman: University of Oklahoma Press, 1962.

Dale, Edward Everett, and Morris L. Wardell. *History of Oklahoma.* Englewood Cliffs, N. J.: Prentice-Hall, 1948.

Danker, Donald F., ed. *Man of the Plains: Recollections of Luther North, 1856–1882.* Introduction by George Bird Grinnell. Lincoln: University of Nebraska Press, 1961.

Davies, Wallace Evan. *Patriotism on Parade: The Story of Veterans' and Hereditary Organizations in America, 1783–1900.* Cambridge: Harvard University Press, 1955.

Davis, William C. *Battle at Bull Run: A History of the First Major Campaign of the Civil War.* Baton Rouge: Louisiana State University Press, 1977.

De Barthe, Joe. *Life and Adventures of Frank Grouard.* Edited by Edgar I. Stewart. Norman: University of Oklahoma Press, 1958.

Delo, David Michael. *Peddlers and Post Traders: The Army Sutler on the Frontier.* Salt Lake City: University of Utah Press, 1992.

De Montravel, Peter. *A Hero to His Fighting Men: Nelson A. Miles, 1829–1925.* Kent, Ohio: Kent State University Press, 1998.

De Trobriand, Philippe. *Military Life in Dakota: The Journal of Philippe Régis de Trobriand.* Translated and edited by Lucile M. Kane. St. Paul, Minn.: Alvord Memorial Commission, 1951.

DeVoto, Bernard. *Across the Wide Missouri.* Boston: Houghton Mifflin, 1947.

Dictionary of North Carolina Biography. 5 vols. Chapel Hill: University of North Carolina Press, 1979–1996.

Dobak, William A. *Fort Riley and Its Neighbors: Military Money and Economic Growth, 1853–1895.* Norman: University of Oklahoma Press, 1998.

Dodge, Grenville Mellen. *How We Built the Union Pacific Railway, and Other Railway Papers and Addresses.* Washington, D.C.: GPO, 1910.

Dodge, Richard Irving. *The Black Hills: A Minute Description of the Routes, Scenery, Soil, Climate, Timber, Gold, Geology, Zoölogy, etc. with an Accurate Map, Four Sectional Drawings, and Ten Plates from Photographs, Taken on the Spot.* New York: James Miller, 1875.

———. *The Black Hills Journals of Colonel Richard Irving Dodge.* Edited by Wayne R. Kime. Norman: University of Oklahoma Press, 1996.

———. *The Hunting Grounds of the Great West.* London: Chatto & Windus, 1877 [1876].

———. *The Indian Territory Journals of Colonel Richard Irving Dodge.* Edited by Wayne R. Kime. Norman: University of Oklahoma Press, 2000.

———. *A Living Issue.* Washington, D.C.: F. B. Mohun, 1882.

———. *Our Wild Indians: Thirty-three Years' Personal Experience among the Red Men of the Great West. A Popular Account of Their Social Life, Religion, Habits, Traits, Customs, Exploits, Etc. with Thrilling Adventures and Experiences on the Great Plains and in the Mountains of Our Wide Frontier.* Hartford, Conn.: A. D. Worthington and Co., 1882.

———. *The Plains of North America and Their Inhabitants.* Edited by Wayne R. Kime. Newark: University of Delaware Press, 1989.

———. *The Plains of the Great West and Their Inhabitants.* New York: G. P. Putnam's Sons, 1877.

———. *The Powder River Expedition Journals of Colonel Richard Irving Dodge.* Edited by Wayne R. Kime. Norman: University of Oklahoma Press, 1997.

———. *The Sherman Tour Journals of Colonel Richard Irving Dodge.* Edited by Wayne R. Kime. Norman: University of Oklahoma Press, 2002.

Doubleday, Abner. *My Life in the Old Army. The Reminiscences of Abner Doubleday from the Collections of the New-York Historical Society.* Edited by Joseph E. Chance. Fort Worth: Texas Christian University Press, 1998.

Dunlay, Thomas W. *Wolves for the Blue Soldiers: Indian Scouts and Auxiliaries with the United States Army.* Lincoln: University of Nebraska Press, 1982.

Dunraven, Windham Thomas Wyndham-Quin, Fourth Earl of. *The Great Divide: Travels in the Upper Yellowstone in the Summer of 1874.* New York: Scribner, Welfrod, and Armstrong, 1876.

Dyer, Mrs. D. B. *Fort Reno: or, Picturesque Cheyenne and Arapahoe Army Life Before the Opening of "Oklahoma."* New York: G. W. Dillingham, 1896.

Eisenhower, John S. D. *Agent of Destiny: The Life and Times of General Winfield Scott.* Norman: University of Oklahoma Press, 1997.

Eisenschiml, Otto. *The Celebrated Case of Fitz-John Porter: An American Dreyfus Affair.* Indianapolis: Bobbs-Merrill, 1950.

Ellis, Richard N. *General Pope and U. S. Indian Policy.* Albuquerque: New Mexico University Press, 1970.

Emerson, William K. *Encyclopedia of United States Army Insignia and Uniforms.* Norman: University of Oklahoma Press, 1996.

Emmitt, Robert. *The Last War Trail: The Utes and the Settlement of Colorado.* Norman: University of Oklahoma Press, 1972.

Farrow, Edward S. *Farrow's Military Encyclopedia: A Dictionary of Military Knowledge.* 2nd ed., 3 vols. New York: Military-Naval Publishing Co., 1895.

———. *Mountain Scouting. A Hand-Book for Officers and Soldiers on the Frontier.* New York: The Author, 1881.

Faulk, Odie B., Kenny A. Franks, and Paul F. Lambert, eds. *Early Military Forts and Posts in Oklahoma.* Oklahoma City: Oklahoma Historical Society, 1978.

Fellman, Michael. *Citizen Sherman: A Life of William Tecumseh Sherman.* Lawrence: University Press of Kansas, 1997.

Finerty, John F. *War-Path and Bivouac: or, The Conquest of the Sioux.* Introduction by Oliver Knight. Norman: University of Oklahoma Press, 1961.

Fisher, John S. *A Builder of the West: The Life of William Jackson Palmer.* Caldwell, Idaho: Caxton Press, 1939.

Foner, Jack D. *The United States Soldier between Two Wars: Army Life and Reforms, 1865–1898.* New York: Humanities Press, 1970.

Foote, Shelby. *The Civil War: A Narrative.* 3 vols. New York: Random House, 1958–1974.

Fossett, Frank. *Colorado: Its Gold and Silver Mines and Health and Pleasure Resorts.* 2nd ed. New York: C. G. Crawford, 1880.

Frazer, Robert W. *Forts of the West: Military Forts and Presidios and Posts Commonly Called Forts West of the Mississippi River to 1898.* Norman: University of Oklahoma Press, 1965.

Freeman, George D. *Midnight and Noonday: or, The Incidental History of Southern Kansas and the Indian Territory, 1871–1890.* Edited by Richard L. Lane. Norman: University of Oklahoma Press, 1984.

Frontier Forts of Texas. Introduction by Rupert N. Richardson. Waco, Tex.: Texian Press, 1966.

Fry, James B. *Army Sacrifices, or Briefs from Official Pigeon-Holes. Sketches Based on Official Reports—Grouped Together for the Purpose of Illustrating the Services and Experiences of the Regular Army of the United States on the Indian Frontier.* New York: Van Nostrand, 1879.

———. *The Conkling and Blaine-Fry Controversy in 1866. The Outbreak of the Life-long Feud Between the Two Great Statesmen, Roscoe Conkling and James G. Blaine.* New York: A. G. Sherwood, 1893.

———. *Military Miscellanies.* New York: Brentano's, 1889.

Gaff, Alan, and Maureen Gaff, eds. *Adventures on the Western Frontier: Major General John Gibbon.* Bloomington: Indiana University Press, 1994.

Goetzmann, William H. *Exploration and Empire: The Explorer and the Scientist in the Winning of the American West.* New York: Columbia University Press, 1966.

Gohdes, Clarence. *American Literature in Nineteenth Century England.* Carbondale: Southern Illinois University Press, 1944.

Gould, David B., comp. *Gould's St. Louis Directory for 1876.* St. Louis: Gould, 1876.

Grange, Roger T. *Fort Robinson: Outpost on the Plains.* Lincoln: Nebraska State Historical Society, 1965.

Gray, John S. *Centennial Campaign: The Sioux War of 1876.* Fort Collins, Colo.: Old Army Press, 1976.

Greene, Jerome A. *Morning Star Dawn: The Powder River Expedition and the Northern Cheyennes, 1876.* Norman: University of Oklahoma Press, 2003.

———. *Nez Perce Summer, 1877: The U.S. Army and the Nee-Me-Poo Crisis.* Helena: Montana Historical Society Press, 2000.

———. *Slim Buttes, 1876: An Episode of the Great Sioux War.* Norman: University of Oklahoma Press, 1982.

———. *Yellowstone Command: Colonel Nelson A. Miles and the Great Sioux War, 1876–1877.* Lincoln: University of Nebraska Press, 1991.

Greene, Jerome A., ed. *Battles and Skirmishes of the Great Sioux War, 1876–1877: The Military View.* Norman: University of Oklahoma Press, 1993.

———. *Lakota and Cheyenne: Indian Views of the Great Sioux War, 1876–1877.* Norman: University of Oklahoma Press, 1993.

Grinnell, George Bird. *The Fighting Cheyennes.* Norman: University of Oklahoma Press, 1956.

———. *Two Great Scouts and Their Pawnee Battalion: The Experiences of Frank J. North and Luther H. North, Pioneers in the Great West, 1856–1882, and Their Defence of the Building of the Union Pacific Railroad.* Cleveland: Arthur H. Clark Co., 1928.

Haddock, John A. *The Growth of a Century as Illustrated in the History of Jefferson County, New York, from 1798 to 1894.* Philadelphia: Sherman & Co., 1894.

Hafen, LeRoy R., and Ann W. Hafen, eds. *Powder River Campaigns and Sawyer's Expedition of 1865.* Glendale, Calif.: Arthur H. Clark, 1961.

Hafen, LeRoy R., and Francis Marion Young. *Fort Laramie and the Pageant of the West, 1834–1890.* Glendale, Calif.: Arthur H. Clark, 1967.

Hall, Frank. *History of the State of Colorado.* 4 vols. Chicago: Blakely Printing Co., 1895.

Hamersley, L. R., comp. *Records of Living Officers of the United States Army.* Philadelphia: L. R. Hamersley and Co., 1884.

Hamersley, Thomas H., comp. *Complete Army Register of the United States: For One Hundred Years (1779 to 1879).* 2 vols. Washington, D.C.: T. Hamersley, 1880.

Haywood, C. Robert. *Trails South: The Wagon Road Economy in the Dodge City–Panhandle Region.* Norman: University of Oklahoma Press, 1986.

Hedges, James B. *Henry Villard and the Railways of the Northwest.* New Haven: Yale University Press, 1930.

Hedren, Paul L. *Fort Laramie in 1876: Chronicle of a Frontier Post at War.* Lincoln: University of Nebraska Press, 1988.

———. *Traveler's Guide to the Great Sioux War: The Battlefields, Forts and Related Sites of America's Greatest Indian War.* Helena: Montana Historical Society Press, 1996.

———. *With Crook in the Black Hills: Stanley J. Morrow's 1876 Photographic Legacy.* Boulder, Colo.: Pruett, 1985.

Heiner, Gordon C., Jr. *From Saints to Red Legs. Madison Barracks: The History of a Border Post.* Watertown, N.Y.: A. W. Mauk, [1937].

Heitman, Francis B. *Historical Register and Dictionary of the United States Army.* 2 vols. Washington, D.C.: GPO, 1903.

Hewes, Leslie. *Occupying the Cherokee Country of Oklahoma.* Lincoln: University of Nebraska Press, 1978.

Hill, Edward E. *The Office of Indian Affairs, 1874–1880: Historical Sketches.* New York: Clearwater Publishing Co., 1974.

[Hill, J. M.]. *Miss Margaret Mather under the Managership of J. M. Hill.* Buffalo: Courier Lithograph Co., [1883].

Hirshson, Stanley P. *The White Tecumseh: A Biography of General William T. Sherman.* New York: John Wiley & Sons, 1997.

Hittell, John S. *A History of the City of San Francisco and Incidentally the State of California.* San Francisco: A. L. Bancroft & Co., 1878.

Hoig, Stan. *Fort Reno and the Indian Territory Frontier.* Fayetteville: University of Arkansas Press, 2000.

———. *The Peace Chiefs of the Cheyennes.* Foreword by Boyce D. Timmons. Norman: University of Oklahoma Press, 1980.

———. *Perilous Pursuit: The U.S. Cavalry and the Northern Cheyennes.* Boulder: University Press of Colorado, 2002.

———. *The Sand Creek Massacre.* Norman: University of Oklahoma Press, 1961.

Hollon, Eugene. *Beyond the Cross Timbers: The Travels of Randolph B. Marcy, 1812–1887.* Norman: University of Oklahoma Press, 1957.

———. *The Great American Desert: Then and Now.* New York: Oxford University Press, 1966.

Hooker, William Francis. *The Bullwhacker: Adventures of a Frontier Freighter.* Introduction by David Dary, edited by Howard R. Driggs. Lincoln: University of Nebraska Press, 1988.

Hornaday, William T. *The Extermination of the American Bison.* 2 vols. Washington, D.C.: GPO, 1889.

Hough, Franklin B. *A History of Jefferson County, in the State of New York, from the Earliest Period to the Present Time.* Albany, N.Y.: Joel Munsell; Watertown. N.Y.: Sterling & Riddell, 1854.

Hunt, Elvid, and Walter E. Lorence. *History of Fort Leavenworth, 1827–1937.* Fort Leavenworth: Command and General Staff School Press, 1937.

Hutton, Paul A. *Phil Sheridan and His Army.* Lincoln: University of Nebraska Press, 1985.

Hutton, Paul A., ed. *Soldiers West: Biographies from the Military Frontier.* Introduction by Robert M. Utley. Lincoln: University of Nebraska Press, 1987.

Hyde, George E. *A Life of George Bent, Written from His Letters.* Edited by Savoie Lottinville. Norman: University of Oklahoma Press, 1968.

———. *The Pawnee Indians.* Norman: University of Oklahoma Press, 1974.

———. *Red Cloud's Folk: A History of the Oglala Sioux Indians.* Norman: University of Oklahoma Press, 1957.

———. *Spotted Tail's Folk: A History of the Brulé Sioux.* Norman: University of Oklahoma Press, 1961.

Jackson, Donald. *Custer's Gold: The United States Cavalry Expedition of 1874.* New Haven: Yale University Press, 1966.

Jackson, Helen Hunt. *A Century of Dishonor: A Sketch of the United States Government's Dealings with Some of the Indian Tribes.* Minneapolis: Ross & Haines, 1964.

Jackson, William H. *Descriptive Catalogue of Photographs of North American Indians.* U.S. Geological Survey, Misc. Pub. No. 9. Washington, D.C.: GPO, 1877.

Johnson, Harrison. *Johnson's History of Nebraska.* Omaha: Henry Gibson, 1880.

Johnson, Richard W. *A Soldier's Reminiscences in Peace and War.* Philadelphia: J. B. Lippincott, 1886.

Johnson, Virginia W. *The Unregimented General: A Biography of Nelson A. Miles.* Boston: Houghton Mifflin, 1962.

Jones, Douglas C. *The Treaty of Medicine Lodge: The Story of the Great Treaty Council as Told by Eyewitnesses.* Norman: University of Oklahoma Press, 1966.

Kappler, Charles, ed. *Indian Affairs: Laws and Treaties.* 3 vols. Washington, D.C.: GPO, 1904.

Keim, De Benneville Randolph. *Sheridan's Troopers on the Borders: A Winter Campaign on the Plains.* Philadelphia: Claxton, Remses and Haffelflinger, 1870.

Kennett, Lee. *Sherman: A Soldier's Life.* New York: HarperCollins, 2001.

Kime, Wayne R. *Pierre M. Irving and Washington Irving: A Collaboration in Life and Letters.* Waterloo, Ontario: Wilfrid Laurier University Press, 1978.

King, Charles. *Campaigning with Crook and Stories of Army Life.* New York: Harper and Brothers, 1890.

Knight, Oliver. *Following the Indian Wars: The Story of the Newspaper Correspondents among the Indian Campaigners.* Norman: University of Oklahoma Press, 1960.

———. *Life and Manners in the Frontier Army.* Foreword by Paul L. Hedren. Norman: University of Oklahoma Press, 1993.

Krause, Herbert, and Gary D. Olson. *Prelude to Glory: The Newspaper Accounts of Custer's 1874 Expedition to the Black Hills.* Sioux Falls, S.D.: Brevet Press, 1974.

Kroeker, Marvin E. *Great Plains Command: William B. Hazen in the Frontier West.* Norman: University of Oklahoma Press, 1976.

Laidley, T. T. S. *A Course of Instruction in Rifle Firing.* Philadelphia: J. B. Lippincott, 1879.

Langley, H., comp. *Langley's San Francisco Directory for 1881.* San Francisco: Langley, 1881.

Larson, Robert W. *Red Cloud: Warrior Statesman of the Lakota Sioux*. Norman: University of Oklahoma Press, 1997.

Leckie, William H. *The Military Conquest of the Southern Plains*. Norman: University of Oklahoma Press, 1963.

Lee, Arthur T. *Fort Davis and the Texas Frontier: Paintings by Captain Arthur T. Lee, Eighth U.S. Infantry*. Text by W. Stephen Thomas. College Station: Texas A & M University Press, 1996.

Lee, Robert. *Fort Meade and the Black Hills*. Lincoln: University of Nebraska Press, 1991.

Los Angeles City and County Directory for 1881–82. Los Angeles: L. Whitworth, 1881.

Lowie, Robert H. *Indians of the Plains*. Preface by Raymond J. DeMallie. Lincoln: University of Nebraska Press, 1982.

Ludlow, William. *Report of a Reconnaissance of the Black Hills of Dakota, Made in the Summer of 1874*. Washington, D.C.: GPO, 1875.

Lyman, Horace S. *History of Oregon: The Growth of an American State*. 4 vols. New York: North Pacific Publishing Society, 1903.

McChristian, Douglas C. *An Army of Marksmen: The Development of United States Army Marksmanship in the Nineteenth Century*. Fort Collins, Colo.: Old Army Press, 1981.

———. *The United States Army in the West, 1870–1880: Uniforms, Weapons, and Equipment*. Norman: University of Oklahoma Press, 1995.

McCrea, Tully. *Dear Belle: Letters from a Cadet and Officer to His Sweetheart, 1858–1865*. Edited by Catharine S. Crary. Middleton, Conn.: Wesleyan University Press, 1965.

McDermott, John D. *Gold Rush: The Black Hills Story*. Pierre: South Dakota State Historical Society Press, 2001.

McGillycuddy, Julia B. *McGillycuddy, Agent: A Biography of Dr. Valentine T. McGillycuddy*. Stanford, Calif.: Stanford University Press, 1941.

McGroarty, John S. *History of Los Angeles County*. 3 vols. Chicago: American Historical Society, 1923.

McNitt, Frank. *The Indian Traders*. Norman: University of Oklahoma Press, 1962.

Mallery, Garrick. *Introduction to the Study of Sign Language among the North American Indians*. Washington, D.C.: GPO, 1880.

Manypenny, George W. *Our Indian Wards*. Cincinnati: R. Clarke & Co, 1880.

Marcou, Jules. *Life, Letters, and Works of Louis Agassiz*. 2 vols. New York: Macmillan, 1895.

Marcy, Randolph B. *Border Reminiscences*. New York: Harper & Brothers, 1872.

———. *Thirty Years of Army Life on the Border. Comprising Descriptions of the Indian Nomads of the Plains; Explorations of New Territory; A Trip Across the Rocky Mountains in the Winter; Descriptions of the Habits of Different Animals Found in the West, and the Methods of Hunting Them; With Incidents in the Life of Different Frontier Men, &c &c*. New York: Harper and Brothers, 1866.

Marszalek, John F. *Sherman: A Soldier's Passion for Order*. New York: Vintage Books, 1994.

Mattes, Merrill J. *Indians, Infants, and Infantry: Andrew and Elizabeth Burt on the Frontier*. Lincoln: University of Nebraska Press, 1988.

Meneely, Alexander H. *The War Department, 1861, A Study in Mobilization and Administration*. New York: Columbia University Press, 1928.

Merritt, John I. *Baronets and Buffalo: The British Sportsman in the American West, 1833–1881*. Missoula, Mont.: Mountain Press Publishing Company, 1985.

Miles, Nelson A. *Personal Recollections and Observations*. Introduction by Robert M. Utley. New York: Da Capo Press, 1969.

Miller, William J. *Civil War City: Harrisburg, Pennsylvania, 1861–1865, The Training of an Army*. Shippensburg, Pa.: White Mane Publishing Company, 1990.

Milner, Joe E. *California Joe: Noted Scout and Indian Fighter.* Caldwell, Idaho: Caxton Printers, 1935.

Miner, H. Craig. *West of Wichita: Settling the High Plains of Kansas, 1865–1890.* Lawrence: University Press of Kansas, 1986.

———. *Wichita: The Early Years, 1865–80.* Lincoln: University of Nebraska Press, 1982.

Monnett, John H. *Tell Them We Are Going Home: The Odyssey of the Northern Cheyennes.* Norman: University of Oklahoma Press, 2001.

Moore, John W. *History of North Carolina.* 2 vols. Raleigh, N.C.: Alfred Williams, 1888.

Morris, John W., Charles R. Goins, and Edwin C. McReynolds. *Historical Atlas of Oklahoma.* 3rd ed. Norman: University of Oklahoma Press, 1986.

Morrison, James L., Jr. *"The Best School": West Point, 1833–1866.* London, Ohio: Kent State University Press, 1986.

Morton, J. Sterling. *Illustrated History of Nebraska.* 3 vols. Lincoln: J. North, 1905–1913.

Murdock, Eugene Converse. *Patriotism Limited, 1862–1865: The Civil War Draft and the Bounty System.* Kent, Ohio: Kent State University Press, 1967.

Murray, Robert A. *Military Posts in the Powder River Country of Wyoming, 1865–1894.* Lincoln: University of Nebraska Press, 1968.

Newton, Henry W., and Walter P. Jenney. *Report on the Geology and Resources of the Black Hills of Dakota, with Atlas.* 2 vols. Washington, D.C.: GPO, 1880.

The New York Supplement. Containing the Decisions of the Intermediate and Lower Courts of Record of New York State. Volume 5 (June 6–August 1, 1889). St. Paul, Minn.: West Publishing Co., 1889.

Noel, Thomas J., Paul F. Mahoney, and Richard E. Stevens. *Historical Atlas of Colorado.* Norman: University of Oklahoma Press, 1994.

Nohl, Lessing H., Jr. "Bad Hand: The Military Career of Ranald Slidell Mackenzie, 1871–1889." Ph.D. dissertation, University of New Mexico, 1962.

North Carolina Troops, 1861–1865. A Roster. Volume V. Infantry, 11th–15th Regiments. Raleigh: Division of Archives and History, 1975.

Nowell-Smith, Simon. *International Copyright Laws and the Publisher in the Reign of Queen Victoria.* Oxford: Oxford University Press, 1961.

Nye, Wilbur S. *Carbine and Lance: The Story of Old Fort Sill.* Norman: University of Oklahoma Press, 1937.

———. *Plains Indian Raiders: The Final Phases of Warfare from the Arkansas to the Red River. With Original Photographs by William S. Soule.* Norman: University of Oklahoma Press, 1968.

Odell, George C. D. *Annals of the New York Stage.* 15 vols. New York: Columbia University Press, 1939–1953.

Oliva, Leo E. *Fort Hays, Frontier Army Post, 1865–1889.* Topeka: Kansas State Historical Society, 1980.

———. *Fort Larned and the Santa Fe Trail.* Topeka: Kansas State Historical Society, 1982.

———. *Soldiers on the Santa Fe Trail.* Norman: University of Oklahoma Press, 1967.

Olson, James C. *Red Cloud and the Sioux Problem.* Lincoln: University of Nebraska Press, 1965.

Pabor, William W. *Colorado as an Agricultural State: Its Farms, Fields, and Garden Lands.* New York: Orange Judd, 1883.

Palmer, William J. *The Westward Current of Population in the United States, with a Paper on the Colonies of Colorado in Their Relations to English Enterprise and Settlement. By William A. Bell.* London: Chapman and Hall, 1874.

The Papers of the Order of Indian Wars. Introduction by John M. Carroll. Fort Collins, Colo.: Old Army Press, 1975.

Parker, James. *The Old Army: Memories, 1872–1918.* Philadelphia: Dorrance, 1929.

Parker, Watson. *Gold in the Black Hills.* Norman: University of Oklahoma Press, 1966.

Paul, Rodman W. *The Far West and the Great Plains in Transition, 1859–1890.* Foreword by Martin Ridge. Norman: University of Oklahoma Press, 1998.

———. *Mining Frontiers of the Far West, 1848–1880.* Rev. ed. Albuquerque: University of New Mexico Press, 2001.

Pierce, Michael D. *The Most Promising Young Officer: A Life of Ranald Slidell Mackenzie.* Norman: University of Oklahoma Press, 1993.

Poor, Henry V. *Manual of the Railroads of the United States.* New York: Poor, 1873–1883.

Porter, Joseph C. *Paper Medicine Man: John Gregory Bourke and His American West.* Norman: University of Oklahoma Press, 1986.

Powell, Peter J. *People of the Sacred Mountain: A History of the Northern Cheyenne Chiefs and Warrior Societies.* 2 vols. San Francisco: Harper and Row, 1979.

———. *Sweet Medicine: The Continuing Role of the Sacred Arrows, the Sun Dance, and the Sacred Buffalo Hat in Northern Cheyenne History.* 2 vols. Norman: University of Oklahoma Press, 1969.

Powell, William S. *A North Carolina Gazetteer.* Chapel Hill: University of North Carolina Press, 1968.

Pride, Woodbury F. *History of Fort Riley.* Fort Riley, Kansas: Cavalry School, 1926.

Priest, Loring Benson. *Uncle Sam's Stepchildren: The Reformation of United States Indian Policy, 1865–1887.* New Brunswick, N.J.: Rutgers University Press, 1942.

Prucha, Francis Paul. *American Indian Policy in Crisis: Christian Reformers and the Indian, 1865–1900.* Norman: University of Oklahoma Press, 1976.

———. *The Great Father: The United States Government and the American Indians.* 2 vols. Lincoln: University of Nebraska Press, 1984.

Putnam, George H. *Authors and Publishers: A Manual.* New York: G. P. Putnam's Sons, 1883.

Reber, Bruce. *The United States Army and the Indian Wars in the Trans-Mississippi West, 1860–1898.* Special Bibliography 17. Carlisle Barracks, Pa.: USAMHI, 1978.

Report of the Commission Appointed to Treat with the Sioux Indians for the Relinquishment of the Black Hills. Washington, D.C.: GPO, 1875.

Richardson, Rupert N. *The Comanche Barrier to South Plains Settlement.* Glendale, Calif.: Arthur H. Clark, 1953.

Rickey, Don, Jr. *Forty Miles a Day on Beans and Hay: The Enlisted Soldier Fighting the Indian Wars.* Norman: University of Oklahoma Press, 1963.

Rideing, William H. *Boys in the Mountains and on the Plains: Or, The Western Adventures of Tom Smart, Bob Edge and Peter Small.* New York: Appleton, 1882.

Rister, Carl Coke. *Land Hunger: David L. Payne and the Oklahoma Boomers.* Norman: University of Oklahoma Press, 1942.

Roberts, Robert B. *Encyclopedia of Historic Forts: The Military, Pioneer, and Trading Posts of the United States.* New York: Macmillan, 1988.

Robinson, Charles M., III. *Bad Hand: A Biography of General Ranald S. Mackenzie.* Foreword by Stan Hoig. Austin, Tex.: State House Press, 1993.

———. *General Crook and the Western Frontier.* Norman: University of Oklahoma Press, 2001.

———. *A Good Year to Die: The Story of the Great Sioux War.* New York: Random House, 1995.

Rockwell, Wilson. *The Utes: A Forgotten People.* Denver: Sage Books, 1956.

Rodenbough, Theophilus. *The Army of the United States: Historical Sketches.* New York: Maynard, Merrill & Co., 1896.

Roe, Frances Marie Antoinette. *Army Letters from an Officer's Wife, 1871–1888.* New York: D. Appleton & Co., 1909.

Ruby, Robert H., and John A. Brown. *Half-Sun on the Columbia: A Biography of Chief Moses.* Norman: University of Oklahoma Press, 1965.

———. *The Spokane Indians: Children of the Sun*. Norman: University of Oklahoma Press, 1970.

Ruffin, Thomas. *The Papers of Thomas Ruffin*. Edited by J. J. de R. Hamilton. 4 vols. Raleigh, N.C.: Edwards and Broughton, 1918–1920.

Rusling, James F. *Men and Things I Saw in Civil War Days*. New York: Eaton and Mains, 1899.

Salt Lake City Directory for 1879–80. Salt Lake City, Utah: G. Owen, 1879.

Salvator, Ludwig Louis. *Los Angeles in the Sunny Seventies: A Flower from the Golden Land*. Translated by Marguerite Eyre Wilbur. Los Angeles: Bruce McAllister, 1929.

Sandoz, Mari. *The Buffalo Hunters: The Story of the Hide Men*. New York: Hastings House, 1954.

———. *Cheyenne Autumn*. Lincoln: University of Nebraska Press, 1953.

———. *Crazy Horse, The Strange Man of the Oglalas: A Biography*. New York: Hastings House, 1942.

Sargent, Mary Elizabeth. *They Lie Forgotten: The United States Military Academy, 1856–1861, Together with a Class Album of May, 1861*. Middleton, N.Y.: Prior King Press, 1986.

Savage, James Woodruff. *History of Omaha, Nebraska*. New York: Munsell, 1894.

Schaff, Morris. *The Spirit of Old West Point, 1858–1862*. Boston: Houghton Mifflin, 1909.

Scharf, J. Thomas. *History of St. Louis City and County*. 2 vols. Philadelphia: Louis H. Evarts & Co., 1883.

———. *History of Westchester County, New York, Including Morrisania, Kings Bridge, and West Farms, Which Have Been Annexed to New York City*. 2 vols. Philadelphia: L. E. Preston, 1886.

Schindler, Henry. *Fort Leavenworth, Its Churches and Schools, 1827–1912*. Fort Leavenworth, Kans.: Army Service School Press, 1912.

Schindler, Henry, comp. *A Guide. Description of Fort Leavenworth, Kansas, and the U.S. School of Application for Cavalry and Infantry, and the U.S. Military Prison, Together with Other Useful Information about the Army, and a Directory of Fort Leavenworth, Kansas*. Leavenworth: The Compiler, 1884.

Schmeckebier, Laurence F. *The Office of Indian Affairs: Its History, Activities, and Organization*. Baltimore: Johns Hopkins University Press, 1927.

Schofield, John M. *Forty-Six Years in the Army*. Foreword by William M. Ferraro. Norman: University of Oklahoma Press, 1998.

Schoolcraft, Henry Rowe. *Information Respecting the History, Condition and Prospects of the Indian Tribes of the United States*. 6 vols. Philadelphia: Lippincott, Grambo, 1851–1857.

Schuchert, Charles, and Clara Mae LeVene. *O. C. Marsh, Pioneer in Paleontology*. New Haven: Yale University Press, 1940.

Schuler, Harold H. *Fort Sully: Guns at Sunset*. Vermillion: University of South Dakota Press, 1992.

Schutz, Wallace J., and Walter N. Trenerry. *Abandoned by Lincoln: A Military Biography of General John Pope*. Urbana: University of Illinois Press, 1990.

Seger, John H. *Early Days among the Cheyenne and Arapahoe Indians*. Edited by Stanley Vestal. Norman: University of Oklahoma Press, 1956.

Sherman, William T. *Memoirs of General William T. Sherman*. 2nd ed. 2 vols. New York: D. Appleton, 1886.

———. *Travel Accounts of General William T. Sherman to Spokan [sic] Falls, Washington, Territory, in the Summers of 1877 and 1883*. Fairfield, Wash.: Ye Galleon Press, 1984.

Skaggs, Jimmy M. *The Cattle-Trailing Industry: Between Supply and Demand, 1866–1890*. Norman: University of Oklahoma Press, 1991.

Smith, Sherry L. *Sagebrush Soldier: Private William Earl Smith's View of the Sioux War of 1876*. Norman: University of Oklahoma Press, 1989.

———. *The View from Officers' Row: Army Perceptions of Western Indians*. Tucson: University of Arizona Press, 1990.

Smith, Thomas T. *The U.S. Army and the Texas Frontier Economy, 1845–1900*. College Station: Texas A & M University Press, 1999.

Socolofsky, Homer E., and Huber Self. *Historical Atlas of Kansas*. 2nd ed. Norman: University of Oklahoma Press, 1988.

Some Account of the Blackmore Museum, Salisbury: The Opening Meeting. Devises: Wiltshire Archeological and Natural History Society, [1868].

Sorensen, Alfred R. *History of Omaha from the Pioneer Days to the Present Time*. Omaha: Gibson, Miller, and Richardson, 1889.

Sprague, Marshall. *Massacre: The Tragedy at White River*. Lincoln: University of Nebraska Press, 1957.

Spring, Agnes Wright. *The Cheyenne and Black Hills Stage and Express Routes*. Glendale, Calif.: Arthur H. Clark, 1949.

Stallard, Patricia Y. *Glittering Misery: Dependents of the Indian-Fighting Army*. University of Oklahoma Press, 1992.

Stevens, Edward T. *Flint Chips: A Guide to Pre-historic Archeology, as Illustrated by the Collection in the Blackmore Museum, Salisbury*. London: Bell and Daldy, 1870.

Stone, Wilbur Fiske. *History of Colorado*. 4 vols. Chicago: J. Clarke, 1918–1919.

Storm, Colton. *A Catalogue of the Everett D. Graff Collection of Western Americana*. Chicago: University of Chicago Press for the Newberry Library, 1968.

Strahorn, Robert E. *Gunnison and San Juan. A Late and Reliable Description*. Omaha: The New West, 1881.

———. *The Resources of Montana Territory and Attractions of Yellowstone Park. Facts and Experiences on the Farming, Stock Raising, Lumbering, and Other Industies of Montana and Notes on the Climate, Scenery, Game, Fish, and Mineral Springs, with Full and Reliable Data on Routes, Distances, Rates of Fare, Expenses of Living, Wages, School and Church Privileges, Society, Means of Acquiring Homes, and Other Valuable and Reliable Information Applicable to the Wants of the Capitalist, Homeseeker, or Tourist*. Helena: Montana Legislature, 1879.

Strong, William Emerson. *Canadian River Hunt*. Norman: University of Oklahoma Press, 1960.

Tate, Michael L. *The Frontier Army in the Settlement of the West*. Norman: University of Oklahoma Press, 1999.

Thoreau, Henry David. *The Illustrated Walden*. Edited by J. Lyndon Shanley. Princeton: Princeton University Press, 1973.

Thornton, Richard H. *An American Glossary*. 3 vols. New York: Frederick Ungar, 1962.

Thrapp, Don L. *The Conquest of Apacheria*. Norman: University of Oklahoma Press, 1967.

Tibbles, T. H. *Hidden Power: A Secret History of the Indian Ring, Its Operations, Intrigues, and Machinations*. New York: G. W. Carleton & Co., 1881.

Tidball, John C. *Manual of Heavy Artillery Service*. 2nd ed. Washington, D.C.: J. J. Chapman, 1881.

Trenholm, Virginia Cole. *The Arapahoes, Our People*. Norman: University of Oklahoma Press, 1970.

Trennert, Robert A. *Alternative to Extinction: Federal Indian Policy and the Beginnings of the Reservation System, 1846–1851*. Philadelphia: Temple University Press, 1975.

Trow, John F., comp. *Trow's New York City Directory*. New York: Trow, 1859, 1876–1881, 1888–1894.

Turchen, Lesta V., and James D. McLaird. *The Black Hills Expedition of 1875*. Mitchell, S.D.: Dakota Wesleyan University Press, 1975.

Twenty-seventh Annual Reunion of the Association of Graduates of the United States Military Academy, at West Point, New York. Saginaw, Mich.: Seeman, Peters, 1896.

United States Bureau of Indian Affairs. *Biographical and Historical Index of American Indians and Persons Involved in Indian Affairs*. 8 vols. Boston: G. K. Hall, 1966.

Upton, Emory. *A New System of Infantry Tactics, Double and Single Rank: Adapted to American Topography and Improved Fire-Arms*. New York: D. Appleton, 1873.

Utley, Robert M. *Frontier Regulars: The United States Army and the Indian, 1866–1891*. New York: Macmillan, 1973.

———. *Frontiersmen in Blue: The United States Army and the Indian, 1848–1865.* Lincoln: University of Nebraska Press, 1967.

———. *The Indian Frontier of the American West, 1846–1890.* Albuquerque: University of New Mexico Press, 1961.

———. *The Lance and the Shield: The Life and Times of Sitting Bull.* New York: Henry Holt and Co., 1993.

———. *The Last Days of the Sioux Nation.* New Haven: Yale University Press, 1963.

Vaughn, Jesse W. *Indian Fights: New Facts on Seven Encounters.* Norman: University of Oklahoma Press, 1966.

———. *The Reynolds Campaign on Powder River.* Norman: University of Oklahoma Press, 1961.

———. *With Crook at the Rosebud.* Harrisburg, Pa.: Stackpole Co., 1956.

Walker, Henry Pickering. *The Wagonmasters: High Plains Freighting from the Earliest Days of the Santa Fe Trail to 1880.* Norman: University of Oklahoma Press, 1966.

Wallace, Ernest, and E. Adamson Hoebel. *The Comanches: Lords of the Southern Plains.* Norman: University of Oklahoma Press, 1986.

Warren, Gouverneur K. *Preliminary Report of Explorations in Nebraska and Dakota in the Years 1855, '56, '57.* Washington, D.C.: Government Printing Office, 1858.

Waugh, John C. *The Class of 1846. From West Point to Annapolis: Stonewall Jackson, George McClellan and Their Brothers.* New York: Ballantine Books, 1994.

———. *Reelecting Lincoln: The Battle for the 1864 Presidency.* New York: Da Capo Press, 2001.

Webb, Walter Prescott. *The Great Plains.* Boston: Ginn & Co., 1931.

———. *The Texas Rangers: A Century of Frontier Defense.* Boston: Houghton Mifflin, 1935.

Webb, William Edward. *Buffalo Land: An Authentic Narrative of the Adventures and Misadventures of a Late Scientific and Sporting Party Upon the Great Plains of the West.* Cincinnati and Chicago: E. Hanneford & Co., 1872.

Wellman, Paul I. *Death on the Prairie: The Thirty Years' Struggle for the Western Plains.* Lincoln: University of Nebraska Press, 1987.

Wheeler, Homer W. *Buffalo Days: The Personal Memoir of a Cattleman, Indian Fighter and Army Officer.* Indianapolis: Bobbs-Merrill, 1925.

Wheeler, John H. *Reminiscences and Memoirs of North Carolina and Eminent North Carolinians.* Columbus, Ohio: Columbus Printing Works, 1884.

Wilder, Daniel Webster. *The Annals of Kansas.* Topeka, Kans.: T. Dwight Thatcher, 1885.

Wilhelm, Thomas. *Synopsis of the History of the Eighth U.S. Infantry: The Military Record of Officers Assigned to the Regiment, from Its Organization July 1838 to Sept. 1871.* Davis's Island, New York Harbor: The Regiment, 1871.

Wilkins, Frederick. *Defending the Borders: The Texas Rangers, 1848–1861.* Austin, Tex.: State House Press, 2001.

Willis, Bailey. *A Yanqui in Patagonia: A Bit of Autobiography.* Stanford, Calif.: Stanford University Press, 1947.

Wood, George B., and Franklin Bache. *The Dispensatory of the United States of America.* 16th ed. Philadelphia: J. B. Lippincott, 1892.

Wooster, Robert. *The Military and United States Indian Policy, 1865–1903.* New Haven: Yale University Press, 1988.

———. *Nelson A. Miles and the Twilight of the Frontier Army.* Lincoln: University of Nebraska Press, 1993.

Wright, Muriel H. *A Guide to the Indian Tribes of Oklahoma.* Foreword by Arrell Morgan Gibson. Norman: University of Oklahoma Press, 1986.

Wyckoff, William, and Lary M. Dilsaver, eds. *The Mountainous West: Explorations in Historical Geography.* Lincoln: University of Nebraska Press, 1995.

Young, Harry (Sam). *Hard Knocks: A Life Story of the Vanishing West.* Portland: Wells, 1915.

Index

The following abbreviations are used in the index:

A.T.	Arizona Territory
B.C.	British Columbia
BH	Black Hills
BHE	Black Hills Expedition
CNFCR	Cantonment North Fork Canadian River
D.T.	Dakota Territory
I.T.	Indian Territory
Id.T.	Idaho Territory
M.T.	Montana Territory
N.M.T.	New Mexico Territory
NC	Northern Cheyenne
OWI	*Our Wild Indians*
PNA	*The Plains of North America and Their Inhabitants*
PRE	Powder River Expedition
RID	Richard Irving Dodge
SC	Southern Cheyenne
Tour	General William T. Sherman's Inspection Tour of 1883
U.S.	United States
U.T.	Utah Territory
W.T.	Washington Territory
WTS	William Tecumseh Sherman
Wy.T.	Wyoming Territory

References to illustrations and maps are in *italics*.